AMERICAN INTERNATIONAL LAW CASES

AMERICAN INTERNATIONAL LAW CASES

Fourth Series

2009

Volume 1

Oceana®
NEW YORK

OXFORD
UNIVERSITY PRESS

Oxford University Press, Inc., publishes works that further Oxford University's objective of excellence in research, scholarship, and education.

Published by Oxford University Press, Inc.
198 Madison Avenue, New York, New York 10016

Cataloging-in-Publication information is available from the Library of Congress.

ISBN 978-0-19-975885-2 (2009, Volume 1)

Note to Readers:

This publication is designed to provide accurate and authoritative information in regard to the subject matter covered. It is based upon sources believed to be accurate and reliable and is intended to be current as of the time it was written. It is sold with the understanding that the publisher is not engaged in rendering legal, accounting, or other professional services. If legal advice or other expert assistance is required, the services of a competent professional person should be sought. Also, to confirm that the information has not been affected or changed by recent developments, traditional legal research techniques should be used, including checking primary sources where appropriate.

(Based on the Declaration of Principles jointly adopted by a Committee of the American Bar Association and a Committee of Publishers and Associations.)

TABLE OF CONTENTS

INTRODUCTORY NOTE

In 2009, American courts dealt with a host of cases incorporating international law, including issues such as the federal government's foreign affairs power and human rights abuses in foreign countries. This year's edition of *AILC* includes cases involving these topics, along with dozens of others critical to understanding the current application of international law in domestic courts.

The force of the foreign affairs doctrine was felt last year when the Ninth Circuit Court of Appeals struck down two California statutes on the grounds that the statutes conflicted with the federal government's foreign affairs power. In the first case, *Von Saher v. Norton Simon Museum of Art at Pasadena*, the statute at issue provided a cause of action to recover artwork looted by the Nazis during World War II. The Ninth Circuit found that California exceeded its authority by allowing all Holocaust victims and their heirs to bring action against any museum or gallery located in the United States. Although the court found that regulating property is generally an activity reserved to the state, the statute's broad scope conflicted with the federal government's power over foreign affairs. In the second case, *Movsesian v. Victoria Versicherung AG*, the Ninth Circuit also struck down a California statute on similar grounds. The California statute at issue in *Movsesian* extended the statute of limitations for claims arising out of life insurance policies issued to Armenian Genocide victims. The statute was held unconstitutional because it conflicted with the executive branch's foreign policy of not providing legislative recognition for the Armenian Genocide. These two California cases demonstrate how a federal court struck down a statute even though the statute did not directly conflict with a treaty, executive agreement, or federal statute.

The Alien Tort Statute and Torture Victim Protection Act also produced a series of cases that dealt with human rights abuses occurring outside of the United States. In *Chavez v. Carranza*, the Sixth Circuit Court of Appeals decided in favor of plaintiffs for crimes committed by a former Salvadoran military officer during the civil war in El Salvador. The court found that a Salvadoran law which granted amnesty to the defendant was not applicable because the plaintiffs were bringing action in the United States. In *Saleh v. Titan Corp.*, the U.S. Court of Appeals for the District of Columbia Circuit discussed whether Alien Tort Statute claims against two private military contractors providing services to the United States at the Abu Ghraib military prison were barred by the federal governmental immunity defense exception. Finally, in *Arar v. Ashcroft*, the U.S. District Court for the Eastern District of New York dismissed an action brought by a Canadian citizen who was arrested by U.S. authorities in New York and deported to Syria, where he was held for a year before being released without charges. The plaintiff brought claims under the Torture Victim Protection Act and the Fifth Amendment against U.S. officials for violations of his rights under international law.

HOW TO USE

Each volume of *American International Law Cases (AILC)* contains a *List of Subjects*, a *List of Abbreviations*, and a *Table of Cases* (by volume). The collection of cases for each year is organized around the *List of Subjects*. Subjects are assigned the same number each year with new subjects added as necessary. This numeration system unifies the collection so that the user can easily locate the topic in any edition of *AILC*. The *Table of Contents* for each volume lists only those subjects covered in the particular edition.

The cases are arranged alphabetically under each subject. Individual Subject Table of Contents for each covered subject provides a complete list of cases dealing with the subject. The Subject Table of Contents includes the page references both for cases printed in the particular volume and for those appearing in other volumes of the edition. Cases are printed under the subject heading with the lowest page number but are included in the Subject Table of Contents under every subject to which they are applicable. For example, the 2009 edition of *AILC* includes three cases that have been classified under the "Service of Process" topic. That topic constitutes subcategory "7. Service of Process" under category "III. PROCEDURE" in the volume's *Table of Contents*. The Subject Table of Contents for "Service of Process" cases appears at Volume 4, page 1291, a page that alphabetically lists the cases falling under that subject. The full text of one of those cases (*STX Panocean (UK) Co., Ltd. v. Glory Wealth Shipping Pte Ltd.*) appears in that section. The text of the other two cases listed there, *Oldfield v. Pueblo De Bahia Lora, S.A.*, and *Transfield ER Cape Ltd. v. Industrial Carriers, Inc.*, appears in Volume 2 in the earlier section of the book devoted to the topic and subtopic under which those cases are cross-referenced: "1.A. Jurisdiction: *In Personam*, over Persons & Corporations", also under "category III. Procedure". You will therefore find the text of those cases at Volume 2, pages 627 and 641.

To assist the user in finding particular cases or in researching particular topics, the 2009 edition includes in the last volume of the edition a "Subject Index of Cases" as well as an expanded Consolidated Table of Cases.

– To research cases by topic, use the *Subject Index of Cases*. The *Subject Index of Cases* lists the titles of *all* cases in the year's entire collection, according to subject, with a reference to the volume and page number where each case is reproduced.

– To locate cases by title, use the *Consolidated Table of Cases*. Cases listed in the alphabetical *Consolidated Table of Cases* are referenced to the volume, page, and topical section where they are reproduced as well as to all the topical sections to which they pertain.

LIST OF SUBJECTS

TABLE OF CASES

Each volume has a Table of Cases covering the materials included in that volume. A Consolidated Table of Cases appears in the last volume.

LIST OF ABBREVIATIONS

Significant abbreviations appearing in *American International Law Cases, 2009* are listed below.

A., A.2d	Atlantic Reporter [1885–1938], *Id.,* 2d Series [1938–date].
App. Div.	Appellate Division Reports [N.Y. 1896–1955].
Bevans	Treaties and Other International Agreements of the United States of America [1776–1949], compiled under the direction of Charles I. Bevans.
B.R.	Bankruptcy Reporter [1979–date].
Cal., Cal. 2d	California Reports [1850–1934], *Id.,* 2d Series [1934–date].
Cal. App.	California Appellate Decisions [1905–1940].
Cal. Rptr.	California Reporter [1959–date].
Cir. (1st, 2d, etc.)	Numbered Circuits of United States Courts of Appeal.
C.M.R.	Court Martial Reports [1951–date].
[state] Ct. App.	Court of Appeals [s] (state)
Ct. Cl.	Court of Claims (U.S.) [1863–1982].
Ct. Int'l Trade or C.I.T.	Court of International Trade [1980–date].
Cust. Ct.	Customs Court (U.S.) [1938–1980].
D. (N.D., S.D., etc.)	District Court (N.D. Northern District, S.D. Southern District, etc.).
D.C.	District of Columbia.
E.A.S.	Executive Agreement Series (replaced in 1945 by T.I.A.S.).
F. App'x or Fed. App'x.	Federal Appendix [2001–date].
F., F.2d, F.3d	Federal Reporter [1910–date].
F.P.C.	Federal Power Commission Reports [1931–date].
F.R.D.	Federal Rules Decisions [1938–date].
F. Supp., F. Supp. 2d	Federal Supplement [1933–date].
Fed. Cir.	Federal Circuit.
Fed. Cl.	Federal Claims Reporter [1992–date].
I.L.M.	International Legal Materials.
L. Ed., L. Ed. 2d	Lawyers' Edition, United States Supreme Court Reports [1754–1956], *Id.,* 2d Series [1956–date].

Misc., Misc. 2d	New York Miscellaneous [1892–1955], *Id.,* 2d Series [1956–date].
M.J.	Military Justice Reporter [1975–date].
N.E., N.E.2d	North Eastern Reporter [1885–1936], *Id.,* 2d Series [1934–date].
N.J.	New Jersey Reports [1948–date].
N.J. Eq.	New Jersey Equity [1830–1948].
N.W., N.W.2d	North Western Reporter [1879–1941], *Id.,* 2d Series [1941–date].
N.Y., N.Y.2d, N.Y.3d	New York Court of Appeals Reports [1846–1956], *Id.*, 2d Series [1956–2003], *Id.*, 3d Series [2004–date].
N.Y.S., N.Y.S.2d	New York Supplement [1888–1937], *Id.,* 2d Series [1937–date].
P., P.2d	Pacific Reporter [1883–1931], *Id.,* 2d Series [1931–date].
S. Ct.	Supreme Court Reporter [1882–date].
S.E., S.E.2d	South Eastern Reporter [1887–1839], *Id.,* 2d Series [1939–date].
So., So. 2d	Southern Reporter [1886–1941], *Id.,* 2d Series [1941–date].
Stat.	United States Statutes at Large.
[state] Super. Ct.	Superior Court
[state] Sup. Ct.	Supreme Court (other)
S.W., S.W.2d	South Western Reporter [1886–1928], *Id.,* 2d Series [1928–date].
T.C.	Tax Court (U.S.) [1942–date].
T.I.A.S.	Treaties and Other International Acts Series [1945–date].
T.S.	Treaty Series [1908–1945].
U.N.T.S.	United Nations Treaty Series [1946–date].
U.S.	United States Supreme Court Reports [1774–date] (Official).
U.S.C.M.A.	United States Court of Military Appeals [1951–date].
U.S.T.	United States Treaties and Other International Agreements [1950–date].
W.L.	Westlaw [1986–date].

I. INTERNATIONAL LAW IN GENERAL

1. C.I.L. (Customary International Law)

RABI ABDULLAHI
v.
PFIZER, INC.

562 F.3d 163 (2d Cir. 2009)
Decided January 30, 2009

PETER SAFIRSTEIN (Elaine S. Kusel, Ann M. Lipton, Andrew Wilmar, and Tatiana Rodriguez, on the brief), MILBERG WEISS BERSHAD & SCHULMAN LLP, New York, NY, for Plaintiffs-Appellants Rabi Abdullahi, et al.

RICHARD ALTSCHULER (Ali Ahmad, Cheverly, MD, on the brief), ALTSCHULER & ALTSCHULER, West Haven, CT, for Plaintiffs-Appellants Ajudu Ismaila Adamu, et al.

STEVEN GLICKSTEIN (David Klingsberg, Maris Veidemanis, James D. Herschlein, and Julie B. du Pont, on the brief), KAYE SCHOLER LLP, New York, NY, for Defendant-Appellee Pfizer, Inc.

Before: POOLER, B.D. PARKER, and WESLEY, Circuit Judges.

BARRINGTON D. PARKER, *Circuit Judge*:

This consolidated appeal is from the judgments of the United States District Court for the Southern District of New York (Pauley, *J.*) dismissing two complaints for lack of subject matter jurisdiction under the Alien Tort Statute, 28 U.S.C. § 1350 ("ATS"), and in the alternative, on the ground of *forum non conveniens*. Plaintiffs-Appellants Rabi Abdullahi and other Nigerian children and their guardians sued Defendant-Appellee Pfizer, Inc. under the ATS ("the *Abdullahi* action"). They alleged that Pfizer violated a customary international law norm prohibiting involuntary medical experimentation on humans when it tested an experimental antibiotic on children in Nigeria, including themselves, without their consent or knowledge. Plaintiffs-Appellants Ajudu Ismaila Adamu and others, also children and their guardians who were part of Pfizer's Nigerian drug experiment, brought a similar action against Pfizer, alleging violations of the ATS, the Connecticut Unfair Trade Practices Act ("CUTPA"), and the Connecticut Products Liability Act ("CPLA") ("the *Adamu* action"). Pfizer moved to dismiss both actions for lack of subject matter jurisdiction and on the basis of *forum non coveniens*. The district court granted the motions and both sets of plaintiffs have appealed.

As explained below, we conclude: (1) that the district court incorrectly determined that the prohibition in customary international law against nonconsensual human medical experimentation cannot be enforced through the ATS; (2) that changed circumstances in Nigeria since the filing of this appeal require re-examination of the appropriate forum, albeit on the basis of a legal analysis different from that employed by the district court; and (3) that the district court incorrectly applied Connecticut's choice of law rules in the *Adamu* action. Consequently, we reverse and remand the cases to the district court for further proceedings.

BACKGROUND

A. Pfizer's Trovan Test in Nigeria

On review of a district court's grant of a motion to dismiss, we assume as true the facts alleged in the complaints, construing them in the light most favorable to the appellants. *See Vietnam Ass'n for Victims of Agent Orange v. Dow Chem. Co.*, 517 F.3d 104, 115 (2d Cir. 2008). The central events at issue in these cases took place in 1996, during an epidemic of bacterial meningitis in northern Nigeria.[1] The appellants allege that at that time, Pfizer, the world's largest pharmaceutical corporation, sought to gain the approval of the U.S. Food and Drug Administration ("FDA") for the use on children of its new antibiotic, Trovafloxacin Mesylate, marketed as "Trovan." They contend that in April 1996, Pfizer, dispatched three of its American physicians to work with four Nigerian doctors to experiment with Trovan on children who were patients in Nigeria's Infectious Disease Hospital ("IDH") in Kano, Nigeria. Working in concert with Nigerian government officials, the team allegedly recruited two hundred sick children who sought treatment at the IDH and gave half of the children Trovan and the other half Ceftriaxone, an FDA-approved antibiotic the safety and efficacy of which was well-established. Appellants contend that Pfizer knew that Trovan had never previously been tested on children in the form being used and that animal tests showed that Trovan had life-threatening side effects, including joint disease, abnormal cartilage growth, liver damage, and a degenerative bone condition. Pfizer purportedly gave the children who were in the Ceftriaxone control group a deliberately low dose in order to misrepresent the effectiveness of Trovan in relation to Ceftriaxone. After approximately two weeks, Pfizer allegedly concluded the experiment and left without administering follow-up care. According to the appellants, the tests caused the deaths of eleven children, five of whom had taken Trovan and six of whom had

---

1 Bacterial meningitis is a serious and sometimes fatal infection of the fluids surrounding the spinal cord and the brain. Centers for Disease Control and Prevention, Meningococcal Disease: Frequently Asked Questions (May 28, 2008), http://www.cdc.gov/meningitis/bacterial/faqs.htm.

taken the lowered dose of Ceftriaxone, and left many others blind, deaf, paralyzed, or brain-damaged.

Appellants claim that Pfizer, working in partnership with the Nigerian government, failed to secure the informed consent of either the children or their guardians and specifically failed to disclose or explain the experimental nature of the study or the serious risks involved. Although the treatment protocol required the researchers to offer or read the subjects documents requesting and facilitating their informed consent, this was allegedly not done in either English or the subjects' native language of Hausa. The appellants also contend that Pfizer deviated from its treatment protocol by not alerting the children or their guardians to the side effects of Trovan or other risks of the experiment, not providing them with the option of choosing alternative treatment, and not informing them that the non-governmental organization Medecins Sans Frontieres (Doctors Without Borders) was providing a conventional and effective treatment for bacterial meningitis, free of charge, at the same site.[2]

The appellants allege that, in an effort to rapidly secure FDA approval, Pfizer hastily assembled its test protocol at its research headquarters in Groton, Connecticut, and requested and received permission to proceed from the Nigerian government in March 1996. At the time, Pfizer also claimed to have secured approval from an IDH ethics committee. Appellants allege, however, that the March 1996 approval letter was backdated by Nigerian officials working at the government hospital well after the experiments had taken place and that at the time the letter was purportedly written, the IDH had no ethics committee.[3] Appellants also contend that the experiments were condemned by doctors, including one on Pfizer's staff at the time of the Kano trial.

In 1998, the FDA approved Trovan for use on adult patients only. After reports of liver failure in patients who took Trovan, its use in America was eventually restricted to adult emergency care. In 1999, the European Union banned its use.

---

2 The appellants further allege that Pfizer failed to follow its protocol in ways that might have mitigated the harm suffered by the children. They contend that Pfizer violated the protocol by administering Trovan orally even though oral absorption is difficult for sick children; conducting no testing prior to administering the drug to determine whether Nigeria's strain of meningitis might be responsive to Trovan; failing to determine that the children in the test had meningitis; and failing to either exclude from the experiment children with liver or joint problems or to test for such problems, even though Trovan was known to exacerbate them. Although Pfizer's protocol called for children receiving Trovan to be switched to Ceftriaxone if they did not respond well to Trovan, Pfizer allegedly did not conduct regular blood tests of the children or switch those who suffered from Trovan-related side effects to Ceftriaxone.

3 A Nigerian physician who was the principal investigator for the test allegedly admitted that his office created the backdated approval letter when the FDA conducted an audit of the experiment in 1997.

B. The Proceedings Below

In August 2001, the *Abdullahi* plaintiffs sued Pfizer under the ATS, alleging that the experiments violated international law. In September 2002, the district court granted Pfizer's motion to dismiss the *Abdullahi* claims on the ground of *forum non conveniens*, conditioned on Pfizer's consent to litigation in Nigeria. *Abdullahi v. Pfizer, Inc.*, No. 01 Civ. 8118 (WHP), 2002 U.S. Dist. LEXIS 17436, 2002 WL 31082956, at *12 (S.D.N.Y. Sept. 17, 2002) ("*Abdullahi I*"). It found that Nigeria was an adequate alternative forum despite plaintiffs' contentions about corruption in the Nigerian court system. 2002 U.S. Dist. LEXIS 17436, [WL] at *8–10. The district court denied Pfizer's motion to dismiss under Rule 12(b)(6), Fed. R. Civ. P., concluding that the plaintiffs adequately alleged that Pfizer's collusion with the Nigerian government made it a state actor. 2002 U.S. Dist. LEXIS 17436, [WL] at *5–6.

Meanwhile, another group of children and guardians involved in the Trovan experiment sued in the Federal High Court in Kano, alleging claims under Nigerian law. That case, *Zango v. Pfizer International, Inc.*, [2001] Suit No. FHC/ K/CS/204/2001 (Nigeria), was dismissed in 2003 after plaintiffs voluntarily discontinued the suit following the removal from the bench of the first judge assigned to the action and the second judge's decision to decline jurisdiction for personal reasons. *Abdullahi v. Pfizer, Inc.*, No. 01 Civ. 8118 (WHP), 2005 U.S. Dist. LEXIS 16126, 2005 WL 1870811, at *5 (S.D.N.Y. Aug. 9, 2005) ("*Abdullahi III*"). On appeal to this Court from the district court's dismissal in *Abdullahi I*, the *Abdullahi* appellants argued that the dismissal of the *Zango* litigation was a result of rampant corruption, which indicated that the Nigerian judicial system could not provide an adequate alternative forum for their action. Given an inconclusive record regarding the events leading to the dismissal of the *Zango* lawsuit, we vacated the judgment and remanded for further fact-finding on *forum non conveniens. See Abdullahi v. Pfizer, Inc.*, 77 F. App'x 48, 53 (2d Cir. 2003) (summary order) ("*Abdullahi II*").

In November 2002, following the dismissal of the *Zango* lawsuit, a number of the *Zango* plaintiffs filed the *Adamu* action. They alleged that in planning the Trovan experiment in Connecticut and in conducting the tests in Nigeria without informed consent, Pfizer violated the CUTPA, the CPLA, and the ATS. Eventually, the *Adamu* action was transferred to the Southern District of New York and consolidated with the *Abdullahi* action. Pfizer then moved to dismiss both cases for failure to state a claim under the ATS and on the basis of *forum non conveniens*. It also moved to dismiss in *Adamu* on the ground that Connecticut choice of law principles require the application of Nigerian law, which bars suit under CUTPA and the CPLA.

The district court granted the motions. *See Abdullahi III*, 2005 U.S. Dist. LEXIS 16126, 2005 WL 1870811; *Adamu v. Pfizer, Inc.*, 399 F. Supp. 2d 495 (S.D.N.Y. 2005). In *Abdullahi III*, Judge Pauley held that while "[p]laintiffs correctly state that non-consensual medical experimentation violates the law of nations and, therefore, the laws of the United States," they failed to identify a source of international law that "provide[s] a proper predicate for jurisdiction under the ATS." 2005 U.S. Dist. LEXIS 16126, 2005 WL 1870811, at *9, 14. Noting that "a decision to create a private right of action is one better left to legislative judgment in the great majority of cases," he concluded that "[a] cause of action for Pfizer's failure to get any consent, informed or otherwise, before performing medical experiments on the subject children would expand customary international law far beyond that contemplated by the ATS." 2005 U.S. Dist. LEXIS 16126, [WL] at *13–14 (internal quotation marks omitted).

With regard to the *forum non conveniens* analysis, the district court declined to accept plaintiffs' submissions concerning Pfizer's alleged bribery of Nigerian officials on the ground that they were not based on personal knowledge. 2005 U.S. Dist. LEXIS 16126, [WL] at *16–17. Finding that the plaintiffs had failed to submit specific evidence that the Nigerian judiciary would be biased against its own citizens in an action against Pfizer, the district court alternatively held that Nigeria was an adequate alternate forum. 2005 U.S. Dist. LEXIS 16126, [WL] at *16, 18.

Several months later, the district court also granted Pfizer's motion to dismiss the *Adamu* case. *Adamu*, 399 F. Supp. 2d 495. It relied on its *Abdullahi III* decision to hold that the plaintiffs could not establish jurisdiction under the ATS. *Id.* at 501. The district court also incorporated the *forum non conveniens* analysis from *Abdullahi III* to find that Nigeria is an adequate forum. *Id.* at 504. Applying the public and private interest factors set forth in *Gulf Oil Corp. v. Gilbert*, 330 U.S. 501, 508–09, 67 S. Ct. 839, 91 L. Ed. 1055 (1947), *superseded by statute on other grounds as recognized in Cowan v. Ford Motor Co.,* 713 F.2d 100, 103 (5th Cir. 1983), the court found that while public interest factors did not support either forum, private interest factors weighed in favor of dismissal. *Adamu*, 339 F. Supp. 2d. at 505–06. The district court also dismissed the *Adamu* plaintiffs' Connecticut law claims, concluding that, under Connecticut choice of law principles, the action was governed and barred by Nigerian law. *Id.* at 503.

The *Abdullahi* and *Adamu* plaintiffs appealed. Since then, a tectonic change has altered the relevant political landscape. In May 2007, the state of Kano brought criminal charges and civil claims against Pfizer, seeking over $2 billion in damages and restitution.[4] Around the same time, the federal government of Nigeria sued Pfizer and several of its employees, seeking $7 billion in damages.[5] None of these cases seek compensation for the subjects of the tests, who are the appellants

4 Tina Akannam, *Nigeria: Pfizer—Case Adjourned Till May 27*, Vanguard, April 30, 2008, http://allafrica.com/stories/200804300470.html; Joe Stephens, *Pfizer Faces Criminal Charges in Nigeria*, The Washington Post, May 30, 2007, at A10, available at http://www.washingtonpost.com/wp-dyn/content/article/2007/05/29/AR2007052902107.html.

5 Jonathan Clayton, *Pfizer Under Fire After Drug Trial*, TimesOnline, June 27, 2007, http://business.timesonline.co.uk/tol/business/industry_sectors/health/article1990908.ece; *Nigeria Sues Drugs Giant Pfizer*, BBC News, June 5, 2007, http://news.bbc.co.uk/2/hi/africa/6719141.stm.

before this Court. Pfizer then notified this Court that in light of these recent developments, which it believed required further consideration by the district court, it would not seek affirmance on the basis of *forum non conveniens*.

DISCUSSION

The district court dismissed both actions based on its determination that it lacked subject matter jurisdiction because plaintiffs failed to state claims under the ATS. We review dismissal on this ground *de novo*. *Rweyemamu v. Cote*, 520 F.3d 198, 201 (2d Cir. 2008). "To survive dismissal, the plaintiff[s] must provide the grounds upon which [their] claim rests through factual allegations sufficient 'to raise a right to relief above the speculative level.'" *ATSI Commc'ns, Inc. v. Shaar Fund, Ltd.*, 493 F.3d 87, 98 (2d Cir. 2007) (quoting *Bell Atl. Corp. v. Twombly*, 550 U.S. 544, 127 S. Ct. 1955, 1965, 167 L. Ed. 2d 929 (2007)).[6]

I. The Alien Tort Statute

The Alien Tort Statute, 28 U.S.C. § 1350, provides that "[t]he district courts shall have original jurisdiction of any civil action by an alien for a tort only, committed in violation of the law of nations or a treaty of the United States." Included in the Judiciary Act of 1789, the statute provided jurisdiction in just two cases during the first 191 years after its enactment. *See Taveras v. Taveraz*, 477 F.3d 767, 771 (6th Cir. 2007). In the last thirty years, however, the ATS has functioned slightly more robustly, conferring jurisdiction over a limited category of claims.

We first extensively examined the ATS in *Filartiga v. Pena-Irala*, 630 F.2d 876 (2d Cir. 1980), where we held that conduct violating the law of nations is actionable under the ATS "only where the nations of the world have demonstrated that the wrong is of mutual, and not merely several, concern, by means of express international accords." *Id.* at 888. Following *Filartiga*, we concluded that ATS claims may sometimes be brought against private actors, and not only state officials, *see Kadic v. Karadzic*, 70 F.3d 232, 239 (2d Cir. 1995), when the tortious activities violate norms of "universal concern" that are recognized to extend to the conduct of private parties—for example, slavery, genocide, and war crimes, *id.* at 240. This case involves allegations of both state and individual action. In *Flores v. Southern Peru Copper Corp.*, 414 F.3d 233 (2d Cir. 2003), we clarified that "the law of nations" in the ATS context "refers to the body of law known as customary international law," which "is discerned from myriad decisions made in numerous and varied international and domestic arenas" and "does not stem from any single, definitive, readily-identifiable source." *Id.* at 247–48. These principles are rejected in their entirety by our dissenting colleague. In *Flores*, we concluded that ATS jurisdiction is limited to alleged violations of "those clear and unambiguous rules

---

6 *Twombly* instituted a flexible "plausibility standard," not limited to antitrust cases, which requires the amplification of facts in certain contexts. *Iqbal v. Hasty*, 490 F.3d 143, 155–58 (2d Cir. 2007).

by which States universally abide, or to which they accede, out of a sense of legal obligation and mutual concern." *Id.* at 252. Applying this standard, we held that the appellants' claim that pollution from mining operations caused lung disease failed to state a violation of customary international law. We reasoned that the "right to life" and the "right to health" were insufficiently definite to constitute binding customary legal norms and that there was insufficient evidence to establish the existence of a narrower norm prohibiting intranational pollution. *Id.* at 254–55.

In 2004, the Supreme Court comprehensively addressed the ATS for the first time in *Sosa v. Alvarez-Machain*, 542 U.S. 692, 124 S. Ct. 2739, 159 L. Ed. 2d 718. Justice Souter, writing for the majority, clarified that the ATS was enacted to create jurisdiction over "a relatively modest set of actions alleging violations of the law of nations" and with "the understanding that the common law would provide a cause of action." *Id.* at 720, 723. The Supreme Court confirmed that federal courts retain a limited power to "adapt[] the law of nations to private rights" by recognizing "a narrow class of international norms" to be judicially enforceable through our residual common law discretion to create causes of action. *Id.* at 728–29. It cautioned, however, that courts must exercise this power with restraint and "the understanding that the door [to actionable violations] is still ajar subject to vigilant doorkeeping," permitting only those claims that "rest on a norm of international character accepted by the civilized world and defined with a specificity comparable to the features of the 18th-century paradigms [the Supreme Court has] recognized." *Id.* at 725, 729. These 18th-century paradigms consist of offenses against ambassadors, violations of the right to safe passage, and individual actions arising out of piracy. *Id.* at 724. The common theme among these offenses is that they contravened the law of nations, admitted of a judicial remedy, and simultaneously threatened serious consequences in international affairs. *Id.* at 715. Lower courts are required to gauge claims brought under the ATS against the current state of international law, but are permitted to recognize under federal common law only those private claims for violations of customary international law norms that reflect the same degree of "definite content and acceptance among civilized nations" as those reflected in the 18th-century paradigms. *Id.* at 732–33. The Supreme Court in *Sosa* also counseled that "the determination whether a norm is sufficiently definite to support a cause of action should (and, indeed, inevitably must) involve an element of judgment about the practical consequences of making that cause available to litigants" in federal courts. *Id.*

In this way *Sosa* set a "high bar to new private causes of action" alleging violations of customary international law. *Id.* at 727. A federal court can recognize one only if a plaintiff identifies the violation of a norm of customary international law that, as defined by the sources of such law that United States courts "have long, albeit cautiously, recognized," *id.* at 733–34 (referencing *The Paquete Habana*, 175 U.S. 677, 700, 20 S. Ct. 290, 44 L. Ed. 320 (1900)), is sufficiently specific, universal, and obligatory to meet the standards established by *Sosa*. *See Sosa*, 542 U.S.

at 732 (citing with approval Tel-*Oren v. Libyan Arab Republic*, 233 U.S. App. D.C. 384, 726 F.2d 774, 781 (D.C. Cir. 1984) (Edwards, J., concurring), and *In re Estate of Marcos, Human Rights Litig.*, 25 F.3d 1467, 1475 (9th Cir. 1994)). Applying these principles, the Supreme Court held that the plaintiff, a Mexican national who sued a fellow Mexican national under the ATS for allegedly aiding in his illegal abduction by agents of the U.S. Drug Enforcement Agency, had failed to allege the violation of a customary international law norm with the required precision. *Sosa*, 542 U.S. at 738. The Supreme Court found that the practical consequences of recognizing a general and broad customary international law prohibition of arbitrary detention in a case involving "a single illegal detention of less than a day, followed by the transfer of custody to lawful authorities and a prompt arraignment" would be "breathtaking" and inappropriate. *Id.* at 736, 738.

Since *Sosa*, this Court has reviewed three judgments dismissing claims under the ATS. In *Khulumani v. Barclay National Bank, Ltd.*, 504 F.3d 254 (2d Cir. 2007) (per curiam), we held that the ATS conferred jurisdiction over multinational corporations that purportedly collaborated with the government of South Africa in maintaining apartheid because they aided and abetted violations of customary international law. *Id.* at 260. In *Vietnam Ass'n for Victims of Agent Orange v. Dow Chemical Co.*, 517 F.3d 104 (2d Cir. 2008), we concluded that the ATS did not support a claim that the defendants violated international law by manufacturing and supplying Agent Orange and other herbicides used by the United States military during the Vietnam War. *Id.* at 123. We reasoned that the sources of law on which the appellants relied did not define a norm prohibiting the wartime use of Agent Orange that was both universal and sufficiently specific to satisfy the requirements of *Sosa*. *Id.* at 119–23. Similarly, in *Mora v. People of the State of New York*, 524 F.3d 183 (2d Cir. 2008), we held that the norm at issue—one that prohibits the detention of a foreign national without informing him of the requirement of consular notification and access under Article 36(1)(b)(3) of the Vienna Convention on Consular Relations—was insufficiently universal to support a claim under the ATS. *Id.* at 208–09.

Turning now to this appeal, and remaining mindful of our obligation to proceed cautiously and self-consciously in this area, we determine whether the norm alleged (1) is a norm of international character that States universally abide by, or accede to, out of a sense of legal obligation; (2) is defined with a specificity comparable to the 18th-century paradigms discussed in *Sosa*; and (3) is of mutual concern to States.

A. The Prohibition of Nonconsensual Medical Experimentation on Humans

Appellants' ATS claims are premised on the existence of a norm of customary international law prohibiting medical experimentation on non-consenting human subjects. To determine whether this prohibition constitutes a universally accepted norm of customary international law, we examine the current state of international law by consulting the sources identified by Article 38 of the Statute of the International

Court of Justice ("ICJ Statute"), to which the United States and all members of the United Nations are parties. *Flores*, 414 F.3d at 250; *see, e.g., United States v. Yousef*, 327 F.3d 56, 100–01 (2d Cir. 2003). Article 38 identifies the authorities that provide "competent proof of the content of customary international law." *Flores*, 414 F.3d at 251. These sources consist of:

> (a) international conventions, whether general or particular, establishing rules expressly recognized by the contesting states;
>
> (b) international custom, as evidence of a general practice accepted as law;
>
> (c) the general principles of law recognized by civilized nations;
>
> (d) . . . judicial decisions and the teachings of the most highly qualified publicists of the various nations, as subsidiary means for the determination of rules of law.

Statute of the International Court of Justice, art. 38(1), June 26, 1945, 59 Stat. 1055, 1060, T.S. No. 993 [hereinafter ICJ Statute].

The appellants ground their claims in four sources of international law that categorically forbid medical experimentation on non-consenting human subjects: (1) the Nuremberg Code, which states as its first principle that "[t]he voluntary consent of the human subject is absolutely essential"; (2) the World Medical Association's Declaration of Helsinki, which sets forth ethical principles to guide physicians world-wide and provides that human subjects should be volunteers and grant their informed consent to participate in research; (3) the guidelines authored by the Council for International Organizations of Medical Services ("CIOMS"), which require "the voluntary informed consent of [a] prospective subject"; and (4) Article 7 of the International Covenant on Civil and Political Rights ("ICCPR"), which provides that "no one shall be subjected without his free consent to medical or scientific experimentation."[7]

The district court found that "non-consensual medical experimentation violates the law of nations and, therefore, the laws of the United States" and cited the Nuremberg Code for support. *Abdullahi III,* 2005 U.S. Dist. LEXIS 16126, 2005 WL 1870811, at *9. It then noted that "[w]hile federal courts have the authority to imply the existence of a private right of action for violations of *jus cogens* norms of international law, federal courts must consider whether there exist special

---

7 These sources are located respectively at (1) *United States v. Brandt*, 2 Trials of War Criminals Before the Nuremberg Military Tribunals Under Control Council Law No. 10, 181 (1949) [hereinafter Nuremberg Trials]; (2) World Med. Ass'n, *Declaration of Helsinki: Ethical Principles for Medical Research Involving Human Subjects*, art. 20, 22, G.A. Res. (adopted 1964, amended 1975, 1983, 1989, 1996, and 2000), http://www.wma.net/e/policy/pdf/17c.pdf [hereinafter Declaration of Helsinki]; (3) Council for International Organizations of Medical Services [CIOMS], International Ethical Guidelines for Biomedical Research Involving Human Subjects, guideline 4 (3rd ed. 2002), *superseding id.* at guideline 1 (2nd ed. 1993); (4) International Covenant on Civil and Political Rights, art. 7, Dec. 19, 1966, 999 U.N.T.S. 171 [hereinafter ICCPR].

factors counseling hesitation in the absence of affirmative action by Congress." *Id.* (internal citations and quotation marks omitted). The district court then separately analyzed the four sources of international law that prohibit nonconsensual medical experimentation on humans and the Universal Declaration of Human Rights. 2005 U.S. Dist. LEXIS 16126, [WL] at *11–13. It found that with the exception of the Nuremberg Code, these sources contain only aspirational or vague language lacking the specificity required for jurisdiction. 2005 U.S. Dist. LEXIS 16126, [WL] *12–13. It also determined that because the United States did not ratify or adopt any of these authorities except the ICCPR, and because even the ICCPR is not self-executing, none of them create binding international legal obligations that are enforceable in federal court. 2005 U.S. Dist. LEXIS 16126, [WL] at *11–13. Finally, the district court concluded that the plaintiffs failed to provide a proper predicate for ATS jurisdiction because none of the sources independently authorizes a private cause of action and the inference of such a cause of action is a matter best left to Congress. 2005 U.S. Dist. LEXIS 16126, [WL] at *13–14.[8]

The district court's approach misconstrued both the nature of customary international law and the scope of the inquiry required by *Sosa*. It mistakenly assumed that the question of whether a particular customary international law norm is sufficiently specific, universal, and obligatory to permit the recognition of a cause of action under the ATS is resolved essentially by looking at two things: whether each source of law referencing the norm is binding and whether each source expressly authorizes a cause of action to enforce the norm. But *Sosa*, as we have seen, requires a more fulsome and nuanced inquiry. Courts are obligated to examine how the specificity of the norm compares with 18th-century paradigms, whether the norm is accepted in the world community, and whether States universally abide by the norm out of a sense of mutual concern. By eschewing this inquiry, the district court did not engage the fact that norms of customary international law are "discerned from myriad decisions made in numerous and varied international and domestic arenas" and "[do] not stem from any single, definitive, readily-identifiable source." *Flores*, 414 F.3d at 247–48.

The district court also inappropriately narrowed its inquiry in two respects. First, it focused its consideration on whether the norm identified by the plaintiffs is set forth in conventions to which the United States is a party, and if so, whether these treaties are self-executing or executed by federal legislation. While adoption of a self-executing treaty or the execution of a treaty that is not self-executing may provide the best evidence of a particular country's custom or practice of recognizing a norm, *see Flores*, 414 F.3d at 257, the existence of a norm of customary international law is one determined, in part, by reference to the custom or practices of many States, and the broad acceptance of that norm by the international community.

8 The district court interchangeably refers to the 'lack of jurisdiction' or 'lack of subject matter jurisdiction' over plaintiffs' claims, the plaintiffs' failure to state an ATS claim, and their failure to identify a norm that permits the inference of a cause of action.

Agreements that are not self-executing or that have not been executed by federal legislation, including the ICCPR, are appropriately considered evidence of the current state of customary international law. *See Khulumani,* 504 F.3d at 284 (Katzmann, J., concurring) (noting that "[w]hether a treaty that embodies [a norm of customary international law] is self-executing is relevant to, but is not determinative of, [the] question" of whether the norm permits ATS jurisdiction). A formal treaty, moreover, is not the lone primary source of customary international law. The ICJ Statute permits, and *Sosa* encourages, among other things, that courts consider "international custom, as evidence of a general practice accepted as law." ICJ Statute, *supra*, at art. 38(1); *Sosa*, 542 U.S. at 734 ("[W]here there is no treaty, and no controlling executive or legislative act or judicial decision, resort must be had to the customs and usages of civilized nations.") (quoting *The Paquete Habana*, 175 U.S. at 700).

Second, the district court's consideration of whether each source of law creates binding legal norms failed to credit the fact that even declarations of international norms that are not in and of themselves binding may, with time and in conjunction with state practice, provide evidence that a norm has developed the specificity, universality, and obligatory nature required for ATS jurisdiction. *See Filartiga*, 630 F.2d at 883 ("[A non-binding] Declaration creates an expectation of adherence, and insofar as the expectation is gradually justified by State practice, a declaration may by custom become recognized as laying down rules binding upon the States.") (internal quotation marks omitted). The district court should have considered a greater range of evidence and weighed differently the probative value of the sources on which the appellants relied.

In sum, it was inappropriate for the district court to forego a more extensive examination of whether treaties, international agreements, or State practice have ripened the prohibition of nonconsensual medical experimentation on human subjects into a customary international law norm that is sufficiently (i) universal and obligatory, (ii) specific and definable, and (iii) of mutual concern, to permit courts to infer a cause of action under the ATS. *See Sosa*, 542 U.S. at 732–35. We now proceed with such an examination.

i. Universality

The appellants must allege the violation of a norm of customary international law to which States universally subscribe. *See Sosa*, 542 U.S. at 732; *Vietnam Ass'n for Victims of Agent Orange,* 517 F.3d at 117. The prohibition on nonconsensual medical experimentation on human beings meets this standard because, among other reasons, it is specific, focused and accepted by nations around the world without significant exception.

The evolution of the prohibition into a norm of customary international law began with the war crimes trials at Nuremberg. The United States, the Soviet Union, the United Kingdom and France "acting in the interest of all the United Nations," established the International Military Tribunal ("IMT") through entry into the London Agreement of August 8, 1945. M. Cheriff Bassiouni et al., *An Appraisal of Human Experimentation in International Law and Practice: The Need for International Regulation of Human Experimentation*, 72 J. Crim. L. & Criminology 1597, 1640 & n.220 (1981) (internal quotation marks omitted). Annexed to the London Agreement was the London Charter, which served as the IMT's Constitution. *See* Agreement for the Prosecution and Punishment of the Major War Criminals of the European Axis Powers, with annexed Charter of the International Military Tribunal art. 2, Aug. 8, 1945, 59 Stat. 1544, 82 U.N.T.S. 279. According to the Charter, the IMT had the "power to try and punish persons who, acting in the interests of the European Axis countries, whether as individuals or as members of organisations, committed," among other offenses, war crimes and crimes against humanity. *Id.* at art. 6.

The IMT tried 22 "major" Nazi war criminals leaving "lower-level" war criminals, including "[l]eading physicians . . . and leading German industrialists," to be tried in subsequent trials by U.S. military tribunals acting "under the aegis of the IMT." United States Holocaust Memorial Museum, *War Crimes Trials*, Holocaust Encylopedia (2008), http://www.ushmm.org/wlc/article.php?lang=en&ModuleId=10005140. The law that authorized the creation of the U.S. military tribunals, Control Council Law No. 10, was enacted in 1945 by the Allied Control Council, *see id.*, an authority through which the London Agreement signatories exerted joint-control over Germany, *see* Encyclopedia Britannica, Germany, Encyclopedia Britannica Online (2009), http://search.eb.com/eb/article-58214. Control Council Law No. 10 stated that its purpose was to "give effect to the terms of . . . the London Agreement . . . and the [London] Charter," and "to establish a uniform legal basis in Germany for the prosecution of war criminals." Allied Control Council No. 10, preamble, (Dec. 20, 1945), http://avalon.law.yale.edu/imt/imt10.asp. Law No. 10 expressly incorporated the London Agreement, identifying it as an "integral part[] of this Law." *Id.* at art. I. Law No. 10 also authorized military tribunals of the occupying powers to prosecute individuals for the same crimes over which the IMT had jurisdiction, including war crimes and crimes against humanity, *see id.* at arts. II–III, and made military tribunal prosecutions subject to the IMT's right of first refusal, *see id.* at art. III. Consequently, the U.S. military tribunals effectively operated as extensions of the IMT, *see* Telford Taylor, *Final Report to the Secretary of the Army on the Nuernberg War Crimes Trials Under Control Council Law No. 10* 7, 107 (1949) [hereinafter *Report on Nuernberg War Crimes Trials], available at* http://www.loc.gov/rr/frd/Military_Law/pdf/NT_final-report.pdf (explaining that "the trials under Law No. 10 were to be a means of carrying out such 'declarations of criminality' . . . as the International Military Tribunal might make" and that "[t]he first [IMT] trial and the 12 following [military tribunal] trials . . . form a single sequence based on common principles"), and Control Council Law No. 10 served to implement the commitments undertaken in the London Agreement, *see id.* at 7 (noting that "the two documents supplemented each other" and "[m]ajor criminals not tried under the one could be tried under the other").

In August 1947, Military Tribunal 1, staffed by American judges and prosecutors and conducted under American procedural rules, *see* George J. Annas, *The Nuremberg Code in U.S. Courts: Ethics versus Expediency, in The Nazi Doctors and the Nuremberg Code* 201, 201 (George J. Annas & Michael A. Grodin eds., 1992), promulgated the Nuremberg Code as part of the tribunal's final judgment against fifteen doctors who were found guilty of war crimes and crimes against humanity for conducting medical experiments without the subjects' consent, *Brandt*, 2 Nuremberg Trials, at 181–82. Among the nonconsensual experiments that the tribunal cited as a basis for their convictions were the testing of drugs for immunization against malaria, epidemic jaundice, typhus, smallpox and cholera. *Id.* at 175–178. Seven of the convicted doctors were sentenced to death and the remaining eight were sentenced to varying terms of imprisonment. *Id.* at 298–300. The tribunal emphasized that

> [i]n every single instance appearing in the record, subjects were used who did not consent to the experiments; indeed, as to some of the experiments, it is not even contended by the defendants that the subjects occupied the status of volunteers.

Id. at 183. The judgment concluded that "[m]anifestly human experiments under such conditions are *contrary to the principles of the law of nations* as they result from usages established among civilized peoples, from the laws of humanity, and from the dictates of public conscience." *Id.* (emphasis added and internal quotation marks omitted). The Code created as part of the tribunal's judgment therefore emphasized as its first principle that "[t]he voluntary consent of the human subject is absolutely essential." *Id.* at 181.

The American tribunal's conclusion that action that contravened the Code's first principle constituted a crime against humanity is a lucid indication of the international legal significance of the prohibition on nonconsensual medical experimentation. As Justices of the Supreme Court have recognized, "[t]he medical trials at Nuremberg in 1947 deeply impressed *upon the world* that experimentation with unknowing human subjects is morally and legally unacceptable." *United States v. Stanley*, 483 U.S. 669, 687, 107 S. Ct. 3054, 97 L. Ed. 2d 550 (1987) (Brennan, J., concurring in part and dissenting in part) (emphasis added); *see also id.* at 709–10 (O'Connor, J., concurring in part and dissenting in part).

Moreover, both the legal principles articulated in the trials' authorizing documents and their application in judgments at Nuremberg occupy a position of special importance in the development of bedrock norms of international law. United States courts examining the Nuremberg judgments have recognized that "[t]he universal and fundamental rights of human beings identified by Nuremberg—rights against genocide, enslavement, and other inhumane acts . . . —are the direct ancestors of the universal and fundamental norms recognized as *jus cogens*," from which no derogation is permitted, irrespective of the consent or practice of a given State. *Siderman de Blake v. Republic of Arg.*, 965 F.2d 699, 715 (9th Cir. 1992) (cited in *Sampson v. F.R.G.*, 250 F.3d 1145, 1150 (7th Cir. 2001)). As Telford Taylor, who first served as an assistant to Justice Robert Jackson during his time as Chief

Prosecutor for the IMT and then became Chief of Counsel for War Crimes on the Nuremberg trials held under the authority of Control Council Law No. 10, explained, "Nuernberg was based on enduring [legal] principles and not on temporary political expedients, and this fundamental point is apparent from the reaffirmation of the Nuernberg principles in Control Council Law No. 10, and *their application and refinement* in the 12 judgments rendered under that law during the 3-year period, 1947 to 1949." Taylor, *Report on Nuernberg War Crimes Trials*, at 107 (emphasis added).

Consistent with this view, the Code's first principle has endured: "[S]ignificant world opinion has not come to the defense of the nature or manner in which the experiments were conducted in the Nazi concentration camps." Bassiouni et al., *supra*, at 1641. Rather, since Nuremberg, states throughout the world have shown through international accords and domestic law-making that they consider the prohibition on nonconsensual medical experimentation identified at Nuremberg as a norm of customary international law.[9]

In 1955, the draft International Covenants on Human Rights was revised to add a second sentence to its prohibition of torture and cruel, inhuman or degrading treatment or punishment. The addition provided that "[i]n particular, no one shall be subjected without his free consent to medical or scientific experimentation involving risk, where such is not required by his state of physical or mental health." Annotations on the text of the draft International Covenants on Human Rights, at 31, U.N. GAOR, 10th Sess., Annexes, agenda item 28 (II), U.N. Doc. A/2929 (July 1, 1955). The clause was later revised to offer the simpler and sweeping prohibition that "no one shall be subjected without his free consent to medical or scientific experimentation." ICCPR, *supra*, at art. 7. This prohibition became part of Article 7 of the ICCPR, which entered into force in 1976, and is legally binding

9 The Fourth Geneva Convention, which entered into force in 1950 and provides protection to civilians in the time of war, elaborates on the application of the norm during armed conflict. Article 32 of the convention prohibits civilian or military agents of the state parties from conducting "medical or scientific experiments not necessitated by the medical treatment of the protected person." Geneva Convention Relative to the Protection of Civilian Persons in Time of War art. 32, Aug. 12, 1949, 6 U.S.T. 3516, 75 U.N.T.S. 287. According to the commentary, "[p]rotected persons must not in any circumstances be used as 'guinea pigs' for medical experiments." *Commentary on the Geneva Conventions of 12 August 1949: IV Geneva Convention Relative to the Protection of Civilian Persons in Time of War* 224 (Oscar Uhler & Henri Coursier eds., 1958). This commentary explains that the prohibition is directly related to the first principle of the Nuremberg Code since "[i]n prohibiting medical experiments on protected persons, the Diplomatic Conference wished to abolish for ever the criminal practices from which thousands of persons suffered in the death camps of the [second] world war." The practices involved human medical experiments that were objectionable because they were nonconsensual. *See Brandt*, 2 Nuremberg Trials, at 183. The convention is legally-binding on 194 states that have ratified it without reservation to Article 32. *See* International Committee of the Red Cross, Geneva Conventions of 12 August 1949 State Parties, Signatories, Reservations and Declarations, http://www.icrc.org/ihl.nsf/WebSign?ReadForm&id=375&ps=P.

on the more than 160 States-Parties that have ratified the convention without reservation to the provision.[10] By its terms this prohibition is not limited to state actors; rather, it guarantees individuals the right to be free from nonconsensual medical experimentation by any entity—state actors, private actors, or state and private actors behaving in concert.

Its status as a norm that states conceive as legally binding-and therefore part of customary international law-is confirmed by Article 2 of the accord, which requires that "[e]ach State Party . . . undertake[] to respect and to ensure to all individuals within its territory and subject to its jurisdiction the rights recognized in the present Covenant." ICCPR art. 2(1). The international community's recognition in the ICCPR of its obligation to protect humans against nonconsensual medical experimentation, regardless of the source of the action, is powerful evidence of the prohibition's place in customary international law.

It is clear that, as the court mentioned in *Sosa*, the Universal Declaration of Human Rights and the ICCPR themselves could not establish the relevant, applicable rule of international law in that case. *Sosa*, 542 U.S. at 754. Nonetheless, the ICCPR, when viewed as a reaffirmation of the norm as articulated in the Nuremberg Code, is potent authority for the universal acceptance of the prohibition on nonconsensual medical experimentation. As we discuss below, *see infra* pp. 28–30, the fact that the prohibition on medical experimentation on humans without consent has been consciously embedded by Congress in our law and reaffirmed on numerous occasions by the FDA demonstrates that the United States government views the norm as the source of a binding legal obligation even though the United States has not ratified the ICCPR in full.[11]

In 1964, the World Medical Association adopted the Declaration of Helsinki, which enunciated standards for obtaining informed consent from human subjects. It provided that in clinical research combined with professional care, "[i]f at all possible, consistent with patient psychology, the doctor should obtain the patient's freely given consent after the patient has been given a full explanation," and that non-therapeutic clinical research on a person "cannot be undertaken without his

---

10 Although certain States-Parties to the ICCPR have made reservations or declarations with respect to Article 7's prohibition of torture and cruel, inhuman or degrading treatment or punishment, we are not aware of any similar qualification by a State-Party to the prohibition of medical or scientific experimentation without the free consent of human subjects. *See* Office of the United Nations High Commissioner for Human Rights, International Covenant on Civil and Political Rights, Declarations and Reservations, http://www2.ohchr.org/english/bodies/ratification/docs/DeclarationsReservationsICCPR.pdf.

11 *Khulumani* makes clear that treaties that the United States has neither signed nor ratified-let alone treaties like the ICCPR that the United States has signed but not ratified-may evidence a customary international law norm for ATS purposes where the treaty has been ratified widely and it is clear that the reason for the United States's failure to subscribe to the treaty was unrelated to the particular norm in question. *See Khulumani*, 504 F.3d at 276, 276 n.9 (Katzmann, J., concurring).

free consent, after he has been fully informed." World Med. Ass'n, *Declaration of Helsinki: Code of Ethics of the World Medical Association*, art. III(3a), G.A. Res. (1964), http://www.pubmedcentral.nih.gov/picrender.fcgi?artid=1816102&blobtype=pdf. The Declaration has since been amended five times. The informed consent provision now provides that "subjects must be volunteers and informed participants in the research project." Declaration of Helsinki, *supra*, at art. 20. The Declaration also requires that "[i]n any research on human beings, each potential subject must be adequately informed of the aims, methods, . . . anticipated benefits and potential risks of the study, and the discomfort it may entail" and that researchers "obtain the subject's freely-given informed consent, preferably in writing." *Id.* at art. 22.

Although the Declaration itself is non-binding, since the 1960s, it has spurred States to regulate human experimentation, often by incorporating its informed consent requirement into domestic laws or regulations. *See* Delon Human & Sev S. Fluss, The World Medical Association's Declaration of Helsinki: Historical and Contemporary Perspectives, 8–11 (July 24, 2001) (fifth draft), http://www.wma.net/e/ethicsunit/pdf/draft_historical_contemporary_perspectives.pdf (describing legal and regulatory developments in Australia, Belgium, Brazil, China, Israel, Japan, New Zealand, Norway, Switzerland, and the United States following the Declaration of Helsinki). Currently, the laws and regulations of at least eighty-four countries, including the United States, require the informed consent of human subjects in medical research.[12] That this conduct has been the subject of domestic legislation is not, of course, in and of itself proof of a norm. *See Flores*, 414 F.3d at 249. However, the incorporation of this norm into the laws of this country and this host of others is a powerful indication of the international acceptance of this norm as a binding legal obligation, where, as here, states have shown that the norm is of mutual concern by including it in a variety of international accords.

The history of the norm in United States law demonstrates that it has been firmly embedded for more than 45 years and—except for our dissenting colleague-its validity has never been seriously questioned by any court. Congress mandated patient-subject consent in drug research in 1962. Bassiouni et al., *supra*, at 1624 (citing 21 U.S.C. § 355(i) (1976)). In response, the FDA promulgated its first regulations requiring the informed consent of human subjects. Tellingly, the sources on which our government relied in outlawing non-consensual human medical experimentation were the Nuremberg Code and the Declaration of Helsinki, which suggests the government conceived of these sources' articulation of the norm as a binding legal obligation. Bassiouni et al., *supra*, at 1625–26 (citing 21 C.F.R.

12 The Department of Health and Human Services has compiled the laws, regulations, and guidelines governing human subjects research in eighty-four countries. See Office of Human Research Prot., Dep't of Health & Human Servs., International Compilation of Human Subject Research Protections (2008), http://www.hhs.gov/ohrp/international/HSPCompilation.pdf. It is uncontested that all of the countries identified in this compilation require informed consent to medical experimentation.

§ 310.102(h) (1980)).[13] Today, FDA regulations require informed consent to U.S. investigators' research, whether conducted domestically or in a foreign country, used to support applications for the approval of new drugs. *See* 21 C.F.R. §§ 50.20, 50.23–.25, 50.27, 312.20, 312.120 (2008); 45 C.F.R. §§ 46.111, 46.116–.117 (2008).

The importance that the United States government attributes to this norm is demonstrated by its willingness to use domestic law to coerce compliance with the norm throughout the world. United States law requires that, as a predicate to FDA approval of any new drug, both American and foreign sponsors of drug research involving clinical trials, whether conducted here or abroad, procure informed consent from human subjects. 21 C.F.R. §§ 312.20, 312.120 (2008); *see also* Dep't of Health & Human Servs., Office of Inspector Gen., The Globalization of Clinical Trials 5 (2001), http://www.oig.hhs.gov/oei/reports/oei-01-00-00190.pdf. Sponsors conducting research under an Investigational New Drug Application ("IND") are obligated to adhere to FDA regulations, which require informed consent. 21 C.F.R. § 312.20 (2008); The Globalization of Clinical Trials, *supra*, at 5. Prior to April 2008, sponsors conducting research under non-IND guidelines were obligated to adhere to the ethical principles of the 1989 version of the Declaration of Helsinki or the host country's regulations, whichever offered greater protection to the human subject. 21 C.F.R. § 312.120 (2007); The Globalization of Clinical Trials, *supra*, at 5. The April 2008 revisions to the non-IND guidelines reaffirmed the informed consent requirement. Human Subject Protection: Foreign Clinical Studies Not Conducted Under an *Investigational New Drug Application*, 73 Fed. Reg. 22,800, 22,801, 22,803, 22,804, 22,816 (Apr. 28, 2008) (codified at 21 C.F.R. pt. 312). Foreign clinical studies not conducted under an IND must now comply with the Good Clinical Practice guidelines ("GCP") promulgated by the *International Conference on Harmonisation of Technical Requirements for Registration of Pharmaceuticals for Human Use*, 62 Fed. Reg. 25,692 (May 9, 1997), which require informed consent to medical experimentation. 21 C.F.R. § 312.120 (2008).

---

13 The importance of informed consent to medical experimentation was reinforced with the passage of the National Research Act in 1974, which established the National Commission for the Protection of Human Subjects of Biomedical and Behavioral Research. *See* National Research Act, Pub. L. 93-348, 88 Stat. 342 (codified as amended in scattered sections of 42 U.S.C.). This body issued the *Belmont Report: Ethical Principles and Guidelines for the Protection of Human Subjects of Research* in 1979, which identifies basic ethical principles governing biomedical and behavioral research on human subjects and requires informed consent. Nat'l Comm'n for the Prot. of Human Subjects of Biomedical & Behavioral Research, The Belmont Report: Ethical Principles and Guidelines for the Protection of Human Subjects of Research, part C (1) (1979), *available* at http://ohsr.od.nih.gov/guidelines/belmont.html#goc. Soon afterwards, the Department of Health, Education and Welfare (later renamed the Department of Health and Human Services) promulgated stricter regulations for ensuring informed consent in research conducted or supported by federal departments or agencies. *See* U.S. Dep't of Health & Human Servs., Guidelines for the Conduct of Research Involving Human Subjects at the National Institutes of Health, 17–18 (5th ed. 2004), http://ohsr.od.nih.gov/guidelines/GrayBooklet82404.pdf (referencing 45 C.F.R. pt. 46, subpt. A (1981)).

Additional international law sources support the norm's status as customary international law. The European Union embraced the norm prohibiting nonconsensual medical experimentation through a 2001 Directive passed by the European Parliament and the Council of the European Union. The Directive accepted the informed consent principles of the 1996 version of the Declaration of Helsinki. Council Directive 2001/20/EC, preamble (2), 2001 O.J. (L 121) 37 (EC) [hereinafter 2001 Clinical Trial Directive]. It also required member States to adopt rules protecting individuals incapable of giving informed consent and permitting clinical trials only where "the trial subject or, when the person is not able to give informed consent, his legal representative has given his written consent after being informed of the nature, significance, implications and risks of the clinical trial." *Id.* at art. (1), (2)(d). The Directive further required all member States to implement by 2004 domestic laws, regulations, and administrative provisions to comply with its informed consent requirements. *Id.* at art. 22(1).

Since 1997, thirty-four member States of the Council of Europe have also signed the Convention on Human Rights and Biomedicine, a binding convention and a source of customary international law. Convention for the Protection of Human Rights and Dignity of the Human Being with regard to the Application of Biology and Medicine: Convention on Human Rights and Biomedicine, art. 5, 15–16, *opened for signature* Apr. 4, 1997, E.T.S. No. 164, http://conventions.coe.int/Treaty/en/Treaties/html/164.htm [hereinafter Convention on Human Rights and Biomedicine]; Convention on Human Rights and Biomedicine, Chart of Signatures and Ratifications as of Aug. 8, 2008, http://conventions.coe.int/Treaty/Commun/ChercheSig.asp?NT=164&CM=8&DF=8/8/2008&CL=ENG. It provides that an "intervention in the health field may only be carried out after the person concerned has given free and informed consent to it" and that the informed consent of human subjects is required for their involvement in medical research. Convention on Human Rights and Biomedicine, *supra*, at art. 5.[14] In 2005, the General Conference of the United Nations Educational, Scientific and Cultural Organization (UNESCO) adopted the Universal Declaration on Bioethics and Human Rights, which requires "the prior, free, express and informed consent of the person concerned" for research-oriented treatments. Universal Declaration on Bioethics and Human Rights, UNESCO Gen. Conf. Res., at art. 6, 33rd Sess., 33 C/Resolution 36, (Oct. 19, 2005).

This history illustrates that from its origins with the trial of the Nazi doctors at Nuremburg through its evolution in international conventions, agreements, declarations, and domestic laws and regulations, the norm prohibiting nonconsensual medical experimentation on human subjects has become firmly embedded and has

---

14 States-Parties to the Convention on Human Rights and Biomedicine are also required to afford "appropriate judicial protection" to prevent or end infringements of the rights protected by the Convention, including the right to informed consent to medical experimentation. Convention on Human Rights and Biomedicine, *supra*, at art. 23.

secured universal acceptance in the community of nations. Unlike our dissenting colleague's customary international law analysis, which essentially rests on the mistaken assumption that ratified international treaties are the only valid sources of customary international law for ATS purposes, *see* Dissent at 19–20, we reach this conclusion as a result of our review of the multiplicity of sources—including international conventions, whether general or particular, and international custom as identified through international agreements, declarations and a consistent pattern of action by national law-making authorities-that our precedent requires us to examine for the purpose of determining the existence of a norm of customary international law. Our dissenting colleague's reasoning fails to engage the incompatibility of nonconsensual human testing with key sources of customary international law identified in Article 38 of the ICJ's statute, most importantly international custom, as evidence of a general practice accepted as law, as well as the general principles of law recognized by civilized nations. *See supra* p. 15.

ii. Specificity

Sosa requires that we recognize causes of action only to enforce those customary international law norms that are no "less definite [in] content . . . than the historical paradigms familiar when [the ATS] was enacted." *Sosa*, 542 U.S. at 732. The norm prohibiting nonconsensual medical experimentation on human subjects meets this requirement. In *United States v. Smith*, 18 U.S. (5 Wheat) 153, 159–61, 5 L. Ed. 57 (1820), Justice Story found that "whatever may be the diversity of definitions, . . . all writers concur, in holding, that robbery or forcible depredations upon the sea . . . is piracy." *Id.* at 161. We have little trouble concluding that a norm forbidding nonconsensual human medical experimentation is every bit as concrete—indeed even more so—than the norm prohibiting piracy that Story describes, or interference with the right of safe conducts and the rights of ambassadors, which together are the paradigmatic norms identified in *Sosa. Id.* at 724. The Nuremberg Code, Article 7 of the ICCPR, the Declaration of Helsinki, the Convention on Human Rights and Biomedicine, the Universal Declaration on Bioethics and Human Rights, the 2001 Clinical Trial Directive, and the domestic laws of at least eighty-four States all uniformly and unmistakably prohibit medical experiments on human beings without their consent, thereby providing concrete content for the norm.[15] The appellants allege that Pfizer knowingly and purposefully conducted such experiments on a large scale. Whatever uncertainty may exist at the margin is

---

15 At the fringe, disagreement exists over certain aspects of informed consent including, for example, the way to best secure consent from illiterate or otherwise vulnerable populations, *see, e.g.*, Daniel W. Fitzgerald et al., *Comprehension During Informed Consent in a Less-Developed Country*, 360 The Lancet 1301, 1301–02 (2002), and whether informed consent is possible in double-blind experiments in which some subjects are given placebos, *see, e.g.*, Timothy S. Jost, *The Globalization of Health Law: The Case of Permissibility of Placebo-Based Research*, 26 Am. J. L. & Med. 175, 183–86 (2000). These debates do not disturb the specificity of the basic norm at issue or the unanimity of world opinion against medical experimentation on human subjects without their consent.

irrelevant here because appellants allege a complete failure on the part of Pfizer and the Nigerian government to inform appellants of the existence of the Trovan experiments. These allegations, if true, implicate Pfizer and the Nigerian government in conduct that is at the core of any reasonable iteration of the prohibition against involuntary medical experimentation. While the prohibition in question applies to the testing of drugs without the consent of human subjects on the scale Pfizer allegedly conducted, we do not suggest that it would extend to instances of routine or isolated failures by medical professionals to obtain informed consent, such as those arising from simple negligence. The allegations in the complaints involve anything but a doctor's routine or erroneous failure to obtain such consent from his patient.

iii. Mutual Concern

Customary international law proscribes only transgressions that are of "mutual" concern to States—"those involving States' actions performed . . . towards or with regard to the other." *Flores*, 414 F.3d at 249 (differentiating matters of "mutual" concern from those of "several" concern, in which "States are separately and independently interested"). Conduct that States have prohibited through domestic legislation is also actionable under the ATS as a violation of customary international law when nations of the world have demonstrated "by means of express international accords" that the wrong is of mutual concern. *Filartiga*, 630 F.2d at 888. An important, but not exclusive, component of this test is a showing that the conduct in question is "capable of impairing international peace and security." *Flores*, 414 F.3d at 249. Appellants have made both of these showings.

As we have seen, States throughout the world have entered into two express and binding international agreements prohibiting nonconsensual medical experimentation: the ICCPR and the Convention on Human Rights and Biomedicine. The entry of over 160 States into these agreements and the European Union's passage of the 2001 Clinical Trial Directive demonstrates that States have not only acted independently to outlaw large-scale, nonconsensual drug testing on humans, but they have also acted in concert to do so. In other words, acting out of a sense of mutual concern, "the nations [of the world] have made it their business, both through international accords and unilateral action," to demonstrate their intention to eliminate conduct of the type alleged in the complaints. *Filartiga*, 630 F.2d at 889.

The administration of drug trials without informed consent on the scale alleged in the complaints poses a real threat to international peace and security. Over the last two decades, pharmaceutical companies in industrialized countries have looked to poorer, developing countries as sites for the medical research essential to the development of new drugs. *See* James V. Lavery, *Putting International Research Ethics Guidelines to Work for the Benefit of Developing Countries*, 4 Yale J. Health Pol'y L. & Ethics 319, 320–21 (2004); The Globalization of Clinical Trials, *supra*, at 8.[16] Pharmaceutical companies recognize the potential benefits of drug trials to poor nations and have sought to promote access to medicines and health care in underserved populations through philanthropy and partnership with governments and NGOs. *See, e.g.*, PhRMA, Press Releases: Worldwide Pharmaceutical Industry Launches Global Health Progress Initiative to Expand Efforts to Improve Health in Developing Countries (April 16, 2008), http://www.phrma.org/news_room/press_releases/global_health_progress_initiative_launched_to_improve_health_in_developing_countries/ (describing initiative by worldwide pharmaceutical industry to "further access to medicines; build capacity of health workers in developing nations; advocate for global action to address health challenges; and continue R&D to develop new tools to fight diseases that plague the developing world"); PhRMA, Profile2008: Pharmaceutical Industry 42 (2008), http://www.phrma.org/files/2008%20Profile.pdf (describing contributions by American pharmaceutical companies to the promotion of global access to medicines and health care). This trend offers the possibility of enormous health benefits for the world community. Life-saving drugs can potentially be developed more quickly and cheaply, and developing countries may be given access to cutting edge medicines and treatments to assist underresourced and understaffed public health systems, which grapple with life-threatening diseases afflicting their populations.[17]

The success of these efforts promises to play a major role in reducing the cross-border spread of contagious diseases, which is a significant threat to international peace and stability. The administration of drug trials without informed consent on the scale alleged in the complaints directly threatens these efforts because such conduct fosters distrust and resistance to international drug trials, cutting edge medical innovation, and critical international public health initiatives in which

---

16 In the United States, for example, the number of foreign clinical investigators conducting drug research under an IND increased sixteen-fold in the 1990s. Globalization of Clinical Trials, *supra*, at 6.

17 These benefits are well acknowledged. *See, e.g.*, Remigius N. Nwabueze, *Ethical Review of Research Involving Human Subjects in Nigeria: Legal and Policy Issues*, 14 Ind. Int'l & Comp. L. Rev. 87, 102 (2003) (recognizing that clinical trials at times provide the only access to innovative and effective health care in developing countries); David Wendler, et al., *The Standard of Care Debate: Can Research in Developing Countries Be Both Ethical and Responsive to those Countries' Health Needs?*, 94 Am. J. Pub. Health 923, 923 (2004) (noting dramatic inequalities in health care world-wide and the potential of drug research to better care for the world's poor).

Doctors Without Borders, the WHO, and other international health organizations, for example, have called for increased corporate research interest in developing countries. Sonia Shah, *Globalizing Clinical Research*, The Nation, June 13, 2002, at 3, http://www.thenation.com/doc/20020701/shah. Ruth Faden, a bioethicist at Johns Hopkins, stated, "What we need, if anything, is more health research in the developing world, not less." *Id.* An HIV researcher observed that even when companies test drugs geared for patients in the developed world through trials in developing countries, the testing "brings benefits to the patients. They get special attention and potential therapy." *Id.*

pharmaceutical companies play a key role. This case itself supplies an exceptionally good illustration of why this is so. The Associated Press reported that the Trovan trials in Kano apparently engendered such distrust in the local population that it was a factor contributing to an eleven month-long, local boycott of a polio vaccination campaign in 2004, which impeded international and national efforts to vaccinate the population against a polio outbreak with catastrophic results.[18] According to the World Health Organization, polio originating in Nigeria triggered a major international outbreak of the disease between 2003 and 2006, causing it to spread across west, central, and the Horn of Africa and the Middle East, and to re-infect twenty previously polio-free countries.[19]

The administration of drug trials without informed consent also poses threats to national security by impairing our relations with other countries. Seven of the world's twelve largest pharmaceutical manufacturers—a group that includes Pfizer—are American companies. *Global 500*, Fortune, July 21, 2008, http://money.cnn.com/magazines/fortune/global500/2008/industries/21/index.html.

Consequently, American companies are likely to be sponsors of medical experiments on human subjects abroad.[20] As this case illustrates, the failure to secure consent for human experimentation has the potential to generate substantial anti-American animus and hostility. Unsurprisingly, as noted above, *see supra* p. 30, our government actively attempts to prevent this practice in foreign countries. For example, federal law requires that data generated from testing on human subjects abroad that is used to seek regulatory approval for a given drug must, at minimum,

---

18 Salisu Rabiu, *Pfizer Asks Nigeria Court to Dismiss Case*, The Associated Press, July 4, 2007, http://origin.foxnews.com/printer_friendly_wires/2007Jul04/0,4675,NigeriaPfizer,00.html (reporting that the boycott of the Kano polio vaccination program is believed to have "set back global eradication" of polio and to have "caus[ed] an outbreak that spread the disease across Africa and into the Middle East"). The boycott also impaired the efforts of American pharmaceutical companies to contribute to polio eradication by donating over 130 million doses of polio vaccine to sixteen African countries since 1997. PhRMA, Global Partnerships: Humanitarian Programs of the Pharmaceutical Industry in Developing Nations 4 (2004), http://www.phrma.org/files/Global_Partnerships_2004.pdf.

19 World Health Organization, Poliomyelitis in Nigeria and West/Central Africa, June 18, 2008, http://www.who.int/csr/don/2008_06_18/en/.

Other examples of the link between the cross-border spread of contagious disease and international peace and stability come to mind, such as the outbreak of anti-U.S. riots in South Korea as a result of fear that imported American beef will spread mad cow disease to that country. *See* Choe Sang-Hun, *South Korea Lifts Ban on U.S. Beef*, New York Times, June 26, 2008, http://www.nytimes.com/2008/06/26/world/asia/26korea.html.

20 FDA data suggests the industry trend is to use foreign research to support applications for new drug approvals in the United States. Since 1990 there has been an explosion in the number of foreign clinical investigators conducting drug research that sponsors use for this purpose. In 1990, there were 271 foreign investigators conducting research in 28 countries in the FDA database. By 1999, the number had grown to 4,458 investigators working in 79 countries. Globalization of Clinical Trials, *supra*, at i.

be the result of testing conducted consistent with the requirements of informed consent. Consequently, the US government denies access to the US market for any new drug unless the drug's research data is generated in a manner consistent with the customary international law norm prohibiting drug trials on human subjects without informed consent.

For these reasons, we hold that the appellants have pled facts sufficient to state a cause of action under the ATS for a violation of the norm of customary international law prohibiting medical experimentation on human subjects without their consent. In such an instance, ATS jurisdiction exists over plaintiffs' claims. The district court determined that the norm existed, but concluded that because no single source recognizing the norm was legally binding on the United States and created a private cause of action, it could not infer such a right under the ATS. Presumably, on this basis, it simultaneously held that there was no subject matter jurisdiction over plaintiffs' claims. Under *Sosa*, this approach was not correct. *Sosa* makes clear that the critical inquiry is whether the variety of sources that we are required to consult establishes a customary international law norm that is sufficiently specific, universally accepted, and obligatory for courts to recognize a cause of action to enforce the norm. Nothing in *Sosa* suggests that this inquiry can be halted if some of the sources of international law giving rise to the norm are found not to be binding or not to explicitly authorize a cause of action.

We believe that the issues raised by this appeal regarding customary international law are framed by our analysis and by that of our dissenting colleague. He contends that our analysis is created from "whole cloth." Dissent at 1. We believe that his approach to customary international law is unselfconsciously reactionary and static. The approach does not accommodate itself to the normative world that, by their commitments and conduct over the past fifty years, states—including our own—have shown they believe to exist.

B. State Action

A private individual will be held liable under the ATS if he "acted in concert with" the state, i.e., "under color of law." *Kadic*, 70 F.3d at 245. In making this determination, courts look to the standards developed for finding state action in claims brought under 42 U.S.C. § 1983. *Id.* Under § 1983, state action may be found when "there is such a 'close nexus between the State and the challenged action' that seemingly private behavior 'may be fairly treated as that of the State itself.'" *Brentwood Acad. v. Tenn. Secondary Sch. Athletic Ass'n,* 531 U.S. 288, 295, 121 S. Ct. 924, 148 L. Ed. 2d 807 (2001) (quoting *Jackson v. Metropolitan Edison Co.,* 419 U.S. 345, 351, 95 S. Ct. 449, 42 L. Ed. 2d 477 (1974)). That nexus may exist "where a private actor has operated as a willful participant in joint activity with the State or its agents," *Gorman-Bakos v. Cornell Coop. Extension of Schenectady County*, 252 F.3d 545, 551–52 (2d Cir. 2001) (quoting *Loce v. Time Warner Entertainment Advance/ Newhouse Partnership*, 191 F.3d 256, 266 (2d Cir. 1999)), or "acts together with state officials or with significant state aid," *Kadic*, 70 F.3d at 245. Pfizer meets this test.

The Appellants have alleged that the Nigerian government was involved in all stages of the Kano test and participated in the conduct that violated international law. They allege that the Nigerian government provided a letter of request to the FDA to authorize the export of Trovan, arranged for Pfizer's accommodations in Kano, and facilitated the nonconsensual testing in Nigeria's IDH in Kano. Despite overcrowding due to concurrent epidemics, the Nigerian government extended the exclusive use of two hospital wards to Pfizer, providing Pfizer with control over scarce public resources and the use of the hospital's staff and facilities to conduct the Kano test, to the exclusion of MSF.

The unlawful conduct is alleged to have occurred in a Nigerian facility with the assistance of the Nigerian government and government officials and/or employees from the IDH and Aminu Kano Teaching Hospital. Pfizer's research team in Kano was comprised of three American physicians, Dr. Abdulhamid Isa Dutse (a physician in the Aminu Kano Teaching Hospital), and three other Nigerian doctors. The American and Nigerian members of Pfizer's team allegedly jointly administered the Kano test. Finally, in addition to assisting with the Kano test, Nigerian officials are alleged to have conspired to cover up the violations by silencing Nigerian physicians critical of the test and by back-dating an "approval letter" that the FDA and international protocol required to be provided prior to conducting the medical experiment. In addition to these allegations, the Adamu plaintiffs explicitly allege that the Nigerian government "was intimately involved and contributed, aided, assisted and facilitated Pfizer's efforts to conduct the Trovan test," "acted in concert with Pfizer," and, according to a Nigerian physician involved in the Trovan experimentation, appeared to "back[]" the testing. At the pleading stage, these contentions meet the state action test because they adequately allege that the violations occurred as the result of concerted action between Pfizer and the Nigerian government.

II. Forum Non Conveniens

As an alternative to dismissal for failure to state a claim under the ATS, the district court dismissed the actions on the ground of *forum non conveniens*. Appellants raised this issue on appeal. Ordinarily, we review a *forum non conveniens* dismissal for abuse of discretion. *Norex Petroleum Ltd. v. Access Indus., Inc.*, 416 F.3d 146, 153 (2d Cir. 2005). Since filing this appeal, however, Pfizer has notified the Court that in light of recent developments, in particular the initiation of proceedings by the federal government of Nigeria and the state of Kano against Pfizer and certain of its employees, it would not seek affirmance of the judgment on the basis of *forum non conveniens*. The appellants agreed and also requested that the issue be remanded. We accede to this request.

Although we are not now called upon definitively to review the district court's application of *forum non conveniens*, in view of the frequency with which this issue has arisen and remained unsettled in this case, we offer additional guidance to assist the parties and the district court. The three-step analysis set forth in

Iragorri v. United Techs. Corp., 274 F.3d 65, 71–75 (2d Cir. 2001) (en banc), applies. In this litigation, the second step of the analysis, which requires the district court to consider the adequacy of the alternative forum, is pivotal. Dismissal is not appropriate if an adequate and presently available alternative forum does not exist. *Norex*, 416 F.3d at 159. A forum in which defendants are amenable to service of process and which permits litigation of the dispute is generally adequate. *Id.* at 157. Such a forum may nevertheless be inadequate if it does not permit the reasonably prompt adjudication of a dispute, if the forum is not presently available, or if the forum provides a remedy so clearly unsatisfactory or inadequate that it is tantamount to no remedy at all. *Piper Aircraft Co. v. Reyno*, 454 U.S. 235, 254–55, 102 S. Ct. 252, 70 L. Ed. 2d 419 & n.22 (1981); *USHA (India), Ltd. v. Honeywell Int'l, Inc.*, 421 F.3d 129, 136 (2d Cir. 2005); *Norex*, 416 F.3d at 160.

The defendant bears the burden of establishing that a presently available and adequate alternative forum exists, and that the balance of private and public interest factors tilts heavily in favor of the alternative forum. *USHA (India), Ltd.*, 421 F.3d at 135*; PT United Can Co. v. Crown Cork & Seal Co., Inc.*, 138 F.3d 65, 74 (2d Cir. 1998). Absent a showing of inadequacy by a plaintiff, "considerations of comity preclude a court from adversely judging the quality of a foreign justice system." *PT United Can Co.*, 138 F.3d at 73. Accordingly, while the plaintiff bears the initial burden of producing evidence of corruption, delay or lack of due process in the foreign forum, the defendant bears the ultimate burden of persuasion as to the adequacy of the forum. *See, e.g., Norex*, 416 F.3d at 159–160.

When the district court granted Pfizer's motion, it identified the pivotal issue as whether the plaintiffs produced sufficient evidence to show that Nigeria is an inadequate alternative forum. *Abdullahi III*, 2005 U.S. Dist. LEXIS 16126, 2005 WL 1870811, at *15. Having found that they had not, it concluded that Nigeria was an adequate forum. 2005 U.S. Dist. LEXIS 16126, [WL] at *16–18. In so doing, the district court omitted an analysis of whether Pfizer discharged its burden of persuading the court as to the adequacy and present availability of the Nigerian forum and improperly placed on plaintiffs the burden of proving that the alternative forum is inadequate. *Cf. DiRienzo v. Philip Servs. Corp.*, 294 F.3d 21, 30 (2d Cir. 2002) (holding that it is error not "to hold defendants to their burden of proof" of the *Gilbert* factors). On remand, the district court will have an opportunity to reassess this issue, as well as the relationship between Fed. R. Civ. P. 44.1 and the Federal Rules of Evidence.

III. Choice of Law

The district court dismissed the *Adamu* plaintiffs' claims under the Connecticut Unfair Trade Practices Act and the Connecticut Products Liability Act on the ground that Connecticut choice of law principles applied and called for the application of Nigerian law. *Adamu*, 399 F. Supp. 2d at 501–03. "We review the district court's choice of law *de novo*." *Fin. One Pub. Co. Ltd. v. Lehman Bros. Special Fin., Inc.*, 414 F.3d 325, 331 (2d Cir. 2005).

The district court correctly determined that Connecticut choice-of-law rules applied because it was obligated to apply the state law that would have been applicable if the case had not been transferred from Connecticut to New York. *See Van Dusen v. Barrack*, 376 U.S. 612, 639, 84 S. Ct. 805, 11 L. Ed. 2d 945 (1964). Under Connecticut law, *lex loci delicti*, "the doctrine that the substantive rights and obligations arising out of a tort controversy are determined by the law of the place of injury," typically applies. *O'Connor v. O'Connor*, 201 Conn. 632, 637, 519 A.2d 13 (1986). *Lex loci delicti* would require the application of Nigerian law because the *Adamu* plaintiffs' injuries are alleged to have occurred there. Connecticut, however, has conspicuously retreated from a rigid application of the doctrine. The Connecticut Supreme Court held that *lex loci delicti* does not apply to a tort claim when doing so would undermine expectations of the parties or an important state policy, produce an arbitrary and irrational result, or where "reason and justice" counsel for the application of a different principle. *Id.* at 637, 648, 650. In such cases, Connecticut courts are required to apply the "most significant relationship" analysis set forth in the *Restatement (Second) of Conflict of Laws* §§ 6 & 145 (1971) [hereinafter Restatement (Second)]. *O'Connor*, 201 Conn. at 649–50.

Section 145 (1) of the Restatement provides that "[t]he rights and liabilities of the parties with respect to an issue in tort are determined by the local law of the state which, with respect to that issue, has the most significant relationship to the occurrence and the parties under the principles stated in § 6." *Restatement (Second)* § 145(1). Section 6(2), in turn, provides that where a state is not guided by a statutory directive on choice of law,

> the factors relevant to the choice of the applicable rule of law include
>
> (a) the needs of the interstate and international systems,
>
> (b) the relevant policies of the forum,
>
> (c) the relevant policies of other interested states and the relative interests of those states in the determination of the particular issue,
>
> (d) the protection of justified expectations,
>
> (e) the basic policies underlying the particular field of law,
>
> (f) certainty, predictability and uniformity of result, and
>
> (g) ease in the determination and application of the law to be applied.

Restatement (Second) § 6(2). The Connecticut Supreme Court has determined that Section 145(2) provides courts with guidance regarding the evaluation of the policy choices set out in Sections 145(1) and 6(2). *O'Connor*, 201 Conn. at 652. Section 145(2) assists with the application of the principles of Section 6 to tort cases by calling for consideration of:

> (a) the place where the injury occurred,
>
> (b) the place where the conduct causing the injury occurred,

(c) the domicil, residence, nationality, place of incorporation and place of business of the parties, and

(d) the place where the relationship, if any, between the parties is centered.

Restatement (Second) § 145(2). These factors are "to be evaluated according to their relative importance with respect to the particular issue." *Id.*

The district court correctly decided to apply Sections 6 and 145 of the Restatement rather than *lex loci delicti*. It applied the factors in Section 145(2) to determine whether Connecticut or Nigeria has the most significant relationship to the conduct at issue, which it identified as "Pfizer's failure to inform the children or their parents about the potential problems with Trovan, and the administration of Trovan and low dosage of Ceftriaxone." *Adamu*, 399 F. Supp. 2d at 503 (citations omitted). It reasoned that "the Nigerian contacts to this litigation are stronger than Connecticut's" and noted in particular that both the plaintiffs' injuries and Pfizer's alleged conduct occurred in Nigeria, that the plaintiffs were Nigerian residents, and that "the parties' relationship is centered" in Nigeria. *Id.* It determined that most of the factors of Section 145(2) point toward applying Nigerian law and that the "sole basis" for the applicability of Connecticut law was that "Pfizer performed research and development with respect to Trovan and planned the experiment in Connecticut." *Id.* For these reasons, it concluded that Nigeria's interests were superior and that its law should apply. *Id.*

Although the district court correctly identified some of the pertinent factors, it ultimately erred in its application of the "most significant relationship" test because it did not factor into its Section 145(2) analysis the integral factors set out in Section 6(2). It did not, for example, discuss "the relevant policies of the forum" or "the relevant policies of other interested states and the relative interests of those states in the determination of the particular issue." Restatement (Second) § 6(2)(b)–(c). Nor did it analyze what "justified expectations" existed that could have prompted Pfizer reasonably to believe that its conduct in Connecticut would not expose it to Connecticut law, or how Pfizer would have been disadvantaged by litigating these claims in Connecticut. *Id.* § 6(2)(d). Finally, the district court did not evaluate its own ability to determine and apply Connecticut, as opposed to Nigerian, law. *Id.* § 6(2)(g). For these reasons, we vacate the dismissal of the state law claims and remand to the district court for further consideration.

CONCLUSION

For the foregoing reasons, we REVERSE the judgments of the district court and REMAND for further proceedings.

DISSENT

WESLEY, *Circuit Judge*, dissenting:

The majority has undertaken to define a "firmly established" norm of international law, heretofore unrecognized by any American court or treaty obligation, on the basis of materials inadequate for the task. In deviating from our settled case law, the majority *identifies* no norm of customary international law, it creates a new norm out of whole cloth. Because the majority's analysis misconstrues—rather than vindicates—customary international law, I respectfully dissent.

Proceeding with "extraordinary care and restraint," *Flores v. S. Peru Copper Corp.,* 414 F.3d 233, 248 (2d Cir. 2003), this Court has upheld jurisdiction under the Alien Tort Statute, 28 U.S.C. § 1350 ("ATS"), in only a handful of cases alleging violations of the most firmly established international law norms, *see Kadic v. Karadzic*, 70 F.3d 232, 241–43 (2d Cir. 1995) (genocide and war crimes); *Amerada Hess Shipping Corp. v. Argentine Republic,* 830 F.2d 421, 426 (2d Cir. 1987), *rev'd on other grounds*, 488 U.S. 428, 109 S. Ct. 683, 102 L. Ed. 2d 818 (1989) (free passage of neutral ship in international waters); *Filartiga v. Pena-Irala*, 630 F.2d 876, 878 (2d Cir. 1980) (state-administered torture). In *Sosa v. Alvarez-Machain*, the Supreme Court identified three such "paradigmatic" norms, namely "violation of safe conducts, infringement of the rights of ambassadors, and piracy." 542 U.S. 692, 724, 124 S. Ct. 2739, 159 L. Ed. 2d 718 (2004). Rather than declare that list exhaustive for purposes of the ATS, the Court held that "any claim based on the present-day law of nations [must] rest on a norm of international character accepted by the civilized world and defined with a specificity comparable to the features of the 18th-century paradigms we have recognized." *Id.* at 725. Accordingly, we are charged with "vigilant doorkeeping" when reviewing ATS claims to ensure that they rest on "a narrow class of international norms" comparable to the paradigms identified by the Supreme Court. *Id.* at 729.

The majority identifies three criteria that must be satisfied before a violation of international law can be actionable under the ATS: that the norm is (1) specific and definable, (2) universally adhered to out of a sense of legal obligation, and (3) a matter of mutual concern, namely a matter "involving States' actions performed towards or with regard to the other." *Flores*, 414 F.3d at 249 (internal quotation and alterations omitted). I agree with the methodology used by the majority to determine whether a norm falls within the jurisdictional grant of the ATS, but I do not agree with their conclusion that a norm against non-consensual medical experimentation on humans by private actors is (1) universal and obligatory or (2) a matter of mutual concern.

The majority relies on eight sources of customary international law to support its determination that a norm against non-consensual medical experimentation on humans by private actors is universal and obligatory. However, this evidence falls far short of the quantum necessary to establish the existence of such a norm: (1) the

International Covenant on Civil and Political Rights has been described by the Supreme Court as a "well-known international agreement[] that despite [its] moral authority, ha[s] little utility," in defining international obligations, *Sosa*, 542 U.S. at 734, and moreover, it does not apply to private actors, such as the Defendant in this action; (2) the Council of Europe's Convention on Human Rights and Biomedicine—a regional convention—was not ratified by the most influential nations in the region, such as France, Germany, Italy, the Netherlands, Russia and the United Kingdom, and it was promulgated on April 4, 1997, one year *after* the conduct at issue in this litigation; (3) the UNESCO Universal Declaration of Bioethics and Human Rights of 2005 and (4) the European Parliament Clinical Trial Directive of 2001 both also post-date the relevant time period by several years; (5) the Declaration of Helsinki issued by the World Medical Association, a private entity, and (6) the International Ethical Guidelines for Research Involving Human Subjects promulgated by the Council for International Organizations for Medical Sciences, another private entity, "express[] the sensibilities and the asserted aspirations and demands of some countries or organizations" but are not "statements of universally-recognized legal obligations," *Flores*, 414 F.3d at 262; (7) states' domestic laws, which, unsupported by express international accords, are not "significant or relevant for purposes of customary international law," *id.* at 249; and (8) the so-called Nuremberg Code, a statement of principles that accompanied a criminal verdict, possesses at best "subsidiary" value as a judicial decision, Statute of the International Court of Justice art. 38, June 26, 1945, 59 Stat. 1031, 33 U.N.T.S. 993 ("ICJ Statute"). Taken together, this evidence falls short of charting the existence of a universal and obligatory international norm actionable against non-government actors under the ATS.[1]

In support of its determination that non-consensual medical experimentation by private actors is a matter of mutual concern, the majority reasons that non-consensual medical experiments breed distrust of medical interventions and thereby accelerate the spread of infectious diseases across international borders. It is not enough, however, that tortious conduct could create some sort of international consequence. In order for conduct to be a matter of mutual concern, it must "threaten[] serious consequences in international affairs." *Sosa*, 542 U.S. at 715. Such is the case when an ambassador is assaulted, for example, because the assault "impinge[s] upon the sovereignty of the foreign nation and if not adequately redressed could rise to an issue of war." *Id.* Non-consensual medical experimentation by private actors simply does not present the same grave risk of serious consequences in international affairs and is therefore not a matter of mutual concern.

---

1 Even if we were to conclude that such a norm applied to state actors and that private entities could be held liable if they act under color of law, Plaintiffs have not pleaded sufficient state involvement to impose liability on Pfizer under that theory. *See* Part III *infra*.

For these reasons, I conclude that non-consensual medical experimentation by private actors, though deplorable, is not actionable under international law and would therefore affirm the district court's dismissal of Plaintiffs' complaints.

DISCUSSION

I. Universal and Legally Obligatory Adherence

In order for a principle to become a norm of customary international law, states must universally abide by it out of a sense of legal obligation, and not merely aspiration. *See Flores*, 414 F.3d at 248. It might seem obvious, but before one can determine whether a principle is universally followed, one must define the principle in question. Like domestic law, international law is not a monolith—a unitary set of rules applying indiscriminately to all actors that come within its reach. To the contrary, international law consists of rules that govern only states, rules that apply to private parties—individuals and corporations—and other rules that regulate both evenhandedly. *See, e.g., Restatement (Third) of Foreign Relations of the United States* § 101 (1987) ("Restatement (Third)"). As a result, the Supreme Court has required courts deciding whether a principle is a customary international law norm to consider "whether international law extends the scope of liability for a violation of a given norm to the perpetrator being sued, if the defendant is a private actor such as a corporation or individual." *Sosa*, 542 U.S. at 732 n.20; *see also id.* at 760 (Breyer, J., concurring) ("The norm must extend liability to the type of perpetrator (*e.g.*, a private actor) the plaintiff seeks to sue.").

The majority lists the norm at issue here as the prohibition of "medical experimentation on non-consenting human subjects," Maj. Op. at 15, and proceeds to analyze that norm without regard to the alleged violator, *see id.* at 15–40. Put another way, the majority's analysis would be no different if Plaintiffs had sued the Nigerian government, instead of, or in addition to, Pfizer. Such a broad, simplified definition ignores the clear admonitions of the Supreme Court—and conflicts with prior decisions of this Court—that a customary international law norm cannot be divorced from the identity of its violator. The majority's analysis omits this critical consideration. As a result, the majority opinion presents only half of the equation. To my mind, the majority should have asked whether customary international law prohibits *private actors* from medical experimentation on non-consenting human subjects. That question must be answered in the negative.

A. The Majority's Sources of Customary International Law

In *Flores*, we explained some of the difficulties inherent in determining what offenses violate customary international law:

> Customary international law is discerned from myriad decisions made in numerous and varied international and domestic arenas. Furthermore, the relevant evidence of customary international law is widely dispersed and generally unfamiliar to lawyers and judges. These difficulties are compounded by the fact that customary international law . . . does not stem from any single, definitive, readily-identifiable source.

414 F.3d at 247–48. We have consistently looked to the ICJ Statute as the starting point for determining the proper sources of international law. *See, e.g., id.* at 250–51; *United States v. Yousef,* 327 F.3d 56, 100–03 (2d Cir. 2003). That statute lists: (1) "international conventions, whether general or particular, establishing rules expressly recognized by the contesting states"; (2) "international custom, as evidence of general practice accepted as law"; (3) "the general principles of law recognized by civilized nations"; and, in certain circumstances (4) "judicial decisions and the teachings of the most highly qualified publicists of the various nations, as subsidiary means for the determination of rules of law." ICJ Statute art. 38.

The ability to pick and choose from this seemingly limitless menu of sources presents a real threat of "creative interpretation." *Flores*, 414 F.3d at 248; *see also Amerada Hess*, 830 F.2d at 429 (Kearse, J., dissenting). To mitigate this risk, and to prevent courts from becoming "roving commission[s]," *Flores*, 414 F.3d at 262, we have, in our cases, methodically assessed the weight and relative influence of not only each class of sources listed in the ICJ Statute, but many individual sources within each class. The near-infinite list of international law sources makes adherence to this precedent of paramount importance, for our analysis demonstrates that not every source of international law carries equal weight.

Instead of following and applying our framework, the majority substitutes in its place a compelling narrative. Over the course of only a few pages, the majority employs several sources that it believes demonstrate a customary norm against medical experimentation by non-state entities and weaves them together to reach its conclusion. *See* Maj. Op. at 15–35. Nowhere does the majority examine these sources in the context required by *Sosa*. The majority does not discuss the weight of these sources, how they collectively demonstrate a customary norm, or how evidence supporting that norm compares with our ATS precedent. Had they done so, I am hopeful that my colleagues would reach the same conclusion that I do—that medical experimentation by private actors, while reprehensible, is not actionable under international law.

1. Treaties & Conventions

In *Flores*, we noted that treaties are the strongest evidence of customary international law because they "create *legal obligations* akin to contractual obligations on the States parties to them." 414 F.3d at 256. "[W]e look primarily to the formal lawmaking and official actions of States . . . as evidence of the established practices of States." *Yousef*, 327 F.3d at 103. But not all treaties are equal. Although "[a]ll treaties that have been ratified by at least two States provide some evidence of the custom and practice of nations . . . a treaty will only constitute *sufficient proof* of a norm of customary international law if an overwhelming majority of States have ratified the treaty." *Flores*, 414 F.3d at 256. Moreover, the "evidentiary weight to be afforded to a given treaty varies greatly depending on (i) how many, and which, States have ratified the treaty, and (ii) the degree to which those

States actually implement and abide by the principles set forth in the treaty." *Id.* at 256–57. For instance, treaties ratified by the United States are of greater evidentiary value if they are either self-executing or executed through acts of Congress. *See, e.g., id. at 257; Khulumani v. Barclay Nat'l Bank Ltd.,* 504 F.3d 254, 284 (2d Cir. 2007) (Katzmann, J., concurring).

The majority relies primarily on two treaties.

a. International Covenant on Civil and Political Rights

The International Covenant on Civil and Political Rights, Dec. 9, 1966, S. Exec. Doc. E, 95-2, 999 U.N.T.S. 171, 6 I.L.M. 368 (ratified by the United States June 8, 1992) ("ICCPR") "guarantees a broad spectrum of civil and political rights to individuals within signatory nations." *United States v. Duarte-Acero*, 296 F.3d 1277, 1282 (11th Cir. 2002). One of those rights—to be free of non-consensual medical or scientific experimentation—is stated in Article 7.

The ICCPR is not appropriate evidence of customary international law for at least two reasons. First, the Supreme Court in Sosa explicitly described the ICCPR as a "well-known international agreement[] that, despite [its] moral authority, ha[s] *little utility* under the standard set out in this opinion," because the "United States ratified [it] on the express understanding that it was not self-executing and so did not itself create obligations enforceable in the federal courts." 542 U.S. at 734–35 (emphasis added).

Second, whatever limited weight the ICCPR has with regard to state action, it does nothing to show that a norm prohibiting involuntary medical experimentation applies to non-state entities. In citing its seemingly universal language, the majority overlooks the ICCPR's operative section, which requires that "[e]ach State Party . . . undertake[] to respect and to ensure to all individuals within its territory and subject to its jurisdiction the rights recognized in the present Covenant." ICCPR art. 2(1). Thus, despite its broad text, the ICCPR by its own terms, only governs "the relationship between a State and the individuals within the State's territory." *Duarte-Acero*, 296 F.3d at 1283. Because the ICCPR only creates obligations flowing from a state to persons within its territory, a non-state actor cannot be said to have violated it. Thus, the ICCPR was relevant in *Filartiga* (decided before the Supreme Court limited its utility), in the context of state-administered torture of one of its citizens in contravention of one of the rights guaranteed by states in the ICCPR. *See* 630 F.2d at 884. But whatever its evidentiary value had Plaintiffs sued the Nigerian government, the ICCPR clearly has none where the question is whether international law includes a norm actionable against a *private corporation.*

b. Convention on Human Rights and Biomedicine

The second treaty cited by the majority is the Convention on Human Rights and Biomedicine, Apr. 4, 1997, E.T.S. No. 164 (the "Convention"), promulgated by the Council of Europe. *See* Maj. Op. at 31–32. Articles 5[2] and 16[3] of the Convention require that the subject of scientific research give his or her informed consent, which may be withdrawn at any time.

The first problem with the majority's reliance on the Convention is that it is a regional agreement not signed by the most influential states in the region. Membership in the Council of Europe is limited to European states. *See* Statute of the Council of Europe, art. 4, May 5, 1949, E.T.S. No. 1. It is difficult to see how the Convention demonstrates the *universality* of the medical experimentation principle when its signatories are limited to one continent. The majority also notes that the Convention has been signed by thirty-four states, *see* Maj. Op. at 31, but overlooks that it has only been ratified by twenty-two, and a treaty only evidences the customs and practices of states that have ratified it. *Flores*, 414 F.3d at 256. Lastly, and perhaps more importantly, the Convention is lacking even as evidence of a European norm, since it has not been ratified by the more influential European states, including France, Germany, Italy, the Netherlands, Russia and the United Kingdom, and a treaty's evidentiary value increases along with the influence in international affairs of the states that have ratified it. *See id.* at 257; Convention on Human Rights and Biomedicine, Chart of Signatures and Ratifications as of December 23, 2008, http://conventions.coe.int/Treaty/Commun/ChercheSig.asp?NT=164&CM=8&DF=12/23/2008&CL=ENG ("Convention Ratifications Chart").

A second, more fundamental problem with the majority's reliance on the Convention is that it was promulgated *after* the conduct at issue here. I know of no authority for an international ex post facto definition of the law of nations by later signed treaties. *Cf. Vietnam Ass'n for Victims of Agent Orange v. Dow Chem. Co.,* 517 F.3d 104, 118 (2d Cir. 2008) ("The United States did not ratify the 1925 Geneva Protocol until 1975. Accordingly, the Protocol cannot be said to have constituted

---

2 Article 5—General rule

> An intervention in the health field may only be carried out after the person concerned has given free and informed consent to it. This person shall beforehand be given appropriate information as to the purpose and nature of the intervention as well as on its consequences and risks. The person concerned may freely withdraw consent at any time.

3 Article 16—Protection of persons undergoing research

> Research on a person may only be undertaken if all the following conditions are met:
>
> i. there is no alternative of comparable effectiveness to research on humans;
>
> ii. the risks which may be incurred by that person are not disproportionate to the potential benefits of the research;
>
> iii. the research project has been approved by the competent body after independent examination of its scientific merit, including assessment of the importance of the aim of the research, and multidisciplinary review of its ethical acceptability;
>
> iv. the persons undergoing research have been informed of their rights and the safeguards prescribed by law for their protection;
>
> v. the necessary consent as provided for under Article 5 has been given expressly, specifically and is documented. Such consent may be freely withdrawn at any time.

'a treaty of the United States,' 28 U.S.C. § 1350, during the period relevant to this appeal."). Plaintiffs allege that the Trovan testing occurred in March and April of 1996, but the Convention was not opened for signature until April 4, 1997, and did not bind any state until Slovakia's ratification on January 15, 1998. *See* Flores, 414 F.3d at 256 ("A State only becomes bound by—that is, becomes a party to—a treaty when it ratifies the treaty."); Convention Ratifications Chart. The Convention is without import to this inquiry. Two other post-1996 sources cited by the majority, the 2005 UNESCO Universal Declaration on Bioethics and Human Rights and the 2001 European Parliament Clinical Trial Directive share equal evidentiary irrelevance for the same reason.

2. Multinational Declarations of Principle

Plaintiffs and the majority cite several multinational declarations, including the World Medical Association's Declaration of Helsinki and the International Ethical Guidelines for Research Involving Human Subjects promulgated by the Council for International Organizations of Medical Sciences ("CIOMS Guidelines"), as additional evidence that the prohibition against non-consensual medical experimentation applies to non-state actors. In doing so, the majority somehow overlooks our decisions in *Flores* and *Yousef.*

In *Flores*, plaintiffs sought to demonstrate customary international law by reference to multinational declarations. In response, we noted that a declaration, "which may be made by a multinational body, or by one or more States, customarily is a 'mere general statement of policy [that] is unlikely to give rise to . . . obligation[s] in any strict sense.'" 414 F.3d at 262 (quoting *1 Oppenheim's International Law* 1189 (Sir Robert Jennings & Sir Arthur Watts, eds., 9th ed. 1996)) (alterations in original). "Such declarations are almost invariably political statements—expressing the sensibilities and the asserted aspirations and demands of some countries or organizations—rather than statements of universally-recognized legal obligations." *Id.* As a result, we concluded that "such declarations *are not proper evidence of customary international law.*" *Id.* (emphasis added).

In *Flores*, the declarations we rejected were put forth by international governmental bodies, the Organization of American States and the United Nations Conference on Environment and Development. *Id.* at 263. Here, the two declarations embraced by the majority were put forward by entirely private organizations—hardly evidence of the state of international law. The Declaration of Helsinki was adopted by the World Medical Association, a group comprised not of member states, but of physicians and private national medical associations. "The World Medical Association (WMA) is an international organization representing physicians. . . . [and] has always been an independent confederation of free professional associations." *See* The World Medical Association, "About the WMA," http://www.wma.net/e/about/index.htm. The express terms of the Declaration of Helsinki make it abundantly clear that it is hortatory, and not obligatory: "The World Medical Association (WMA) has developed the Declaration of Helsinki as a statement of ethical principles . . . ." *See* World Med. Ass'n, *Declaration of Helsinki: Ethical Principles for Medical Research Involving Human Subjects* art. A(1), June 1964. Similarly, CIOMS is "an international non-governmental, non-profit organization." CIOMS, "What is CIOMS?", http://www.cioms.ch/jan2008_what_is_cioms.pdf.

Treating these well-meaning, aspirational, but private, declarations as sources of international law runs counter to our observation in *Yousef* that "no private person—or group of men and women such as comprise the body of international law scholars—*creates* the law." 327 F.3d at 102. This is so for good reason. As we have seen in our ATS jurisprudence, international custom gives rise to legally enforceable obligations. To include the political statements of private organizations in the select and conscribed group of sources capable of creating international law would enfranchise non-democratic, unaccountable entities with governmental authority. As a result, these declarations are "not proper evidence of customary international law." *Flores*, 414 F.3d at 262.

The majority focuses its lens on one line in *Filartiga* for the proposition that a "declaration may by custom become recognized as laying down rules binding upon the States." Maj. Op. at 19 (quoting *Filartiga*, 630 F.2d at 883). In *Filartiga*, we were discussing a *United Nations declaration*, which though not binding, "creates an expectation of adherence" because it "specif[ies] with great precision the obligations of member nations." 630 F.2d at 883. The declarations relied on by the majority were not put forth by a governmental body such as the United Nations but by wholly private organizations, incapable of creating legally binding obligations.

3. State Practice

The majority also points to the great number of states that, in their respective domestic laws, require informed consent in medical research. That many countries have prohibited private actors from conducting medical experiments or treatments without informed consent is certainly commendable and worthy of praise, but not "significant or relevant for purposes of customary international law."[4] *See Flores*, 414 F.3d at 249. For it is only when states prohibit domestic action as a result of "express international accords" that a wrong becomes a violation of customary international law. *See Filartiga*, 630 F.2d at 888 (quoting *IIT v. Vencap, Ltd.*, 519 F.2d 1001, 1015 (2d Cir. 1975) (Friendly, J.)). No such international accord exists here.

Moreover, "substantive uniformity" among states' domestic laws is only a starting point for demonstrating international custom through individual state practice, which should also reflect a "procedural" consensus among states on how that behavior should be prosecuted—criminally and civilly. *See Sosa*, 542 U.S. at 761–62 (Breyer, J, concurring). As Justice Breyer noted in his *Sosa* concurrence, the states of the world have reached both substantive and procedural agreement

---

4 Reliance on states' domestic laws also raises questions of mutuality, discussed *infra* at Part II.

with respect to only a handful of certain international law norms made actionable against non-state entities. *See id.*; Part I(B) *infra*. Non-consensual medical testing is not among them.

4. The Nuremberg Code

The majority centers its analysis around the Nuremberg Code, but, in the process, critically misstates its genesis and status in international law. *See* Maj. Op. at 20–24. Because the Code is a *sui generis* source of international law, its context is vital to understanding what it is—and what it is not.

The Nuremberg trials are unquestionably one of this country's greatest and most enduring contributions to the field of international law. As early as 1943, the Allied powers contemplated bringing Nazi war criminals to justice after the conclusion of the Second World War. At the October 1943 Moscow Conference, the United States, United Kingdom and Soviet Union issued

a joint "Statement on Atrocities," warning that:

> At the time of granting of any armistice to any government which may be set up in Germany, those German officers and men and members of the Nazi party who have been responsible for or have taken a consenting part in the above atrocities, massacres and executions will be sent back to the countries in which their abominable deeds were done in order that they may be judged and punished according to the laws of these liberated countries and of free governments which will be erected therein.

Moscow Declaration Statement of Atrocities, Oct. 30, 1943, 9 U.S. Dept of State Bull. 310 (signed by President Roosevelt, Prime Minister Churchill and Premier Stalin). The statement added that German criminals "whose offenses have no particular geographical localization . . . will be punished by joint decision of the government of the Allies." *Id.*

Following victory in Europe and the surrender of Germany, the Allies executed the London Charter on August 8, 1945, establishing an International Military Tribunal to try the "major war criminals," London Charter, Agreement for the Prosecution and Punishment of the Major War Criminals of the European Axis, art. 3, Aug. 8, 1945, 59 Stat. 1544, 82 U.N.T. S. 279, and leaving the door open for other war criminals to be tried in any other "national or occupation court" that might be established, *id.* art. 6. Alongside the London Charter, the Allies promulgated the Charter of the International Military Tribunal and formed a four-member tribunal with one member appointed by each of the Allies, with jurisdiction over "the major war criminals" accused of committing three crimes: crimes against peace,[5] war

5 "Crimes Against Peace" were defined as "planning, preparation, initiation or waging of a war of aggression, or a war in violation of international treaties, agreements or assurances, or participation in a common plan or conspiracy for the accomplishment of any of the foregoing." Charter of the International Military Tribunal art. 6(a).

crimes,[6] and crimes against humanity.[7] Charter of the International Military Tribunal, arts. 2, 6, Aug. 8, 1945, 59 Stat. 1544, 82 U.N.T.S. 279. It was the International Military Tribunal that conducted the celebrated trial that resulted in the convictions of 19 of 22 defendants, including high-ranking Nazi officials Hermann Goering, Rudolf Hess, and Karl Doenitz. *See generally* Robert H. Jackson, Final Report to the President on the Nuremberg Trials (Oct. 7, 1946). But the Nuremberg Code was adopted by a different tribunal in a different trial.

Four months after the London Charter established the International Military Tribunal, the Allied Control Council, the joint allied entity that governed post-war Germany, enacted Control Council Law No. 10, which authorized each of the occupying Allies, within its own "Zone of Occupation," to arrest and prosecute "persons within such Zone suspected of having committed a crime,"[8] subject to a right of first refusal by the International Military Tribunal. Allied Control Council Law No. 10 art. III, §§ 1,3 (Dec. 20, 1945), *in 1 Trials of War Criminals Before the Nuernberg Military Tribunals Under Control Council Law No.* 10, XVIII (William S. Hein & Co., Inc. 1997) (1949), *available at* http://www.loc.gov/rr/frd/Military_law/pdf/NT_war-criminals_Vol-I.pdf ("*1 Trials of War Criminals*").

The first of the American trials arising under Control Council Law No. 10 was the "Medical Case" against German doctors. On October 25, 1946, the American Office of Military Government for Germany enacted General Order 68, constituting Military Tribunal 1, comprised of three American military judges and one alternate judge. *Id.* at 5. That same day, Brigadier General Telford Taylor, Chief of Counsel for War Crimes, signed an indictment in *United States v. Karl Brandt, et al.* charging 23 defendants with war crimes, crimes against humanity, and conspiracy, and charging 10 of the defendants with membership in the "SS," an organization declared criminal by the International Military Tribunal. *Id.* at 8–18. These charges were premised, primarily, on the defendants' forced medical experiments, which

6 "War Crimes" were defined as "violations of the laws or customs of war. Such violations shall include, but not be limited to, murder, ill-treatment or deportation to slave labor or for any other purpose of civilian population of or in occupied territory, murder or ill-treatment of prisoners of war or persons on the seas, killing of hostages, plunder of public or private property, wanton destruction of cities, towns or villages, or devastation not justified by military necessity." Charter of the International Military Tribunal art. 6(b).

7 "Crimes Against Humanity" were defined as "murder, extermination, enslavement, deportation, and other inhumane acts committed against any civilian population, before or during the war; or persecutions on political, racial or religious grounds in execution of or in connection with any crime within the jurisdiction of the Tribunal, whether or not in violation of the domestic law of the country where perpetrated." Charter of the International Military Tribunal art. 6(c).

8 In addition to the three crimes listed in the Charter of the International War Tribunal, Control Council Law No. 10 added a fourth—"Membership in categories of a criminal group or organization declared criminal by the International Military Tribunal." Control Council Law No. 10 art. II, § (d).

constituted war crimes when performed on prisoners of war, and crimes against humanity when conducted on Nazi concentration camp prisoners.

At the conclusion of the Medical Case, 16 of the 23 defendants were convicted of one or more of the charges, and seven were ultimately sentenced to death. Along with their verdict, the military judges enumerated ten principles that came to be known as the Nuremberg Code, the first of which states that in medical experiments, the "voluntary consent of the human subject is absolutely essential." *2 Trials of War Criminals Before the Nuernberg Military Tribunals Under Control Council Law No. 10*, 181 (William S. Hein & Co., Inc. 1997) (1949), *available at* http://www.loc.gov/rr/frd/Military_law/pdf/NT_war-criminals_Vol-II.pdf ("*2 Trials of War Criminals*").

My colleagues contend that the Code flowed naturally from the principles of law espoused in the London Charter. They are quite right, of course, that Control Council Law No. 10 was modeled after the London Charter and the American and International military tribunals shared largely the same general international law and procedural frameworks. The London Charter identified and defined certain international law offenses—Crimes Against Humanity, Crimes Against Peace, and War Crimes—while each of the twelve trials before the American military tribunal concerned a unique and horrific context for the commission of those crimes, ranging from medical experimentation on prisoners to the use of slave labor. For example, the definitions of Crimes Against Humanity and War Crimes under which the Nazi doctors were tried in the Medical Case were virtually identical to those of the London Charter. However, the majority overlooks the fact that the Nuremberg Code dealt not with these general principles of law, but instead with the very specific issue of permissible medical experimentation. The ethical principles espoused in the Code had no forebears in either the London Charter or the judgment of the International Military Tribunal. They were developed exclusively in the Medical Case.

I recite this history not to suggest that the Nuremberg Code is not an extraordinary or groundbreaking document, but rather to demonstrate the difficulty inherent in measuring its evidentiary weight, as it does not fit neatly into any of the categories this Court has identified for sources of international law. For one thing, the Code was developed by the United States military and announced by an American military court. *See United States v. Stanley*, 483 U.S. 669, 687, 107 S. Ct. 3054, 97 L. Ed. 2d 550 (1987) (Brennan, J., dissenting). Certainly, the Code is not a treaty and did not immediately bind any state. Under the framework of the ICJ Statute—and, accordingly, this Court—because it was part of a criminal verdict, its closest analogue is a judicial decision, but judicial decisions are only "subsidiary," rather than primary, sources of customary international law. *See* ICJ Statute art. 38; Maj. Op. at 15. I agree with my colleagues that the Code has had significant import—influence that continues to this day. The Code surely has evidentiary value in our inquiry, but there is nothing to indicate that the Code establishes a norm of international law prohibiting non-consensual medical experimentation or treatment by private actors, or compensates for the virtually non-existent evidentiary value of the other sources cited by the majority.

Conscious of our obligation to measure the weight of the sources of international law in the aggregate, what is the sum of the sources that serve as the cornerstone of the majority's conclusion? The ICCPR, characterized by the Supreme Court as being of "little utility," *Sosa*, 542 U.S. at 734, which, in any event, does not apply to private actors; a pair of private organizations' declarations that our Circuit precedent tells us "are not proper evidence of customary international law," *Flores*, 414 F.3d at 262; one regional convention and two multinational declarations that post-date the critical time period and are thus completely irrelevant; states' domestic laws untethered to any international agreement that we are told is not "significant or relevant for purposes of customary international law," *id.* at 249; and the Nuremberg Code, a document whose evidentiary value is unclear.

Simply put, the evidence here does not compare with the sources put forward in the few cases where we have held a principle to be a norm of customary international law. Exercising "extraordinary care and restraint," *see id.* at 248, we have only upheld ATS jurisdiction in cases where the evidence of customary international law was entirely overwhelming.[9] In *Filartiga*, we were persuaded by the fact that the "international consensus surrounding torture has found expression in *numerous* international treaties and accords." 630 F.2d at 883 (emphasis added). There, the State Department—"the political branch with principal responsibility for conducting the international relations of the United States," *Flores*, 414 F.3d at 262—had expressly announced that the prohibition against torture had ripened into a norm of customary international law.[10] *Filartiga*, 630 F.2d at 884. In *Kadic*, we observed that genocide was included in section 404 of the Restatement and that the Convention on the Prevention and Punishment of the Crime of Genocide had been ratified by more than 120 nations, including the United States, 70 F.3d at 240–42, while international criminalization of war crimes was established by four Geneva Conventions, ratified by more than 180 nations, including the United States, *id.* at 242–43. In *Amerada-Hess*, it was similarly obvious that Argentina's Falkland War attack on an American ship violated one of the oldest customary international

9 The majority purports to include our recent decision in *Khulumani v. Barclay National Bank Ltd.*, 504 F.3d 254 (2d Cir. 2007) (per curiam) in this select group, stating that it "held that the ATS conferred jurisdiction over multinational corporations that purportedly collaborated with the government of South Africa in maintaining apartheid because they aided and abetted violations of customary international law." Maj. Op. at 13–14. To the contrary, *Khulumani* did not confer jurisdiction and did not make any determination on whether plaintiffs had stated a violation of international law. It merely held that the district court erred in concluding that the ATS did not convey jurisdiction for "aiding and abetting violations of customary international law," and remanded for consideration of whether plaintiffs had alleged such a violation that the defendants could have been liable for aiding and abetting. *See Khulumani*, 504 F.3d at 260.

10 Indeed, the Supreme Court later declared that in ATS actions, "federal courts should give serious weight to the Executive Branch's view of the case's impact on foreign policy." *Sosa*, 542 U.S. at 733 n.21.

law norms. 830 F.2d at 423–24. We cited a variety of international accords establishing the right of a neutral ship to free passage. *Id.* at 424. After tracing the norm to Blackstone, we concluded that it was "beyond controversy that attacking a neutral ship in international waters . . . violates international law." *Id.*

In those cases, the evidence of international acceptance of each norm with respect to each defendant was "clear and unambiguous." *Flores*, 414 F.3d at 252. In each case, the nations of the world gathered to ratify in universal numbers treaties that specifically prohibited genocide, war crimes, torture, and attacks on neutral ships—not in generalized human rights agreements but in accords with those discrete norms as their exclusive subjects.

My colleagues contend that I look only to the presence (or, in this case, the absence) of a globally ratified treaty as the exclusive source of an international law norm. Far from it—we have held that customary international law "does not stem from any single, definitive, readily-identifiable source." *Id.* at 248. However, the great weight of ATS jurisdiction must rest upon a foundation sturdy enough to support it. Just as it would be error to stubbornly require one source of sufficient strength to bear that burden on its own, the majority is equally mistaken in its attempt to employ a series of extraordinarily weak sources to secure a purported norm of customary international law. Our case law makes clear that even when viewed collectively, these sources are incapable of carrying the weight placed upon them by my colleagues.

B. Restatement § 404

Nor does Plaintiffs' purported norm resemble the select few norms for which international law extends liability to private actors. Although the law of nations in general does not "confine[] its reach to state action," *see Kadic*, 70 F.3d at 239, courts must still consider whether the specific norm at issue does. In *Kadic*, we noted that the Restatement (Third) of Foreign Relations Law of the United States differentiates between "those violations that are actionable when committed by a state[11] and a more limited category of violations" that apply with equal force to private actors. *Id.* at 240 (citing Restatement (Third) §§ 404, 702). Section 404 of

---

11 Section 702 provides:

> A state violates international law if, as a matter of state policy, it practices, encourages, or condones
>
> (a) genocide,
>
> (b) slavery or slave trade,
>
> (c) the murder or causing the disappearance of individuals,
>
> (d) torture or other cruel, inhuman, or degrading treatment or punishment,
>
> (e) prolonged arbitrary detention,
>
> (f) systematic racial discrimination, or
>
> (g) a consistent pattern of gross violations of internationally recognized human rights.

the Restatement authorizes universal criminal jurisdiction over non-state entities "for certain offenses recognized by the community of nations as of universal concern, such as piracy, slave trade, attacks on or hijacking of aircraft, genocide, war crimes, and perhaps certain acts of terrorism, even where [no other basis of jurisdiction] is present."[12] Universal jurisdiction, not to be confused with universal acceptance of a norm for ATS purposes, "permits a State to prosecute an offender of any nationality for an offense committed outside of that State and without contacts to that State." *Yousef*, 327 F.3d 56 at 103.

The plaintiffs in *Kadic* alleged that Radovan Karadzic, the "president" of the self-proclaimed republic of Srpska violated several international law norms, notably bans on genocide, war crimes and torture. 70 F.3d at 236-37. Treating Karadzic as a non-state actor, we reviewed not only the Restatement, but a host of relevant international accords, leading us to conclude that by their own terms, the norms prohibiting genocide and war crimes applied to private individuals, while torture and summary execution "are proscribed by international law only when committed by state officials or under color of law." *Id.* at 241-43. We added that the "'color of law' jurisprudence of 42 U.S.C. § 1983 is a relevant guide to whether a defendant has engaged in official action for purposes of jurisdiction under the [ATS]." *Id.* at 245.

Five years later, we again determined whether an international law norm applied only to state actors. *See Bigio v. Coca-Cola Co.,* 239 F.3d 440 (2d Cir. 2000). Building on *Kadic*, we held that ATS jurisdiction over a non-governmental entity requires the violation of a norm "listed as an 'act of universal concern' in § 404 or . . . sufficiently similar to [those] acts for us to treat them as though they were incorporated into § 404 by analogy," or conduct committed under color of law. *Id.* at 448. In affirming the district court's dismissal, we determined that the act at issue—discriminatory expropriation of property—is much more like the acts listed in section 702 than those in section 404, and that the complaint did not allege that Coca-Cola acted in concert with Egyptian state officials. *Id.* at 447–49. However, unlike in *Kadic*, we saw no need to look beyond the Restatement to any sources of international law in order to conclude that the norm did not apply to non-state entities. *Compare id.* at 448, *with Kadic*, 70 F.3d at 241–43. It is equally clear that section 404 of the Restatement does not reveal a norm of customary international law prohibiting non-consensual medical experimentation by *private actors*.

12 The Court explained its application of a criminal law provision to a civil statute by noting that a comment to section 404 "permits states to establish appropriate civil remedies such as the tort actions authorized by the [ATS]." *Kadic*, 70 F.3d at 240 (citation omitted). More specifically, "jurisdiction on the basis of universal interests has been exercised in the form of criminal law, but international law does not preclude the application of non-criminal law on this basis, for example, by providing a remedy in tort or restitution for victims of piracy." Restatement (Third) § 404 cmt. b.

To reiterate, section 404 lists only five specific acts for which universal criminal jurisdiction over private actors exists: piracy, genocide, slave trade, war crimes, and attacks on aircrafts. *See also Vietnam Ass'n for Victims of Agent Orange,* 517 F.3d at 116 (describing these five as comprising "the list of principles that may be said to have ripened into universally accepted norms of international law" (internal quotation marks omitted)). If anything, this Court has been even more stringent, holding that in spite of the Restatement, federal courts could not try an alleged airline bomber under customary international law principles of universal jurisdiction.[13] *See Yousef,* 327 F.3d at 103–08. Regardless, there is no dispute that none of the five acts in section 404 encompasses non-consensual medical experimentation. Instead, Plaintiffs argue that it is "sufficiently similar" to those acts to support its application to a private corporation.[14] *See Bigio*, 239 F.3d at 448. This Court has never had occasion to consider what types of acts are "sufficiently similar" to the section 404 acts except to conclude in *Bigio* that discriminatory expropriation was not among them. *Id.* For similar reasons, neither is non-consensual medical experimentation.

Universal jurisdiction originated with prosecutions of piracy more than 500 years ago. *See Yousef,* 327 F.3d at 104; *United States v. Lei Shi*, 525 F.3d 709, 723 (9th Cir. 2008). As we explained in *Yousef,* piracy is universally punishable not because it is uniquely heinous but "because of the threat that piracy poses to orderly transport and commerce between nations and because the crime occurs statelessly on the high seas." 327 F.3d at 104. By 1822, it was beyond "doubt . . . that vessels and property in the possession of pirates may be lawfully seized on the high seas by [any] person, and brought in for adjudication." *United States v. the La Jeune Eugenie*, 26 F. Cas. 832, 843, F. Cas. No. 15551 (C.C.D. Mass. 1822) (No. 15,551); *see also United States v. Smith*, 18 U.S. (5 Wheat) 153, 163, 5 L. Ed. 57 (1820) (Story, J.) (discussing the bases for universal jurisdiction over piracy).

Private actors trading slaves (as opposed to those engaging in slavery in general) are subject to universal criminal jurisdiction because the early treaties that formed

13 Yousef was charged with placing a bomb aboard a Philippine Airlines jet flying from the Philippines to Japan. 327 F.3d at 81, 88. After holding that customary international law could not support universal jurisdiction, we observed that "treaties may diverge broadly from customary international law," *id.* at 108, and upheld jurisdiction under 18 U.S.C. § 32, the statute implementing the "extradite or prosecute" provision of the Montreal Convention for the Suppression of Unlawful Acts Against the Safety of Civil Aviation (Sabotage) art. 7, Sept. 23, 1971, 24 U.S.T. 565, 974 U.N.T.S. 177 ("The Contracting State in the territory of which the alleged offender is found shall, if it does not extradite him, be obliged, without exception whatsoever and whether or not the offence was committed in its territory, to submit the case to its competent authorities for the purpose of prosecution."), *id.* at 108–10.

14 I note the tension between our holding in *Bigio* that acts can, at least in theory, be incorporated into § 404 by analogy for ATS purposes, *see* 239 F.3d at 448, and our statement in *Yousef* that the "strictly limited set of crimes subject to universal jurisdiction cannot be expanded by drawing an analogy between some new crime . . . and universal jurisdiction's traditional subjects" for purposes of exercising criminal jurisdiction, *see* 327 F.3d at 103–04.

the basis for customary international law considered the slave trade akin to piracy. For example, the 1841 Treaty of London provided that:

> Their Majesties the Emperor of Austria, the King of Hungary and Bohemia, the King of Prussia, and the Emperor of all the Russias, engage to prohibit all trade in slaves, either by their respective subjects, or under their respective flags, or by means of capital belonging to their respective subjects; and *to declare such traffic piracy*. Their Majesties further declare that any vessel which may attempt to carry on the Slave Trade, shall, by that fact alone, lose all right to the protection of their flag.

Treaty for the Suppression of the African Slave Trade art. I, Dec. 20, 1841, 92 Consol. T.S. 437 (emphasis added), *reprinted in* M. Cherif Bassiouni & Edward M. Wise, *Aut Dedere Aut Judicare: The Duty to Extradite or Prosecute in International Law* 132–33 (1995); *see also* Kenneth C. Randall, *Universal Jurisdiction Under International Law*, 66 TEX. L. REV. 785, 798 (1988) ("Currently, states can recognize universal jurisdiction over slave trading by . . . customary law."). Although we declined to hold in *Yousef* that the principle had ripened into a customary norm, attacks on airliners logically fit into this class because, like the high seas, airspace is stateless and extraterritorial.

After World War II, universal criminal jurisdiction was extended to private actors—including many of the Nazi defendants prosecuted under Control Council Law No. 10—accused of crimes against humanity such as war crimes and genocide because, like piracy, "'there is . . . a lack of any adequate judicial system operating on the spot where the crime takes place—in the case of piracy it is because the acts are on the high seas and in the case of war crimes because of a chaotic condition or irresponsible leadership in time of war.'" *Yousef*, 327 F.3d at 105 (quoting Willard B. Cowles, *Universality of Jurisdiction Over War Crimes*, 33 CAL. L. REV. 177, 194 (1945)); *see also Flores*, 414 F.3d at 244 n.18 ("Customary international law rules proscribing crimes against humanity, including genocide, and war crimes, have been enforceable against individuals since World War II.").

In *Yousef*, we concluded that these acts share two common traits: they "(1) are universally condemned by the community of nations, and (2) by their nature occur either outside of a State or where there is no State capable of punishing, or competent to punish, the crime." 327 F.3d at 105.

Non-consensual medical experimentation is not "sufficiently similar" to these crimes to warrant its incorporation into section 404 by analogy. Plaintiffs acknowledge that the acts listed in section 404 share "a particular quality of crossing international boundaries," a quality that they argue that medical experimentation shares "because of the universal uses of medical research and the common practice of physicians to travel to crisis areas to deliver humanitarian aid." But the mere crossing of an international border does not give rise to universal jurisdiction over non-state actors. We made this clear in *Yousef*, where we rejected universal jurisdiction over an individual accused of bombing of an aircraft leaving the Philippines for Japan. 327 F.3d at 98, 103. As we held, universal criminal jurisdiction over private actors is only appropriate for acts which, "by their nature," are beyond state sovereignty. *Id.* at 105. Here, Pfizer's alleged actions occurred exclusively within Nigeria, and medical experimentation is not a crime which, by its nature, is incapable of state punishment. Plaintiffs' argument to the contrary is belied by the state and federal civil and criminal actions pending against Pfizer in Nigeria. *See* Maj. Op. at 9.

As in *Bigio*, medical experimentation more closely resembles the acts for which only state actors may be held responsible. Plaintiffs compare medical experimentation with slavery. Yet, under the Restatement, while anyone may be prosecuted for engaging in the slave trade, slavery itself is only actionable against state actors. *See* Restatement (Third) § 702(b) ("A state violates international law if, as a matter of state policy, it practices, encourages, or condones . . . slavery . . ."). Medical experimentation resembles slavery in its grievous exploitation of unconsenting and unwilling subjects; it also resembles torture in its infliction of horrific physical and emotional pain. However, both the Restatement and this Court have recognized that the norm against torture reaches only state actors. *See Kadic*, 70 F.3d at 243–44; Restatement (Third) § 702(d); *see also* Convention Against Torture and Other Cruel, Inhuman or Degrading Treatment or Punishment art 1, Dec. 10, 1984, S. Treaty Doc. No. 100-20, 1465 U.N.T.S. 85 ("CAT") (defining torture as being "inflicted by or at the instigation of or with the consent or acquiescence of a public official or other person acting in an official capacity.").[15]

One of the fundamental attributes of sovereignty is a state's authority to exercise criminal jurisdiction over persons accused of committing crimes within its territory. The crimes listed in section 404 are not the extraordinary exceptions because they are singularly reprehensible or deserving of condemnation. Few would argue that piracy, for which private actors may be prosecuted universally but which requires neither an act of violence nor the infliction of physical injury,[16] is more heinous than torture or slavery, practices made actionable only against state entities. Rather, by definition, these crimes occur in locations where, or during times when, sovereignty, and *a fortiori* criminal jurisdiction, are incapable of being exercised. Because medical experimentation is entirely *intranational* and fully subject to domestic criminal jurisdiction, it is not "sufficiently similar" to those acts listed in section 404, and cannot be incorporated by analogy as to reach private, non-state actors.

The defendants in the Medical Case were not charged with conducting nonconsensual medical tests per se. Rather, those tests, when conducted on prisoners

---

15 It should be noted that while universal criminal jurisdiction under the CAT does exist for torturers, those torturers must, by definition, be state actors. *See* CAT arts. 4, 7, 8.

16 *See*, e.g., United Nations Convention on the Law of the Sea part VII, art. 101, Dec. 10, 1982, S. Treaty Doc. No. 103-39, 1833 U.N.T.S. 3 (stating that piracy may consist of "any illegal acts of violence or detention, or any act of depredation . . . .")

of war and members of a discrete civilian population imprisoned in concentration camps, constituted "war crimes" and "crimes against humanity," offenses for which customary international law has imposed individual responsibility. *See Flores*, 414 F.3d at 244 n.18. Unlike the Defendant in this action, the Nazi doctors convicted by the American military tribunal were not private actors. Each convicted defendant held a position of authority in either the medical services or the military of the Third Reich.[17] *See 1 Trials of War Criminals* 29. Moreover, the atrocities for which they were convicted victimized state prisoners in state-administered concentration camps, according to the Indictment, "for the benefit of the German Armed Forces." *Id.* at 11–14. It is difficult to imagine a more egregious example of the violation of a customary international law norm or a more appropriate case for ATS jurisdiction.

The majority today authorizes the exercise of ATS jurisdiction over an entirely private corporation for violating a previously unrecognized norm of international law. In doing so, my colleagues accept proof far weaker than in any other case where this Court has identified a norm of customary international law, and, apparently, overlook the fact that this purported norm in no way resembles those few norms enforceable against private entities. When tasked by the Supreme Court with "vigilant doorkeeping" to ensure that the list of actionable international norms remains "narrow," *Sosa*, 542 U.S. at 729, we must be no less demanding than we have been in the past. Under that standard, the evidence put forward by Plaintiffs does not establish a norm of customary international law actionable against private actors. I believe that the majority's decision departs from our settled case law and lowers considerably our previously high bar for ATS jurisdiction.

II. Mutuality

There are many principles on which most states of the world community agree. Most find support and enforcement in the richly diverse legal systems in place around the globe. But universal acceptance as a normative principle is not enough to gain entrance into the "law of nations." The norm must not only be universal, it must touch on matters that are "of mutual, and not merely several, concern." *Filartiga*, 630 F.2d at 888. Matters are of mutual concern when they "affect[] the relationship between states or between an individual and a foreign state, and [are] used by those states for their common good and/or dealings inter se." IIT, 519 F.2d at 1015. On the other hand, matters of several concern are those "in which States are separately and independently interested." *Flores*, 414 F.3d at 249. For example, as we noted in *Flores*, "murder of one private party by another, universally proscribed by the

17 All but three of the 23 defendants were doctors. *1 Trials of War Criminals* 29. The three that were not were colonels or senior colonels in the Nazi SS. *1 Trials of War Criminals* 8, 29. Of the 20 doctors, all but one "held positions in the medical services of the Third Reich." *1 Trials of War Criminals* 29. The lone exception, Adolf Pokorny, a specialist in skin and venereal diseases, was acquitted of all charges. *1 Trials of War Criminals 10*; *2 Trials of War Criminals* 292–94.

domestic law of all countries . . . is not actionable under the [ATS] as a violation of customary international law because 'the nations of the world' have not demonstrated that this wrong is of mutual, and not merely several, concern." *Id.* (quotation marks omitted). The majority concludes that non-consensual medical experimentation by one private party on another is a matter of mutual concern. I disagree.

We have consistently held that the best evidence that states consider a matter to be of mutual concern is the fact that they have agreed to be bound "by means of express international accords." *Filartiga*, 630 F.2d at 888; *see Flores*, 414 F.3d at 249; *Khulumani*, 504 F.3d at 274 n.7 (Katzmann, J., concurring). The majority points to the ICCPR, the Convention on Human Rights and Biomedicine, and the 2001 Clinical Trial Directive as evidence that "States throughout the world have entered into . . . express and binding international agreements prohibiting nonconsensual medical experimentation." *See* Maj. Op. at 35. But those agreements fail to demonstrate mutuality for the same reason they fail to demonstrate universality—the ICCPR does not address acts by non-state actors and the other two were not in force at the time of the alleged misconduct. Whatever international consensus has been reached as to non-consensual medical experimentation by private actors has not yet "found expression in numerous treaties and accords," *cf. Filartiga*, 630 F.2d at 883. The majority cites no worldwide, multi-continental, universally applicable "Convention Against Medical Experimentation," because, at the moment, none exists. That fact alone distinguishes this case from *Filartiga, Amerada-Hess*, and *Kadic*.

In the absence of a binding global treaty, the majority seeks to demonstrate mutuality of concern by describing the downstream effects of non-consensual medical experimentation. In essence, the majority contends that non-consensual medical experiments feed distrust among their victims, which, in turn, engenders a general reluctance to seek future medical attention or vaccination, which, in turn, helps accelerate the spread of infectious diseases across international borders. *See* Maj. Op. at 36–39. Indeed, I would concede that the majority may be quite right. But a smaller, more interdependent world community has not been employed by the Supreme Court (or any other court to my knowledge) to convert claims such as those presented here into violations of the law of nations. In fact, the majority's theory would be no different when evaluating the medical malpractice of Pfizer's research physicians or the strict products liability for its allegedly defective drug, but malpractice and products liability are among the quintessential subjects of domestic law.

It is not enough that a wrong could create international ramifications; in order for it to be a matter of mutual concern, it must "threaten[] serious consequences in international affairs." *Sosa*, 542 U.S. at 715. The Supreme Court listed three historical mutual wrongs as guideposts to frame this inquiry: infringement of the rights of ambassadors, the violation of safe conducts and piracy. *Id.* at 715, 720. An assault against an ambassador "impinged upon the sovereignty of the foreign nation and if not adequately redressed could rise to an issue of war." *Id.* at 715. The 18th century safe-conduct document was the historical equivalent of the modern passport, "which entitles a bearer with a valid visa to safe passage to, within, and out of a foreign land pursuant to a treaty or an agreement negotiated by his or her sovereign and the host sovereign." *Taveras v. Taveraz*, 477 F.3d 767, 773 (6th Cir. 2007) (quoting Thomas H. Lee, *The Safe-Conduct Theory of the Alien Tort Statute*, 106 Colum. L. Rev. 830, 874 (2006)). Thus, "the purpose of the doctrine of safe conducts under the law of nations is to protect the safety and security of the person and property of the journeying alien bearing the safe conduct privilege (and consequently to preserve commercial and diplomatic relationships between the alien's host and home countries)." *Id.* at 773–74. This is still true today—a passport issued by the United States contains an official request from the Secretary of State to an authority of another sovereign state: "The Secretary of State of the United States of America hereby requests all whom it may concern to permit the citizen/national of the United States named herein to pass without delay or hindrance and in case of need to give all lawful aid and protection." Breaches of customary international law impair the normal expectations that nations have in dealing with other nations. They must threaten serious consequences in international affairs because the norms were, and still are, the foundation for states' formal relationships with one another.

Piracy does not fit squarely with the other two *Sosa* historical paradigms, but the threat to international affairs posed by piracy needs no detailed exegesis. Suffice it to say that one of the young Republic's first military tests was its campaign against the Barbary Pirates, *see, e.g.*, Act For the Protection of the Commerce and Seamen of the United States Against the Tripolitan Cruisers, ch. IV, § 2, 2 Stat. 129, 130 (1802) (authorizing President Jefferson to instruct the armed forces to "seize and make prize of all vessels, goods and effects, belonging to the Bey of Tripoli . . . and also to cause to be done all such other acts of precaution or hostility as the state of war will justify, and may, in his opinion, require."), and piracy continues to threaten serious consequences in international affairs today, *see* S.C. Res. 1851, P 2, U.N. Doc. S/RES/1851 (Dec. 16, 2008) (calling upon states "to take part actively in the fight against piracy and armed robbery at sea off the coast of Somalia").

We have accepted no lesser showing in our case law. The threat posed by genocide is so great that states are empowered to request "the competent organs of the United Nations to take such action under the Charter of the United Nations as they consider appropriate for the prevention and suppression of acts of genocide." Convention on the Prevention and Punishment of the Crime of Genocide art. 8, Dec. 9, 1948, 102 Stat. 3045, 78 U.N.T.S. 277. The Geneva Conventions collectively establish, and obligate contracting parties to follow, the laws of war—almost by definition a matter of international affairs. *See Kadic*, 70 F.3d at 242–43. On the other hand, because international law does not define torture to include acts by private entities, torturous conduct by non-state actors—while criminalized domestically—is not a matter of mutual concern. *Id.* at 243–44.

Demonstrating that a wrong is a matter of mutual concern must necessarily be difficult. The Supreme Court has only opened the door for ATS jurisdiction over a "narrow set of violations of the law of nations, admitting of a judicial remedy and at the same time threatening serious consequences in international affairs." *Sosa*, 542 U.S. at 715. The nations of the world have not yet demonstrated that non-consensual medical experimentation by non-state actors "is of mutual, and not merely several, concern, by means of express international accords." *Filartiga*, 630 F.2d at 888. Nor does it threaten serious consequences in international affairs in the same manner or to the same extent as the historical paradigms listed by the Supreme Court or their modern counterparts identified by this Court. Without either showing, I cannot agree with the majority that non-consensual medical experimentation by *private actors* is a matter of mutual concern.

III. State Action

The fact that medical experimentation by private actors is not a subject of customary international law does not end the inquiry. If international law supports state liability but not private liability, a private actor may still be liable if he or she "acted under color of law." In that regard, we are told to employ our 42 U.S.C. § 1983 jurisprudence in the inquiry. *See Bigio*, 239 F.3d at 448; *Kadic*, 70 F.3d at 245. As an initial matter, this requires that the law of nations includes a norm actionable against states, which, in the instant case, is far from certain. But even assuming, for argument's sake, that international law prohibits states from conducting non-consensual medical tests, Plaintiffs have not demonstrated that Pfizer acted under the color of law.

This issue requires a bit of procedural context. In 2002, Pfizer moved to dismiss Plaintiffs' complaint in *Abdullahi* on the grounds that (1) Plaintiffs had not alleged that Pfizer was a state actor, and (2) the alternate ground of forum non conveniens. *See Abdullahi v. Pfizer, Inc.*, No. 01 Civ. 8118, 2002 U.S. Dist. LEXIS 17436, 2002 WL 31082956, at *12 (S.D.N.Y. Sept. 17, 2002). Judge Pauley granted the forum non conveniens motion, but denied the state action motion, concluding that Plaintiffs "sufficiently allege[d] that the former Nigerian government and Pfizer were joint participants in the Trovan treatment." 2002 U.S. Dist. LEXIS 17436, [WL] at *6. Plaintiffs appealed the district court's dismissal, and Pfizer cross-appealed from the court's denial of its motion to dismiss on state action. *See Abdullahi v. Pfizer, Inc.*, 77 Fed. Appx. 48 (2d Cir. 2003). On appeal, we vacated the district court's judgment of dismissal, and did not reach Pfizer's cross-appeal, noting that our intervening decision in *Flores* might have some application on remand. *Id.* at 53. Back before Judge Pauley, Pfizer filed a new motion to dismiss, arguing that Plaintiffs failed to state a claim under the substantially different ATS landscape which now included the Supreme Court's decision in *Sosa* and our decision in *Flores*. *See Abdullahi v. Pfizer, Inc.*, No. 01 Civ. 8118, 2005 U.S. Dist. LEXIS 16126, 2005 WL 1870811, at *3 (S.D.N.Y. Aug. 9, 2005). Both of these decisions made clear that the identity of the defendant is a critical component of whether a principle is a norm of customary international law. Without addressing or affirming its previous conclusion finding sufficient allegations of state action, the district court granted Pfizer's motion to dismiss, holding that medical experimentation was not actionable under the law of nations. 2005 U.S. Dist. LEXIS 16126, [WL] at *18. On appeal to this Court, both parties addressed the issue of state action in their briefs. The majority concludes that Plaintiffs' allegations of state action were sufficient to defeat a motion to dismiss. *See* Maj. Op. at 41–43. I cannot agree.

In their twin complaints, which total 628 paragraphs, Plaintiffs make only four allegations concerning the role of the Nigerian government in the Trovan experiments: (1) in order for the FDA to authorize the export of Trovan, "Pfizer obtained the required letter of request from the Nigerian government"; (2) the government "arrang[ed] for Pfizer's accommodation in Kano"; (3) the government acted "to silence Nigerian physicians critical of [Pfizer's] test"; and (4) the government "assign[ed] Nigerian physicians to assist in the project."[18] Elsewhere in their complaints, Plaintiffs note in conclusory fashion that a Nigerian doctor did not publicly object to the Trovan study because it "seemed to have the backing of the Nigerian government."

In their brief to this Court, Plaintiffs seek to bolster their complaints by describing the role of "Nigerian government doctors" at the allegedly government-owned hospital that hosted the study. However, the portions of the complaints that they cite do not support their contentions. Nowhere in their complaints did Plaintiffs allege that the hospital was, in fact, government owned or administered, nor did they allege that the four Nigerian doctors working with Pfizer were employed by the government, and our review of a decision to grant a motion to dismiss "is limited to the facts as asserted within the four corners of the complaint" and any attached documents. *McCarthy v. Dun & Bradstreet Corp.,* 482 F.3d 184, 191 (2d Cir. 2007).

These bare allegations are plainly insufficient to survive a motion to dismiss for lack of state action. The Supreme Court's case law on state action is hardly a model of clarity, but certain principles are well-settled. As a threshold matter, the conduct alleged attributable to the state must be defined with the requisite specificity. "When analyzing allegations of state action, we begin 'by identifying the specific conduct of which the plaintiff complains,'" *Tancredi v. Metro. Life Ins. Co.,* 316 F.3d 308, 312 (2d Cir. 2003) (quoting *Am. Mfrs. Mut. Ins. Co. v. Sullivan*, 526 U.S. 40, 51, 119 S. Ct. 977, 143 L. Ed. 2d 130 (1999)), and in most cases, a finding of state action "must be premised upon the fact that the State is *responsible*" for that specific conduct, *Horvath v. Westport Library Ass'n*, 362 F.3d 147, 154

18 Plaintiffs also initially allege that the government backdated a letter of approval for the test, but then allege that the letter was in fact created by a "Nigerian physician whom Pfizer says was its principal investigator."

(2d Cir. 2004) (internal quotation omitted). Determining state action in these cases "requires tracing the activity to its source to see if that source fairly can be said to be the state." *Leshko v. Servis*, 423 F.3d 337, 340 (3d Cir. 2005); *see also Hadges v. Yonkers Racing Corp.*, 918 F.2d 1079, 1082–83 (2d Cir. 1990). As we recently stated, when confronted with a motion to dismiss, it "is not enough . . . for a plaintiff to plead state involvement in *some activity* of the institution alleged to have inflicted injury upon a plaintiff; rather, the plaintiff must allege that the state was involved with the *activity that caused the injury* giving rise to the action." *Sybalski v. Indep. Group Home Living Program, Inc.*, 546 F.3d 255, 257–58 (2d Cir. 2008) (internal quotations omitted).

Here, that activity was not, as the majority apparently concludes, conducting the Trovan trials in general, but rather administering the drug without informed consent. Although Plaintiffs allege that the Nigerian government requested the import of Trovan and arranged for Pfizer's accommodations and some medical staff in Kano, they do not allege that the government or any government employee played any role in either administering Trovan without consent or deciding to do so in the first instance. The Supreme Court has described "the typical case raising a state-action issue" as one in which "a private party has taken the decisive step that caused the harm to the plaintiff, and the question is whether the State was sufficiently involved to treat that decisive conduct as state action." *NCAA v. Tarkanian*, 488 U.S. 179, 192, 109 S. Ct. 454, 102 L. Ed. 2d 469 (1988). Plaintiffs have not alleged any facts that would indicate that the answer here is "yes."

Plaintiffs' complaints are more noteworthy for what they do not allege than what they do. They have not suggested that Pfizer was exercising any delegated state authority, *cf. West v. Atkins*, 487 U.S. 42, 108 S. Ct. 2250, 101 L. Ed. 2d 40 (1988), or that the Nigerian government "knowingly accept[ed] the benefits derived from [the unlawful] behavior," *Tarkanian*, 488 U.S. at 192. Plaintiffs have not alleged that Pfizer *conspired* with government officials to deprive the subjects of their rights, *cf. Fries v. Barnes*, 618 F.2d 988, 991 (2d Cir. 1980), nor have they alleged that the Nigerian government exercised any coercive power over Pfizer, *cf. Brentwood Acad. v. Tenn. Secondary Sch. Athletic Ass'n*, 531 U.S. 288, 296, 121 S. Ct. 924, 148 L. Ed. 2d 807 (2001). In fact, Plaintiffs did not allege that any Nigerian government officials even knew about the non-consensual tests, because if Nigerian government doctors were somehow involved in the study, Plaintiffs did not specify what role, if any, they played.

The case of *Beanal v. Freeport-McMoRan, Inc.*, 969 F. Supp. 362 (E.D. La. 1997), *aff'd* 197 F.3d 161 (5th Cir. 1999), is instructive. In *Beanal*, plaintiffs seeking to recover under the ATS sought to establish state action on the basis of the Indonesian military's involvement in allegedly actionable conduct. The court rejected that argument, holding that plaintiffs had not "alleged whether the military personnel helped enforce Freeport's policies or merely observed . . . the violative conduct." *Id.* at 378. Broad conclusory statements of state involvement are not sufficient to establish state action; "there must be some allegation indicating that the troops jointly cooperated in the conduct, jointly participated in the conduct, influenced the conduct or played an integral part in the deprivation of human rights." *Id.* at 379. The same is true here.[19] Plaintiffs' allegations are inadequate.

Even without alleging that the State "coerced or even encouraged" the act complained of, Plaintiffs can still survive a motion to dismiss if "the relevant facts show pervasive entwinement to the point of largely overlapping identity between the State and the entity that the plaintiff contends is a state actor." *Horvath*, 362 F.3d at 154 (quotation omitted). This line of cases revolves around the relationship between the state and the actor, as opposed to the specific act. Showing "overlapping identity" is highly uncommon, and most often arises where a private actor is performing one of the few functions traditionally and exclusively reserved to the state or is controlled by a state entity. State assistance by itself is insufficient—the relevant question is whether the *decisionmakers* were ostensibly state actors. We answered that question in the affirmative in *Horvath*, where half of the putatively private defendant's trustees were state appointees. *Id.* at 153. But the assistance alleged by Plaintiffs—helping to procure a ward in a hospital and arranging for the assistance of a handful of doctors—is not enough to clear this hurdle. Using government property, government staff, and even government funds does not make a private entity a state actor when its decisions are made independently of the state. *See Yeo v. Town of Lexington*, 131 F.3d 241, 254 (1st Cir. 1997) (en banc).

Plaintiffs' generalized allegations (unsupported by factual allegations) that the government acted to silence critics of the test are no more helpful. They do not allege who these government officials were, how they acted to silence critics, or when in the sequence of events this conduct occurred. Such a "merely conclusory allegation that a private entity acted in concert with a state actor does not suffice to state a § 1983 claim against the private entity." *Ciambriello v. County of Nassau*, 292 F.3d 307, 324 (2d Cir. 2002).

At most, Plaintiffs' complaints alleged that the Nigerian government acquiesced to or approved the Trovan program in general without knowing its disturbing details. That it approved the program is hardly surprising—in the midst of a widespread epidemic, the Nigerian government likely welcomed help from every entity offering it, but "[m]ere approval of or acquiescence in the initiatives of a private party is not sufficient to justify holding the State responsible for those initiatives." *Blum v. Yaretsky*, 457 U.S. 991, 1004–05, 102 S. Ct. 2777, 73 L. Ed. 2d 534 (1982). Plaintiffs have not demonstrated that Pfizer acted "under the color of law" such

---

19 The case relied upon by the district court is entirely distinguishable. *See Nat'l Coal. Gov't of the Union of Burma v. Unocal, Inc.*, 176 F.R.D. 329 (C.D. Cal. 1997). There, plaintiffs survived a motion to dismiss by alleging that Unocal and the Burmese government were joint venturers and partners in a pipeline, with the Burmese government retaliating against protesters with military action and forced labor imposed by the Burmese military with Unocal's knowledge. *Id.* at 348. There, as opposed to here, the state committed the unlawful acts.

that it can be held liable for the Nigerian government's alleged violation of the "law of nations."

* * * *

Plaintiffs' allegations paint a vivid picture of the unspeakable pain and suffering of dozens of innocent children. The issue on this appeal, however, is not whether Pfizer's alleged conduct was "wrong," or even whether it is legally actionable, but whether it falls within both the "narrow class" of international norms for which ATS jurisdiction exists, and the even smaller subset of those norms actionable against non-state actors. Our Court and the Supreme Court have made it pellucidly clear that ATS jurisdiction must be reserved only for acts that the nations of the world collectively determine interfere with their formal relations with one another—including those rare acts by private individuals that are so serious as to threaten the very fabric of peaceful international affairs. I cannot agree with my colleagues that Pfizer's alleged conduct poses the same threat or is so universally and internationally proscribed as to fit within that narrow class.

I respectfully dissent.

RAMCHANDRA ADHIKARI
v.
DAOUD & PARTNERS

Case No. 09-cv-1237 (S.D. Tex. 2009)
Decided Nov. 3, 2009

Agnieszka M. Fryszman, Matthew K. Handley, Maureen E. McOwen, Cohen Milstein et al., Washington, DC, Paul L. Hoffman, Schonbrun Desimone et al., Venice, CA, Andrew S. Golub, Dow Golub Remels & Beverly LLP, Houston, TX, for Plaintiffs.

Aundrea Kristine Frieden, Gibbs & Bruns LLP, Michael W. Mengis, Baker & Hostetler LLP, Houston, TX, Christopher Tayback, Scott Watson, Quinn Emanuel Urquhart Oliver and Hedges LLP, Loura L. Alaverdi, Peter W. James, Loura L. Alaverdi, Baker and Hostetler, Los Angeles, CA, David B. Rivkin, Jr., Lee A. Casey, Carlos Ramos-Mrosovsky, Lee A. Casey, Baker and Hostetler LLP, Washington, DC, for Defendants.

MEMORANDUM AND ORDER

KEITH P. ELLISON, District Judge.

Pending before the Court is the Motion to Dismiss Plaintiffs' First Amended Complaint ("FAC", Doc. No. 58) filed by Defendants Kellogg Brown & Root, Inc.; Kellogg Brown & Root Services, Inc.; KBR, Inc.; KBR Holdings, LLC; Kellogg Brown & Root, LLC; KBR Technical Services, Inc.; Kellogg Brown & Root International, Inc.; Service Employees International, Inc.; and Overseas Administration Services, Ltd. ("KBR" collectively) (Doc. No. 138). For the following reasons, KBR's Motion must be granted in part and denied in part.

I. Background

For purposes of this Motion to Dismiss, the Court accepts the factual allegations in Plaintiffs' FAC as true. *Frame v. City of Arlington,* 575 F.3d 432, 434 (5th Cir. 2009). This case is brought by Plaintiff Buddi Prasad Gurung ("Gurung") and the surviving family members of twelve other men: Prakash Adhikari, Ramesh Khadka, Lalan Koiri, Mangal Limbu, Jeet Magar, Gyanendra Shrestha, Budham Sudi,

Manoj Thakur, Sanjay Thakur, Bishnu Thapa, and Jhok Bahadur Thapa ("Deceased" collectively). All Plaintiffs are Nepali citizens and currently reside in Nepal.

Defendant Daoud & Partners ("Daoud") is a Jordanian corporation. Daoud has entered into a number of contracts with the United States for the provision of services at military bases, including Al Asad Air Base in Iraq. (FAC ¶ 22.) Defendant KBR is a business conglomerate including a parent corporation with its principal place of business in Houston, Texas, and several divisions, subsidiaries, and associated partnerships with pecuniary interests in the outcome of this case. One such KBR subsidiary serves as a contractor with the United States government to perform specific duties at United States military facilities in Iraq. (FAC ¶¶ 23–29.)

The gravamen of the FAC is that, in an effort to fulfill their contractual obligations, Defendants "willfully and purposefully formed an enterprise with the goal of procuring cheap labor and increasing profits" and thereby engaged in human trafficking. (FAC ¶ 54.) Plaintiffs allege that the Deceased, whose ages ranged from 18 to 27, were recruited from their several places of residence in August of 2004 by Moonlight Consultant Pvt, Ltd. ("Moonlight"), a recruiting company based in Nepal. (*Id.* ¶ 62.) Most of the men were told that they would be employed by a luxury hotel in Amman, Jordan. (*Id.* ¶ 63.) Some were told that that they would be working in an American camp. (*Id.*) Although there is no indication that they were told where the camp would be, their family members assumed they were going to the United States. (*Id.*) All of the men were led to believe that they would not be placed in a dangerous location, and that if they found themselves in a dangerous area, they would be sent home at the employer's expense. (*Id.*) They were promised a salary of approximately $500 per month. (*Id.* ¶ 64.) The men and their families incurred substantial debt to pay the brokerage fees in seeking out this employment (*Id.* ¶ 65.)

After they were recruited, Plaintiffs were then transferred to the custody of a Jordanian job brokerage company that operates in Amman called Morning Star for Recruitment and Manpower Supply ("Morning Star"). (*Id.* ¶ 66.) The men were held in Jordan by Daoud and agents of Daoud; all of the men were required to turn over their passports to Daoud. (*Id.* ¶¶ 67–68.) It was there that they first discovered that they were actually being sent to Iraq to work on Al Asad Air Base, north of Ramadi, Iraq. (*Id.* ¶ 70.) Several of the men phoned relatives in Nepal, expressing concern and fear about their futures. (*Id.* ¶¶ 70–71.) At least one of the Deceased informed his family that he and the other men were being kept in a dark room and were unable to see. (*Id.* ¶ 72.) In Jordan, the men were also informed that they would be paid only three quarters of what they were initially promised. (*Id.* ¶ 73.) Daoud transported the Deceased into Iraq on or about August 19, 2004, via an unprotected automobile caravan of seventeen vehicles. (*Id.* ¶ 75.) They traveled along the Amman-to-Baghdad highway, which was known to be a highly dangerous. (*Id.* ¶¶ 76–81.) Daoud was aware of the significant and well-known risks involved in traveling on this highway at the time Plaintiffs were thus transported. (*Id.*) No security was provided for the caravan. (*Id.* ¶ 81.)

As they were nearing Al Asad base, the two lead cars in which the Deceased were being transported were stopped by a group of men who later revealed themselves to be members of the Ansar al-Sunna Army, an insurgent group in Iraq. (*Id.* ¶¶ 81–83.) The men told the drivers to leave the Deceased at the checkpoint, and that the Americans would come from the base to pick them up. (*Id.* ¶ 81.)

Between August 20 and August 24, the Ansar al-Sunna Army posted an internet statement that it had captured the Deceased, posted pictures of the Deceased, and sent a video of ten of the Deceased to the Foreign Ministry of Nepal. (*Id.* ¶¶ 83–86.) Many of the family members of the Deceased saw the images broadcast on Nepali television. In the video, the Deceased described their trip to Iraq, stating that they "were kept as captives in Jordan at first" and were not allowed to return home. (*Id.*) They all stated that they were forced to go to Iraq, and were visibly very frightened. (*Id.*)

On or about August 31, 2004, international media outlets broadcasted video of the Ansar al-Sunna Army executing the Deceased. (*Id.* ¶ 86.) The group beheaded one of the men, and shot the other eleven men in the back of their heads. (*Id.*)

Like the Deceased, Plaintiff Gurung was recruited from his residence in Nepal. (*Id.* ¶ 91.) He was sent to Delhi, India for twenty days and then went on to Amman, Jordan for another twenty days. (*Id.*) Gurung was transported to Iraq in one of the cars of the caravan in which the Deceased were also traveling. (*Id.* ¶ 92.) Gurung's car was not captured by the insurgents, and he arrived at Al Asad base as scheduled. (*Id.* ¶ 93.) There, he was supervised by KBR in his duties as a warehouse loader/unloader. (*Id.*) Upon learning about the death of the Deceased, Gurung became frightened and expressed his desire to return to Nepal. He was told by both Daoud and KBR that he could not leave until his work in Iraq was complete. (*Id.*) After fifteen months, during which he experienced frequent mortar fire without protection, Gurung was permitted to return to Nepal. (*Id.* ¶¶ 95–96.)

Plaintiffs allege that KBR knew or should have known prior to August 2004 of the circumstances under which the men were being brought to Iraq to work for them. KBR was repeatedly told by the workers brought to Iraq from India, Sri Lanka, and Nepal that they did not want to come to Iraq and that they were not informed in advance that they were being brought there. (*Id.* ¶ 98.) Furthermore, Daoud was previously involved in an incident in which eighteen Indian laborers were forcibly kept in a camp in Fallujah where they worked, although they had quit their jobs months before. (*Id.* ¶ 102.)

In addition, KBR knew of complaints made by the workers during their time in Iraq regarding their safety and security, and the provision of food, water, and health care. (*Id.* ¶ 100.) Finally, Plaintiffs allege that KBR had the authority to terminate all subcontractors who mistreated employees, unlawfully compelled employees to perform work, or unlawfully compelled employees to remain somewhere against their will. (*Id.* ¶ 101.)

Pursuant to these allegations, Plaintiffs bring causes of action against Defendants under the Trafficking Victims Protection Reauthorization Act ("TVPRA"), 18 U.S.C. § 1595; the Racketeering Influenced and Corrupt Organizations Act ("RICO"), 18 U.S.C. § 1962(c), as well as conspiracy to violate the same; the Alien Tort Statute ("ATS"), 28 U.S.C. § 1350; and various common law claims including, in particular, negligence claims against KBR. KBR now moves to dismiss these actions pursuant to Federal Rule of Civil Procedure 12(b)(1), claiming that this Court lacks subject matter jurisdiction to hear these claims, and Rule 12(b)(6), alleging that Plaintiffs have failed to state a claim upon which relief can be granted. This case was initially filed in the United States District Court for the Central District of California, but was transferred to this Court pursuant to KBR's motion.

II. Standard of Review

A. FED.R.CIV.P. 12(b)(1)

The court must dismiss a case when the plaintiff fails to establish subject matter jurisdiction. FED.R.CIV.P. 12(b)(1). "It is incumbent on all federal courts to dismiss an action whenever it appears that subject matter jurisdiction is lacking." *Stockman v. Federal Election Comm'n,* 138 F.3d 144, 151 (5th Cir.1998). A case is properly dismissed for lack of subject matter jurisdiction when the court lacks the statutory or constitutional power to adjudicate the case. *Home Builders Ass'n of Mississippi, Inc. v. City of Madison, Miss.,* 143 F.3d 1006, 1010 (5th Cir.1998) (internal quotation marks and citation omitted). The burden of establishing federal jurisdiction rests on the party seeking the federal forum. *Stockman,* 138 F.3d at 151.

B. FED.R.CIV.P. 12(b)(6)

A court may dismiss a complaint for "failure to state a claim upon which relief can be granted." FED.R.CIV.P. 12(b)(6). When considering a Rule 12(b)(6) motion to dismiss, a court must "accept the complaint's well-pleaded facts as true and view them in the light most favorable to the plaintiff." *Johnson v. Johnson,* 385 F.3d 503, 529 (5th Cir.2004). "To survive a Rule 12(b)(6) motion to dismiss, a complaint 'does not need detailed factual allegations,' but must provide the plaintiff's grounds for entitlement to relief-including factual allegations that when assumed to be true 'raise a right to relief above the speculative level.' " *Cuvillier v. Taylor,* 503 F.3d 397, 401 (5th Cir.2007) (citing *Bell Atl. Corp. v. Twombly,* 550 U.S. 544, 555, 127 S.Ct. 1955, 167 L.Ed.2d 929 (2007)). That is, "a complaint must contain sufficient factual matter, accepted as true, to 'state a claim to relief that is plausible on its face.' " *Ashcroft v. Iqbal,* 556 U.S. ——, 129 S.Ct. 1937, 1949, 173 L.Ed.2d 868 (2009) (quoting *Twombly,* 550 U.S. at 570, 127 S.Ct. 1955). A claim has facial plausibility when the plaintiff pleads factual content that allows the court to draw the reasonable inference that the defendant is liable for the misconduct alleged. *Id.* (citing *Twombly,* 550 U.S. at 556, 127 S.Ct. 1955). The plausibility standard is not akin to a "probability requirement," but asks for more than a sheer possibility that a defendant has acted unlawfully. *Id.* A pleading that offers "labels and conclusions" or "a formulaic recitation of the elements of a cause of action" will not be sufficient. *Id.* at 1949 (quoting *Twombly,* 550 U.S. at 555, 127 S.Ct. 1955).

III. TVPRA

A. Extraterritoriality

KBR's first objection to Plaintiffs' claims under the TVPRA is that this Court lacks jurisdiction to hear these claims under the principle of extraterritoriality. Although 18 U.S.C. Section 1596 grants U.S. courts "extra-territorial jurisdiction over any offense (or any attempt or conspiracy to commit an offense) under Sections 1581, 1583, 1584, 1589, 1590, or 1591," which comprise the substantive provisions of the TVPRA, KBR points out that this provision had not been enacted at the time that the alleged offenses occurred. Thus, argues KBR, Plaintiffs are relying on substantive provisions of the TVPRA that were not applicable outside of U.S. territory during the period in question. Although Section 1596 now grants this Court jurisdiction to hear extraterritorial claims under the TVPRA, KBR argues that the presumption against retroactive application of statutes bars this Court from relying on Section 1596 to adjudicate events occurring before its enactment.

A statute that impairs vested substantive rights under existing laws or creates new obligations or duties with respect to events already past are subject to a presumption against retroactivity. *Hughes Aircraft Co. v. United States ex rel. Schumer,* 520 U.S. 939, 947, 117 S.Ct. 1871, 138 L.Ed.2d 135 (1997) (citations omitted). In *Hughes Aircraft,* the Court found that an amendment to the jurisdictional provision of the False Claims Act ("FCA") permitting certain private parties, in addition to the government, to bring suits, could not be applied retroactively. *Id.* at 949, 117 S.Ct. 1871. The Court reasoned that, because these private plaintiffs had different incentives for bringing suit than did government officials, applying the provision retroactively subjected defendants to new disability. *Id.*

Subsequently, however, in *Republic of Austria v. Altmann,* 541 U.S. 677, 124 S.Ct. 2240, 159 L.Ed.2d 1 (2004), the Court held that an amendment to the Foreign Sovereign Immunities Act ("FSIA") that effectively enlarged federal court jurisdiction to hear certain claims against foreign sovereigns could be applied retroactively because it did not affect substantive rights. The Court distinguished *Hughes Aircraft,* stating:

> When a "jurisdictional" limitation adheres to the cause of action in this fashion-when it applies by its terms regardless of where the claim is brought-the limitation is essentially substantive. In contrast, the FSIA simply limits the jurisdiction of federal and state courts to entertain claims against foreign sovereigns. The Act does not create or modify any causes of action.

Id. at 695 n. 15, 124 S.Ct. 2240. The Court then looked to the purpose of FSIA and went on to explain that "[t]he principal purpose of foreign sovereign immunity has never been to permit foreign states and their instrumentalities to shape their conduct in reliance on the promise of future immunity from suit in United States courts." *Id.* at 696, 124 S.Ct. 2240.

The instant proceeding is more analogous to *Republic of Austria* than to *Hughes Aircraft.* As with *Republic of Austria,* this Court does not deprive Defendants of any vested right in applying Section 1596 to the events alleged in Plaintiffs' FAC. The Defendants do not now, nor did they in 2004, have the right to traffic human beings at home or abroad. Furthermore, unlike the jurisdictional provision at issue in *Hughes Aircraft,* Section 1596 does not create any additional duties for, or obligations upon, Defendants. Regardless of the extent of this Court's jurisdiction to hear claims, the passage of the TVPRA plainly created an express public duty to refrain from acts of trafficking. That a defendant, subject to the laws of the United States, chose to commit a criminal act in a location where this Court may not have had jurisdiction does not alter the criminality of the act itself. Section 1596, which explicitly recognizes this Court's jurisdiction over extraterritorial TVPRA claims, only enlarges jurisdiction of courts within the United States, but does not change the operative substantive laws. Thus, the concerns surrounding retroactive application of this statute do not apply.

Furthermore, to find that Section 1596 did not apply retroactively would contravene the purpose of the TVPRA. While the substantive provisions of the TVPRA, which were in place when the alleged acts took place, did not explicitly apply extraterritorially until the passage of Section 1596, human trafficking is by nature an "international" crime; it is difficult clearly to delineate those trafficking acts which are truly "extraterritorial" and those which sufficiently reach across U.S. borders. Accordingly, the thrust of the TVPRA would be severely undermined by a holding that U.S. defendants who gained commercial advantage in this country through engaging in illegal human trafficking were free from liability, so long as the trafficking acts themselves took place outside of American borders. Therefore, the Court finds that the traditional presumption against the retroactive application of statutes would contravene the clear purpose of the TVPRA, and would inappropriately absolve those who could in fact be guilty of violating its provisions.

KBR further contends that, by choosing to extend jurisdiction over alleged TVPRA criminal offenses but declining expressly to include Section 1595, which allows for civil remedies under the TVPRA, Congress manifested its intent not to authorize extraterritorial civil claims. (Def. Mot. at 16.) This argument is unavailing. Section 1596 identifies the substantive criminal provisions of the TVPRA and expands the circumstances under which they can be enforced. The civil remedies authorized by Section 1595 attach when any claim is properly brought before a court of law. In this case, therefore, Section 1595 remedies are triggered because, as discussed above, Plaintiffs bring this case pursuant to this Court's statutorily granted jurisdiction. This is consistent with the structure of the statute, which contains substantive criminal provisions enforceable through civil remedies. To hold that the jurisdictional grant of Section 1596 excludes the remedies provided in Section 1595 would be both illogical and in contravention of the purpose of the statute.

Finally, KBR argues that to hold that Section 1596 applies retroactively would violate constitutional guarantees against ex post facto laws, because the TVPRA is a criminal statute that merely "piggy-backs" civil remedies. (Def. Mot. at 16.) The Ex Post Facto Clause's prohibition is triggered only by a statute that criminally punishes an act that was not criminal when committed, makes the punishment for a crime more burdensome after its commission, or deprives a criminally charged person of a defense that was available when the act was committed. *Wilson v. Lensing,* 943 F.2d 9 (5th Cir.1991) (citing *Collins v. Youngblood,* 497 U.S. 37, 110 S. Ct. 2715, 111 L.Ed.2d 30 (1990)). Changes in the manner in which a criminal case is adjudicated, as opposed to changes in the substantive law of crimes, do not violate the Ex Post Facto Clause. *Collins,* 497 U.S. at 45, 110 S.Ct. 2715.

Here, as previously discussed, the kind of human trafficking in which Plaintiffs claim that Defendants engaged was criminal at the time that the alleged incidents occurred. Section 1596 did nothing to alter or expand the criminality of the actions themselves. Therefore, a conclusion that Section 1596 applies to this case does not violate the Ex Post Facto Clause of the Constitution.

B. Sufficiency of Pleadings

KBR also contends that Plaintiffs' TVPRA allegations fail because they do not allege facts sufficient to support their claims. Under *Iqbal* and *Twombly,* a plaintiff must plead facts in its complaint that make the allegations facially plausible. *Iqbal,* 129 S.Ct. at 1949. Pleadings that offer no more than conclusory allegations and which track the language of the statute itself are insufficient. *Id.* (quoting *Twombly,* 550 U.S. at 555, 127 S.Ct. 1955).

In this case, Plaintiffs' pleadings meet the *Iqbal* standard. Plaintiffs have sufficiently alleged facts to make out claims under Section 1595 and the substantive provisions of the TVPRA.[1] Plaintiffs' complaint alleges that KBR actively participated in and knowingly benefited from a venture that involved forced labor and trafficking. (FAC ¶¶ 97–103.) Plaintiffs further allege facts that make these claims plausible. In the FAC, they allege that the Deceased were misled and deceived into working in a dangerous area, held in a dark room, had their passports taken away,

1 18 U.S.C. Section 1595(a) provides: "An individual who is a victim of a violation may bring a civil action against the perpetrator (or whoever knowingly benefits, financially or by receiving anything of value from participation in a venture which that person knew or should have known has engaged in an act in violation of this chapter) in an appropriate district court of the United States and may recover damages and reasonable attorneys fees." Thus, in this case, Plaintiffs must allege and provide support for the contention that Defendants participated in or knowingly benefited from forced labor (Section 1589) or trafficking (Section 1590).

and were transported against their will along a knowingly dangerous route, all while being told that they could not return to their home country. They further allege that KBR knew this was occurring, both through statements and complaints made by laborers brought to Iraq, as well as through previously publicized complaints and incidents involving Daoud. *Id.* They also allege that KBR deliberately formed an enterprise with the purpose of trafficking cheap labor to U.S. military installations in Iraq in order to earn a profit, and that they performed concrete acts to further this purpose. (FAC ¶¶ 131–36.) Whether these allegations, if proven, will lead to a Plaintiffs' verdict is irrelevant at this stage. Under *Iqbal,* all that is required at this pleading stage is that the claims made by Plaintiffs are plausible, not that they show probability of success. By providing significant, though not indisputable, factual support for their allegations of trafficking, Plaintiffs meet that burden in this case.

IV. Alien Tort Statute

KBR also avers that Plaintiffs' claims under the Alien Tort Statute ("ATS") fail because they do not allege state action, they are not cognizable under *Sosa v. Alvarez-Machain,* 542 U.S. 692, 732, 124 S.Ct. 2739, 159 L.Ed.2d 718 (2004), and they are preempted by claims brought under the TVPRA.

A. State Action

While some circuits require that any claims brought under the Alien Tort Statute allege state action, other circuits have explicitly recognized exceptions to this requirement. In *Kadic v. Karadzic,* 70 F.3d 232, 239 (2d Cir.1995), the Second Circuit held that, for certain categories of action, including genocide, the scope of the law of nations is not confined solely to state action but reaches conduct of private individuals. Other circuits have since elaborated upon this finding. *See Sinaltrainal v. Coca-Cola Co.,* 578 F.3d 1252, 1266–67 (11th Cir.2009) (stating that "plaintiffs need not plead state action for claims of torture and murder perpetrated in the course of war crimes"); *Abdullahi v. Pfizer, Inc.,* 562 F.3d 163, 188 (2d Cir.2009) (finding that a private individual will be held liable under the ATS if he "acted in concert with" the state, that is, "under color of law") (citations omitted); *Abagninin v. AMVAC Chem. Corp.,* 545 F.3d 733, 741 (9th Cir.2008) (holding that the district court correctly found that defendants were not "States or State-like organizations" for purposes of international law or crimes against humanity under ATS); *Doe v. Unocal Corp.,* 963 F. Supp. 880, 891–892 (C.D.Cal.1997) (noting that "forced labor, is among the handful of crimes . . . to which the law of nations attributes individual liability" such that state action is not required). The Fifth Circuit has yet to address this precise issue.

In light of this precedent, this Court recognizes that the state action requirement under the ATS is not absolute. KBR argues that, to the extent that courts have recognized any exception to the state action requirement for ATS claims, they have done so only in instances where the crimes alleged by the plaintiff were so grave as to rise to the level of war crimes or genocidal acts. According to KBR, the crimes alleged here fall significantly short of this level. Plaintiffs do not deny that courts have regularly required that claims brought under the ATS allege some form of state action. Rather, they argue that state action is a requirement only for claims for which state action is an element of the law of nations violation that gives rise to the ATS claim. In other words, whether a claim against a private individual is actionable under the ATS is determined by the nature and requirements of the underlying offense. This argument is consistent with the widely accepted notion that slave trade, which is traditionally carried out by private actors, does not require state action in order to constitute a violation of the law of nations. *See, e.g.,* RESTATEMENT (THIRD) OF FOREIGN RELATIONS LAW § 404; Supplementary Convention on the Abolition of Slavery, the Slave Trade and Institutions and Practices Similar to Slavery, 1956, art. 3 § 1, Sept. 7, 1956, 18 U.S.T. 3201, 226 U.N.T.S. 3 (prescribing penalties for "persons" convicted of various forms of slavery). Plaintiffs' argument finds further support in recent ATS case law. *See Kadic v. Karadzic,* 70 F.3d 232, 241 (2d Cir.1995) (finding that, because evolving standards of international law govern who is within the ATS jurisdictional grant, courts must examine the offense of which the private defendant is accused in determining ATS actionability); *Beanal v. Freeport-McMoRan, Inc.,* 969 F. Supp. 362, 371 (E.D.La.1997) (finding that state action is not required for all international torts covered by the ATS, as certain conduct, like genocide, violates the law of nations whether committed by a state or private actor).

This Court finds Plaintiffs' arguments and reasoning to be based on sound principle. Although, as Plaintiffs point out, federal courts of appeal have explicitly found exceptions to the state action requirement only in the context of genocide or war crimes, this Court recognizes that internationally accepted prohibitions on those acts are not limited to states, but also extend to private individuals. Accordingly, ATS claims for violations of those offenses do not require state action. The law cited above makes it clear that the state action requirement is not inherent to the ATS; rather, its frequent and consistent application by courts for claims brought under the ATS stems from the fact that, for the majority of crimes recognized as universal norms and international law, the accused actor must be a state. Thus, to the extent that Plaintiffs can show that *private* acts of trafficking have become universally prohibited, the ATS state action requirement does not apply.

As elaborated upon further below, Plaintiffs have in fact met that burden. It is apparent from the findings of both judicial and academic authorities, discussed later in this Memorandum and Order, that human trafficking and forced labor, whether committed by states or private individuals, have been recognized as violations of *jus cogens* norms, and therefore fall within the jurisdictional grant of the ATS.

B. Cognizable under *Sosa*

Claims cognizable under the ATS statute are those that are "specific, universal, and obligatory" international legal norms. *Sosa v. Alvarez-Machain,* 542 U.S. 692, 732, 124 S.Ct. 2739, 159 L.Ed.2d 718 (2004). In *Sosa,* the Court stated that, when deciding whether an alleged norm of international law is sufficiently definite that violation thereof will support cause of action under the ATS, the court, in absence of any treaty, or of any controlling executive or legislative act or judicial decision, must resort to

> the customs and usages of civilized nations and, as evidence of these, to works of jurists and commentators, who by years of labor, research and experience, have made themselves peculiarly well acquainted with the subjects of which they treat. Such works are resorted to by judicial tribunals, not for the speculations of their authors concerning what the law ought to be, but for trustworthy evidence of what the law really is.

Id. at 734, 124 S.Ct. 2739 (quoting *The Paquete Habana,* 175 U.S. 677, 700, 20 S.Ct. 290, 44 L.Ed. 320 (1900)). Furthermore, "the determination whether a norm is sufficiently definite to support a cause of action should (and, indeed, inevitably must) involve an element of judgment about the practical consequences of making that cause available to litigants in the federal courts." *Id.* at 732–33, 124 S.Ct. 2739. The existence of a norm or customary international law is one determined, in part, by reference to the custom or practices of many states and the broad acceptance of that norm by the international community. *Abdullahi v. Pfizer, Inc.,* 562 F.3d 163, 176 (2d Cir.2009). Furthermore, whether the treaty that embodies the alleged crimes is self-executing is relevant to, but not determinative of, the question of whether the norm permits ATS jurisdiction. *Id.* It is important to distinguish between those claims that are not actionable under the ATS because this Court lacks jurisdiction, from those that should be dismissed due to insufficient pleadings. *See John Roe I v. Bridgestone Corp.,* 492 F. Supp. 2d 988, 1006 (S.D.Ind.2007) (finding that "to establish subject matter jurisdiction under the ATS it should be sufficient that plaintiffs allege an arguable violation of the law of nations," which is different from whether they adequately plead a violation of the law of nations).

Plaintiffs cite to several documents of international consensus that prohibit the modern forms of forced labor alleged in the FAC. (FAC ¶ 170.) Plaintiffs also point to numerous international conventions which prohibit human trafficking. (*Id.*) Numerous courts within the United States have found trafficking, forced labor, and involuntary servitude cognizable under ATS. *See, e.g., Licea v. Curacao Drydock Co., Inc.,* 584 F. Supp. 2d 1355 (S.D.Fla.2008) (finding that alleged forced labor and international human trafficking of plaintiff by operator of a drydock facility constituted violations of international law); *In re World War II Era Japanese Forced Labor Litigation,* 164 F. Supp. 2d 1160, 1179 (N.D.Cal.2001) (holding that forced labor violates the law of nations); *Doe v. Unocal Corp.,* 963 F. Supp. 880, 892 (C.D.Cal.1997) (allegations that defendants participated and benefited from forced labor sufficient to establish jurisdiction under the ATS).

The Court finds this sufficient to establish that the trafficking and forced labor alleged in this FAC qualify as universal international norms under *Sosa,* such that they are actionable under ATS. The Declaration of Professor William J. Aceves, in which he describes the overwhelming consensus regarding the status of forced labor and trafficking as international crimes, only provides further support for this conclusion. (Pl. Resp., Ex. 15.)[2] In their FAC, Plaintiffs allege that they were deceived and coerced into traveling to Iraq to work for KBR, thereby making them victims of human trafficking and forced labor. Whether these crimes have been sufficiently pled is a separate issue with no bearing upon this Court's jurisdiction to consider the claims. Thus, this Court has jurisdiction to consider Plaintiffs' ATS claims.

C. TVPRA Preemption

KBR further alleges that Plaintiffs' ATS claims are preempted by those brought pursuant to the TVPRA. Because few courts have addressed preemption specifically in the context of the TVPRA, it is helpful to look to the case law addressing this very issue with respect to the Torture Victim Protections Act ("TVPA").

There is a clear divide among circuits as to the preemptive effect of the TVPA on claims brought under ATS. According to some circuits, the enactment of the TVPA did not diminish the scope of the ATS in any way. *See Kadic v. Karadzic,* 70 F.3d 232, 241 (2d Cir.1995) ("[t]he scope of the Alien Tort Act remains undiminished by enactment of the Torture Victim Act"); *Aldana v. Del Monte Fresh Produce, Inc.,* 416 F.3d 1242, 1250 (11th Cir.2005) (finding that plaintiff may bring distinct claims under both the TVPA and the ATS). The Seventh Circuit, however, disagrees with this finding. *See Enahoro v. Abubakar,* 408 F.3d 877, 885 (7th Cir.2005) (finding that creation of a specific statutory cause of action under the TVPA preempts ATS claims).

We choose to adopt the reasoning of the Second and Ninth Circuits in holding that the TVPRA and the ATS provide separate and distinct causes of action for the alleged crimes. Particularly at this preliminary stage in the litigation, Plaintiffs should be given the chance to proceed on both theories in order to assess over the course of discovery which best captures the nature of the events that took place, and the remedies that are sought.

---

2 The Court has considered Defendant's Motion to Strike Professor Aceve's Declaration (Doc. No. 148). In light of the fact that *Sosa* anticipates that courts may look to jurists and commentators for evidence as to the content of international law, *Sosa*, 542 U.S. at 734, 124 S.Ct. 2739, and that courts routinely use declarations of academic experts to assist them in deciding upon subject matter jurisdiction under the ATS, this Court finds that this Motion should be denied. Nonetheless, based on the international agreements and case law cited by Plaintiffs, the Court finds that Professor Aceve's Declaration is not necessary to its determination that the crimes alleged in Plaintiffs' FAC create actionable claims under the ATS.

V. RICO Claims

KBR objects to Plaintiffs' RICO claims on numerous grounds. Each of these objections will be considered in turn:

A. Subject Matter Jurisdiction

KBR first asserts that this Court lacks subject matter jurisdiction over these claims, because RICO does not allow for subject matter jurisdiction over alleged foreign conduct with only foreign effects.[3] Courts have created two basic tests for subject matter jurisdiction in RICO actions that involve activity abroad: the "conduct" test, which in essence asks whether the fraudulent conduct that forms the alleged violation occurred in the United States, and the "effects" test, which asks whether conduct outside the United States has had a substantial adverse effect on American investors or securities markets. *Robinson v. TCI/US W. Commc'ns Inc.,* 117 F.3d 900, 905 (5th Cir.1997).

1. Extraterritorially Indictable RICO offenses

As a preliminary matter, Plaintiffs argue that the predicate acts of which the FAC alleges Defendants are guilty are extraterritorially indictable, thereby making the conduct/effects analysis unnecessary with respect to their RICO claims. RICO applies to any act that is indictable under specified provisions of Title 18, including 18 U.S.C. Sections 1589, 1590, and 1592, the offense alleged here. 18 U.S.C. § 1961. Plaintiffs aver that the Military Extraterritorial Jurisdiction Act ("MEJA"), 18 U.S.C. § 3261, renders the offenses on which their RICO claims are predicated extraterritorially indictable, thereby removing the extraterritoriality concerns of the alleged RICO violations. MEJA provides:

> Whoever engages in conduct outside the United States that would constitute an offense punishable by imprisonment for more than 1 year if the conduct had been engaged in within the special maritime and territorial jurisdiction of the United States while employed by or accompanying the Armed Forces outside the United States . . . shall be punished as provided for that offense."

3 In their Response, Plaintiffs aver that extraterritorial concerns do not apply in this case, because the Al Asad base is "subject to the exclusive control and authority of the United Nations Multinational Force-Iraq," citing *Rasul v. Bush*, 542 U.S. 466, 480, 124 S.Ct. 2686, 159 L.Ed.2d 548 (2004). (Pl. Resp. at 13–14.) While the Court has misgivings about the applicability of *Rasul* to the specific circumstances of this case, we find it unnecessary to reach this question. As a significant portion of the events and conduct that make up the alleged RICO violation took place outside of the Al Asad base, we find that, regardless of the status of the base, it is necessary to perform an extraterritorial RICO analysis. Furthermore, because we do not reach this question, we also find it unnecessary to consider KBR's Motion to Strike the declaration of Maureen E. McOwen and the exhibit attached thereto-a chart comparing U.S. jurisdiction and control at U.S. military bases in Iraq, Cuba, and Bermuda. The Court did not consider this evidence in its analysis.

18 U.S.C. § 3261(a). KBR does not controvert Plaintiffs' assertion that, if the offenses upon which the RICO claims are predicated are extraterritorially indictable, then extraterritoriality concerns do not apply to their RICO claims. Instead, KBR attempts to limit MEJA's applicability to those federal statutes that reference the "special maritime and territorial jurisdiction" of the United States. This Court finds that imposing such a limitation is inappropriate. As Plaintiffs point out, MEJA indictments have been issued and upheld for violations of federal statutes of general applicability, or those enacted pursuant to Congress's enumerated powers as opposed to U.S. special maritime and territorial jurisdiction. (*See* Pl. Supp. Brief, Doc. No. 167, at 7.) Sections 1589, 1590, and 1592, as federal laws of general applicability, could, under MEJA, therefore also extend extraterritorially to parties employed by the United States Armed Forces, including KBR. This Court therefore holds that, because the alleged predicate offenses can be indicted extraterritorially, the RICO allegations at issue here are not subject to extraterritoriality limitations indicated in the conduct and effects tests. Nonetheless, because of MEJA's novelty and the relatively limited contexts in which it has been applied, we will now proceed through the conduct and effects analysis so as to avoid resting our jurisdictional finding on a relatively murky area of the law.

2. Conduct Test

As to the conduct test, circuits are divided as to the nature of the conduct necessary to establish jurisdiction. The Second and District of Columbia Circuits have adopted a more restrictive position in which the domestic conduct must have been "of material importance" to or have "directly caused the acts complained of." *Robinson,* 117 F.3d at 905 (citing *Itoba Ltd. v. Lep Gr. PLC,* 54 F.3d 118, 122 (2d Cir.1995); *Zoelsch v. Arthur Andersen & Co.,* 824 F.2d 27, 31–33 (D.C.Cir.1987); *Psimenos v. E.F. Hutton & Co.,* 722 F.2d 1041, 1045–46 (2d Cir.1983); *IIT v. Cornfeld,* 619 F.2d 909, 918–21 (2d Cir.1980) (remaining citations omitted)). The Third, Eighth, and Ninth Circuits, on the other hand, generally require some "lesser quantum of conduct," and look to whether the domestic conduct is significant to, rather than the direct cause of, the alleged crimes. *Id.* (citing *Butte Mining PLC v. Smith,* 76 F.3d 287, 290-91 (9th Cir.1996); *Grunenthal GmbH v. Hotz,* 712 F.2d 421, 424–25 (9th Cir.1983); *Cont'l Grain (Australia) Pty. Ltd. v. Pac. Oilseeds, Inc.,* 592 F.2d 409, 420–21 (8th Cir.1979); *SEC v. Kasser,* 548 F.2d 109, 114 (3d Cir.1977); *Travis v. Anthes Imperial, Ltd.,* 473 F.2d 515, 524 (8th Cir.1973)). In *Robinson,* the Fifth Circuit expressly adopted the more restrictive test of the Second Circuit. *Id.* at 906. Thus, in evaluating the case at hand, we look to whether KBR's domestic conduct was of material importance to, or the direct cause of, the crimes alleged by Plaintiffs.

Here, we cannot find that the conduct test is met. Although, as Plaintiffs point out, it seems that much of the decision making as to KBR contracting was within the United States, the Court finds these actions significantly remote from the alleged acts of trafficking, which occurred between and among Nepal, Jordan, and Iraq.

Indeed, according to KBR in its Motion to Transfer Venue (Doc. No. 39), it was only the umbrella contract governing KBR's operation of various military bases in Iraq that was managed in the United States; KBR's subsequent subcontract with Daoud was executed in Iraq. (Def. Mot., Doc. No. 39, at 11.) Plaintiffs offer no facts or evidence to contradict this assertion; this Court therefore accepts it as true. Because the RICO allegations primarily involve the decision making structure between and among KBR, Daoud, and other parties located abroad who are not named in this litigation, we cannot say that the management decisions made in the United States were the direct cause of, or were material to, the alleged harms experienced by Plaintiffs. Thus, the conduct test is not met in this case.

3. Effects Test

We must now look to whether Plaintiffs have satisfied the effects test for extraterritorial jurisdiction. The effects test provides for jurisdiction whenever there are "substantial effects within the United States." *North South Fin. Corp. v. Al-Turki,* 100 F.3d 1046, 1051 (2d Cir.1996). The court in *North South Finance* was careful to distinguish between substantial effects and "remote and indirect effects." *Id.*

KBR cites to several cases to support its contention that Plaintiffs must be actually injured within the United States for the effects test to be met. However, unlike the circumstances of those cases, this case does not involve fraudulent acts concerning securities in which the harms are primarily economic in nature. (Def. Mot. at 5.) *See Norex Petrol. Ltd. v. Access Indus., Inc.,* 540 F. Supp. 2d 438 (S.D.N.Y.2007); *Interbrew v. Edperbrascan Corp.,* 23 F. Supp. 2d 425 (S.D.N.Y.1998). The RICO statute is designed to punish organized criminal activity, the effects of which can be physical and/or economic in nature. That these foreign Plaintiffs experienced the physical effects of the alleged RICO crimes outside of this country is therefore not dispositive in determining whether the effects test has been met, if the economic harms of the alleged violation did reach across American borders.

Accordingly, this Court must examine the domestic effects and determine if they were, in fact, sufficiently substantial. The effects that Plaintiffs allege in this case are that "the supply of cheap labor benefited the RICO participants, which disadvantaged their competitors for [Department of Defense] contracts and impacted the U.S. labor market, and the jobs were not offered to U.S. workers." (Pl. Resp. at 16.) In addition, Plaintiffs point to the fact that the alleged RICO enterprise passed money through the U.S. banking system, and that the contracts were funded by U.S. taxpayers. *Id.*

Taking these allegations as true, as the Court must, this case presents a large American business allegedly engaged in racketeering activity. More specifically, we note that the FAC describes an American defendant engaged in labor trafficking on a systematic, widespread scale. The American defendant gained substantial economic benefit through this activity, and this gain occurred at the expense of other American companies bidding for the same government contracts. Finally, the alleged racketeering activity occurred in furtherance of a public purpose, namely the U.S. occupation in Iraq. Regardless of whether these allegations prove true, this Court nonetheless finds that Plaintiffs have sufficiently alleged substantial effects within the United States such that this court may exercise jurisdiction over these claims.

B. RICO Standing

KBR further objects to Plaintiffs' RICO claims on the grounds that Plaintiffs lack RICO standing. A plaintiff has RICO standing if he has been "injured in his business or property by the conduct constituting the violation." *Sedima, S.P.R.L. v. Imrex Co.,* 473 U.S. 479, 483, 105 S.Ct. 3275, 87 L.Ed.2d 346 (1985). Lost property is not equated with legally protected property rights in procedural due process analysis; what is required is a legal entitlement to business relations unhampered by schemes prohibited by the RICO predicate statutes. *Mendoza v. Zirkle Fruit Co.,* 301 F.3d 1163, 1168 (9th Cir.2002). Plaintiffs in this case allege that, as a result of KBR's conduct, Plaintiffs were compelled to pay out-of-pocket fees to Defendants, suffered a reduction in promised wages, and were prevented from obtaining alternative employment. (FAC ¶¶ 65, 69, 73, 74.)

We find these allegations of financial loss sufficient to establish RICO standing. The Fifth Circuit has recognized that alleged victims of trafficking violations have RICO standing for claims of denied wages. *See Abraham v. Singh,* 480 F.3d 351 (5th Cir.2007) (reaching the question of whether RICO allegations based on alleged trafficking were sufficiently pled). Thus, the Deceased, in addition to Gurung, would have had standing to bring these claims for relief had they survived.

Instead, Plaintiffs, aside from Gurung, bring this case on behalf of their deceased relatives. The most persuasive authority as to whether the family members of the Deceased have standing to assert these claims is from the Fourth Circuit. It has expressly upheld a number of district court opinions finding that RICO claims survive the death of the injured party. *Faircloth v. Finesod,* 938 F.2d 513, 518 (4th Cir.1991) (noting that "civil RICO claims do not abate upon the death of the injured party") (citing cases). Although the Fifth Circuit has yet to address this precise issue, we find no reason to reject this principled reasoning.

In addition, there is proximate causation in this case, because the allegations assert financial losses resulting from Defendants' alleged acts of trafficking, not from the untimely death of the Deceased at the hands of terrorists. It is clear from this case, and others brought in other circuits, that the statutory requirements for standing under RICO are not so rigorous as to render Plaintiffs' allegations inadequate.

C. Statute of Limitations

KBR also objects to Plaintiffs' RICO claims as a violation of the four-year statute of limitations. This limitation begins to run as soon as Plaintiffs "knew or should have known about this injury." *Rotella v. Wood,* 147 F.3d 438, 439–40 (5th Cir.1998), *aff'd,* 528 U.S. 549, 555–58, 120 S.Ct. 1075, 145 L.Ed.2d 1047 (2000).

Here, KBR alleges that the statute of limitations began to run on either August 19, 2004, or August 24, 2004, the day that the laborers were informed that they were being taken to Iraq, and the day that the Foreign Ministry received the video in which ten of the Deceased stated that they were forcibly taken to Iraq, respectively. Thus, KBR alleges that Plaintiffs, in bringing this action on August 27, 2008, missed the statute of limitation by three days.

This Court takes note of the fact that more typical cases under RICO involve acts of ongoing securities fraud in which the plaintiffs are not subject to any form of restricted movement, and are often sophisticated participants in commerce. Here, the Deceased were killed before having any significant contact with their family members regarding the circumstances that led them into the custody of terrorists. We cannot assume that, on August 24, 2004 the day the video was sent to the Nepali government, the family members of the Deceased were immediately aware of it or knew of the facts presented in Plaintiffs' RICO claims. In fact, as Plaintiffs point out in their Response, the alleged trafficking enterprise was deliberately concealed by at least some of Defendants, who deceived both Plaintiffs' families as well as the Nepali government into thinking that the men were being taken to Jordan. Such concealment is further evidence of the improbability that the families of the Deceased were sufficiently certain as to their sons' situations to initiate legal proceedings on August 24. (Pl. Resp. at 24.) In addition, Gurung has alleged that, although he was working in Iraq for some time, he was not permitted to leave or travel such that he could take legal action upon realizing that he was the victim of trafficking. We cannot find, in light of the restrictions placed upon his freedom of movement, that the statute of limitations began to run while Gurung was still being held in Iraq. *Cf. Wallace v. Kato,* 549 U.S. 384, 388, 127 S.Ct. 1091, 166 L.Ed.2d 973 (2007) (finding that the limitations for a Section 1983 action began to run when the alleged false imprisonment ended).

Accordingly, this Court cannot find, on the present record, that August 19 and 24, 2004 are the relevant dates from which the statute of limitations should be measured. On August 19, 2004, the men themselves became aware that they were being sent to Iraq, but were prevented from acting upon this knowledge because of the continuing acts of trafficking. On August 24, 2004, it became known to the Nepali government that the Deceased had been captured, but the family members presumably remained unaware of the circumstances that brought them to that tragic situation. This Court finds that, in light of the notably small margin by which KBR asserts that the limitation has been breached, we can conclusively find that Plaintiffs did not become aware of their injuries until after August 27, 2004, and thus there is no statute of limitations violation in this case.

D. Plaintiffs Failure to Plead a Violation under Section 1962(c)

In order successfully to bring an action under RICO, Plaintiffs must allege (1) conduct (2) of an enterprise (3) through a pattern (4) of racketeering activity. *Sedima, S.P.R.L. v. Imrex Co.,* 473 U.S. 479, 496, 105 S.Ct. 3275, 87 L.Ed.2d 346 (1985).

1. Allegations of an Association-In-Fact Enterprise

KBR contends that Plaintiffs failed adequately to allege an association-in-fact enterprise. In the recent case of *Boyle v. United States,* ____ U.S. ____, 129 S.Ct. 2237, 173 L.Ed.2d 1265 (2009), the Supreme Court clarified the pleading standard for alleging an association-in-fact under RICO. There, the Court found that the enterprise was required to have structure, but it need not have an ascertainable structure beyond that inherent in the pattern of racketeering activity in which it engaged. *Boyle,* 129 S.Ct. at 2244. In other words, it need not have a hierarchical structure or a chain-of-command. *Id.* An association-in-fact is merely "a group of persons associated together for a common purpose of engaging in a course of conduct." *Id.* at 2243–44. By alleging that the alleged RICO enterprise acted to fulfill Department of Defense contracts through engaging in a "pattern of racketeering activity for the common illegal purpose of providing trafficked labor at a low cost," Plaintiffs have alleged that KBR was part of a unit that, even absent any decision making structure, worked cooperatively and illegally to achieve that goal. (FAC ¶¶ 132–33.) That they allege no facts to suggest that KBR had any actual contact with Moonlight or Morningstar is of no moment; the allegations that KBR actively associated themselves with Daoud is enough to establish that they were acting as part of an enterprise to achieve a common purpose: the provision of cheap labor for the fulfillment of the government contract.

2. "Racketeering Activity"

Racketeering activity must consist of two or more predicate acts that "amount to or pose a threat of continued criminal activity." *H.J. Inc. v. Nw. Bell Tel. Co.,* 492 U.S. 229, 239, 109 S.Ct. 2893, 106 L.Ed.2d 195 (1989). One method of alleging continuity is to show that the offenses are part of an entity's "regular way of doing business." *Id.* at 241–43, 109 S.Ct. 2893. The Court finds that Plaintiffs have sufficiently alleged that KBR regularly employed laborers brought to Iraq against their will. Aside from Plaintiff Gurung, who was in Iraq for the full fifteen months of his contract, Plaintiffs name another Nepali laborer, Sarad Sapkota, who was allegedly brought to Iraq against his will in 2003. (FAC ¶ 98.) They further allege that Sapkota was brought there with ninety other laborers from Sri Lanka and Nepal, who were there under similar circumstances. (*Id.* ¶ 99.) We find these allegations sufficiently plead that bringing in cheap laborers against their will was part and parcel of KBR's operation at Al Asad base. Thus, the pleading requirements for continuity are met.

KBR further alleges that Plaintiffs have not met the standard of *Iqbal* and *Twombly* in alleging the predicate acts necessary for a RICO claim. As KBR points out, the predicate crimes that Plaintiffs allege in their complaint involve the common elements of coercion, deception, and force. (Def. Mot. at 12.)

In accordance with the finding that Plaintiffs have sufficiently pled a violation of the TVPRA, this Court also finds that the predicate acts under RICO have been sufficiently alleged. That Plaintiffs were deceived over the course of their journey to Iraq is made clear; they were all told they would be employed at either a hotel in Jordan or in an area where there would be no danger to their lives. (FAC ¶ 63.) Plaintiffs also allege elements of force and coercion. Plaintiffs incurred extreme financial debt to arrange their promised employment opportunities, they were required to turn over their passports when they arrived in Jordan, and were kept in a room so dark they were unable to see. (FAC ¶ 65, 68, 72.) Plaintiff Gurung was specifically told in Iraq, upon expressing his fear and desire to return home, that he could not leave until his employment was over. (FAC ¶ 94.) The fact that physical force is not explicitly alleged in the Complaint should not be given the weight that KBR assigns it. "Conduct other than the use, or threatened use, of law or physical force may, under some circumstances, have the same effect as the more traditional forms of coercion-or may even be more coercive." *U.S. v. Mussry,* 726 F.2d 1448, 1453 (9th Cir.1984). That these factual allegations may not be sufficient conclusively to prove the elements of force or coercion is irrelevant; what is significant to the Court at this stage is that they make the predicate acts alleged by Plaintiff plausible.

3. Sufficiency of Plaintiffs' pleadings under Section 1962(d)

To be guilty of a RICO conspiracy, the conspirator must agree "to the objective of a violation of RICO; he need not agree personally to violate the statute." *U.S. v. Marmolejo,* 89 F.3d 1185, 1196 (5th Cir.1996). "A conspirator must intend to further an endeavor which, if completed, would satisfy all the elements of a substantive criminal offense, but it suffices that he adopt the goal of furthering or facilitating the criminal endeavor." *Salinas v. United States,* 522 U.S. 52, 65, 118 S.Ct. 469, 139 L.Ed.2d 352 (1997).

This case, Plaintiffs allege that, in subcontracting with Daoud, KBR willfully entered into an agreement with another party to benefit from and to further the goal of procuring cheap labor and increasing profits. Plaintiffs point out that the predicate acts alleged in their briefs required recruitment, transportation, retention, and supervision. Plaintiffs further allege KBR's knowledge of the recruiting and transporting, and their active participation in the retention and supervision. (FAC ¶¶ 94–102.) These allegations sufficiently allege a violation under 18 U.S.C. Section 1962(d).

4. Vicarious Liability Under RICO

KBR also seeks to dismiss Plaintiffs' alternative theory of KBR's vicarious RICO liability for the actions of Daoud. At this preliminary stage, the FAC does allege facts that would establish an agency relationship between KBR and Daoud. Plaintiffs point out that a contractual relationship existed between KBR and Daoud. KBR is correct that a contract does not automatically create a principal-agent relationship. *See Texaco Exploration & Prod., Inc. v. AmClyde Engineered Prods. Co.,* 448 F.3d 760, 778–79 (5th Cir.2006); *Avondale Indus. v. Int'l Marine Carriers,*

15 F.3d 489, 494 (5th Cir.1994). However, because the only burden on Plaintiff at this pleading stage is one of plausibility, the contractual relationship between KBR and Daoud, combined with Plaintiffs' additional allegations that "KBR had the authority to supervise, prohibit, control, and/or regulate Daoud personnel," meet the *Iqbal* standard in establishing a principal-agent relationship. (FAC ¶ 206.)

VI. Negligence Claims

KBR avers that Plaintiffs' common law negligence claims should be dismissed as violating the applicable two-year statute of limitations.[4] Because the limitations period on Plaintiffs' negligence claims is two years shorter than that under RICO, the rationale used there will not apply to these claims.

Plaintiffs argue that this Court should invoke the "extraordinary circumstances" doctrine to apply equitable tolling to these negligence claims. (Pl. Resp. at 24–25.) It is true that, in cases of violent civil war or authoritarian regimes, courts have applied equitable tolling to claims brought by plaintiffs unable to vindicate their legal rights because of unrest and instability. *See Jean v. Dorelien,* 431 F.3d 776, 780 (11th Cir.2005) (citing cases). However, such cases differ in material respects. Most notably, they involve civil unrest at the hands of authoritarian governments that directly prohibited the plaintiffs from bringing their claims to light. *See, e.g., Hilao v. Estate of Marcos,* 103 F.3d 767, 773 (9th Cir.1996) (tolling statute of limitations for claims of torture, disappearance, and summary execution against former Philippine dictator Ferdinand Marcos until he left power and the country regained democratic rule); *Doe v. Saravia,* 348 F. Supp. 2d 1112, 1146–48 (E.D.Cal.2004) (tolling statute of limitations during and after El Salvadorian civil war due to fear of retaliation from military, government, and death squads if plaintiffs were to bring litigation in United States); *Doe v. Unocal Corp.,* 963 F. Supp. 880, 897 (C.D.Cal.1997) (stating that ATCA and TVPA claims "should be tolled" during Burmese dictatorship based on plaintiffs' alleged inability to "obtain access to judicial review" in Burma and the "threat of reprisal from [the government]" if plaintiffs attempted to access courts in the United States). While Plaintiffs point out that Nepal was mired in a civil war between the Nepali government and Maoist rebels that lasted until November of 2006, they allege no facts which suggest that this war had a direct and significant impact on the ability of litigants to bring civil claims, particularly against an American company with no connections to the fighting. They allege nothing to suggest that Plaintiffs were prohibited from traveling or were otherwise cut off from the information necessary for them to learn of Defendants' actions for two full years following the death of their sons. Indeed, the "limited contact with the outside world" which Plaintiffs do allege seems more a product of Plaintiffs' geographic location and economic circumstances, rather than

4 California Code of Civil Procedure Section 335.1 and Texas Civil Practice and Remedies Code Section 16.003 impose an identical two-year limitations period for personal injuries attributable to the wrongful act or neglect of another.

the civil conflict itself. Geographic location and personal hardship cannot provide the sole basis for tolling an otherwise applicable statute of limitations.

In addition, because Plaintiffs maintain the possibility of legal recourse through their human rights claims under the TVPRA, the ATS, and RICO, this Court cannot view this as a compelling case for equitable tolling of Plaintiffs' negligence claims under state law. Barring these claims on statute of limitations grounds does not leave Plaintiffs without legal recourse. Thus, in light of the two-year statute of limitations, this Court finds that Plaintiffs' negligence claims against KBR must be dismissed.

VII. Conclusion

In light of the foregoing, KBR's Motion to Dismiss is hereby **GRANTED IN PART** and **DENIED IN PART.**

IT IS SO ORDERED.

LAWRENCE BELKIN
v.
ISLAMIC REPUBLIC OF IRAN

667 F. Supp. 2d 8 (D.D.C. 2009)
Decided September 30, 2009

Emil Hirsch, Paul L. Knight, Nossanam LLP/O'Connor & Hannan, LLP, Washington, DC, for Plaintiff.

OPINION, FINDINGS OF FACT, AND CONCLUSIONS OF LAW

PAUL L. FRIEDMAN, District Judge.

This matter is before the Court on plaintiff Lawrence Belkin's motion, individually and as next of kin of Gail Belkin, for default judgment under Rule 55 of the Federal Rules of Civil Procedure, based on the sworn affidavits, exhibits, and other evidence submitted to the Court in support of the entry of a default judgment. This case arises from the 1996 killing of plaintiff's wife in Israel as the result of a suicide bombing allegedly sponsored by the defendants and carried out by the Palestinian Islamic Jihad.

I. Procedural History

1. On April 20, 2006, plaintiff filed his complaint in this Court seeking, among other things, compensation for his emotional distress and economic loss due to the wrongful death of his wife, Gail Belkin.

2. In accordance with the relevant provision of the Foreign Sovereign Immunities Act, 28 U.S.C. § 1608(a), and 22 C.F.R. § 93.2, plaintiff caused the complaint, summons and Notice of Suit, along with translations of each, to be served on each defendant, namely the Islamic Republic of Iran ("Iran"), Iran's Ministry of Information and Security ("MOIS"), and the Islamic Revolutionary Guard Corp of Iran ("IRGC").

3. Service of process was initially attempted on each defendant in Tehran, Iran via DHL pursuant to 28 U.S.C. § 1608(a)(3) on July 6, 2006 and on August 18, 2006. The DHL packages were refused on August 26, 2006, and the return receipt was returned unexecuted on August 28, 2006. Docket No. 5.

4. At plaintiff's request, the summonses were reissued on November 1, 2006, and on December 12, 2006 only as to Iran and MOIS, whereupon the Clerk of the Court was requested to assist with service of process under 28 U.S.C. § 1608(a)(4). Docket No. 8.

5. Service of process was further attempted via diplomatic channels pursuant to 28 U.S.C. § 1608(a)(4) on Iran and MOIS. On December 11, 2006, plaintiff made a request to the Clerk of the Court by letter. The Clerk of the Court transmitted the service documents to the State Department on January 25, 2007. Docket No. 9. The documents were transmitted to Iran's Ministry of Foreign Affairs via the Embassy of Switzerland on April 22, 2007 under cover of diplomatic notes, numbers 1069-IE and 1070-IE. The Iranian Ministry of Foreign Affairs returned the documents after being served, but service was effective as of April 22, 2007 under 28 U.S.C. § 1608(c)(1). Docket No. 10; *see also* Plaintiff's Exhibit 1.[1]

6. Defendants' answer was due on June 21, 2007. Defendants Iran and MOIS failed to enter any appearance and failed to respond by that date. To date, no responses have been made by either defendant.

7. On July 2, 2007, plaintiff requested the Clerk of this Court to enter a default, which was entered by the Clerk on July 6, 2007. Docket No. 12. On July 27, 2007, plaintiff moved for default judgment. Docket No. 14. On December 7, 2007, plaintiff made his evidentiary submission consisting of affidavits, videotapes, and documents to the Court. Plaintiff submitted proposed findings of fact and conclusions of law.

8. On March 28, 2008, prior to the Court ruling on plaintiff's motion for default judgment, plaintiff moved for leave to file a First Amended Complaint under the authority of Section 1083 of the National Defense Authorization Act for Fiscal Year 2008 ("NDAA"), Pub. L. 110-181, which was signed by the President and enacted into law on January 28, 2008. The First Amended Complaint was lodged with the motion.

9. The Court granted leave to file the First Amended Complaint on June 17, 2008. The Amended Complaint added three additional causes of action under federal common law. They are Wrongful Death (Count II), Solatium (Count III), and Intentional Infliction of Emotional Distress (Count IV-A).[2]

---

1 Because there was no service on the IRGC, they will be dismissed from this action.

2 The Amended Complaint deleted the previously made claims for damages under the District of Columbia's Survival Act and for loss of consortium. Counts I and II of the First Amended Complaint charge the defendants with wrongful death, Count I under District of Columbia law and Count II under federal common law. Count III charges loss of solatium under federal common law. Count IV and Count IV-A charge the intentional infliction of emotional distress, Count IV under District of Columbia law and Count IV-A under federal common law. Counts V through IX charge wrongful death, aggravated assault, violations of human dignity, and

10. Plaintiff continues to rely on his previously filed evidentiary submission in support of his renewed motion for default judgment (Docket No. 20) on the Amended Complaint. On a motion for default judgment brought against a foreign sovereign or its agencies or instrumentalities, the claimant must establish his claim or right to relief by evidence satisfactory to the court. *See* 28 U.S.C. § 1608(e). The evidentiary submission was filed on December 7, 2007, and a courtesy copy delivered to Chambers. The Court finds that these evidentiary submissions are sufficient to establish plaintiff's claims.

II. Findings of Fact

1. Plaintiff Lawrence Belkin is a United States citizen, born and raised in Pennsylvania. After graduating from the University of Michigan in 1969, he served three years in the United States Army and then four more years in the Army Reserve. After his active duty discharge, he attended graduate school in North Carolina where he received Masters Degrees in both Architecture and Regional Planning. He worked in North Carolina from 1973 until mid-1981 when he moved to Israel and opened his own architectural design firm. Plaintiff's Exhibit 2 ¶¶ 1–5 ("Belkin Declaration").

2. When Mr. Belkin moved from North Carolina to Israel in 1981, he no longer maintained any residences or substantial contacts with any particular state in the United States. At the time he considered Israel to be his permanent residence. He did maintain general contacts with the United States government, including by filing his United States income tax returns each year while he resided in Israel. Belkin Declaration ¶ 6.

3. Mr. Belkin married Gail Belkin on March 23, 1995. Gail Belkin had been born in Rhodesia and also lived in South Africa before she immigrated to Israel. English was her native language. By profession, she was a cosmetician and ran a successful business. She became a citizen and resident of Israel. At the time of her death, she was 48 years of age and had two adult daughters from a previous marriage. Belkin Declaration ¶ 10.

4. At the time of his marriage to Gail Belkin, Mr. Belkin was a widower with two children. His first wife died suddenly six years earlier in Israel when her car collided with a truck. As a result of the loss of his first wife, the evidence submitted supports the factual assertion that Mr. Belkin felt compelled to be the best husband he could be to his new wife, and he was very close to her. He made it a point to tell her every day how much he loved her, and often told her how he dreaded the thought of losing her through death as he did his first wife. Gail Belkin was to be his companion for the rest of his life. Belkin Declaration ¶ 8.

violations of international treaty obligations under the laws of Israel. Count X charges defendants with violation of customary international law (*jus cogens*).

A. The March 4, 1996 Bombing Incident

5. On the afternoon of March 4, 1996, Gail Belkin, her mother, and one of her daughters went shopping for a wedding dress in the Dizengoff Center Shopping Mall in Tel Aviv, Israel, as her daughter was engaged to be married. After a time, the daughter remained in the mall shopping by herself while Gail Belkin and her mother went outside. At approximately 4:00 p.m. on March 4, 1996, a suicide bomber affiliated with the Shaqaqi faction of the Palestinian Islamic Jihad ("PIJ") detonated a 40-pound bomb that he was carrying just outside the doors of the shopping mall in the vicinity of Gail Belkin and her mother. Gail Belkin and her mother, plus eleven others, mostly women and children, were killed in the blast. 125 other individuals were injured. *Id.;* Plaintiff's Exhibit 3, Expert Report of Dr. Patrick Clawson ("Clawson Report") at 5, 8.[3]

6. The PIJ suicide bomber was identified as Ramez abed el Kader Machmad Abid, a resident of the Chan-Yuness refugee camp in Gaza. He was a known activist in the PIJ with the Shaqaqi faction. The police investigation determined that Abid had been smuggled into Israel that day by a truck driver traveling from Gaza to Tel Aviv. Clawson Report at 6, 8. *See* Plaintiff's Exhibit 4, Israeli Police Report, Event 27126 ("Israeli Police Report").

7. Abid carried the bomb in a black bag with two carrying handles. The main explosive was approximately 15 kilograms of TNT, around which was packed number 10 nails so as to cause maximum pain, suffering, and death to anyone in the vicinity of the detonation. The explosion was triggered by power from 9 volt batteries. When he arrived at the Dizengoff Center, Abid attached the bag to his shoulders. *Id.*

8. The truck driver who drove Abid into Tel Aviv, Said Bin Hussain Sulimany, was subsequently indicted and prosecuted for smuggling Abid into Israel for the equivalent of $1,100, and for assisting in murder and sabotage. Sulimany, who was convicted of providing support to terrorists, admitted that he knew Abid was a PIJ member and that he was paid the equivalent of $1,100 by a PIJ leader to smuggle Abid into Tel Aviv. Clawson Report at 6.

9. Both the PIJ and Hamas claimed responsibility for the Dizengoff Center bombing.[4] There is evidence that Hamas provided the bomb and that the PIJ provided the

3 Dr. Patrick Clawson has provided sworn expert testimony concerning the PIJ, Iran, MOIS and the IRGC in numerous cases before this Court. In *Heiser v. Islamic Republic of Iran*, Dr. Clawson is described as a "renowned scholar of Middle Eastern politics, who has studied and written about Iran for years. In over 20 cases, Dr. Clawson has provided this Court with reliable and credible testimony regarding the involvement of Iran, MOIS and IRGC in sponsoring and organizing acts of terrorism carried out against citizens of the United States." *See Heiser v. Islamic Republic of Iran*, 466 F. Supp. 2d 229, 265 (D.D.C.2006).

4 Hamas, which is the popular name for the Islamic Resistance Movement (Harakat alMuqawama al-Islamiya), is an organization that has been supported over the years by the Islamic Republic

suicide bomber and facilitated his transportation to Tel Aviv where the bomb was detonated. The PIJ and Hamas are known to have collaborated in other terrorist bombings, including an April 6, 1994 incident where the suicide bomber in a car-bomb attack on a bus in Afala, Israel was a member of the PIJ, but the bomb was provided by Hamas. *Id.* at 6–7.

10. The context for the PIJ's bombing of the Dizengoff Center was the ongoing peace discussions between Palestinian President Yassar Arafat and Israel. Iran, as well as its agents, Hamas and the PIJ, was strongly opposed to any kind of recognition of Israel and sought by violence the rejection of the Middle East peace process. On February 28, 1996, Iranian Vice President Habibi met with Hamas leaders and PIJ leaders (including Ramadan Abdallah Shallah) in Damascus, Syria. It was reported that Habibi stressed the continuation of Iran's support for the Palestinian oppositionists working against the peace agreement. Plaintiff's Exhibit 5, *Patterns of Global Terrorism, 1996;* Clawson Report at 4. This statement and meeting occurred in the middle of several major bombings in Israel, including two February 25, 1996 bombings: one of a bus in Jerusalem and the other of a soldier rest station in Ashkelon, plus a subsequent bombing of another bus in Jerusalem on March 3, 2006.[5] There is strong evidence that the Dizengoff Center bombing was actually planned to occur on February 25, 1996 in coordination with the two other bombings that did occur that day, but it did not occur because the truck driver, who was paid to drive the suicide bomber Abid into Tel Aviv, failed to show up that day. Dr. Clawson opined that it was reasonable to conclude that at their meeting of February 28, 1996, Iran's Vice President Habibi discussed with PIJ leader Shallah Iran's support for the PIJ's suicide bombings against the Israelis. The Dizengoff Center bombing happened a few days later. *Id.* Credible reports describe how Iran pledged to increase support based on major terror killings carried out by the PIJ. Clawson Report at 2.

11. The autopsy of Gail Belkin was performed by forensic pathologists Yehuda Hiss, M.D. and R. Nachman, M.D. They found that she had suffered first and

of Iran, primarily through Iran's Ministry of Information and Security ("MOIS"), and its Revolutionary Guard Corps. There are numerous opinions by judges of this Court which have found that Iran not only is a major source of support for Hamas, both financially and in terrorist training, but also that Iran fully knew of the purposes and objectives of Hamas and approved of them. *See, e.g., Bennett v. Islamic Republic of Iran*, 507 F. Supp. 2d 117, 124 (D.D.C.2007); *Campuzano v. Islamic Republic of Iran*, 281 F. Supp. 2d 258, 262 (D.D.C.2003); *Stern v. Islamic Republic of Iran*, 271 F. Supp. 2d 286 (D.D.C.2003); *Mousa v. Islamic Republic of Iran*, 238 F. Supp. 2d 1, 3 (D.D.C.2001); *Weinstein v. Islamic Republic of Iran*, 184 F. Supp. 2d 13 (D.D.C.2002); *Eisenfeld v. Islamic Republic of Iran*, 172 F. Supp. 2d 1, 5 (D.D.C.2000); *see also In re Abu Marzook*, 924 F. Supp. 565 (S.D.N.Y.1996).

5 This bus bombing in Israel has spawned four terrorism cases in this Court: *Bodoff v. Islamic Republic of Iran*, 424 F. Supp. 2d 74 (D.D.C.2006); *Mousa v. Islamic Republic of Iran*, 238 F. Supp. 2d 1 (D.D.C.2001); *Weinstein v. Islamic Republic of Iran*, 184 F. Supp. 2d 13 (D.D.C.2002); *Eisenfeld v. Islamic Republic of Iran*, 172 F. Supp. 2d 1 (D.D.C.2000).

second degree burns on her head, neck, trunk, and limbs. There were numerous lacerations in those same areas. Most significantly, the force of the explosion caused fractures of her cranial and facial bones as well as her ribs. It was the opinion of the forensic pathologists that the cause of Gail Belkin's death was the detonation of explosives. Plaintiff's Exhibit 6, Autopsy Report.

12. As a result of the death of Gail Belkin, her estate suffered economic losses. This loss is based on a projected work history of 19 additional years to retirement age and then receipt of a pension for 15 years to her life expectancy of 82.7 years, based on the Israeli Bureau of Statistics life expectancy tables. The total lost wages for those 34 years as reduced to present value is $376,848. She also had funeral expenses totaling $3,710, for a total of $380,558. *See* Plaintiff's Exhibit 10, Economic Report of Dov Weinstein, CPA ("Weinstein Report").

13. Lawrence Belkin suffered severe emotional distress as the result of the bombing and gruesome death of his wife. While not present at the Dizengoff Center at the actual time of the bomb's detonation, he learned about the bombing very shortly after it occurred, and he was immediately filled with anxiety knowing that his wife was then at the shopping center. His fear and concern increased with each passing minute when he did not hear from his wife.

14. The entire country of Israel was at a heightened state of tension and fear as the result of the spate of bombings that had recently happened and which took the lives of numerous innocent civilians, many of them children. The anxiety immediately increased with the television media immediately broadcasting photographs of the massive damage at the area around the Center. Mr. Belkin was sickened as he watched the special crews of workers scouring the scene for every piece of human flesh that could be recovered, in accordance with Jewish law. *See* Belkin Declaration ¶ 10; *see also* Plaintiff's Exhibit 7 (DVD of Israeli news showing post-bombing activity outside the Dizengoff Center).

15. Lawrence Belkin's anxiety further increased with each call to a hospital which responded that it had no information about a Gail Belkin. The hospitals told him he should consider calling the morgue. Within hours of the bombing, he was taken to the morgue to view the body of a woman believed to be his wife. The body was so severely injured in the blast that he could not identify his own wife while viewing it. He was only able to identify the jewelry that she was wearing, particularly her distinctive wedding ring which he had given to her. Belkin Declaration ¶ 11.

16. For over two years after his wife's death, Lawrence Belkin attended group therapy sessions to deal with his grief and emotions. The program was operated by the Israeli government and all of the participants were spouses of victims of terrorism. Even into 2004, eight years after Gail Belkin's murder, he was treated by his physician for "Generalized Anxiety Disorder" which was attributed to Gail Belkin's death and his experiences in Israel. On occasion, he still experiences an overwhelming sense of anxiety associated with the events of his wife's death. Belkin Declaration ¶¶ 12–14.

17. In 2001, Lawrence Belkin decided to move back to the United States to an environment of greater quiet and less intensity. He currently resides in the Commonwealth of Virginia. Belkin Declaration ¶ 14.

B. The Palestinian Islamic Jihad

18. The Palestinian Islamic Jihad was founded by Sunni Islamic fundamentalist Fathi Shaqaqi in the 1970s. Almost from the outset, PIJ leaders have proudly proclaimed their close connection with the Iranian government. In 1981, Fathi Shaqaqi wrote a book about his admiration for the Islamic Republic of Iran. Particularly remarkable about the PIJ's long affiliation with Iran is how they have always worked together cooperatively notwithstanding the longstanding disagreements between the Sunni and Shia Muslim factions, on both religious and socio-economic grounds. PIJ leaders traveled frequently to Iran, often being shown in the Iranian media meeting with top officials in the Iranian government. The PIJ actively defended Iran and its ideology to Sunni extremists who were put off by Iran's Shiite majority. Clawson Report at 2–3; Plaintiff's Exhibit 8, Dr. Clawson's testimony in *Flatow v. Islamic Republic of Iran,* Civil Action No. 97-396 (March 3, 1998) ("Clawson Testimony") at 146–147.

19. After the 1987 outbreak of a Palestinian popular uprising against Israel, the PIJ was the group which most loudly and openly proclaimed the need for terrorist attacks on Israeli civilians at a time when most other Palestinian extremists thought such attacks were unwise tactics. The Shaqaqi faction of the PIJ was relatively small, numbering a few hundred members, but it was particularly violent. For the next 12 years, the PIJ had few activities other than carrying out terrorist acts (unlike other terrorist groups such as Hamas and Hezbollah which also undertook charitable and political activities). Clawson Report at 2–4; Clawson Testimony at 148; Plaintiff's Exhibit 9, testimony of terrorism expert Harry B. Brandon in *Flatow v. Islamic Republic of Iran,* Civ. Action No. 97-396 ("Brandon Testimony") at 174.

20. The PIJ has been found responsible for many other terrorist attacks in Israel, including the April 9, 1995 bus bombing in which Alisa Flatow was killed and Seth Haim was severely injured. *See Flatow v. Islamic Republic of Iran,* 999 F. Supp. 1 (D.D.C.1998); *Haim v. Islamic Republic of Iran,* 425 F. Supp. 2d 56 (D.D.C.2006).

C. Iran's Support for the PIJ

21. In the mid-1990s, Iran had an urgent desire to disrupt the Middle East peace process which appeared to be moving forward at that time. Iran considered terrorist activities in Israel and the murder of Israeli civilians carried out by the PIJ as an effective means of damaging relations between Israel and the Palestinian Authority. According to Dr. Clawson, by supporting the PIJ, Iran enhanced its standing with radical Islamic extremists, especially among Sunni Muslims who would otherwise be hostile to the Shiite Islamic Republic of Iran. Iran provided the PIJ not only with financing, but also with advanced military training and munitions technology that

allowed the PIJ to evolve into a dangerous and effective terrorist organization. Clawson Report at 2.

22. In 1990, after Fathi Shaqaqi arrived in Damascus, PIJ operatives began training at Hezbollah camps in Lebanon under the supervision of Iranian Revolutionary Guards stationed in that country and carried out some joint operations with Hezbollah against Israeli forces in south Lebanon.

23. The strong consensus among scholars of Palestinian extremism is that from 1988 until about 2000, the PIJ was heavily dependent on Iranian government support. Several experts, including Dr. Reuvan Paz and Harry B. Brandon, the former Chief of the FBI's Counterterrorism Section, opined in 1998 that the Iranian government was virtually the sole support of the PIJ. While in a 1994 interview of Fathi Shaqaqi by Arab journalists, Shaqaqi denied the accepted figure that the PIJ was receiving $20,000,000 that year from Iran, he did admit receiving $3,000,000 to support PIJ terrorism. Clawson Report at 4–5 (citing testimony from Dr. Paz); Brandon Testimony at 176.

24. The Iranian Ministry of Information and Security, during the 1990s and beyond, acted as a conduit for the Islamic Republic of Iran's provision of funds and training to the Shaqaqi faction for its terrorist activities in the Gaza strip region. Clawson Report at 5.

25. The PIJ's dependence on Iran deepened after the 1995 death of Fathi Shaqaqi.[6] Shaqaqi's successor Shallah faced the challenge of showing that the PIJ was still an important force, especially as the larger Hamas organization had stepped up its terroristic activities. In the weeks prior to the Dizengoff bombing, Hamas had stepped up its activities to undermine Arafat and the Palestinian Authority. On the day before the Dizengoff bombing, in response to Israeli pressure following the spate of suicide bombings, Arafat outlawed paramilitary organizations including Hamas and the PIJ, and Palestinian police arrested 800 Islamic militants and seized large quantities of explosives. Clawson Report at 4.

26. *The Patterns of Global Terrorism* was an annual report by the State Department based on statistical data on significant international terrorist incidents (the State Department now publishes similar information in its *Country Reports on Terrorism*). *The Patterns of Global Terrorism* report for 1996, the year in which the bombing that killed plaintiff's wife occurred, stated: "Iran remained the premier state sponsor of terrorism in 1996 . . . Iran continued to provide support—including money, weapons and training—to a variety of terrorist groups, such as Hezbollah, Hamas and the Palestine Islamic Jihad ("PIJ")." Plaintiff's Exhibit 5.

27. Iran was designated a state sponsor of terrorism in 1984 and has been on the State Department's list of state sponsors of terrorism ever since. *See Dammarell v.*

6 Fathi Shaqaqi was shot and killed on October 26, 1995 by an unknown professional assassin, generally believed to be an Israeli operative.

Islamic Republic of Iran, 404 F. Supp. 2d 261, 273–74 (D.D.C.2005); *see also* 22 C.F.R. § 126.1(d) (2008); 31 C.F.R. § 596.201 (2009); Determination Pursuant to Section 6(I) of the Export Administration Act of 1979—Iran, 49 Fed.Reg. 2836 (Jan. 23, 1984).

28. The Ministry of Information and Security ("MOIS"), Iran's intelligence service, is a major Iranian agency designated by Iran to help organize Iranian government support to the PIJ. MOIS operates both within and beyond Iranian territory. With approximately 30,000 agents, MOIS is the largest intelligence agency in the Middle East. MOIS acted as a conduit for Iran's provision of funds and training to the Shaqaqi faction of the PIJ for its terrorist activities. Iran's intelligence services facilitate and direct terrorist attacks. MOIS's provision of material support and resources for terrorism is conducted with the approval of the highest levels of the Iranian regime. Clawson Report at 5, 7; *accord, Haim v. Islamic Republic of Iran,* 425 F. Supp. 2d at 61; *Flatow v. Islamic Republic of Iran,* 999 F. Supp. at 11.[7]

29. Another means by which Iranian support for terrorism is carried out is through the Iranian Revolutionary Guard Corps ("IRGC"), the activities of which are carefully controlled by the Iranian government. Since 1988, scores of PIJ operatives from the West Bank and Gaza have received Iranian military and terrorist training at bases run by the IRGC in Lebanon and in Iran itself. Iran has provided the PIJ with explosives and weapons, as well as the training required to use such weapons. It is reasonably believed that these weapons came from IRGC stocks or through IRGC channels. Clawson Report at 7–8.

30. Dr. Clawson opined, to a reasonable degree of certitude, that the Islamic Republic of Iran, through its agencies MOIS and the IRGC, provided funding and training to the PIJ both before and after March 4, 1996 in order to facilitate the PIJ's ability to carry out terroristic activities, including suicide bombings, and particularly the suicide bombing on March 4, 1996 of the Dizengoff Center. Such training would include how to operate explosive devices and how to achieve maximum death and destruction. Iran, through MOIS and the IRGC, would have provided funding to carry out terrorist attacks, including payment for smuggling the suicide bomber through Israeli security to the place of detonation. Clawson Report at 8.

---

7 Although not necessary to the resolution of this case, the Court may take judicial notice of facts and conclusions made by Judge Lamberth in the *Flatow* and *Haim* cases. While the event underlying those two cases occurred eleven months prior to the event in this matter, the longstanding relationship between Iran and the PIJ found by the Court in those two cases (that were decided eight years apart) is relevant to this case, particularly so because they are so consistent. *See Heiser v. Islamic Republic of Iran*, 466 F. Supp. 2d at 262–263; *Haim v. Islamic Republic of Iran*, 425 F. Supp. 2d at 60; *Flatow v. Islamic Republic of Iran*, 999 F. Supp. at 14; FED.R.EVID. 201(e).

III. Conclusions of Law

A. Jurisdiction

The Foreign Sovereign Immunities Act ("FSIA") establishes the general principle that foreign states are immune from suit in United States courts. The statute also sets out certain exceptions to the rule for limited categories of cases. Thus, the FSIA provides the sole basis for asserting jurisdiction over foreign sovereigns. *Argentine Republic v. Amerada Hess Shipping Corp.,* 488 U.S. 428, 434, 109 S. Ct. 683, 102 L.Ed.2d 818 (1989). A party may not generally bring an action for money damages in U.S. courts against a foreign state. 28 U.S.C. § 1604. The "state-sponsored terrorism" exception, now set forth at 28 U.S.C. § 1605A and formerly at 28 U.S.C. § 1605(a)(7), removed a foreign state's immunity from suits for money damages brought in U.S. courts where plaintiffs seek damages against the foreign state for personal injury or death caused by "an act of torture, extrajudicial killing, aircraft sabotage, hostage taking, or the provision of material support or resources" for such an act if such act or provision of material support "is engaged in by an official, employee, or agent of such foreign state while acting within the scope of his or her office, employment or agency." 28 U.S.C. § 1605A(a)(1); *see Heiser v. Islamic Republic of Iran,* 466 F. Supp. 2d at 304.

On January 28, 2008, the National Defense Authorization Act for Fiscal Year 2008 ("NDAA"), Pub. L. No. 110-181, repealed Section 1605(a)(7) of Title 28 and replaced it with a new section codified at Section 1605A of the same title. *See Simon v. Republic of Iraq,* 529 F.3d 1187, 1189 (D.C.Cir.2008), *rev'd on other grounds,* ___ U.S. ___, 129 S. Ct. 2183, 173 L.Ed.2d 1193 (2009).[8]

Section 1083(c)(3) of the NDAA, in relevant part, authorizes a plaintiff who has "timely commenced" a "related action" under Section 1605(a)(7), to bring "any other action arising out of the same act or incident," provided that "the [new] action is commenced" within 60 days of "the date of the enactment of [the NDAA]." *Simon v. Republic of Iraq,* 529 F.3d at 1192. The NDAA was enacted on January 28, 2008. Plaintiff Lawrence Belkin commenced this "related action" on March 28, 2008, within the 60-day window of the NDAA.

In order to subject a foreign sovereign to suit under Section 1605A, a plaintiff must show that: (1) the foreign sovereign was designated by the State Department as a "state sponsor of terrorism" when the acts occurred and remains so designated when the matter was refiled, 28 U.S.C. § 1605A(a)(2)(A)(i)(I); (2) that the victim or claimant was a U.S. national at the time the acts took place, *see* 28 U.S.C.

8 Where a pending action was brought under 28 U.S.C. § 1605(a)(7) and is not refiled under Section 1605A, the district courts retain jurisdiction pursuant to § 1605(a)(7) over cases that were pending under that section when Congress enacted the NDAA. *See Simon v. Republic of Iraq*, 529 F.3d at 1192.

§ 1605A(a)(2)(A)(ii)(I); and (3) that the foreign sovereign engaged in conduct that falls within the ambit of the statute. *See* 28 U.S.C. § 1605A(a)(1).[9]

Each of the requirements is met in this case. First, defendant Iran has been designated a state sponsor of terrorism continuously since January 19, 1984, and was so designated at the time of the attack. *See* 22 C.F.R. § 126.1(d) (2008); 31 C.F.R. § 596.201 (2009). Second, the plaintiff was a United States citizen when the murder of the decedent occurred and at the time plaintiff filed this action. Finally, defendant Iran's persistent financial and organizational material support of the entity or entities that committed an extrajudicial killing and the provisions of material support has been established and it falls squarely within the ambit of the statute.[10] Defendants MOIS and the IRGC are political subdivisions of the State of Iran, and therefore are treated as members of the State of Iran itself. *Roeder v. Islamic Republic of Iran,* 333 F.3d 228, 234 (D.C.Cir.2003), *cert. denied,* 542 U.S. 915, 124 S. Ct. 2836, 159 L.Ed.2d 287 (2004); *see also Salazar v. Islamic Republic of Iran,* 370 F. Supp. 2d 105, 116 (D.D.C. 2005) (analogizing the IRGC to the MOIS for purposes of liability, and concluding that both must be treated as the State of Iran itself). Therefore, the same determinations that apply to the conduct of MOIS and the IRGC apply to the conduct of Iran.

B. Service of Process

Personal jurisdiction exists over a non-immune sovereign as long as service of process has been made under Section 1608 of the FSIA. *See Stern v. Islamic Republic of Iran,* 271 F. Supp. 2d at 298 (D.D.C.2003); *see also* Fed.R.Civ.P. 4(j). Service of the original complaint was effected on all three Defendants under 28 U.S.C. § 1608(a)(4). *See* Plaintiff's Exhibit 1. Plaintiff did not serve the amended complaint on defendants. Where changes made in an amended complaint are "not substantial," the requirement of Rule 5(a)(2) of the Federal Rules of Civil Procedure that a pleading that states a new claim for relief against a party in default must be served on that party is not applicable. *See* FED.R.CIV.P. 5(a)(2); *see also Blais v. Islamic Republic of Iran,* 459 F. Supp. 2d 40, 46 (D.D.C.2006); *Dammarell v. Islamic Republic of Iran,* 370 F. Supp. 2d 218, 224 (D.D.C.2005). Plaintiff's amended complaint did not substantially change the allegations in the original complaint and did not add new defendants. The causes of action are essentially the same, but, as explained below, are now available under another source of law—namely, Section 1605A. The Court will not require the plaintiff to serve the

9 Section 1605A expanded the potential class of plaintiffs by including any member of the armed forces or any employee or contractor of the U.S. government, regardless of nationality. *See* 28 U.S.C. § 1605A(a)(2)(A)(ii)(II) and (III).

10 The FSIA utilizes the same definition of "extrajudicial killing" as the Torture Victim Protection Act of 1991, which defines an "extrajudicial killing" as "a deliberate killing not authorized by a previous judgment pronounced by a regularly constituted court affording all judicial guarantees which are recognized as indispensable by civilized people." *See* 28 U.S.C. § 1605A(h)(7); *Peterson v. Islamic Republic of Iran*, 264 F. Supp. 2d 46, 61 (D.D.C.2003).

amended complaint. *See Blais v. Islamic Republic of Iran,* 459 F. Supp. 2d at 46 (amended FSIA complaint which added causes of action based on state substantive law as well as the federal statutory scheme need not be served on foreign sovereign in default); *Dammarell v. Islamic Republic of Iran,* 370 F. Supp. 2d at 224. Accordingly, this Court has *in personam* jurisdiction over defendants Iran, MOIS and the IRGC.

C. Legal Standard for FSIA Default Judgment

In an action over which subject matter jurisdiction exists by virtue of the "terrorism exception" of 28 U.S.C. § 1605A, "[n]o judgment by default shall be entered by a court of the United States or of a state against a foreign state . . . unless the claimant establishes his claim or right to relief by evidence satisfactory to the court." 28 U.S.C. § 1608(e); *see Roeder v. Islamic Republic of Iran,* 333 F.3d at 232–33. In default judgment cases, plaintiffs may present such evidence in the form of affidavits or declarations rather than through live witnesses testifying in open court. *Bodoff v. Islamic Republic of Iran,* 424 F. Supp. 2d at 82; *Campuzano v. Islamic Republic of Iran,* 281 F. Supp. 2d 258, 268 (D.D.C.2003). Upon evaluation, the Court may accept any uncontroverted evidence presented by plaintiffs as true. *Heiser v. Islamic Republic of Iran,* 466 F. Supp. 2d at 255 (citing *Campuzano v. Islamic Republic of Iran,* 281 F. Supp. 2d at 268). This Court accepts and credits the uncontested evidence and testimony submitted by plaintiff and his witnesses in this case as true. Not only have the defendants in this action not objected to such evidence or even appeared to contest it, but the Court finds the evidence submitted by plaintiff to be relevant and highly probative of the claims asserted.

D. Governing Law

The FSIA, as amended, creates a federal cause of action against foreign states, for which both compensatory and punitive damages may be awarded, for personal injury or death caused by an extrajudicial killing or by the provision of material support or resources by the foreign state, among other acts. *See* 28 U.S.C. § 1605A(a)(1) and (c)(1); *see also Simon v. Republic of Iraq,* 529 F.3d at 1190. This area of law has been in flux. In 2004, the court of appeals held that while the FSIA waived sovereign immunity for state sponsors of terrorism, it did not "create[ ] a private right of action against a foreign government." *Cicippio-Puleo v. Islamic Republic of Iran,* 353 F.3d 1024, 1033 (D.C.Cir.2004). In the same year, the court of appeals also held that FSIA plaintiffs cannot state a claim against foreign states under the "generic common law" but must "identify a particular cause of action arising out of a specific source of law." *Acree v. Republic of Iraq,* 370 F.3d 41, 59 (D.C.Cir.2004). These decisions left FSIA plaintiffs with the option of suing foreign officials for damages in their personal capacities, a cause of action which was created by the Flatow Amendment, P. L. 104-208, 110 Stat. 3009-172 (published as a note to 28 U.S.C. § 1605), or to advance claims against the foreign state based on a specific, non-federal source of law, such as the law of the U.S. state that is or was the domicile of the injured party or decedent. *See Gates v. Syrian Arab Republic,* 580 F. Supp. 2d 53, 65 (D.D.C. 2008).

Section 1605A of the NDAA changed the mechanism for recovery by creating a federal private right of action against foreign state sponsors of terrorism for compensatory damages for economic loss, solatium, and pain and suffering, as well as for punitive damages. *See* 28 U.S.C. § 1605A(a) and (c); *Acosta v. Islamic Republic of Iran,* 574 F. Supp. 2d 15, 25 (D.D.C.2008). Now that Congress has created an express federal cause of action, neither the Court nor plaintiff need rely on state tort theories of recovery for plaintiff's claims. *See Gates v. Syrian Arab Republic,* 580 F. Supp. 2d at 65–66 ("By providing for a private right of action and by precisely enumerating the types of damages recoverable, Congress has eliminated the inconsistencies that arise in these cases when they are decided under state law.").

E. Vicarious Liability for the Torts Committed by the PIJ

One of the substantive bases of the defendants' liability is that at a minimum they engaged in the "provision of material support and resources" to the PIJ, which carried out the terrorist bombing of the Dizengoff Center and caused the death of Gail Belkin. The acts of another may render a party liable "under theories of vicarious liability, such as conspiracy, aiding and abetting and inducement." *Haim v. Islamic Republic of Iran,* 425 F. Supp. 2d at 69. This Court finds that civil conspiracy provides a basis of liability for defendants Iran and MOIS and, accordingly, it declines to reach the issue of whether they might also be liable on other theories of liability. *See Acosta v. Islamic Republic of Iran,* 574 F. Supp. 2d at 26; *Heiser v. Islamic Republic of Iran,* 466 F. Supp. 2d at 266–68.

The elements of civil conspiracy consist of (1) an agreement between two or more persons or entities; (2) to participate in an unlawful act or in an otherwise lawful act in an unlawful manner; (3) that an injury or death or other damages was caused by an unlawful overt act performed by one of the parties to the agreement and (4) pursuant to or in furtherance of the common scheme. *See Acosta v. Islamic Republic of Iran,* 574 F. Supp. 2d at 27 (*citing Halberstam v. Welch,* 705 F.2d 472, 477 (D.C.Cir.1983)).

It is axiomatic that the "agreement" element "may be inferred from conduct." *Bodoff v. Islamic Republic of Iran,* 424 F. Supp. 2d at 84 (*citing Weishapl v. Sowers,* 771 A.2d 1014, 1023 (D.C.2001)); *see also Haim v. Islamic Republic of Iran,* 425 F. Supp. 2d at 69. Based on the evidence submitted to this Court, most notably the Clawson Report, plaintiffs have established that Iran, MOIS, the IRGC and the PIJ acted in concert because they had agreed to commit high profile terrorism activities to promote Iran's brand of revolutionary Islamic ideology and to further the goal of damaging Israel and its citizens as well as United States' interests whenever possible. Clawson Report at 3–4. Such agreement also may be inferred from the substantial financial support and training that Iran, MOIS and the IRGC provided to the PIJ. *See id.* at 2–4. The very "'sponsorship of terrorist activities inherently involves conspiracy to commit terrorist acts.'" *Bodoff v. Islamic Republic of Iran,* 424 F. Supp. 2d at 84 (quoting *Flatow v. Islamic Republic of Iran,* 999 F. Supp. at 27).

The evidence also clearly establishes that the PIJ carried out the sequence of conduct that killed the decedent. *See* Clawson Report at 5–7. Dr. Clawson's Report also demonstrates to the satisfaction of this Court that the torts alleged by plaintiffs were carried out in "furtherance of the scheme" between the PIJ, Iran, MOIS, the IRGC, and likely Hamas, to disrupt the Middle Eastern peace talks. *See id.* at 6. For these reasons, each of the four elements of civil conspiracy is established under District of Columbia law, with regard to the defendants and the PIJ perpetrators. *See also Valore v. Islamic Republic of Iran,* 478 F. Supp. 2d 101, 108–09 (D.D.C.2007) (civil conspiracy basis for vicarious liability established with respect to Iran and MOIS' provision of "material support and resources to Hezbollah" to bomb U.S. Marine barracks in Beirut).

F. Solatium and Intentional Infliction of Emotional Distress

Count III of the First Amended Complaint seeks damages for solatium under 28 U.S.C. § 1605A(c). Counts IV and IV-A of that complaint seek damages for intentional infliction of emotional distress, under both the common law of the District of Columbia and under Section 1605A(c). The courts in this jurisdiction have generally viewed solatium and intentionally inflicted emotional distress claims as being closely connected. *See, e.g., Surette v. Islamic Republic of Iran,* 231 F. Supp. 2d 260, 267 n. 5 (D.D.C.2002) ("In the context of FSIA cases, this Court has recognized the claim of solatium as . . . indistinguishable from the claim of intentional infliction of emotional distress"). Plaintiff recognizes that there can be but one award of damages for the claims made in Counts III, IV and IV-A. Because section 1605A explicitly makes damages for solatium available, the Court will proceed under this theory of recovery. *See* 28 U.S.C. § 1605A(c).

A claim of solatium is a claim for the mental anguish, bereavement and grief that those with a close personal relationship to a decedent experience as the result of the decedent's death, as well as the harm caused by the loss of the decedent, society and comfort. *Dammarell v. Islamic Republic of Iran,* 281 F. Supp. 2d 105, 196–97 (D.D.C.2003); *Elahi v. Islamic Republic of Iran,* 124 F. Supp. 2d 97, 110 (D.D.C.2000). Acts of terrorism are by their very definition extreme and outrageous and intended to cause the highest degree of emotional distress. *Stethem v. Islamic Republic of Iran,* 201 F. Supp. 2d 78, 89 (D.D.C.2002). Prior to the *Cicippio-Puleo* decision, courts regularly recognized the distress of spouses of terrorism victims by awarding solatium damages to such spouses. *See Weinstein v. Islamic Republic of Iran,* 184 F. Supp. 2d 13, 23 (D.D.C. 2002); *Higgins. v. Islamic Republic of Iran,* 2000 WL 33674311 at *7–8 (D.D.C. Sept. 21, 2000); *see also Alejandre v. Republic of Cuba,* 996 F. Supp. 1239, 1249 (S.D.Fla.1997). The Court will award damages to Mr. Belkin under Count III.

G. Plaintiff's Wrongful Death Claims

Count I alleges wrongful death under District of Columbia law (16 D.C.Code § 2701); Count II alleges wrongful death under 28 U.S.C. § 1605A(c); and Count V alleges wrongful death under Israeli law. Each of these counts seek essentially the same remedy—compensation for economic losses in the form of lost wages, benefits, retirement pay and funeral expenses incurred as the result of the extra-judicial killing of Gail Belkin under the direction of defendants. Plaintiff recognizes that only one recovery for these economic damages is permissible. Section 1605A(c) explicitly provides for economic damages for a death caused by a foreign state sponsor of terrorism. *See* 28 U.S.C. § 1605A(a). Accordingly the Court will award damages under Count II. *See Gates v. Syrian Arab Republic,* 580 F. Supp. 2d at 69.

IV. Damages

A. Compensatory Damages[11]

To obtain damages against defendants in an FSIA action, the plaintiff must prove that the consequences of the defendants' conduct were "'reasonably certain' (i.e., more likely than not) to occur, and must prove the amount of the damages by a 'reasonable estimate consistent with this [Circuit's] application of the American rule on damages.'" *Salazar v. Islamic Republic of Iran,* 370 F. Supp. 2d at 115–16 (quoting *Hill v. Republic of Iraq,* 328 F.3d 680, 681 (D.C.Cir.2003) (internal quotations omitted)). Because there have been so many cases in this District where family members have been killed by terrorist bombings, this Court is by no means writing on a proverbial "clean slate" in fashioning a damages remedy in this case. To the contrary, this Court is guided by remedial approaches and formulas, utilized in similar cases. *Prevatt v. Islamic Republic of Iran,* 421 F. Supp. 2d 152, 160 (D.D.C. 2006); *Haim v. Islamic Republic of Iran,* 425 F. Supp. 2d at 71.

In determining the appropriate award of damages for solatium, the Court may look to prior decisions awarding damages for intentional infliction of emotional distress as well as to decisions regarding solatium. *See Acosta v. Islamic Republic of Iran,* 574 F. Supp. 2d at 29. While the loss suffered by a spouse is difficult to quantify, courts typically award between $8 million and $12 million for the emotional distress resulting from the death of a spouse. *See, e.g., id.* at 30 ($8 million to wife of target of terrorist assassination); *Heiser v. Islamic Republic of Iran,* 466 F. Supp. 2d at 293 (relying on solatium cases to find that range of compensatory damages for spouses is $8–12 million); *Greenbaum v. Islamic Republic of Iran,* 451 F. Supp. 2d 90, 107–108 (D.D.C.2006) ($9 million to husband of woman killed by suicide bomber); *Salazar v. Islamic Republic of Iran,* 370 F. Supp. 2d at 116 (awarding $10 million to the widow of a bombing victim); *Kerr v. Islamic Republic of Iran,*

11 Plaintiff has withdrawn his punitive damages demand. *See* Plaintiff's Proposed Findings of Fact and Conclusions of Law in Support of Renewed Motion for Default Judgment at 31–32.

245 F. Supp. 2d 59, 64 (D.D.C.2003) (award of $10 million to the widow of a torture and hostage taking victim). One recent award to a spouse was for $30 million. *See Estate of Bayani v. Islamic Republic of Iran,* 530 F. Supp. 2d 40, 46 (D.D.C.2007) ($30 million awarded to spouse whose husband was tortured and executed).

Based upon the wealth of cases involving immediate family members of civilians killed in terrorist bombings, this Court awards solatium damages of $10 million to plaintiff in his capacity as the husband of the decedent. The Court believes this award is appropriate in this case as it is not unlike the awards to other spouses whose wives or husbands were killed in suicide bombings. *See Greenbaum v. Islamic Republic of Iran,* 451 F. Supp. 2d at 107–08. The Court believes, however, that this plaintiff in particular is entitled to this higher award due to the extreme shock he experienced when he had to view his wife's severely disfigured body shortly after the bombing occurred. Such a shocking experience is one that he will never be able to put out of his mind and that will long continue to cause pain and anxiety. For that reason, the Court will award plaintiff $10 million on his solatium claim.

To compute the economic damages associated with plaintiff's death, plaintiff has submitted a report from forensic economic expert Dov Weinstein, Plaintiff's Exhibit 10, Weinstein Report. The Weinstein Report bases its calculations on reasonable and well-founded assumptions about the likely earnings of Gail Belkin had she survived. *Id.* Mr. Weinstein concluded that Mrs. Belkin would have worked for 19 more years and then, based on her life expectancy, received a pension for 15 additional years. Based upon this forensic evidence, the lost wages of Gail Belkin reduced to present value would be $376,848. *See Gates v. Syrian Arab Republic,* 580 F. Supp. 2d at 69 (computing present value of the anticipated earnings of victims of terrorism to award economic damages pursuant to Section 1605A(c)). The additional amount of $3,710 is for Mrs. Belkin's funeral expenses. *See* Findings of Fact ¶ 12. Accordingly, the Court awards plaintiff wrongful death damages in the amount of $376,848 and $3,710, for a total of $380,558.

B. Prejudgment Interest

Plaintiff requests prejudgment interest for his solatium claim (formerly his IIED claim). "It is within this Court's discretion to award plaintiffs prejudgment interest from the date of the bombing . . . until the date of final judgment . . . [c]ourts in this Circuit have awarded prejudgment interest in cases where plaintiffs were delayed in recovering compensation for their injuries—including, specifically, where such injuries were the result of targeted attacks perpetrated by foreign defendants." *Pugh v. Socialist People's Libyan Arab Jamahiriya,* 530 F. Supp. 2d 216, 263 (D.D.C.2008) (relying on *Oldham v. Korean Air Lines Co.,* 127 F.3d 43, 54 (D.C.Cir.1997); and *Forman v. Korean Air Lines Co.,* 84 F.3d 446, 450 (D.C.Cir. 1996)); *see also Ben-Rafael v. Islamic Republic of Iran,* 540 F. Supp. 2d 39, 59 (D.D.C.2008). The Court agrees that prejudgment interest is appropriate in this case and awards plaintiff prejudgment interest on his solatium claim computed at a rate of six percent per annum on a simple interest basis from March 4, 1996 to the present.

C. Other Causes of Action Asserted in the Complaint

In light of these Findings of Fact and Conclusions of Law, it is not necessary for the Court to address the other claims asserted by the plaintiff under either Israeli law or under customary international law. *See Beaty v. Republic of Iraq,* 480 F. Supp. 2d 60, 92–93 (D.D.C.2007). (Count X).

V. Conclusion

For the reasons explained above, the Court will award judgment for plaintiff on Counts II and III of his amended complaint and will dismiss the remaining counts. Because plaintiff has established a right to damages as a direct and proximate result of defendants' extreme and outrageous conduct and because the evidence in the record amply supports the allegations in the complaint, a judgment consistent with these findings will be entered against defendants Iran and MOIS in the amount of $10 million for solatium, plus prejudgment interest at the rate of six percent per annum, dated to March 4, 1996 when Gail Belkin was murdered, as well as $376,858 in lost wages and $3,710 in funeral and burial costs under plaintiff's wrongful death claim.

An Order in accordance with these Findings of Fact and Conclusions of Law shall issue as of the date of this Opinion.

CLAUDE CASSIRER
v.
KINGDOM OF SPAIN

580 F.3d 1048 (9th Cir. 2009)
Decided September 8, 2009

William M. Barron of Alston & Bird, LLP, New York City, New York; Anthony A. De Corso of Beck, De Corso, Daly, Kreindler & Harris, for defendant-appellant the Kingdom of Spain.

Thaddeus J. Stauber and Walter T. Johnson of Nixon Peabody, LLP, Los Angeles, California, for defendant-appellant Thyssen-Bornemisza Collection Foundation.

Stuart R. Dunwoody of Davis Wright Tremaine, LLP, Los Angeles, California, for plaintiff-appellee Claude Cassirer.

Before: Thomas G. Nelson, Sandra S. Ikuta, and N. Randy Smith, Circuit Judges. Opinion by Judge N.R. Smith; Partial Concurrence and Partial Dissent by Judge Ikuta.

N.R. SMITH, Circuit Judge:

Claude Cassirer ("Cassirer") filed this action in federal district court against the Kingdom of Spain ("Spain") and the Thyssen-Bornemisza Collection Foundation (the "Foundation")[1] to recover a Camille Pissarro painting now on display at the Foundation's museum in Madrid, Spain. Cassirer alleges that the painting was taken from his grandmother in violation of international law in 1939 by an agent of the government of Nazi Germany. On appeal, Appellants challenge the district court's denial of their respective motions to dismiss for lack of (1) personal jurisdiction, (2) standing, (3) a justiciable case or controversy, and (4) subject matter jurisdiction based on sovereign immunity.

We dismiss this appeal with regard to Appellants' challenges to personal jurisdiction, standing, and the existence of a justiciable case or controversy. We lack appellate jurisdiction because there has been no final judgment and these issues are not immediately appealable under the collateral order doctrine.

1 When referred to collectively, Spain and the Foundation are referred to as "Appellants."

However, under the collateral order doctrine, we have jurisdiction to consider the issue of sovereign immunity. *Gupta v. Thai Airways Int'l, Ltd.*, 487 F.3d 759, 763, 764 n.6 (9th Cir. 2007). We consider for the first time whether the expropriation exception of the Foreign Sovereign Immunities Act ("FSIA"), 28 U.S.C. § 1605(a)(3), applies when the foreign state (against whom a claim is made) is not the entity that expropriated the property in violation of international law. We hold that it does. We also hold that advertising and promotional activity, purchase and sale of goods and services, and the exchange of artwork with persons and entities, all within the United States, are sufficient to constitute "commercial activity in the United States" under § 1605(a)(3). Finally, based on guidance in our recent decision in *Sarei v. Rio Tinto, PLC,* 550 F.3d 822, 832 (9th Cir. 2008) (*en banc*) (plurality opinion), we remand to the district court to determine, in the first instance, whether the circumstances of this case warrant judicial imposition of an exhaustion requirement.

I. Background

For the purposes of this appeal, we take the factual allegations in this case as true.[2] At the heart of the present dispute is the *Rue Saint-Honore, apres-midi, effet de pluie* (the "Painting"), an oil painting by the French impressionist master Camille Pissarro. The Painting was originally purchased in 1898 by Cassirer's great-grandfather, Julius Cassirer, a member of a wealthy Jewish family living in Germany. The Painting remained in the family for the next forty years. First passing upon Julius's death to his son, Fritz, and later to Fritz's widow, Lilly Cassirer.

In 1939, as persecution of Jews living in Nazi Germany increased, Lilly and her new husband sought official permission to leave Germany and take their possessions, which included the Painting. Before granting permission, the Nazi government appointed Munich art dealer Jakob Scheidwimmer as the official appraiser to evaluate the works of art that Lilly wished to take with her. After his appraisal, Scheidwimmer refused to allow Lilly to take the Painting out of Germany and demanded that she sell it to him for approximately $360. Because she feared she would not be allowed to leave Germany, she relinquished the Painting, knowing that she would never receive the funds she was promised.[3]

---

2 In reviewing the district court's denial of a motion to dismiss, we accept all well-pleaded factual allegations in the complaint as true, *Altmann v. Republic of Austria*, 317 F.3d 954, 962 (9th Cir. 2002) (citing *Zimmerman v. City of Oakland*, 255 F.3d 734, 737 (9th Cir. 2001)), *amended by* 327 F.3d 1246 (9th Cir. 2003), *aff'd by* 541 U.S. 677, 124 S. Ct. 2240, 159 L. Ed. 2d 1 (2004), and determine whether the factual content "allows the court to draw the reasonable inference that the defendant is liable for the misconduct alleged," *Ashcroft v. Iqbal*, 129 S. Ct. 1937, 1949, 173 L. Ed. 2d 868 (2009).

3 Lilly's sister, who remained in Germany, was later imprisoned in the Theresienstadt extermination camp, where she was subsequently killed. Lilly died in 1962, never having recovered the Painting or learned of its whereabouts.

Scheidwimmer traded the Painting to another art dealer who, also persecuted by the Nazis, fled Germany and took the Painting to Holland. After Germany invaded Holland, the Gestapo confiscated the Painting and returned it to Germany, where it was sold at auction to an anonymous purchaser in 1943. The Painting surfaced at a New York gallery in 1952 and was then sold to a private collector in St. Louis. It was sold again in 1976 to an unknown dealer, who subsequently sold it to Baron Hans-Heinrich Thyssen-Bornemisza (the "Baron"), a resident of Switzerland and one of the world's foremost private art collectors.

In 1988, Spain paid the Baron $50 million to lease his collection for ten years. Five years into the lease, Spain paid the Foundation approximately $327 million to purchase the Baron's entire collection, including the Painting. Under the terms of the purchase, Spain provided the Foundation a palace in Madrid, free of charge, for use as the Thyssen-Bornemisza Museum (the "Museum"). In addition, the purchase agreement requires that the collection be exhibited at the Museum in Spain and sets limits regarding loans to other art institutions. If the collection is not used in accordance with the purchase agreement or if the Foundation ceases to exist, Spain will become the owner of the collection.[4]

In 2000, Claude Cassirer,[5] the grandson and heir of Lilly Cassirer, discovered that the Painting was on display in Madrid at the Museum. He petitioned Spain's Minister for Education, Culture and Sports (who was also chair of the Foundation's Board), requesting the return of the Painting. His request was denied. In July 2003, five United States Congressmen wrote to the Minister, again requesting that Appellants return the Painting to Cassirer. The request was again denied. Cassirer never attempted to obtain the Painting through judicial proceedings in Spain.

On May 10, 2005, Cassirer filed suit against the Foundation and Spain in the Central District of California. On February 28, 2006, the Foundation filed a motion to dismiss, contending that the district court lacked subject matter and personal jurisdiction and that venue did not lie in the Central District of California. While the Foundation's motion was pending, Cassirer moved the court for leave to conduct jurisdictional discovery.

On April 5, 2006, the district court reviewed, as a question of law, whether the expropriation exception to sovereign immunity in § 1605(a)(3) of the FSIA applied to a sovereign entity that was not alleged to have taken property in violation of international law. After receiving further briefing from the parties, the district court ruled that § 1605(a)(3) requires only that property was seized in violation of

---

4 Under Spanish law, at least two-thirds of the Foundation's Board of Directors must be representatives of Spain, who are nominated and removed freely by the Spanish government through royal decree. Currently, Spain's Minister of Culture, Secretary of State for Culture, Secretary of State for Budget and Expenses, and Undersecretary of Culture all sit as *ex officio* members of the Foundation's Board.

5 Claude Cassirer is a United States citizen and resident of California.

international law, not that the foreign sovereign itself violated international law. The district court also granted sixty days to conduct discovery for the purpose of determining whether the Foundation conducted "commercial activity in the United States within the meaning of the FSIA."

On June 9, 2006, Spain filed its own motion to dismiss, contending lack of subject matter jurisdiction due to sovereign immunity and various other grounds. On August 30, 2006, after hearing argument, the district court issued a Memorandum and Order denying both the motions to dismiss. The district court held that 1) Cassirer presented a case or controversy against both the Foundation and Spain; 2) Cassirer was not required to exhaust judicial remedies; 3) § 1605(a)(3) of the FSIA applies to the Foundation and Spain, despite Cassirer's admission that neither took the Painting in violation of international law (affirming its earlier decision on this point); 4) the Foundation and Spain engage in commercial activity in the United States within the meaning of § 1605(a)(3), such that they are not entitled to sovereign immunity; 5) under the language of the FSIA, personal jurisdiction exists over the Foundation and Spain by virtue of the fact that subject matter jurisdiction existed; and 6) venue is proper in the Central District of California. *See Cassirer v. Kingdom of Spain*, 461 F. Supp. 2d 1157 (C.D. Cal. 2006).

The Appellants brought this timely interlocutory appeal. Cassirer subsequently filed a Motion to Dismiss, contending that this court lacks appellate jurisdiction over any issues other than whether the Appellants are entitled to sovereign immunity.

II. Jurisdiction

We first address the issue of appellate jurisdiction raised by Cassirer. We have jurisdiction to review "final decisions" of the district court. 28 U.S.C. § 1291. "Final decisions end the litigation on the merits and leave nothing for the court to do but execute the judgment." *Am. States Ins. Co. v. Dastar Corp.,* 318 F.3d 881, 884 (9th Cir. 2003) (internal quotations and alterations omitted). Typically, a district court's denial of a motion to dismiss is not final for purposes of 28 U.S.C. § 1291. *See Marx v. Government of Guam,* 866 F.2d 294, 296 (9th Cir. 1989). Under the "collateral order doctrine," we may nonetheless review that "small category of decisions" that are "conclusive [because they] resolve important questions separate from the merits, and that are effectively unreviewable on appeal from the final judgment in the underlying action." *Swint v. Chambers County Comm'n*, 514 U.S. 35, 42, 115 S. Ct. 1203, 131 L. Ed. 2d 60 (1995) (citation omitted).

"[T]he denial of a claim of lack of [personal] jurisdiction is not an immediately appealable collateral order." *Van Cauwenberghe v. Biard*, 486 U.S. 517, 526–27, 108 S. Ct. 1945, 100 L. Ed. 2d 517 (1988); *Batzel v. Smith*, 333 F.3d 1018, 1023 (9th Cir. 2003) (orders denying motions to dismiss for lack of personal jurisdiction are not final and are not appealable under the collateral order doctrine). Therefore, we do not have jurisdiction to review the district court's denial of Appellants' motions to dismiss for lack of personal jurisdiction, and we dismiss this appeal with regard to that issue.

Likewise, we dismiss the appeal with regard to the issues of standing and Article III case or controversy. The district court's order denying Appellants' motion to dismiss on these issues is fully reviewable on appeal from a final judgment. Therefore, we hold that such a denial is not immediately appealable as a collateral order.[6] *See Swint*, 514 U.S. at 42 (to be immediately appealable under collateral order doctrine, decision must be effectively unreviewable on appeal from the final judgment in the underlying action).[7]

We have jurisdiction to review the district court's order as it pertains to sovereign immunity. "[A]n order denying immunity under the FSIA is appealable under the collateral order doctrine," because sovereign immunity is immunity from suit, which is effectively lost if a case is erroneously permitted to go to trial. *Gupta*, 487 F.3d at 763, 764 n.6.

III. Sovereign Immunity Under the FSIA

The primary issue before us is whether Appellants are entitled to sovereign immunity under the FSIA, such that the district court lacks subject matter jurisdiction. The existence of subject matter jurisdiction under the FSIA is a question of law

---

6 *See also, e.g., Moniz v. City of Ft. Lauderdale*, 145 F.3d 1278, 1281 n.3 (11th Cir. 1998) (question of standing is not a final decision under the collateral order doctrine); *Triad Assocs., Inc. v. Robinson*, 10 F.3d 492, 496–97 n.2 (7th Cir. 1993) (denial of a motion to dismiss for lack of standing does not qualify as a final judgment and is not immediately appealable); *Crymes v. DeKalb County, Ga.*, 923 F.2d 1482, 1484 (11th Cir. 1991) (observing that denial of motion to dismiss on ripeness grounds is not immediately appealable); *Shanks v. City of Dallas*, 752 F.2d 1092, 1099 n.9 (5th Cir. 1985) (case or controversy considerations are not appealable under the collateral order exception because they obviously "involve considerations that are emeshed in the legal issues surrounding [the merits of the] cause of action"); *City of Detroit v. Grinnell Corp.*, 495 F.2d 448, 474–75 (2d Cir. 1974) (question of ripeness and standing are not immediately appealable under collateral order doctrine), *abrogated on other grounds by Goldberger v. Integrated Res., Inc.*, 209 F.3d 43 (2d Cir. 2000).

7 In *Swint*, the Supreme Court left open the possibility that we might exercise pendent appellate jurisdiction when we properly have jurisdiction over one ruling and "related rulings that are not themselves independently appealable" are "inextricably intertwined," or when review of the related ruling is "necessary to ensure meaningful review of the [issue over which the court has jurisdiction]," *Swint*, 514 U.S. at 50–51, and we have done so under some circumstances. *See Idaho Watersheds Project v. Hahn*, 307 F.3d 815, 824 (9th Cir. 2002); *Hook v. Ariz. Dep't of Corr.*, 107 F.3d 1397, 1401–02 (9th Cir. 1997). We decline to do so here, however. Whether Appellants are "persons" within the meaning of the *Due Process Clause* for purposes of personal jurisdiction is not inextricably intertwined with our determination of sovereign immunity. Likewise, whether the case involves a case or controversy against Spain does not relate to or necessarily involve our consideration of sovereign immunity. Further, because we can resolve the sovereign immunity issue without reaching the merits of Appellants' challenge to Article III case or controversy and standing, we do not exercise pendent appellate jurisdiction under Swint. Accordingly, we dismiss this appeal as to these issues.

reviewed de novo. *Adler v. Fed. Republic of Nigeria,* 107 F.3d 720, 723 (9th Cir. 1997). A district court's factual findings on jurisdictional issues are reviewed for clear error. *Id.*

A. The FSIA Provides Limited Exceptions to Sovereign Immunity

The district court has original jurisdiction of any non-jury civil action against a foreign state, including its agencies and instrumentalities.[8] *See* 28 U.S.C. § 1330(a). Under the FSIA, however, foreign states are immune from the jurisdiction of United States courts, subject only to the specific exceptions in §§ 1605, 1607, and specified existing international agreements. *See id.* at § 1604.[9] Thus, the sole basis for obtaining jurisdiction over a foreign state in federal court is the existence of an exception to the FSIA. *Argentine Republic v. Amerada Hess Shipping Corp.,* 488 U.S. 428, 439, 109 S. Ct. 683, 102 L. Ed. 2d 818 (1989). The FSIA exceptions include "waiver of immunity, § 1605(a)(1), commercial activities occurring in the United States or causing a direct effect in this country, § 1605(a)(2), property expropriated in violation of international law, § 1605(a)(3), inherited, gift, or immovable property located in the United States, § 1605(a)(4), non-commercial torts occurring in the United States, § 1605(a)(5), and maritime liens, § 1605(b)." *Id.*

B. The Expropriation Exception

Cassirer contends that neither the Foundation nor Spain is entitled to sovereign immunity due to the "expropriation exception" of § 1605(a)(3).[10] Section 1605(a)(3) provides that a "foreign state shall not be immune . . . in any case . . . in which rights in property taken in violation of international law are in issue . . . ." The issue regarding the applicability of this exception arises because the statute uses the passive voice and does not expressly require that the foreign state (against whom the claim is made) be the entity that took the property in violation of international law. Appellants invite us to read such a requirement into the statute. The parties agree that Germany, and not Spain, allegedly took the Painting in violation of

---

8 Section 1603(a) defines "foreign state" to include "a political subdivision of a foreign state or an agency or instrumentality of a foreign state . . ."

9 Section 1604 provides: "Subject to existing international agreements to which the United States is a party at the time of enactment of this Act a foreign state shall be immune from the jurisdiction of the courts of the United States and of the States except as provided in sections 1605 to 1607 of this chapter." 28 U.S.C. § 1604.

10 Section 1605(a)(3) provides: "A foreign state shall not be immune from the jurisdiction of courts of the United States or of the States in any case . . . in which rights in property taken in violation of international law are in issue and that property or any property exchanged for such property is present in the United States in connection with a commercial activity carried on in the United States by the foreign state; or that property or any property exchanged for such property is owned or operated by an agency or instrumentality of the foreign state and that agency or instrumentality is engaged in a commercial activity in the United States." 28 U.S.C. § 1605(a)(3).

international law. Therefore, under the construction urged by Appellants, the expropriation exception could not apply. We disagree.

We find § 1605(a)(3) to be unambiguous. Where "the intent of Congress is clear and unambiguously expressed by the statutory language," that is normally the end of the statutory analysis. *Zuni Pub. Sch. Dist. No. 89 v. Dep't of Educ.,* 550 U.S. 81, 93, 127 S. Ct. 1534, 167 L. Ed. 2d 449 (2007). We hold that the plain language of § 1605(a)(3) does not require that the foreign state (against whom the claim is made) be the entity who expropriated the property in violation of international law.

Our holding is consistent with the legislative history.[11] In reviewing Congress's intent in enacting the FSIA, we consider § 1602, which sets forth Congress's findings and purpose. This section expresses Congress's understanding that foreign states are not immune from suit "insofar as their commercial activities are concerned."[12] In explaining § 1602, the House Report states that Congress is adopting the restrictive theory of sovereign immunity, that is, "[T]he sovereign immunity of foreign states should be 'restricted' to cases involving acts of a foreign state which are sovereign or governmental in nature, as opposed to acts which are either commercial in nature or those which private persons normally perform." H.R. Rep. No. 94-1487, at 14 (1976), *reprinted in* 1976 U.S.C.C.A.N. 6604, 6613.

Consistent with the restrictive theory of sovereign immunity described in § 1602 and the House Report, the exceptions in § 1605(a) apply to situations in which foreign states act more like private persons or are engaged in commercial activities. The plain language of § 1605(a)(3) is entirely consistent with Congress's intent, because § 1605(a)(3) gives a court jurisdiction over a foreign state in cases involving stolen property only if the foreign state (or its agency) is engaged in a commercial activity in the United States.

Citing *In re Republic of Philippines,* 309 F.3d 1143 (9th Cir. 2002), Appellants argue that § 1605(a)(3) applies only when the foreign state against whom the claim is leveled actually took property in violation of international law. *Republic of Philippines* required us to interpret the exception in § 1605(a)(4), which provides

---

11 Under appropriate circumstances, we may consider legislative history even when the plain language is clear. We do this, however, only where the legislative history "*clearly* indicates that Congress meant something other than what it said." *Carson Harbor Vill., Ltd. v. Unocal Corp.,* 270 F.3d 863, 877 (9th Cir. 2001) (emphasis added).

12 In its statement of "Findings and declaration of purpose," 28 U.S.C. § 1602 provides:

> The Congress finds that the determination by United States courts of the claims of foreign states to immunity from the jurisdiction of such courts would serve the interests of justice and would protect the rights of both foreign states and litigants in United States courts. Under international law, states are not immune from the jurisdiction of foreign courts insofar as their commercial activities are concerned, and their commercial property may be levied upon for the satisfaction of judgments rendered against them in connection with their commercial activities. Claims of foreign states to immunity should henceforth be decided by courts of the United States and of the States in conformity with the principles set forth in this chapter.

that a foreign state loses its immunity in any case "in which rights in property in the United States acquired by succession or gift or rights in immovable property situated in the United States are in issue." We construed the statute as applying only to rights in property in the United States acquired by succession or gift *by the foreign state*. In reaching this conclusion, we relied on language in the House Report which stated:

> There is general agreement that a foreign state may not claim immunity when the suit against it relates to rights in property, real or personal, obtained by gift or inherited by the foreign state and situated or administered in the country where the suit is brought . . . The reason is that, in claiming rights in a decedent's estate or obtained by gift, *the foreign state claims the same right which is enjoyed by private persons*.

Republic of Philippines, 309 F.3d at 1151 (quoting H.R. Rep. No. 94-1487) (emphasis added). In other words, to effectuate Congress's intent to grant courts jurisdiction over foreign states only when they act more like private persons, we read "by the foreign state" into § 1605(a)(4). Under this reading, courts gain jurisdiction over a foreign state only if the state acted like a private person and by claiming rights in a decedent's estate or obtaining a gift. Contrary to Appellant's argument, our interpretation of § 1605(a)(4) in *Republic of Philippines* is entirely consistent with a plain language reading of § 1605(a)(3). It is not necessary to read "by the foreign state" into § 1605(a)(3) to achieve consistency with the restrictive theory of sovereign immunity. The plain language of § 1605(a)(3) already grants courts jurisdiction over foreign states only if they act like a private person by engaging in commercial activities. *Republic of Philippines* therefore provides no justification to depart from the plain language of § 1605(a)(3).

Because nothing in the plain language of the FSIA or the legislative history requires us to read additional language into the statute, we hold that the expropriation exception to sovereign immunity found in § 1605(a)(3) does not require that the foreign state against whom the claim is made be the foreign state that took property in violation of international law.

C. Commercial Activity in the United States

For the expropriation exception to apply, the FSIA also requires "that property or any property exchanged for such property is owned or operated by an agency or instrumentality of the foreign state and that agency or instrumentality is engaged in a commercial activity in the United States." 28 U.S.C. § 1605(a)(3). The Foundation admits that it is an "agency or instrumentality" of Spain and that it owns the Painting. We agree with the district court that the Foundation has engaged in sufficient commercial activity in the United States to satisfy § 1605(a)(3).

As defined in the FSIA, "commercial activity"

> means either a regular course of commercial conduct or a particular commercial transaction or act. The commercial character of an activity shall be determined by reference to the nature of the course of conduct or particular transaction or act, rather than by reference to its purpose.

28 U.S.C. § 1603(d). "The central question is whether the activity is of a kind in which a private party might engage." *Siderman de Blake v. Republic of Argentina*, 965 F.2d 699, 708 (9th Cir. 1992) (internal quotation marks omitted).

In *Siderman*, we concluded that Argentina conducted commercial activity in the United States, because (1) it advertised an expropriated hotel in the United States; (2) it solicited guests through its United States agent (Argentina's national airline); (3) numerous Americans stayed at the hotel; and (4) the hotel accepted all major American credit cards. *Id.* at 712–13.

Likewise, in *Altmann*, we concluded that authoring, promoting, and distributing books and other publications in the United States to exploit expropriated paintings were "sufficient to constitute 'commercial activity' for the purpose of satisfying the FSIA." *Altmann*, 317 F.3d at 959.

In this case, after allowing limited jurisdictional discovery, the district court found that the Foundation engaged in commercial transactions in the United States, including transacting business as a purchaser and a seller of goods and services and as an advertiser in distributing marketing and other commercial promotional materials. *Cassirer v. Kingdom of Spain*, 461 F. Supp. 2d 1157, 1173–75 (C.D. Cal. 2006). For example, the Foundation made numerous purchases of books, posters, post cards, and related materials from United States businesses in New York, California, and Washington, D.C. The Foundation also purchased books about Nazi expropriation of great works of art[13] and a book presumably about the works of Pissaro. *Id.* at 1173. The Foundation sold posters and books to United States residents and businesses, and licensed the reproduction of images to various United States businesses. *Id.* The Foundation also admitted that it worked with U.S. entities to secure goods to be sold in the Museum gift shop, including paying U.S. citizens to write for its exhibit catalogs. *Id.* Further, it admitted that it has shipped gift shop items to purchasers in the United States. *Id.* Notably, the Foundation sold a poster of the Painting at issue in this case to individuals in both California and North Carolina. The California purchaser resides in the Central District of California and used her American Express credit card to consummate the transaction. *Id.*

The Foundation also solicited, recruited, and commissioned writers and speakers from the United States to provide services at the Museum. *Id.* The Foundation facilitated the production of a film on the Foundation collection, featuring the Painting, which it knew would be presented in-flight on Iberia Airlines flights to and from the United States. *Id.* at 1174.

The Foundation placed advertisements in magazines that are distributed in the United States and sent press releases, brochures, and general information to

---

13 The district court noted, "As particularly ironic examples, the Foundation purchased through Amazon.com *The Lost Museum: The Nazi Conspiracy to Steal the World's Greatest Works of Art*, . . . and from the American Association of Museums in Washington, DC purchased a volume on *Museum Policy and Procedure for Nazi Era Issues*." Cassirer, 461 F. Supp. 2d at 1173 (internal citations omitted).

TourEspana and the Spanish National Tourist Offices in the United States. For example, the Foundation advertised in news publications such as *Newsweek, Time Magazine*, and the *New Yorker. Id.* It also distributes its Museum bulletin, "Perspectives," to individuals in the United States, including two in the Central District of California. *Id.*

The Foundation also contracted with museums in the United States to loan its artwork to the U.S. institutions or to borrow artwork for display in the Foundation Museum in Spain. *Id.* at 1174–75.

The record supports the district court's factual findings, which are not clearly erroneous. Cassirer has produced numerous examples of the Foundation's commercial activity in the United States that are "of a kind in which a private party might engage." *Siderman*, 965 F.2d at 708 (internal quotation marks omitted). Much of that activity was connected with the Painting. Thus, Cassirer has adequately demonstrated that the Foundation has engaged in sufficient commercial activity in the United States to satisfy § 1605(a)(3).

IV. Exhaustion of Remedies

Cassirer unsuccessfully petitioned the Foundation for return of the Painting, but Cassirer has not alleged that he made recourse to the Spanish or German judiciaries to settle his claim to the Painting.[14] Thus, Spain argues that § 1605(a)(3) cannot apply, because Cassirer has not exhausted judicial remedies in the foreign forum. The district court held that the plain language of § 1605(a)(3) of the FSIA contains no "exhaustion-of-foreign-remedies requirement" and therefore the court refused to impose such a requirement on Cassirer. *Cassirer*, 461 F. Supp. 2d at 1164. Whether the FSIA, specifically § 1605(a)(3), requires exhaustion is a matter of statutory interpretation and an issue of first impression.

"Of paramount importance to any exhaustion inquiry is congressional intent." *McCarthy v. Madigan,* 503 U.S. 140, 144, 112 S. Ct. 1081, 117 L. Ed. 2d 291 (1992) (citing *Patsy v. Board of Regents of Florida,* 457 U.S. 496, 501, 102 S. Ct. 2557, 73 L. Ed. 2d 172 (1982) (internal quotation marks omitted)), *superceded by statute as stated in Booth v. Churner,* 532 U.S. 731, 732, 121 S. Ct. 1819, 149 L. Ed. 2d 958 (2001).[15] "Where Congress specifically mandates, exhaustion is required." *Id.* (citing *Colt Independence Joint Venture v. FSLIC*, 489 U.S. 561,

---

14 The record does not indicate what, if any, judicial actions have been brought in Germany. We note that there is some indication in publicly available material that, in 1958, the West German government may have acknowledged Lilly Cassirer to be the legal owner of the Painting, conceding that she retained the full rights of ownership. See Emma Daly, *American Says Painting in Spain is Holocaust Loot*, N.Y. Times, Feb. 10, 2003, at E1.

15 Although these decisions generally involve the exhaustion of administrative remedies, we have previously approached exhaustion of claims invoking international law in a manner consistent with our application of exhaustion in other domestic contexts. *See Sarei*, 550 F.3d at

579, 109 S. Ct. 1361, 103 L. Ed. 2d 602 (1989); Patsy, 457 U.S. at 502 n.4). "But where Congress has not clearly required exhaustion, sound judicial discretion governs." *McCarthy*, 503 U.S. at 144 (citing *McGee v. United States,* 402 U.S. 479, 483 n.6, 91 S. Ct. 1565, 29 L. Ed. 2d 47 (1971)). To discern the intent of Congress, "'[w]e look first to the plain language of the statute, construing the provisions of the entire law, including its object and policy.'" *United States v. $493,850.00 in U.S. Currency,* 518 F.3d 1159, 1167 (9th Cir. 2008) (quoting *Carson Harbor Vill., Ltd. v. Unocal Corp.,* 270 F.3d 863, 877 (9th Cir. 2001)).

As the district court noted, the FSIA is silent as to any exhaustion requirement. The legislative history is also devoid of any enlightening reference to exhaustion.[16] Accordingly, we hold that Congress has not clearly required exhaustion for claims brought under the FSIA. This, however, does not end our analysis.

To determine whether an action brought against a foreign state (invoking an exception to the FSIA) requires exhaustion, it is important to put into context what the FSIA is and what it is not. The FSIA is not a source of substantive law and does not create any causes of actions. Rather, it is a jurisdictional statute incorporating international law principles to guide U.S. courts in determining when a foreign state is or is not entitled to sovereign immunity. *See* § 1602. In other words, claims brought in U.S. courts, against foreign states, for violations of international law depend on the applicability of an exception to the FSIA for jurisdiction.

831–32 ("[E]xhaustion under the [Alien Torts Statute] should be approached consistently with exhaustion principles in other domestic contexts.").

16 Cassirer's argument that Congress's prior inclusion of an arbitration requirement in § 1605 (a)(7)(B)(i) evidences an intent to exclude an exhaustion requirement from § 1605(a)(3) is not persuasive. A mandatory arbitration requirement, although similar, is not the same as an exhaustion-of-local-remedies requirement. The phrase "local remedies" has been "interpreted broadly, [to include] the whole system of legal protection, as provided by municipal law, not only the courts and tribunals but also the use of procedural facilities which municipal law makes available to litigants." Restatement (Third) of Foreign Relations Law § 713, Reporters' Note 5 (citing *Ambatielos Case (Greece v. United Kingdom)*, 1951, 12 R. Int'l Arb. Awards 91, 120, 122) (internal quotation marks omitted). Therefore, one might fulfil an arbitration requirement without exhausting local remedies.

Further, § 1605(a)(7)(B)(i) was enacted approximately twenty years after § 1605(a)(3). Thus, the *exclusio unius* doctrine does not apply. *See Cipollone v. Liggett Group, Inc.,* 505 U.S. 504, 520, 112 S. Ct. 2608, 120 L. Ed. 2d 407 (1992) (noting that "the views of a subsequent Congress form a hazardous basis for inferring the intent of an earlier one") (internal quotation marks omitted). For this reason, we disagree with the D.C. Circuit's suggestion that the inclusion of § 1605(a)(7)(B)(i) "strengthens the inference that its omission from a closely related section must have been intentional." *Agudas Chasidei Chabad v. Russian Fed'n,* 528 F.3d 934, 948, 381 U.S. App. D.C. 316 (D.C. Cir. 2008) (suggesting, but not deciding, that § 1605(a)(3) does not impose an exhaustion requirement).

Congress has since repealed the arbitration requirement of § 1605(a)(7). *See* National Defense Authorization Act for Fiscal Year 2008, Pub. L. No. 110-181, div. A, § 1083(b)(1)(A)(iii), 122 Stat. 3, 341 (2008) (repealing 28 U.S.C. § 1605(a)(7)).

Such claims, however, depend on the law of nations to define the substantive rights embodied in any cause of action. The Supreme Court has similarly recognized the Alien Tort Statute (ATS), 28 U.S.C. § 1350, to be a jurisdictional statute that creates no new causes of action and relies on the common law and the present-day law of nations to define substantive rights. *See Sosa v. Alvarez-Machain*, 542 U.S. 692, 724, 124 S. Ct. 2739, 159 L. Ed. 2d 718 (2004) ("[T]he ATS is a jurisdictional statute creating no new causes of action . . .).[17]

The doctrine of exhaustion of domestic remedies is a "well-established rule of customary international law." *See Sarei*, 550 F.3d at 829 (quoting *Interhandel Case (Switz. v. U.S.)*, 1959 I.C.J. 6, 26 (Mar. 29)). This rule generally provides that a state is not required to consider a claim, made by a person against a foreign state, and alleging a violation of international law "until that person has exhausted domestic remedies, unless such remedies are clearly sham or inadequate, or their application is unreasonably prolonged." *See Sarei*, 550 F.3d at 829 (citing Restatement (Third) of Foreign Relations Law § 713 cmt. f & § 703 cmt. d)). Because United States courts import well-settled principles of international law to define substantive rights in cases brought under the FSIA, there are logical arguments suggesting that courts should also import the well-settled limitations to such causes of action, including the doctrine of exhaustion of remedies. *Cf. Sarei*, 550 F.3d at 833–35 (Bea, J., concurring) (discussing exhaustion in the context of the ATS); *Sarei*, 487 F.3d at 1231–45 (Bybee, J., dissenting) (same). Nonetheless, where Congress has not clearly required exhaustion, we have not (and likely cannot) impose exhaustion as an absolute jurisdictional requirement. *See Sarei*, 550 F.3d at 824 ("[W]e decline to impose an absolute requirement of exhaustion in ATS cases."). *See also Sampson v. Federal Republic of Germany*, 250 F.3d 1145, 1153–54 (7th Cir. 2001) ("[A]lthough international law is 'part of our law,' it does not follow that federal statutes must be read to reflect the norms of international law.") (citation omitted).

The jurisdiction of federal courts derives from and is circumscribed exclusively by Article III of the United States Constitution and by federal statutes enacted by Congress. *See Karcher v. May,* 484 U.S. 72, 77, 108 S. Ct. 388, 98 L. Ed. 2d 327 (1987) ("The power of federal courts to hear and decide cases is defined by Article III of the Constitution and by the federal statutes enacted thereunder."); *Sheldon v. Sill*, 49 U.S. (8 How.) 441, 448–49, 12 L. Ed. 1147 (1850) ("Congress, having the power to establish the courts, must define their respective jurisdictions. . . . Courts created by statute can have no jurisdiction but such as the statute confers."). In the domestic context, we have acknowledged that statutory exhaustion requirements

17 The ATS provides that "[t]he district courts shall have original jurisdiction of any civil action by an alien for a tort only, committed in violation of the law of nations or a treaty of the United States." 28 U.S.C. § 1350.

are jurisdictional in nature. *See Sarei*, 550 F.3d at 828 & n.6 (gathering cases).[18] Where Congress requires exhaustion, a failure to exhaust available remedies typically deprives the federal court of jurisdiction. Such is not necessarily the case, however, when international norms, and not Congress, purport to circumscribe jurisdiction by requiring exhaustion of remedies. International law may define the substantive rights of parties in actions permitted by the FSIA, but it cannot compel or restrict Article III jurisdiction. *Cf. Sampson*, 250 F.3d at 1152 ("[I]nternational law itself does not mandate Article III jurisdiction over foreign sovereigns."). Absent clear Congressional intent, we cannot incorporate exhaustion as an absolute requirement merely because international law would require it. An absolute exhaustion requirement amounts to an absolute limitation on the jurisdiction of federal courts. To impose such a requirement would, in essence, usurp the Constitutional power vested in Congress and cede foreign lawmakers and jurists with power to limit the jurisdiction of United States federal courts.

Neither Congress nor this court have imposed an absolute exhaustion of remedies requirement in cases brought against foreign states under an exception to the FSIA. Yet, where principles of international comity and rules of customary international law require exhaustion, we exercise sound judicial discretion and consider exhaustion on a prudential, case-by-case basis. *See Sarei*, 550 F.3d at 828. *In Sarei*, we held that domestic prudential standards and core principles of international law require a district court to consider exhaustion in appropriate cases. *Id.* at 824 (citing *Sosa*, 542 U.S. at 733 n.21).[19] Under our prudential approach, when a defendant affirmatively pleads failure to exhaust remedies, the district court must, as

---

18 *See, e.g., Coit Independence Joint Venture v. FSLIC*, 489 U.S. 561, 579, 109 S. Ct. 1361, 103 L. Ed. 2d 602 (1989) (establishing that "exhaustion of administrative remedies is required where Congress imposes an exhaustion requirement by statute"); *Weinberger v. Salfi*, 422 U.S. 749, 764–67, 95 S. Ct. 2457, 45 L.Ed.2d 522 (1975) (holding 42 U.S.C. § 405(h) of the Social Security Act contains a jurisdictional exhaustion requirement); *Barron v. Ashcroft*, 358 F.3d 674, 677 (9th Cir. 2004) (holding that exhaustion of administrative remedies under 8 U.S.C. § 1252(d)(1) is a jurisdictional requirement, and failure to exhaust deprives the court of subject-matter jurisdiction); *Platte River Whooping Crane Critical Habitat Maint. Trust v. FERC*, 876 F.2d 109, 112–13, 277 U.S. App. D.C. 350 (D.C. Cir. 1989) (interpreting Federal Power Act statute, 16 U.S.C. § 825(b), to provide a jurisdictional exhaustion requirement); *Dhangu v. INS*, 812 F.2d 455, 460 (9th Cir. 1987) (stating that exhaustion of administrative remedies with the BIA is a jurisdictional requirement); *Lindsey v. U.S.*, 448 F. Supp. 2d 37, 51 (D.D.C. 2006) (interpreting provision of the Internal Revenue Code, 26 U.S.C. § 7422(a), as imposing a jurisdictional exhaustion requirement).

19 Justice Breyer, joined by Justice Souter, indicated, in dicta, that they would likely read § 1605(a)(3) to require exhaustion. Concurring in *Republic of Austria v. Altmann*, Justice Breyer wrote "a plaintiff may have to show an absence of remedies in the foreign country sufficient to compensate for any taking. . . . A plaintiff who chooses to litigate in this country in disregard of the postdeprivation remedies in the expropriating state may have trouble showing a tak[ing] in violation of international law." *Republic of Austria v. Altmann*, 541 U.S. 677, 714, 124 S. Ct. 2240, 159 L. Ed. 2d 1 (2004) (Breyer, J., concurring) (internal quotation marks omitted).

a discretionary matter, determine in the first instance whether to impose such a requirement on a plaintiff. *Id.* at 832.

Although *Sarei* addressed exhaustion in the context of the ATS, where Congress has not clearly adopted or rejected exhaustion as a jurisdictional prerequisite, our formulation of prudential exhaustion applies equally to cases brought against foreign states (and their instrumentalities) under the FSIA.[20] In this case, Appellants have asserted that Cassirer failed to exhaust available remedies in Spain or Germany. Although the district court correctly concluded that the FSIA does not require exhaustion of remedies, the court erred by failing to conduct a prudential exhaustion analysis.[21]

On remand, the district court should be guided by the principles we outlined in *Sarei*. Summarizing the *Sarei* framework generally, we first note that the district court need only consider exhaustion to the extent the defendant has affirmatively pleaded Cassirer's failure to exhaust local remedies. *See Sarei*, 550 F.3d at 832 ("The defendant bears the burden to plead and justify an exhaustion requirement, including the availability of local remedies.") (citation omitted). Second, the court must consider whether Congress has clearly required exhaustion for the specific claims asserted in the complaint. If, as in this case, Congress has not imposed or rejected such a requirement, the court must then determine whether the applicable substantive law would require exhaustion.[22] Third, the court must consider whether

---

20 We respectfully disagree with the concurring-and-dissenting opinion's conclusion that *Sarei* is not on point. As in *Sarei*, the substantive claims here are based on alleged violations of international law. Both the ATS (at issue in *Sarei*) and the FSIA are jurisdictional statutes, and Congress has not expressly required or rejected exhaustion in either. With regard to principles of prudential exhaustion, the only meaningful difference between the international tort claims in *Sarei* and the claims made in the present case (and the only reason the FSIA is at issue) is that the defendant here is a sovereign foreign state. That is, if the defendant here were a private party, there could be little doubt that *Sarei* would apply. That the defendant is a foreign state does not undermine the applicability of *Sarei*. Rather, that fact and the principles of international comity weigh strongly in favor of the district court's consideration of exhaustion of local remedies on a prudential basis.

21 Contrary to the concurring-and-dissenting opinion's assertion, we are not writing an absolute exhaustion requirement into the FSIA. Nor are we absolutely precluding an exhaustion requirement where one might ordinarily be required by the applicable international law and justified under the circumstances. We do not hold that the district court must impose an exhaustion requirement in this case. Rather, we direct the district court (in the absence of clear Congressional intent otherwise) to examine the record before it, the applicable substantive law, and various equitable factors and then to carefully weigh whether to require exhaustion of local remedies on the claims before it. Where Congress has neither clearly imposed or rejected exhaustion as a prerequisite to exercising jurisdiction against a foreign state, the district court has discretion to consider exhaustion on a prudential basis. *See Sarei*, 550 F.3d at 828.

22 Although exhaustion is, generally, a well-established rule of international law, it may not be firmly established in all areas of international law. *See Sarei*, 550 F.3d at 844 (Reinhardt, J., dissenting) (discussing exhaustion in the context of international human rights).

the defendant has met its burden to show the availability of local remedies and that such remedies have not been exhausted. *Id.* The plaintiff may rebut a showing of unexhausted remedies abroad by demonstrating the futility of exhaustion ("by showing that the local remedies were ineffective, unobtainable, unduly prolonged, inadequate, or obviously futile."). *Id.* (citations omitted). Finally, the court may, in its sound discretion, impose or waive exhaustion after assessing the availability, effectiveness, and possible futility of any unexhausted remedies in light of various prudential factors, including but not limited to: (1) the need to safeguard and respect the principles of international comity and sovereignty, (2) the existence or lack of a significant United States "nexus,"[23] (3) the nature of the allegations and the gravity of the potential violations of international law, and (4) whether the allegations implicate matters of "universal concern" for which a state has jurisdiction to adjudicate the claims without regard to territoriality or the nationality of the parties. *See id.* at 830–31.

V. Conclusion

We dismiss this appeal with regard to the issues of personal jurisdiction, standing, and Article III case or controversy. We affirm the district court with regard to its statutory interpretation of 28 U.S.C. § 1605(a)(3). We likewise affirm the district court's conclusion that the Foundation engaged in sufficient commercial activity within the United States to satisfy the requirements of § 1605(a)(3). We reverse the

---

23 The concurring-and-dissenting opinion would limit the reach of *Sarei* by suggesting that prudential exhaustion applies only in cases where there is a weak nexus with the United States. Therefore, the concurring-and-dissenting opinion suggests that, if an FSIA exception to sovereign immunity applies, then prudential exhaustion should not be considered because the claim necessarily has a strong nexus with the United States. We respectfully disagree. First, we do not read *Sarei* to hold that exhaustion may *only* be considered where there is a weak nexus to the United States. As we explained in *Sarei*, "The lack of a significant U.S. 'nexus' is an *important* consideration in evaluating whether plaintiffs should be required to exhaust their local remedies in accordance with the principle of international comity." *Sarei*, 550 F.3d at 831 (emphasis added). That is, courts should "carefully consider the question of exhaustion," particularly where the nexus is weak and where the claims "do not involve matters of 'universal concern.'" *See id.*

Second, some of the exceptions to sovereign immunity under the FSIA require little (if any) nexus with the United States. *See, e.g.*, § 1605(a) (1) (exception to sovereign immunity where there is an explicit or implicit waiver of immunity by the foreign state); § 1605(a)(6) (exception to sovereign immunity for actions to enforce an agreement made by the foreign state with or for the benefit of a private party to submit to arbitration); § 1605(b) (exception to sovereign immunity for a suit in admiralty brought to enforce a maritime lien against a vessel or cargo of the foreign state which maritime lien is based upon a commercial activity of the foreign state). *But see, e.g.*, §§ 1605(a)(2) – (5) (generally requiring that the foreign state have engaged in some commercial activity within or having direct impact in the United States). Thus, we cannot say that a claim's nexus with the United States is necessarily strong any time an exception to sovereign immunity applies. In some cases, a relatively isolated or weak nexus may be sufficient to subject a foreign state to jurisdiction. Yet a weak nexus may also weigh in favor of requiring exhaustion of local remedies in the appropriate case.

district court, however, with regard to exhaustion of remedies and we remand for the limited purpose to determine in the first instance whether to impose an exhaustion requirement on Cassirer.

AFFIRMED in part, REVERSED in part, and REMANDED.

Each party shall bear its own cost.

DISSENT

IKUTA, J., concurring in part and dissenting in part:

I concur in Sections I, II and III. I disagree with Section IV, however, because in my view we should not take it upon ourselves to write an exhaustion requirement into the Foreign Sovereign Immunities Act ("FSIA") when Congress has chosen not to. In enacting the FSIA, Congress created uniform and clear standards for litigants seeking to bring lawsuits against foreign sovereigns, and there is no indication that Congress contemplated that courts would impose an additional exhaustion requirement on litigants. Moreover, our case law on prudential exhaustion in the context of the Alien Tort Statute ("ATS") is both inapposite and non-binding. Because imposing a judge-made exhaustion requirement here is contrary to Congressional intent and does nothing more than create a trap for the unwary, I respectfully dissent.

I.

As always, we begin with the plain language of the statute. *Prince v. Jacoby*, 303 F.3d 1074, 1079 (9th Cir. 2002). As the majority acknowledges, the FSIA does not include an exhaustion requirement. Maj. Op. at 12711–12.

Nor is there any evidence that Congress intended to require plaintiffs to exhaust their remedies in a foreign nation before bringing suit under the FSIA. To the contrary, as explained below, the history of the FSIA indicates that Congress intended to create a comprehensive scheme governing lawsuits in federal courts against a foreign sovereign that would establish once and for all a plaintiff's rights, thereby eliminating inconsistency and uncertainty.

Before the enactment of the FSIA, federal courts "deferred to the decisions of the political branches—in particular, those of the Executive Branch—on whether to take jurisdiction over actions against foreign sovereigns and their instrumentalities." *Verlinden B.V. v. Cent. Bank of Nig.*, 461 U.S. 480, 486, 103 S. Ct. 1962, 76 L. Ed. 2d 81 (1983) (citing *The Schooner Exchange v. M'Faddon*, 11 U.S. 116, 7 *Cranch* 116, 3 L. Ed. 287 (1812)). Before 1952, the Executive Branch generally asked federal courts to recognize the sovereign immunity of friendly sovereigns in all lawsuits. *Id.* In 1952, however, the State Department changed course, and announced that the Executive Branch had adopted the "restrictive theory" of sovereign immunity,[1] under which the Executive Branch would request courts to recognize sovereign immunity only in "suits involving the foreign sovereign's public acts," and not in "cases arising out of a foreign state's strictly commercial acts." *Id.* at 487.

1 *See* Letter from Jack B. Tate, Acting Legal Adviser, Department of State, to Acting Attorney General Philip B. Perlman (May 19, 1952), *reprinted in* 26 Dep't of State Bull. 984–85 (1952).

Judicial application of the restrictive theory "proved troublesome" however. *Id.* Foreign sovereigns often put diplomatic pressure on the State Department to recommend that courts recognize sovereign immunity in cases not fitting the restrictive theory, and the Executive Branch's involvement in judicial immunity determinations proved inconsistent. *Id.* These problems resulted in a lack of uniform, predictable standards regarding when federal courts would exercise jurisdiction in lawsuits against foreign sovereigns. *See id.* at 487–88; *see also Republic of Austria v. Altmann*, 541 U.S. 677, 690–91, 124 S. Ct. 2240, 159 L. Ed. 2d 1 (2004).

Seeking to remedy these problems, Congress passed the FSIA in 1976. *Id.* at 691. The statute's purpose was "to free the Government from the case-by-case diplomatic pressures, to clarify the governing standards, and to assure litigants that decisions are made on purely legal grounds and under procedures that insure due process." *Verlinden*, 461 U.S. at 488 (internal quotation marks omitted) (citing H.R. REP. NO. 94-1487, at 7 (1976), *reprinted in* 1976 U.S.C.C.A.N. 6604, 6605).

The FSIA "codif[ied], as a matter of federal law, the restrictive theory of sovereign immunity," and created "a comprehensive set of legal standards governing claims of immunity in every civil action against a foreign state or its political subdivisions, agencies, or instrumentalities." *Id.* Section 2 of the FSIA added § 1330(a) to Title 28, thereby conferring on federal courts subject matter jurisdiction "as to any claim for relief in personam with respect to which the foreign state is not entitled to immunity either under sections 1605–1607 of this title or under any applicable international agreement." 28 U.S.C. § 1330(a) (2006).[2] Section 1604 provides foreign sovereigns with a presumption of immunity,[3] and §§ 1604 and 1330(a) "work in tandem: § 1604 bars federal and state courts from exercising jurisdiction when a foreign state *is* entitled to immunity, and § 1330(a) confers jurisdiction on district courts to hear suits brought by United States citizens and by aliens when a foreign state is *not* entitled to immunity" by operation of an exception in §§ 1605 to 1607. *Argentine Republic v. Amerada Hess Shipping Corp.*, 488 U.S. 428, 434, 109 S. Ct. 683, 102 L. Ed. 2d 818 (1989). The exceptions to immunity in §§ 1605 to 1607 (including actions based on specified commercial activities, rights in personal and real property under certain conditions, and enforcement of certain

---

2 The full text of § 1330(a) states:

> The district courts shall have original jurisdiction without regard to amount in controversy of any nonjury civil action against a foreign state as defined in section 1603(a) of this title as to any claim for relief in personam with respect to which the foreign state is not entitled to immunity either under sections 1605–1607 of this title or under any applicable international agreement.

28 U.S.C. § 1330(a).

3 28 U.S.C. § 1604 (2006) states:

> Subject to existing international agreements to which the United States is a party at the time of enactment of this Act a foreign state shall be immune from the jurisdiction of the courts of the United States and of the States except as provided in sections 1605 to 1607 of this chapter.

agreements, among others) generally require "some form of substantial contact with the United States." *Verlinden*, 461 U.S. at 490 (citing 28 U.S.C. § 1605).

If a foreign state is not entitled to sovereign immunity under the FSIA, it is treated like any other private individual litigant (with the exception that punitive damages are unavailable),[4] because the state is acting as a private party rather than a sovereign exercising power over its own citizens. *See Republic of Arg. v. Weltover, Inc.*, 504 U.S. 607, 614, 112 S. Ct. 2160, 119 L. Ed. 2d 394 (1992) ("A foreign state engaging in 'commercial' activities does not exercise powers peculiar to sovereigns; rather, it exercises only those powers that can also be exercised by private citizens." (internal quotation marks and alterations omitted)); *see also Permanent Mission of India to the U.N. v. City of New York*, 551 U.S. 193, 200–01, 127 S. Ct. 2352, 168 L. Ed. 2d 85 (2007) (holding that a foreign sovereign is not immune from an action for declaratory relief regarding tax liens on the sovereign's real property, and stating that "property ownership is not an inherently sovereign function"); *Weltover*, 504 U.S. at 614 (holding that sovereign immunity does not apply "when a foreign government acts, not as a regulator of a market, but in the manner of a private player within that market").

The FSIA "governs the types of actions for which foreign sovereigns may be held liable in a court in the United States," *Verlinden*, 461 U.S. at 496–97, but it does not focus on international law claims. Rather, it "merely opens United States courts to plaintiffs with pre-existing claims against foreign states[.]" *Altmann*, 541 U.S. at 695; *see also id.* at 704 (Scalia, J., concurring) (noting that plaintiff's claims were based primarily in California law and explaining that "the FSIA affects substantive rights only accidentally, and not as a necessary and intended consequence of the law"). The FSIA treats claims arising under international law the same as claims arising under federal or state law, granting federal courts jurisdiction over foreign sovereigns in circumstances that meet the requirements of §§ 1605 to 1607, while granting immunity "in those cases involving alleged violations of international law that do not come within one of the FSIA's exceptions." *Amerada Hess*, 488 U.S. at 439, 443 (holding that federal courts lacked jurisdiction over a Liberian corporation's suit against Argentina for damage to an oil tanker during war between Great Britain and Argentina, because the FSIA was the sole source of jurisdiction over a foreign state, and it did not authorize jurisdiction in that case); *see also Saudi Arabia v. Nelson*, 507 U.S. 349, 361, 113 S. Ct. 1471, 123 L. Ed. 2d 47 (1993) (holding district court lacked jurisdiction over claims against Saudi Arabia for wrongful arrest, imprisonment, and torture because the "conduct boils down to abuse of the power of its police by the Saudi Government, and however monstrous such abuse undoubtedly may be, a foreign state's exercise of the power of its police has long been understood for purposes of the restrictive theory as peculiarly sovereign in nature").

---

4 *See* 28 U.S.C. § 1606 (2006).

In short, the FSIA established clear and comprehensive standards regarding the limited situations in which Congress deemed it appropriate to allow plaintiffs to sue foreign sovereigns in federal courts. Plaintiffs may bring such suits only in cases having a substantial connection to the United States and involving claims relating to a sovereign's private or commercial activities. The purpose of this comprehensive framework was to rectify the inconsistency and lack of uniformity that had previously beleaguered litigants. The Supreme Court has emphasized "the importance of developing a uniform body of law in this area," and that the FSIA's "standards control in the courts of the United States and of the States." *Verlinden*, 461 U.S. at 489 (internal quotation marks omitted).[5]

II.

Given Congress's intent to establish a uniform and consistent framework for jurisdiction over and litigation involving foreign sovereigns, and given that Congress chose not to include an exhaustion requirement in the FSIA, there appears to be little room for federal courts to impose a new, judge-made requirement on top of the statutory requirements already in the FSIA itself. "[F]ederal courts are vested with a virtually unflagging obligation to exercise the jurisdiction given them," *McCarthy v. Madigan*, 503 U.S. 140, 146, 112 S. Ct. 1081, 117 L. Ed. 2d 291 (1992) (internal quotation marks omitted), and courts have no authority to devise an additional exhaustion requirement when a statute clearly sets out the prerequisites for federal jurisdiction, *see Darby v. Cisneros*, 509 U.S. 137, 138, 113 S. Ct. 2539, 125 L. Ed. 2d 113 (1993).

A.

In imposing a judge-made exhaustion requirement on litigants in the FSIA context, the majority relies primarily on cases addressing exhaustion of administrative remedies. Maj. Op. at 12710–11 (citing *McCarthy*, 503 U.S. at 145; *Coit Independence Joint Venture v. FSLIC*, 489 U.S. 561, 579, 109 S. Ct. 1361, 103 L. Ed. 2d 602 (1989); *Patsy v. Bd. of Regents of Fla.*, 457 U.S. 496, 501, 102 S. Ct. 2557, 73 L. Ed. 2d 172 (1982); *McGee v. United States*, 402 U.S. 479, 483 n.6, 91 S. Ct. 1565, 29 L. Ed. 2d 47 (1971)). Because the reasoning in these cases is based on considerations of separation of powers, administrative efficiency and expertise, and other agency-related concerns, they provide little assistance in determining whether an exhaustion requirement should be imposed in the FSIA context. *See, e.g., McCarthy*, 503 U.S. at 145 ("[T]he exhaustion doctrine recognizes the notion, grounded in deference to Congress'[s] delegation of authority to coordinate branches of Government, that agencies, not the courts, ought to have primary responsibility for the programs that Congress has charged them to administer."); *accord McGee*, 402

5 The Court has further explained that "Congress'[s] intention to enact a comprehensive statutory scheme is also supported by the inclusion in the FSIA of provisions for venue, 28 U.S.C. § 1391(f), removal, § 1441(d), and attachment and execution, §§ 1609–1611." *Amerada Hess*, 488 U.S. at 435 n.3.

U.S. at 484 (noting that the task for courts in deciding the applicability of the administrative exhaustion requirement is "whether allowing all similarly situated registrants to bypass the administrative avenue in question would seriously impair [the agency's] ability to perform its functions") (internal quotation marks and modifications omitted).

To the extent it is appropriate to look to these cases for guidance, they do not support the majority's conclusion. Rather, they counsel exercising caution and considering carefully whether an exhaustion requirement is consistent with congressional intent. In both *McCarthy* and *Patsy*, the Supreme Court looked first for an indication that Congress intended to impose exhaustion requirements upon plaintiffs. *See McCarthy*, 503 U.S. at 144 ("[A]ppropriate deference to Congress'[s] power to prescribe the basic procedural scheme under which a claim may be heard in a federal court requires fashioning of exhaustion principles in a manner consistent with congressional intent and any applicable statutory scheme."); *Patsy*, 457 U.S. at 501–02 ("[T]he initial question whether exhaustion is required should be answered by reference to congressional intent; and a court should not defer the exercise of jurisdiction under a federal statute unless it is consistent with that intent."). The Court has rarely discerned such an intent, and indeed has in general declined to require claimants to exhaust administrative remedies when it is not required by statute. *See, e.g., Darby*, 509 U.S. at 138 (holding that courts may not impose a prudential exhaustion requirement on litigants under the Administrative Procedure Act when "neither the statute nor agency rules specifically mandate exhaustion as a prerequisite to judicial review."); *McCarthy*, 503 U.S. at 149 (holding that a prisoner was not required to exhaust the Bureau of Prisons' administrative procedure before making a *Bivens* claim for money damages); *Coit*, 489 U.S. at 565 (holding that creditors were not required to exhaust the Federal Home Loan Bank Board's administrative claims procedure before bringing suit against a federal bank); *Patsy*, 457 U.S. at 516 (holding that a plaintiff claiming discriminatory treatment was not required to exhaust state administrative remedies before bringing a § 1983 claim in federal court).[6]

---

6 Only one of the cases cited by the majority held that a claimant must exhaust administrative remedies before initiating suit in federal court, and that case arose in the unique context of the federal Selective Service system. *McGee v. United States*, 402 U.S. at 485. Before requiring exhaustion, the Court undertook "a discrete analysis of the particular default in question, to see whether there is a governmental interest compelling enough to justify the forfeiting of judicial review." *Id.* (internal quotation marks omitted). In this context, the Court determined that a deliberate flouting of the administrative processes would undermine "the scheme of decisionmaking that Congress has created," and "jeopardize the interest in full administrative fact gathering and utilization of agency expertise." *Id.* at 484, 486; *see also McKart v. United States*, 395 U.S. 185, 195, 89 S. Ct. 1657, 23 L. Ed. 2d 194 (1969) ("In Selective Service cases, the exhaustion doctrine must be tailored to fit the peculiarities of the administrative system Congress has created.").

Nothing in these administrative law cases suggests that a court should require exhaustion in the FSIA context, where allowing plaintiffs immediate access to federal courts does not raise any risk of undermining the Congressional scheme. To the contrary, imposing an exhaustion requirement not contemplated by Congress is inconsistent with Congress's intent to have the FSIA's "comprehensive jurisdictional scheme" provide litigants with "clear guidelines" that were previously lacking. *Altmann*, 541 U.S. at 699, 700; *see also* Darby, 509 U.S. at 147 (refusing to impose additional exhaustion requirements under the APA, noting that doing so would "transform [the APA provision] from a provision designed to remove obstacles to judicial review of agency action into a trap for unwary litigants." (internal quotation marks omitted)). When Congress seeks to create such uniformity and clear standards for litigants, *see Verlinden*, 461 U.S. at 488, the administrative law cases cited by the majority counsel that we should defer to Congressional intent and decline to impose a new exhaustion requirement that will create a trap for unwary plaintiffs. *Cf. El Paso Natural Gas Co. v. Neztsosie*, 526 U.S. 473, 485–86, 119 S. Ct. 1430, 143 L. Ed. 2d 635 (1999) (holding that imposing a prudential exhaustion requirement was inappropriate where Atomic Energy Act gave district courts original jurisdiction over certain types of cases, and imposing such a requirement "would invite precisely the mischief . . . that the Act sought to avoid").

B.

Nor is the majority's assertion that *Sarei* compels us to write an exhaustion requirement into the FSIA persuasive. Maj. Op. at 12715–16; *see Sarei v. Rio Tinto, PLC*, 550 F.3d 822 (9th Cir. 2008) (en banc) (plurality op.). First, the lead opinion in *Sarei*, which adopts the principle of prudential exhaustion for purposes of the Alien Tort Statute (ATS), is a plurality opinion that is not binding on subsequent panels. *See Nevius v. Sumner,* 105 F.3d 453, 460 n.6 (9th Cir. 1996).

Second, even as persuasive authority, *Sarei* is not on point. In *Sarei*, the plaintiffs (who were aliens) brought a lawsuit under the ATS charging a British corporation with violations of customary international law regarding matters of universal concern stemming from its operations in Papua New Guinea. *Sarei*, 550 F.3d at 825–26.[7] As noted by the plurality, this lawsuit had no nexus of any kind with the United States. *Id.* at 831. The *Sarei* plurality was concerned that the ATS gave

---

7 Specifically, the plaintiffs brought claims alleging:

> (1) crimes against humanity resulting from the blockade; (2) war crimes for murder and torture; (3) violation of the rights to life, health, and security of the person resulting from the environmental damage; (4) racial discrimination in destroying villages and the environment, and in working conditions; (5) cruel, inhuman, and degrading treatment resulting from the blockade, environmental harm, and displacement; (6) violation of international environmental rights resulting from building and operating the mine; and (7) a consistent pattern of gross violations of human rights resulting from destruction of the environment, racial discrimination, and [Papua New Guinea] military activities.

Sarei, 550 F.3d at 825–26.

courts potentially sweeping jurisdiction over civil tort actions raising customary international law claims that lacked any nexus to the United States. *Id.* In order to cabin this supposed limitless jurisdictional reach, the plurality adopted the Supreme Court's suggestion in *Sosa v. Alvarez-Machain,* 542 U.S. 692, 733 n.21, 124 S. Ct. 2739, 159 L. Ed. 2d 718 (2004), that federal courts consider adopting a prudential exhaustion requirement as a jurisdiction-limiting principle in the appropriate circumstances. *Sarei*, 550 F.3d at 824. *Sarei* held that prudential exhaustion is appropriate in cases "where the United States 'nexus' is weak" particularly "with respect to claims that do not involve matters of 'universal concern.'" *Id.* at 831.

The concerns expressed by the *Sarei* plurality are not at issue in the FSIA context. There is no analogous concern about unlimited jurisdiction due to the lack of a nexus with the United States: Unlike the ATS (in which courts must create jurisdiction-limiting principles), the FSIA does not give federal courts jurisdiction unless the claim has a nexus to the United States as required by § 1605. In enacting the FSIA, "Congress was aware of concern that our courts might be turned into small international courts of claims, open to all comers to litigate any dispute which any private party may have with a foreign state anywhere in the world." *Verlinden*, 461 U.S. at 490 (internal quotation marks and alteration omitted). The FSIA "protect[s] against this danger not by restricting the class of potential plaintiffs, but rather by enacting substantive provisions requiring some form of substantial contact with the United States." *Id.* (citing 28 U.S.C. § 1605).[8] Although the Supreme Court recognized that the implications of vast, unchecked federal jurisdiction under the ATS would be "breathtaking," *Sosa*, 542 U.S. at 736, these concerns are simply not present under the FSIA.

Moreover, the concern that jurisdictional overreaching under the ATS could have a negative effect on foreign relations, *see Sosa*, 542 U.S. at 727, are not present in the FSIA context. The FSIA's jurisdictional reach is consistent with that exercised by foreign nations over the United States. Indeed, the Supreme Court noted that Congress "join[ed] the majority of other countries by adopting the 'restrictive theory' of sovereign immunity[.]" *Permanent Mission of India*, 551 U.S. at 199; *see also Alfred Dunhill of London, Inc. v. Republic of Cuba,* 425 U.S. 682, 702, 96 S. Ct. 1854, 48 L. Ed. 2d 301 & n.15 (1976) (explaining that the United States adopted the restrictive view in part based "on the fact that this approach has been accepted by a large and increasing number of foreign states in the international

8 The Supreme Court has acknowledged that certain provisions of the FSIA do not (on their face) require a nexus to the United States. For example, the Court explained that "Section 1605(a)(1), which provides that sovereign immunity shall not apply if waived, may be seen as an exception to the normal pattern of the Act, which generally requires some form of contact with the United States." *Verlinden*, 461 U.S. at 491 n.15. In noting "[w]e need not decide whether, by waiving its immunity, a foreign state could consent to suit based on activities wholly unrelated to the United States," *id.*, the Court hinted that such a nexus might nevertheless be necessary in order for a federal court to have jurisdiction over a foreign sovereign under the FSIA.

community," and listing countries). Further, the Supreme Court has recognized that "subjecting foreign governments to the rule of law in their commercial dealings presents a much smaller risk of affronting their sovereignty than would an attempt to pass on the legality of their governmental acts." *Id.* at 703–04. Here, Cassirer's case is a property dispute with Spain in its role as a private party, not as a sovereign exercising power over its own citizens.[9]

In sum, while the *Sarei* plurality strove to fill in both procedural and substantive gaps in the ATS to cabin its potentially unlimited jurisdiction and avoid impinging on relations with foreign sovereigns, *see Sosa*, 542 U.S. at 727, applying the FSIA's clear language does not require the same creative approach. In creating the FSIA's comprehensive and detailed scheme, Congress expressed its intent that foreign sovereigns meeting the statutory criteria be subject to suit in federal court, and did not invite us to read in anything more. *See* 28 U.S.C. § 1602 ("Claims of foreign states to immunity should henceforth be decided by courts of the United States and of the States *in conformity with the principles set forth in this chapter*." (emphasis added)); *Amerada Hess*, 488 U.S. at 434 (concluding that "the text and structure of the FSIA demonstrate Congress'[s] intention that the FSIA be the *sole basis* for obtaining jurisdiction over a foreign state in our courts" (emphasis added)).

III.

Nothing in the statutory language, history, or the Supreme Court's interpretation of the FSIA suggests that we should read an exhaustion requirement into the statute. Doing so will tend to defeat Congress's goal of achieving consistency and uniformity in suits against foreign sovereigns. The concerns addressed by the *Sarei* plurality are entirely distinguishable, and in any event, the plurality's decision to write an exhaustion requirement into the ATS is not binding on us. There is no need to create judge-made law in this context, and therefore, I would refrain from doing so. I respectfully dissent.

---

9 Contrary to the majority's assertion, Cassirer does not bring claims "based on non-domestic, international law," Maj. Op. at 12715 n.20, but rather brings state common-law claims of conversion. Indeed, allegations similar to those in Cassirer's complaint have been made, and adjudicated, in lawsuits between two private persons. *See, e.g., DeWeerth v. Baldinger*, 836 F.2d 103 (2d Cir. 1987) (painting owner's heir brought conversion suit against good-faith purchaser for return of oil painting by Claude Monet, allegedly stolen during the Second World War).

JANE DOE
v.
EMMANUEL CONSTANT

354 F. App'x 543 (2d Cir. 2009)
Decided December 1, 2009

FOR DEFENDANT-APPELLANT: EMMANUEL CONSTANT, Pro se, Coxsackie, NY.

FOR PLAINTIFFS-APPELLEES:DANIEL G. PANCOTTI, Sonnenschein Nath & Rosenthal LLP, New York, NY (on the brief); Ivor E. Samson, Sonnenschein Nath & Rosenthal LLP, San Francisco, CA; Natasha Fain, Center for Justice & Accountability, San Francisco, CA; Jennifer Green, Center for Constitutional Rights, New York, NY.

PRESENT: ROSEMARY S. POOLER, RICHARD C. WESLEY, Circuit Judges, JOHN F. KEENAN,* District Judge.

* John F. Keenan, of the United States District Court for the Southern District of New York, sitting by designation.

SUMMARY ORDER

UPON DUE CONSIDERATION IT IS HEREBY ORDERED, ADJUDGED, AND DECREED that the order of the district court be AFFIRMED.

Defendant-Appellant Emmanuel Constant, *pro se,* appeals the district court's denial of his Federal Rules of Civil Procedure 60(b)(4) motion for relief from the court's entry in August 2006 of a default judgment against him, finding him liable under the Alien Tort Statute ("ATS"), 28 U.S.C. § 1350, and the Torture Victim Protection Act ("TVPA"), 28 U.S.C. § 1350 (note), for attempted extrajudicial killing, torture, and crimes against humanity, and awarding Plaintiffs-Appellees Jane Does I, II, III ("Plaintiffs") $19 million in compensatory and punitive damages. We assume the parties' familiarity with the underlying facts, the procedural history of the case, and the issues on appeal.

As an initial matter, because Constant did not argue before the district court that Plaintiffs failed to adequately plead violations of the law of nations under the ATS, or that the district court's default judgment violated his due process rights, we decline to consider those arguments. *See Singleton v. Wulff*, 428 U.S. 106, 120–21, 96 S. Ct. 2868, 49 L. Ed. 2d 826 (1976) (recognizing the well-established general rule that a court of appeals will generally not consider an issue raised for the first time on appeal); *see also Virgilio v. City of New York*, 407 F.3d 105, 116 (2d Cir. 2005) (citing *Westinghouse Credit Corp. v. D'Urso,* 371 F.3d 96, 103 (2d Cir. 2004)).[1]

We review *de novo* the district court's denial of a motion to vacate a default judgment under Rule 60(b)(4), recognizing that "a deferential standard of review is not appropriate because if the underlying judgment is void, it is a *per se* abuse of discretion for a district court to deny a movant's motion to vacate the judgment under Rule 60(b)(4)." *Burda Media, Inc. v. Viertel*, 417 F.3d 292, 298 (2d Cir. 2005) (quoting *State St. Bank & Trust Co. v. Inversiones Errazuriz Limitada,* 374 F.3d 158, 178 (2d Cir. 2004)). However, to the extent the district court's denial of a Rule 60(b)(4) motion turns on findings of fact, we review those findings for clear error. *See Luckett v. Bure*, 290 F.3d 493, 496 (2d Cir. 2002) (reviewing factual findings for clear error, but reviewing conclusions of law based on those findings *de novo*). "In the context of a Rule 60(b)(4) motion, a judgment may be declared void for want of jurisdiction only when the court plainly usurped jurisdiction . . . [i.e.,] when there is a total want of jurisdiction and no arguable basis on which it could have rested a finding that it had jurisdiction." *Central Vermont Public Service Corp. v. Herbert,* 341 F.3d 186, 190 (2d Cir. 2003) (internal quotations omitted); *accord Nemaizer v. Baker*, 793 F.2d 58, 65–66 (2d Cir. 1986).

I. Subject Matter Jurisdiction

Constant argues that the district court's judgment is void because the court lacked subject matter jurisdiction to enter a default judgment, given that: (1) Plaintiffs' claims were untimely; (2) Plaintiffs failed to exhaust other available remedies; (3) some of Plaintiffs' claims were barred by *res judicata;* and (4) Plaintiffs failed to present sufficient evidence that he acted under color of law to render him liable under the ATS or the TVPA. However, only this last claim of error potentially implicates the district court's subject matter jurisdiction, as the first three are

---

1 Even if we considered these arguments, they are unavailing. Constant fails to present anything but conclusory allegations in support of his due process claim. As to the other claim, Plaintiffs adequately pleaded violations of the law of nations under the ATS. *See Kadic v. Karadzic*, 70 F.3d 232, 239 (2d Cir. 1995) (complaint alleging violations of the law of nations is adequately pleaded if "the defendant's alleged conduct violates well-established, universally recognized norms of international law" (internal quotations omitted)); *see also Sosa v. Alvarez-Machain*, 542 U.S. 692, 732, 124 S. Ct. 2739, 159 L. Ed. 2d 718 (2004) (torture is a violation of the law of nations (citing *Filartiga v. Pena-Irala,* 630 F.2d 876, 890 (2d Cir. 1980)); *Presbyterian Church of Sudan v. Talisman Energy, Inc.*, 582 F.3d 244, 256 (2d Cir. 2009) (crimes against humanity may be asserted under the ATS); *Flores v. Southern Peru Copper Corp.*, 414 F.3d 233, 249 (2d Cir. 2003) (recognizing that extrajudicial killings "violate customary international law"—i.e., the law of nations—and would be actionable under the ATS).

merely affirmative defenses. *See United States v. Walsh,* 700 F.2d 846, 855–56 (2d Cir. 1983) (timeliness under a statute of limitations is not jurisdictional, but is an affirmative defense that may be forfeited or waived); *Jean v. Dorelien*, 431 F.3d 776, 781 (11th Cir. 2005) ("[T]he exhaustion requirement pursuant to the TVPA is an affirmative defense."); *Scherer v. Equitable Life Assurance Society of the United States*, 347 F.3d 394, 398 (2d Cir. 2003) (holding that, as an affirmative defense, *res judicata* does not—except in rare circumstances not applicable here—affect a court's jurisdiction).

In *Kadic,* this Court held that the ATS "confers federal subject-matter jurisdiction when the following three conditions are satisfied: (1) an alien sues (2) for a tort (3) committed in violation of the law of nations (*i.e.,* international law)." *Kadic*, 70 F.3d at 238. Constant only challenges the third prong of this standard—namely, that Plaintiffs failed to sufficiently allege that his actions were committed under color of law; the other two prongs are not in dispute. However, this argument fails. A review of Plaintiffs' complaint indicates that Plaintiffs alleged sufficient facts to demonstrate that, for purposes of establishing jurisdiction under the ATS, Constant's actions were sufficiently intertwined with those of the Haitian government to constitute state action. *See id.* at 245 ("The 'color of law' jurisprudence of 42 U.S.C. § 1983 is a relevant guide to whether a defendant has engaged in official action for purposes of jurisdiction under the Alien Tort Act."); *see also Lugar v. Edmondson Oil Co.,* 457 U.S. 922, 937, 102 S. Ct. 2744, 73 L. Ed. 2d 482 (1982) (holding that an individual acts under color of law under § 1983 where she acts with state officials or with significant state aid).

Here, Plaintiffs alleged that Constant founded the *Front Revolutionnaire Pour L'Avancement et le Progres d'Haiti* ("FRAPH") in 1993, and worked in concert with the Haitian military to terrorize and repress the civilian population. Plaintiffs further alleged that FRAPH members received weapons, training, and financial support from the Haitian military, and that, at the time Plaintiffs were victimized by FRAPH troops, Constant exercised command and control over FRAPH forces, which operated as an extension of the Haitian armed forces and under the auspices of the Haitian political police, the latter of which reported directly to the commander of the Haitian armed forces. Additionally, the district court's findings of fact confirmed these allegations. Based on testimony from the evidentiary hearing, the district court concluded that: (1) "Constant was at all times the de facto leader of FRAPH and was active in its daily operations"; (2) "[h]e communicated regularly with top commanders in the armed forces, and received funding from the military to support FRAPH activities"; and (3) "[FRAPH] exacted widespread violence against opponents of the military regime, including . . . plaintiffs Jane Does I, II, and III . . . [by] raid[ing] neighborhoods populated by Aristide supporters, raping and abducting its targets." Based on these allegations, Plaintiffs clearly pled sufficient facts to satisfy the color of law requirement under the ATS to vest the district court with subject matter jurisdiction over their claims.

For similar reasons, Plaintiffs also alleged sufficient facts to vest the district court with subject matter jurisdiction over their TVPA claims. Unlike the ATS, the TVPA expressly "renders liable only those individuals who have committed torture or extrajudicial killing 'under actual or apparent authority, or color of law, of any foreign nation.'" *Kadic*, 70 F.3d at 245 (quoting TVPA, 28 U.S.C. § 1350 (note) § 2(a)). However, like under the ATS, "in construing the term[] . . . 'color of law,' courts are instructed to look to . . . jurisprudence under 42 U.S.C. § 1983." *Id.* Accordingly, because Plaintiffs pled sufficient facts to demonstrate that Constant acted under color of law for purposes of the ATS, they also satisfied this requirement under the TVPA, and thus the district court had subject matter jurisdiction to consider Plaintiffs' claims under both statutes.

II. Personal Jurisdiction

Constant's argument that the district court lacked personal jurisdiction to enter a default judgment is without merit. As a general matter, there is no dispute that Constant received personal service of the summons and complaint in January 2005, and therefore had actual notice of the district court proceedings; his only argument is that service was improper because the summons misstated the full name of the FRAPH and incorrectly indicated that he was a "commander" of the group. However, Rule 4(a)(1)(B) of the Federal Rules of Civil Procedure provides only that a summons "be directed to the defendant," and this rule is "to be liberally construed, to further the purpose of finding personal jurisdiction in cases in which the party has received actual notice." *Grammenos v. Lemos,* 457 F.2d 1067, 1070 (2d Cir. 1972); *see also McGann v. State of New York,* 77 F.3d 672, 674 (2d Cir. 1996). Thus, because Constant received actual notice, and because any defects in the summons were purely clerical, service of process was sufficient to vest the district court with personal jurisdiction.

As a final matter, Constant argues that the district court should have construed his motion as brought pursuant to Rule 60(b)(6) and, as construed, granted the motion on the basis of "extraordinary circumstances"—namely, that he was incarcerated when the default judgment was entered, and that his attorney was allegedly "grossly negligent" in failing to respond to Plaintiffs' summons and complaint. Neither of these arguments have merit. "[A] Rule 60(b)(6) motion requires extraordinary circumstances which typically do not usually exist where the applicant fails to more for relief promptly." *Grace v. Bank Leumi Trust Co. of N.Y.,* 443 F.3d 180, 190 n.8 (2d Cir. 2006) (quotation marks omitted). Here, Constant did not file his motion until more than a year after the district court entered default judgment, and, despite his assertion of attorney misconduct, he presented no evidence in support of this basis for relief apart from the conclusory allegation that his counsel failed to file a notice of appearance in the district court. Moreover, although he asserts that his incarceration should have been considered by the district court, Constant was not in prison at the time he received service of process; indeed, Constant did not enter prison until July 2006, more than a year and a half after service was made, and less than a month before the district court entered a default judgment. Therefore, Constant failed to demonstrate extraordinary circumstances, and, to the extent his motion could have been construed as brought under Rule 60(b)(6), the district court's refusal to grant the motion was not an abuse of discretion. *See Aczel v. Labonia*, 584 F.3d 52, 61 (2d Cir. 2009) ("A motion seeking [Rule 60(b)(6)] relief is addressed to the sound discretion of the district court with appellate review limited to determining whether that discretion has been abused." (quoting *Nemaizer*, 793 F.2d at 61–62)).

Accordingly, in light of the above, it cannot be said that the district court "plainly usurped [its] jurisdiction" by entering a default judgment, and the court's denial of Constant's Rule 60(b)(4) motion was therefore correct.

We have considered all of Constant's remaining claims of error and found them to be without merit. Accordingly, there is no basis on which to challenge the judgment of the district court.

For the foregoing reasons, the order of the district court is hereby AFFIRMED.

JESUS MARIA LOPEZ
v.
MICHAEL WALLACE

325 F. App'x 782 (11th Cir. 2009)
Decided April 24, 2009

Jesus Maria Lopez, Appellant, *Pro se*, GLENNVILLE, GA.

Before CARNES, BARKETT and WILSON, Circuit Judges.

PER CURIAM:

Jesus Maria Lopez, a *pro se* Colombian citizen incarcerated in a Georgia prison, appeals the dismissal of his civil claim under the Alien Tort Statute, 28 U.S.C. § 1350, alleging a violation of his rights under Article 36 of the Vienna Convention on Consular Relations ("VCCR").[1] On June 19, 2007, Lopez filed a *pro se* suit against his trial and appellate attorneys, the assistant district attorneys who prosecuted him, and the police officers who arrested and interrogated him. Lopez maintained that he was asserting "a Federal Alien Tort action authorized by 42 U.S.C. [§] 1983 to redress the deprivation, under color of International Treaty, of rights secured by Article 36 of the VCCR and Laws of the United States," and that the district court had jurisdiction pursuant to 28 U.S.C. §§ 1331, 1343, and 1350. Lopez alleged that on the day of his arrest, January 17, 2001, his arresting officers refused his request to contact the Colombian consulate, in violation of his right to such notification under the VCCR. Lopez further alleged that his attorneys and the district attorneys were aware of this violation but failed to do anything about it. Lopez sought a declaration that his VCCR rights had been violated, an injunction ordering the defendants to inform non-citizens of their right to consular notification, and damages.

1 Article 36 of the VCCR provides that signatory States shall inform an alien's consulate when he is arrested or imprisoned, and the arresting State shall inform the alien of his right to consulate contact. VCCR, art. 36(1)(b), Apr. 24, 1963, 21 U.S.T. 77, 101, T.I.A.S. No. 6820.

The district court *sua sponte* dismissed Lopez's complaint pursuant to 28 U.S.C. § 1915A(b)(1)[2] for failure to state a § 1983 claim, concluding that the VCCR did not provide Lopez with judicially enforceable rights. Lopez filed a motion for reconsideration, which the district court denied on the grounds that (1) even if Lopez did possess an individual right to consular notification under the VCCR, he could not show actual harm arising from the violation of that right; and (2) Lopez's § 1983 action was frivolous because it was filed after the two-year statute of limitations had run. Lopez appealed the court's dismissal of his § 1983 complaint and denial of his motion to reconsider.

We affirmed in part and vacated and remanded in part. We held that irrespective of whether the VCCR grants individual rights that are enforceable under § 1983, the district court was correct in holding that Lopez's claim would be time-barred. We went on to note, however, that neither the district court's *sua sponte* order dismissing Lopez's complaint nor its order denying his motion to reconsider had addressed whether the complaint stated a claim under § 1350 or whether § 1350's ten-year statute of limitations, which had not run, should have been applied. Accordingly, we remanded the case for consideration of whether Lopez's complaint stated a § 1350 claim, and, assuming that it did, whether that claim could survive § 1915A review.

On remand, the district court dismissed Lopez's complaint for failure to state a claim under either § 1983 or § 1350, citing our recently published decision in *Gandara v. Bennett*, 528 F.3d 823 (11th Cir. 2008), in which we held that the VCCR does not contain rights or remedies individually enforceable through § 1983. On appeal, Lopez argues essentially that because the VCCR is self-executing and creates judicially enforceable rights, he may enforce those rights pursuant to the "remedial structure" of § 1350.[3] We disagree.[4]

In *Gandara*, we held that Article 36 of the VCCR does not confer judicially enforceable individual rights and that violations of the VCCR are properly addressed by and between the states themselves. 528 F.3d at 829. Our holding applies irrespective of whether an individual petitioner attempts to enforce Article 36 pursuant to § 1983 or § 1350. *See Gandara*, 528 F.3d at 830 n.1 (Rodgers, J., specially concurring) (noting that the petitioner had filed his claim under the VCCR

---

2 Section 1915A provides for a screening process whereby a judge reviews as soon as possible any suit filed by a prisoner against a government entity or officer and may dismiss the suit for, among other things, failure to state a claim.

3 Section 1350 provides that "[t]he district courts shall have original jurisdiction of any civil action by an alien for a tort only, committed in violation of the law of nations or a treaty of the United States."

4 We review *de novo* a *sua sponte* dismissal for failure to state a claim, pursuant to § 1915A(b)(1). *Leal v. Georgia Dep't of Corr.*, 254 F.3d 1276, 1279 (11th Cir. 2001). We liberally construe *pro se* pleadings, holding them to a less stringent standard than attorney-drafted pleadings. *Tannenbaum v. United States*, 148 F.3d 1262, 1263 (11th Cir. 1998).

pursuant to both § 1983 and § 1350). Lopez may not use § 1350 to create an individual cause of action under the VCCR where we have found there to be none. *See Sosa v. Alvarez-Machain*, 542 U.S. 692, 124 S. Ct. 2739, 159 L. Ed. 2d 718 (2004) (dismissing alien's § 1350 action alleging he had been abducted in Mexico by U.S. agents in violation of the extradition treaty between the U.S. and Mexico and customary international law on the grounds that § 1350 is jurisdictional and authorizes suits based only on a limited number of offenses recognized at the time of its enactment or universally recognized today). Therefore, the district court did not err in dismissing Lopez's complaint for failure to state a claim under § 1350.

AFFIRMED.

McKESSON CORP.
v.
ISLAMIC REPUBLIC OF IRAN

Case No. 82-0220 (D.D.C. 2009)
Decided November 23, 2009

MEMORANDUM OPINION

RICHARD J. LEON, District Judge.

The plaintiff, McKesson Corporation ("McKesson"), a U.S. company, alleges that the defendant, Islamic Republic of Iran ("Iran"), expropriated McKesson's interest in an Iranian dairy and illegally withheld dividends. In its 27-year history, this case has reached the United States Court of Appeals five times. Most recently, the Court of Appeals remanded to this Court to consider three specific issues: (1) Does McKesson have a cause of action under Iranian law?; (2) Does customary international law provide a cause of action in light of *Sosa v. Alvarez-Machain,* 542 U.S. 692 (2004)?; and (3) Does the act of state doctrine apply in this case? Upon review of the parties' submissions and the extensive record in this case, this Court concludes that McKesson does have a cause of action under Iranian law, that customary international law continues to provide McKesson with a cause of action, even in light of *Sosa,* and that the act of state doctrine does not apply in this case.

BACKGROUND[1]

In 1960, McKesson and a group of Iranian investors joined together to create Pak Dairy ("Pak"). During the Iranian Revolution in 1979, however, McKesson

1 For additional background, see the previous Court of Appeals's decisions, *Foremost-McKesson, Inc. v. Islamic Republic of Iran,* 905 F.2d 438 (D.C. Cir. 1990) (*"McKesson I"*); *McKesson Corp. v. Islamic Republic of Iran,* 52 F.3d 346 (D.C. Cir. 1995) (*"McKesson II"*); *McKesson HBOC, Inc. v. Islamic Republic of Iran,* 271 F.3d 1101 (D.C. Cir. 2001) (*"McKesson III"*); *McKesson HBOC, Inc. v. Islamic Republic of Iran,* 320 F.3d 280 (D.C. Cir. 2003) (*"McKesson IV"*); and *McKesson Corp. v. Islamic Republic of Iran,* 539 F.3d 485 (D.D.C. 2008) (*"McKesson V"*), as well as previous decisions issued by Judge Flannery and this Court, *McKesson Corp. v. Islamic Republic of Iran,* No. 82-220, 1997 WL 361177 (D.D.C. June 23, 1997) (*"McKesson 1997"*); *McKesson Corp. v. Islamic Republic of Iran,*

personnel at Pak fled the country, and the Iranian government took control of Pak's Board of Directors. *See McKesson 2007,* 520 F.Supp.2d at 40. In 1982, McKesson sued Iran in this Court alleging that Iran had expropriated its 31 % interest in Pak and illegally withheld dividends. *See id.*

In 1997, after years of litigation and two appeals to our Circuit Court, Judge Flannery, who was previously assigned this case, found Iran liable for expropriating McKesson's equity interest and for withholding the dividends. *See id.* at 41–42 n.1. Following a trial from January 18 though February 17, 2000, Judge Flannery held that McKesson was entitled to $20,071,159.14 in total damages, which includes the amount of the expropriated property and interest, for violating customary international law and the 1955 Treaty of Amity, Economic Relations, and Consular Rights ("Treaty of Amity" or "the Treaty") between the United States and Iran. *McKesson 2000,* 116 F.Supp.2d at 35–36, 43 (citing Treaty of Amity, art. XXI(I), Aug. 15, 1955, 8 U.S.T. 899). In 2001, the Court of Appeals affirmed the judgment in part and remanded for another trial on two particular factual issues. *McKesson III,* 271 F.3d at 1110. After extensive discovery and motions practice with regard to these two factual issues, this Court conducted a three week bench trial on these issues in 2007. Once again, McKesson prevailed at trial under the Treaty, and this Court reinstated the 2000 judgment against Iran. *McKesson 2007,* 520 F.Supp.2d at 40. On appeal, the Court of Appeals declined to revisit this Court's jurisdiction under the commercial activities exception of the Foreign Sovereign Immunities Act ("FSIA"),[2] but, contrary to its previous decisions, held that the Treaty of Amity does not provide McKesson with a cause of action. *McKesson V,* 539 F.3d at 491. The Court of Appeals, however, remanded the case to this Court for consideration of the previously noted three legal issues.

ANALYSIS

I. McKesson has a cause of action under Iranian law

McKesson brings several causes of action under Iranian law.[3] Iran, however, not only fails to address the merits of McKesson's Iranian law claims, but concedes

---

116 F.Supp.2d 13 (D.D.C. 2000) (*"McKesson 2000"*); and *McKesson Corp. v. Islamic Republic of Iran,* 520 F.Supp.2d 38 (D.D.C. 2007) (*"McKesson 2007"*).

2 Although McKesson argues Iran violated the law of takings, jurisdiction in this case is predicated on the commercial activities exception, 28 U.S.C. § 1605(a)(2), not the takings exception of FSIA, 28 U.S.C. § 1605(a)(3). *See McKesson III,* 271 F.3d at 1103.

3 Specifically, McKesson alleges Iran has violated the Civil Responsibility Act of Iran, which is based on the laws of Switzerland, (Katirai Appendix A [Dkt #898-2] at 6), and allows an injured party to recover damages caused by the negligent or intentional act of another; the Commercial Code of Iran, Article 90, which requires that shareholders receive annual dividends equal to 10% of net profits; and the Civil Code of Iran, which provides a remedy for property "alienated from the possession of its owner except in accordance with a legal order." (*See* McKesson's Mem. of Points and Authorities [Dkt. #898] ("McKesson") at 12–30.)

that McKesson has, at least, a cause of action under the Commercial Code of Iran (although not one for a taking). (Iran's Mem. of Points and Authorities [Dkt. #901] ("Iran") at 22.)[4] This Court thus concludes that McKesson has a cause of action under Iranian law.[5]

Rather than contending that McKesson does not have a cause of action under Iranian law, Iran argues that the Treaty of Amity requires McKesson to bring its suit in an Iranian court. (*Id.* at 15.) The Treaty, however, does not require this. In fact, the relevant Treaty provision states, in part:

> Nationals and companies of either High Contracting Party shall have freedom of access to the courts of justice and administrative agencies within the territories of the other High Contracting Party, in all degrees or jurisdiction, both in defense and pursuit of their rights, to the end that prompt and impartial justice shall be done.

Treaty of Amity, art. III, cl. 2. Iran asserts this provision is an "unambiguous provision show[ing] that the parties agreed that their home country courts [in this instance, Iranian courts] would hear disputes brought privately by the investors of the other country." (Iran at 3.) I disagree. Indeed, it is difficult, if not impossible, to comprehend how a provision stating that companies in the United States and Iran *must* have access to the courts of the other country "both in defense and pursuit of their rights" requires McKesson to file its suit in Iran, much less how it requires it "unambiguous[ly]."

Previous decisions in this case also support the conclusion that this Treaty provision is not one that establishes exclusive jurisdiction. As our Court of Appeals itself stated in 2001, although this provision "suggests that one party will receive protections within the territory of the other party, it doesn't say that those protections

---

4 Iran argues that the Commercial Code of Iran precludes other Iranian law causes of action. (Iran at 22.) However, Iran does not point to anything in the Commercial Code, another Iranian law, or case establishing this. Additionally, as McKesson's expert explains, Iranian laws generally do not preempt other laws unless they do so explicitly or are clearly in conflict with the other laws. In fact, the Supreme Court of Iran, sitting en banc, has held that a plaintiff was entitled to seek compensation under *both* the Islamic Criminal Law *and* the Civil Responsibility Act. (McKesson's Reply to Iran's Mem. of Points and Authorities [Dkt. #905] ("McKesson Reply"), Ex. A, Supp. Legal Opinion of Mahmoud Katirai ("Katirai Supp.") at 2 n.2 (citing Deliberation and Decisions of the Supreme Court, En Banc, Year 1375 (March 21, 1996– March 20, 1997), p. 168).) Thus, Iran has failed to establish that the Commercial Code precludes other causes of action.

Iran further argues that the Iranian government cannot be sued under the Commercial Code of Iran. (Iran at 26.) This argument also fails, as, again, Iran has not cited to any law establishing or even suggesting this. Furthermore, under FSIA, a "foreign state shall be liable in the same manner and to the same extent as a private individual under like circumstances." 28 U.S.C. § 1606.

5 McKesson argues this Court should determine Iran's liability and damages under Iranian causes of action. However, as this discussion is outside the scope of the Court of Appeals's narrow remand, and Iran has not addressed the merits of McKesson's Iranian law claims, the Court does not address Iran's liability and damages at this time.

can *only* be enforced in the territory of the other party," *McKesson III,* 271 F.3d at 1108 (citing *McKesson* 1997, 1997 WL 361177 at 13–14) (emphasis added). In sum, the Treaty does not contain an exclusive-jurisdiction provision, and it does not preclude McKesson from bringing its Iranian-based cause of action in this Court.

Furthermore, contrary to Iran's argument, the Treaty does not preempt other causes of action merely because it provides McKesson with remedies, such as diplomacy and a suit before the International Court of Justice. *See* Treaty Art. XXI. As a matter of U.S. law, a treaty does not preempt other causes of action absent "clear and convincing evidence" in a treaty's "language, negotiation[,] . . . drafting history," that the treaty precludes judicial review of claims not stemming from it. *Cardenas v. Smith,* 733 F.2d 909, 918–19 (D.C. Cir. 1984). Iranian law regarding treaty preemption is less clear. Iran offers the Court little guidance regarding treaty preemption law, yet McKesson's expert notes that treaties generally do not preempt other causes of action unless they are explicitly exclusive, or clearly inconsistent with each other. (McKesson Reply, Ex. A., Katirai Supp. at 3–4.)

Not surprisingly, Iran has failed to provide this Court with any authority to support its argument that the Treaty of Amity preempts other remedies. And its failure to do so is especially problematic, in light of U.S. law that Iran "bears a heavy burden" to establish by "clear and convincing evidence" an "intent to restrict access to the courts." *Cardenas,* 733 F.2d at 919. Simply put, the Treaty does *not* provide that McKesson must bring its action in an Iranian court and does *not* preempt Iranian law, thus this Court can hear McKesson's Iranian causes of action.[6] Indeed, hearing McKesson's Iranian causes of action is especially appropriate in light of the post-revolutionary Iranian judicial system's incapability of affording an adequate remedy[7] and this Court's previous finding that "it is hard to imagine . . . that less

---

6 *See Randall v. Arabian Am. Oil Co.,* 778 F.2d 1146, 1150 (5th Cir. 1985) (finding jurisdiction to hear a case brought under Saudi Arabian labor law); *Basch v. Westinghouse Elec. Corp.,* 777 F.2d 165, 169–72 (4th Cir. 1985) (affirming a judgment was based on Iranian *causes of action); Matter ofOi! Spill by Amoco Cadiz Off the Coast of France on March 15, 1978,* 954 F.2d 1279, 1313–23 (7th Cir. 1992) (applying French law); *Nikbin v. Islamic Republic of Iran,* 517 F.Supp.2d 416, 426 (D.D.C. 2007) (concluding "that under Iranian law, although certainly not under United States law, lashing represents a lawful sanction"); *see also* Fed. R. Civ. P. 44.1. (providing that in "determining foreign law," courts "may consider any relevant material or source, including testimony, whether or not submitted by a party or admissible under the Federal Rules of Evidence").

7 *See McKesson 2007,* 520 F.Supp.2d at 54 (finding that Iran "affords our citizens (and companies) *no* realistic legal process through which to vindicate [their] rights"); *Rockwell Int'l Sys., Inc. v. Citibank, N.A.,* 719 F.2d 583, 587–88 (2d Cir. 1983); *McDonnell Douglas Corp. v. Islamic Republic of Iran,* 758 F.2d 341, 345 (8th Cir. 1985) (refusing to enforce a forum selection clause because litigation in Iran would "be so gravely difficult and inconvenient that [the plaintiff] will for all practicable purposes be deprived of his day in court" (internal quotation omitted)).

evidence has ever delayed the awarding of so much, to one so deserving, for so long!" *McKesson 2007,* 520 F.Supp.2d. at 42.

II. McKesson also has a cause of action under customary international law

In *Sosa,* the plaintiff alleged that the U.S. Drug Enforcement Administration instigated his abduction from Mexico for a criminal trial in the United States, and he sought a remedy, in part, under the Alien Tort Statute ("ATS"). 542 U.S. at 697. The Supreme Court found that although the ATS was "in its terms only jurisdictional," it nevertheless "enabled federal courts to hear claims in a very limited category defined by the law of nations and recognized at common law." *Id.* at 712.

This Court finds that, like the ATS, the commercial activities exception to the Foreign Sovereign Immunities Act is more than a jurisdictional statute. This Court finds Congress enacted the commercial activities exception on an understanding that courts would apply causes of action based on customary international law. *See Aquamar, S.A. v. Del Monte Fresh Produce,* 179 F.3d 1279, 1294–95 (11th Cir. 1999) (noting that Congress intended for courts to look to international law when interpreting FSIA's terms). As Judge Flannery himself noted in 1997, "[c]ustomary international law is a part of the law of the United States, and must be ascertained and enforced by federal courts." *McKesson* 1997, 1997 WL 36117 at * 15. The Supreme Court in *Sosa* emphasized that "[f]or two centuries [the Supreme Court] ha[s] affirmed that the domestic law of the United States recognizes the law of nations," 542 U.S. at 729. FSIA was enacted against this backdrop, and Congress intended for courts to use FSIA to apply customary international law. As the Supreme Court has held, "[t]he language and history of the FSIA clearly establish that the Act was not intended to affect the substantive law determining the liability of a foreign state or instrumentality, or the attribution of liability among instrumentalities of a foreign state." *First Nat'l City Bank v. Banco Para El Comercio Exterior de Cuba,* 462 U.S. 611, 620 (1983). Even in *Sosa,* the Supreme Court acknowledged the validity of customary international law absent congressional authorization, stating that while it "would welcome any congressional guidance in exercising jurisdiction with such obvious potential to affect foreign relations, *nothing Congress has done is a reason/or us to shut the door to the law o/nations entirely.*" 542 U.S. at 731 (emphasis added). Thus, this Court finds that, in enacting the commercial activities exception, Congress, in essence, demonstrated its intention that courts hear causes of action involving customary international law violations.

More specifically, this Court finds that Congress intended for courts to hear causes of action for expropriation. Unlike the cause of action the plaintiff sought in *Sosa, see* 542 U.S. at 725, the international norm against expropriation in this case is, as Iran concedes, widely accepted by the civilized world, (Iran at 31 (acknowledging "there is some consensus on the general proposition that uncompensated expropriation of alien property is wrongful under at least some circumstances . . .")).

Additionally, the norm against expropriation is also defined with specificity. As Judge Flannery noted in 1997, a cause of action for expropriation under customary international law is incorporated in the Restatement (Third) of the Foreign Relations Law of the United States, which provides that "a state is responsible under international law for injury resulting from a taking by the state of property that (1) is not for a public purpose, or (2) is discriminatory, or (3) is not accompanied by provision for just compensation." *McKesson 2007,* 1997 WL 36117 at *15 (citing Restatement § 712). Additionally, international treaties routinely incorporate international norms against uncompensated expropriation and require compensation for the full value of the taken property. (*See* McKesson at 53 (citing numerous Treaties of Friendship, Commerce, and Navigation); *id.* at 55–57 (citing bilateral investment treaties).)

Indeed, at least with respect to the takings exception to the foreign sovereign immunities act, 28 U.S.C. § 1605(a)(3), (but not the commercial activities exception at issue here), courts have determined, in *post-Sosa* cases, that plaintiffs can bring a cause of action for takings in violation of international law. *See Agudas Chasidei Chabad v. Russian Federation,* 528 F.3d 934, 943 (D.C. Cir. 2008); *see also Cassirer v. Spain,* 580 F.3d 1048, 1060 (9th Cir. 2009) (noting that claims under the Foreign Sovereign Immunities Act, like under the ATS, "depend on the law of nations to define the substantive rights embodied in any cause of action").

Furthermore, congressional intent that courts hear implied causes of action for expropriation under customary international law is evinced by the Second Hickenlooper Amendment, addressed further below, which Congress passed *to ensure* that courts would hear causes of action for expropriation against foreign states. *See* 22 U.S.C. § 2370(e)(2). Based on the foregoing, this Court will not, as a result of *Sosa,* disturb its previous decision to imply in the commercial activities exception a cause of action under customary international law.

III. The act of state doctrine does not apply in this case

Finally, our Court of Appeals has asked this Court to address whether the act of state doctrine applies to this case, noting that "[t]he doctrine must be addressed before this litigation is completed because if it applies Iran cannot be held liable." *McKesson V,* 539 F.3d at 491. In applying the act of state doctrine, "the judiciary's interest in hearing a case involving commercial activity is balanced with the desire to avoid matters of foreign affairs controlled by the executive or legislative branches." *Malewicz v. Amsterdam,* 517 F.Supp.2d 322, 337 (D.D.C. 2007) (internal quotation omitted). Courts "should be mindful that the decision to deny judicial relief to a party should not be made lightly." *Id.* (internal quotation omitted).

Iran, as the party asserting the act of state defense, has the burden of proving the act of state doctrine applies to bar McKesson from seeking relief in this Court. *Agudas Chasidei Chabad of United States v. Russian Federation,* 528 F.3d 934, 951 (D.C. Cir. 2008). Iran has failed to meet its burden. To the extent that Iran is liable under Iranian law, it is in its non-sovereign capacity and the act of state doctrine does not apply. Furthermore, to the extent Iran is liable for expropriation, the Second Hickenlooper Amendment prevents the act of state doctrine from applying. How so?

The act of state doctrine does not apply unless and until the Court declares invalid a sovereign public act. *See W.S. Kirkpatrick & Co., Inc. v. Envtl. Tectonics Corp., Int'l,* 493 U.S. 400, 405 (1990); *Malewicz,* 517 F.Supp.2d at 337–38. Contrary to McKesson's argument, an act may be a sovereign act of state "even if a court has jurisdiction over the foreign sovereign pursuant to the commercial activity exception to the FSIA." *Virtual Defense and Development Int'l Inc. v. Moldova,* 133 F.Supp.2d 1, 7 (D.D.C. 1999).

As has been found previously in this case, Iran's denial of dividends was an act "commercial in nature," as "Iran never issued a formal declaration nationalizing Pak Dairy" and "McKesson's claims are akin to a corporate dispute between majority and minority shareholders," *McKesson* 1997, No. 82-220, 1997 WL 361177 at *10 n.17. Unfortunately for the defendant, the act of state doctrine does *not* apply to preclude this Court from inquiring into the validity of such commercial acts.[8] Furthermore, to the extent Iran's acts were not commercial in nature, McKesson's claim is one for expropriation, and Congress has provided, in essence, that the act of state doctrine cannot be used to preclude a court from hearing a case involving a taking by a foreign government in violation of international law. *See* 22 U.S.C. § 2370(e)(2) (the "Second Hickenlooper Amendment"). As a result, the act of state doctrine does not apply in this case.

CONCLUSION

For all of the above reasons, McKesson has causes of action under Iranian law and an implied cause of action under customary international law for expropriation. Additionally, the act of state doctrine does not prevent this Court from hearing McKesson's claims.

8 *See Malewicz,* 517 F.Supp.2d at 339 (finding a government's acquisition of paintings to be a commercial act and noting that while the act was "official" in the sense that it was taken by a government employee acting in his official capacity, "it was not an action taken by right of sovereignty," because "any private person or entity could have purchased the paintings for display in a public or private museum" (internal quotation omitted)); *Virtual Defense,* 133 F.Supp.2d at 8 (finding a government's selling of military aircraft is not a sovereign act of state).

JAMES H. O'BRYAN
v.
HOLY SEE

556 F.3d 361 (6th Cir. 2009)
Decided February 10, 2009

ARGUED: Jeffrey S. Lena, LAW OFFICES OF JEFFREY S. LENA, Berkeley, California, for Appellant.

William F. McMurry, McMURRY & ASSOCIATES, Prospect, Kentucky, for Appellees.

Lewis Yelin, UNITED STATES DEPARTMENT OF JUSTICE, Washington, D.C., for Intervenor.

ON BRIEF: Jeffrey S. Lena, LAW OFFICES OF JEFFREY S. LENA, Berkeley, California, R. Gregg Hovious, John David Dyche, FULTZ, MADDOX, HOVIOUS & DICKENS, Louisville, Kentucky, for Appellant.

William F. McMurry, Adrienne W. Kim, McMURRY & ASSOCIATES, Prospect, Kentucky, Douglas H. Morris II, Lea A. Player, MORRIS & PLAYER, Prospect, Kentucky, for Appellees.

Lewis Yelin, Douglas N. Letter, UNITED STATES DEPARTMENT OF JUSTICE, Washington, D.C., for Intervenor.

Before: MARTIN, GIBBONS, and GRIFFIN, Circuit Judges.

AMENDED OPINION

JULIA SMITH GIBBONS, Circuit Judge.

Defendant Holy See appeals the district court's denial, in part, of its motion to dismiss all of plaintiffs' claims due to lack of subject matter jurisdiction. The Holy See contends that the district court has no subject matter jurisdiction over plaintiffs' claims because the Holy See is immune from suit as a foreign state pursuant to the Foreign Sovereign Immunities Act ("FSIA"), 28 U.S.C. § 1602 et seq. Plaintiffs James H. O'Bryan, Donald E. Poppe, and Michael J. Turner ("plaintiffs") cross-appeal the district court's partial grant of the Holy See's motion to dismiss. Plaintiffs claim that the FSIA does not immunize the Holy See from suit on the grounds alleged in their complaint and thus the district court does in fact have subject matter jurisdiction in this case. The United States as intervenor and *amicus* supports the position of the Holy See with respect to the Holy See's status as a foreign state and the constitutionality of the FSIA. For the following reasons, we affirm the decision of the district court.

I.

On June 4, 2004, plaintiffs, who claim to have been victims of sexual abuse by Roman Catholic clergy, filed a class action suit against the Holy See. The Holy See is both a foreign state and an unincorporated association and the central government of an international religious organization, the Roman Catholic Church. The United States has recognized the Holy See as a foreign sovereign since 1984. According to their complaint, plaintiffs consist of representatives for two separate classes. James H. O'Bryan and Donald E. Poppe serve as the representatives of Class I, which "consists of all persons who have not previously brought claims against an agent or servant of the Defendant, Holy See, in the United States . . . arising out of sexual abuse he or she suffered at the hands of a Roman Catholic priest, cleric, bishop, archbishop, cardinal, agent or employee . . . ." Michael J. Turner serves as the representative of Class II, which "consists of all persons who have previously brought claims against an agent or servant of the Defendant, Holy See, in the United States . . . arising out of sexual abuse he or she suffered at the hands of a Roman Catholic priest, cleric, agent or employee . . . ." All three representatives were residents of Kentucky and citizens of the United States at the time of the alleged sexual abuse by local Catholic priests.

As representatives, the plaintiffs allege the following underlying facts in support of their suit.

> Plaintiff, James H. O'Bryan, was sexually abused, molested and assaulted by a Roman Catholic priest in the 1920s, while Plaintiff was under the care, custody, authority, control and influence of an abusive Roman Catholic priest, which authority was granted to him by the Defendant, Holy See.
>
> Plaintiff, Donald E. Poppe, was sexually abused, molested and assaulted by a Roman Catholic priest in the 1960s, while Plaintiff was under the care, custody, authority, control and influence of an abusive Roman Catholic priest, which authority was granted to him by the Defendant, Holy See.
>
> Plaintiff, Michael J. Turner, was sexually abused, molested and assaulted by a Roman Catholic priest in the mid 1970s, while Plaintiff was under the care, custody, authority, control and influence of an abusive Roman Catholic priest, which authority was granted to him by the Defendant, Holy See.

In all cases, plaintiffs allege that the sexual molestation in question "occurred while the abusive Roman Catholic priest, agent, servant or employee was acting within the scope of his employment, as part of an agency relationship with the

Defendant, Holy See, and the misconduct was committed with the apparent authority arising from this employment and/or agency relationship."

Plaintiffs' claims regarding the liability of the Holy See stem, in large part, from their allegations regarding the purported policy of the Holy See towards accusations of sexual abuse leveled against clergy:

> [T]he Holy See has mandated that all allegations of childhood sexual abuse be kept under a cloak of complete secrecy, even if that secrecy violated state, federal, or international law. In March, 1962, the Holy See privately circulated a document containing a set of procedural norms for dealing with the solicitation of sex in confession, clergy sex with minors, homosexual relations, and bestiality. This document [the "1962 Policy"]—an official legislative text issued by the Congregation of the Holy Office and specifically approved by Pope John XXIII—imposes the highest level of secrecy on the handling of clergy sexual abuse matters. . . . This secret document was first discovered and made public in July, 2003 by news media in the United States and throughout the world. The policies of the Holy See expressed in this and other documents require bishops in the United States to, among other things, refuse to report childhood sexual abuse committed by priests to criminal or civil authorities, even where such failure to report would itself be a criminal offense.

(Plaintiff's Complaint, Introduction.) On behalf of Class I, plaintiffs outline in their complaint the following causes of action:[1] violation of customary international law of human rights; negligence; breach of fiduciary duty; and the tort of outrage/intentional infliction of emotional distress. In addition, plaintiffs advance claims of deceit and misrepresentation against the Holy See "in its capacity as an Unincorporated Association and Head of an International Religious Organization Only." Finally, plaintiffs, on behalf of Class I, request injunctive relief.

On behalf of Class II, plaintiffs outline in their complaint the following causes of action: violation of customary international law of human rights; negligence; breach of fiduciary duty; and the tort of outrage/intentional infliction of emotional distress. In addition, plaintiffs advance claims of deceit and misrepresentation against the Holy See "in its capacity as an Unincorporated Association and Head of an International Religious Organization Only." Finally, plaintiffs, on behalf of Class II, request injunctive relief.

Plaintiffs assert in their complaint that federal subject matter jurisdiction exists in this case on a number of grounds. First, plaintiffs advance claims of federal jurisdiction under the FSIA, 28 U.S.C. § 1602 et seq. Assuming that the Holy See is a "foreign state" within the meaning of 28 U.S.C. § 1603, plaintiffs claim that federal jurisdiction attaches because (1) the Holy See has waived its immunity

---

1 Plaintiffs also plead a separate cause of action titled "Respondeat Superior Liability." However, *respondeat superior* is not a cause of action. It is a basis for holding the Holy See responsible for the acts of its agents. Thus, *respondeat superior* will factor in to our discussion of the other claims advanced by plaintiffs but will not be treated separately.

pursuant to 28 U.S.C. § 1605(a)(1); (2) the Holy See was acting in a commercial capacity pursuant to 28 U.S.C. § 1605(a)(2); or (3) the money damages that are sought are for personal injuries stemming from the Holy See's tortious conduct pursuant to 28 U.S.C. § 1605(a)(5).

Alternatively, assuming that the Holy See is not a "foreign state" within the meaning of 28 U.S.C. § 1603, plaintiffs assert that this court has subject matter jurisdiction pursuant to 28 U.S.C. §§ 1331 and 1332 and supplemental jurisdiction pursuant to 28 U.S.C. § 1367.

On April 4, 2005, the Holy See filed a motion to dismiss on the grounds that the plaintiffs' complaint failed to state a claim upon which relief can be granted, lack of subject matter jurisdiction, lack of personal jurisdiction, insufficient process and insufficient service of process. In its memorandum and opinion of October 7, 2005, the district court addressed the Holy See's claim that the service of process had been insufficient. In doing so, the district court began its analysis by determining that the Holy See was in fact a "foreign state" within the meaning of the FSIA. In turn, the district court found that plaintiffs had not satisfied the service of process requirements under the FSIA, 28 U.S.C. § 1608(a). However, the district court found that because the plaintiffs had made good faith attempts to perfect service of process, it would grant them an additional 60 days in which to perfect service. *O'Bryan v. Holy See*, 490 F. Supp 2d 826, 832 (W.D. Ky. 2005) ("*O'Bryan I*").

On January 10, 2007, the district court determined that plaintiffs had perfected service of process and therefore went on to consider the Holy See's motion to dismiss on the grounds that there was no subject matter jurisdiction in the instant case. In its memorandum and opinion, the district court determined that while subject matter jurisdiction did not exist for a number of plaintiffs' claims, a number of the plaintiffs' claims fell within the exceptions to the immunities granted foreign states under FSIA. In doing so, the district court concluded that plaintiffs had sufficiently pled that the clergy in the United States were Holy See's employees; in turn, because the Holy See had declined to provide evidence to the contrary, the district would presume that the clergy in question were in fact Holy See employees. However, the district court remained "open to reconsidering its decision that the United States-based bishops, archbishops, and other clergy of the Roman Catholic Church are employees of the Holy See for purposes of FSIA if further contrary evidence emerges during the litigation." The district court summarized its holdings as follows:

> In summary, this Court will dismiss the Plaintiffs' negligence claim that Defendant Holy See failed to provide safe care of children entrusted to the clergy. The Court also will dismiss Plaintiffs' deceit and misrepresentation claims. However, the Court will deny Defendant's motion to dismiss as to the failure to report and failure to warn negligence claims and as to all other claims asserted against the Holy See at this time. Therefore, the following claims remain against the Holy See: negligent failure to report, negligent failure to warn, breach of fiduciary duty (insofar as that breach involved the failure to report and the failure to warn), outrage and emotional distress, violations of the customary law of human rights, and claims under the doctrine of respondeat superior.

The Holy See appealed the district court's order denying, in part, its motion to dismiss and plaintiffs subsequently cross-appealed. In their Final Second Brief, the plaintiffs argued, for the first time, that the application of the FSIA to the Holy See violated the *Establishment Clause*. Because the plaintiffs' new contentions amounted to a challenge of the FSIA's constitutionality, the United States, pursuant to 28 U.S.C. § 2403(a), intervened as a matter of right to defend the constitutionality of the FSIA. The United States also intervened as an *amicus curiae* supporting the position of the Holy See regarding its status as a foreign sovereign. The United States took no position on the applicability of the statutory exceptions to immunity with respect to plaintiffs' claims.

II.

Because "sovereign immunity is an immunity from trial, not just a defense to liability on the merits, the denial of a claim of sovereign immunity is immediately appealable under the collateral order doctrine as a final decision, pursuant to 28 U.S.C. § 1291." *Keller v. Cent. Bank of Nig.*, 277 F.3d 811, 815 (6th Cir. 2002). This court "review[s] de novo questions of subject matter jurisdiction." *Bauer v. RBX Indus.*, 368 F.3d 569, 578 (6th Cir. 2004) (citing *Caudill v. N. Am. Media Corp.*, 200 F.3d 914, 916 (6th Cir. 2000)). However, "[a] district court's decision to exercise supplemental jurisdiction over state law claims that are related to the federal question claim is reviewed only for abuse of discretion." *Harper v. Auto Alliance Int'l, Inc.*, 392 F.3d 195, 200 (6th Cir. 2004).

III.

As stated in 28 U.S.C. § 1604, "a foreign state shall be immune from the jurisdiction of the courts of the United States and of the States except as provided in sections 1605–1607 of this chapter." However, the FSIA does not itself define the term "foreign state." *See, e.g., Ungar v. Palestinian Liberation Org.*, 402 F.3d 274, 283 (1st Cir. 2005).

In determining whether a particular entity constitutes a "foreign state" courts typically adopt one of two approaches. A number of courts have looked to the criteria enumerated in Restatement (Third) of the Foreign Relations Law of the United States § 201: "Under international law, a state is an entity that has a defined territory and a permanent population, under the control of its own government, and that engages in, or has the capacity to engage in, formal relations with other such entities." *See Estate of Klieman v. Palestinian Auth.*, 424 F. Supp. 2d 153, 158–59 (D.D.C. 2006) (collecting cases); *see also Ungar*, 402 F.3d at 283 (noting that FSIA's legislative history makes it clear that the "objective of the bill was to codify sovereign immunity doctrine as recognized by international law and to ensure that this international standard would be applied in federal litigation"); *Morgan Guar. Trust Co. v. Republic of Palau,* 924 F.2d 1237, 1243 (2d Cir. 1991) (relying primarily on the Restatement standard for determining whether the appellee was a "foreign state" under FSIA). However, as the First Circuit noted in *Ungar*, "the Restatement standard . . . is not inevitably correct. It may be argued that a foreign state, for purposes of the FSIA, is an entity that has been recognized as a sovereign by the United States government." 402 F.3d at 284 n.6. Regardless, as the court noted in *Ungar*, when both standards lead to the same conclusion, courts need not choose as "all roads lead to Rome." *Id.*

In this case, there is no dispute that the United States recognized the Vatican in 1984,[2] and there is no dispute between the parties that the *State of the Vatican* is a foreign state within the meaning of FSIA. (Appellee's Br. 21 ("The Holy See, as State of the Vatican, meets the[] requirements [of the Restatement Standard]")). *See also Dale v. Colagiovanni*, 337 F. Supp. 2d 825, 832 (S.D. Miss. 2004) (vacated on other grounds) (treating the Vatican as a foreign state for the purposes of the FSIA); *English v. Thorne*, 676 F. Supp. 761, 764 (S.D. Miss. 1987) (same).[3]

Plaintiffs, however, contend that the "Holy See . . . . *as the head of the Roman Catholic Church*, . . . has no defined territory and no permanent population, and thus does not" satisfy the definition of "foreign state" under the Restatement's standard. (Appellee's Br. 21 (emphasis added)).

Plaintiffs' argument remains somewhat obscure. As noted, plaintiffs admit that the Holy See, as State of the Vatican, is a foreign state within the meaning of FSIA. Thus, they do not dispute that the entity recognized by the United States government as a foreign state is indeed a foreign sovereign. Instead, plaintiffs appear to advance one of two arguments. The first possible interpretation of plaintiffs' argument is that they ask this court to conceive of the Holy See as two separate entities—first, a foreign sovereign, recognized by the United States government, and second, an unincorporated head of an international religious organization (Appellee's Br. 21 ("The Holy See, as State of the Vatican, meets the[] requirements [of the

---

2 *See, e.g., Ams. United for Separation of Church & State v. Reagan*, 786 F.2d 194, 197 (3d Cir. 1986) (noting that diplomatic relations between the United States and the Vatican began in 1984).

3 Plaintiffs argue that because the conduct in question preceded the United States' recognition of the Holy See as a foreign sovereign, this court should not apply FSIA. This argument also fails. First, as a general principle of international law, "recognition is retroactive in effect and validates all the actions and conduct of the government so recognized from the commencement of its existence." *Oetjen v. Cent. Leather Co.*, 246 U.S. 297, 303, 38 S. Ct. 309, 62 L. Ed. 726 (1918). More importantly, "the principal purpose of foreign sovereign immunity has never been to permit foreign states and their instrumentalities to shape their conduct in reliance on the promise of future immunity from suit in United States courts. Rather, such immunity reflects current political realities and relationships, and aims to give foreign states and their instrumentalities some *present* 'protection from the inconvenience of suit as a gesture of comity.'" *Republic of Austria v. Altmann*, 541 U.S. 677, 696, 124 S. Ct. 2240, 159 L. Ed. 2d 1 (2004) (emphasis in original) (holding that FSIA can be retroactive in application) (quoting *Dole Food Co. v. Patrickson*, 538 U.S. 468, 479, 123 S. Ct. 1655, 155 L. Ed. 2d 643 (2003)). Thus, the purpose of FSIA is to grant immunity based upon the current relationship between the United States and the relevant foreign sovereign. Because the United States currently has diplomatic relations with the Holy See, foreign sovereign immunity applies even to prior conduct.

Restatement Standard]," but the "Holy See . . . . as the head of the Roman Catholic Church, . . . has no defined territory and no permanent population, and thus does not" satisfy the definition of "foreign state" under the Restatement's standard")). Alternatively, they ask this court not to consider the Holy See, a single entity, a foreign sovereign in this case because the Holy See was acting in a non-sovereign capacity when it engaged in the conduct alleged in plaintiffs' complaint. Compl. P. 22 ("At the same time, and wholly distinct and separate from its role and activities as a sovereign, [the Holy See] is an unincorporated association and head of the Roman Catholic Church, an international religious organization.").

Plaintiffs' argument fails under either construction. With respect to the first alternative—the two-entity alternative—the district court correctly noted that "[p]laintiffs cite no authority for the proposition that the Holy See may be sued in a separate, non-sovereign function as an unincorporated association and as head of an international religious organization." *O'Bryan I*, 490 F. Supp. 2d at 830. To the contrary, courts have generally treated the Holy See as a foreign state for purposes of the FSIA. *See Dale*, 337 F. Supp. 2d at 832 (treating the Vatican as a foreign state for the purposes of the FSIA); *English*, 676 F. Supp. at 764 (concluding that the Vatican is a foreign state for the purposes of the FSIA); *Doe v. Holy See*, 434 F. Supp. 2d 925, 933 (D. Or. 2006) (applying FSIA's foreign state status to the Holy See). Consequently, we reject plaintiffs' contention that they are not suing the Holy See that has been recognized by the United States government, but a parallel non-sovereign entity conjured up by the plaintiffs.

The structure and intent of the FSIA also counsel us to reject the plaintiffs' alternative capacity approach. As the Supreme Court has explained, by enacting FSIA, Congress intended to adopt the "restrictive theory" of sovereign immunity, "under which 'the immunity of the sovereign is recognized with regard to sovereign or public acts (*jure imperii*) of a state, but not with respect to private acts (*jure gestionis*).'" *Permanent Mission of India to the U.N. v. City of New York*, 551 U.S. 193, 127 S. Ct. 2352, 2357, 168 L. Ed. 2d 85 (2007) (quoting *Alfred Dunhill of London, Inc. v. Republic of Cuba*, 425 U.S. 682, 711, 96 S. Ct. 1854, 48 L. Ed. 2d 301 (1976)).

In order to implement the "restrictive theory" of sovereign immunity and limit immunity to sovereign acts but not private acts, Congress crafted exceptions to FSIA. *See* 28 U.S.C. 1605(a). For example, "[t]he 'commercial activity' exception of the FSIA withdraws immunity in cases involving essentially private commercial activities of foreign sovereigns that have an impact within the United States." *Commercial Bank of Kuwait v. Rafidain Bank*, 15 F.3d 238, 241 (2d Cir. 1994); *see also Orient Mineral Co. v. Bank of China*, 506 F.3d 980, 983 (10th Cir. 2007) ("The FSIA's commercial activity exceptions, however, permit a foreign sovereign to be sued in a court within the United States, to the same extent as any private individual . . . ."). In this way, Congress constructed the FSIA to immunize foreign sovereigns acting in a public capacity, while ensuring that essentially private activities would be actionable under the FSIA exceptions.

For these reasons, the Supreme Court has stated "[w]e think that the text and structure of the FSIA demonstrate Congress' intention that the FSIA be the sole basis for obtaining jurisdiction over a foreign state in our courts." *Argentine Republic v. Amerada Hess Shipping Corp.*, 488 U.S. 428, 434, 109 S. Ct. 683, 102 L. Ed. 2d 818 (1989); *accord Am. Telecom Co., L.L.C. v. Republic of Leb.*, 501 F.3d 534, 538 (6th Cir. 2007). This conclusion stems from the FSIA's rule-plus-exceptions structure; if a party believes that the foreign state was not acting in its capacity as a sovereign, but instead in its private capacity, then the party can seek redress via one of the FSIA's exceptions.

Thus, if plaintiffs believe that the Holy See acted in a private capacity, then the plaintiffs are limited to arguing that an exception to the FSIA applies; such claims cannot serve as reasons to avoid the FSIA altogether. The exceptions to FSIA capture all instances where Congress has deemed conduct, if pursued by a foreign sovereign, sufficiently private so as to eliminate foreign sovereign immunity. In turn, the alternative-capacity argument can only succeed to the extent that it identifies conduct that fits within one of the exceptions outlined under FSIA. *See* 28 U.S.C. § 1605(a).[4]

This argument misapprehends the nature of the court's inquiry. Plaintiffs do not ask this court to contravene the executive branch's recognition of the Holy See as a foreign sovereign. Instead, they either ask this court to determine that they can rightfully bring suit against a parallel religious entity that also goes by the name "Holy See" or that the conduct of the Holy See rendered it a private actor *in this case*. Courts routinely determine whether incorporated entities satisfy the criteria necessary to be considered an agency or instrumentality of a recognized foreign state pursuant to 28 U.S.C. § 1603(b) without becoming entangled in a non-justiciable political question. *See, e.g., Gould, Inc. v. Pechiney Ugine Kuhlmann*, 853 F.2d 445 (6th Cir. 1988) (agreeing with the district court's determination that the corporation in question could qualify for foreign sovereign immunity status because the majority owner of the corporation was a foreign state) (abrogated on other grounds by *Republic of Arg. v. Weltover, Inc.*, 504 U.S. 607, 112 S. Ct. 2160, 119 L. Ed. 2d 394 (1992)); *Gen. Elec. Capital Corp. v. Grossman*, 991 F.2d 1376 (8th Cir. 1993) (same).

---

4 Both the Holy See and the United States argue that this court should refrain from making a determination regarding whether the Holy See is a foreign sovereign because such an issue is a non-justiciable political question. They rely on the following language: "It has been specifically decided that 'Who is the sovereign, de jure or de facto, of a territory is not a judicial, but is a political question, the determination of which by the legislative and executive departments of any government conclusively binds the judges, as well as all other officers, citizens and subjects of that government.'" *Oetjen*, 246 U.S. at 302 (quoting *Jones v. United States*, 137 U.S. 202, 212, 11 S. Ct. 80, 34 L. Ed. 691 (1890)); *see also United States v. Belmont*, 301 U.S. 324, 328, 57 S. Ct. 758, 81 L. Ed. 1134 (1937) ("[T]hat who is the sovereign of a territory is not a judicial question, but one the determination of which by the political departments conclusively binds the courts; and that recognition by these departments is retroactive and validates all actions and conduct of the government so recognized from the commencement of its existence.").

And courts can consider the conduct of the Holy See in order to determine whether the type of conduct alleged should cause the Holy See to lose its sovereign immunity. *See* 28 U.S.C. § 1605(a).

IV.

We next consider the plaintiffs contention that the FSIA, as applied to the Holy See, violates the *Establishment Clause.*

"Issues that are not squarely presented to the trial court are considered waived and may not be raised on appeal." *Thurman v. Yellow Freight Sys*., 90 F.3d 1160, 1172 (6th Cir. 1996). Similarly, "vague references fail to clearly present the objection in the district court so as to preserve the issue for appellate review." *Bldg. Serv. Local 47 Cleaning Contractors Pension Plan v. Grandview Raceway,* 46 F.3d 1392, 1399 (6th Cir. 1995).

Plaintiffs contend that they preserved their constitutional claims by articulating them in their response to the Holy See's motion to dismiss. However, plaintiffs' response brief includes no such constitutional claims. Plaintiffs' response to *the Holy See's* First Amendment challenges cannot preserve plaintiffs' own Establishment Clause claim. Thus, plaintiffs waived their constitutional challenges to the FSIA.[5]

V.

We next address the Holy See's contention that the district court misapplied the FSIA's burden-shifting process.

In the proceedings before the district court, the Holy See filed a motion to dismiss for lack of subject matter jurisdiction pursuant to Federal Rule of Civil Procedure 12(b)(1). This motion presented a facial attack to plaintiffs' complaint.

As this court has previously noted, "Rule 12(b)(1) motions to dismiss for lack of subject-matter jurisdiction generally come in two varieties: a facial attack or a factual attack." *Gentek Bldg. Prods. v. Sherwin-Williams Co*., 491 F.3d 320, 330 (6th Cir. 2007) (citing *Ohio Nat'l Life Ins. Co. v. United States*, 922 F.2d 320, 325 (6th Cir. 1990)). "A facial attack on the subject-matter jurisdiction alleged in the complaint questions merely the sufficiency of the pleading." *Id.* And, "[w]hen reviewing a facial attack, a district court takes the allegations in the complaint as true. . . . If those allegations establish federal claims, jurisdiction exists." *Id.* However, "conclusory allegations or legal conclusions masquerading as factual conclusions will not suffice to prevent a motion to dismiss." *Mezibov v. Allen*, 411 F.3d 712, 716 (6th Cir. 2005).

---

5 Although this court "may exercise [its] discretion to review an issue not raised below in exceptional cases or particular circumstances, or when the rule would produce a plain miscarriage of justice," *United States v. Chesney*, 86 F.3d 564, 567–68 (6th Cir. 1996) (internal quotation marks and citation omitted), we see no such exceptional circumstances in this case.

Applying the standards under 12(b)(1) to the FSIA context is complicated by FSIA's burden-shifting process. "The party claiming FSIA immunity bears the initial burden of proof of establishing a prima facie case that it satisfies the FSIA's definition of a foreign state; once this prima facie case is established, the burden of production shifts to the non-movant to show that an exception applies." *Keller*, 277 F.3d at 815. The party claiming immunity under FSIA retains the burden of persuasion throughout this process. *Id.*

The Holy See contends that this burden-shifting process was misapplied by the district court. In addressing the Holy See's motion to dismiss, the district court explained that "once the *asserted allegations* bring claims within the statutory exceptions to FSIA, the burden then shifts to the party asserting immunity to prove that the exceptions do not apply." *O'Bryan v. Holy See*, 471 F. Supp. 2d 784, 791 (W.D. Ky. 2007) ("*O'Bryan II*") (citing *Siderman de Blake v. Republic of Arg.*, 965 F.2d 699, 707–08 (9th Cir. 1992)) (emphasis in original). The Holy See, however, argues that the burden-shifting analysis, because of its reliance on evidence from the parties, cannot be applied to a facial motion to dismiss, which simply attacks the legal sufficiency of the complaint.

Federal courts have consistently applied the FSIA's burden-shifting process to facial motions to dismiss; in doing so, courts simply look to the general standards for evaluating motions to dismiss pursuant to Rule 12(b)(1) and take the factual allegations of the plaintiff as true. *See, e.g., Siderman de Blake*, 965 F.2d at 708 n.9 (noting that "even if the [plaintiffs] had presented nothing more than the allegations in their complaint . . . it would have been incumbent upon [defendant] to respond to those allegations"); *Kilburn v. Socialist People's Libyan Arab Jamahiriya*, 363 U.S. App. D.C. 87, 376 F.3d 1123, 1127 (D.C. Cir. 2004) ("[I]f the defendant challenges only the legal sufficiency of the plaintiff's jurisdictional allegations, then the district court should take the plaintiff's factual allegations as true and determine whether they bring the case within any of the [FSIA] exceptions to immunity invoked by the plaintiff.") (quoting *Phoenix Consulting, Inc. v. Republic of Angl.,* 342 U.S. App. D.C. 145, 216 F.3d 36, 40 (D.C. Cir. 2000)); Doe, 434 F. Supp. 2d at 933 ("If the foreign state makes [the "foreign state"] showing, the burden of production shifts to the plaintiff to show, *either by the allegations in the complaint* or by extrinsic evidence, that at least one of the FSIA exceptions applies. Once the plaintiff offers evidence that an exception to immunity applies, the party claiming immunity bears the burden of proving by a preponderance of the evidence that the exception does not apply." (internal citations and quotation marks omitted; emphasis added)).

We conclude that the district court correctly applied the FSIA's burden shifting process. It accurately described the process. *O'Bryan II,* 471 F. Supp. 2d at 790–91. It considered the allegations in plaintiffs' complaint that a number of exceptions to FSIA immunity applied and concluded that the tortious act exception did in fact apply. *O'Bryan II*, 471 F. Supp. 2d at 792. As the district court correctly noted, the Holy See could still retain immunity if it could "prove that the exceptions do not apply." *Id.* at 791. Such proof would presumably amount to a "factual attack" pursuant to Rule 12(b)(1). *Cf. Gentek Bldg. Prods.*, 491 F.3d at 330 ("Where . . . there is a factual attack on the subject-matter jurisdiction alleged in the complaint, no presumptive truthfulness applies to the allegations.").

VI.

Because the plaintiffs can only bring suit against the Holy See in its capacity as a foreign sovereign, the district court has subject matter jurisdiction over the dispute only if the Holy See is "not entitled to immunity [under any of the FSIA exceptions]." *See* 28 U.S.C. § 1330(a). Title 28 U.S.C. § 1605(a) provides the following relevant exceptions to a foreign state's immunity under the FSIA:

> (a) A foreign state shall not be immune from the jurisdiction of courts of the United States or of the States in any case –
>
> (1) in which the foreign state has waived its immunity either explicitly or by implication, notwithstanding any withdrawal of the waiver which the foreign state may purport to effect except in accordance with the terms of the waiver;[6]
>
> (2) in which the action is based upon a commercial activity carried on in the United States by the foreign state; or upon an act performed in the United States in connection with a commercial activity of the foreign state elsewhere; or upon an act outside the territory of the United States in connection with a commercial activity of the foreign state elsewhere and that act causes a direct effect in the United States;
>
> . . .
>
> (5) not otherwise encompassed in paragraph (2) above, in which money damages are sought against a foreign state for personal injury or death, or damage to or loss of property, occurring in the United States and caused by the tortious act or omission of that foreign state or of any official or employee of that foreign state while acting within the scope of his office or employment; except this paragraph shall not apply to—
>
> (A) any claim based upon the exercise or performance or the failure to exercise or perform a discretionary function regardless of whether the discretion be abused, or
>
> (B) any claim arising out of malicious prosecution, abuse of process, libel, slander, misrepresentation, deceit, or interference with contract rights . . . .

The district court determined that the "commercial activity" exception did not apply, *O'Bryan II*, 471 F. Supp. 2d at 789, a determination that the plaintiffs contest in their cross-appeal.[7] The district court also found that it had subject matter

---

6 While plaintiffs raised the waiver exception in their complaint, they have abandoned this argument in their briefs before this court.

7 The Holy See argues that this court has no jurisdiction to hear plaintiffs' cross-appeal. This court has jurisdiction to hear the Holy See's appeal because the "denial of sovereign immunity is immediately appealable under the collateral order doctrine as a final decision, pursuant to

jurisdiction over some of the plaintiffs' claims under the "tortious act" exception, *id.* at 792, a determination that the Holy See now appeals. We will consider the application of the various exceptions to sovereign immunity under the FSIA in turn.

a. The Commercial Activity Exception

As noted above, the commercial activity exception reads as follows:

> A foreign state shall not be immune from the jurisdiction of courts of the United States or of the States in any case . . . in which the action is based upon a commercial activity carried on in the United States by the foreign state; or upon an act performed in the United States in connection with a commercial activity of the foreign state elsewhere; or upon an act outside the territory of the United States in connection with a commercial activity of the foreign state elsewhere and that act causes a direct effect in the United States . . . .

28 U.S.C. § 1605(a)(2). "A 'commercial activity' means either a regular course of commercial conduct or a particular commercial transaction or act. The commercial character of an activity shall be determined by reference to the nature of the course of conduct or particular transaction or act, rather than by reference to its purpose." 28 U.S.C. § 1603(d). In addition, "the commercial activity relied upon by plaintiff for jurisdictional purposes must be also the activity upon which the lawsuit is based; that is, there must be a connection between that activity and the act complained of in the lawsuit." *Gould*, 853 F.2d at 452 (citing *Riedel v. Bancam*, S.A., 792 F.2d 587, 591 (6th Cir. 1986)).

---

28 U.S.C. § 1291." *Keller*, 277 F.3d at 815. In order to hear plaintiffs' cross-appeal, this court would have to exercise pendent jurisdiction: "The doctrine of pendent appellate jurisdiction allows an appellate court, in its discretion, to exercise jurisdiction over issues that are not independently appealable when those issues are 'inextricably intertwined' with matters over which the appellate court properly and independently has jurisdiction." *Chambers v. Ohio Dep't of Human Servs.*, 145 F.3d 793, 797 (6th Cir. 1998). "A pendent appellate claim can be regarded as 'inextricably intertwined' with a properly reviewable claim only if the pendent claim 'is coterminous with, or subsumed in, the claim before the court on interlocutory appeal.'" *Id.* (quoting *Law v. Nat'l Collegiate Athletic Ass'n,* 134 F.3d 1025, 1028 (10th Cir. 1998)). To be sure, "[t]he 'inextricably intertwined' requirement of pendent appellate jurisdiction is not meant to be loosely applied as a matter of discretion; rather, such jurisdiction only may be exercised when the appealable issue at hand cannot be resolved without addressing the non appealable collateral issue." *Id.*

Despite this strict standard for pendent jurisdiction, we conclude that pendent jurisdiction should be exercised in this case. Plaintiffs seek to challenge the district court's ruling on the applicability of the commercial activity exception of the FSIA. The ultimate issue of this interlocutory appeal—whether the Holy See is immune from suit pursuant to the FSIA—also hinges on a finding that this exception does not apply. Moreover, given the relatedness of the two exceptions, judicial economy would counsel hearing these two issues together. *Cf. Rendall-Speranza v. Nassim*, 323 U.S. App. D.C. 280, 107 F.3d 913 (D.C. Cir. 1997) (exercising pendent appellate jurisdiction pursuant to an interlocutory appeal of the denial of sovereign immunity under the FSIA).

The Supreme Court has further analyzed the statutory definition of commercial activity, stating that

> [W]hen a foreign government acts, not as regulator of a market, but in the manner of a private player within it, the foreign sovereign's actions are "commercial" within the meaning of the FSIA. Moreover, because the Act provides that the commercial character of an act is to be determined by reference to its "nature" rather than its "purpose," the question is not whether the foreign government is acting with a profit motive or instead with the aim of fulfilling uniquely sovereign objectives. Rather, the issue is whether the particular actions that the foreign state performs (whatever the motive behind them) are the type of actions by which a private party engages in trade and traffic or commerce.

Republic of Arg., 504 U.S. at 614 (internal quotation marks and citations omitted). By "withdraw[ing] immunity in cases involving essentially private commercial activities," the commercial activity exception "reflects the 'restrictive' theory of sovereign immunity that underlies the FSIA." *Commercial Bank of Kuwait v. Rafidain Bank,* 15 F.3d 238, 241 (2d Cir. 1994).

The Supreme Court applied the *Weltover* standard in *Saudi Arabia v. Nelson*, 507 U.S. 349, 113 S. Ct. 1471, 123 L. Ed. 2d 47 (1993). In *Nelson*, the plaintiff, a United States citizen and a former employee of the Saudi government, had allegedly been imprisoned and tortured by Saudi officials for reporting defects regarding hospital equipment to a Saudi government commission. Upon release, the plaintiff filed suit against the Saudi government, alleging, *inter alia*, that the government was negligent in its failure to warn him of the undisclosed dangers of his employment position (*i.e.* the likelihood of being imprisoned and tortured). *Id.* at 352–54. In finding that the Saudis' conduct was not commercial in nature, the Supreme Court analyzed Nelson's claims as follows:

> [T]he intentional conduct alleged here (the Saudi Government's wrongful arrest, imprisonment, and torture of Nelson) could not qualify as commercial under the restrictive theory. The conduct boils down to abuse of the power of its police by the Saudi Government, and however monstrous such abuse undoubtedly may be, a foreign state's exercise of the power of its police has long been understood for purposes of the restrictive theory as peculiarly sovereign in nature . . . . Exercise of the powers of police and penal officers is not the sort of action by which private parties can engage in commerce.

Id. at 361–62. Indeed, directly addressing Nelson's attempt to advance a failure-to-warn theory of the case, the Supreme Court responded:

> [T]his is merely a semantic ploy. For aught we can see, a plaintiff could recast virtually any claim of intentional tort committed by sovereign act as a claim of failure to warn, simply by charging the defendant with an obligation to announce its own tortious propensity before indulging it. To give jurisdictional significance to this feint of language would effectively thwart the Act's manifest purpose to codify the restrictive theory of foreign sovereign immunity.

Id. at 363.

The analysis in *Weltover* and *Nelson* points to two distinct limitations on the application of the commercial activity exception. First, the activity must be of the type in which private individuals engage; if the activities in question are not private, but sovereign in nature, then the commercial activity exception will not apply. This flows from the purpose of the commercial activity exception - to encapsulate the restrictive theory of sovereign immunity, which grants immunity for the public, not private, actions of a sovereign. *Permanent Mission of India to the UN v. City of New York*, 551 U.S. 193, 127 S. Ct. 2352, 2357, 168 L. Ed. 2d 85 (2007) (quoting *Alfred Dunhill of London, Inc. v. Republic of Cuba*, 425 U.S. 682, 711, 96 S. Ct. 1854, 48 L. Ed. 2d 301 (1976)); *see also City School of Detroit v. Government of France*, 1990 U.S. Dist. LEXIS 19577, at *9–*10 (E.D. Mich. 1990) (concluding that the commercial activity exception did not apply because "[t]he granting of accreditation to a private school by a foreign government is by its very nature a sovereign function, incapable of being performed by a private individual [and] . . . the welfare and education of its citizenry is . . . an area where sovereign activity is typically asserted").

Second, the *Weltover* and *Nelson* cases also instruct courts to avoid the artful pleading of plaintiffs and look to the core of the activities alleged to be commercial in nature. Thus, the Southern District of New York has explained that "*Nelson* rest[s] on a broader principle, directing district courts first to ascertain the claim's gravamen to determine whether the FSIA plaintiff is simply using creative nomenclature as a semantic ploy to shroud the true essence of its theory and obtain jurisdiction over a claim that Congress did not intend to be brought against a foreign sovereign." *Leutwyler v. Office of Her Majesty Queen Rania Al Abdullah,* 184 F. Supp. 2d 277, 299 (S.D.N.Y. 2001) (internal quotation marks and citation omitted). District courts have applied both limiting principles in instructive contexts.

Employing this principle, the District of Oregon has recently considered the commercial activity exception in circumstances similar to our own. In *Doe v. Holy See*, the district court of Oregon considered the applicability of the commercial activity exception to claims against the Holy See stemming from the alleged abuse of the plaintiff by his priest, a Holy See employee. 434 F. Supp. 2d at 937–47. After a lengthy analysis of the term "commercial activity" under the FSIA, the district court stated as follows:

> [T]he Supreme Court has counseled courts not to lose sight of the ultimate issue: whether the true essence of the complaint is commercial. *Nelson*, 507 U.S. at 363. Here, plaintiff's complaint does not allege property damage, breach of contract for goods or services, product liability, copyright infringement, an indebtedness yet unpaid on a loan or other transaction, or any other theory whose true essence is commercial. Instead, at the heart of plaintiff's complaint is the injury inflicted by a sexually abusive priest at plaintiff's church, a claim clearly sounding in tort.

Id. at 942. In other words, the *Doe* Court did not rely on the public-private inquiry, but instead it examined the "gravaman" of the claims advanced by the plaintiff. *See Leutwyler*, 184 F. Supp. 2d at 299. Regardless of how the plaintiff phrased his complaint, none of the allegations truly sounded in commercial activity, and thus the commercial activity exception did not apply. *Doe*, 434 F. Supp. 2d at 947.

Both limiting principles apply to plaintiffs' attempt to invoke the commercial activity exception in our own case. On one front, all of the claims advanced by plaintiffs stem from the promulgation of the purported 1962 Policy by the Holy See. Indeed, in arguing that the discretionary function exception did not apply, plaintiffs themselves emphasize the force of the purported policy and the potential for sanction if Holy See employees chose not to comply.

In addition, the gravaman of plaintiffs' claims is the tortious conduct of priests which was allegedly facilitated by the tortious conduct of Holy See employees. Thus to allow plaintiffs to obtain jurisdiction under the commercial activity exception through a semantic ploy would allow them to "obtain jurisdiction over a claim that Congress did not intend to be brought against a foreign sovereign." *See Leutwyler*, 184 F. Supp. 2d at 299. We therefore conclude that the commercial activity exception does not apply.

b. The Tortious Act Exception

Pursuant to the FSIA, a plaintiff can establish subject matter jurisdiction over a foreign sovereign under the tortious act exception if there has been a tortious act (1) "occurring in the United States"; (2) "caused by [a] tortious act or omission"; (3) where the alleged acts or omissions were those of a "foreign state or of any official or employee of that foreign state"; and (4) those acts or omissions were done within the scope of tortfeasor's employment. *See* 28 U.S.C. § 1605(a)(5).

Because, however, there are exceptions to the tortious act exception, our inquiry does not end here. If the tortious act in question was either (1) "based upon the exercise or performance or the failure to exercise or perform a discretionary function" or (2) "ar[o]s[e] out of . . . misrepresentation [or] deceit . . ." then the foreign sovereign retains its immunity. 28 U.S.C. § 1605(a)(5)(A),(B).

In determining whether the tortious act exception applies, courts, as a rule, apply state substantive law: "where state law provides a rule of liability governing private individuals, the FSIA requires the application of that rule to foreign states in like circumstances." *First Nat'l City Bank v. Banco Para El Comercio Exterior De Cuba,* 462 U.S. 611, 622 n.11, 103 S. Ct. 2591, 77 L. Ed. 2d 46 (1983); *see also Pescatore v. PAN AM*, 97 F.3d 1, 12 (2d Cir. 1996) (stating that "the FSIA thereby operates as a 'pass-through' to state law principles"). Thus, "[a]s a general rule, state law should provide a cause of action against a foreign nation in a section 1605(a)(7) claim [under the Tortious Act Exception]." *Damarrell v. Islamic Republic of Iran,* 2005 U.S. Dist. LEXIS 5343, at *55 (D.D.C. 2005). Therefore, to determine the applicability of the tortious act exception, we must consider the elements of the exception, applying Kentucky state law where applicable.[8]

---

8 As noted above, the class representatives all resided in the state of Kentucky at the time of the alleged abuse. "[I]n FSIA cases, we use the forum state's choice of law rules to resolve

However, the choice of law inquiry is complicated by the fact that the case before is us is a class action suit. Under *Phillips Petroleum Co. v. Shutts*, 472 U.S. 797, 105 S. Ct. 2965, 86 L. Ed. 2d 628 (1985), due process requirements apply to nationwide class action lawsuits, requiring courts to engage in individualized choice of law analysis for each plaintiff's claims and not just named plaintiffs. *Id.* at 822–23.

But the individualized choice of law analysis is only necessary once the class seeks certification. While the class remains a putative class, courts focus on the application of the forum's choice of law rules to the named plaintiffs. *Cunningham v. PFL Life Ins. Co.*, 42 F. Supp. 2d 872, 883 (N.D. Iowa 1999) ("[I]t is important to note that at this point in the litigation, the Court has not certified the Plaintiffs as class representatives. Accordingly, the Court will not make a choice of law determination that will bind the putative class in this Order. This Order only contemplates the claims of the named Plaintiffs . . . ."); *cf. Rakes v. Life Investors Ins. Co. of Am.*, 2007 U.S. Dist. LEXIS 52719, at *33 (N.D. Iowa July 20, 2007) ("[I]n the case at bar the court has not yet certified Plaintiffs as class representatives. Therefore, nothing in this order may be construed as a non-individualized choice-of-law determination that binds all 150,000 putative members of the Class."). We, in the instant case, need not engage in such an individualized choice of law analysis because plaintiffs have not yet sought certification.

i. Elements of the Tortious Act Exception

(a) "Occurring in the United States"

"Section 1605(a)(5) is limited by its terms . . . to those cases in which the damage to or loss of property occurs in the United States." *Amerada Hess Shipping Corp.*, 488 U.S. at 439 (emphasis omitted). Thus, in contrast to the commercial activity exception, a tortious act having "direct effects" in the United States will not satisfy the requirements of the tortious activity exception. *Id.* at 441. Courts in both the Second and D.C. Circuits have interpreted this requirement to mean that the "entire tort" must occur in the United States. *See, e.g., Asociacion de Reclamantes v. United Mexican States*, 237 U.S. App. D.C. 81, 735 F.2d 1517, 1524–25 (D.C. Cir. 1984) (rejecting application of the tortious activity exception because "the entire tort would not have occurred [in the United States]"); *Kline v. Kaneko*, 685 F. Supp. 386, 391 (S.D.N.Y. 1988) ("If the non-commercial tort exception is to apply, the entire tort must be committed in the United States."); *see also Burnett v. Al Baraka Inv. & Dev. Corp. (In re Terrorist Attacks),* 349 F. Supp. 2d 765, 795

'all issues,' except jurisdictional ones." *Karaha Bodas Co. v. Perusahaan Pertambangan Minyak Dan Gas Bumi Negara*, 313 F.3d 70, 85 (2d Cir. 2002). According to Kentucky's choice of law rules, Kentucky law would apply where Kentucky is the state where the relevant acts or omissions occurred. *See, e.g., Vaughn v. United States*, 1997 U.S. App. LEXIS 35795, at *9 n.2 (6th Cir. Dec. 16, 1997) (applying Kentucky law in a case arising under the Federal Tort Claims Act).

(S.D.N.Y. 2005) (collecting Second Circuit cases). *But see Olsen v. Gov't of Mexico*, 729 F.2d 641, 646 (9th Cir. 1984) (abrogated on other grounds by *Joseph v. Office of Consulate Gen. of Nig.*, 830 F.2d 1018, 1026 (1987)) ("[I]f plaintiffs allege at least one entire tort occurring in the United States, they may claim under section 1605(a)(5).").

We join the Second and D.C. Circuits in concluding that in order to apply the tortious act exception, the "entire tort" must occur in the United States. This position finds support in the Supreme Court's decision in *Amerada Hess Shipping*: "the exception in § 1605(a)(5) covers only torts occurring within the territorial jurisdiction of the United States." 488 U.S. at 441. Moreover, the purpose of the tortious activity exception is limited: "Congress' primary purpose in enacting § 1605(a)(5) was to eliminate a foreign state's immunity for traffic accidents and other torts committed in the United States, for which liability is imposed under domestic tort law." *Id.* at 439–40 (citing H.R. Rep., at 14). Thus, it seems most in keeping with both Supreme Court precedent and the purposes of the FSIA to grant subject matter jurisdiction under the tortious activity exception only to torts which were entirely committed within the United States.

(b) Caused by an Act or Omission

In Kentucky, "[l]iability for a negligent act follows a finding of proximate or legal cause," which is defined as "a finding of causation in fact, i.e., substantial cause, and the absence of a public policy rule of law which prohibits the imposition of liability." *Deutsch v. Shein*, 597 S.W.2d 141, 143–44 (Ky. 1980). "In order to be a legal cause of another's harm, it is not enough that the harm would not have occurred had the actor not been negligent. . . . The negligence must also be a substantial factor in bringing about the plaintiff's harm." *Id.* (quoting Restatement of Torts (Second) § 431, cmt. a).

(c) Official or Employee of a Foreign State

Kentucky law appears to have adopted the Restatement (Third) of Agency § 7.07 definition of employee when addressing claims of vicarious liability: "an employee is an agent whose principal controls or has the right to control the manner and means of the agent's performance of work . . . ." *Papa John's Int'l, Inc. v. McCoy*, 244 S.W.3d 44, 2008 Ky. LEXIS 16, at *16 (Ky. 2008) (quoting Restatement (Third) of Agency § 7.07).[9] In addition, "the fact that work is performed gratuitously does not relieve a principal of liability." *Id.*

---

9 The Holy See contends that plaintiffs failed to identify specifically which clergy engaged in the relevant tortious conduct. As a result, the Holy See seizes upon the language in the complaint which names the "Louisville Corporation" as one of the agents of the Holy See having engaged in the tortious conduct; in turn, the Holy See argues that all of the allegations in the complaint can only be analyzed interms of the actions of the Louisville Corporation. And, the Holy See believes that corporate law prevents holding it liable for the actions of another corporate entity. However, this analysis begins with a faulty premise. Plaintiffs pled repeatedly

(d) Scope of Employment

"State law, not federal common law, governs whether an officer's or employee's action is within the scope of employment in determining the applicability of the FSIA." *Moran v. Kingdom of Saudi Arabia,* 27 F.3d 169, 173 (5th Cir. 1994) (applying Mississippi law) (citing *First Nat'l City Bank v. Banco Para el Comercio Exterior de Cuba,* 462 U.S. 611, 622 n.11, 103 S. Ct. 2591, 77 L. Ed. 2d 46 (1983)); *see also, e.g.,* Doe, 434 F. Supp. 2d at 944 (applying Oregon law); *Robinson v. Gov't of Malay.,* 269 F.3d 133, 145 (2d Cir. 2001) (applying New York law); *Randolph v. Budget Rent-A-Car,* 97 F.3d 319, 326–27 (9th Cir. 1996) (applying California law). Because the conduct alleged by the named plaintiffs occurred in Kentucky, Kentucky law applies to the instant case.

Under Kentucky law, for alleged conduct to be considered within the scope of employment "the conduct must be of the same general nature as that authorized or incidental to the conduct authorized." *Osborne v. Payne*, 31 S.W.3d 911, 915 (Ky. 2000). Thus, "[u]nder the doctrine of respondeat superior, an employer can be held vicariously liable for an employee's tortious actions if committed in the scope of his or her employment." *Papa John's Int'l*, 244 S.W.3d 44, 2008 Ky. LEXIS 16, at *28–*29. "In the area of intentional torts, the focus is consistently on the purpose or motive of the employee in determining whether he or she was acting within the scope of employment." *Id.* at *29. However, "[a] principal is not liable under the doctrine of respondeat superior unless the intentional wrongs of the agent were calculated to advance the cause of the principal or were appropriate to the normal scope of the operator's employment." *Osborne*, 31 S.W.3d at 915. Applying these principles, the Kentucky Supreme Court ruled that a priest's adulterous conduct could not be considered within the scope of his employment, even though the underlying conduct was intentional. *Osborne*, 31 S.W.3d at 915.

ii. Exceptions to the Tortious Act Exception

(a) Discretionary Function Exception to the Tortious Act Exception

The FSIA does not define "discretionary functions." To interpret the FSIA's discretionary function exception, courts typically apply the interpretation of the discretionary function exception of the Federal Tort Claims Act (the "FTCA"), because "[n]ot only does the language of the FSIA discretionary function exception replicate that of the [FTCA], 28 U.S.C. § 2680(a), but the legislative history

---

that the tortious acts of which they complain were also committed by priests, clerics, bishops, archbishops, cardinals, agents and employees. General allegations against employees are sufficient for the purposes of notice pleading: "a complaint that generally alleges an employer's negligence need not specifically identify each employee involved to hold the employer liable under respondeat superior." *Cornejo-Ramirez v. James G. Garcia, Inc.*, 2000 U.S. Dist. LEXIS 20064, at *13 (D. Ariz. 2000) (also noting "[t]he court is required to examine Plaintiffs' complaint under the standard set forth in Fed R. Civ. P. 8(f) that 'all pleading shall be so construed as to do substantial justice'").

of the FSIA, in explaining section 1605(a)(5)(A), directs us to the FTCA." *Olsen*, 729 F.2d at 646 (citing H.R. Rep. at 21); *see also Rodriguez v. Republic of Costa Rica*, 297 F.3d 1, 8 (1st Cir. 2002); *Office of Consulate Gen. of Nig.*, 830 F.2d at 1026 (9th Cir. 1987).

In determining whether particular conduct falls under the FTCA's, and in turn under the FSIA's, discretionary function exception, courts apply the two part *Berkovitz* test:

> The first inquiry is whether the challenged action involved an element of choice or judgment, for it is clear that the exception "will not apply when a federal statute, regulation, or policy specifically prescribes a course of action for an employee to follow." If choice or judgment is exercised, the second inquiry is whether that choice or judgment is of the type Congress intended to exclude from liability - that is, whether the choice or judgment was one involving social, economic or political policy.

Vickers v. United States, 228 F.3d 944, 949 (9th Cir. 2000) (internal citations omitted) (quoting *Berkovitz v. United States*, 486 U.S. 531, 536, 108 S. Ct. 1954, 100 L. Ed. 2d 531 (1988)); *Rodriguez*, 297 F.3d at 9 (applying the two-part *Berkovitz* test to the FSIA's discretionary function exception). The Supreme Court in *Berkovitz* explained the rationale behind the discretionary function exception:

> The basis for the discretionary function exception was Congress' desire to prevent judicial 'second-guessing' of legislative and administrative decisions grounded in social, economic, and political policy through the medium of an action in tort. The exception, properly construed, therefore protects only governmental actions and decisions based on considerations of public policy.

Berkovitz, 486 U.S. at 536–37 (internal quotation marks and citation omitted).

A number of courts have applied the *Berkovitz* test to cases of negligent hiring, concluding that the selection of employees, officials and officers typically falls within the scope of the FTCA's discretionary function exception. *See, e.g., United States v. Gaubert*, 499 U.S. 315, 332–34, 111 S. Ct. 1267, 113 L. Ed. 2d 335 (1991) (finding that the negligent selection of directors and officers falls squarely under the FTCA's discretionary function exception); *Burkhart v. Washington Metro. Area Transit Auth.*, 324 U.S. App. D.C. 241, 112 F.3d 1207, 1217 (D.C. Cir. 1997) ("The hiring, training, and supervision choices that [the defendant] faces are choices susceptible to policy judgment. The hiring decisions of a public entity require consideration of numerous factors, including budgetary constraints, public perception, economic conditions, individual backgrounds, office diversity, experience and employer intuition." (internal quotation marks and citation omitted)); *Tonelli v. United States*, 60 F.3d 492, 496 (8th Cir. 1995) ("The post office's choice between several potential employees involves the weighing of individual backgrounds, office diversity, experience and employer intuition. These multi-factored choices require the balancing of competing objectives, and are of the nature and quality that Congress intended to shield from tort liability." (internal quotation marks and citation omitted)); *cf. Carlyle v. United States, Dep't of Army*, 674 F.2d 554, 557 (6th Cir. 1982) ("Any decision to supervise [army recruits] only by means of letters and not to place personnel in the Hotel was a discretionary function and outside federal jurisdiction.").

(b) Arising Out of Misrepresentation or Deceit Exceptions to the Tortious Act Exception

The scope of the misrepresentation or deceit exception to the tortious act exception is an unsettled matter. Courts generally have looked to the definition of misrepresentation in the FTCA as a guide for defining the term under the FSIA, relying on the legislative history of the FSIA for such comparison. *See, e.g., Cabiri v. Gov't of the Republic of Ghana,* 165 F.3d 193, 200 n.4 (2d Cir. 1999) ("The FSIA House Report provides that 'the exceptions provided in subparagraph[] . . . (B) of section 1605(a)(5) correspond to many of the claims with respect to which the U.S. Government retains immunity under the [FTCA], 28 U.S.C. 2680(a) and (h).") (quoting H.R. Rep. at 21); *see also De Sanchez v. Banco Central de Nicar.*, 770 F.2d 1385, 1398 (5th Cir. 1985).

In addition, both the Second and Ninth Circuits have dismissed claims against foreign sovereigns where the foreign sovereign allegedly provided false or misleading information regarding the whereabouts of the plaintiffs' relatives. *See Cabiri*, 165 F.3d 193, 200 (dismissing claim "for emotional injury caused by the refusal of a foreign state, however nefarious, to give its citizens in the United States full or truthful information concerning its operations"); *Kozorowski v. Russian Fed'n*, No. 93-16388, 1997 U.S. App. LEXIS 26266 (9th Cir. Sept. 19, 1997) (dismissing claims of intentional infliction of emotional distress, fraud and deceit, conspiracy and other claims because they were premised on the Soviet Union's failure to disclose its role in the 1940 massacre of Polish soldiers and therefore arose out of misrepresentation and deceit).

iii. Application of the Tortious Act Exception to the Instant Case

The difficulty in applying the elements of the tortious act exception to plaintiffs' complaint is the manner in which plaintiffs have pled their claims. In their complaint, plaintiffs advance the following claims: violation of customary international law of human rights, negligence, breach of fiduciary duty, tort of outrage/infliction of emotional distress, deceit and misrepresentation.[10] In each of their claims, plaintiffs base their theories of liability not only on the actions of the Holy See itself, but also on the acts of the Holy See's agents and employees. As a result, we must analyze each claim to see not only which claims survive, but which *parts* of each claim survive.

---

10 *See supra*, n.1.

Looking first to the fourth requirement for the application of the tortious act exception, the Kentucky Supreme Court's holding in *Osborne*, 31 S.W.3d at 915, leads to the inescapable conclusion that the alleged acts of sexual abuse were not done while the alleged tortfeasors were acting within the scope of their employment. Thus, the tortious act exception to the FSIA's grant of immunity cannot apply to permit suit against the Holy See for sexual abuse by its clergy, even if the other requirements for its application are met.

Furthermore, as per the FSIA's explicit terms, in order for the tortious act exception to apply, the tortious acts in question must have occurred in the United States. Therefore, any portion of plaintiffs' claims that relies upon acts committed by the Holy See abroad cannot survive. For example, the tortious act exception to the FSIA's grant of immunity would not include any theory of liability premised on the Holy See's own negligent supervision because such acts presumably occurred abroad; moreover, a direct claim leveled against the Holy See for promulgating the 1962 Policy would not fall within the tortious act exception because it too presumably occurred abroad. In turn, plaintiffs cannot pursue claims based upon the alleged sexual abuse of priests or based upon the acts of the Holy See that occurred abroad.[11]

These conclusions are not wholly dispositive, however, of the claims against the Holy See. As noted before, plaintiffs' claims are not based solely on the conduct of the Holy See itself or the allegedly abusive conduct of priests. All of plaintiffs' claims also advance theories of liability premised on the conduct of Holy See employees in the United States engaged in the supervision of the allegedly abusive priests. These portions of plaintiffs' claims meet the four requirements for application of the tortious act exception.

First and contrary to the Holy See's protestations, plaintiffs have pled both that the relevant archbishops, bishops and other Holy See personnel had knowledge of the alleged sexual abuse of priests and that they failed to act on that knowledge. In doing so, it would seem that the complaint also pleads that conduct of the archbishops, bishops and other Holy See personnel were a substantial factor in causing plaintiffs' damages, satisfying Kentucky's causation requirements.

In addition, and as already noted, tortious acts committed by bishops, archbishops and other Holy See personnel while engaged in the supervision of allegedly abusive priests satisfy the requirements of the FSIA's tortious act exception that the tortious act occur in the United States and within the scope of employment.

---

11 Plaintiffs appear to have agreed with these applications of the tortious act exception: "The Plaintiffs do not seek to hold the Defendant vicariously liable for the acts of its priests; rather, they seekto hold the Defendant vicariously liable for the acts of its bishops and archbishops who, following the directives of the Defendant, permitted childhood sexual abuse to occur." Indeed, the alleged torts committed by the bishops and archbishops occurred entirely within the United States. Moreover, complying with the alleged 1962 Policy would fall within the scope of the bishops' and archbishops' employment.

Also, for the conduct of bishops and archbishops and other Holy See personnel to serve as a basis for jurisdiction under the tortious act exception, these bishops, archbishops and Holy See personnel must have been employees of the Holy See. As noted above, under Kentucky law, this inquiry focuses on the degree of control exercised by the employer over the individual or individuals in question. In their complaint, plaintiffs allege facts that demonstrate that the Holy See exercised a significant degree of control over the bishops and archbishops accused of having committed the tortious acts in question. Taking these allegations as true, plaintiffs have sufficiently pled the employee element of the tortious activity exception.[12]

Thus, the portions of plaintiffs' claims that are based upon the conduct of bishops, archbishops and Holy See personnel while supervising allegedly abusive clergy satisfy all four requirements of the tortious act exception: this conduct served as a substantial cause of the alleged abuse; the conduct occurred in the United States; the conduct was within the scope of employment; and these individuals were, according to the pleadings, Holy See employees.

However, although the four requirements are met for these claims, we must still consider whether either of the two exceptions to the tortious act exception applies and prevents its application: the discretionary-function exception and the arising-out-of misrepresentation-or-deceit exception.

According to the allegations in plaintiffs' complaint, theories of liability premised upon the supervision of the allegedly abusive clergy do not implicate the discretionary function exception to the tortious act exception because the terms of the supervision were not discretionary. According to the complaint, the 1962 Policy "impose[d] the highest level of secrecy on the handling of clergy sexual abuse matters." Plaintiffs contend that this required secrecy prohibited Holy See personnel from, among other things, reporting childhood sexual abuse to government authorities. *Id.* Thus, following the 1962 Policy cannot, on the pleadings in plaintiffs' complaint, be deemed discretionary. We now apply these general conclusions to each of the plaintiffs' remaining claims.[13]

1) **Violation of Customary International Law of Human Rights** (Class I Claim II, Class II Claim I): Plaintiffs plead this claim against the Holy See itself, stating that

> [t]he instructions, mandates and dictates of the Defendant, Holy See in the United States prohibiting the disclosure of the identity and existence of pedophiles and sexual predators under its control, thereby placing children in a position of peril, is a gross violation of well-established, universally recognized norms of international law of human rights.

---

12 As noted above, the district court also correctly employed the FSIA burden-shifting analysis in connection with this inquiry.

13 *See supra* n.1.

This claim does not survive against the Holy See as it pertains to the actual promulgation of the 1962 Policy because the promulgation itself occurred abroad. However, this claim does survive against the Holy See as it pertains to the conduct of its employees who, pursuant to the 1962 Policy, violated the terms of the relevant international laws through their tortious supervisory conduct over the allegedly abusive clergy.

2) **Negligence** (Class I Claim III, Class II Claim II): Plaintiffs present three grounds for negligence in their complaint: failure to provide "safe care"; failure to "warn"; and failure to report. The failure to warn and failure to report prongs of the negligence claim survive because they are premised on the conduct of Holy See employees who were allegedly negligent in their supervision of abusive clergy. However, the claims of negligence against the Holy See for its own conduct cannot survive because such negligence would not have occurred in the United States. Furthermore, the claim of failure to provide safe care does not survive. As the district court noted, the failure to provide safe care amounts to a claim for negligent hiring. *O'Bryan II*, 471 F. Supp 2d at 793. And, as outlined above, claims of negligent hiring fall within the discretionary function exception. Indeed, the 1962 Policy, even according to plaintiffs' allegations, only required Holy See employees not to disclose information regarding sexual misconduct, not to actually hire individuals who had engaged in prior sexual misconduct.

3) **Breach of Fiduciary Duty** (Class I Claim IV, Class II Claim III): Plaintiffs plead this claim against the Holy See itself, stating that "a special legal relationship existed between the Plaintiffs and the Defendant Holy See, in the nature of a fiduciary relationship, which was carried out by and through priests, clerics, and administrators under the absolute control of the Defendant . . . ." In turn, plaintiffs contend that the "Defendant breached fiduciary duties owed to the Plaintiffs," premised upon the "duty to warn parents" and the "duty to report known or suspected perpetrators. This claim survives against the Holy See for the actions of its supervising employees occurring in the United States. As has already been emphasized, the claim cannot survive against the Holy See itself for its own failures to warn or report because such tortious conduct would have occurred abroad.

4) **Tort of Outrage/Infliction of Emotional Distress** (Class I Claim V, Class II Claim IV): Plaintiffs plead this claim against the Holy See itself, stating:

> The acts and omissions of the Defendant, Holy See alleged herein, including the concealment of its policy of harboring and protecting its abusive priests, agents and employees from public disclosure and prosecution and directives prohibiting the reporting of child sexual abuse to authorities . . . is conduct which is so outrageous and extreme in degree, as to go beyond all possible bounds of decency, so as to be regarded as utterly atrocious in a civilized society.

This claim cannot survive against the Holy See as it pertains to the actual promulgation of the 1962 Policy because the promulgation itself occurred abroad. In addition, it cannot survive against the Holy See for the conduct of its allegedly abusive priests because the acts of alleged abuse did not occur within the scope of employment. In contrast, this claim does survive against the Holy See as it pertains to the conduct of its employees who, pursuant to the 1962 Policy, violated the terms of the relevant international laws through their tortious supervisory conduct over the allegedly abusive clergy.[14]

We next turn to considering whether the surviving theories of liability, as outlined above, are precluded by the other exception to the tortious act exception: whether they arise out of misrepresentation or deceit.

In contrast to *Cabiri* and *Kozorowski*, plaintiffs' claims are not best characterized as stemming directly from the misinformation disseminated by the Holy See. Instead, plaintiffs' claims are more akin to claims of negligent supervision as employees of the Holy See are alleged to have provided inadequate supervision over those under its care. In this way, these claims resemble other negligent supervision claims more than they resemble claims brought by the plaintiffs in *Cabiri* and *Kozorowski*. *See, e.g., Williams v. Ky. Dep't of Educ.*, 113 S.W.3d 145, 148 (Ky. 2003) (addressing claims of negligent supervision on the part of high school faculty which resulted in the death of a student and noting that "[i]t is well established in this jurisdiction that a school teacher can be held liable for injuries caused by negligent supervision of his/her students"); *see also Yanero v. Davis,* 65 S.W.3d 510, 528–31 (Ky. 2001); *Nelson v. Turner,* No. 2007CA-000489-MR, 256 S.W.3d 37, 2008 Ky. App. LEXIS 177 (Ky. Ct. App. June 6, 2008). We therefore conclude that, at this stage of the litigation, the plaintiffs' claims of violation of customary international law of human rights, negligence, and breach of fiduciary duty should not be dismissed for "arising out of . . . misrepresentation [or] deceit." *See* 28 U.S.C. § 1605(a)(5)(B). We do however dismiss the last two claims advanced by plaintiffs in their complaint (Class I Claims VI and VII, Class II Claims V and VI) as they do arise out of misrepresentation or deceit.[15]

---

14 It also appears that the plaintiffs have abandoned this claim by stating in their response to the Holy See's motion to dismiss "[t]he Plaintiffs' complaint also identifies claims for intentional infliction of emotional distress . . . . Plaintiffs are no longer pursuing those claims." (Plaintiffs' Response to the Holy See's Motion to Dismiss at 6 n.9).

15 In addition, plaintiffs' complaint states that it pursues these claims against the Holy See "in its capacity as an Unincorporated Association and Head of an International Religious Organization Only." As a result, because we have determined above that the Holy See cannot be sued in such a capacity, these claims would appear to no longer be relevant. Moreover, plaintiffs admit as much in their Response to the Holy See's motion to dismiss. Plaintiffs' Response to the Holy See's Motion to Dismiss at 6 n.9 (stating that "the complaint alleges claims for deceit . . . and misrepresentation . . . . Those latter causes of action were expressly brought against the Defendant only in its capacity as an unincorporated association and head of an international religious organization. In light of the [district] Court's previous ruling that such capacity does not apply here, those claims are no longer at issue).

In conclusion, we also note that we believe the foregoing analysis to be consistent with the analysis of the district court in *O'Bryan II*.

VII.

For the foregoing reasons, we affirm the district court's partial grant of defendant's motion to dismiss.

THE PRESBYTERIAN CHURCH OF SUDAN
v.
TALISMAN ENERGY, INC.

582 F.3d 244 (2d Cir. 2009)
Decided October 2, 2009

Paul L. Hoffman, Schonbrun DeSimone Seplow Harris & Hoffman, Venice, CA, (Adrienne J. Quarry, Schonbrun DeSimone Seplow Harris & Hoffman, Venice, CA; Carey D'Avino, Stephen Whinston, and Keino Robinson, Berger & Montague, P.C., Philadelphia, PA; Lawrence Kill, John O'Connor, and Stanley Bowker, Anderson Kill & Olick, P.C., New York, NY; Daniel E. Seltz, Steven E. Fineman, and Rachel Geman, Lieff, Cabraser, Heimann & Bernstein, LLP, New York, NY, on the brief), for Plaintiffs-Appellants.

Marc J. Gottridge (Joseph P. Cyr, Scott W. Reynolds, Andrew M. Behrman, on the brief), Lovells, New York, NY, for Defendant-Appellee.

Ralph Steinhardt, Professor of Law, George Washington University Law School, Washington, DC, (William J. Aceves, Professor of Law, California Western School of Law, San Diego, CA, on the brief) for Amici Curiae International Law Scholars in Support of Appellants.

Richard L. Herz (Marco B. Simons, on the brief), Earthrights International, Washington, DC, for Amicus Curiae Earthrights International in Support of Plaintiffs-Appellants and Reversal.

Judith Brown Chomsky and Michael Poulshock, Law Office of Judith Brown Chomsky, Elkins Park, PA, and Jennifer M. Green and Katherine Gallagher, Center for Constitutional Rights, New York, NY, for Amicus Curiae on Civil Conspiracy and Joint Criminal Enterprise in Support of Plaintiffs-Appellants and in Support of Reversal of the District Court's Opinion.

Terrence P. Collingsworth, Derek Baxter, and Natacha Thys, International Labor Rights Fund, Washington, DC, for Amicus Curiae International Labor Rights Fund in Support of Plaintiffs-Appellants.

Mark Diamond, Counsel for Amici Curaie, New York, NY, for Amici Curiae Lexiuste Cajuste, Neris Gonzalez, Zenaida Velásquez Rodriguez, and Francisco Calderon in Support of Plaintiffs-Appellants Urging Reversal.

Renee C. Redman, Legal Director, American Civil Liberties Union Foundation of Connecticut, Hartford, CT, for Amici Curiae Canadian Parliamentarians in Support of the Appellants.

Jonathan W. Cuneo and R. Brent Walton, Cuneo Gilbert & LaDuca, LLP, Washington, DC, for Amici Curiae The Rt. Reverand Keith L. Ackerman, SSC, Bishop, Diocese of Quincy, the Episcopal Church; Christian Solidarity International-USA; Coalition for the Defense of Human Rights; Family Research Council; Institute on Religion & Democracy; Renew Network; Servant's Heart; Sudan Advocacy Action Forum; Sudan Sunrise; and Trinity Presbytery's Sudan Ministry in Support of Appellants.

Lewis S. Yelin, Attorney, Appellate Staff, Civil Division, U.S. Department of Justice, Washington, DC, (Michael J. Garcia, United States Attorney, and David S. Jones, Assistant United States Attorney, Southern District of New York, New York, NY, John B. Bellinger III, Legal Advisor, Department of State, Washington, DC, Jeffrey S. Bucholtz, Acting Assistant Attorney General, and Douglas N. Letter and Robert M. Loeb, Attorneys, Appellate Staff, Civil Division, U.S. Department of Justice, Washington, DC, on the brief), for Amicus Curiae United States.

Samuel Estreicher, NYU School of Law, New York, NY, (Michael D. Ramsey, University of San Diego School of Law, San Diego, CA on the brief), for Amici Curiae Professors of International Law, Federal Jurisdiction and the Foreign Relations Law of the United States in Support of Defendant-Appellee.

Karen M. Asner and Milana Salzman, White & Case LLP, New York, NY, for Amicus Curiae the Government of Canada in Support of Dismissal of the Underlying Action.

Robin S. Conrad and Amar D. Sarwal, National Chamber Litigation Center, Inc., Washington, DC, and John Townsend Rich, Paul R. Friedman, and William F. Sheehan, Goodwin Proctor LLP, Washington, DC, for Amicus Curiae the Chamber of Commerce of the United States of America in Support of Defendant-Appellee Talisman Energy, Inc. and in Support of Affirmance.

Daniel J. Popeo and Richard A. Samp, Washington Legal Foundation, Washington, DC, for Amici Curiae Washington Legal Foundation and Allied Educational Foundation in Support of Defendant/Appellee, Urging Affirmance.

James J. Dillon, Foley Hoag LLP, Boston, MA, Janet Walker, Professor of Law, Osgood Hall Law School of York University, Toronto, Ontario, Canada, and H. Scott Fairley, Theall Group LLP, Toronto, Ontario, Canada, for Amici Curiae the Canadian Chamber of Commerce; the Mining Association of Canada; the Canadian Association of Petroleum Producers; and the Prospectors and Developers Association of Canada in Support of Defendant-Appellee.

James J. Dillon, Foley Hoag LLP, Boston, MA, for Amici Curiae The National Foreign Trade Council; The Independent Petroleum Association of America; and The United States Council for International Business in Support of Defendant-Appellee.

Christopher Greenwood, CMG, QC, Essex Court Chambers, London, United Kingdom, for Amicus Curiae Professor Christopher Greenwood, CMG, QC, in Support of Defendant-Appellee.

James Crawford, Whewell Professor of International Law, University of Cambridge, Cambridge, United Kingdom, for Amicus Curiae Professor James Crawford in Support of Defendant-Appellee.

Before: JACOBS, Chief Judge, LEVAL and CABRANES, Circuit Judges.

DENNIS JACOBS, Chief Judge:

Plaintiffs-Appellants are Sudanese who allege that they are victims of human rights abuses committed by the Government of the Sudan in Khartoum ("the Government") and that Talisman Energy, Inc. ("Talisman"), a Canadian corporation, aided and abetted or conspired with the Government to advance those abuses that facilitated the development of Sudanese oil concessions by Talisman affiliates. Plaintiffs appeal from a judgment of the United States District Court for the Southern District of New York (Cote, *J.*) dismissing their claims under the Alien Tort Statute ("ATS"), 28 U.S.C. § 1350.

We hold that under the principles articulated by the United States Supreme Court in *Sosa v. Alvarez-Machain,* 542 U.S. 692, 124 S. Ct. 2739, 159 L.Ed.2d 718 (2004), the standard for imposing accessorial liability under the ATS must be drawn from international law; and that under international law, a claimant must show that the defendant provided substantial assistance with the purpose of facilitating the alleged offenses. Applying that standard, we affirm the district court's grant of summary judgment in favor of Talisman, because plaintiffs presented no evidence that the company acted with the purpose of harming civilians living in southern Sudan.

It becomes necessary to set out at some length the background of the hostilities in the Sudan; the history of the oil enterprise, its facilities and corporate structure; the security measures taken by the enterprise and by the Government; the injuries and persecutions alleged; and the extent and nature of Talisman's connection to the human rights abuses.

BACKGROUND

A. Civil War in the Sudan

At the time Sudan obtained its independence from Britain and Egypt in 1956, civil war broke out between the Arab-dominated Islamic regime in the north, and the non-Muslim African population in the south.[1] In 1972, the two sides reached a power-sharing agreement in Addis Ababa, Ethiopia, after which relative stability ensued until an anti-Government uprising in 1983.

In 1991, southern rebels fractured, and the factions fought the Government and each other, with large-scale displacement and death among civilians.

In April 1997, the Government signed the Khartoum Peace Agreement ("KPA") with several (but not all) of the southern rebel groups. The KPA provided for religious freedom, a cease-fire, sharing of resources and power between the north and south, creation of a "Coordinating Council" of factions in southern Sudan, and the consolidation of most of the rebel militias into the South Sudan Defense Force ("SSDF"), which was aligned with the Government, but with a measure of autonomy and control in the south. The benefits of this agreement were short-lived: the SSDF split into warring factions by 1998, and competing militia groups continued fighting each other and the Government. This violence continued throughout the time that Talisman operated in the Sudan.

B. Oil Development in the Sudan

After Chevron discovered oil in southern Sudan in 1979, the Government granted development rights to foreign companies for six numbered "blocks."

In August 1993, a Canadian company named State Petroleum Company ("SPC") purchased the rights to develop blocks 1, 2, and 4. In 1994, SPC was acquired by, and became a wholly owned subsidiary of, another Canadian company, Arakis Energy Corporation ("Arakis").

In December 1996, SPC formed a consortium with three other companies: China National Petroleum Corporation ("CNPC"), Petronas Carigali Overseas SDN BHD ("Petronas"), and Sudapet, Ltd. ("Sudapet") (collectively "the Consortium"), which were wholly owned by China, Malaysia, and the Republic of the Sudan, respectively. The Consortium members signed agreements among themselves and with the Government concerning oil exploration, production, and development, as well as the construction of a pipeline from the Consortium's concession area to the Red Sea. More than half of the Consortium's profits accrued to the Government.

The Consortium members conducted operations through a Mauritius corporation, called the Greater Nile Petroleum Operating Company Limited ("GNPOC"), which was owned 40% by CNPC, 30% by Petronas, 25% by SPC, and 5% by Sudapet.

---

1 The facts are set forth in detail in the district court's summary judgment decision. *See Presbyterian Church of Sudan v. Talisman Energy, Inc.*, 453 F. Supp. 2d 633, 641–61 (S.D.N.Y.2006). We recount only those facts that bear upon the disposition of the appellate issues.

C. Talisman's Purchase of Arakis

In October 1998, Talisman acquired Arakis and its 25% stake in GNPOC. The purchase of Arakis was effectuated through Talisman's indirect subsidiary, State Petroleum Corporation B.V., which was later renamed "Talisman (Greater Nile) B.V." ("Greater Nile") on December 10, 1998. Greater Nile was a wholly-owned subsidiary of Goal Olie-en-Gasexploratie B.V., which at the time was wholly owned by British companies. The British companies were wholly owned subsidiaries of Talisman Energy (UK) Limited, which was a direct and wholly owned subsidiary of Talisman.

Before purchasing Arakis, Talisman engaged in several months of due diligence: meetings between senior Talisman executives and governmental and security officials in the Sudan; conversations with GNPOC employees and visits to GNPOC development sites; reports on security conditions in the country; round-table discussions in Canada with representatives of non-governmental organizations, church groups, and other stakeholders; and consultations with representatives of the British government, which controlled the Sudan in condominium with Egypt from 1899 to 1956.

Among their many meetings, Talisman CEO Jim Buckee and other Talisman officers met with Riek Machar ("Machar"), then the First Assistant to the President of the Sudan and head of the Southern Sudan Coordinating Council ("SSCC") and the SSDF. Sudanese officials, including Machar and Unity State Governor Taban Deng Gai, provided assurances concerning safety, security, and peace.

Robert Norton, the head of security for Arakis in the Sudan from 1994 to 1998, advised Talisman that the oil fields were protected both by the military and by Government-sponsored militias. Norton opined that, though Talisman's assistance would greatly advance oil exploration, it would tip the military balance in favor of the Government. Norton believed that Talisman should not invest in the Sudan.

A representative of Freedom Quest International also discouraged Talisman from investing in the Sudan, warning senior Talisman officials that GNPOC and the Government used the Sudanese military to expel civilian populations from villages in order to create a *"cordon sanitaire"* ("buffer zone") around oil fields.

D. Security Arrangements for GNPOC

Because GNPOC's operations took place amidst civil war, security arrangements were made for Consortium personnel in coordination with the Government and military forces. Plaintiffs contend that these arrangements resulted in the persecution of civilians living in or near the oil concession areas.

In May 1999, GNPOC and the Government built all-weather roads traversing the oil concession areas and linking the concessions to military bases. To protect GNPOC's employees and equipment, these roads served the dual purposes of moving personnel for oil operations and facilitating military activities. According to plaintiffs, these roads enabled the military to operate year-round in areas prone to seasonal flooding, enhancing the military's ability to launch attacks.

In 1999–2000, GNPOC upgraded two airstrips in the concessions—Heglig and Unity—for the safety and convenience of GNPOC personnel. The improvements also had the effect of supporting military activity, because the Government began using the airstrips to supply troops, take defensive action, and initiate offensive attacks.

Heglig, in particular, was used extensively by the military. Talisman employees saw outgoing flights by helicopter gunships and Antonov bombers. One Talisman security advisor observed 500-pound bombs being loaded on Government-owned Antonov bombers at Heglig and regular bombing runs from the airstrip. At both Heglig and Unity, GNPOC personnel refueled military aircraft, sometimes with GNPOC's own fuel.

During the time that Greater Nile was a member of the Consortium, it employed former soldiers as security advisors who traveled throughout the concession areas, coordinated with Mohammed Mokhtar (the former Sudanese Army colonel who served as head of GNPOC security), and wrote detailed reports for senior Talisman officials.[2]

Talisman CEO Buckee was aware of the military's activities from GNPOC airstrips. In February 2001, he wrote to Sudanese Minister of National Defense Major General Bakri Hassan Saleh urging restraint in the Government's military activities and warning that whatever "the military objectives may be, the bombings are [universally] construed as violations of international humanitarian law." Greater Nile employees expressed concern to Mokhtar and Government officials about bombers and helicopter gunships using the airstrips.

Notwithstanding occasional breaks, the military continued to use the facilities. After a missile attack on the Heglig facility in August 2001, Buckee dropped his objection to the presence of helicopter gunships, and a Greater Nile security officer wrote to the Government emphasizing the need for security at GNPOC's facilities.

E. Buffer Zone Strategy

At the heart of plaintiffs' complaint is the allegation that the Government created a "buffer zone" around GNPOC facilities by clearing the civilian population to secure areas for exploration. Witness testimony and internal Talisman reports show evidence of forced displacement. For example, a 2002 Greater Nile report

2 Talisman argues that security reports prepared for Greater Nile are inadmissible because of "multiple levels of hearsay lurking" in the documents and the absence of a hearsay exception allowing for their admission. We do not reach this question, because even assuming the reports would be admissible in their entirety, they would not defeat summary judgment.

describing the "buffer zone" around the Heglig camp explained that "[t]he remaining nomads . . . are being 'encouraged' to complete their move through the area as soon as possible. The area within the security ring road while not a sterile area as found on security operations elsewhere . . . is moving in that direction." A 1999 security report stated that "[t]he military strategy, driven it appears by the GNPOC security management, is to create a buffer zone, i.e. an area surrounding both Heglig and Unity camps inside which no local settlements or commerce is allowed."

F. Greater Nile Inquiry into Expanding its Exploration Area

Greater Nile explored options for drilling new wells within GNPOC's concession, but outside the small area secured by the military in which production was ongoing. Greater Nile considered expanding exploration notwithstanding its knowledge of the Government's buffer zone strategy. According to plaintiffs, decisions about where to explore "were based upon technical analysis of geological formations performed by Talisman employees in Calgary," without regard to the human consequences of expansion.

G. Plaintiffs' Injuries

The individual plaintiffs remaining in the case consist of current or former residents of southern Sudan who were injured or displaced by Government forces in attacks on communities in Blocks 1, 2, and 5A. The plaintiffs were subjected to assaults by foot soldiers, attackers on horseback, gunships, and bombers. They testified at depositions, with varying degrees of certainty, as to whether the attacks were perpetrated by the Government.

The Presbyterian Church of Sudan asserts claims based on the destruction of its churches by the Government. Plaintiffs Rev. James Koung Ninrew, Chief Tunguar Kueigwong Rat, and Chief Gatluak Chiek Jang testified to seeing churches burned in the Government's attacks.

H. Procedural History

In November 2001, the Presbyterian Church of Sudan and four individual plaintiffs purporting to represent a class of thousands of southern Sudanese filed a complaint against Talisman in the United States District Court for the Southern District of New York. Plaintiffs filed an amended complaint in February 2002 naming additional plaintiffs and adding the Government as a defendant. Plaintiffs' amended complaint alleged that Talisman (1) directly violated, (2) aided and abetted the Government of Sudan in violating, and (3) conspired with the Government of Sudan to violate customary international law related to genocide, torture, war crimes, and crimes against humanity. Plaintiffs subsequently abandoned the claim of direct liability and elected to proceed against Talisman only on the claims of aiding and abetting and conspiracy.

1. Talisman's Motions to Dismiss

The case was initially assigned to Judge Allen Schwartz. In March 2003, Judge Schwartz issued a lengthy decision denying Talisman's motion to dismiss on numerous jurisdictional grounds. *Presbyterian Church of Sudan v. Talisman Energy, Inc.*, 244 F. Supp. 2d 289 (S.D.N.Y. 2003).

The case was reassigned to Judge Denise Cote after Judge Schwartz died in March 2003. Plaintiffs filed a Second Amended Class Action Complaint in August 2003, which added plaintiffs.[3]

After the Supreme Court's decision in *Sosa,* and our decision in *Flores v. Southern Peru Copper Corp.*, 414 F.3d 233 (2d Cir.2003), defendants moved for judgment on the pleadings arguing that the decisions changed the landscape for ATS claims and required reconsideration of the conclusions that [i] corporations can be liable for violating the ATS, and [ii] accessorial liability is recognized under the ATS. By decision dated June 13, 2005, the district court denied Talisman's motion. *Presbyterian Church of Sudan v. Talisman Energy, Inc.*, 374 F. Supp. 2d 331 (S.D.N.Y.2005).

Talisman again moved for judgment on the pleadings based on a letter from the United States Attorney, with attachments from the Department of State and Embassy of Canada expressing concern with the litigation. *Presbyterian Church of Sudan v. Talisman Energy, Inc.*, No. 01 Civ. 9882(DLC), 2005 WL 2082846, at *1 (S.D.N.Y. Aug.30, 2005). The Department of State advised that "considerations of international comity and judicial abstention may properly come into play" in view of Canada's objections to the litigation and the United States government's determination that Canadian courts were capable of adjudicating plaintiffs' claims. *Id.* at *2. Canada argued that the court's exercise of jurisdiction [i] infringed on its sovereignty, [ii] chilled its ability to use "trade support services as 'both a stick and carrot in support of peace,'" and [iii] violated traditional restraints on the exercise of extraterritorial jurisdiction. *Id.* at *1–2.

In August 2005, the district court denied Talisman's motion. *Id.* at *9. As to dismissal on comity grounds, the court found an insufficient nexus between Canada's foreign policy and the specific allegations in the complaint because the litigation did not require judging Canada's policy of constructive engagement with the Sudan, but "merely" judging "whether Talisman acted outside the bounds of customary international law while doing business in Sudan." *Id.* at *5–8. The court also observed that Canadian courts are unable to consider civil suits for violations of the law of nations. *Id.* at *7.

3 On August 27, 2004, after the submission of relevant discovery, the district court again denied a motion to dismiss for lack of personal jurisdiction. *Presbyterian Church of Sudan v. Talisman Energy, Inc.*, No. 01 Civ. 9882(DLC), 2004 WL 1920978 (S.D.N.Y. Aug.27, 2004).

As to dismissal on political question grounds, the court emphasized that the State Department letter did not explicitly declare that the lawsuit would interfere with United States policy toward the Sudan or Canada, and the court concluded therefore that exercising jurisdiction would not unduly intrude on the authority of the executive branch.[4] *Id.* at *8.

2. Motions to Amend and for Summary Judgment

In April 2006, plaintiffs filed a Proposed Third Amended Class Action Complaint. Later that month (before the district court ruled on plaintiffs' motion), Talisman moved for summary judgment as to all claims. On September 12, 2006, the district court granted Talisman's motion. *See Presbyterian Church of Sudan v. Talisman Energy, Inc.,* 453 F. Supp. 2d 633 (S.D.N.Y.2006).

The district court first considered whether international law recognized conspiracy liability. The court held that "the offense of conspiracy is limited to conspiracies to commit genocide and to wage aggressive war" and that international law does not recognize the doctrine of liability articulated in *Pinkerton v. United States,* 328 U.S. 640, 646–47, 66 S. Ct. 1180, 90 L.Ed. 1489 (1946). *Presbyterian Church of Sudan,* 453 F. Supp. 2d at 663, 665. The court observed that plaintiffs never brought a claim for "wag[ing] aggressive war" and that they had abandoned their genocide claim. *Id.* at 665. Nonetheless, the court addressed the genocide claim and held that plaintiffs could not be made liable for a co-conspirator's conduct solely because that conduct was foreseeable. *Id.*

The district court next considered plaintiffs' claim that Talisman aided and abetted genocide, war crimes, and crimes against humanity. The court undertook to define the elements of aiding and abetting liability under the ATS, and concluded that they must be derived from international law. The court comprehensively surveyed international law and held that:

> To show that a defendant aided and abetted a violation of international law, an ATS plaintiff must show:
>
> 1) that the principal violated international law;
>
> 2) that the defendant knew of the specific violation;

---

4 In 2005, the district court denied two motions for class certification on the ground that plaintiffs failed to satisfy the "predominance requirement." *Presbyterian Church of Sudan v. Talisman Energy, Inc.,* 226 F.R.D. 456, 482–85 (S.D.N.Y.2005); *Presbyterian Church of Sudan v. Talisman Energy, Inc.,* No. 01 Civ. 9882(DLC), 2005 WL 2278076, at *1 (S.D.N.Y. Sep.20, 2005). The court explained that all class members would have to show "that the injuries for which they are claiming damages were actually caused by [a Government campaign in the south]," which would require individual, fact-intensive inquiries, given the numerous factions of rebel groups and the fog of war. *Presbyterian Church of Sudan,* 226 F.R.D. at 482. Moreover, "damages to class members occurred over more than four years, a territory of many hundreds of square miles, . . . [and] through at least 142 separate incidents." *Presbyterian Church of Sudan,* 2005 WL 2278076, at *3.

> 3) that the defendant acted with the intent to assist that violation, that is, the defendant specifically directed his acts to assist in the specific violation;
>
> 4) that the defendant's acts had a substantial effect upon the success of the criminal venture; and
>
> 5) that the defendant was aware that the acts assisted the specific violation.

Id. at 668.

As to plaintiffs' genocide claim, the court held that whether or not genocide was taking place, plaintiffs had presented no evidence that Talisman was aware of the genocide, or, if it was, that Talisman intended to further it. *Id.* at 669–70.

As to war crimes and crimes against humanity, the court identified the kinds of "substantial assistance" that Talisman allegedly provided in aid of these violations: "(1) upgrading the Heglig and Unity airstrips; (2) designating areas 'south of the river' in Block 4 for oil exploration; (3) providing financial assistance to the Government through the payment of royalties; (4) giving general logistical support to the Sudanese military; and (5) various other acts." *Id.* at 671–72.

The court determined that the airstrips at Unity and Heglig were owned and operated by GNPOC—not Talisman—and that there was no evidence that Talisman upgraded or improved the airstrips. *Id.* at 673. Moreover, even if plaintiffs could show that Talisman was involved, there is no evidence that it upgraded the airstrips with the intention that the Government would use them for missions that violate human rights. *Id.* at 674.

As to designating areas "south of the river" for exploration, the court determined that preliminary discussions about expanding operations did not violate international humanitarian law and that there was no evidence Talisman was involved in such discussions, let alone that it considered the expansion as a pretext for attacking civilians. *Id.* at 675.

As to Talisman's payment of royalties to the Government, the court found no admissible evidence of the relationship between oil profits and military spending. *Id.* Nonetheless, the court assumed the relationship, and held that such payments were not enough to establish liability in the absence of evidence that Talisman "specifically directed" payments to military procurement or that it intended to aid attacks. *Id.* at 676.

As to the construction of all-weather roads and the provision of fuel to the military, the court concluded that the assistance was provided by GNPOC, not Talisman, which had a limited presence on the ground. *Id.* at 676–77.

Finally, the court addressed plaintiffs' allegations that Talisman assisted the Government by "using its community development program as a cover for gathering military intelligence" and by publicly denying knowledge of human rights violations. The court ruled that there was no admissible evidence of the former allegation, and concluded that the latter did not constitute "substantial assistance" in violation of international humanitarian law. *Id.* at 677.

Although not necessary for deciding Talisman's motion, the court ruled on whether plaintiffs could show that their injuries were caused by attacks initiated from GNPOC airfields, finding that only three plaintiffs were "arguably" attacked with GNPOC assistance, *id.* at 677, and that there was an absence of admissible evidence as to which Government aircraft flew particular missions, *id.* at 678.

Further, plaintiffs' motion to amend the complaint was denied on the ground that plaintiffs could not show good cause to amend three years after the deadline for amendment set forth in the scheduling order. *Id.* at 680. The court went on, however, to discuss the merits of the amended complaint and whether it could survive a motion for summary judgment (given that the discovery period had closed). The court conducted a comprehensive choice of law analysis, and concluded that [i] there was no basis for applying domestic federal law to plaintiffs' claims against foreign corporations, *id.* at 681–83, and [ii] plaintiffs could not pierce the corporate veils of Talisman's subsidiaries or hold GNPOC or the subsidiaries liable on theories of joint venture or agency, *id.* at 683–89.

Having prevailed on summary judgment, Talisman moved for partial judgment pursuant to Federal Rule of Civil Procedure 54(b), so that it could achieve finality in the case notwithstanding the Government's failure to enter an appearance. The district court granted Talisman's motion and entered judgment in favor of Talisman. *See Presbyterian Church of Sudan v. Talisman Energy, Inc.,* No. 01 Civ. 9882(DLC), 2006 WL 3469542, at *2 (S.D.N.Y. Dec.1, 2006). This appeal followed.

DISCUSSION

Plaintiffs argue that, in granting summary judgment, the district court drew inferences in favor of Talisman, excluded plaintiffs' evidence from consideration, and failed to hold Talisman responsible for human rights abuses committed by its partners and agents. This Court "review[s] *de novo* the district court's grant of summary judgment, drawing all factual inferences in favor of the non-moving party." *Paneccasio v. Unisource Worldwide, Inc.,* 532 F.3d 101, 107 (2d Cir.2008).

I.

The ATS provides that "[t]he district courts shall have original jurisdiction of any civil action by an alien for a tort only, committed in violation of the law of nations or a treaty of the United States." 28 U.S.C. § 1350. Although the statute was passed as part of the Judiciary Act of 1789, it provided jurisdiction in only one case in its first 170 years. *Sosa,* 542 U.S. at 712, 124 S. Ct. 2739. Invocation of the statute became more frequent after the issuance of *Filártiga v. Peña-Irala,* 630 F.2d 876 (2d Cir.1980), which held "that deliberate torture perpetrated under color of official authority violates universally accepted norms of the international law of human rights, regardless of the nationality of the parties," and that the ATS "provides federal jurisdiction" over torture claims. *Id.* at 878. The torturer was likened to the pirate and slave trader of old, "an enemy of all mankind." *Id.* at 890.

Filártiga held "that courts must interpret international law not as it was in 1789, but as it has evolved and exists among the nations of the world today." *Id.* at 881. At the same time, *Filártiga* cautioned restraint: "[t]he requirement that a rule command the 'general assent of civilized nations' to become binding upon them all is a stringent one." *Id.* "It is only where the nations of the world have demonstrated that the wrong is of mutual, and not merely several, concern, by means of express international accords, that a wrong generally recognized becomes an international law violation within the meaning of the statute." *Id.* at 888.

In *Kadic v. Karadzic,* 70 F.3d 232 (2d Cir.1995), we concluded "that certain forms of conduct violate the law of nations whether undertaken by those acting under the auspices of a state or only as private individuals." *Id.* at 239. *Kadic* recognized that claims for genocide and war crimes against individuals could proceed without state action. *Id.* at 244.

In *Flores,* we surveyed the state of ATS case law and engaged in a detailed analysis of the ATS and related principles of international law. *Flores* distilled three elements required to state a claim under the ATS: "plaintiffs must (i) be 'aliens,' (ii) claiming damages for a 'tort only,' (iii) resulting from a violation 'of the law of nations' or of 'a treaty of the United States.'" 414 F.3d at 242 (quoting 28 U.S.C. § 1350). We again issued a caution: "in determining what offenses violate customary international law, courts must proceed with extraordinary care and restraint." *Id.* at 248. The decisive issue in this case is whether accessorial liability can be imposed absent a showing of purpose. To answer this question "'we look primarily to the formal lawmaking and official actions of States and only secondarily to the works of scholars as evidence of the established practices of States.'"[5] *Id.* at 250 (quoting *United States v. Yousef,* 327 F.3d 56, 103 (2d Cir.2003)). After a thorough review of these sources, *Flores* concluded that the alleged prohibition

---

5 *Flores* cited Article 38 of the Statute of the International Court of Justice, which provides that courts should look to the following sources of international law:

> a. international conventions, whether general or particular, establishing rules expressly recognized by the contesting states;
>
> b. international custom, as evidence of a general practice accepted as law;
>
> c. the general principles of law recognized by civilized nations;
>
> d. subject to the provisions of Article 59, judicial decisions and the teachings of the most highly qualified publicists [i.e., scholars or "jurists"] of the various nations, as subsidiary means for the determination of rules of law.

414 F.3d at 251 (italics omitted)(quoting Statute of the International Court of Justice, June 26, 1945, art. 38, 59 Stat. 1055, 33 U.N.T.S. 993).

on "*intranational* pollution" and "rights to life and health [were] insufficiently definite to constitute rules of customary international law." *Id.* at 254–55.

The United States Supreme Court has analyzed the ATS only once. In *Sosa,* the Court explained that the ATS "was intended as jurisdictional in the sense of addressing the power of the courts to entertain cases concerned with a certain subject," 542 U.S. at 714, 124 S. Ct. 2739, and that "[t]he jurisdictional grant is best read as having been enacted on the understanding that the common law would provide a cause of action for the modest number of international law violations with a potential for personal liability at the time," *id.* at 724, 124 S. Ct. 2739. Claims "based on the present-day law of nations" should be recognized only if "accepted by the civilized world and defined with a specificity comparable to the features of the 18th-century paradigms" contemporary with enactment of the ATS. *Id.* at 725, 124 S. Ct. 2739.

Sosa cited five reasons for courts to exercise "great caution" before recognizing violations of international law that were not recognized in 1789:

> First, . . . the [modern] understanding that the law is not so much found or discovered as it is either made or created[;] . . . [s]econd, . . . an equally significant rethinking of the role of the federal courts in making it[;] . . . [t]hird, [the modern view that] a decision to create a private right of action is one better left to legislative judgment in the great majority of cases[;] . . . [f]ourth, . . . risks of adverse foreign policy consequences[; and] . . . fifth[,] . . . [the lack of a] congressional mandate to seek out and define new and debatable violations of the law of nations.

Id. at 725–28, 124 S. Ct. 2739. Thus, under *Sosa,* "the determination whether a norm is sufficiently definite to support a cause of action should (and, indeed, inevitably must) involve an element of judgment about the practical consequences of making that cause available to litigants in the federal courts." *Id.* at 732–33, 124 S. Ct. 2739.

We have applied *Sosa* in four opinions addressing ATS claims. In three of them, we considered whether *Sosa* permitted recognition of particular offenses. In *Vietnam Ass'n for Victims of Agent Orange v. Dow Chemical Co.,* 517 F.3d 104 (2d Cir. 2008), we held that the manufacture and supply of an herbicide used as a defoliant (with collateral damage) did not violate international law: "[i]nasmuch as Agent Orange was intended for defoliation and for destruction of crops only, its use did not violate . . . international norms . . . , since those norms would not necessarily prohibit the deployment of materials that are only secondarily, and not intentionally, harmful to humans." *Id.* at 119–20.

Mora v. New York, 524 F.3d 183 (2d Cir.2008), held that detention without notice of consular rights (in violation of Article 36(1)(b)(third) of the Vienna Convention on Consular Relations) did not violate a "wellaccepted" international law norm. *Id.* at 208–09. But a divided panel held in *Abdullahi v. Pfizer, Inc.,* 562 F.3d 163 (2d Cir.2009), "that the prohibition in customary international law against nonconsensual human medical experimentation can[] be enforced through the ATS." *Id.* at 169.

In the fourth case—*Khulumani v. Barclay National Bank Ltd.,* 504 F.3d 254 (2d Cir.2007)—we ruled in a per curiam opinion that "in this Circuit, a plaintiff may plead a theory of aiding and abetting liability under the [ATS]." *Id.* at 260.

II.

Plaintiffs assert that Talisman aided and abetted (and conspired with) the Government in the commission of three violations of international law: [i] genocide, [ii] war crimes, and [iii] crimes against humanity. All three torts may be asserted under the ATS. *Kadic,* 70 F.3d at 236 ("[W]e hold that subject-matter jurisdiction exists[, and] that [defendant] may be found liable for genocide, war crimes, and crimes against humanity. . . ."); *see also Sosa,* 542 U.S. at 762, 124 S. Ct. 2739 (Breyer, J., concurring in part and concurring in judgment)(describing a "subset" of "universally condemned behavior" for which "universal jurisdiction exists," including "torture, genocide, crimes against humanity, and war crimes"); *Flores,* 414 F.3d at 244 n. 18 ("Customary international law rules proscribing crimes against humanity, including genocide, and war crimes, have been enforceable against individuals since World War II.").

In *Kadic,* we defined "genocide" and "war crimes." *Kadic* adopted the definition of genocide from the Convention on the Prevention and Punishment of the Crime of Genocide art. 2, Dec. 9, 1948, 102 Stat. 3045, 78 U.N.T.S. 277 ("Genocide Convention"), which defines genocide as:

> any of the following acts committed with intent to destroy, in whole or in part, a national, ethnical, racial or religious group, as such:
>
> (a) Killing members of the group;
>
> (b) Causing serious bodily or mental harm to members of the group;
>
> (c) Deliberately inflicting on the group conditions of life calculated to bring about its physical destruction in whole or in part;
>
> (d) Imposing measures intended to prevent births with the group;
>
> (e) Forcibly transferring children of the group to another group.

Kadic, 70 F.3d at 241 (quoting Genocide Convention).

As to war crimes, *Kadic* applied the definition from Common Article 3 of the Geneva Convention, which "applies to 'armed conflict[s] not of an international character'" and requires "'each Party to the conflict'" to adhere to the following:

> Persons taking no active part in the hostilities . . . shall in all circumstances be treated humanely, without any adverse distinction founded on race, colour, religion or faith, sex, birth or wealth, or any other similar criteria.
>
> To this end, the following acts are and shall remain prohibited at any time and in any place whatsoever with respect to the above-mentioned persons:
>
> (a) violence to life and person, in particular murder of all kinds, mutilation, cruel treatment and torture;

(b) taking of hostages;

(c) outrages upon personal dignity, in particular humiliating and degrading treatment;

(d) the passing of sentences and carrying out of executions without previous judgment pronounced by a regularly constituted court. . . .

Kadic, 70 F.3d at 243 (alterations in original)(quoting Convention Relative to the Protection of Civilian Persons in Time of War art. 3, August 12, 1949, 6 U.S.T. 3516, 75 U.N.T.S. 287). This standard applies to "all 'parties' to a conflict—which includes insurgent military groups." *Id.*

We have never defined "crimes against humanity." Here, the district court adopted a generally serviceable definition, which the parties do not challenge and which we therefore, for purposes of this case, need not evaluate or edit: "[c]rimes against humanity include murder, enslavement, deportation or forcible transfer, torture, rape or other inhumane acts, committed as part of a widespread [or] systematic attack directed against a civilian population."[6] *Presbyterian Church of Sudan,* 453 F. Supp. 2d at 670.

Talisman does not contest that the enumerated torts are cognizable under the ATS. At issue is whether plaintiffs' claim that Talisman aided and abetted these offenses (and conspired to do them) is actionable under the ATS absent evidence that Talisman acted with the purpose of advancing the abuses, and, if proof of purpose is an element, whether the evidence supports such a finding.

III.

There is no allegation that Talisman (or its employees) personally engaged in human rights abuses; the allegation is that Talisman was complicit in the Government's abuses.

That allegation places in issue the standard for aiding and abetting liability under the ATS.[7] This question was presented to a prior panel, which held, in a brief per curiam opinion, that "in this Circuit, a plaintiff may plead a theory of aiding and abetting liability under the [ATS]." *Khulumani,* 504 F.3d at 260. However, the panel fractured as to the standard for pleading such liability.

---

6 The district court used the phrase "widespread and systematic," but plaintiffs argue that this was error, and that "and" should be replaced by "or." (Pls.' Br. 65). We assume for purposes of this appeal that plaintiffs' formulation is correct.

7 We address aiding and abetting liability—a concept typically associated with the criminal law—because customary international law norms prohibiting genocide, war crimes, and crimes against humanity have "been developed largely in the context of criminal prosecutions rather than civil proceedings." *John Doe I v. Unocal Corp.,* 395 F.3d 932, 949 (9th Cir.2002); *see also Khulumani,* 504 F.3d at 270 n. 5 (Katzmann, J., concurring) ("[O]ur case law . . . has consistently relied on criminal law norms in establishing the content of customary international law for purposes of the [ATS].").

Judge Katzmann, concurring, was of the view "that a defendant may be held liable under international law for aiding and abetting the violation of that law by another when the defendant (1) provides practical assistance to the principal which has a substantial effect on the perpetration of the crime, and (2) does so with the purpose of facilitating the commission of that crime." *Id.* at 277 (Katzmann, J., concurring). Judge Korman noted that (were he not dissenting on other grounds) he would have concurred with Judge Katzmann. *Id.* at 333 (Korman, J., concurring in part and dissenting in part). Both judges observed that the standard for aiding and abetting liability under the ATS must derive from international law sources. *Id.* at 268 (Katzmann, J., concurring); *id.* at 331 (Korman, J., concurring in part and dissenting in part).

Judge Hall's closely reasoned concurring opinion concluded that *Sosa*'s reliance on international law applied to the question of recognizing substantive offenses, but not to the issue of secondary liability. On that issue, he found that "*Sosa* at best lends Delphian guidance," largely in dicta. *Id.* at 286 (Hall, J., concurring). Citing "a hornbook principle that international law does not specify the means of its domestic enforcement," *id.* (internal quotation marks omitted), Judge Hall turned to the Restatement (Second) of Torts § 876(b), which states that the aiding and abetting standard should be [i] knowing [ii] encouragement [iii] that facilitated the substantive violation. *Id.* at 287–89.

The upshot of this split is that notwithstanding the agreement of two judges, Judge Katzmann's view did not constitute a holding and is therefore not binding precedent. In this unusual circumstance, the issue remains live. This opinion draws substantially from Judge Katzmann's concurring opinion, and adopts his proposed rule as the law of this Circuit.

Judge Katzmann began by choosing the source of law that should provide the basis for an aiding and abetting standard.[8] He observed that this Court has "repeatedly emphasized that the scope of the [ATS's] jurisdictional grant should be determined by reference to international law." *Id.* at 269 (Katzmann, J., concurring)(citing *Kadic,* 70 F.3d at 238; *Flores,* 414 F.3d at 248; *Filártiga,* 630 F.2d at 887). Similarly, footnote 20 of *Sosa,*[9] while nominally concerned with the liability of non-state actors, supports the broader principle that the scope of liability for ATS violations should be derived from international law. *Id.* Judge Katzmann concluded that, while domestic law might provide guidance on whether to recognize a

---

8 Judge Katzmann's individual opinion contains a thorough discussion of aiding and abetting principles. This opinion sets forth only so much of Judge Katzmann's analysis as is necessary to provide the context of our holding. For an extended discussion of the aiding and abetting issue, see *Khulumani,* 504 F.3d at 268–77 (Katzmann, J., concurring).

9 A consideration related to whether the ATS provides jurisdiction over a norm is "whether international law extends the scope of liability for a violation of a given norm to the perpetrator being sued, if the defendant is a private actor such as a corporation or individual." *Sosa,* 542 U.S. at 732 n. 20, 124 S. Ct. 2739.

violation of international norms, it cannot render conduct actionable under the ATS. *Id.* at 270.

Judge Katzmann's research "revealed no source of international law that recognizes liability for aiding and abetting a violation of international law but would not authorize the imposition of such liability on a party who acts with the purpose of facilitating that violation (provided, of course, that the *actus reus* requirement is also satisfied)." *Id.* at 277. While liability had been imposed in certain cases under a less-stringent knowledge standard, *see, e.g., id.* at 277 n. 12 (citing *Prosecutor v. Vasiljevic,* Case No. IT-98-32-A, Appeal Judgment, ¶ 102(ii) (Feb. 24, 2004)), Judge Katzmann cited *Sosa*'s requirement that a norm obtain universal acceptance, and adopted the standard set forth in the Rome Statute: "that a defendant may be held liable under international law for aiding and abetting the violation of that law by another when the defendant (1) provides practical assistance to the principal which has a substantial effect on the perpetration of the crime, and (2) does so with the purpose of facilitating the commission of that crime." *Id.* at 277.

We agree that *Sosa* and our precedents send us to international law to find the standard for accessorial liability. Plaintiffs argue that aiding and abetting liability is a matter ordinarily left to the forum country, where (in this venue) the principle is broad and elastic. But such an expansion would violate *Sosa*'s command that we limit liability to "violations of . . . international law . . . with . . . definite content and acceptance among civilized nations [equivalent to] the historical paradigms familiar when § 1350 was enacted." 542 U.S. at 732, 124 S. Ct. 2739. Recognition of secondary liability is no less significant a decision than whether to recognize a whole new tort in the first place.

Thus, applying international law, we hold that the *mens rea* standard for aiding and abetting liability in ATS actions is purpose rather than knowledge alone. Even if there is a sufficient international consensus for imposing liability on individuals who *purposefully* aid and abet a violation of international law, *see Khulumani,* 504 F.3d at 276 (Katzmann, J., concurring); *cf. id.* at 333 (Korman, J., concurring in part and dissenting in part), no such consensus exists for imposing liability on individuals who *knowingly* (but not purposefully) aid and abet a violation of international law.

Indeed, international law at the time of the Nuremberg trials recognized aiding and abetting liability only for purposeful conduct. *See United States v. von Weizsaecker (The Ministries Case), in* 14 *Trials of War Criminals Before the Nuremberg Military Tribunals Under Control Council Law No. 10,* at 662 (William S. Hein & Co., Inc.1997)(1949)(declining to impose criminal liability on a bank officer who made a loan with the knowledge, but not the purpose, that the borrower would use the funds to commit a crime). That purpose standard has been largely upheld in the modern era, with only sporadic forays in the direction of a knowledge standard. *See Khulumani,* 504 F.3d at 276 (Katzmann, J., concurring)(noting that some international criminal tribunals have made overtures toward a knowledge standard but that the Rome Statute of the International Criminal Court adopts a purpose standard); *see also id.* at 332–37 (Korman, J., concurring in part and dissenting in part). Only a purpose standard, therefore, has the requisite "acceptance among civilized nations," *Sosa,* 542 U.S. at 732, 124 S. Ct. 2739, for application in an action under the ATS. *See generally Flores,* 414 F.3d at 248 ("[I]n order for a principle to become part of customary international law, States must universally abide by it."); *see also Yousef,* 327 F.3d at 92, 105–08; *Kadic,* 70 F.3d at 239; *Filártiga,* 630 F.2d at 888.

IV.

Plaintiffs allege that Talisman conspired with the Government to commit human rights abuses and argue that the district court failed to apply conspiracy principles from United States law to violations of international law under the ATS. In particular, plaintiffs urge application of the *Pinkerton* doctrine, 328 U.S. at 646–47, 66 S. Ct. 1180.[10] Whether conspiracy claims are cognizable under international law is a question of first impression in this Circuit.

As a matter of first principles, we look to international law to derive the elements for any such cause of action.[11] *See* Sec. III, *supra.* In so doing, we must distinguish between the inchoate crime of conspiracy (which requires an agreement and overt acts, but no completed deed) and conspiracy as a theory of accessorial liability for completed offenses.

As to conspiracy as an inchoate offense, the Supreme Court held in *Hamdan v. Rumsfeld,* 548 U.S. 557, 610, 126 S. Ct. 2749, 165 L.Ed.2d 723 (2006), that "the only 'conspiracy' crimes that have been recognized by international war crimes tribunals (whose jurisdiction often extends beyond war crimes proper to crimes against humanity and crimes against the peace) are conspiracy to commit genocide and common plan to wage aggressive war." Plaintiffs did not plead the waging of aggressive war, and while they did plead genocide, it is pled as a completed offense, not an inchoate one.

---

10 "[U]nder *Pinkerton,* a defendant may be found 'guilty on a substantive count without specific evidence that he committed the act charged if it is clear that the offense had been committed, that it had been committed in the furtherance of an unlawful conspiracy, and that the defendant was a member of that conspiracy.'" *United States v. Bruno,* 383 F.3d 65, 89 (2d Cir.2004) (quoting *United States v. Miley,* 513 F.2d 1191, 1208 (2d Cir. 1975)).

11 Plaintiffs argue that federal conspiracy law should apply to ATS claims. *See, e.g., Cabello v. Fernandez-Larios,* 402 F.3d 1148 (11th Cir. 2005) (applying domestic law to ATS conspiracy claim). Judge Cote rejected that approach, holding that *Sosa* required applying international law. *Presbyterian Church,* 453 F. Supp. 2d at 665 n. 64. We agree with Judge Cote. Moreover, plaintiffs would fare no better if we adopted their preferred definition of conspiracy, because that definition (derived from domestic law) also requires proof "that . . . [the defendant] joined the conspiracy *knowing of at least one of the goals of the conspiracy and intending to help accomplish it.*" *Cabello,* 402 F.3d at 1159 (emphasis added).

The analog to a conspiracy as a completed offense in international law is the concept of a "joint criminal enterprise." *See Hamdan,* 548 U.S. at 611 n. 40, 126 S. Ct. 2749. Even assuming, without deciding, that plaintiffs could assert such a theory in an ATS action, an essential element of a joint criminal enterprise is "a criminal intention to participate in a common criminal design." *Prosecutor v. Tadic,* Case No. IT-94-1-A, Appeal Judgment, ¶ 206 (July 15, 1999)(basing that finding on numerous precedents from criminal tribunals established in the aftermath of Word War II). Therefore, under a theory of relief based on a joint criminal enterprise, plaintiffs' conspiracy claims would require the same proof of *mens rea* as their claims for aiding and abetting.

In any event, plaintiffs have not established that "international law [universally] recognize[s] a doctrine of conspiratorial liability that would extend to activity encompassed by the *Pinkerton* doctrine." *Presbyterian Church of Sudan,* 453 F. Supp. 2d at 663.

V.

Therefore, in reviewing the district court's grant of summary judgment to Talisman, we must test plaintiffs' evidence to see if it supports an inference that Talisman acted with the "purpose" to advance the Government's human rights abuses.

The district court's observations are well-considered and apt. "The activities which the plaintiffs identify as assisting the Government in committing crimes against humanity and war crimes generally accompany any natural resource development business or the creation of any industry." *Presbyterian Church of Sudan,* 453 F. Supp. 2d at 672. None of the acts was inherently criminal or wrongful. "[T]he plaintiffs' theories of substantial assistance serve essentially as proxies for their contention that Talisman should not have made any investment in the Sudan, knowing as it did that the Government was engaged in the forced eviction of non-Muslim Africans from lands that held promise for the discovery of oil." *Id.* In sum:

> The plaintiffs essentially argue that Talisman understood that the Government had cleared and would continue to clear the land of the local population if oil companies were willing to come to the Sudan and explore for oil, and that[,] understanding that to be so, Talisman should not have come. They have no evidence that Talisman (or [Greater Nile] or GNPOC) participated in any attack against a plaintiff and no direct evidence of Talisman's illicit intent, so they wish to argue that Talisman's knowledge of the Government's record of human rights violations, and its understanding of how the Government would abuse the presence of Talisman, is a sufficient basis from which to infer Talisman's illicit intent when it designated areas for exploration, upgraded airstrips or paid royalties.

Id. at 672–73.

Plaintiffs argue that the district court's analysis was flawed because it assumed that "ordinary development activities cannot constitute aiding and abetting."

This argument misconstrues the district court's analysis, which does not rely on any categorical or blanket principle precluding liability; rather, the court conscientiously looked at each specific activity to determine if it satisfied the aiding and abetting standard. A *de novo* review of plaintiffs' evidence confirms the soundness of the district court's ruling.

As a threshold matter, Talisman did not manage oil operations in the Sudan: its indirect subsidiary Greater Nile was a 25% shareholder in GNPOC, the corporation responsible for developing the concessions. The rest of the GNPOC shares were held by entities from China, Malaysia, and the Sudan. This attenuation between the plaintiffs' allegations and the named defendant (the only entity over which the district court had personal jurisdiction) raises knotty issues concerning control, imputation, and veil piercing (among other things). Nevertheless, we will assume for most purposes that plaintiffs could surmount these hurdles;[12] so we proceed to the allegations of aiding and abetting and conspiring to commit human rights abuses.

The district court classified four kinds of "substantial assistance" that Talisman provided (or is alleged to have provided) to the Government: "(1) upgrading the Heglig and Unity airstrips; (2) designating areas 'south of the river' in Block 4 for oil exploration; (3) providing financial assistance to the Government through the payment of royalties; [and] (4) giving general logistical support to the Sudanese military."[13] *Presbyterian Church of Sudan,* 453 F. Supp. 2d at 671–72. We take these up one by one.

1. Talisman helped build all-weather roads and improved airports, notwithstanding awareness that this infrastructure might be used for attacks on civilians. There is no doubt that roads and airports are necessary features of a remote facility for oil extraction: they are used for transporting supplies, bringing workers to the work site, and assuring evacuation in the event of emergency.

There is evidence that Talisman (partially) financed the road-building, from its Calgary headquarters, and helped build other infrastructure, notwithstanding awareness of the Government's activity. But obviously there are benign and constructive purposes for these projects and (more to the point) there is no evidence that any of this was done for an improper purpose. Consistent with plaintiffs' effort

12 We will also assume, without deciding, that corporations such as Talisman may be held liable for the violations of customary international law that plaintiffs allege. Because we hold that plaintiffs' claims fail on other grounds, we need not reach, in this action, the question of "whether international law extends the scope of liability" to corporations. *Sosa,* 542 U.S. at 732 n. 20, 124 S. Ct. 2739.

13 The district court also addressed plaintiffs' allegations that Talisman assisted the Government by "using its community development program as a cover for gathering military intelligence" and by publicly denying knowledge of human rights violations. *Presbyterian Church of Sudan,* 453 F. Supp. 2d at 677. Plaintiffs do not raise the former point on appeal and we agree with the district court that publicly denying knowledge of abuses is not "substantial assistance."

to show that GNPOC personnel had knowledge of the Government's human rights abuses, plaintiffs adduce evidence that senior Talisman officials protested to the Government and that security reports shared with senior Talisman officials expressed concern about the military's use of GNPOC airstrips. Since, however, the proper test of liability is purpose (not knowledge), all this evidence of knowledge (and protest) cuts against Talisman's liability.

Even if Talisman built roads or improved the airstrips with the intention that the military would also be accommodated, GNPOC had a legitimate need to rely on the military for defense. It is undisputed that oil workers in that tumultuous region were subjected to attacks: rebel groups viewed oil installations and oil workers as enemy targets; an e-mail from a Talisman employee describes rebel attacks and the placement of mines in work areas; rebels launched a nighttime mortar attack against a Heglig camp where 700 oil workers were living; and in Block 5A the attacks caused that concessionaire (Lundin Oil AB) to close down operations for an extended period. In these circumstances, evidence that GNPOC was coordinating with the military supports no inference of a purpose to aid atrocities.

2. At one point, Greater Nile was worried that the Government would terminate GNPOC's concession on lands south of its existing operations unless GNPOC began to exploit them, and consideration was given to an expansion. Plaintiffs contend that this consideration violated international law. However, the evidence shows that this expansion south did not occur during the time any Talisman affiliate was in the Sudan, and contemplation does not amount to "substantial assistance" in violation of international law.

3. The royalties paid by GNPOC may have assisted the Government in its abuses, as it may have assisted any other activity the Government wanted to pursue. But there is no evidence that GNPOC or Talisman acted with the purpose that the royalty payments be used for human rights abuses.

4. GNPOC provided fuel for military aircraft taking off on bombing missions, and some of the fuel was paid for by GNPOC rather than the Government. This evidence is insufficient to defeat summary judgment for two reasons. First, there is no showing that Talisman was involved in such routine day-to-day GNPOC operations as refueling aircraft. Second, there is no evidence that GNPOC workers provided fuel for the purpose of facilitating attacks on civilians; to the contrary, an e-mail from a Talisman employee to his supervisor, which plaintiffs use to show that the military refueled at a GNPOC airstrip, expresses anger and frustration at the military using the fuel.

Plaintiffs' primary argument is that Talisman supported the creation of a buffer zone around its oil fields, understanding that the Government was displacing huge numbers of civilians from oil-rich regions, decimating as it went the population of southern Sudan. As evidence, plaintiffs cite statements in Greater Nile security memoranda, including this one: "[t]he military strategy, driven it appears by the GNPOC security management, is to create a buffer zone, i.e., an area surrounding both Heglig and Unity camps inside which no local settlements or commerce is allowed."[14]

Plaintiffs repeatedly cite the forced displacement of people from the oil fields, but they do not allege that such displacement in itself is a violation of international law. That is understandable, because a government has power to regulate use of land and resources. Resource extraction in particular is by nature land-intensive: land is needed for exploration and engineering, equipment, rigs or mines, offices and dormitories in remote areas, transportation infrastructure, and so on. Under the best circumstances, these facilities might require relocation from a development area. But GNPOC was not operating in the best of circumstances. Sudan's oil was located in an area heavily contested in a civil war, in a region of the country that had suffered through four decades of violence before Talisman arrived. The oil facilities came under frequent rebel attack and oil workers were killed during the relevant time. Safe operation of the oil facilities therefore required tightened security; and displacing civilians from an "area within the security ring road" was not in itself unlawful.

It is therefore not enough for plaintiffs to establish Talisman's complicity in depopulating areas in or around the Heglig and Unity camps: plaintiffs must establish that Talisman acted with the purpose to assist the Government's violations of customary international law.

Plaintiffs have provided evidence that the Government violated customary international law; but they provide no evidence that Talisman acted with the purpose to support the Government's offenses. Plaintiffs do not suggest in their briefs that Talisman was a partisan in regional, religious, or ethnic hostilities, or that Talisman acted with the purpose to assist persecution. To the contrary, the actions of the Sudanese government threatened the security of the company's operations, tarnished its reputation, angered its employees and management, and ultimately forced Talisman to abandon the venture.

Plaintiffs argue that they need no direct evidence of purpose because "'[genocidal intent may] be inferred from a number of facts and circumstances, such as the general context, the perpetration of other culpable acts systematically directed against the same group, the scale of atrocities committed, the systematic targeting of victims on account of their membership of a particular group, or the repetition of destructive and discriminatory acts.'" *Presbyterian Church of Sudan v. Talisman Energy, Inc.*, 226 F.R.D. 456, 479 (S.D.N.Y.2005)(alterations in original) (quoting *Prosecutor v. Jelisec,* No. IT-95-10-A, Appeals Chamber Judgment, ¶ 101 (July 5, 2001)). True, intent must often be demonstrated by the circumstances, and there may well be an ATS case in which a genuine issue of fact as to a defendant's intent

14 Talisman argues that this statement (and others cited by plaintiffs) references an area of 5km and 8km around the Heglig and Unity camps, respectively, not a zone covering the entirety of the concession area.

to aid and abet the principal could be inferred; but in this case, there were insufficient facts or circumstances suggesting that Talisman acted with the purpose to advance violations of international humanitarian law.

The reports that plaintiffs rely upon to prove knowledge also show that Greater Nile security personnel and GNPOC workers were upset by the Government's actions and possible attacks on civilians. For example, several reports address the company's efforts to relieve the plight of internally displaced persons, which included stockpiling tons of relief supplies and distributing food, water, medicine, and mosquito nets.

There is evidence that southern Sudanese were subjected to attacks by the Government, that those attacks facilitated the oil enterprise, and that the Government's stream of oil revenue enhanced the military capabilities used to persecute its enemies. But if ATS liability could be established by knowledge of those abuses coupled only with such commercial activities as resource development, the statute would act as a vehicle for private parties to impose embargos or international sanctions through civil actions in United States courts. Such measures are not the province of private parties but are, instead, properly reserved to governments and multinational organizations.

VI.

Plaintiffs argue that the district court failed to consider portions of the summary judgment record and failed to afford the parties an opportunity to argue evidentiary issues. We reject these contentions. The district court did not make a "wholesale blanket ruling" excluding plaintiffs' evidence and did not exclude evidence in contravention of the Federal Rules of Evidence. Moreover, plaintiffs have cited no relevant authority holding that a district court is confined to a particular evidentiary procedure in ruling on a summary judgment motion.

A district court deciding a summary judgment motion "has broad discretion in choosing whether to admit evidence." *Raskin v. Wyatt Co.*, 125 F.3d 55, 65 (2d Cir.1997). "The principles governing admissibility of evidence do not change on a motion for summary judgment." *Id.* at 65–66. "Rule 56(e) provides that affidavits in support of and against summary judgment shall set forth such facts as would be *admissible in evidence.* Therefore, only admissible evidence need be considered by the trial court in ruling on a motion for summary judgment." *Id.* at 66 (internal quotation marks and citations omitted). It is difficult to see how a court can decide a summary judgment motion without deciding questions of evidence:

> Because the purpose of summary judgment is to weed out cases in which "there is no genuine issue as to any material fact and . . . the moving party is entitled to a judgment as a matter of law," it is appropriate for district courts to decide questions regarding the admissibility of evidence on summary judgment. Although disputes as to the validity of the underlying data go to the weight of the evidence, and are for the fact-finder to resolve, questions of admissibility are properly resolved by the court.

> The resolution of evidentiary questions on summary judgment conserves the resources of the parties, the court, and the jury.

Id. (citations omitted)(alterations in original); *see also LaSalle Bank Nat. Ass'n v. Nomura Asset Capital Corp.,* 424 F.3d 195, 205–06 (2d Cir.2005)("Even on summary judgment, a district court has wide discretion in determining which evidence is admissible, [and] we review its evidentiary rulings for manifest error." (internal quotation marks and citations omitted)(alterations in original)).

At the outset of the summary judgment opinion in this case, the district court observed that

> plaintiffs have not distinguished between the admissible and inadmissible. The plaintiffs repeatedly describe 'Talisman' as having done this or that, when the examination of the sources to which they refer reveals that it is some other entity or an employee of some other company that acted. They assert that this or that event happened, when the documents to which they refer consist of hearsay embedded in more hearsay. Indeed, most of the admissible evidence is either statements made by or to Talisman executives, and the plaintiffs' descriptions of their own injuries, with very little admissible evidence offered to build the links in the chain of causation between the defendant and those injuries.

Presbyterian Church of Sudan, 453 F. Supp. 2d at 639. Plaintiffs argue that this prefatory language amounts to an evidentiary ruling and bespeaks a disregard of the plaintiffs' evidence in whole. However, the district court set aside its concerns about the evidence in describing the facts of the case: "In order to describe as fairly as possible the evidence the plaintiffs present, the description of events that follows is largely taken from the documents on which the plaintiffs have placed the greatest reliance, without a careful analysis of the admissibility of this evidence." *Id.* at 641–42.

In weighing evidence of questionable admissibility, the district court often noted Talisman's evidentiary objection, and sometimes expressed a view of the objection; but the court never made a blanket exclusion of evidence.

Plaintiffs focus on four specific "exclusions":

1. Congressional findings included in the Sudan Peace Act stating that genocide was taking place in the Sudan and that oil profits were contributing to the misery. *See* Pub.L. No. 107-245, 116 Stat. 1504 (codified at 50 U.S.C. § 1701). This was not excluded; the court described the congressional findings and Talisman's objections, and explained that in any case plaintiffs had no proof of Talisman's intent. *Presbyterian Church of Sudan,* 453 F. Supp. 2d at 669–70.

2. Evidence from plaintiffs' experts about the relationship between oil profits and military spending. The district court conceded that "plaintiffs have evidence from which a jury could find that Talisman believed that the Government used oil revenues to buy armaments, even if Talisman did not have any direct evidence or

knowledge of that fact." *Id.* at 676. The district court nonetheless concluded that was not enough, because plaintiffs had not "identified evidence sufficient to support a finding that when Talisman (or [Greater Nile] or GNPOC) paid royalties, it 'specifically directed' those payments to the Government's procurement of weaponry to target civilians and displace them." *Id.*

3. Security reports by Greater Nile personnel (who monitored threats to GNPOC workers) recording the military's use of airstrips to conduct bombing runs and other military operations. The district court described these reports in great detail in the background section of its opinion, and explained that the reports painted a complex picture of the situation. Whatever the significance of the information in the reports, there is no question that they were accounted for in the district court's analysis.

4. A declaration from the head of security for Arakis (Robert Norton), stating that he had warned Talisman at the time it purchased Arakis about likely civilian displacement. The district court excluded this declaration because the witness had testified at an earlier deposition that he was unaware of any displacement. *Presbyterian Church of Sudan,* 453 F. Supp. 2d at 647 & n. 11. The district court explained "[a] witness may not use a later affidavit to contradict deposition testimony in an effort to defeat a motion for summary judgment." *Presbyterian Church of Sudan,* 453 F. Supp. 2d at 647 (citing *Bickerstaff v. Vassar Coll.,* 196 F.3d 435, 455 (2d Cir. 1999)). Plaintiffs contend that only declarations from parties contradicting earlier deposition testimony are inadmissible, and that Norton's declaration did not fit within this rule. We need not decide this question, because [i] there was other evidence of Talisman's knowledge of displacement of civilians and [ii] Talisman's notice of this displacement is not enough to show an illicit purpose.

Plaintiffs cite *United States v. McDermott,* 245 F.3d 133 (2d Cir.2001), and *United States v. Carson,* 52 F.3d 1173 (2d Cir.1995), for the proposition that a party must make a specific and contemporaneous objection to the admission of trial evidence under Federal Rule of Evidence 103(a)(1). This non-controversial proposition is irrelevant, because the case never went to trial and because Talisman is not objecting to the district court's admission of trial evidence.

Finally, plaintiffs rely on an unpublished opinion from the Eleventh Circuit which reversed a district court's striking of fifty passages from a response to a motion for summary judgment. *Mack v. ST Mobile Aerospace Eng'g, Inc.,* 195 Fed.Appx. 829 (11th Cir.2006). The district court in that case: [i] failed to give the parties an opportunity to argue the merits of the objections; [ii] failed to analyze and rule on each objection; and [iii] offered only a "blanket declaration that 'the statements at issue are inadmissible hearsay, double hearsay, opinion, speculation and/or conjecture.'" *Id.* at 842–43. Moreover, nothing in the submission could be "inadmissible hearsay evidence because the passages [were] not evidence at all—they [were] the plaintiffs' *arguments* in their responsive pleading." *Id.* at 842 (emphasis in original). *Mack* is easily distinguishable. First, the district court in this case explained its reasons for excluding evidence. Second, the district court in *Mack* struck pleadings, not evidence. Third, the Eleventh Circuit reversed in part because it determined (after addressing several specific strikes) that the district court's evidentiary rulings were wrong on the merits. Plaintiffs have pointed to no incorrect rulings in this case (with the possible exception of the Norton declaration, which is not material as to purpose).[15]

In conclusion, there is no evidence that the district court improperly failed to consider plaintiffs' evidence.

VII.

Two weeks before Talisman moved for summary judgment, plaintiffs filed a Proposed Third Amended Class Action Complaint. In denying plaintiffs' motion to amend, the district court explained that the Second Amended Complaint sought to hold Talisman liable for its own acts, while the proposed pleading, "[w]hen stripped to its essentials, seeks to hold Talisman liable for the actions of GNPOC." *Presbyterian Church of Sudan,* 453 F. Supp. 2d at 679. Thus, while the Second Amended Complaint alleged that Talisman aided and abetted the Government, the Third Amended Complaint alleged that Talisman aided and abetted GNPOC and Greater Nile. *Id.*

The district court ruled that, to plead new theories of liability three years after the deadline for amendment specified in the scheduling order, plaintiffs were required to show good cause for delay and the exercise of due diligence. *Id.* at 680 (citing Fed.R.Civ.P. 16; *Grochowski v. Phoenix Constr.,* 318 F.3d 80, 86 (2d Cir. 2003); *In re Wireless Tel. Servs. Antitrust Litig.,* 02 Civ. 2673(DLC), 2004 WL 2244502, at *5 (S.D.N.Y. Oct. 6, 2004)). The court found that plaintiffs failed to show good cause, and that "[i]t could even be said that the plaintiffs acted in bad faith in waiting until the eve of summary judgment practice to file the motion to amend." *Id.* at 680.

Once the deadline for amendment in a scheduling order has passed, leave to amend may be denied "where the moving party has failed to establish good cause." *Parker v. Columbia Pictures Indus.,* 204 F.3d 326, 340 (2d Cir.2000). "[A] finding of 'good cause' depends on the diligence of the moving party." *Id.* We review a district court's denial of leave to amend for abuse of discretion.

Plaintiffs argue that they filed the Third Amended Complaint as promptly as they could at the conclusion of discovery. But the district court concluded that it was

15 Plaintiffs also rely on *Halbrook v. Reichhold Chemicals, Inc.,* 735 F. Supp. 121, 128 (S.D.N.Y.1990), in which the district court denied summary judgment on a sexual harassment claim. *Halbrook* is inapposite because the court in that case deferred ruling on trial evidence given its denial of summary judgment. The court did not articulate a general rule for considering evidence on summary judgment.

unreasonable for plaintiffs to hold the proposed amendment until discovery ended. Plaintiffs also argue that the proposed amendment would not have required new discovery and that the dates in the scheduling order were irrelevant because the theories pled in the Third Amended Complaint were already in the case. However, the Second Amended Complaint reads as if Talisman operated directly in the Sudan with no intervening subsidiaries and it does not allege that Talisman acted through GNPOC. While references to GNPOC are sprinkled throughout the Second Amended Complaint, the gravamen is that Talisman conspired directly with the Sudanese government. Thus, the Third Amended Complaint, which alleged that Talisman aided and abetted GNPOC and that it conspired with Greater Nile, substantially revised plaintiffs' theory.

It is true that the issue of joint venture liability was mentioned early in the case by Judge Schwartz in a 2003 decision denying Talisman's motion to dismiss on the ground that GNPOC was a necessary party. In that decision, the district court considered and rejected a number of arguments as to why the litigation could not proceed without GNPOC. Judge Schwartz explained that "nearly every paragraph describes alleged unlawful acts by Talisman, not GNPOC." *Presbyterian Church of Sudan,* 244 F. Supp. 2d at 352. In a footnote, the district court added that "[t]o the extent that the Amended Complaint alleges acts by GNPOC, . . . Talisman may potentially be held liable for the acts of other GNPOC members under a theory of joint venture liability." *Id.* at 352 n. 50 (citation omitted)

Plaintiffs cite this footnote as evidence that the district court and Talisman were aware from early in the litigation that plaintiffs might proceed against Greater Nile and GNPOC on theories of joint liability. But Judge Cote observed that the Third Amended Complaint "dramatically alter[ed] the plaintiffs' theories of liability and the focus of the entire case," *Presbyterian Church of Sudan,* 453 F. Supp. 2d at 680, and Talisman vigorously contests the idea that the substance of the amended complaint was already understood to be part of the case. The district court supervised this case for three years before the filing of plaintiffs' motion and was thoroughly familiar with the facts and allegations, having written several lengthy opinions in the matter. We owe deference to the district court's analysis.

The district court also denied leave to amend on the alternative ground that amendment would be futile. The court assessed whether plaintiffs could pierce the corporate veils of GNPOC and subsidiaries between GNPOC and Talisman: the court held plaintiffs could not pierce and that Talisman could not be liable on theories of joint venture or agency. *Id.* at 683–89.

We have not considered what law would be applied in seeking to pierce a corporate veil in the ATS context, and this case does not require us to reach the question. The district court discussed the issue in an abundance of caution; but we have no occasion to do so given our affirming the denial of leave to amend on good-faith grounds.

Finally, plaintiffs argue that even absent amended pleading, the district court should have considered their agency, joint venture, and veil piercing theories. We disagree. The district court concluded that these theories were insufficiently pled, and our independent review of the Second Amended Complaint supports the district court's conclusion.[16]

CONCLUSION

For the foregoing reasons, the judgment of the district court is affirmed.

---

16 Plaintiffs also appeal from the denial of their motions for class certification. Because we affirm the district court's grant of summary judgment as to all claims against Talisman, we do not reach that issue.

RACHEL ROTHSTEIN
v.
UBS AG

647 F. Supp. 2d 292 (E.D.N.Y. 2009)
Decided August 23, 2009

Robert Joseph Tolchin, Robert J. Tolchin, Esq., New York, NY, Nathaniel A. Tarnor, Tarnor, PLLC, Washington, DC, for Plaintiffs.

Daniel Lucas Cantor, Jonathan Rosenberg, O'Melveny & Myers LLP, New York, NY, for Defendant.

OPINION AND ORDER

JED S. RAKOFF, District Judge.

The sympathy one feels for the plaintiffs in this case cannot disguise the fact that their counsel has attempted to stretch the law beyond all recognizable limits. Accordingly on March 6, 2009, the Court issued a "bottom-line" Order granting defendant's motion to dismiss with prejudice plaintiffs' claims that defendant UBS AG ("UBS") aided and abetted international terrorism (Count One) and aided and abetted violations of customary international law (Count Two).[1] This Opinion and Order sets forth the reasons for that ruling and directs the entry of final judgment.

The plaintiffs here are forty-five victims and/or families of victims of violence perpetrated by the terrorist organizations Hamas and Hezbollah in the form of a bombing in Jerusalem, Israel on July 30, 1997; a bombing in Jerusalem, Israel on September 4, 1997; a bombing near Neve Yamin, Israel on March 28, 2001; a bombing in Jerusalem, Israel on August 9, 2001; a bombing in Jerusalem, Israel on December 1, 2001; a rocket attack on Safed, Israel on July 13, 2006; and further rocket attacks on Safed, Israel between July 13, 2006 and July 22, 2006. Defendant UBS, a large international bank, concededly had no direct involvement in

---

1 Plaintiffs had previously withdrawn their other claims, which were for negligence under Israeli law (Count Three), for breach of statutory duty under Israeli law (Count Four), and for aiding and abetting these violations under Israeli law (Count Five). *See* Order, October 17, 2008.

those attacks. But plaintiffs allege that UBS indirectly assisted the Government of Iran in financially supporting Hamas and Hezbollah and consequently is liable to plaintiffs for compensatory and punitive damages pursuant to 18 U.S.C. § 2333 of the Antiterrorism Act (Count One) and under customary international law (Count Two).

The plaintiffs premise these assertions on the admissions made by UBS itself when, in June, 2003, it disclosed that it had transferred U.S. currency to Iran and to Iranian "counterparties," in violation of regulations issued by the U.S. Office of Foreign Asset Control ("OFAC"). Am. Compl. ¶¶ 72, 82. In connection with these violations, UBS paid a $100 million civil monetary penalty to the U.S. government in May, 2004. *See id.* ¶ 82. Building on these admissions, plaintiffs allege that the Iranian government is a recognized sponsor of terrorism and has funded and supported Hamas, Hezbollah, and other Palestinian terrorist organizations; that these terrorist organizations require U.S. cash dollars to carry out their activities; and that UBS's involvement in banknote transactions with Iranian counterparties had the effect of providing U.S. cash dollars to the Iranian government, which, in turn, supplied the aforementioned terrorist organizations with U.S. cash dollars that were used to facilitate terrorist acts. This indirect facilitation, plaintiffs argue, makes UBS liable to plaintiffs for the harms they suffered at the hands of the terrorist groups.

This extended chain of inferences, however, is far too attenuated to provide plaintiffs with sufficient standing to bring this action under federal law. *See Allen v. Wright*, 468 U.S. 737, 750, 104 S. Ct. 3315, 82 L.Ed.2d 556 (1984) (standing requires that the injury be "fairly traceable" to the alleged actions of the defendant); *Simon v. E. Ky. Welfare Rights Org.*, 426 U.S. 26, 42–43, 96 S. Ct. 1917, 48 L.Ed.2d 450 (1976) (standing is not established where injury results from "the independent action of some third party not before the court"); *see also Bell Atlantic Corp. v. Twombly*, 550 U.S. 544, 545, 127 S. Ct. 1955, 167 L.Ed.2d 929 (2007) (from a pleading perspective, "[f]actual allegations must be enough to raise a right to relief above the speculative level"); *Ashcroft v. Iqbal*, ___ U.S. ___, 129 S. Ct. 1937, 1949–50, 173 L.Ed.2d 868 (2009) (affirming *Twombly*).

Specifically, plaintiffs, to establish standing here, must at a minimum allege facts that show a proximate causal relationship between UBS's transfers of funds to Iran and Hamas' and Hezbollah's commission of the terrorist acts that caused plaintiffs' injuries. This they have entirely failed to do.

Among many other deficiencies in the causal chain, the First Amended Complaint ("Am. Compl.") does not allege that UBS is a primary or even relatively significant source of U.S. banknotes for the Iranian government. Moreover, cash dollars have multiple legitimate uses besides funding terrorism, and, as the amended complaint itself states, "[U.S.] cash dollars are a universally accepted currency and means of payment." Am. Compl. ¶ 55. Further still, there are no specific allegations showing that the terrorist groups here in question raise their funds from monies transferred from Iran. Without multiplying examples, the point is that plaintiffs' allegations here are far too speculative to provide the plausible indication of proximate causation necessary to establish plaintiffs' standing in this case.

Plaintiffs point to two cases in the Eastern District of New York that they claim support the adequacy of their inferential pleadings: *Strauss, et al. v. Credit Lyonnais*, S.A., No. 06-CV-0702, 2006 WL 2862704 (E.D.N.Y. Oct. 5, 2006) and *Linde, et al. v. Arab Bank*, PLC, 384 F. Supp. 2d 571 (E.D.N.Y.2005). But, quite aside from the fact that these cases (and other relied on by plaintiffs) were decided before the more stringent pleading standards of Twombly and Iqbal were promulgated by the Supreme Court, both cases involved direct involvement between the defendant banks and the terrorist organizations or "fronts" those organizations directly controlled. No such direct relationships are alleged here. Plaintiffs' claims must therefore be dismissed for lack of standing.

Plaintiffs' alleged claims must also be dismissed for the independent reason that they fail to state a legal claim. Count One is brought under the private right of action provision of the Antiterrorism Act, which provides in pertinent part that

> [a]ny national of the United States injured in his or her person property, or business *by reason of* an act of international terrorism, or his or her estate, survivors, or heirs, may sue therefor in any appropriate district court of the United States. . . .

18 U.S.C. § 2333(a) (emphasis supplied).

The "by reason of" language, ultimately derived from the Clayton Antitrust Act of 1914, 15 U.S.C. §§ 12-27, 52-53, has typically been construed to be synonymous with "proximate cause." *See, e.g. Holmes v. Sec. Investor Prot. Corp.*, 503 U.S. 258, 266, 112 S. Ct. 1311, 117 L.Ed.2d 532 (1992) (in the context of Racketeer Influenced and Corrupt Organizations Act ("RICO")); *id.* at 268, 112 S. Ct. 1311 ("a plaintiff's right to sue under § 4 [of the Clayton Act] required a showing that the defendant's violation not only was a 'but for' cause of his injury, but was the proximate cause as well") (citing *Associated Gen. Contractors of Cal., Inc. v. Carpenters*, 459 U.S. 519, 534, 103 S. Ct. 897, 74 L.Ed.2d 723 (1983)); *Anza v. Ideal Steel Supply Corp.*, 547 U.S. 451, 457, 126 S. Ct. 1991, 164 L.Ed.2d 720 (2006) (citing *Holmes* in the context of RICO); *Bridge v. Phoenix Bond & Indem. Co.*, ___ U.S. ___, 128 S. Ct. 2131, 2143–44, 170 L.Ed.2d 1012 (2008) (discussing the role of reliance in assessing proximate cause under Holmes in the RICO context). If the allegations here are so speculative and attenuated as to deprive plaintiffs of standing, it follows a fortiori that they fail to adequately plead causation.

Furthermore, assuming *arguendo* that a defendant in a private action brought under the Antiterrorism Act can be held liable on an aiding and abetting theory,[2] such a

2 But *see Boim v. Holy Land Foundation for Relief and Development*, 549 F.3d 685, 689 (7th Cir.2008) ("statutory silence on the subject of secondary liability means that there is none; and section 2333(a) does not mention aiders and abettors or other secondary actors").

theory would here require adequate allegations that the defendant not only knew that its funds would be used to sponsor terrorist acts by Hamas and Hezbollah, but also intended to do so. *See, e.g.*, *Boim v. Quranic Literacy Institute and Holy Land Foundation for Relief and Development*, 291 F.3d 1000, 1023 (7th Cir.2002) (requiring plaintiffs to "prove that the defendants knew of Hamas' illegal activities, that they desired to help those activities succeed, and they engaged in some act of helping the illegal activities"); *Boim v. Holy Land Foundation for Relief and Development*, 511 F.3d 707, 716 (7th Cir.2007) (reaffirming elements of aiding and abetting as stated in the first Boim case); *Stutts, et al. v. De Dietrich Group, et al.*, No. 03-CV-4058, 2006 WL 1867060 (E.D.N.Y. June 30, 2006).

No such allegations are remotely made here. In fact, the Court cannot discern any substantive allegation in the amended complaint that adequately alleges intent in any form. Courts in this circuit have dismissed aiding and abetting claims under the Antiterrorism Act precisely for failure to allege knowledge and intent. *See, e.g.*, *Weiss v. Nat'l Westminster Bank PLC*, 453 F. Supp. 2d 609, 621–22 (E.D.N.Y.2006); *Stutts*, at 6; *see also Khulumani v. Barclay Nat'l Bank Ltd.*, 504 F.3d 254, 289 (2d Cir.2007), aff'd mem. by an equally divided court sub nom. *Am. Isuzu Motors, Inc. v. Ntsebeza*, ___ U.S. ___, 128 S. Ct. 2424, 171 L.Ed.2d 225 (2008) (holding in a concurring opinion by Judge Hall that a claim for aiding and abetting requires proof that the defendant knew that the "tools, instrumentalities, or services" it provided would be used to commit an unlawful act).

As for the second cause of action for aiding and abetting violations under customary international law, while customary international law is considered part of federal common law, *see The Paquete Habana*, 175 U.S. 677, 700, 20 S. Ct. 290, 44 L.Ed. 320 (1900), there is a well-established "presumption in favor of preemption of federal common law whenever it can be said that Congress has legislated on the subject." *In re Oswego Barge Corp.*, 664 F.2d 327, 335 (2d Cir.1981). Thus, the second cause of action is swallowed by the first. Moreover, aiding and abetting under customary international law requires the same knowledge and intent as elsewhere, and, as noted, plaintiffs here fail to adequately plead such knowledge and intent. *See Khulumani*, 504 F.3d at 277; *see also Presbyterian Church of Sudan v. Talisman Energy, Inc.*, 453 F. Supp. 2d 633, 669 (S.D.N.Y.2006) (requiring scienter to establish a claim of aiding and abetting in violation of international law).

Accordingly, for the foregoing reasons, the Clerk of the Court is directed to enter final judgment dismissing the plaintiffs' amended complaint in its entirety.

SO ORDERED.

ALEXIS HOLYWEEK SAREI
v.
RIO TINTO PLC

650 F. Supp. 2d 1004 (C.D. Cal. 2009)
Decided July 31, 2009

Brent R. Walton, Elaine T. Byszewski, Kevin P. Roddy, Hagens Berman Sobol Shapiro LLP, Los Angeles, CA, Jeffrey T. Sprung, Shayne C. Stevenson, Steve W. Berman, Hagens Berman Sobol Shapiro, Joel D. Cunningham, Paul Luvera, Luvera Barnett Brindley Beninger & Cunningham, Seattle, WA, for Plaintiff.

Anthony L. Press, Charles Ernest Patterson, Morrison & Foerster, Los Angeles, CA, Jack W. Londen, James J. Brosnahan, Morrison & Foerster, San Francisco, CA, Shayne C. Stevenson, Hagens Berman Sobol Shapiro, Seattle, WA, Peter J. Stern, Morrison and Foerster LLP, Tokyo, Japàn, Amanda Quester, Vincent M. Garvey, Federal Trade Commission, Washington, DC, for Defendants.

ORDER RE: PRUDENTIAL EXHAUSTION

MARGARET M. MORROW, District Judge.

Plaintiffs, who are current and former residents of the island of Bougainville in Papua New Guinea ("PNG"), filed this putative class action in 2000 against defendants Rio Tinto plc and Rio Tinto Limited under the Alien Tort Claims Act ("ATCA" or "ATS"), 28 U.S.C. § 1350. Plaintiffs allege that defendants' mining operations on Bougainville destroyed the island's environment, harmed the health of its people, and incited a ten-year civil war, during which thousands of civilians died or were injured. They assert that defendants are guilty of war crimes and crimes against humanity, as well as racial discrimination and environmental harm that violates international law.

In December 2008, an en banc panel of the Ninth Circuit Court of Appeals remanded the action to this court for the limited purpose of ascertaining whether, as an initial, prudential matter, exhaustion should be required. *See Sarei v. Rio Tinto, PLC,* 550 F.3d 822 (9th Cir.2008) (en banc) ("*Rio Tinto IV*"); *id.* at 825 n. 1 (McKeown, J.) ("As a prudential matter, in this case there is a certain logic to considering exhaustion before considering threshold grounds that may 'deny[] audience to a case on the merits'" (citation omitted; alteration original)).

I. Procedural Background

The factual background of this dispute is detailed extensively in the court's prior order on defendants' motion to dismiss; that discussion is incorporated by reference in this order. *See Sarei v. Rio Tinto,* 221 F. Supp. 2d 1116, 1121-27 ("*Rio TintoI*"); *see also Rio Tinto IV,* 550 F.3d at 825–26 (McKeown, J.) (factual and procedural overview). The court provides a brief summary of the procedural history of the action as relevant to the issue on remand below.

A. Plaintiffs' Lawsuit and *Rio Tinto I*

On November 2, 2000, Alexis Holyweek Sarei, a California resident who lived in Bougainville between 1973 and 1987, and twenty-one individuals who then resided in Bougainville or elsewhere in PNG, filed this putative class action against Rio Tinto pic and Rio Tinto Limited (collectively "Rio Tinto"). Shortly thereafter, plaintiffs filed a first amended complaint asserting claims under the Alien Tort Claims Act, 28 U.S.C. § 1350.[1] The amended complaint pled claims for crimes against humanity; war crimes/murder; violation of the rights to life, health, and security of the person; racial discrimination; cruel, inhuman, and degrading treatment; violation of international environmental rights; and a consistent pattern of gross violations of human rights.[2] The pleading also alleged claims for negligence, public nuisance, private nuisance, strict liability, equitable relief, and medical monitoring.[3] Plaintiffs contend that Rio Tinto's mining operations destroyed Bougainville's environment and the health of its residents. They also assert that, because the mine was a joint venture between Rio Tinto and the PNG government, and because Rio Tinto's threats led PNG to use military force against the Bougainvilleans, it is responsible for human rights violations and war crimes committed during Bougainville's civil war.

On January 26, 2001, Rio Tinto filed a motion to dismiss plaintiffs' complaint,[4] asserting that the court lacked subject matter jurisdiction because plaintiffs had failed to state a cognizable claim under the Alien Torts Claim Act. Alternatively, it argued that the action should be dismissed on *forum non conveniens* grounds, as either Papua New Guinea or Australia was a more appropriate forum. Finally, Rio Tinto challenged plaintiffs' claims as nonjusticiable under the act of state, political question, and international comity doctrines.

---

1 First Amended Class Action Complaint for Violations of the Alien Tort Claims Act [28 U.S.C. § 1350], Docket No. 7 (Dec. 6, 2000).

2 *See id.,* ¶¶ 210–66.

3 *See id.,* ¶¶ 267–93.

4 Notice of Motion and Motion to Dismiss for Failure to State a Claim, Docket No. 18 (Jan. 26, 2001).

In July 2002, the court issued a final order on Rio Tinto's motion to dismiss,[5] which, *inter alia,* addressed its threshold argument that the action should be dismissed because plaintiffs had not exhausted remedies available locally in PNG. *Rio Tinto I,* 221 F. Supp. 2d at 1132–33. Comparing the ATCA and the Torture Victims Protection Act ("TVPA"), the court concluded that there was no explicit statutory requirement that plaintiffs exhaust local remedies before filing suit in federal court under the ATCA, and no indication in the legislative history that Congress intended to impose such a requirement on ATCA claims. *Id.* at 1132–38. The court next considered Rio Tinto's alternative argument, namely, that exhaustion of local remedies is a well-established principle of international law and should be required of an ATCA plaintiff pleading a "violation of the law of nations." *Id.* at 1138–39. The court concluded that "the ATCA does not adopt wholesale all principles of international law," but instead "creates a domestic cause of action for violations of international law," which "need not impose the same conditions on a plaintiff's right to sue as international law or the domestic law of other nations." *Id.* at 1139. Consequently, the court held that plaintiffs were not required to exhaust remedies available in PNG, or show that doing so would be futile, before filing an ATCA suit in federal court. *Id.*

B. *Sosa, Rio Tinto II* and *Rio Tinto III*

The parties filed cross-appeals. Plaintiffs challenged the court's dismissal of their ATCA claims on jurisdictional and political question grounds, while Rio Tinto maintained that the ATCA required exhaustion of local remedies. The appeal was argued and submitted on September 8, 2003; the panel withdrew the submission, however, on December 11, 2003, to await the Supreme Court's opinion in *Sosa v. Alvarez-Machain,* 542 U.S. 692, 124 S. Ct. 2739, 159 L.Ed.2d 718 (2004).

In *Sosa,* the Supreme Court held that the ATCA "is a jurisdictional statute creating no new causes of action." It noted, however, that the statute "was intended to have practical effect the moment it became law," and thus provided a "cause of action for [a] modest number of international law violations with a potential for personal liability." *Id.* at 724, 124 S. Ct. 2739. Consistent with this view of the statute, the Court held that "courts should require any claim based on the present-day law of nations to rest on a norm of international character accepted by the civilized world and defined with a specificity comparable to the features of the 18th-century paradigms" it identified when tracing the ATCA's history. *Id.* at 725, 124 S. Ct. 2739. The Court observed in dicta that it "would certainly consider" an exhaustion requirement "in an appropriate [ATCA] case." *Id.* at 733 n. 21, 124 S. Ct. 2739.

Following *Sosa,* in June 2005, the parties reargued their cross-appeals in this case and the matter was resubmitted. In August 2006, a three-judge panel of the Ninth

5 *See* Amended Order Granting Defendants' Motion to Dismiss, 221 F. Supp. 2d 1116 (C.D.Cal.2002). The court had previously issued an order on the motion in March 2002. (*See* Order, Docket No. 131 (Mar. 23, 2002).)

Circuit affirmed in part, reversed in part, and remanded. *See Sarei v. Rio Tinto, PLC,* 456 F.3d 1069 (9th Cir.2006) ("*Rio Tinto II*"), withdrawn and superseded on rehearing in part by *Sarei v. Rio Tinto, PLC,* 487 F.3d 1193 (9th Cir.2007) ("*Rio Tinto III*") (Fisher, J.). Rio Tinto petitioned for rehearing and rehearing en banc. Its petition was initially granted in part; the merits panel's majority and dissenting opinions were withdrawn and superseded by *Rio Tinto III.*

In *Rio Tinto III,* the panel considered Rio Tinto's contention that an exhaustion requirement should be read into the ATCA. *Id.* at 1213–23. Examining congressional intent—of "paramount importance" in any exhaustion inquiry—the court concluded that the ATCA's "legislative history stopped] short of a broad and unambiguous statement that Congress believed that the satisfaction of the international exhaustion rule was *required* as a matter of U.S. domestic law before an ATCA claim could be heard in a U.S. court." *Id.* at 1214, 1217. Noting that the TVPA targeted only torture and extrajudicial killing claims, the panel observed that in "addressing causes of action based on norms of customary international law, Congress . . . treated different kinds of substantive claims differently—a caution against importing an across-the-board exhaustion requirement into ATCA based on what Congress did in the TVPA." *Id.* at 1217–18.

Finding no support for a statutory exhaustion requirement in the text or legislative history of the ATCA, the court next assessed whether exhaustion was warranted as a matter of judicial discretion. Ultimately, it concluded that "the balance tips against judicially engrafting an exhaustion requirement onto a statute where Congress has declined to do so, and in an area of international law where the Supreme Court has called for the exercise of judicial caution rather than innovation." *Id.* at 1219.[6]

---

6 The court offered four reasons why it declined to require exhaustion as a matter of judicial discretion in every ATCA case. First, it noted that "the international norm of exhaustion does not speak to the hybrid situation [in an ATCA case] where a domestic court in a sovereign country, rather than an international tribunal, is charged with adjudicating violations of customary international law through the vehicle of a civil suit." *Id.* at 1220. Second, it concluded that international exhaustion was procedural rather than substantive, and noted that the Supreme Court had not addressed whether the methodology it employed in *Sosa* to identify substantive international norms within ATCA's jurisdictional grant also applied to procedural and other nonsubstantive customary law norms. *Id.* at 1221. Third, the court found defendants' argument that an exhaustion requirement could improve compliance with international human rights law by providing an incentive for nations to improve their legal systems "fairly speculative," and posited the "alternative and perhaps equally plausible hypothesis" that foreign court judgments against rights-abusing defendants could place pressure "from above" on the state where the human rights abuses had occurred. *Id.* at 1222 (quoting ELLEN LUTZ & KATHRYN SIKKINK, THE JUSTICE CASCADE: THE EVOLUTION AND IMPACT OF HUMAN RIGHTS TRIALS IN LATIN AMERICA, 2 CHI. J. INT'L. 1, 4 (2001); *id.* at 24–25, 30). Finally, in a nod to the unique nature of the ATCA, the Ninth Circuit concluded that importing a blanket exhaustion requirement into the ATCA "by judicial fiat" was inadvisable, "especially when Congress has not seen fit to do so when it had the opportunity." *Rio Tinto III,* 487 F.3d at 1223.

Judge Bybee wrote a lengthy dissent expressing the view that exhaustion of local remedies should be required before a U.S. court exercises jurisdiction over ATCA claims. *Id.* at 1224–46 (Bybee, J., dissenting). Judge Bybee observed that exhaustion "is a well-established principle of international law," and one the United States "has long recognized." *Id.* at 1231. In addition, he referenced various international tribunals and treaties requiring exhaustion. *Id.* at 1232–33. After discussing whether exhaustion was procedural or substantive, *id.* at 1233–36, and concluding that the exhaustion requirement was sufficiently well-defined to be easily applied by the courts, *id.* at 1236–38, Judge Bybee argued that, at the very least, courts "should recognize exhaustion as a prudential principle required by our domestic law [] for the same reasons that we require exhaustion of state, tribal and administrative remedies." *Id.* at 1238.[7]

C. *Rio Tinto IV*

Following the decision in *Rio Tinto III,* Rio Tinto filed a second petition for hearing en banc, which asserted that exhaustion ought to be required. The petition was granted. *See Sarei v. Rio Tinto, PLC,* 499 F.3d 923 (9th Cir.2007). The case was argued and submitted on October 11, 2007. On December 16, 2008, the en banc court remanded the case "for the limited purpose to determine in the first instance whether to impose an exhaustion requirement on plaintiffs." *Rio Tinto IV,* 550 F.3d at 832 (McKeown, J.).

Judge McKeown, who authored the plurality opinion, concluded that the *Sosa* Court's statement that exhaustion should be considered in an "appropriate" ATCA case indicated that exhaustion ought to be approached "as a prudential principle." *Id.* at 827. Juxtaposing "prudential" or judicially-imposed exhaustion with statutory exhaustion requirements, she explained that the former "originated [in the United States] in habeas corpus cases to serve a gatekeeping function," i.e., to prevent unnecessary conflicts between the federal and state courts, which are "equally bound to guard and protect [constitutional] rights." *Id.* at 828 (citation omitted). In this context, and in the tribal court context as well, Judge McKeown stated, the principle of prudential exhaustion is "grounded in principles of comity," specifically respect for another, potentially conflicting sovereign. *Id.* at 828–29. Judge McKeown compared the prudential exhaustion requirement in these areas

---

7 Judge Bybee identified three reasons for imposing a prudential exhaustion requirement: (1) the requirement would demonstrate respect for the tribunals or other dispute resolution processes of a sovereign nation, *id.* at 1238–40; (2) it would give other countries "the opportunity to address their own conflicts and craft their own solutions," and would "encourage creative political solutions" that cannot readily be achieved through litigation, *id.* at 1240–41; and (3) it would foster more accurate fact-finding by requiring that the initial round(s) of litigation occur, when possible, where the claims arose, *id.* at 1242. In addition, he noted, an exhaustion requirement would "preserve" the courts' role in a government of separated powers. *Id.* at 1242. Examining this action. Judge Bybee concluded that it was "a textbook case for exhaustion." *Id.* at 1245–46.

with the exhaustion of local remedies rule that is part of international law, and concluded that the international rule too was motivated by concerns regarding comity. *Id.* at 829–30.

Judge McKeown next discussed the considerations animating exhaustion. She noted that cases like this one "simultaneously appeal to two divergent impulses that have traditionally played out in our country's international affairs and have been imported into our legal system. The first impulse is to safeguard and respect the principle of comity. . . . The second is the American role in establishing collective security arrangements that support international institutions, including international tribunals. . . . Both impulses draw from the recognition that we need a complement to our domestic system, because we are but one member in a community of nations." *Id.* at 830–31.

The interplay of these concerns informs the prudential exhaustion analysis that the plurality directed be conducted here:

> "The lack of a significant U.S. 'nexus' [in this case] is an important consideration in evaluating whether plaintiffs should be required to exhaust their local remedies in accordance with the principle of international comity. . . . [On the other hand, s]ome of the [plaintiffs'] claims— torture, crimes against humanity, and war crimes—may implicate matters of 'universal concern,' generally described as offenses 'for which a state has jurisdiction to punish without regard to territoriality or the nationality of the offenders.'" *Id.* at 831 (citations omitted).

Observing that the mere existence of universal jurisdiction did not necessarily mean that it should be exercised, Judge McKeown concluded that "in ATS cases where the United States 'nexus' is weak, courts should carefully consider the question of exhaustion, particularly—but not exclusively—with respect to claims that do not involve matters of 'universal concern.'" *Id.*

Several members of the en banc panel wrote separately to express their views regarding exhaustion in the ATCA context.[8] Judge Bea, joined by Judge Callahan, concurred in the limited remand, but opined that the ATCA mandated application of a traditional exhaustion analysis in every case. *Id.* at 833–37 (Bea, J., concurring). Emphasizing the *Sosa* Court's explanation that the ATCA "simply provides

---

8 Judge Ikuta, joined by Judge Kleinfeld, dissented to express her view that "in the absence of direction from Congress, [courts] cannot read the ATS as authorizing an extension of jurisdiction to disputes lacking any nexus to United States territory, citizens, or interests." 550 F.3d at 840 (Ikuta, J., dissenting) (citing *Sosa,* 542 U.S. at 726, 124 S. Ct. 2739). Judge Reinhardt, joined by Judges Pregerson, Berzon, and Rawlinson, dissented. *Id.* at 841–46 (Reinhardt, J., dissenting). He argued that the *Sosa* Court had not "counseled" the court to adopt prudential exhaustion in the ATCA context, or "signaled" that it believed such a requirement was appropriate. *Id.* at 841. Consequently, Judge Reinhardt maintained, the court should refrain from imposing such a requirement before the Supreme Court had "had the opportunity to decide itself after the issue is properly presented to it." *Id.* at 841. Citing evidence that many putative class members feared returning to PNG, Judge Reinhardt also concluded that this case was not an "appropriate" one in which to require exhaustion. *Id.*

a forum for hearing existing causes of action that arise under the law of nations," Judge Bea argued that "it makes more sense to interpret the [ATCA] as incorporating the whole of the law of nations: the rights it grants *and* the limitations it places on those rights." *Id.* at 833; *id.* at 835 ("But if exhaustion *is* raised [in a particular case], and so the case *is* appropriate, it would seem *Sosa* indicated the Court would consider exhaustion as a *requirement.* 'Deference to the political branches,' on the other hand, is not required, but only *'possible,'* and then only on a case-specific—i.e., prudential—basis"). Such an exhaustion requirement, he stated, would include standard exceptions for futility or ineffectiveness. *Id.* at 836 ("In other words, as *part* of the law of nations's exhaustion requirement, the futility excuse is *also* incorporated into the ATS's statutory exhaustion requirement. Thus, a statutorily required two-step exhaustion analysis would permit Sarei to prosecute his ATS claims without exhausting his local remedies in Papua New Guinea if he can prove that local remedies there are ineffective, unobtainable, unduly prolonged, inadequate, or otherwise futile to pursue").[9] Echoing Judge Bybee's dissent in *Rio Tinto III,* Judge Bea contended that "[a] mandatory requirement of exhaustion of local remedies, except where futile or otherwise unavailable, allows our courts to play the role the ATS intended them to play: an ultimate venue for claimed violations of the law of nations when those claimed violations cannot or will not be cured by the courts of the country in which the injuries occurred." *Id.*[10]

In the end, seven of the eleven members of the en banc panel declined to impose an exhaustion *requirement* in every ATCA case.[11] Six, however, agreed to remand the case to this court for the limited purpose of having the court consider whether to impose a *prudential* exhaustion requirement. *Id.* at 832 n. 10 (McKeown, J.).[12]

---

9 *See id.* at 836 (Bea, J., concurring) ("I wish to make clear that a statutory exhaustion requirement does not mean a plaintiff must prove in every case that he *has* exhausted his local remedies. Rather, it means a district court must conduct a two-step exhaustion analysis, in the process considering whether first, local remedies exist, and second, whether local exhaustion would be futile, unduly prolonged, or subject to one of the other exceptions recognized in customary international law. If so, local exhaustion requirements may be excused").

10 Judge Bea noted that the "one aspect" of Judge Bybee's *Rio Tinto III* dissent with which he disagreed was the latter's "speculation] as to whether there was an additional, prudential basis for exhaustion" in the ATCA context. *Id.* at 834 n. 3. Judge Bea opined that "the elements that go into a prudential consideration, such as 'nexus' or international comity, [] should [not] be left to individual and potentially discordant trial court determinations." This was particularly true, he noted, because "[t]he facts underpinning these prudential considerations are generally undisputed; the determinations primarily involve judicial policy with regard to international relations." *Id.* Consequently, Judge Bea opposed imposition of an initial, prudential exhaustion inquiry and argued for conducting a mandatory two-step exhaustion analysis in every ATCA case. *Id.*

11 *See Rio Tinto IV,* 550 F.3d at 824 (plurality authored by Judge McKeown joined by Judges Schroeder and Silverman); *id.* at 841 (dissent authored by Judges Reinhardt joined by Judges Pregerson, Berzon, and Rawlinson).

12 The judges who concurred in the limited remand were Judges McKeown, Schroeder, Silverman; Judges Bea and Callahan, *id.* at 833 (Bea, J., concurring) ("I concur in the plurality's conclusion

II. Discussion

A. Prudential Exhaustion in Alien Tort Claims Act Cases

Where, as in the case of the ATCA, Congress has not clearly required exhaustion, sound judicial discretion governs. *See McCarthy v. Madigan,* 503 U.S. 140, 144, 112 S. Ct. 1081, 117 L.Ed.2d 291 (1992), superseded by statute as stated in *Booth v. Churner,* 532 U.S. 731, 732, 121 S. Ct. 1819, 149 L.Ed.2d 958 (2001). "Judicially-imposed or prudential exhaustion is not a prerequisite to the exercise of jurisdiction, but rather is 'one among related doctrines—including abstention, finality, and ripeness—that govern the timing of federal-court decisionmaking.'" *Rio Tinto IV,* 550 F.3d at 828 (McKeown, J.) (quoting *McCarthy,* 503 U.S. at 144, 112 S. Ct. 1081).

As noted, in *Sosa,* the Supreme Court recognized that imposing a prudential exhaustion requirement might be warranted in "appropriate" ATCA cases. *Sosa,* 542 U.S. at 733 n. 21, 124 S. Ct. 2739. Citing this observation, the *Rio Tinto IV* plurality held that "[w]here the 'nexus' to the United States is weak, courts should carefully consider the question of exhaustion, particularly—but not exclusively—with respect to claims that do not involve matters of 'universal concern.'" *Rio Tinto IV,* 550 F.3d at 824 (McKeown, J.). In conducting this analysis, the plurality directed that courts balance two competing interests. *Id.* at 830. On the one hand, they must "safeguard and respect the principle of comity." *Id.*; *see also Sosa,* 542 U.S. at 761, 124 S. Ct. 2739 (Breyer, J., concurring) ("I would ask whether the exercise of jurisdiction under the ATS is consistent with those notions of comity that lead each nation to respect the sovereign rights of other nations by limiting the reach of its laws and their enforcement"). On the other hand, "[t]he nature of certain allegations and the gravity of the potential violations of international law [ ] trigger the second impulse: [U.S. courts'] historical commitment to upholding customary international law." *Rio Tinto IV,* 550 F.3d at 831 (McKeown, J.). In analyzing prudential exhaustion in the ATCA context, therefore, courts must ask questions typically associated with the doctrine of international comity, while at the same time evaluating the universality of plaintiffs' claims.

Following the en banc court's remand, the court received briefs from the parties and held a hearing at which they presented their respective positions concerning the nature of the inquiry the court had been asked to conduct. The parties disagreed regarding the meaning of the plurality's direction that the court "determine in the first instance whether to impose an exhaustion requirement on plaintiffs." *Id.* at 832. Plaintiffs argued that the court had been directed solely to decide, as a threshold matter, whether a prudential exhaustion requirement should be imposed in this

---

that the district court erred by failing to conduct an exhaustion analysis, and I agree a limited remand is the preferable solution"); and Judge Kleinfeld, *id.* at 840 (Kleinfeld, J., concurring) ("I concur in the result reached by Judge McKeown's opinion, limited remand for consideration of whether exhaustion should be required. I do so because we must provide some clear direction to the district court, and only a result adopted by a majority can do so").

case; they asserted that if the court answered that question yes, it should not conduct the traditional two-step exhaustion analysis but should return the matter forthwith to the circuit court.[13] Focusing on the plurality's discussion of the standard two-step exhaustion analysis as a "framework for evaluating exhaustion," Rio Tinto countered that it should be permitted to "justify an exhaustion requirement," which plaintiffs could rebut by demonstrating the futility of exhaustion. Specifically, it asserted that the court "should weigh the 'animating considerations' of U.S. nexus and matters of 'universal concern' and determine 'whether to impose an exhaustion requirement on plaintiffs'" only *after* considering "the availability and adequacy of remedies" in Papua New Guinea.[14]

While, based on the language of the plurality opinion, the matter is not free from doubt, the court ultimately concluded that the plurality wished it to determine, as an initial threshold inquiry, whether it was appropriate to impose a prudential exhaustion requirement in this case.[15] It therefore solicited briefs that addressed the factors identified in the plurality opinion as relevant to this determination—i.e., nexus and universality, as informed by general notions of comity—and that refrained from arguing factors relevant in applying the traditional two-step exhaustion analysis—i.e., the availability of local remedies, and whether plaintiffs should be excused from exhausting local remedies because they "are ineffective, unobtainable, unduly prolonged, inadequate, or otherwise futile to pursue," *Rio Tinto IV*, 550 F.3d at 833 n. 1 (Bea, J., concurring).[16] The court further determined that, if it concluded a prudential exhaustion requirement should be imposed with respect to any of plaintiffs' claims, it would conduct the traditional two-step exhaustion analysis before returning the matter to the circuit court so that the appellate court

---

13 Plaintiffs' Status Report and Request for Briefing Schedule, Docket No. 201 (Jan. 14, 2009).

14 Rio Tinto's Response to Plaintiffs' Status Report and Request for Briefing Schedule, Docket No. 204 (Mar. 6, 2009) at 3–7.

15 *Rio Tinto IV*, 550 F.3d at 833 n. 1 (Bea, J., concurring) ("[T]he district court must, in its discretion, choose whether [exhaustion is in fact required], depending on considerations such as whether [plaintiffs'] claims have a close nexus to the United States, affect principles favoring international comity and advancement of international institutions, and implicate notions of customary international law"); *see id.* at 832 (McKeown, J.) ("We remand to the district court for the limited purpose to determine in the first instance *whether* to impose an exhaustion requirement on plaintiffs" (emphasis added)); *see also id.* at 836 (Bea, J., concurring) ("[A] statutory exhaustion requirement . . . means a district court must conduct a two-step exhaustion analysis. . . . But this is different from the plurality's prudential exhaustion doctrine, which grants district courts discretion to decide whether or not to consider exhaustion in the first place"); *id.* at 837 n. 7 ("[I]t appears the plurality holds the district court here has discretion not to conduct a two-step exhaustion analysis should it find one unnecessary due to prudential considerations").

16 In its brief, Rio Tinto prematurely raised arguments regarding access to witnesses and evidence in PNG. (Rio Tinto Opening Brief at 15–18.) For the reasons stated, these matters will be considered, if at all, after the threshold inquiry as to whether exhaustion should be prudentially required in this case has been completed.

would have a full and complete record in deciding whether plaintiffs should be required to pursue local remedies as to any claim.[17]

B. Whether Exhaustion Should be Prudentially Required in This Case

1. Strength of the Nexus Between Plaintiffs' Claims and the United States

In *Rio Tinto IV,* Judge McKeown made the following observation with respect to the nexus between plaintiffs' claims and the United States:

> "This [case] . . . lacks the traditional bases for exercising our sovereign jurisdiction to prescribe laws, namely nationality, territory, and effects within the United States. *See* RESTATEMENT (THIRD) [FOREIGN RELATIONS LAW OF THE UNITED STATES] § 403(2) at cmt. d [(1987)] (stating jurisdiction is appropriately exercised with respect to activity outside the state that has or intends to have substantial effect within the state's territory). The lack of a significant U.S. 'nexus' is an important consideration in evaluating whether plaintiffs should be required to exhaust their local remedies in accordance with the principle of international comity." *Rio Tinto IV,* 550 F.3d at 831.

Examining the accepted bases for jurisdiction to prescribe set forth in section 402 of the Restatement, Rio Tinto adds that plaintiffs' claims have nothing to do with "conduct that, wholly or in substantial part, takes place within [U.S.] territory," RESTATEMENT § 402(1)(a); that they do not implicate "the status of persons, or interests in things, present within its territory," *id.,* § 402(1)(b); and that they are not premised on "conduct outside [the U.S.'s] territory that has or is intended to have substantial effect within its territory," *id.* § 402(1)(c).[18] Defendants also argue that no U.S. national is a party to this action, such that there might be a basis for

---

17 *See Rio Tinto IV,* 550 F.3d at 837 (Bea, J., concurring) ("I would require the district court to consider (1) whether Sarei had local remedies and exhausted them and (2) whether such exhaustion would be futile or otherwise inadequate—not merely require the court to decide whether to conduct this two-step analysis [as does the plurality]"); *id.* at 841 (Reinhardt, J., dissenting) ("The plurality opinion remands this action to the district court to consider whether this is a case in which prudential exhaustion analysis should be applied, and, if so, whether plaintiffs should be required to exhaust their remedies in Papua New Guinea before proceeding further in the district court"); *see also id.* at 832 (McKeown, J.) ("As a preliminary matter, to 'exhaust,' it is not sufficient that a plaintiff merely initiate a suit, but rather, the plaintiff must obtain a final decision of the highest court in the hierarchy of courts in the legal system at issue, or show that the state of the law or availability of remedies would make further appeal futile. [ ] Another basic element is that the remedy must be available, effective, and not futile. [ ] To measure effectiveness, a court must look at the circumstances surrounding the access to a remedy and the ultimate utility of the remedy to the petitioner. . . . A judgment that cannot be enforced is an incomplete, and thus ineffective, remedy. The adequacy determination will also necessarily include an assessment of any delay in the delivery of a decision" (citations omitted)).

18 Rio Tinto Opening Brief at 3.

exercising jurisdiction to prescribe under section 402(2).[19] Finally, Rio Tinto asserts that plaintiffs' allegations do not involve "conduct outside [U.S.] territory by persons not its nationals that is directed against the security of the state or against a limited class of other state interests," RESTATEMENT § 402(3).[20]

In response, plaintiffs assert that "[a]ny challenge to the sufficiency of nexus in this case must be made with the understanding that every ATS case will involve claims by an alien for a tort committed in violation of the law of nations."[21] They argue that "[w]hat Rio asks this Court to do is defer to factors articulated in the Restatement in order to determine the wisdom and legitimacy of the ATS itself."[22] Because the ATCA provides jurisdiction in U.S. courts when (1) an alien sues (2) for a tort (3) committed in violation of the law of nations, plaintiffs contend that "[a]ny threshold requirements suggested for jurisdiction by the Restatement that are in tension with the very language of the ATS cannot seriously be considered."[23] Given these requirements for stating a claim under the ATCA, plaintiffs maintain that "neither [their] citizenship status [ ], nor [their] physical location [ ] at the time they suffered violations of customary international law, is determinative on the question of 'nexus' to the United States."[24] Plaintiffs also observe that the Ninth Circuit has held that courts "are constrained by what § 1350 shows on its face: no

---

19 This section states, in relevant part, that "a state has jurisdiction to prescribe law with respect to . . . the activities, interests, status, or relations of its nationals outside as well as within its territory." Restatement § 402(2). Although, as noted, plaintiffs allege that Sarei is a lawful permanent resident ("LPR") of the United States, Rio Tinto asserts that LPR status is not synonymous with the term "U.S. national," and thus that Sarei's residence does not provide a basis for plaintiffs to invoke jurisdiction to prescribe under this section. (Rio Tinto Opening Brief at 3 n. 2 (citing 8 U.S.C. § 1101(a)(3); *Perdomo-Padilla v. Ashcroft,* 333 F.3d 964, 967–71 (9th Cir.2003); and RESTATEMENT § 212).) Additionally, Rio Tinto contends that, as a corporation's nationality "is that of the state under whose law it is organized," RESTATEMENT § 213; *id.* § 402 cmt. e, Rio Tinto plc is a British corporation, and Rio Tinto Limited is an Australian corporation. (Rio Tinto Opening Brief at 3 n. 1.) It also notes that neither corporation maintains a principal place of business in the United States, which is one basis for assessing "nationality" in the context of diversity jurisdiction. (*Id.*)

20 Rio Tinto Opening Brief at 3.

21 Plaintiffs' Reply at 10.

22 *Id.* at 11.

23 *Id.* (citing *Wiwa v. Royal Dutch Petroleum Co.,* 626 F. Supp. 2d 377, 381–82 (S.D.N.Y. 2009)) (quoting *Kadic v. Karadzic,* 70 F.3d 232, 238 (2d Cir.1995) (identifying the "first," "second," and "third" "ATS conditions")); *see also id.* at 12 ("Jurisdictional requirements of the ATS itself cannot logically be weighed as factors held against Plaintiffs in determining whether a sufficient nexus exists—the ATS is not itself under scrutiny").

24 *Id.* at 12; *see also* Plaintiffs' Opening Brief at 18–21; *id.* at 21 ("[N]either the citizenship status of the Plaintiffs, nor the physical location of Plaintiffs at the time they suffered violations of customary international law, is determinative on the question of 'nexus' to the United States. Were these considerations determinative, the ATS would have no force or effect, and the legion of precedential case law permitting foreign plaintiffs to litigate under the ATS for offenses committed abroad would be swept away. The holding in *Sosa* precludes Rio

limitations as to the citizenship of the defendant, or the locus of the injury." *In re Estate of Ferdinand E. Marcos Human Rights Litigation (Trajano v. Marcos),* 978 F.2d 493, 500 (9th Cir.1992).

Plaintiffs contend that, rather than focusing on the Restatement factors, the nexus inquiry must examine the ties Rio Tinto has to the United States as well as the "strong United States interest in vindicating international human rights violations" committed by companies acting abroad.[25] Plaintiffs argue that Rio Tinto is a multinational mining group that has its largest concentration of assets in the United States; that has operations in at least fifty countries worldwide, including the United States; that owns a California corporation, U.S. Borax; that obtained much of the original funding for its Panguna mining operations in PNG from the Bank of America; and that maintains American Depository Receipt facilities at the Bank of New York.[26] Put differently, plaintiffs argue that the presence of adequate minimum contacts between Rio Tinto and the United States for personal jurisdiction purposes demonstrates that this case has an adequate "nexus" to the United States.

The court concludes that "nexus" is most sensibly evaluated in the ATCA context by consideration of a spectrum or range (weakest to strongest) of contacts or connections, not as an absolute. In assessing where on that spectrum a particular ATCA case falls, courts should consider the Restatement factors outlined above, other pertinent connections between the United States and the parties and/or claims, and the scope and purpose of the ATCA itself.[27] Viewed in this manner, the parties' positions are reconcilable and reflect a variety of factors, all of which are properly considered in testing the strength of the "nexus" between an ATCA plaintiff or his claims and a United States forum.

---

from arguing that extraterritorial torts affecting non-citizens cannot be adjudicated here [in the United States] under the ATS").

25 *Id.* at 21 (quoting *Presbyterian Church of Sudan v. Talisman Energy, Inc.,* 244 F. Supp. 2d 289, 339 (S.D.N.Y.2003)).

26 *Id.* at 21–24.

27 None of the concurring or dissenting members of the *Rio Tinto IV* en banc panel endorsed or joined in Judge McKeown's analysis regarding the weight to be afforded the Restatement factors in evaluating nexus. Consequently, it does not appear that her views regarding the subject are binding on remand. *See, e.g., Alperin v. Vatican Bank,* 410 F.3d 532, 552 n. 13 (9th Cir.2005) ("Abiding by the rule that when 'no single rationale explaining the result enjoys the assent of five Justices, the holding of the Court may be viewed as that position taken by those Members who concurred in the judgments on the narrowest grounds,'" *Marks v. United States,* 430 U.S. 188, 193, 97 S. Ct. 990, 51 L.Ed.2d 260 (1977) (internal quotation marks omitted)). As a result, the plurality's analysis serves as a useful starting point in evaluating "nexus," but does not preclude consideration of other factors. The court concurs with the plurality that the Restatement factors are relevant; it also finds persuasive plaintiffs' arguments that the specific purpose and jurisdictional requirements of the ACTA (e.g., that suit be filed by an alien) caution against limiting the nexus inquiry to the Restatement factors, or applying them in an overly rigid fashion.

The *Rio Tinto IV* plurality commented that the nexus between plaintiffs' claims here and the United States appeared to be weak given that Rio Tinto is a foreign corporation; that the acts in question occurred exclusively on foreign soil; and that the violations alleged were directed at aliens, virtually all of whom have no connection with the United States. *See Rio Tinto IV,* 550 F.3d at 831 (McKeown, J.) ("The lack of a significant United States 'nexus' to the allegations here stimulates the comity response. These claims involve a foreign corporation's complicity in acts on foreign soil that affected aliens (though at least one of them—Sarei—has enjoyed the status of a lawful permanent resident of this country for some time now)").[28] Balanced against these factors are Rio Tinto's connections to the United States. The court agrees with plaintiffs that these merit consideration, although it does not agree that they are dispositive in assessing the strength of the "nexus" between this dispute and an American forum. This is particularly true since most of Rio Tinto's connections to the United States have nothing to do with plaintiffs' claims.[29]

Plaintiffs represent that the government of PNG and the Autonomous Bougainville Government, now established on that island,[30] have confirmed that they do not oppose the court's exercise of ATCA jurisdiction over plaintiffs' claims; they present several letters sent by PNG and Bougainvillean officials to the U.S. ambassador to PNG confirming this fact.[31] These submissions show that, as early as 2003,

---

28 Plaintiffs note that Sarei's wife is a putative class member acting on behalf of her deceased son, who was killed in the Bougainville conflict. They assert that Mrs. Sarei is a United States citizen, and that her son was as well. (Plaintiffs' Opening Brief at 18 n. 25.)

29 Rio Tinto concedes that its "ownership of U.S. companies might be relevant to nexus if those companies were involved in the challenged conduct." (Rio Tinto Reply at 8.)

30 Under the Bougainville Peace Agreement signed August 30, 2001, Bougainville's autonomy will increase over time, as it will "operat[e] under a home-grown Bougainville Constitution with a right to assume increasing control over a wide range of powers, functions, personnel and resources on the basis of guarantees contained in the National [PNG] Constitution." *See* Bougainville Peace Agreement at 1, available at http://www.google.com/#hl=en&q=bougainville + peace + agreement&aq=O&oq=bougainville + peace + &aqi=g4&fp=kEOCV11PqvM (last visited July 2, 2009). A referendum on independence from Papua New Guinea will take place between 2015 and 2020. *See, e.g., Asia: Explosive Mines; Bougainville,* THE ECONOMIST (LONDON), Feb. 9, 2008, at 61. In June 2005, an Autonomous Bougainville Government was elected and assumed power. *See, e.g.,* LLOYD JONES, ISLAND READY FOR SELF-RULE, Courier Mail (Australia), June 15, 2005, at 12. More recently, the Autonomous Government of Bougainville and PNG signed a memorandum of understanding, which contemplates that PNG will transfer power over minerals and oil and gas resources to Bougainville, as well as lift a moratorium on mining to boost economic development. *See, e.g.,* ELISABETH BEHRMANN, PNG'S BOUGAINVILLE PAVING WAY FOR COPPER, GOLD EXPLORATION, DOW JONES NEWSWIRES, May 2, 2008. The entity created by the Bougainville government to oversee these resources—the Bogenvil Resources Development Corporation, Ltd. ("BRDC")—will not deal with Panguna-related mining issues, however, as they remain politically volatile. *Id.*

31 Plaintiffs' Opening Brief at 13–14 ("In 2002, both the U.S. Government and the PNG Government expressed opposition to the litigation proceeding in the United States. Since the

the PNG government advised the United States that it neither "support[ed] nor den[ied] the constitutional rights of [its] citizens [to] tak[e] whatever action they deem[ed] necessary" with respect to the claims asserted in this suit.[32] In 2005 and again in 2009, PNG officials reaffirmed this position, explaining that the PNG government was "not a party to this case," and did "not see the case presently before the courts in the U.S. affecting diplomatic and bilateral relations between our two countries." The government also stated that it did not believe the lawsuit "affect[ed] the peace process on the island of Bougainville."[33] In a letter to the U.S. ambassador to PNG, the Acting Chief Administrator for the Autonomous Bougainville Government communicated his government's belief that "the case should be heard and decided by courts in the United States as the citizens have exercised their rights to have the case heard there."[34] The Administrator noted that "if the case is not heard [in the U.S.], [this] will result in further delays, frustrations and likelihood of prejudices to [the] rights and interests of Plaintiffs and us all."[35] Finally, he commented that the Bougainville government did "not see the case presently in U.S. Courts adversely affecting any relations between [it] and [the] United States."[36]

The fact that PNG and the Autonomous Bougainville Government do not oppose litigation of plaintiffs' claims in the United States does not strengthen the nexus between the claims and the United States. Similarly, evidence that the United States no longer opposes litigation in this forum[37] does not change the fact that the

---

end of the conflict, however, . . . the government of Papua New Guinea [has] confirmed that it [does] not oppose the litigation and that it would not effect diplomatic or bilateral relations. The Autonomous Bougainville Government agrees and takes the view that the case 'should be heard and decided by courts in the United States'" (record citations omitted)). *See* Berman Decl., Exh. A (letter from Patrick Koles, Acting Chief Administrator for the Autonomous Bougainville Government, to Leslie Rowe, Ambassador at the United States Embassy in Papua New Guinea (May 26, 2009)); B (letter from Margaret L. Elias, the Chief Secretary to Government of Papua New Guinea to Leslie Rowe, Ambassador at the United States Embassy in Papua New Guinea (February 11, 2009)); C (letter from Joshua Kalinoe, then-Chief Secretary to Government of Papua New Guinea to Robert Fitts, then-Ambassador at the United States Embassy in Papua New Guinea (March 30, 2005)); and D (letter from Joshua Kalinoe, then-Chief Secretary to Government of Papua New Guinea to Susan Jacobs, then-Ambassador at the United States Embassy in Papua New Guinea (February 6, 2003)).

32 Berman Decl., Exh. D.

33 Berman Decl, Exhs. B & C.

34 Berman Decl., Exh. A.

35 *Id.*

36 *Id.*

37 In September 2006, the U.S. government submitted an *amicus curiae* brief to the Ninth Circuit, in which it explained:

> "At the request of the district court, in November 2001, the Government filed a statement of interest, presenting the State Department's views about the effect this litigation would have on the Bougainville peace process and the conduct of the United States' foreign relations.

nexus between the claims and the United States is weak in terms of nationality, territory, and effects within this country.

Rio Tinto argues that, given the fact that "[i]nternational law imposes a duty on all states to provide effective judicial processes and remedies for the violation of norms reflecting matters of universal concern," comity requires that the United States "respect . . . PNG as a co-equal sovereign" and "allow PNG to fulfill its obligation" to adjudicate the claimed human rights violations.[38] It asserts the United States and its courts "cannot ignore [this] obligation [to respect another nation's sovereignty simply because that nation] 'consents]' to a U.S. forum." Ultimately, Rio Tinte concludes that, since no "government can[ ] opt out of its sovereign duty to provide remedies for violations of customary international law," the fact that PNG and the Autonomous Bougainville Government do not oppose litigation of the case in this court does not preclude imposition of a prudential exhaustion requirement or application of the traditional two-step exhaustion analysis.[39]

The court agrees with Rio Tinto insofar as it asserts that the consent or non-opposition of PNG and the Autonomous Bougainville Government to having the litigation proceed in this forum does not strengthen the nexus between plaintiffs' claims and the United States. To the extent Rio Tinto suggests that comity considerations and international law obligations *require* the United States to defer to another sovereign's initial adjudication of claims involving matters of universal concern, however, it adopts the position taken by Judges Bybee and Bea in their

---

> That statement was based on the State Department's assessment of the Government's foreign relations interests and the peace process as they existed in 2001, which are different from the interests and circumstances that exist today."

(*See* Rio Tinto's Supplemental Request for Judicial Notice in Support of Reply Brief on the Limited Remand Issue, Exh. 46 ("Brief for the United States as Amicus Curiae Supporting Panel Rehearing or Rehearing En Banc") at 14 n. 3.) Moreover, when pressed by the en banc panel to state whether continued adjudication of the action would negatively affect foreign relations PNG or other U.S. interests, a representative of the Executive Branch confirmed that the U.S. government did not believe the case raised any "case-specific" political questions or unduly sensitive foreign affairs. (*See* Statement of the United States Government (Robert Loeb, Department of Justice) at oral argument before Ninth Circuit en banc panel (audio file located at http://www.ca9.uscourts.gov/media/view_subpage.php?pk_id=0000001917), at 45:45 to 47:10 of oral argument (detailing government's then-current position regarding U.S. interests in this case).)

38 Rio Tinto Opening Brief at 5. Rio Tinto asserts that "[b]oth PNG and the U.S. have ratified the International Covenant on Civil and Political Rights ('ICCPR'), undertaking the obligation to provide and enforce remedies for persons whose rights recognized under international law are violated." (*Id.* at 4.)

39 *Id.*; *see also* Rio Tinto Reply at 13–14 ("A foreign government cannot, by writing a letter, avoid its obligation to adjudicate the claims of its citizens respecting human rights. . . Comity means respecting PNG's duty to adjudicate these matters in its own courts in the first instance. That the current PNG government may or may not object to a U.S. court taking on this very difficult case has no relevance to the comity analysis underlying the exhaustion inquiry").

respective opinions.[40] Seven of the eleven judges who were members of the *Rio Tinto IV* en banc court rejected imposing a mandatory exhaustion requirement, however, and the plurality directed that the court "consider" whether exhaustion ought to be required in this action as a prudential matter.[41] Given the outcome of the en banc proceedings, Rio Tinto's argument that exhaustion is required is not persuasive.[42]

---

40 *Compare, e.g.,* Rio Tinto Opening Brief at 6–7 ("Our national interest is that [universally accepted] norms be enforced, but not that the U.S. be the enforcing nation. The U.S. has no greater claim to the authority to enforce the norms of international law than other nations that are willing and able to do so") and Rio Tinto Reply at 14 ("Nor would the U.S. commitment to effective enforcement of international law be served by inquiring, case by case, into the foreign government's motives or preferences. The institutional interests at stake are best served by respecting each jurisdiction's duty to enforce claims based on customary international law") with *Rio Tinto III,* 487 F.3d at 1238–40 (Bybee, J., dissenting) ("First, requiring exhaustion of local remedies will promote respect for foreign tribunals or other processes for dispute resolution, such as commissions or political records. . . . Exhaustion recognizes the possibility of legislative, executive or judicial acts in another nation; it thus respects the processes by which another nation has constituted itself and is worthy to be considered part of the community of nations. . . . Taking up cases that can be handled domestically aggravates diplomatic and local tensions because it interferes with local control and stirs up unnecessary publicity. . . . By accepting jurisdiction over foreign suits that, can be appropriately handled locally, the federal courts embroil the nation in a kind of judicial 'imperialism' that suggests the United States does not respect or recognize a foreign government's ability to administer justice" (citations omitted)) and *Rio Tinto IV,* 550 F.3d at 836–37 (Bea, J., concurring) ("A mandatory requirement of exhaustion of local remedies, except where futile or otherwise unavailable, allows our courts to play the role the ATS intended them to play: an ultimate venue for claimed violations of the law of nations when those claimed violations cannot or will not be cured by the courts of the country in which the injuries occurred. The requirement simultaneously prevents our unelected judiciary . . . from assuming the role of a roving sheriff in recurring, internecine disputes involving claims of inequity and oppression outside the United States" (citations omitted)).

41 Alternatively, Rio Tinto argues that the reasoning of decisions imposing prudential exhaustion in tribal and administrative law contexts "support[s] imposing an exhaustion requirement." (Rio Tinto Opening Brief at 26–30.) As with Rio Tinto's positions regarding comity, this argument overlooks the scope of the *Rio Tinto IV* plurality's remand, which, rather than *requiring* that the court impose an exhaustion requirement, directed the court to *consider* whether such a requirement was warranted *in this case,* given the weak nexus between plaintiffs' claims and the United States, principles of international comity, and the extent to which plaintiffs' claims involve matters of universal concern.

42 At the hearing, Rio Tinto's counsel argued that the nexus-universal concern inquiry could be conceptualized as a matrix. He opined that one quadrant of the matrix represented cases in which there was no (or very weak) nexus, and asserted that although, in such cases, jurisdiction lies to adjudicate violations of universal norms, an exhaustion requirement *must* be imposed. (*See* Reporter's Transcript of Proceedings ("RT"), Monday, July 6, 2009, at 19:22-20:8; *id.* at 37:7–16.) This argument is unavailing in light of *Rio Tinto IV.* The *Rio Tinto IV* plurality concluded that the nexus in this case was weak or nonexistent. It nonetheless evaluated the universality of the concerns raised by plaintiffs' claims, and discussed the need to balance the universality of the concerns against the nexus. Based on the language of the plurality opinion, the court concludes that the *Rio Tinto IV* plurality implicitly rejected defendants' position where nexus is weak, an exhaustion requirement must always be imposed. Had the plurality

In sum, weighing the Restatement factors, the nature of Rio Tinto's contacts with the United States, and the relationship between the United States and plaintiffs and their claims, the court agrees with the en banc plurality that the nexus between plaintiffs' claims and the United States is weak.[43]

2. Matters of "Universal Concern"

"In ATS cases where the United States 'nexus' is weak, courts should carefully consider the question of exhaustion, particularly—but not exclusively—with respect to claims that do not involve matters of 'universal concern.'" *Rio Tinto IV,* 550 F.3d at 831 (McKeown, J.). Matters of "universal concern" are offenses "for which a state has jurisdiction to punish without regard to territoriality or the nationality of offenders." *Kadic v. Karadzic,* 70 F.3d 232, 240 (2d Cir.1995); *see also* Restatement § 404 ("A state has jurisdiction to define and prescribe punishment for certain offenses recognized by the community of nations as of universal concern . . . even where none of the bases of jurisdiction indicated in § 402 [nationality, territory, and in-country effects] is present").

As the second step in evaluating whether exhaustion of some or all of plaintiffs' claims ought to be required as a prudential matter, therefore, the court examines the ATCA claims pleaded in the first amended complaint to ascertain whether they

---

adopted or accepted defendants' analysis, it would have held that exhaustion was required once the court determined that the nexus was weak or nonexistent. It did not do so. Attempting to carry out the mandate of the Ninth Circuit's opinion, the court likewise declines to impose this type of exhaustion requirement.

43 This does not mean that every ATCA case will have a weak or relatively weak nexus with the United States simply because plaintiffs are aliens alleging violations of international law. Contrary to plaintiffs' assertions, the nexus inquiry does not necessarily undermine the scope or purpose of the ACTA, nor conflict with the elements of an ATCA claim. In a given case, certain of the Restatement factors might well weigh in favor of a finding that nexus was strong, or at least less attenuated than it is here. Violations of international law alleged by ACTA plaintiffs might have a substantial, direct, and foreseeable effect on the United States, for example, because there had been an influx of immigrants to the country seeking refuge from human rights abuses occurring elsewhere. This would result in a much stronger connection between the United States and "those whom [its] regulation [through adjudication] was designed to protect." Several of the Restatement factors, in fact, speak to the second factor the plurality identified as relevant to the prudential exhaustion analysis—i.e., the universality of the concerns implicated by plaintiffs' claims. *See* RESTATEMENT § 403(2) (identifying as relevant factors "the character of the activity to be regulated, the importance of regulation to the regulating state, the extent to which other states regulate such activities, and the degree to which the desirability of such regulation is generally accepted; . . . the importance of the regulation to the international political, legal, or economic system; . . . [and] the extent to which the regulation is consistent with the traditions of the international system"). Finally, even if a court determines that exhaustion ought be required as a prudential matter in a given ATCA case, defendants must still show that local remedies are available and that exhaustion will not be futile. Thus, a finding that nexus is weak does not necessarily mean that American courts will refuse to hear every ATCA case involving foreigners alleging torts against foreign corporations on foreign soil.

involve matters of "universal concern."[44] In doing so, the court finds instructive, but not controlling, the list of offenses denominated matters of universal concern in section 404 of the Restatement. Section 404 specifically states that the list set forth therein is not exhaustive. *See* Restatement § 404 ("A state has jurisdiction to define and prescribe punishment for certain offense recognized by the community of nations as of universal concern, *such as*. . ." (emphasis added)); *id.,* cmt. a ("Universal jurisdiction for additional offenses is provided by international agreements. . .")[45] Moreover, although evaluating whether to require prudential exhaustion—as envisioned by the plurality—is a separate inquiry from subject matter jurisdiction under the ACTA, neither the statute itself[46] nor cases interpreting it limit the claims that are actionable under the ATCA to the matters of universal concern identified in section 404. Therefore, while the Restatement offers some guidance in evaluating the second prong of the plurality's prudential exhaustion test, it is not the sole source to which the court looks in assessing whether the claims asserted in this suit implicate matters of "universal concern."

Other useful reference points include Judge Reinhardt's observation that "heinous offenses like genocide, crimes against humanity, and war crimes" fall within ATCA jurisdiction because they violate specific "'norm[s] of international character accepted by the civilized world'" that all nations have an interest in remedying. *Rio Tinto IV,* 550 F.3d at 845 (Reinhardt, J., dissenting) (citing *Sosa,* 542 U.S. at

---

44 Rio Tinto argues that, following the Supreme Court's decision in *Ashcroft v. Iqbal,* ___ U.S. ___, 129 S. Ct. 1937, 173 L.Ed.2d 868 (2009), plaintiffs' complaint does not sufficiently plead that it aided and abetted violations of matters of universal concern. (Rio Tinto Opening Brief at 20–26.) This argument is unavailing for at least two reasons. First, Rio Tinto ignores the *limited* nature of the question before the court on remand, namely, whether as a prudential matter, an exhaustion requirement should be imposed in this case. An attack on the sufficiency of plaintiffs' pleadings, or the merits of their aiding and abetting claims, is beyond the scope of the remand. Cf. *Rio Tinto III,* 487 F.3d at 1200 (explaining that the initial jurisdictional inquiry in an ATCA case does not evaluate "[w]hether the cause of action [will] turn[ ] out to be well founded in law and fact," quoting *Bell v. Hood,* 327 U.S. 678, 683 n. 2, 66 S. Ct. 773, 90 L.Ed. 939 (1946)). Second, *Iqbal* addressed a narrow issue: what pleading standard had to be satisfied to state a claim against an individual government official for purposeful discrimination in *Bivens* and § 1983 suits. Nothing in *Iqbal* suggests that the pleading standard it articulates applies to ATCA claims; indeed, after *Twombly,* courts appear divided over the pleading standards applicable to § 1350 claims involving accomplice liability. *See generally* AMANDA SUE NICHOLS, Note, ALIEN TORT STATUTE ACCOMPLICE LIABILITY CASES: SHOULD COURTS APPLY THE PLAUSIBILITY PLEADING STANDARD OF BELL ATLANTIC V. TWOMBLY?, 76 FORDHAM L.REV. 2177 (2008).

45 *See also*, *e.g.*, GEORGE K. WALKER, PRINCIPLES FOR COLLECTIVE HUMANITARIAN INTERVENTION TO SUCCOR OTHER COUNTRIES' IMPERILED INDIGENOUS NATIONALS, 18 AM. U. INT'L L.REV. 35, 77 (2002) ("The § 404 list is not exclusive, and certainly today would include crimes against humanity" (footnote omitted)).

46 In the years since *Sosa* was decided, Congress has not accepted Justice Souter's invitation to provide guidance regarding the scope of claims that are actionable under the ACTA. *See Sosa,* 542 U.S. at 731, 124 S. Ct. 2739. Hence, that decision and the standards it articulates for determining whether a particular claim is cognizable under the ACTA control.

742, 124 S. Ct. 2739 (Breyer, J., concurring)). All relevant sources indicate that, while the two inquiries are not coextensive, evaluating whether a claim involves a matter of "universal concern" for purposes of deciding whether to impose a prudential exhaustion requirement overlaps to some extent with the analysis required to ascertain whether a claim falls within ATCA jurisdiction, i.e., whether it is sufficiently "specific, universal, and obligatory." *In re Estate of Marcos Human Rights Litigation* (*Hilao v. Estate of Marcos*), 25 F.3d 1467, 1475 (9th Cir.1994).

Although the primary focus of this prong of the prudential exhaustion analysis is universality, the specificity of a norm, and the extent to which nations feel obliged to follow it, inform a decision regarding its universality. It is thus appropriate to look to ATCA jurisprudence, "the works of jurists on public law, [ ] the general practice of nations, [and] court decisions that discuss and enforce international law," *Rio Tinto I,* 221 F. Supp. 2d at 1131 (citations omitted), as well as the types of claims listed in section 404 of the Restatement, in evaluating whether a particular claim involves matters of "universal concern." Because a court evaluating the universality of a particular norm in the ATCA context must be sensitive to that norm "as it has evolved and exists among the nations of the world today," *Kadic,* 70 F.3d at 238 (citing *Filartiga v. Pena-Irala,* 630 F.2d 876, 887 (2d Cir.1980)), the court examines each of plaintiffs' claims in turn to ascertain whether it can currently be considered "universal."[47]

(a) Crimes Against Humanity

Plaintiffs' first ATCA claim alleges that Rio Tinto "acted jointly and willfully with PNG and the government of Australia to institute a blockade of Bougainville," which constituted "genocide because it foreseeably resulted in the killing of natives, caused serious bodily harm, [and] was deliberately calculated to destroy plaintiffs and their way of life."[48] Plaintiffs also assert that the "instigation of

---

47 An approach that evaluates each claim in the operative complaint separately comports with prudential exhaustion practice in contexts such as habeas. *See, e.g., King v. Ryan,* 564 F.3d 1133, 1138 (9th Cir.2009) ("Habeas petitioners have long been required to adjudicate their claims in state court—that is, 'exhaust' them—before seeking relief in federal court. This requirement is 'grounded in principles of comity[,] as it gives states the first opportunity to address and correct alleged violations of state prisoner's federal rights.' The current statutory exhaustion requirement prevents a federal court from granting habeas relief 'unless it appears that . . . the applicant has exhausted the remedies available in the courts of the State.' In 1982, the U.S. Supreme Court interpreted the exhaustion rule in the habeas context as requiring 'total exhaustion' of 'mixed' petitions—that is, those petitions that contain both exhausted and unexhausted claims. *Rose* [*v. Lundy,* 455 U.S. 509, 102 S. Ct. 1198, 71 L.Ed.2d 379 (1982),] required district courts to dismiss a mixed petition, 'leaving the prisoner with the choice of returning to state court to exhaust his claims or of amending or resubmitting the habeas petition to present only exhausted claims to the district court'" (citations omitted)).

48 First Amended Complaint, ¶¶ 211, 213.

the blockade and denial of medical treatment and other necessities that caused severe pain and suffering, as well as death, constitute acts of official torture."[49]

Both before and after *Sosa,* federal courts have recognized claims for certain crimes against humanity, including genocide and torture, as sufficiently universal to give rise to jurisdiction under the ATCA.[50] *See, e.g., Bowoto v. Chevron Corp.,* 557 F. Supp. 2d 1080, 1084–85 (N.D.Cal.2008) ("The case at bar[ ] considers whether common law claims of torture and summary execution can be pled against *corporations* under the ATS. . . . The Court finds that plaintiffs' claims for torture and summary execution may be brought under the ATS . . ."); *Mujica v. Occidental Petroleum Corp.,* 381 F. Supp. 2d 1164, 1183 (C.D.Cal.2005) (finding that a claim alleging crimes against humanity, based on the forced displacement of civilians, gave rise to ATCA jurisdiction); *see also Kadic,* 70 F.3d at 239–42 ("The Executive Branch has emphatically restated in this litigation its position that private persons may be found liable under the Alien Tort Act for acts of genocide, war crimes, and other violations of international humanitarian law. . . . In the aftermath of the atrocities committed during the Second World War, the condemnation of genocide as contrary to international law quickly achieved broad acceptance by the community of nations. . . . [F]rom its incorporation into international law, the proscription of genocide has applied equally to state and non-state actors"); *Tel-Oren v. Libyan Arab Republic,* 726 F.2d 774, 791 n. 20 (D.C.Cir.1984) (Edwards, J., concurring) ("On the basis of international covenants, agreements and declarations, commentators have identified at least four acts that are now subject to unequivocal international condemnation: torture, summary execution, genocide and slavery" (citations omitted)).[51] Genocide, moreover, is one of the matters of "universal concern" identified in section 404 of the Restatement, and both genocide and crimes against humanity are among the "heinous crimes" mentioned by Judge Reinhardt in his dissent. As pled, therefore, plaintiffs' first claim for crimes against humanity amounting to genocide and torture implicates matters of universal concern.

---

49 *Id.,* ¶ 214.

50 The specificity of a plaintiff's torture allegations is relevant in assessing whether the particular conduct on which a claim is based gives rise to ATCA jurisdiction. *See, e.g., Kiobel v. Royal Dutch Petroleum Co.,* 456 F. Supp. 2d 457, 465 (S.D.N.Y.2006) ("*Sosa* leaves unclear what conduct is included within 'torture.'[ ] However, dictum in *Sosa* suggests that at least some forms of torture continue to provide a basis for actionable claims under the ATS").

51 *See also, e.g., Rio Tinto IV,* 550 F.3d at 831 (McKeown, J.) ("Some of the claims— torture, crimes against humanity, and war crimes—may implicate matters of 'universal concern' . . ."); *Rio Tinto III,* 487 F.3d at 1202 ("Plaintiffs here have alleged several claims asserting *jus cogens* violations that form the least controversial core of modern ATCA jurisdiction, including allegations of war crimes, crimes against humanity and racial discrimination"); *Rio Tinto I,* 221 F. Supp. 2d at 1150–51 ("Genocide is a recognized crime against humanity").

(b) War Crimes

Plaintiffs' second claim alleges that Rio Tinto's actions during the hostilities that occurred in Bougainville violated the international law of war and the Geneva Convention Relative to the Protection of Civilian Persons in Time of War, Article III.[52] War crimes are one of the matters of "universal concern" listed in section 404 of the Restatement, and federal courts have long recognized that alleged violations of the law of war give rise to an actionable ATCA claim. *See, e.g., Vietnam Ass'n for Victims of Agent Orange v. Dow Chemical Co.,* 517 F.3d 104, 116 (2d Cir.2008) ("While not exhaustive, the list of principles that may be said to have 'ripened into universally accepted norms of international law' [ ] includes the proscriptions against piracy, slave trade, attacks on or hijacking of aircraft, genocide, and war crimes" (citing *Kadic* and RESTATEMENT § 404)); *Kadic,* 70 F.3d at 242–43 ("After the Second World War, the law of war was codified in the four Geneva Conventions, which have been ratified by more than 180 nations, including the United States [ ]. Common article 3, which is substantially identical in each of the four Conventions, applies to 'armed conflict[s] not of an international character.' . . . Thus, under the law of war as codified in the Geneva Conventions, all 'parties' to a conflict . . . are obliged to adhere to these most fundamental requirements of the law of war. The liability of private individuals for committing war crimes has been recognized since World War I and was confirmed at Nuremberg. . . and remains today an important aspect of international law. [ ] The District Court has jurisdiction pursuant to the Alien Tort Act over appellants' claims of war crimes and other violations of international humanitarian law" (footnotes and citations omitted)); *Jane Doe I v. Islamic Salvation Front (FIS),* 993 F. Supp. 3, 8 (D.D.C.1998) ("This court concludes that the acts of the FIS alleged by Plaintiffs are proscribed by international law against both state and private actors, as evidenced by Common Article 3. Accordingly, Plaintiffs have properly alleged subject matter jurisdiction under the ATCA"). Plaintiffs' second claim, therefore, also involves a matter of "universal concern."

(c) Environmental Tort Claims

The first amended complaint includes two distinct environmental tort claims: the third claim alleges violations of the rights to life, health, and security while the sixth alleges violations of international environmental rights.

Plaintiffs allege that the right to life "is specifically applicable to cases involving severe environmental harm";[53] that the right to health "constitutes a norm of customary international law";[54] and that international law recognizes "that harm which threatens human life or health necessarily implicates a violation of the right to

---

52 First Amended Complaint, ¶¶ 220–21.

53 First Amended Complaint, ¶ 227.

54 *Id.,* ¶ 228.

security of the person."[55] They assert that Rio Tinto violated their rights to life and health "by appropriating land owned by indigenous people for the purpose of opening a mine, [and by] knowingly emitting and depositing volatile and highly toxic mine waste onto the land and into the water, thus destroying rivers and land that provided a way of life for the native people."[56]

In *Rio Tinto I,* the court concluded that, although various international law treaties and/or agreements reference the rights to life and health, and some address the impact environmental degradation has on those rights, there was insufficient international consensus regarding the type of conduct that violated the rights for purposes of ACTA jurisdiction. *Rio Tinto I,* 221 F. Supp. 2d at 1158.[57] Additionally, the court considered relevant in assessing the universality of the rights the fact that the United States had refused to ratify at least one of the treaties that recognize them. *Id.* at 1157–58. Ultimately, the court was unable to conclude that the rights to life and health were rights that other nations universally recognized could be violated through conduct harmful to the environment. *Id.* at 1158 (citing *Aguinda v. Texaco, Inc.,* No. 93 Civ. 7527(VLB), 1994 WL 142006, 7 (S.D.N.Y. Apr. 11, 1994) ("Not all conduct which may be harmful to the environment, and not all violations of environmental laws, constitute violations of the law of nations")); *see also, e.g., Beanal v. Freeport-McMoran, Inc.,* 197 F.3d 161, 167 (5th Cir.1999) (rejecting plaintiffs' reliance on "several sources of international environmental law to show that the alleged environmental abuses caused by Freeport's mining activities are cognizable under international law," the court explained that "Beanal fails to show that these treaties and agreements enjoy universal acceptance in the international community. The sources of international law cited by Beanal and the *amici* merely refer to a general sense of environmental responsibility and state abstract rights and liberties devoid of articulable or discernable standards and regulations to identify practices that constitute international environmental abuses or torts").

Since *Rio Tinto I,* federal courts have continued to hold that, at present, claims that environmental damage or destruction has injured or threatened individuals' rights to life and health are not sufficiently specific to give rise to ATCA jurisdiction. Courts so holding have recognized that this lack of specificity, and nations' differing interpretations of the conduct that violates the rights, undercuts any claim that they are universal. This is because nations cannot universally subscribe to a principle that is without concrete content. *See, e.g., Bowoto,* 557 F. Supp. 2d at 1095 ("The right to life, liberty and security of person are widely recognized as fundamental human rights. However, these international instruments do not purport to

55 *Id.,* ¶ 229.

56 *Id.,* ¶ 230.

57 The court also found that the rights were not sufficiently specific to support ATCA jurisdiction. *Rio Tinto I,* 221 F. Supp. 2d at 1158.

define these rights nor is there ATS jurisprudence upholding or defining such claims"); *Kiobel v. Royal Dutch Petroleum Co.,* 456 F. Supp. 2d 457, 467 (S.D.N.Y.2006) ("Defendants argue that there is no particular or universal understanding of the civil and political rights [to life, liberty, security and association] covered by Plaintiffs' claim, and thus, pursuant to *Sosa,* these 'rights' are not actionable under the ATS. [ ] The Court agrees"); *In re Agent Orange Product Liability Litigation,* 373 F. Supp. 2d 7, 129 (E.D.N.Y.2005) ("In the developing area of international environmental law, the United States and other nations have tended to treat protection of the environment on an ad-hoc, situationby-situation and case-by-case basis" (citations omitted)); *see also Flores v. Southern Peru Copper Corp.,* 414 F.3d 233, 254–55 (2d Cir.2003) (holding, in a suit where Peruvian residents alleged that pollution from an American mining company's operations had caused severe, deadly lung disease, that general statements regarding the rights to life and health "are boundless and indeterminate. They express virtuous goals understandably expressed at a level of abstraction needed to secure the adherence of States that disagree on many of the particulars regarding how actually to achieve them. . . . For the foregoing reasons, plaintiffs have failed to establish the existence of a customary international law 'right to life' or 'right to health'"); *id.* at 266 ("Because plaintiffs have failed to submit evidence sufficient to establish that intranational pollution violates customary international law, the District Court properly granted defendant's motion to dismiss"); *Presbyterian Church of Sudan v. Talisman Energy, Inc.,* 244 F. Supp. 2d 289, 340 (S.D.N.Y. 2003) ("[I]t is well-established that environmental damage, without more, generally does not violate international law" (citations omitted)).

As a result, the court concludes that plaintiffs' third claim that Rio Tinto's alleged environmental destruction of Bougainville violated their rights to life, health, and security of the person is based on international law norms that have not, as yet, achieved the status of matters of "universal concern."[58]

Plaintiffs' sixth claim alleges that international law "has recognized a minimum right to a safe environment as a customary norm."[59] In *Rio Tinto I,* the court concluded that some of the authorities cited in the complaint as support for this claim, particularly the Rio Declaration and the Stockholm declaration, undermined plaintiffs' position that defendants' conduct violated recognized international law. *Rio Tinto I,* 221 F. Supp. 2d at 1159. It also evaluated the additional bases for the environmental tort claims that plaintiffs had raised in their opposition to defendants' motion to dismiss. *Id.* at 1160. These included the "principle of sustainable

58 As the court noted in *Rio Tinto I,* where the conduct alleged to violate the rights to life, health and security of the person is torture, summary execution or disappearance, courts have recognized the universal nature of the claim. *See Rio Tinto I,* 221 F. Supp. 2d at 1158 n. 174. This is consistent with the court's conclusion that plaintiffs' crimes against humanity claim involves matters of "universal concern."

59 First Amended Complaint, ¶ 255.

development," a concept the court found insufficiently "specific, universal, and obligatory" to support a claim for violation of the law of nations. It noted, in fact, that plaintiffs' expert conceded the principle might be "'too broad a concept to be legally meaningful.'" *Id.*

The court next considered whether plaintiffs' allegations stated a claim for violation of the United Nations Convention on the Law of the Sea ("UNCLOS"), and whether, if so, such a claim fell within its jurisdiction under the ACTA. Ultimately, the court held that "[b]ecause UNCLOS reflects customary international law, plaintiffs may base an ATCA claim upon it." *Id.* at 1162.

While the UNCLOS may reflect customary international law that is specific and obligatory, the court concludes—for purposes of applying the second prong of the prudential exhaustion analysis—that it is not a "matter of universal concern" in the same manner that *jus cogens* norms such as genocide, torture or crimes against humanity are.[60] This conclusion is bolstered by the fact that the United States has signed but not yet ratified UNCLOS. For these reasons, the court finds that plaintiffs' international environmental rights claims, including those premised on the UNCLOS, involve norms "where aspiration has not yet ripened into obligation," *Alvarez-Machain v. United States,* 331 F.3d 604, 620 (9th Cir.2003), reversed on other grounds sub. nom. *Sosa v. Alvarez-Machain,* 542 U.S. 692, 124 S. Ct. 2739, 159 L.Ed.2d 718 (2004). It thus concludes that the claims do not implicate matters of "universal concern."

(d) Racial Discrimination

Plaintiffs' fourth ATCA claim for racial discrimination alleges that Rio Tinto "viewed the people of Bougainville as inferior due to their color and culture and, therefore, intentionally violated their rights."[61] It also asserts that Rio Tinto had

---

60 This conclusion is further supported by the fact that significant disagreement exists among developed and developing nations as to the appropriate reach of international environmental regulation. *See, e.g.*, Andrew P. Morriss & Roger E. Meiners, Borders and the Environment, 39 Envtl. L. 141, 142–45 (2009) ("One group of environmental protection advocates, typically those in developed countries with relatively stringent environmental protection laws, argues that countries with less stringent protection laws should raise their standards to the higher, developed-world standards. . . . The second reaction, also largely by environmental groups from wealthy nations, has been to call for international institutions to set standards for environmental protection to eliminate a 'race to the bottom' among jurisdictions. The Kyoto Protocol, for example, attempts to set levels of carbon dioxide emissions by signatories. Similarly, the World Trade Organization (WTO) has been moving gradually to include environmental standards as a regular part of trade agreements. Such agreements also tend to emphasize the need for less-developed countries to impose more stringent environmental standards domestically. The third reaction, largely from interest groups and governments in emerging nations focused on improving the economic welfare of the poor, is to argue that developing countries should not be expected to bear the burden of restricting emissions to the same degree as developed economies").

61 First Amended Complaint, ¶ 239.

"a deliberate policy of systematic racial discrimination against plaintiffs."[62] Plaintiffs contend that, because defendants acted under color of law in concert with the PNG government, their "discriminatory acts [] constitute governmental action."[63]

As the court noted in *Rio Tinto I,* "it is well-settled that racial discrimination is a violation of the law of nations." Many courts have held, in fact, that discrimination "violates a *jus cogens* norm." *Rio Tinto I,* 221 F. Supp. 2d at 1152 (citations omitted).[64] Racial discrimination is proscribed by international law only when committed by state officials or under color of law, however. *Id.* at 1153 (citing Restatement § 702 ("[a] *state* violates international law if, as a matter of state policy, it practices, encourages, or condones . . . systematic racial discrimination")); *see also, e.g., Bigio v. Coca-Cola Co.,* 239 F.3d 440, 448 (2d Cir.2000) ("However reprehensible, [] racial or religious discrimination . . . are included only in [§ 702] of the Restatement, which describe[s] conduct that violates international law when undertaken by a *state actor"* (citations omitted)); *In re South African Apartheid Litigation,* 617 F. Supp. 2d 228, 250 (S.D.N.Y. 2009) ("Racial discrimination is a violation of customary law when it is practiced systematically as a matter of state policy" (footnotes and internal quotations omitted)).

While the *Bigio* court held that "neither racial or religious discrimination in general nor the discriminatory expropriation of property in particular is listed as an act 'of universal concern' in [section] 404 or is sufficiently similar to the listed acts for us to treat them as though they were incorporated into [section] 404 by analogy," *Bigio,* 239 F.3d at 448, it did so in the context of concluding that a private company could not be sued for discrimination under the ACTA when it had not acted in concert with state officials. *See also Iwanowa v. Ford Motor Co.,* 67 F. Supp. 2d 424, 444 (D.N.J.1999) ("The *Kadic* Court further noted that section 702 [of the Restatement]. . . identifies violations that are actionable when committed by a state, whereas section 404 of the Restatement lists a more limited category of violations of universal concern").

Although the plurality opinion directed the court to weigh nexus against the universality of the concerns underlying plaintiffs' claims in assessing whether to impose a prudential exhaustion requirement, *Rio Tinto IV,* 550 F.3d at 824, 831,

---

62 *Id.,* ¶ 238.

63 *Id. See also Rio Tinto I,* 221 F. Supp. 2d at 1151–52 ("Plaintiffs contend that, given PNG's substantial financial interest in the Panguna Mine, defendants acted under color of state authority in discriminating against the people of Bougainville"); *see id.* at 1154 (noting that plaintiffs alleged "that PNG made its governmental power of eminent domain available to Rio Tinto so that it could build the mine, and that, because of its profit participation in the mine, PNG took no steps to control or minimize the negative impact of Rio Tinto's mining operations").

64 *Jus cogens* norms "proscribe a limited set of activities so universally condemned by the international community that they cannot be undertaken under any circumstances." *Hirsh v. State of Israel,* 962 F. Supp. 377, 381 (S.D.N.Y.1997) (internal quotations omitted).

and although it cited section 404 of the Restatement as defining matters of "universal concern," *id.,* for the reasons stated earlier, the court does not believe that the plurality intended that the definition set forth in section 404 strictly control the prudential exhaustion analysis.

The court is mindful, moreover, of the panel's decision in *Rio Tinto III,* which held that "[a]cts of racial discrimination are violations of *jus cogens* law." *Rio Tinto III,* 487 F.3d at 1209 (citing *Siderman de Blake v. Republic of Argentina,* 965 F.2d 699, 717 (9th Cir.1992), for the proposition that "the Foreign Relations Law Restatement 'identifies] jus cogens norms prohibiting . . . systematic racial discrimination'"); *see Siderman de Blake,* 965 F.2d at 715 ("Courts seeking to determine whether a norm of customary international law has attained the status of *jus cogens* . . . must . . . determine whether the international community recognizes the norm as one 'from which no derogation is permitted'"); *Presbyterian Church of Sudan,* 244 F. Supp. 2d at 306 ("The Amended Complaint is rife with accusations which, if proven true, would constitute behavior manifestly in violation of the most basic rules of international law and, indeed, of civilized conduct. Such acts violate peremptory norms, or *jus cogens.* . . . Violations of *jus cogens* norms constitute violations of obligations owed to all ('*erga omnes*'). In other words, states may exercise universal jurisdiction over acts committed in violation of *jus cogens* norms"). Because racial discrimination violates a *jus cogens* norm, the court concludes that it should be treated as a matter of universal concern for purposes of evaluating whether to impose a prudential exhaustion requirement with respect to plaintiffs' fourth ACTA claim.

(e) Cruel, Inhuman, and Degrading Treatment

Plaintiffs' fifth claim for cruel, inhuman, and degrading treatment ("CIDT") asserts that, by subjecting plaintiffs to inhumane treatment causing "lasting emotional, psychological and physical trauma," Rio Tinto violated Article 16 of the Convention Against Torture and Other Cruel, Inhuman or Degrading Treatment or Punishment ("CAT").[65] Specifically, plaintiffs alleged that "Rio's blockage, massive environmental destruction, and seizure of property for Rio's purposes constitutes cruel, inhuman and degrading treatment."

In its original motion to dismiss, Rio Tinto did not argue that plaintiffs' CIDT claim should be dismissed. Examining its subject matter jurisdiction to hear the claim *sua sponte,* the court noted that it was not based on allegations of torture and that plaintiffs had not "articulated a specific, universal and obligatory norm underlying th[e] claim." *Rio Tinto I,* 221 F. Supp. 2d at 1163 n. 190 (citing *Forti v.*

65 First Amended Complaint, ¶¶ 249-50, 252. Article 16 of the CAT provides: "Each State Party shall undertake to prevent in any territory under its jurisdiction other acts of cruel, inhuman or degrading treatment or punishment which do not amount to torture as defined in article I, when such acts are committed by or at the instigation of or with the consent or acquiescence of a public official or other person acting in an official capacity."

Suarez-Mason, 672 F. Supp. 1531, 1543 (N.D.Cal.1987), superseded by statute on other grounds as stated in *Papa v. United States,* 281 F.3d 1004 (9th Cir.2002); *Forti v. Suarez-Mason,* 694 F. Supp. 707, 712 (N.D.Cal.1988); and *Hilao v. Estate of Marcos,* 103 F.3d 789, 794–95 (9th Cir. 1996)).

More recently, however, federal courts have begun to recognize that "there exists a universal, definable, and obligatory prohibition against cruel, inhuman, or degrading treatment or punishment," and that CIDT "is therefore actionable under the ATCA." *Aldana v. Del Monte Fresh Produce, N.A., Inc.,* 452 F.3d 1284, 1285 (11th Cir.2006) (Barkett, J., dissenting). *See also, e.g., Doe v. Qi,* 349 F. Supp. 2d 1258, 1321–22 (N.D.Cal.2004) (stating that CIDT has been condemned by numerous sources of international law and holding that where the conduct alleged in a particular case to constitute CIDT is sufficiently egregious, it gives rise to jurisdiction under the ATCA); *Tachiona v. Mugabe,* 234 F. Supp. 2d 401, 437 (S.D.N.Y.2002) ("Despite the absence of a distinct definition for what constitutes cruel, inhuman or degrading treatment, various authorities and international instruments make clear that this prohibition is conceptually linked to torture by shades of misconduct discernible as a continuum. . . . That it may present difficulties to pinpoint precisely where on the spectrum of atrocities the shades of cruel, inhuman, or degrading treatment bleed into torture should not detract from what really goes to the essence of any uncertainty: that, distinctly classified or not, the infliction of cruel, inhuman or degrading treatment by agents of the state, as closely akin to or adjunct of torture, is universally condemned and renounced as offending internationally recognized norms of civilized conduct").

Acknowledging that there "is no widespread consensus regarding the elements of cruel, inhuman and degrading treatment," one California district court has concluded that CIDT claims "may be brought under ATS if the specific conduct alleged by the plaintiffs has been universally condemned as cruel, inhuman, or degrading." *Bowoto,* 557 F. Supp. 2d at 1093–94 (citing *Qi,* 349 F. Supp. 2d at 1322; and *Xuncax v. Gramajo,* 886 F. Supp. 162, 187 (D.Mass.1995)).

"Cruel, inhuman, or degrading treatment or punishment is defined as acts which inflict mental or physical suffering, anguish, humiliation, fear and debasement, which fall short of torture." *Aldana,* 452 F.3d at 1285 n. 1 (Barkett, J., dissenting) (citing the CAT). The principal difference between torture and CIDT is "the intensity of the suffering inflicted." Restatement, § 702, Reporter's Note 5 (quoting *Ireland v. United Kingdom,* 25 Pub. Eur. Ct. Hum. Rts., ser. A. para. 167 (1978)); *see also Wiwa v. Royal Dutch Petroleum Co.,* No. 96 CIV. 8386(KMW), 2002 WL 319887, 8 (S.D.N.Y. Feb. 28, 2002) ("International law considers 'cruel, inhuman or degrading treatment' as a general category of prohibited conduct of which 'torture is at the extreme end'").

Here, plaintiffs' CIDT claim is based on a wide range of conduct, including seizure of Bougainvilleans' property and displacement from their homes, environmental damage, and the Rio Tinto's alleged role in the blockade of the island during the civil war. Some of this conduct may implicate matters of universal concern (e.g., the medical blockade), while some does not (e.g., damage to the environment). The CIDT claim that plaintiffs have asserted is thus in many respects different from those that courts have found "closely akin to . . . torture," and based on conduct that is "universally condemned and renounced as offending internationally recognized norms of civilized conduct." *Tachiona,* 234 F. Supp. 2d at 437; *see id.* at 438 (holding that Zimbabwean ruling party's public dragging of dead victims' bodies before their homes, kin and neighbors, constituted CIDT because it was an affront to their human dignity and caused their families severe emotional distress); *see also In re South African Apartheid Litigation,* 617 F. Supp. 2d at 264 (holding that plaintiffs had adequately alleged a CIDT claim under an aiding and abetting theory against automobile companies' security personnel who "provided information about anti-apartheid activists to the South African Security Forces, facilitated arrests, provided information to be used by interrogators, and even participated in interrogations").

As noted, several courts have stated that CIDT is actionable "if the specific conduct alleged by the plaintiffs has been universally condemned as cruel, inhuman, or degrading." *Bowoto,* 557 F. Supp. 2d at 1093–94; *Qi,* 349 F. Supp. 2d at 1321–22 (stating that where the conduct alleged in is sufficiently egregious, a CIDT claim is actionable). Because multiple elements of plaintiffs' CIDT claim do not involve conduct that has been universally condemned as cruel, inhuman, or degrading, the court concludes that the specific CIDT claim plaintiffs assert does not exclusively involve matters of universal concern.

(f) Consistent Pattern of Gross Violations of Human Rights

Plaintiffs' final ACTA claim alleges that the repeated human rights abuses in which Rio Tinto engaged violated an international law norm forbidding "infringements of recognized human rights that are not violations when committed singly or sporadically."[66] Specifically, plaintiffs contend that "Rio's consistent abuse of [plaintiffs], both in terms of destruction of the environment, its racial discrimination and its participation in the military efforts to reopen the mine, violate international law."[67]

Like their claim that Rio Tinto caused environmental damage that violated their rights to life and health, plaintiffs' allegation that the company engaged in a "consistent pattern" of human rights violations suffers from a lack of specificity that undermines the notion that there is a universal consensus condemning the conduct. Although neither party argued the question in *Rio Tinto I,* the court recognized as much, observing that "plaintiffs' claim for gross violations of human rights is not based on any specific provision of international law that is universally recognized."

---

66 First Amended Complaint, ¶ 264 (citing Restatement § 702(g), cmt. m).

67 *Id.,* ¶ 265.

Rio Tinto I, 221 F. Supp. 2d at 1163 n. 190. Post-Sosa jurisprudence, though limited, appears to affirm this conclusion. *See, e.g., Bowoto,* 557 F. Supp. 2d at 1096 ("Plaintiffs appear to concede that their claim of consistent patterns of gross violations of human rights cannot survive scrutiny after *Sosa* and instead choose to focus on their independent causes of action . . . Accordingly, the court grants defendants' motion for summary judgment as to plaintiffs' eighth cause of action").

Like plaintiffs' CIDT claim, moreover, their consistent pattern claim rests on a wide range of conduct, some of which may involve matters of "universal concern" and some of which does not. For this reason, and because there is a high probability that different countries will have different definitions of what constitutes a "consistent pattern of gross violations of human rights," the court believes that plaintiffs' seventh and final ACTA claim does not involve matters of "universal concern."

3. Balancing Nexus and Matters of "Universal Concern"[68]

As alleged in the first amended complaint, plaintiffs' claims for crimes against humanity, war crimes, and racial discrimination implicate matters of

68 For the most part, Rio Tinto's briefs, exhibits and the declaration of its expert, Duke Law Professor Madeline Morris, argue that a nation's commitment to enforcing international law norms of "universal concern" is not inconsistent with that nation requiring exhaustion of adequate and available local remedies. (*See* Rio Tinto Opening Brief at 7–14, 18–20; Rio Tinto Reply at 3–6; Expert Declaration of Madeline Morris.) While interesting, Rio Tinto's survey of the role exhaustion plays in enforcing international human rights in international and foreign tribunals is tangential to the threshold inquiry the plurality directed the court to undertake—i.e., balancing the nexus between the United States and plaintiffs' claims against the universality of the claims. For this reason, the court has not directly referenced the information in this order. It observes, however, that the arguments advanced by Rio Tinto are not without controversy, and that, to the extent they imply that exhaustion ought to be required in every ATCA case, they have been expressly rejected by seven members of the *Rio Tinto IV* en banc panel. In his *Rio Tinto IV* dissent, in fact, Judge Reinhardt addressed many of these contentions. He noted that "[t]he scope of the exhaustion rule is less-settled . . . in the realm of international human rights [than in the arena of diplomatic protection, where it developed, since international human rights]. . . law recognizes the primacy of the fundamental rights of individuals and the interest of states other than the victims' own in guaranteeing such universal human rights." *Id.* at 843. Given that the ATCA vests jurisdiction in U.S. court only for "heinous offences like genocide, crimes against humanity, and war crimes," and that "[individuals have an interest in obtaining a remedy for such injustices and the United States has an interest in punishing the *'hostis humani generis,* an enemy of mankind,'" Judge Reinhardt argued that "the individual and institutional interests in an ATS case weigh heavily against requiring exhaustion." *Id.* at 845. Additionally, he noted:

> "The exhaustion principle is even less established in the enforcement of international human rights norms in domestic courts against individuals and corporations, than in supranational tribunals against states. Exhaustion under international law governs the *vertical* or *hierarchical* relationship of courts—such as the relationship of international tribunals like the International Court of Justice and the Inter-American Court of Human Rights to domestic courts. . . . And when a case is brought in such international tribunals, the defendant is often the state. . . . In adjudicating ATS claims, however, United States courts sit in *horizontal*, not vertical,

"universal concern." "Individuals have an interest in obtaining a remedy for such injustices and the United States has an interest in punishing the *'hostis humani generis,* an enemy of all mankind.'" *Rio Tinto IV,* 550 F.3d at 845 (Reinhardt, J., dissenting) (quoting *Filartiga,* 630 F.2d at 890). While the nexus between plaintiffs' claims and the United States is weak, the court believes that this consideration is outweighed by the "heinous" nature of the allegations on which the claims are based, and for that reason concludes that it should not, as a prudential matter, impose an exhaustion requirement with respect to the claims.

By contrast, plaintiffs' remaining claims, as pled, implicate norms that are not universal. This fact, coupled with the weakness of the nexus between the claims and the United States, weighs in favor of conducting a traditional two-step exhaustion analysis with respect to these claims. As masters of their complaint, plaintiffs can choose whether to bypass this additional step by amending their complaint to allege only universal claims that do not warrant exhaustion.[69] If plaintiffs wish to proceed with all of the claims alleged in the first amended complaint, however, the court will examine the availability of remedies and the futility of requiring exhaustion as respects plaintiffs' claims for violation of their rights to health, life, and security of the person; cruel, inhuman, and degrading treatment; international environmental violations; and a consistent pattern of gross human rights violations.[70]

III. Conclusion

For the reasons stated, the court finds it inappropriate to impose a prudential exhaustion requirement with respect to plaintiffs' claims for crimes against humanity, war crimes, and racial discrimination. Should plaintiffs' wish to pursue their ATCA claims for violation of the rights to health, life, and security of the person; cruel, inhuman, and degrading treatment; international environmental violations;

---

relationship with courts of other countries that might exercise its jurisdiction over the same questions of international law as against individual defendants. The more appropriate point of comparison is therefore whether courts of other nations have imposed such a requirement before exercising universal jurisdiction. It appears that, for the most part, they have not." *Id.* at 844 (citations omitted).

69 For the most part, the claims as to which the court imposes a prudential exhaustion requirement are those it concluded it lacked subject matter jurisdiction to hear under ACTA in *Rio Tinto I.* The only exception is plaintiffs' sixth claim to the extent it alleges a violation of international law as reflected in UNCLOS. As to that claim, the court held that it gave rise to jurisdiction under the ACTA. Here, the court concludes that the claim does not address matters of sufficiently universal concern to overcome the weak nexus between this country and plaintiffs and their claims such that conducting a traditional exhaustion analysis is warranted.

70 Although not entirely clear, it appears that the panel and en banc decisions in the Ninth Circuit leave intact the court's earlier dismissal of the claims for violation of the rights to life, health and security of the person; cruel, inhuman and degrading treatment (albeit this dismissal was with leave to amend); environmental harm under the principle of sustainable development; and a consistent pattern of gross human rights violations.

and a consistent pattern of gross human rights violations, the court will conduct the traditional two-step exhaustion analysis with respect to those claims before returning the matter to the Ninth Circuit.[71] Plaintiffs are directed to file a status report indicating whether they intend to pursue these claims on or before Monday, August 31, 2009. If plaintiffs do elect to pursue these claims, the court will issue a briefing schedule and set a hearing date for the traditional two-step exhaustion analysis.

71 At the hearing, plaintiffs expressed a desire to amend their cruel, inhuman, and degrading treatment claim to ensure that the claim is based on underlying norms that have been found to be matters of universal concern in past ATCA litigation. If plaintiffs wish to proceed in this fashion, they are directed to advise the court of this fact in the report that they are directed to file below. Because the matter is before the court on limited remand from the Ninth Circuit, the court does not believe it is appropriate to permit amendment of the pleadings at this stage. Rather, the court will permit plaintiffs to abandon their cruel, inhuman, and degrading treatment claim as *currently* pled without prejudice to their right to file an amended complaint if and when the matter is returned from the Ninth Circuit. Any new claim would be subject to whatever exhaustion procedure the Ninth Circuit adopts after further consideration of this matter.

SINALTRAINAL
v.
COCA-COLA COMPANY

578 F.3d 1252 (11th Cir. 2009)
Decided August 11, 2009

Daniel M. Kovalik, United Steelworkers of America, Pittsburgh, PA, Terrence P. Collingsworth, Washington, DC, for Plaintiffs-Appellants.

Robert M. Brochin, Morgan, Lewis & Bockius, Miami, FL, for Coca-Cola Co., Panamerican Beverages Co., LLC, Panamco, LLC, Panamco Industrail De Gaseosas, S.A.,

William P. McCaughan, Kirkpatrick Lockhart, Preston Gates Ellis, LLP, Miami, FL, Faith E. Gay, Sanford Ian Weisburst, Quinn Emanuel Urquhart Oliver & Hedges, New York City, J. Noah Hagey, Quinn Emanuel Urquhart Oliver & Hedges, LLP, for Richard I. Kirby.

Paul L. Hoffman, Schonbrun, De Simone, Seplow, Harris & Hoffman, LLP, Venice, CA, for EarthRights Intern., Colombian Institute of Intern. Law, George Washington University Law School Intern., Amici Curiae.

Peter Bowman Rutledge, Athens, GA, for Nat. Foreign Trade Council, Chamber of Commerce of USA, U.S. Council for Inter. Business, Nat. Ass'n of Manufacturers, Organization for Intern. Investment, Amici Curiae.

Jack Landman Goldsmith, III, Newton, MA, for Nat. Business Ass'n of Colombia, Amicus Curiae.

Before TJOFLAT, BLACK and COX, Circuit Judges.

BLACK, Circuit Judge:

The main question presented by this appeal is whether Plaintiffs-Appellants (Plaintiffs) have sufficiently pled factual allegations in their complaints to survive a motion to dismiss. In four consolidated cases, Plaintiffs, who were trade union leaders, brought suit under, *inter alia,* the Alien Tort Statute (ATS), 28 U.S.C.

§ 1350,[1] and the Torture Victims Protection Act (TVPA), 28 U.S.C. § 1350 note, alleging their employers—two bottling companies in Colombia[2]—collaborated with Colombian paramilitary forces[3] to murder and torture Plaintiffs. Plaintiffs' complaints named a number of defendants, including The Coca-Cola Company (Coca-Cola USA) and its subsidiary, Coca-Cola de Colombia, S.A., (Coca-Cola Colombia). Coca-Cola USA and Coca-Cola Colombia (the Coca-Cola Defendants) were allegedly connected to the Colombian bottlers, and their respective employees, through a series of alter ego and agency relationships.

In two separate opinions the district court found it lacked subject matter jurisdiction over Plaintiffs' ATS and TVPA claims. *See Sinaltrainal v. Coca-Cola Co.,* 256 F. Supp. 2d 1345 (S.D.Fla.2003) (*Sinaltrainal I*); *In re Sinaltrainal Litig.,* 474 F. Supp. 2d 1273 (S.D.Fla.2006) (*Sinaltrainal II*). The ATS is discussed in greater detail below, but briefly, it provides district courts with original jurisdiction over "any civil action by an alien for a tort only, committed in violation of the law of nations or a treaty of the United States." 28 U.S.C. § 1350. The TVPA establishes a cause of action for victims of torture and extrajudicial killing "under actual or "apparent authority, or color of law, of any foreign nation." 28 U.S.C. § 1350 note § 2(a). We address whether the four complaints sufficiently allege a violation of the law of nations under the ATS, and torture and extrajudicial killing under color of law under the TVPA, to survive a motion to dismiss. For the reasons stated below, we affirm the district court.

I. Background

Plaintiffs initially filed a single complaint against the Coca-Cola Defendants, Bebidas y Alimentos de Urabá, S.A., Richard Kirby, Panamco Colombia, S.A., Panamerican Beverages Company, LLC, and Panamco, LLC (collectively, Defendants). The complaint alleged the systematic intimidation, kidnapping, detention, torture, and murder of Colombian trade unionists at the hands of paramilitary forces, who allegedly worked as agents of the Defendants. Defendants jointly moved to dismiss the complaint under Rule 12(b)(1) for lack of subject matter jurisdiction. Plaintiffs then amended their complaint by filing four separate complaints, which became the *Gil* case, the *Galvis* case, the *Leal* case, and the

---

1 The statute is also known as the Alien Tort Claims Act (ATCA), *see, e.g., Cabello v. Fernandez-Larios,* 402 F.3d 1148, 1151 (11th Cir. 2005), and the Alien Tort Act (ATA), *see, e.g., Aldana v. Del Monte Fresh Produce, N.A., Inc.,* 416 F.3d 1242, 1246 (11th Cir.2005).

2 The two bottler-employers are Bebidas y Alimentos de Urabá, S.A., and Panamco Colombia, S.A. Also named as defendants along with the bottler-employers are their respective parent companies and owners. Richard Kirby (Bebidas y Alimentos de Urabá's owner) and Panamerican Beverages Company, LLC and Panamco, LLC (Panamco Colombia's owners) were also named as defendants.

3 In one of the four cases, the *Garcia* case, the alleged conspiracy was with local police officials, rather than paramilitary members.

Garcia case.[4] Bottler Bebidas y Alimentos de Urabá and its owner, Richard Kirby (the Bebidas Defendants), were named in the *Gil* complaint, whereas bottler Panamco Colombia and its owners, Panamerican Beverages Company, LLC and Panamco, LLC (the Panamco Defendants), were named in the three other complaints: *Galvis, Leal,* and *Garcia.* None of the Defendants are alleged to be directly liable for the murder and torture alleged in the complaints; rather, according to the *Gil, Galvis,* and *Leal* plaintiffs, the tortious conduct allegedly committed by paramilitary members is imputed to Defendants through conspiracy, agency, and aiding and abetting theories.[5] The *Garcia* plaintiffs allege Defendants are vicariously liable for tortious conduct allegedly committed by the local police.

Brought by the estate of Isidro Segundo Gil, among others, the *Gil* complaint alleges the Bebidas Defendants and the Coca-Cola Defendants hired, contracted with, or otherwise directed paramilitary security forces that murdered, tortured, or silenced leaders of the trade union representing workers at the Bebidas bottling facility. Isidro Segundo Gil, a local union leader, was allegedly murdered by paramilitaries inside the Bebidas bottling plant. Plaintiff Luis Adolfo Cardona, another union leader, allegedly witnessed Gil's murder and was later detained and tortured by the paramilitaries. Events in the *Gil* complaint took place at the Bebidas bottling facility, while the events in the three other complaints took place in three separate bottling facilities operated by Panamco Colombia.

The three other complaints name the Panamco Defendants and the Coca-Cola Defendants. In *Galvis,* the plaintiffs allege local management of the Panamco Colombia facility in Barancabermeja where Juan Carlos Galvis worked conspired with leaders of the local paramilitary to rid the facility of the union. Galvis alleges he received a number of death threats from the paramilitaries for his union activities and while driving in his car, on one occasion, was shot at by a gunman. In *Leal,* plaintiffs allege local management of the Panamco Colombia facility in Cucuta where Jorge Humberto Leal worked conspired with leaders of the local paramilitaries to rid the bottling facility of the union. Leal alleges he was kidnapped, tortured, and threatened by the local paramilitaries for his union activities. In *Garcia,* unlike *Gil, Galvis,* and *Leal,* the plaintiffs allege a conspiracy between the local police, rather than paramilitary officers, and the bottling facilities' management.

4 The original case number was 01-CIV-3208. The *Gil* case was assigned this number, while the other complaints were assigned the following case numbers: 02-CIV-20258, 02-CIV-20259, and 02-CIV-20260. Because these cases were factually related, they were consolidated for pretrial purposes and the *Gil* case was designated as the lead case. *See Sinaltrainal II,* 474 F. Supp. 2d at 1276 & n. 8.

5 A claim for state-sponsored torture under either the ATS or the TVPA may be predicated on indirect liability or direct liability. *Aldana,* 416 F.3d at 1247–48. The ATS permits conspiracy and accomplice liability, and the TVPA permits aiding and abetting liability. *Id.; see also Romero v. Drummond Co., Inc.,* 552 F.3d 1303, 1315 (11th Cir.2008) ("[T]he law of this Circuit permits a plaintiff to plead a theory of aiding and abetting liability under the Alien Tort Statute and the Torture Act.").

The *Garcia* plaintiffs allege the chief of security for the Bucaramanga facility where plaintiffs worked conspired with local police officers to unlawfully arrest, detain, and imprison plaintiffs.

Plaintiffs attempt to connect the Coca-Cola Defendants to the local facilities' management through a series of agency and alter ego relationships. For example, in the *Gil* case, the plaintiffs' layered theory of agency and alter ego liability is as follows: the bottling facility, Bebidas, is responsible for the acts of its employees, including conspiring with local paramilitaries to rid the facility of unions. Bebidas, in turn, is an alter ego or agent of Richard Kirby, Bebidas' owner and manager, such that Kirby is liable for any wrongful conduct by Bebidas employees that resulted in the murder of Gil. Bebidas and Kirby, in turn, are the alter egos or agents of Coca-Cola Colombia because Coca-Cola Colombia is responsible for manufacturing and distributing Coca-Cola products to Bebidas and all other bottlers in Colombia. Coca-Cola Colombia, a wholly-owned subsidiary of Coca-Cola USA, in turn, is an alter ego or agent of Coca-Cola USA because Coca-Cola Colombia is under the management, control, and direction of Coca-Cola USA to the extent that its separateness is illusory.

In *Sinaltrainal I,* the district court held it did not have subject matter jurisdiction over the ATS and TVPA claims against the Coca-Cola Defendants. *See Sinaltrainal I,* 256 F. Supp. 2d at 1355, 1357. The court determined a bottler's agreement, which gave Coca-Cola USA the right to enforce standards necessary to protect Coca-Cola's product in the marketplace, including the use of the trademark, packaging, and quality control, did not give Coca-Cola USA the total control over day-to-day activities that Plaintiffs alleged. It concluded the Coca-Cola Defendants therefore did not have the requisite control to be liable for the actions of Bebidas or its employees.[6] The district court then dismissed the Coca-Cola Defendants for lack of subject matter jurisdiction because the Plaintiffs failed to sufficiently allege the Coca-Cola Defendants violated the law of nations by conspiring with the local paramilitary forces to murder Gil and torture Cardona. *Sinaltrainal I,* 256 F. Supp. 2d at 1354–55. The district court did not dismiss the ATS and TVPA claims against the Bebidas Defendants at that time.[7] *Id.* at 1356, 1360. Subsequently, in *Sinaltrainal II,* the district court examined in detail the allegations in each of the four complaints and determined each fell short of pleading the factual allegations necessary to invoke the court's subject matter jurisdiction under the ATS and the TVPA.

6 The district court discussed the motion to dismiss for lack of subject matter jurisdiction only as it applied to the *Gil* case, but because the other three cases filed identical motions, it stated the holdings in the order would apply to all four cases. *Sinaltrainal I,* 256 F. Supp. 2d at 1347 n. 1.

7 Because the district court discussed the motion to dismiss only as it related to the *Gil* case (in which the Panamco Defendants were not named), the Panamco Defendants sought a clarification of the *Sinaltrainal I* order as it related to the remaining cases. The district court granted the Panamco Defendants' motion for clarification and dismissed the *Galvis* complaint without prejudice.

The district court found the allegations in all four complaints insufficiently pled a conspiracy between the local facilities' management and the paramilitary officers. *Sinaltrainal II,* 474 F. Supp. 2d at 1293–1301.

II. Standard of Review

A district court's decision to grant a motion to dismiss for lack of subject matter jurisdiction pursuant to Rule 12(b)(1) is a question of law we review *de novo. McElmurray v. Consol. Gov't of Augusta-Richmond County,* 501 F.3d 1244, 1250 (11th Cir.2007). A motion to dismiss under Rule 12(b)(1) may assert either a factual attack or a facial attack to jurisdiction. *See id.* at 1251; *Lawrence v. Dunbar,* 919 F.2d 1525, 1528–29 (11th Cir. 1990). A factual attack challenges "the existence of subject matter jurisdiction in fact, irrespective of the pleadings, and matters outside the pleadings, such as testimony and affidavits, are considered." *Lawrence,* 919 F.2d at 1529. In a facial attack, on the other hand, the court examines whether the complaint has sufficiently alleged subject matter jurisdiction. As it does when considering a Rule 12(b)(6) motion to dismiss for failure to state a claim, the court construes the complaint in the light most favorable to the plaintiff and accepts all well-pled facts alleged by in the complaint as true. *McElmurray,* 501 F.3d at 1251 (noting in a Rule 12(b)(1) facial challenge a plaintiff has "safeguards similar to those retained when a Rule 12(b)(6) motion to dismiss for failure to state a claim is raised").

Although it must accept well-pled facts as true, the court is not required to accept a plaintiff's legal conclusions. *Ashcroft v. Iqbal,* 556 U.S. ___, 129 S. Ct. 1937, 1949, 173 L.Ed.2d 868 (2009) (noting "the tenet that a court must accept as true all of the allegations contained in a complaint is inapplicable to legal conclusions"). In evaluating the sufficiency of a plaintiff's pleadings, we make reasonable inferences in Plaintiff's favor, "but we are not required to draw plaintiff's inference." *Aldana v. Del Monte Fresh Produce, N.A., Inc.,* 416 F.3d 1242, 1248 (11th Cir.2005). Similarly, "unwarranted deductions of fact" in a complaint are not admitted as true for the purpose of testing the sufficiency of plaintiff's allegations. *Id.; see also Iqbal,* 129 S. Ct. at 1951 (stating conclusory allegations are "not entitled to be assumed true").

A complaint may be dismissed if the facts as pled do not state a claim for relief that is plausible on its face. *See Iqbal,* 129 S. Ct. at 1950 (explaining "only a complaint that states a plausible claim for relief survives a motion to dismiss"); *Bell Atl. Corp. v. Twombly,* 550 U.S. 544, 561–62, 570, 127 S. Ct. 1955, 1968–69, 1974, 167 L.Ed.2d 929 (2007) (retiring the prior "unless it appears beyond doubt that the plaintiff can prove no set of facts" standard). In *Twombly,* the Supreme Court emphasized a complaint "requires more than labels and conclusions, and a formulaic recitation of the elements of a cause of action will not do." *Twombly,* 550 U.S. at 555, 127 S. Ct. at 1965. Factual allegations in a complaint need not be detailed but "must be enough to raise a right to relief above the speculative level on the assumption that all the allegations in the complaint are true (even if doubtful in fact)." *Id.* at 555, 127 S. Ct. at 1964–65 (internal citations and emphasis omitted).

More recently, in *Iqbal,* the Supreme Court reiterated that although Rule 8 of the Federal Rules of Civil Procedure does not require detailed factual allegations, it does demand "more than an unadorned, the-defendant-unlawfully-harmed-me accusation." *Iqbal,* 129 S. Ct. at 1949. A complaint must state a plausible claim for relief, and "[a] claim has facial plausibility when the plaintiff pleads factual content that allows the court to draw the reasonable inference that the defendant is liable for the misconduct alleged." *Id.* The mere possibility the defendant acted unlawfully is insufficient to survive a motion to dismiss. *Id.* The well-pled allegations must nudge the claim "across the line from conceivable to plausible." *Twombly,* 550 U.S. at 570, 127 S. Ct. at 1974.

III. Discussion

A. Applicable Statutes

1. Alien Tort Statute

The First Congress enacted the ATS as part of the Judiciary Act of 1789. It has received minor amendments since that time[8] and now provides: "The district courts shall have original jurisdiction of any civil action by an alien for a tort only, committed in violation of the law of nations or a treaty of the United States." 28 U.S.C. § 1350. Federal subject matter jurisdiction exists for an ATS claim when the following three elements are satisfied: (1) an alien (2) sues for a tort (3) committed in violation of the law of nations. *See, e.g., Aldana,* 416 F.3d at 1246.

A violation of the law of nations is broadly understood as a violation of the norms of customary international law. In discussing the norms of customary international law, the Supreme Court has noted the limited category of claims that federal courts could entertain at the time the ATS was enacted were "defined by the law of nations and recognized at common law." *Sosa v. Alvarez-Machain,* 542 U.S. 692, 712, 124 S. Ct. 2739, 2754, 159 L.Ed.2d 718 (2004). Offenses against the law of nations principally involved the rights or interests of whole states or nations, and did not necessarily involve the private interests of individuals seeking relief in court. *Id.* at 720, 124 S. Ct. at 2759. As this Court has previously noted, the law of nations are "[t]he standards by which nations regulate their dealings with one another." *Cohen v. Hartman,* 634 F.2d 318, 319 (5th Cir. Unit B Jan.1981)[9] ("[T]he general

8 As it appeared in 1789, the ATS provided federal district courts "shall also have cognizance, concurrent with the courts of the several States, or the circuit courts, as the case may be, of all causes where an alien sues for a tort only in violation of the law of nations or a treaty of the United States." Act of Sept. 24, 1789, ch. 20, § 9, 1 Stat. 77; *see also Sosa v. Alvarez-Machain,* 542 U.S. 692, 712–13, 124 S. Ct. 2739, 2755, 159 L.Ed.2d 718 (2004).

9 In *Bonner v. City of Prichard,* 661 F.2d 1206, 1209 (11th Cir.1981) (en banc), this Court adopted as binding precedent all decisions of the former Fifth Circuit handed down prior to close of business on September 30, 1981.

consensus is that the law [of nations] deals primarily with the relationship among nations rather than among individuals." (internal quotation marks omitted)); *accord In re Estate of Ferdinand E. Marcos Human Rights Litig.*, 978 F.2d 493, 501–02 (9th Cir.1992) ("Only individuals who have acted under official authority or under color of such authority may violate international law. . . .").

At the time of the founding of our nation, the violations of the law of nations that were recognized at common law were understood to include (1) violation of safe conducts, (2) offenses against ambassadors, and (3) piracy. *Sosa,* 542 U.S. at 720, 124 S. Ct. at 2759; *see also* 4 W. Blackstone, Commentaries on the Laws of England 68 (1769).[10] The ATS—which provides "[t]he district courts shall have original jurisdiction"—is unquestionably a jurisdictional statute, yet it also has the "practical effect" of entertaining common law causes of action for the "modest number" of violations of the law of nations. *Sosa,* 542 U.S. at 724, 124 S. Ct. at 2761.

The ATS was rarely employed before the 1980s. Indeed, the "modern line of [ATS] cases" began with *Filártiga v. Peña-Irala,* 630 F.2d 876 (2d Cir.1980). *Sosa,* 542 U.S. at 725, 124 S. Ct. at 2761; *see also Abebe-Jira v. Negewo,* 72 F.3d 844, 846 (11th Cir.1996) (describing *Filártiga* as "[t]he leading case interpreting the Alien Tort Claims Act"). In *Filártiga,* Dr. Joel Filártiga and his daughter, two Paraguayan citizens, brought an action for wrongful death against a Paraguayan police official who allegedly tortured and killed Dr. Filártiga's seventeen-year old son. *Filártiga,* 630 F.2d at 878. The Second Circuit reversed the district court's dismissal for lack of subject matter jurisdiction and held the ATS provided federal jurisdiction for claims involving universally accepted norms of international law. *Id.* The court concluded such universally accepted norms included the right to be free from torture committed by a state official. *Id.* at 880. The court, thus, expanded the ATS beyond the three categories recognized at the founding of the nation.

In *Sosa,* the Supreme Court confirmed the ATS is not only a jurisdictional statute[11]; the ATS also empowers federal courts to entertain "a very limited category"

10 Some commentators have suggested the ATS was enacted "to assure aliens access to federal courts to vindicate any incident which, if mishandled by a state court, might blossom into an international crisis." *Tel-Oren v. Libyan Arab Republic,* 726 F.2d 774, 782 (D.C.Cir.1984) (Edwards, J., concurring).

11 Federal jurisdiction under the ATS exists only when a defendant's alleged conduct violates "well-established, universally recognized norms of international law," *Filártiga,* 630 F.2d at 888. Allegations of a violation of the law of nations, i.e., an offense of universal concern or conduct under color of law that may be imputed to defendants, is a jurisdictional requirement for the ATS. *See Bigio v. Coca-Cola Co.,* 239 F.3d 440, 447 (2d Cir. 2000) ("[I]f the complaint did not plead a violation of the law of nations by [defendant], the district court was without subject matter jurisdiction under the Alien Tort Claims Act. . . ."); *Kadic v. Karadzic,* 70 F.3d 232, 238 (2d Cir.1995) ("[T]he Alien Tort Act requires that plaintiffs plead a 'violation of the law of nations' at the jurisdictional threshold. . . ." (quoting 28 U.S.C. § 1350)); *Filártiga,* 630 F.2d at 887 (noting the ATS requires alleging a violation of the law of nations at the jurisdictional threshold).

of claims. *Sosa,* 542 U.S. at 712, 124 S. Ct. at 2754; *see also Aldana,* 416 F.3d at 1246. Plaintiff Humberto Alvarez-Machain, a Mexican national, brought an action under the ATS against the United States, alleging his abduction from Mexico to stand trial in the United States for a Drug Enforcement Administration agent's torture and murder violated his civil rights. *Sosa,* 542 U.S. at 698–99, 124 S. Ct. at 2746–47. In rejecting his ATS claim, the Supreme Court held "a single illegal detention of less than a day, followed by the transfer of custody to lawful authorities and a prompt arraignment, violates no norm of customary international law so well defined as to support the creation of a federal remedy." *Id.* at 738, 124 S. Ct. at 2769. While not recognizing Alvarez-Machain's claim for a violation of the law of nations, the Court did note the limited category of claims federal court could entertain within the law of nations sphere had expanded beyond the original understanding of the First Congress. Indeed, federal courts have not been precluded from recognizing new claims under the law of nations as an element of the common law, even though the law of nations was originally limited to violation of safe conducts, offenses against ambassadors, and piracy. *Id.* at 724–25, 124 S. Ct. at 2761. The Supreme Court cautioned, however, the judicial power to recognize new law of nations violations "should be exercised on the understanding that the door is still ajar subject to *vigilant doorkeeping.*" *Id.* at 729, 124 S. Ct. at 2764 (emphasis added).

The modern line of ATS cases initially involved state actors violating the law of nations, but subsequent cases have expanded the scope of the ATS to impose liability on private individuals and corporations. In 1995, the Second Circuit held Radovan Karadzic, self-proclaimed leader of an unrecognized Bosnian-Serb entity, could be liable for a violation of the law of nations for ordering a campaign of murder, rape, forced impregnation, and other forms of torture designed to destroy religious and ethnic groups of Bosnian Muslims and Bosnian Croats. *Kadic v. Karadzic,* 70 F.3d 232, 242 (2d Cir.1995). Karadzic argued he was not a state actor because he was not an official of any recognized government. The Second Circuit rejected Karadzic's contention and held acts such as genocide and war crimes "violate the law of nations whether undertaken by those acting under the auspices of a state or only as private individuals." *Id.* at 239; *see also id.* at 244. Indeed, torture and summary execution perpetrated in the course of genocide or war crimes have been found actionable absent state action. *See id.* at 243 ("[T]orture and summary execution—when not perpetrated in the course of genocide or war crimes—are proscribed by international law only when committed by state officials or under color of law.").

This Court has also acknowledged private individuals may be liable for a violation of the law of nations. *See Romero v. Drummond Co., Inc.,* 552 F.3d 1303, 1316 (11th Cir.2008) ("Under the Alien Tort Statute, state actors are the main objects of the law of nations, but individuals may be liable, under the law of nations, for some conduct, such as war crimes, regardless of whether they acted under color of law of a foreign nation."). In addition to private individual liability, we have also recognized corporate defendants are subject to liability under the ATS and may be liable for violations of the law of nations. *See id.* at 1315 ("[T]he law of this Circuit is that [ATS] grants jurisdiction from complaints of torture against corporate defendants."); *Aldana,* 416 F.3d at 1242. In *Romero,* the Colombian subsidiary of an Alabama coal mining company was alleged to have paid paramilitary operatives to torture and assassinate leaders of a Colombian trade union representing workers at the Colombian mine. *Romero,* 552 F.3d at 1309. We rejected defendants' argument that corporate defendants were excluded from either the ATS or the TVPA. *Id.* at 1315.

2. Torture Victim Protection Act

Enacted in 1992, the TVPA provides a cause of action for official torture and extrajudicial killing.[12] The TVPA is broader than the ATS in that the TVPA allows citizens, as well as aliens, to seek remedy in federal court for official torture. S.Rep. No. 102-249, at 5 (1991) ("[W]hile the [ATS] provides a remedy to aliens only, the TVPA . . . extend[s] a civil remedy also to U.S. citizens who may have been tortured abroad."); *see also Flores v. S. Peru Copper Corp.,* 414 F.3d 233, 246–47 (2d Cir.2003). By its terms, the TVPA attaches liability to those individuals[13] who have committed torture or extrajudicial killing "under actual or apparent authority, or color of law, of any foreign nation." To evaluate "actual or apparent authority" and "color of law," this Court has relied on general principles of agency law and 42 U.S.C. § 1983 jurisprudence. *Aldana,* 416 F.3d at 1247; *accord Kadic,* 70 F.3d at 245. To pursue a claim for official torture or extrajudicial killing under the TVPA, the requisite subject matter jurisdiction may be conferred either by the ATS or 28 U.S.C. § 1331. *See Romero,* 552 F.3d at 1315 ("Federal courts are

---

12 In pertinent part, the TVPA provides:

> An individual who, under actual or apparent authority, or color of law, of any foreign nation—
>
> (1) subjects an individual to torture shall, in a civil action, be liable for damages to that individual; or
>
> (2) subjects an individual to extrajudicial killing shall, in a civil action, be liable for damages to the individual's legal representative, or to any person who may be a claimant in an action for wrongful death.

Torture Victim Protection Act of 1991 § 2(a), Pub. L. No. 102-256, 106 Stat. 73 (enacted March 12, 1992) (codified at 28 U.S.C. § 1350 (Historical and Statutory Notes)). The TVPA defines torture as any act (1) "directed against an individual in the offender's custody or physical control[;]" (2) that inflicts "severe pain or suffering[,] . . . whether physical or mental[;]" (3) for the purpose of obtaining information, intimidation, punishment or discrimination. 28 U.S.C. § 1350 note § 3(b)(1). Extrajudicial killing is defined as "a deliberated killing not authorized by a previous judgment pronounced by a regularly constituted court affording all the judicial guarantees which are recognized as indispensable by civilized peoples." 28 U.S.C. § 1350 note § 3(a).

13 This Court has determined "an individual" to whom liability may attach under the TVPA also includes a corporate defendant. *See Romero,* 552 F.3d at 1315 ("Under the law of this Circuit, the Torture Act allows suits against corporate defendants.").

empowered to entertain complaints under the Torture Act when either the Alien Tort Statute or the federal question statute, 28 U.S.C. § 1331, provides jurisdiction.").

This Court, in *Aldana* and *Romero,* squarely considered the state action requirement of the TVPA. In *Aldana,* the plaintiffs alleged Fresh Del Monte Produce, Inc., and its Guatemalan subsidiary hired or established an agency relationship with a private, paramilitary security force to eradicate the local union. *Aldana,* 416 F.3d at 1245. We concluded the state action requirement was satisfied because one public official, a district mayor, was identified by name in the complaint and was alleged to have actively participated in the paramilitary force's armed aggression. *Id.* at 1249 (concluding the complaint could "reasonably be read as depicting the Mayor as an `armed aggressor,' not a mere observer"). On the other hand, in *Romero,* we determined the state action requirement was not satisfied because the plaintiffs failed to allege the paramilitaries enjoyed a "symbiotic relationship" with the state military for the purpose of the alleged assassinations that formed the basis of the complaint. *Romero,* 552 F.3d at 1303. We concluded "there must be proof of a symbiotic relationship between a private actor and the government that involves the torture or killing alleged in the complaint to satisfy the requirement of state action." *Id.* at 1317; *accord Rayburn ex rel. Rayburn v. Hogue,* 241 F.3d 1341, 1348 (11th Cir.2001) ("[T]he symbiotic relationship must involve the specific conduct of which the plaintiff complains." (internal quotation marks omitted)).

B. Plaintiffs' Allegations of Murder and Torture

Plaintiffs contend Colombia has experienced pervasive civil unrest stemming from a longstanding civil war involving armed leftist groups on one side and the Colombian military, as well as right-wing paramilitaries, on the other. Since 1986, when the largest trade union confederation in Colombia was formed, over 4,000 trade unionists have been murdered. Plaintiffs describe the violent persecution of trade unionists in Colombia as reaching "epidemic proportions" for many years. Plaintiffs also contend they do not have access to an independent or functioning legal system in Colombia, because they suggest the country is not governed by the rule of law. It is against this backdrop that Plaintiffs' claims arise. Plaintiffs do not allege any defendant caused or precipitated the violence; rather, Defendants are accused of capitalizing on the hostile environment and conspiring with paramilitaries, or the local police in the case of *Garcia,* to rid their respective bottling facilities of unions.

Plaintiffs each brought claims under the ATS and TVPA.[14] Again, federal subject matter jurisdiction exists for an ATS claim when the following three elements are

14 We need not, and specifically do not, decide whether a heightened pleading standard may be used in evaluating the elements of an ATS or TVPA claim.

satisfied: (1) an alien (2) sues for a tort (3) committed in violation of the law of nations. *Aldana,* 416 F.3d at 1246. In this case, as in most ATS cases, the only issue is whether Plaintiffs have satisfactorily pled a violation of the law of nations. *See Kadic,* 70 F.3d at 238 ("There is no federal subject-matter jurisdiction under the Alien Tort Act unless the complaint adequately pleads a violation of the law of nations (or treaty of the United States)."). A TVPA claim requires the following three elements: (1) an individual (2) committed torture or extrajudicial killing (3) under actual or apparent authority, or color of law, of any foreign nation. 28 U.S.C. § 1350 note § 2(a). Failure to plead any of the elements of a TVPA claim results in a failure to state a claim upon which relief can be granted, *Romero,* 552 F.3d at 1315 ("[D]efects in pleading claims under the Torture Act are not jurisdictional defects[, rather t]hese pleading issues involve stating claims on which relief can be granted and should be raised in motions filed under Federal Rule of Civil Procedure 12(b)(6)."), not a lack of subject matter jurisdiction.

ATS claims generally require allegations of state action because the law of nations are the rules of conduct that govern the affairs of a nation, acting in its national capacity, in relations with another nation, *Cohen,* 634 F.2d at 319, whereas TVPA claims, by statutory definition, always require allegations of "actual or apparent authority, or color of law." *Compare* ATS, 28 U.S.C. § 1350, *with* TVPA, 28 U.S.C. § 1350 note § 2(a); *see also Aldana,* 416 F.3d at 1247 ("State-sponsored torture, unlike torture by private actors, likely violates international law and is therefore actionable under the Alien Tort Act.").[15]

1. Plaintiffs' claims brought under the ATS

For subject matter jurisdiction to entertain Plaintiffs' ATS claims, the complaints must sufficiently plead (1) the paramilitaries were state actors or were sufficiently connected to the Colombian government so they were acting under color of law (or that the war crimes exception to the state action requirement applies)[16] and (2) the Defendants, or their agents, conspired with the state actors, or those acting under color of law, in carrying out the tortious acts. A failure to allege either of these two relationships is fatal to Plaintiffs' ATS claims.

a. Allegations of state action

In *Gil, Galvis,* and *Leal,* paramilitary officers are alleged to have perpetrated murder and torture, which form the basis of their ATS claims. These plaintiffs

15 The ATS and TPVA provide independent actions and neither provides the exclusive remedy for claims of torture, as "a plaintiff may bring distinct claims for torture under each statute." *Aldana,* 416 F.3d at 1250; *see also Romero,* 552 F.3d at 1316 ("The same is true for extrajudicial killing, which is actionable under the Alien Tort Statute if it is 'committed in violation of the law of nations,' 28 U.S.C. § 1350, and under the Torture Act as that Act expressly defines it, [28 U.S.C. § 1350] note § 3(a).").

16 In *Garcia,* which we discuss below, the alleged perpetrators of the torture were the local police. The parties do not dispute that the local police were state actors.

allege the paramilitary are "permitted to exist" and are "assisted" by the Colombian government. Additionally, the plaintiffs allege "[i]t is universally acknowledged that the regular military and the civil government authorities in Colombia tolerate the paramilitaries, allow them to operate, and often cooperate, protect and/or work in concert with them." These plaintiffs also contend the paramilitaries are state actors who had a symbiotic relationship with the Colombian military and thus operated under color of law.

The plaintiffs' conclusory allegation that the paramilitary security forces acted under color of law is not entitled to be assumed true and is insufficient to allege state-sponsored action. *See Iqbal,* 129 S. Ct. at 1951. Colombia's mere "registration and toleration of private security forces does not transform those forces' acts into state acts." *Aldana,* 416 F.3d at 1248. Allegations the Colombian government tolerated and permitted the paramilitary forces to exist are insufficient to plead the paramilitary forces were state actors. The plaintiffs make the naked allegation the paramilitaries were in a symbiotic relationship with the Colombian government and thus were state actors. Nevertheless, in testing the sufficiency of the plaintiff's allegations, we do not credit such conclusory allegations as true. *See Iqbal,* 129 S. Ct. at 1951. We demand allegations of a symbiotic relationship that "involves the torture or killing alleged in the complaint to satisfy the requirement of state action." *Romero,* 552 F.3d at 1317. There is no suggestion the Colombian government was involved in, much less aware of, the murder and torture alleged in the complaints. The plaintiffs' "formulaic recitation," *Twombly,* 550 U.S. at 555, 127 S. Ct. at 1965, that the paramilitary forces were in a symbiotic relationship and were assisted by the Colombian government, absent any factual allegations to support this legal conclusion, is insufficient to state an allegation of state action that is plausible on its face. *See Iqbal,* 129 S. Ct. at 1950.[17]

Our inquiry does not stop here, however, because, under the ATS, the plaintiffs need not plead state action for claims of torture and murder perpetrated in the course of war crimes. *See Kadic,* 70 F.3d at 242–43 (holding war crimes "committed in the course of hostilities" violated fundamental international law and thus were actionable under the ATS).[18] Some acts, such as torture and murder committed in the course of war crimes, violate the law of nations regardless of whether the perpetrator acted under color of law of a foreign nation or only as a private individual. *Romero,* 552 F.3d at 1316; *Kadic,* 70 F.3d at 239, 243 ("[T]orture and

---

17 The *Leal* complaint notes Carlos Castano, the founder and leader of the AUC, Colombia's largest paramilitary group, "lives in hiding and he goes to great pains to keep his whereabouts secret, even from the government." It is unclear the extent to which the AUC act under color of law when its founder and leader "goes to great pains" to keep his location concealed from the Colombian government.

18 On the other hand, torture and murder perpetrated by private actors is actionable under the TVPA only if committed under actual or apparent authority, or color of law. 28 U.S.C. § 1350 note § 2(a). We discuss the TVPA claims in the following section.

summary execution—when not perpetrated in the course of genocide or war crimes—are proscribed by international law only when committed by state officials or under color of law."). The war crimes exception dispenses with the state action requirement for claims under the ATS.

Having failed to connect the paramilitaries with the Colombian government, the plaintiffs advance a second theory and argue the alleged murder and torture occurred during the course of an armed civil conflict, thereby constituting war crimes that negate the need for state action. The plaintiffs suggest the war crimes exception should apply to plaintiffs' murder and torture because, as non-combatants in a civil war, they were targeted for violence to further Defendants' business interests in becoming union-free, and the use of open violence to accomplish this end occurred as a result of a raging civil war.

We conclude the war crimes exception to the state action requirement is not applicable to the plaintiffs because the alleged murder and torture was not committed in the course of a civil war. We reject the plaintiffs' argument that it is sufficient for the purposes of ATS jurisdiction that the violation perpetrated by a non-state actor merely occur during an armed civil conflict. If the war crimes exception to the state action requirement permitted all non-state torture claims occurring during a period of civil disorder, federal courts would be open to lawsuits occurring during any period of civil unrest in a foreign country. The Supreme Court's reminder to exercise "vigilant doorkeeping" persuades us the war crimes exception applies only to claims of non-state torture that were perpetrated in the course of hostilities. *See Sosa,* 542 U.S. at 729, 124 S. Ct. at 2764; *Kadic,* 70 F.3d at 242–43. In this case there is no suggestion the plaintiffs' murder and torture was perpetrated because of the ongoing civil war or in the course of civil war clashes. The civil war provided the background for the unfortunate events that unfolded, but the civil war did not precipitate the violence that befell the plaintiffs.

In sum, the war crimes exception is not applicable to the plaintiffs; thus they must sufficiently allege state action. And as discussed above, the plaintiffs have not sufficiently pled state action. Accordingly, we conclude the district court did not err in dismissing the ATS claims in the *Gil, Galvis,* and *Leal* complaints for lack of federal subject matter jurisdiction.

b. Allegations of conspiracy

In *Garcia,* the complaint alleges a conspiracy between the local police, rather than paramilitary officers, and the bottling facility's management. Plaintiffs Luis Eduardo Garcia, Alvaro Gonzalez, and José Domingo Flores are three members of the local union executive board. In 1995, plaintiffs participated in a 120-hour strike against the Panamco Colombia bottling facility in Bucaramanga, after Panamco reneged on its obligations under a labor agreement with the union. Shortly after the strike, the plaintiffs allege the chief of security for the Bucaramanga facility, José Alejo Aponte, falsely told the local police he found a bomb in the facility, and he accused five members of the local union executive board, including Garcia, Gonzalez, and Flores, of planting the bomb. On March 6, 1996, the police arrested the three men. While in transit to the jail, Flores was repeatedly and brutally beaten by police and was threatened at gun point. As a result of the false charges filed by Aponte, the plaintiffs were incarcerated in a filthy and dangerous Colombian prison for six months. They were released after a regional prosecutor found the charges "to be completely without basis." The plaintiffs allege "Aponte's plan necessarily required the cooperation and complicity of the arresting police officers, since the officers had to be willing to arrest and imprison the union leaders without any evidence of the non-existent bomb." Therefore, "[b]ased on information and belief," the plaintiffs allege Aponte conspired with the arresting police officers to unlawfully arrest, detain, and imprison the plaintiffs.

We reiterate that to state a plausible claim for relief, the plaintiffs must plead "factual content that allows the court to draw the reasonable inference that the defendant is liable for the misconduct alleged." *Iqbal,* 129 S. Ct. at 1949. Rule 8(a)(2) requires "a short and plain statement of the claim showing that the pleader is entitled to relief," in order to "give the defendant fair notice of what the . . . claim is and the grounds upon which it rests." *Twombly,* 550 U.S. at 555, 127 S. Ct. at 1964. At the same time, however, the complaint must plead "more than an unadorned, the-defendant-unlawfully-harmed-me." *Iqbal,* 129 S. Ct. at 1949. Furthermore, unwarranted deductions of fact in a complaint are not admitted as true for the purpose of testing the sufficiency of the allegations. *Aldana,* 416 F.3d at 1248, and the facts as pled must state a claim for relief that is plausible on its face, *see Iqbal,* 129 S. Ct. at 1950.

Here, the *Garcia* plaintiffs' attenuated chain of conspiracy fails to nudge their claims across the line from conceivable to plausible. *Twombly,* 550 U.S. at 570, 127 S. Ct. at 1974. First, while the plaintiffs allege "Aponte's plan necessarily required the cooperation and complicity of the arresting police officers," we are not required to admit as true this unwarranted deduction of fact. Second, the plaintiffs' allegations of conspiracy are "based on information and belief," and fail to provide any factual content that allows us "to draw the reasonable inference that the defendant is liable for the misconduct alleged." *Iqbal,* 129 S. Ct. at 1949. Specifically, these plaintiffs allege "[t]he basis for the conspiracy was either that Aponte arranged to provide payment to the officers for their participation, or that the officers had a shared purpose with Aponte to unlawfully arrest and detain Plaintiffs because they were union officials and had been branded by Panamco officials as leftist guerillas." The premise for the conspiracy is alleged to be either payment of money or a shared ideology. The vague and conclusory nature of these allegations is insufficient to state a claim for relief, and "will not do." *Twombly,* 550 U.S. at 555, 127 S. Ct. at 1965.

Furthermore, the complaint fails to allege when or with whom Aponte entered into a conspiracy to arrest, detain, and harm the plaintiffs. The scope of the conspiracy and its participants are undefined. There are no allegations the treatment the plaintiffs received at the hands of the local police and in prison was within the scope of the conspiracy. Additionally, assuming Aponte even conspired with the local police to arrest the plaintiffs, this action alone is insufficient to form the basis of an ATS claim, *see Sosa,* 542 U.S. at 738, 124 S. Ct. at 2769 (holding "a single illegal detention of less than a day, followed by the transfer of custody to lawful authorities and a prompt arraignment, violates no norm of customary international law so well defined as to support the creation of a federal remedy"), and there is no allegation the subsequent six-month imprisonment and mistreatment was part of the conspiracy. The *Garcia* plaintiffs, thus, fail to state a plausible claim for relief against the Panamco Defendants for a violation of the law of nations. *See* 28 U.S.C. § 1350. We conclude the district court did not err in dismissing the ATS claims in the *Garcia* complaint for lack of subject matter jurisdiction.

2. Plaintiffs' claims brought under the TVPA

Plaintiffs allege the same operative facts that gave rise to ATS violations also gave rise to TVPA violations. It is not uncommon for plaintiffs to assert ATS and TVPA claims together. *See, e.g., Romero,* 552 F.3d at 1309 (asserting ATS and TVPA claims based on the same operative facts); *Aldana,* 416 F.3d at 1246 (same); *Khulumani v. Barclay Nat. Bank Ltd.,* 504 F.3d 254 (2d Cir.2007) (same); *Beanal v. Freeport-McMoran, Inc.,* 197 F.3d 161 (5th Cir.1999) (same). The district court determined there was no subject matter jurisdiction for the ATS claims, and because ATS jurisdiction was lacking, the court concluded the TVPA claims also failed for want of subject matter jurisdiction. *Sinaltrainal II,* 474 F. Supp. 2d at 1301 ("Claims for torture may be entertained [under the TVPA] only if they fall within the jurisdiction conferred by the AT[S]."). We conclude the district court erred in dismissing the TVPA claims for want of subject matter jurisdiction because jurisdiction over the TVPA claims is conferred by 28 U.S.C. § 1331 in this case. *See Romero,* 552 F.3d at 1315. Therefore our inquiry is not whether subject matter jurisdiction is lacking, but whether the TVPA claims state a claim for relief.[19]

---

19 Defendants moved to dismiss Plaintiffs' claims for lack of subject matter jurisdiction; however, the TVPA claims are properly addressed under a motion to dismiss for failure to state a claim for relief. The failure to state a claim for relief presents a purely legal question. *Chudasama v. Mazda Motor Corp.,* 123 F.3d 1353, 1367 (11th Cir. 1997) ("Facial challenges to the legal sufficiency of a claim or defense, such as a motion to dismiss based on failure to state a claim for relief, . . . always present[ ] a purely legal question; there are no issues of fact because the allegations contained in the pleading are presumed to be true." (footnote omitted)). We have discretion to address pure questions of law on appeal, even if such questions are not resolved by the district court. *See Flint Elec. Membership Corp. v. Whitworth,* 68 F.3d 1309, 1314 n. 7 (11th Cir.1995) ("Although the effect of [a recent Eleventh Circuit case] was not resolved in the district court, we have the authority to address this pure question of law on appeal."); *see also Singleton v. Wulff,* 428 U.S. 106, 121, 96 S. Ct. 2868, 2877, 49 L.Ed.2d 826 (1976) ("The matter of what questions may be taken up and resolved for the first time on appeal is one left primarily to the discretion of the courts of appeals, to be exercised on the facts of individual cases."); *Access Now, Inc. v. Southwest Airlines Co.,* 385 F.3d 1324, 1332 (11th Cir.2004) (outlining five general circumstances under which issues may be raised for the first time on appeal).

In other words, relief from a complaint that fails to sufficiently plead the elements of a TVPA claim should be raised in a motion filed under Rule 12(b)(6), rather than 12(b)(1). *See Steel Co. v. Citizens for a Better Env't,* 523 U.S. 83, 96, 118 S. Ct. 1003, 1013, 140 L.Ed.2d 210 (1998) (explaining "the nonexistence of a cause of action was no proper basis for a jurisdictional dismissal"); *see also Williamson v. Tucker,* 645 F.2d 404, 415 (5th Cir. May 20, 1981) ("Judicial economy is best promoted when the existence of a federal right is directly reached and, where no claim is found to exist, the case is dismissed on the merits.").

To survive a motion to dismiss for failure to state a claim upon which relief can be granted on the TVPA claims, Plaintiffs must sufficiently allege (1) the paramilitaries were state actors or were sufficiently connected to the Colombian government so they were acting under color of law and (2) the Defendants, or their agents, conspired with the state actors, or those acting under color of law, in carrying out the state-sponsored torture. *See* 28 U.S.C. § 1350 note § 2(a). Plaintiffs failed to do so. As discussed above, the *Gil, Galvis,* and *Leal* plaintiffs fail to sufficiently plead the paramilitary forces were acting under color of law. Mere toleration of the paramilitary forces does not transform such forces' acts into state acts, *Aldana,* 416 F.3d at 1248; moreover there are no allegations the Colombian government was aware of, much less complicit in, the murder and torture Plaintiffs allege in their complaints. Additionally, the *Garcia* plaintiffs fail to sufficiently allege the Panamco Defendants, or their agents, conspired with the local police in carrying out the alleged torture. The *Garcia* plaintiffs' vague and conclusory allegations of a conspiracy do not state a claim for relief that is plausible on its face, *see Iqbal,* 129 S. Ct. at 1950, and they fail to detail any factual allegations "to raise a right to relief above the speculative level," *Twombly,* 550 U.S. at 555, 127 S. Ct. at 1965. We, therefore, vacate the district court's dismissal of the TVPA claims for want of jurisdiction and instruct the court to dismiss the TVPA claims for failure to state a claim upon which relief can be granted.

IV. Conclusion

Plaintiffs' complaints outline a litany of unfortunate events occurring in a country that Plaintiffs describe as experiencing ongoing civil unrest and lacking a robust legal system. Nevertheless, as explained above, the *Gil, Galvis,* and *Leal* plaintiffs fail to sufficiently plead factual allegations to connect the paramilitary forces, who perpetrated the wrongful acts, with the Colombian government. Furthermore, the *Garcia* plaintiffs fail to sufficiently plead factual allegations to connect the Panamco Defendants to actionable torture. We affirm the dismissal of the ATS claims for lack of subject matter jurisdiction. We vacate the dismissal of the TVPA claims for want of jurisdiction and instruct the district court to enter a dismissal for failure to state a claim upon which relief can be granted.

AFFIRMED IN PART, VACATED AND REMANDED IN PART.

KEN WIWA
v.
ROYAL DUTCH PETROLEUM CO.

626 F. Supp. 2d 377 (S.D.N.Y. 2009)
Decided April 23, 2009

ORDER

KIMBA M. WOOD, District Judge.

Defendants Shell Petroleum, N.V.; Shell Transport and Trading Co., Ltd.; and Brian Anderson ("Defendants") in *Wiwa v. Royal Dutch Petroleum Co.*, 96 Civ. 8386, and *Wiwa v. Brian Anderson*, 01 Civ.1909 (collectively, "*Wiwa*") move, pursuant to Federal Rule of Civil Procedure 12(b)(1), to dismiss for lack of subject matter jurisdiction the claims brought by the *Wiwa* plaintiffs ("Plaintiffs") under the Alien Tort Statute (the "ATS"), 28 U.S.C. § 1350 (Plaintiffs' "ATS claims"). (96 Civ. 8386 D.E. ("96-D.E.") 330.)

For the reasons stated below, the Court DENIES in part and GRANTS in part Defendants' motion.

BACKGROUND

The substance of Plaintiffs' claims and allegations are addressed in detail in the Court's prior orders, familiarity with which is assumed. Here, the Court, provides a summary of the parties' arguments by way of background.

Plaintiffs' ATS claims seek to hold Defendants *vicariously* liable for violations of customary international law ("CIL") committed against Plaintiffs by the Nigerian military government.[1] As discussed below, at Discussion part IV, Plaintiffs may also contend that defendant Brian Anderson ("Anderson") is *directly* liable for violating norms of CIL ("CIL norms").

---

1 Plaintiffs rely on numerous theories of secondary and vicarious liability, including aiding and abetting, principal-agent, conspiracy, and joint participation. For simplicity's sake, the Court here refers to all these types of liability as "vicarious liability."

Defendants argue that the Court lacks subject matter jurisdiction over Plaintiffs' ATS claims for four separate reasons (1) Plaintiffs have failed to establish that their ATS claims plead violations of sufficiently universal, specific, and mutual CIL norms to give rise to the Court's subject matter jurisdiction; (2) the ATS does not grant courts jurisdiction to hear claims that rely on some or all of Plaintiffs' vicarious-liability theories; (3) to the extent that Plaintiffs' ATS claims seek to hold Anderson directly liable, Plaintiffs have failed to establish facts sufficient to justify the Court's subject matter jurisdiction over Plaintiffs' ATS claims against Anderson; and (4) the Court lacks jurisdiction over the ATS claims of plaintiff Blessing Kpuinen ("Kpuinen") because, in 2004, she became a citizen of the United States.[2]

Plaintiffs respond by arguing (1) that all of Plaintiffs' ATS claims are based on sufficiently universal, specific, and mutual CIL norms to survive Defendants' motion; (2) that, in order to establish the Court's subject matter jurisdiction over Plaintiffs' ATS claims, Plaintiffs need demonstrate only that the Nigerian government's tortious conduct *directly* violated these CIL norms, and need not demonstrate that Plaintiffs can hold Defendants *vicariously* liable for that tortious conduct; (3) that Plaintiffs have provided sufficient facts to establish the Court's jurisdiction over Plaintiffs' ATS claims against Anderson; and (4) that Kpuinen's recent change in citizenship does not defeat the Court's jurisdiction over her ATS claims.

The Court concludes that (1) all but one of Plaintiffs ATS claims are based on sufficiently universal, specific, and mutual CIL norms to give rise to an ATS claim; (2) as long as Plaintiffs establish that the Nigerian government's tortious conduct violated these CIL norms, the Court has subject matter jurisdiction over Plaintiffs' ATS claims; (3) Plaintiffs' ATS claims against Anderson survive this motion to dismiss; and (4) the Court has jurisdiction to hear Kpuinen's ATS claims.

DISCUSSION

I. Legal Standard

The ATS "confers federal subject-matter jurisdiction when the following three conditions are satisfied: (1) an alien sues (2) for a tort (3) committed in violation of the law of nations" (respectively, the "first," "second," and "third" "ATS condition"). *Kadic v. Karadzic*, 70 F.3d 232, 238 (2d Cir.1996). Primarily at issue in this order is whether Plaintiffs' ATS claims are based on a violation of the law of nations and thus meet the third ATS condition.

---

2 Defendants move to dismiss Plaintiffs' ATS claims for reasons beyond those stated here. However, as explained below, the Court concludes that it need address only these four arguments in order to resolve Defendants' motion.

A. Sources of the Law of Nations

The law of nations arises from CIL or from binding international agreement. Restatement (Third) of Foreign Relations Law of the United States § 102(1) (1987) ("Restatement"). Here, Plaintiffs' ATS claims are based on violations of CIL norms.

Courts examine the following sources, listed in Article 38 of the Statute of the International Court of Justice ("ICJ Statute"), to determine the existence and substance of a CIL norm

> (a) international conventions, whether general or particular, establishing rules expressly recognized by the contesting states;
>
> (b) international custom, as evidence of a general practice accepted as law;
>
> (c) the general principles of law recognized by civilized nations;
>
> (d) . . . judicial decisions and the teachings of the most highly qualified publicists of the various nations, as subsidiary means for the determination of rules of law.

Abdullahi, 562 F.3d at 175 (quoting *ICJ Statute*, art. 38(1), June 26, 1945, 59 Stat. 1055, 1060 T.S. No. 993).

In determining the existence of a CIL norm, "[a]greements that are not self-executing or that have not been executed by federal legislation . . . are appropriately considered evidence of the current state of customary international law." *Id.* at 176 In addition, "even declarations of international norms that are not in and of themselves binding may, with time and in conjunction with state practice, provide evidence that a norm has developed the specificity, universality, and obligatory nature required for ATS jurisdiction." *Id.*

B. When a CIL Norm Gives Rise to an ATS Claim

In order to give rise to an ATS claim, a CIL norm must meet the three criteria set out in *Sosa v. Alvarez-Machain* ("*Sosa*"), 542 U.S. 692, 732, 124 S. Ct. 2739, 159 L.Ed.2d 718 (2004). Under *Sosa*, a CIL norm must be (1) universally accepted by the civilized world; (2) defined with a specificity comparable to the 18th-century norms regarding piracy, the right of safe passage, and offenses against ambassadors; and (3) abided or acceded to by States out of a sense of legal obligation and mutual concern (collectively, the "Sosa standard"). *See Id.*; *see also Abdullahi v. Pfizer, Inc.*, 562 F.3d 163, 173–74 (2d Cir. 2009).

C. Standard of Review for Rule 12(b)(1) Motion to Dismiss an ATS Claim

Evaluating whether an ATS claim falls within a court's jurisdiction "requires a more searching review of the merits . . . than is required under the more flexible 'arising under' [jurisdictional] formula of 28 U.S.C. § 1331. *Id.* At this jurisdictional threshold, however, a court's more searching review is limited to determining (1) the existence of a CIL norm that meets the Sosa standard (the "legal sufficiency" of Plaintiffs' ATS claims), and, if so, (2) whether the evidence suggests that the CIL norm has been violated (the "factual sufficiency" of Plaintiffs' ATS claims). *See Kadic*, 70 F.3d at 238, 244 (holding that, at the jurisdictional stage, a plaintiff need not demonstrate that he can prove every element of his ATS claim); *cf. Arbaugh v. Y & H Corp.*, 546 U.S. 500, 511, 126 S. Ct. 1235, 163 L.Ed.2d 1097 (2006) ("'Subject matter jurisdiction in federal-question cases is sometimes erroneously conflated with a plaintiffs need and ability to prove the defendant bound by the federal law asserted as the predicate for relief-a merits-related determination'") (quoting 2 J. Moore et al., Moore's Federal Practice § 12.30[1] (3d ed. 2005)).

Defendants' motion challenges both the legal and factual sufficiency of Plaintiffs' ATS claims.[3] When a motion to dismiss under Rule 12(b)(1) challenges the factual sufficiency of a plaintiffs' claims, a court may refer to evidence outside the pleadings. *See Makarova v. U.S.*, 201 F.3d 110, 113 (2d Cir.2000) (citing *Kamen v. American Tel. & Tel. Co.*, 791 F.2d 1006, 1011 (2d Cir.1986)). This may include affidavits or other competent evidence. *See Kamen*, 791 F.2d at 1011. The burden is on the plaintiff to prove, by a preponderance of the evidence, that subject matter jurisdiction exists. *See Makarova* 201 F.3d at 113; *see also Luckett v. Bure*, 290 F.3d 493, 497 (2d Cir.2002); *Scelsa v. City Univ. of N.Y.*, 76 F.3d 37, 40 (2d Cir.1996).

Generally, a court deciding a Rule 12(b)(1) motion to dismiss may make factual determinations. *Grubart v. Great Lakes Dredge & Dock Co.*, 513 U.S. 527, 537, 115 S. Ct. 1043, 130 L.Ed.2d 1024 (1995) ("any litigation of a contested subject-matter jurisdictional fact issue occurs in comparatively summary procedure before a judge alone"). However, where the overlap between jurisdictional and merits evidence "is such that fact-finding on the jurisdictional issue will adjudicate factual issues required by the Seventh Amendment to be resolved by a jury, then the Court must leave the jurisdictional issue for the trial." *Alliance for Envtl. Renewal, Inc. v. Pyramid Crossgates Co.*, 436 F.3d 82, 88 (2d Cir.2006).

II. Whether Plaintiffs' ATS Claims Rely on CIL Norms that Meet the Sosa Standard

In support of their Rule 12(b)(1) motion, Defendants challenge the legal sufficiency of each of Plaintiffs' ATS claims. Defendants' challenge to the legal sufficiency of most of these claims is so unmeritorious as to warrant only summary

---

3 Specifically, Defendants (1) challenge the legal sufficiency of all of Plaintiffs' ATS claims; to the extent that Plaintiffs' ATS claims are otherwise legally sufficient, Defendants further (2) challenge the legal and factual sufficiency of Plaintiffs' ATS claims insofar as those claims seek to hold Defendants' vicariously liable for the Nigerian government's tortious conduct; and (3) challenge the factual sufficiency of Plaintiffs' ATS claims against Anderson. Defendants challenge the Court's jurisdiction over Kpuinen's ATS claims based on the first *Sosa* condition.

treatment.[4] However, Defendants also contend that the CIL norms, on which Plaintiffs' following two ATS claims rely, fail to meet the *Sosa* standard: (1) crimes against humanity, and (2) rights to life, liberty, and security of person and peaceful assembly and association ("rights related to peaceful assembly"). These challenges require more extensive treatment. As explained below, the Court concludes that Plaintiffs establish a CIL norm that meets the *Sosa* standard for crimes against humanity, but fail to do so for rights related to peaceful assembly. Accordingly, the

---

4 Defendants' contention that the Court lacks subject matter jurisdiction over the following ATS claims lacks merit and is treated only summarily: Plaintiffs' ATS claims for (1) summary execution; (2) cruel, inhuman, and degrading treatment ("CIDT"); and (3) arbitrary arrest and detention.

First, the Court finds unpersuasive Defendants' argument that there is no CIL norm against summary execution (also known as extrajudicial killing) that meets the *Sosa* standard. *See* Torture Victims Protection Act ("TVPA"), 28 U.S.C. § 1350 note (defining a federal cause of action for extrajudicial killing as one "not authorized by a previous judgment pronounced by a regularly constituted court affording all the judicial guarantees which are recognized as indispensable by civilized' peoples," unless, under international law, the killing was lawfully carried out by a foreign nation); S.Rep. No. 102-249, at pt. IV.A. (1991) & H.R.Rep. No. 102-367, at pt. III (1991), 1992 U.S.Code Cong. & Admin.News 1991, p. 84 (explaining that the TVPA codifies a universal and defined CIL norm against extrajudicial killing); *see also Geneva Convention Relative to the Treatment of Prisoners of War* ("Geneva Convention"), art. 3, Aug. 12, 1949, 6 U.S.T. 3316, 75 U.N.T.S. 135 (defining extrajudicial killing in similar terms as the TVPA); *Hamdan v. Rumsfeld*, 548 U.S. 557, 633, 126 S. Ct. 2749, 165 L.Ed.2d 723 (2006) (finding that, under customary international law, the "judicial guarantees which are recognized as indispensable by civilized peoples" include, at a minimum, those basic guarantees provided by the Geneva Convention, art. 75, Protocol I); Alston Decl. Ex. A (collecting the statements of over 100 countries describing their policy of providing due process prior to any execution and, for the most part, recognizing that international law obliges them to do so).

The Court's *Kiobel v. Royal Dutch Petroleum Co.*, 456 F. Supp. 2d 457, 464–65 (S.D.N.Y.2006), decision found extrajudicial killing insufficiently well-defined to be actionable under the ATS. The Court's decision in *Kiobel* reflected the inadequate briefing before the Court in that case. *See* 456 F. Supp. 2d at 465. On consideration of the extensive briefing before the Court on this motion, the Court concludes, contrary to its holding in *Kiobel*, that extrajudicial killing is actionable under the ATS.

Second, the Court finds unpersuasive Defendants' argument that the CIL norm against CIDT is insufficiently defined to meet the *Sosa* standard. *See In re South African Apartheid Litigation*, 617 F. Supp. 2d 228, 252–56, 2009 WL 960078, at 9–10 (S.D.N.Y.2009) (defining the elements a plaintiff needs to prove in order to prevail on a CIDT claim); *see also Wiwa v. Royal Dutch Petroleum Co.*, No. 96 Civ. 8386, 2002 WL 319887, at 7–9 (S.D.N.Y. Feb. 28, 2002) (finding CIDT a sufficiently well-defined cause of action).

Third, Defendants argue *either* that *Sosa* held that there is no CIL norm against arbitrary arrest and detention that meets the *Sosa* standard, *or* that the Court should find that there is no CIL norm against arbitrary arrest and detention that is specific enough to meet the *Sosa* standard. This argument likewise lacks merit. *See Kiobel*, 456 F. Supp. 2d at 463, 465–66 (finding the CIL norm against arbitrary arrest and detention sufficiently specific to support ATS claims, and noting that *Sosa*'s holding is "very narrow" and concludes *only* that "'a single detention of less than a day, followed by the transfer of custody to lawful authorities and a prompt arraignment, violates no norm of customary international law so well defined as to support the creation of a federal remedy'").

Court denies Defendants' motion to dismiss Plaintiffs' claims based on crimes against humanity, but grants Defendants' motion to dismiss Plaintiffs' claim based on rights related to peaceful assembly.

A. Crimes Against Humanity

The Court, in a prior order, concluded that Plaintiffs had established an actionable CIL norm barring crimes against humanity. *See Wiwa*, 2002 WL 319887, at 9–10 (the Court's "2002 Order"). The Court's 2002 Order examined the Rome Statute of the International Criminal Court, decisions of international tribunals interpreting CIL norms, as well as reports and commentary issued by the United Nations, to determine that crimes against humanity is a norm that is "customary, obligatory, and well-defined in international jurisprudence." *Id.* In support of their instant motion, Defendants contend that the Court's previous conclusion does not survive the Supreme Court's subsequent decision in Sosa, because (1) under Sosa, the Court's conclusion relied on incompetent sources of international law; and/or (2) the Court, in its 2002 Order, failed to ensure that crimes against humanity are defined with sufficient specificity to meet the Sosa standard. Defendants' contentions are unpersuasive.

1. Sources of International Law

Defendants' argument that, after Sosa, the sources the Court relied upon in its 2002 Order are incompetent lacks merit. *See Abdullahi*, 562 F.3d at 187–88 (holding that, after Sosa, international agreements can still be "appropriately considered evidence of the current state of customary international law" even if they, *inter alia*, are not binding on the United States, and/or are not self-executing); *see also Khulumani*, 504 F.3d at 283 (warning district courts against "overstating the weight we [the Second Circuit] have placed on the self-executing status of a treaty in our consideration of its weight as evidence of [CIL]") (Katzmann, J. concurring, joined by Hall, J.). Indeed, since Sosa was decided, the Court has allowed ATS claims for crimes against humanity to proceed. *See Kiobel*, 456 F. Supp. 2d at 466–67.

Furthermore, even assuming, *arguendo*, that the sources cited in the Court's 2002 Order cannot, on their own, establish a CIL norm that meets the Sosa standard, they are but some of the many sources that condemn crimes against humanity. (*See* Roht-Arriaza Decl. ¶¶ 11-25 (citing sources prohibiting crimes against humanity, including the 1907 preamble to the Hague Convention; the Nuremberg Charter; Control Council Law No. 10, which authorized the creation of the Nuremberg military tribunals; United Nations conventions and resolutions; and the statutes governing the International Criminal Tribunals for Rawanda and Yugoslavia as well as numerous decisions by those Tribunals).) As the Second Circuit has recognized, "[c]ustomary international law rules proscribing crimes against humanity . . . have been enforceable against individuals since World War II." *Flores v. Southern Peru Copper Corp.*, 343 F.3d 140, 151 (2d Cir.2003). Accordingly, the Court finds meritless Defendants' contention that Plaintiffs' crimes against humanity claims do not survive Sosa because Sosa deemed incompetent the sources on which those claims are based.

2. Specificity

Defendants' contention that the CIL norm prohibiting crimes against humanity is insufficiently specific to meet the *Sosa* standard is also unpersuasive. As Judge Cote explains at length in *Presbyterian Church of Sudan v. Talisman Energy Inc.*, 226 F.R.D. 456, 479–81 (S.D.N.Y. 2005), international law sources specifically define the elements a plaintiff must prove in order to prevail on a claim based on crimes against humanity.

Furthermore, although Defendants are correct that there is not universal agreement on every element of a claim based on crimes against humanity, this limited inconsistency does not frustrate the Court's jurisdiction to hear such claims. *See Abdullahi*, 562 F.3d at 184 (finding that a CIL norm whose scope is uncertain at the margins is still sufficiently specific to support an ATS cause of action for "conduct that is at the core of any reasonable iteration" of the CIL norm). All the sources cited by Judge Cote agree that the type of tortious conduct at issue here, including torture, murder, political persecution, and unlawful imprisonment, constitute crimes against humanity. *See Presbyterian Church*, 226 F.R.D. at 479–81. Plaintiffs' ATS claims thus implicate the core of this CIL norm, not its disputed margins. The CIL norm against crimes against humanity is sufficiently specific to meet the Sosa standard.

Accordingly, the Court concludes that Plaintiffs' ATS claims for crimes against humanity are within the Court's subject matter jurisdiction.

B. Rights Related to Peaceful Assembly

The Court's 2002 Order also found that Plaintiffs' ATS claims for rights related to peaceful assembly were based in "well-articulated international norms." *See Wiwa*, 2002 WL 319887, at 10–12. As the Court's 2002 Order observes, at that time "defendants d[id] not dispute that customary international law prohibit[ed] violations" of rights related to peaceful assembly. *Id.* at 10. Now, however, Defendants do so. The Court agrees with Defendants that rights related to peaceful assembly do not meet the *Sosa* standard and thus cannot give rise to an ATS claim.

In the Court's 2002 Order, the Court relied on the definition of the right to peaceful assembly and expression articulated in the United Nation's *Code of Conduct for Law Enforcement Officials*, annex, 34 U.N. GAOR Supp., No. 46, at 186, U.N. Doc. A/34/46 (1979) (the "U.N.'s Code of Conduct"), and the *Basic Principles on the Use of Force and Firearms by Law Enforcement Officials, Eighth United Nations Congress on the Prevention of Crime and the Treatment of Offenders*, principle 9, U.N. Doc. A/CONF. 144/28/Rev. 1, at 112 (1990) (the "U.N.'s Basic Principles"). Plaintiffs now provide several additional decisions by the European Court of Human Rights (the "ECHR") that they contend further define the CIL norm protecting rights related to peaceful assembly. (*See* Roht-Arriaza Decl. 15-16, 19.)

The sources cited in the Court's 2002 Order were promulgated or welcomed by resolutions passed by the United Nations General Assembly (the "U.N. G.A."). Such resolutions can help confirm a CIL norm, but they are not sufficient, on their own, to define such a norm. *Cf. Abdullahi*, 562 F.3d at 176–77 (holding that nonbinding declarations can help establish that a CIL norm meets the Sosa standard, but only when other sources demonstrate that the norms articulated in the non-binding declarations have been broadly incorporated into states' practices).

The four ECHR cases Plaintiffs cite also do not suffice to define the CIL norm protecting rights related to peaceful assembly. First, these cases interpret a regional human rights convention, not one generally open to, and joined by, civilized nations. Thus, these cases do not, on their own, establish international law for the purpose of establishing a court's subject matter jurisdiction over ATS claims. *See supra* pt. I.B. (discussing the sources that determine the existence and substance of a CIL norm, and noting that judicial decisions are only a subsidiary source of CIL norms).

Second, the ECHR's decisions do not otherwise evidence a CIL norm that meets the *Sosa* standard. The ECHR's decisions may help establish that some states have incorporated the norm protecting rights related to peaceful assembly as defined in the U.N.'s Code of Conduct and Basic Principles. Even so, incorporation of this definition by the European states subject to the ECHR is not sufficient to establish an international consensus regarding this definition. Two U.N. resolutions and four ECHR decisions fall far short of the evidence the Second Circuit found sufficient to demonstrate a CIL norm that met the Sosa standard for specificity. *See Abdullahi*, 562 F.3d at 184–85 (finding that a CIL norm meets the Sosa standard for specificity where multiple international agreements (including one that is binding on more than 160 signatory states), as well as the domestic laws of over 80 states, adopt a particular definition of that norm).[5]

The Court concludes that neither the sources cited in the Court's 2002 Order alone, nor those sources supplemented by the ECHR decisions Plaintiffs provide, suffice to demonstrate a CIL norm that is sufficiently specific to meet the Sosa standard.[6] *Accord Bowoto v. Chevron Corp.*, 557 F. Supp. 2d 1080, 1095 (N.D.Cal.2008);

5 A CIL norm may meet the Sosa standard for specificity even if there are fewer, and less persuasive, international law sources defining that norm than were present in *Abdullahi*. However, wherever the outer limit of the Sosa standard for specificity lies, the sources defining the CIL norm protecting rights related to peaceful assembly fall outside of it.

6 Because the Court finds that it lacks subject matter jurisdiction over Plaintiffs' ATS claim based on rights related to peaceful assembly, the Court need not reach Defendants' contention that Plaintiffs Kogbara and Nuate cannot bring such a claim because they were not engaged in peaceful protest when they were harmed.

Kiobel, 456 F. Supp. 2d at 467. Accordingly, the Court dismisses for lack of subject matter jurisdiction Plaintiffs' ATS claims based on rights related to peaceful assembly.

C. Conclusion

For the reasons stated above, the Court (1) denies Defendants' motion to dismiss Plaintiffs' claim based on crimes against humanity, and (2) grants Defendants' motion to dismiss Plaintiffs' claim based on rights related to peaceful assembly.

III. Vicarious-Liability

Defendants purport to challenge the legal and factual sufficiency of Plaintiffs' ATS claims insofar as Defendants argue that the Court has subject matter jurisdiction over Plaintiffs' ATS claims only if Plaintiffs can hold Defendants vicariously liable for the Nigerian government's tortious conduct. Plaintiffs respond that whether they can hold Defendants vicariously liable for the Nigerian government's tortious conduct is irrelevant to determining the Court's subject matter jurisdiction over Plaintiffs' ATS claims. According to Plaintiffs, the Court has jurisdiction over Plaintiffs' ATS claims if Plaintiffs establish that the Nigerian government violated a CIL norm meeting the *Sosa* standard.[7] Plaintiffs contend that whether they can hold Defendants vicariously liable for the Nigerian government's tortious conduct is a purely merits-based question, not also a jurisdictional question. The Court agrees with Plaintiffs that the Court's jurisdiction over Plaintiffs' ATS claims does not turn on whether Plaintiffs can hold Defendants vicariously liable for the Nigerian government's tortious conduct.

There is no clear law on this subject; there is only ambiguous dicta. *See, e.g., Khulumani v. Barclay Nat'l Bank Ltd.*, 504 F.3d 254, 260 (2d Cir.2007) (holding, per curiam, that aiding and abetting liability can be pled in ATS claims but not clearly stating whether a court's subject matter jurisdiction over ATS claims turns on this determination). However, the Second Circuit's recent decision in *Abdullahi*, 562 F.3d 163, persuades the Court that its jurisdiction over Plaintiffs' ATS claims does not turn on whether Plaintiffs can hold Defendants vicariously liable for the Nigerian government's tortious conduct.

The plaintiffs in *Abdullahi*, like the Wiwa Plaintiffs, asserted ATS claims against a corporation. However, the *Abdullahi* plaintiffs alleged that the corporate defendant was *directly*, rather than *vicariously*, liable for violating a CIL norm. In *Abdullahi*, the Second Circuit did not consider, in its *jurisdictional* analysis, whether the corporate defendant could be held liable for violating the CIL norm at issue. Instead, in *Abdullahi*, the Second Circuit *concluded* its jurisdictional analysis

7 Defendants do not contest that, to the extent that Plaintiffs' ATS claims are based on CIL norms that meet the *Sosa* standard, the Nigerian government's tortious conduct violated those norms.

once it established generally that a CIL norm meeting the Sosa standard prohibited the kind of tortious conduct the *Abdullahi* plaintiffs alleged. *After* concluding its jurisdictional analysis, the Second Circuit then turned to the question of whether the corporate defendant could be held liable for violating the CIL norm. *See id.* at 17–18.

If the Second Circuit in *Abdullahi* considered the question of a defendant's *direct* liability for a violation of a CIL norm nonjurisdictional, it follows that the question of a defendant's vicarious liability is also non-jurisdictional.[8]

This conclusion also comports with the Second Circuit's reasoning in *Kadic*, 70 F.3d at 238. In *Kadic*, the Second Circuit concluded its jurisdictional analysis once it had determined that the plaintiff had alleged conduct that violated an actionable CIL norm. *See id.* The Second Circuit specifically stated that a court's jurisdiction over the plaintiff's ATS claims did not turn on whether he could prove every element of those claims, including the *mens rea*, or *actus rea* elements of his ATS claims. *See id.* at 244. Again, if these critical elements of ATS claims are ancillary and non-jurisdictional, then whether a plaintiff can hold a particular defendant vicariously liable for the tortious conduct giving rise to his ATS claim is also an ancillary, non-jurisdictional question.[9] *Id.* at 244.

---

8 Defendants argue that a footnote in *Sosa*, 542 U.S. at 733 n.20, 124 S. Ct. 2739(the "*Sosa* footnote"), holds, to the contrary, that a court must determine, as part of its jurisdictional analysis, whether a plaintiff bringing ATS claims may seek to hold a defendant vicariously liable for the tortious conduct giving rise to those claims. The Court disagrees with Defendants' construction of the *Sosa* footnote.

Sosa held that courts should only recognize federal common law causes of action brought pursuant to the ATS if a plaintiff alleges a violation of a sufficiently universal, specific, and mutually binding CIL norm. *Id.* at 732, 124 S. Ct. 2739. The *Sosa* footnote states that, when a court is making this determination, "a related consideration is whether international law extends the scope of liability for a violation of a given norm to the perpetrator being sued, if the defendant is a private actor such as a corporation or individual." *Id.* at 733 n. 20, 124 S. Ct. 2739. The *Sosa* footnote then cites two cases that considered whether only state actors, or also private actors, could be held *directly* liable for violations of a given CIL norm.

Defendants' construction of the *Sosa* footnote is unpersuasive for three reasons. First, the *Sosa* footnote is merely dictum. Second, the *Sosa* footnote, like the overall decision, is concerned not with the scope of a court's jurisdiction under the ATS, but with what causes of action a court should recognize when exercising that jurisdiction. Third, although the *Sosa* footnote is cast in broad terms, read in context, the *Sosa* footnote is concerned only with who can be held *directly* liable for primary violations of a CIL norm. Even if a court, as part of its jurisdictional analysis pursuant to the ATS, must consider who can be held *directly* liable for violating a CIL norm, it does not follow that a court must also consider whether a defendant can be held *vicariously* liable as part of the court's jurisdictional analysis. (Defendants also misread the Second Circuit's decision in *Kadic v. Karadzic*, 70 F.3d 232, 244 (2d Cir.1996), which also considered only whether a private actor could be held *directly*, not vicariously, liable for violations of a CIL norm.)

9 The logical consequence of the Court's conclusion here is that Defendants' challenge should have been raised in a motion to dismiss for failure to state a claim upon which relief can be

Accordingly, to the extent that Defendants' motion to dismiss challenges Plaintiffs' legal and factual basis for holding Defendants vicariously liable for tortious conduct, Defendants' motion is denied.[10]

IV. Anderson

Defendants challenge the factual sufficiency of Plaintiffs' ATS claims against Anderson. Specifically, Defendants contend that Plaintiffs have failed to establish a factual basis for the Court to assume subject matter jurisdiction over Plaintiffs' ATS claims against Anderson.[11] Defendants argue that Plaintiffs have no evidence that Anderson violated a CIL norm. Defendants' contention implicates the merits of Plaintiffs' ATS claims against Anderson, as well as the Court's jurisdiction over those claims. There are material factual disputes regarding Anderson's involvement in the allegedly tortious conduct. (*Compare, e.g.*, Pls.' Opp'n 29 *with* Anderson's Reply 5-6 (describing conflicting accounts of a meeting between Anderson and plaintiff Owens Wiwa)). Even assuming, *arguendo*, that Defendants raise a jurisdictional, as well as a merits, issue, the facts necessary to resolve this jurisdictional issue are sufficiently intertwined with the merits of Plaintiffs' ATS

---

granted or in a motion for summary judgment, *see* Fed. R. Civ. P. 12(b)(6), 56, rather than in a motion to dismiss for lack of subject matter jurisdiction.

Defendants contend that, should the Court deem non-jurisdictional the question of whether Plaintiffs may hold Defendants vicariously liable for the Nigerian government's tortious conduct, the Court would throw open the courthouse doors to frivolous lawsuits. Because a defendant has ample opportunity to challenge a plaintiff's legal and factual basis for seeking to hold a defendant vicariously liable, for instance by filing the Rule 12(b)(6) or Rule 56 motions described here, the Court finds Defendants' contention unpersuasive.

10 Because the Court deems non-jurisdictional the question of whether Plaintiffs must demonstrate that they can hold Defendants vicariously liable for the Nigerian government's tortious conduct, the Court need not reach the parties' arguments about (1) what law a court looks to in order to determine whether a plaintiff bringing ATS claims may hold a defendant vicariously liable: international law, federal common law, or forum state law; (2) whether, under the source of law the court determines to be applicable, a plaintiff may hold a defendant vicariously liable; and, (3) to the extent that a plaintiff may hold a defendant vicariously liable under the applicable law, whether or not Plaintiffs have provided sufficient evidence of Defendants' vicarious liability.

The Court notes, however, that it finds persuasive Judge Scheindlin's thoughtful treatment of the first two of Defendants' arguments in *In re South African Apartheid Litigation*, 617 F. Supp. 2d at 254–64, 270–74, 2009 WL 960078, at 10–15, 21–22 (looking to international law to determine whether plaintiffs can hold defendants vicariously liable for a government's tortious conduct, but looking to federal common law to develop the specific standard to apply where the international law governing these ancillary issues lacks sufficient specificity).

11 As indicated *supra* note 10, to the extent that Plaintiffs seek to hold Anderson vicariously liable for violating CIL norms, Defendants' contention regarding the sufficiency of Plaintiffs' evidence is not germane to deciding this jurisdictional motion. However, Plaintiffs are unclear as to whether they seek to hold Anderson directly, as well as vicariously, liable for violating CIL norms. The Court thus considers Defendants' contention to the extent that Plaintiffs seek to hold Anderson directly liable for violating CIL norms.

claims against Anderson, and are sufficiently disputed, that the Court must leave the determination of this jurisdictional issue to trial. *See Pyramid Crossgates*, 436 F.3d at 88.

Accordingly, to the extent that Defendants contest the Court's subject matter jurisdiction based on the sufficiency of Plaintiffs' evidence of Anderson's *direct* involvement in violating a CIL norm, Defendants' motion is denied without prejudice and with leave to refile during trial.

V. Kpuinen

Defendants contend that the Court lacks subject matter jurisdiction over Kpuinen's ATS claims because the ATS grants jurisdiction only when an *alien* sues, and Kpuinen has become a United States citizen since bringing this lawsuit.

Defendants' contention is unpersuasive. Defendants rely on decisions that hold that a court's subject matter jurisdiction ceases if a plaintiff, in amending her complaint or filing a pretrial order, abandons the allegations or claims on which the court's jurisdiction was based. *See Rockwell Int'l Corp. v. United States*, 549 U.S. 457, 473–74, 127 S. Ct. 1397, 167 L.Ed.2d 190 (2007) (pretrial order); *Connectu v. Zuckerberg*, 522 F.3d 82, 92–93 (1st Cir.2008) (amended complaint); *United States v. Caremark*, 496 F.3d 730, 735 (7th Cir.2007) (amended complaint). Those cases are inapposite.

Although Kpuinen has amended her complaint five times, she has not abandoned her allegation that she was not a United States citizen (1) at the time she and her husband, on whose behalf she also brings ATS claims, were harmed, or (2) at the time she brought this lawsuit. (*See, e.g.*, Fifth Am. Compl. ¶ 9 (alleging that Kpuinen became a United States citizen in 2004 and was a citizen of Nigeria before that).) Defendants provide no basis for the Court to interpret the ATS to require that a plaintiff remain an alien throughout the duration of her lawsuit, and the Court is not aware of any. Accordingly, the Court finds Defendants' contention that the Court lacks subject matter jurisdiction over Kpuinen's ATS claims unpersuasive.

CONCLUSION

As explained above, the Court GRANTS in part and DENIES in part Defendants' motion. (96-D.E. 330.) Specifically, the Court dismisses Plaintiffs' ATS claim based on rights related to peaceful assembly but otherwise denies Defendants' motion.

SO ORDERED.

IN RE XE SERVICES ALIEN TORT LITIGATION

665 F. Supp. 2d 569 (E.D. Va. 2009)
Decided October 21, 2009

MEMORANDUM OPINION

T.S. ELLIS, III, District Judge.

These five cases, consolidated for purposes of discovery and pretrial motions, present questions unresolved in this circuit concerning the scope and application of the Alien Tort Statute ("ATS") and the Racketeer Influenced and Corrupt Organizations Act ("RICO"). Plaintiffs—all Iraqi nationals or the estates of deceased Iraqi nationals—claim that defendants are liable for various injuries or deaths that occurred in Iraq. Defendants seek dismissal of the cases for lack of federal subject-matter jurisdiction pursuant to Rule 12(b)(1), Fed. R. Civ. P., and for failure to state claims upon which relief may be granted pursuant to Rule 12(b)(6), Fed. R. Civ. P. Defendants also argue for dismissal of the claims because they raise nonjusticiable political questions or, alternatively, on grounds of *forum non conveniens*. The motions have been fully briefed and argued, and are now ripe for disposition.

I.[1]

In these consolidated cases, a total of sixty-four plaintiffs—forty-five Iraqi nationals and the estates of nineteen deceased Iraqi nationals—seek damages for deaths or serious injuries certain plaintiffs suffered when they were allegedly shot or beaten by defendants' employees. All of the alleged shootings or beatings occurred in Iraq.

Named as defendants are eleven business entities, collectively referred to as "Xe defendants," and one individual, Erik Prince, who is alleged to be the owner and

---

1 The facts recited herein are derived largely from plaintiffs' complaints and are, as required at this stage in the proceedings, assumed to be true. *See Revene v. Charles County Comm'rs*, 882 F.2d 870, 872 (4th Cir. 1989); *see also Ashcroft v. Iqbal*, 129 S. Ct. 1937, 1950, 173 L.Ed.2d 868 (2009) ("When there are well-pleaded factual allegations, a court should assume their veracity and then determine whether they plausibly give rise to an entitlement to relief.").

operator of the eleven Xe defendants.[2] The complaints allege that Xe defendants were retained by the United States Department of State to perform security services under contract in Iraq. The complaints further allege that certain plaintiffs were shot or beaten by defendants' employees.

For purposes of ruling on the motions at bar, it is important to summarize briefly the facts alleged with regard to each of the consolidated cases.

A. No. 1:09cv615

Plaintiffs in No. 1:09cv615 are the estate, widow, and two surviving sons of Raheem Khalaf Sa'adoon. Prior to his death, Sa'adoon worked as a security guard for Iraqi Vice President Adel Abdul Mahdi. On December 24, 2006, Andrew Moonen was allegedly an employee of Blackwater, as it was then known.[3] On that day, Moonen attended a Christmas party allegedly attended by several of his Blackwater colleagues. He is said to have consumed an excessive amount of alcohol at the party and thereafter to have left in a state of visible intoxication, armed with his Blackwater-issued Glock handgun. Moonen allegedly became lost and eventually came upon Sa'adoon, who was on guard duty. According to the complaint, Moonen then pulled out his Glock handgun and shot and killed Sa'adoon for no reason. Plaintiffs allege that defendants are liable for Sa'adoon's death. Plaintiffs also accuse Xe defendants of flying Moonen to the United States for the purposes of (i) evading prosecution by Iraqi authorities, and (ii) avoiding promised payments to Sa'adoon's widow.

B. No. 1:09cv616

In No. 1:09cv616, plaintiffs are the estates of Iraqi citizens Ali Hussamaldeen Ibrahim Albazzaz, Kadhum Kayiz Aziz, and Sa'ad Raheem Jarallah. Aziz worked as a security guard for the Iraqi government, while Jarallah was a schoolteacher. The complaint does not specify Albazzaz's occupation. Plaintiffs allege that defendants are liable for Albazzaz's, Aziz's, and Jarallah's deaths, which occurred on September 9, 2007, when unidentified Xe defendants' employees allegedly fired without justification into a crowd near Baghdad's Al Watahba Square.

C. No. 1:09cv617

In No. 1:09cv617, plaintiffs are twenty-two Baghdad residents and the estates of eight deceased former Baghdad residents. Plaintiffs' claims stem from an incident that occurred on September 16, 2007 in Baghdad's Nisoor Square. On that day,

---

2 Xe defendants are: Prince Group, EP Investments LLC, Greystone, Total Intelligence, The Prince Group LLC, Xe, Blackwater Worldwide, Blackwater Lodge and Training Center, Blackwater Target Systems, Blackwater Security Consulting, and Raven Development Group. In addition, plaintiffs in No. 1:09cv615 originally named Andrew Moonen, a former Blackwater employee, as a defendant. Plaintiffs have since settled with Moonen and voluntarily dismissed their claims against him.

3 The entity formerly known as Blackwater now operates under the name Xe Services.

plaintiffs claim that Xe defendants' employees repeatedly fired automatic weapons and detonated grenades into a crowd without justification, thereby causing (i) the deaths of the eight plaintiffs whose estates brought this suit and (ii) the injuries of the remaining twenty-two plaintiffs.

D. No. 1:09cv618

In No. 1:09cv618, plaintiffs are nineteen Baghdad residents and the estates of six deceased former Baghdad residents. According to the complaint, the alleged deaths and injuries occurred in seven separate incidents between March 2005 and April 2008. In all seven incidents, plaintiffs allege that employees of Xe defendants shot or severely beat civilians without justification. Plaintiffs allege that defendants are liable for the deaths of the six decedents and the injuries of the other nineteen plaintiffs. In chronological order, plaintiffs allege:

- On March 22, 2005, Al Qaysi, Hikmat Ali Husein Al Rubae, and one other person were being driven to Baghdad from the Baghdad airport in Al Rubae's BMW automobile when, these plaintiffs allege, Al Qaysi was shot and killed for no reason by Xe defendants' employees. Al Rubae also alleges that Xe defendants' employees shot at him, wounding him and causing damage to his vehicle.
- Husam Hasan Jaber was a Baghdad taxicab operator who, on July 18, 2005, was driving a minibus carrying three passengers. Jaber alleges that Xe defendants' employees shot and wounded Jaber without justification. He further alleges that Xe defendants' employees used exploding ammunition designed to maximize the extent of the injury inflicted and the amount of damage caused. He also claims that Xe defendants' employees fled the scene despite knowing that he had been seriously wounded. Jaber further alleges that he suffered property damage to his minibus as a result of the incident.
- Maulood Mohammed Shathir Husein, a professor of veterinary medicine at the University of Baghdad, claims that in August 2005, he was being driven to the Ministry of Higher Education in Baghdad when his car approached a U.S. military checkpoint. He alleges that vehicles operated by Xe defendants' employees approached the checkpoint at the same time, at which point the employees shot Husein in the leg. According to the complaint, the vehicles operated by Xe defendants' employees left the scene while American military personnel came to Husein's aid.
- Suhad Shakir Fadhil worked in media relations in Baghdad. Her estate alleges that on February 4, 2007, she was driving to her office located near the Iraqi Ministry of Foreign Affairs when Xe defendants' employees shot and killed her without justification. Her estate also alleges that Xe defendants' shooters severely damaged her car.
- On February 7, 2007, Xe defendants' employees shot and killed, without justification, three men—Sabah Salman Hassoon, Azhar Abdullah Ali, and Nibrass

Mohammed Dawood—while the men were working as security guards at the Iraqi Media Network in Central Baghdad. Moreover, these plaintiffs claim that the incident was witnessed by twenty of Xe defendants' employees, and that Xe defendants failed to report the shooting, refused to identify the shooters, and destroyed evidence relating to the incident.

- On July 1, 2007, Xe defendants' employees shot at a minibus containing three families, including small children, for no reason. The shots killed a nine-year-old boy, and wounded a three-month-old baby and the children's mother, father, uncle, and cousin. These plaintiffs allege that other family members in the minibus were also shot at and that they continue to suffer from emotional distress as a result of the incident.
- On April 26, 2008, Safeen Hameed Ahmed Qadir was a photographer covering the opening of a Ford automobile dealership in Iraq's Arbil province. During the event, Qadir attempted to photograph a visiting American dignitary who was being guarded by Xe defendants' employees. Qadir alleges that these employees severely beat him without justification.

E. No. 1:09cv645

Finally, in No. 1:09cv645, plaintiffs are Ali Kareem Fakhri and the estate of Husain Salih Rabea. Rabea was a seventy-two year old man whose occupation is not specified in the complaint. Fakhri was a student at Babylon University College of Biology. These plaintiffs allege that on August 13, 2007, Xe defendants' employees shot at Fakhri and Rabea for no reason, killing Rabea and causing severe emotional distress to Fakhri. They further allege that Xe defendants' employees fled the scene without offering medical aid.

The first four of these consolidated cases were filed on June 2, 2009, and No. 1:09cv645 was thereafter filed on June 10, 2009. On July 14, 2009, defendants moved to dismiss the cases, which were subsequently consolidated for purposes of discovery and pre-trial motions on July 17, 2009. Discovery was stayed pending resolution of defendants' motions. *See In re: Blackwater Alien Tort Claims Act Litigation*, Nos. 1:09cv615, 1:09cv616, 1:09cv617, 1:09cv618, 1:09cv645 (E.D.Va. July 17, 2009) (Order). Oral argument was heard on August 28, 2009.

In all of the cases, plaintiffs accuse defendants of encouraging the killing of Iraqi civilians by fostering a corporate culture in which excessive use of deadly force is unpunished. Specifically, plaintiffs accuse defendants of employing and arming people whom they know to be alcoholics, drug users, or acting under the influence of chemical substances. Moreover, plaintiffs allege that defendants hire individuals known to have engaged in human rights abuses. They claim defendants captured illegal acts by their employees on videotape and subsequently destroyed those tapes. In addition, some plaintiffs claim that defendant Prince has engaged in a pattern of racketeering activities through the commission of illegal acts including murder, tax evasion, destruction of evidence, kidnaping, weapons smuggling, sexual exploitation of minors, and unlawful possession and distribution of controlled substances. These RICO plaintiffs claim they suffered property damage during the commission of the alleged predicate acts and through defendant Prince's alleged control and operation of a RICO enterprise. More specifically, the RICO plaintiffs allege that their vehicles were damaged or destroyed during the course of the killings, which are alleged to be the predicate racketeering acts committed by defendant Prince.

In all of the cases, plaintiffs seek recovery from defendants under the Alien Tort Statute, 28 U.S.C. § 1350, for injuries resulting from the alleged commission of war crimes. In two of the cases, Nos. 1:09cv617 and 1:09cv618, plaintiffs also claim that defendants are liable under the ATS for committing summary executions. In those same two cases, plaintiffs also allege that defendants are civilly liable for RICO violations under 18 U.S.C. § 1964. Moreover, in all of the cases, plaintiffs assert that defendants are liable under nonfederal tort law for (i) assault and battery, (ii) wrongful death, (iii) intentional infliction of emotional distress, (iv) negligent infliction of emotional distress, (v) negligent hiring, training, and supervision, and (vi) tortious spoliation of evidence.

II.

Defendants seek dismissal of all ATS claims on the grounds (i) that the ATS does not recognize claims of war crimes or summary executions, (ii) that ATS liability is limited to state actors, (iii) that the ATS does not recognize claims against corporations, (iv) that plaintiffs have not alleged facts in their complaints sufficient to create a plausible entitlement to relief under the ATS, and (v) that the ATS requires plaintiffs to exhaust their remedies in Iraqi courts before suing under the ATS in the United States. Defendants also argue that even assuming the claims are adequately stated, recovery of punitive damages is not allowed under the ATS. At issue, therefore, are the following questions:

(i) Whether the ATS recognizes causes of action for war crimes and summary executions;

(ii) Whether the ATS recognizes claims brought pursuant to these causes of action against private, non-state actors;

(iii) Whether ATS claims may proceed against corporate defendants;

(iv) Whether plaintiffs have validly stated claims alleging war crimes and summary executions upon which relief may be granted pursuant to the ATS;

(v) Whether plaintiffs must exhaust their remedies in Iraqi courts before they may litigate their ATS claims here; and

(vi) Whether punitive damages are available for ATS claims.

Analysis of plaintiffs' ATS claims properly begins with the statute itself, 28 U.S.C. § 1350. Enacted in 1789 as part of the first Judiciary Act, § 1350's brevity belies the magnitude of its implications. Specifically, the ATS states, in its entirety, that

> [t]he district courts shall have original jurisdiction of any civil action by an alien for a tort only, committed in violation of the law of nations or a treaty of the United States.

28 U.S.C. § 1350. Perhaps because the phrase "law of nations" was considered to be lacking in substance, the statute lay dormant for more than a century and a half. Indeed, so obscure was the import of the ATS, which has been called a "legal Lohengrin" and the "Rip Van Winkle of statutes,"[4] that it formed the basis for federal subject-matter jurisdiction in only one case during its first 170 years of existence.[5] Then, in the 1960s, this statutory Rip Van Winkle awoke, and plaintiffs began asserting ATS claims. These efforts met with varying success.[6] Indeed, ATS jurisprudence during this period is best characterized by confusion and great uncertainty. Then, in 2004, the Supreme Court began to put this house in order when it decided *Sosa v. Alvarez-Machain*, 542 U.S. 692, 124 S. Ct. 2739, 159 L.Ed.2d 718 (2004).

In *Sosa*, a Mexican national brought suit under the ATS after he was abducted in Mexico and brought to the United States for trial by a group of Mexican nationals hired by the U.S. Drug Enforcement Administration for that purpose. The plaintiff alleged that this conduct violated an international norm against arbitrary arrest and detention, and was thus actionable under the ATS. On these facts, the Supreme Court reversed the trial court's award of damages to the plaintiff. The parties hotly disputed whether the ATS, in addition to conferring subject-matter jurisdiction

---

4 *IIT v. Vencap, Ltd.*, 519 F.2d 1001, 1015 (2d Cir.1975) (Friendly, J.) (referring to the ATS as a "legal Lohengrin"); Karen Lin, An Unintended Double Standard of Liability The Effect of the Westfall Act on the Alien Tort Claims Act, 108 Colum. L. Rev. 1718, 1732 (2008) (calling the ATS the "Rip Van Winkle of statutes").

5 The sole case in which the ATS was found to confer jurisdiction was *Bolchos v. Darrel*, 3 F.Cas. 810 (D.S.C.1795) (No. 1607), in which the district judge concluded that it had jurisdiction in admiralty *and* under the ATS to hear a suit for damages brought by a French privateer against the mortgagee of a captured slave ship. *Id.* at 810.

6 *See, e.g.*, *Khedivial Line, S.A.E. v. Seafarers' Int'l Union*, 278 F.2d 49 (2d Cir.1960) (finding no ATS jurisdiction for claim of violation of non-treaty right of access to ports); *Abdul-Rahman Omar Adra v. Clift*, 195 F. Supp. 857 (D.Md.1961) (finding that the unlawful taking of custody over a child by one parent through fraudulent use of a foreign passport violates the law of nations within the meaning of the ATS); *IIT v. Vencap*, 519 F.2d 1001 (2d Cir. 1975) (holding that the Eighth Commandment is not part of the law of nations); *Filartiga v. Pena-Irala*, 630 F.2d 876 (2d Cir. 1980) (concluding that the ATS confers jurisdiction over tort claims for torture); *Tel-Oren v. Libyan Arab Republic*, 726 F.2d 774, 791–95 (D.C.Cir.1984) (Edwards, J., concurring) (finding that torture by non-state actors does not violate the law of nations within the meaning of the ATS); *In re Estate of Marcos Human Rights Lit.*, 25 F.3d 1467 (9th Cir. 1994) (holding that actions against former Philippine president for torture, summary execution, and disappearance were cognizable under the ATS); *Kadic v. Karadzic*, 70 F.3d 232 (2d Cir. 1995) (holding that genocide by non-state actor falls within ATS jurisdiction).

over certain claims to federal courts, created a substantive cause of action for violations of the law of nations. The Supreme Court answered the question, somewhat ambiguously, in the affirmative. Specifically, Justice Souter's majority opinion stated that while the ATS is "in its terms only jurisdictional," it also "enable[s] federal courts to hear claims in a very limited category defined by the law of nations and recognized at common law."[7] 542 U.S. at 713, 124 S. Ct. 2739. According to the *Sosa* majority, the ATS recognizes claims alleging violations of binding customary international norms with no "less definite content and acceptance among civilized nations" today than the historical paradigms of offenses against ambassadors, violations of safe conduct, and piracy had at the time of the ATS's enactment in 1789. *Id.* at 732, 124 S. Ct. 2739. Applying this principle to the facts presented, the Sosa majority consulted a variety of sources,[8] concluding ultimately that the ATS did not confer jurisdiction over the plaintiffs claim. *Id.* at 736–38, 124 S. Ct. 2739. In reaching this result, the majority found that while various international treatises and resolutions condemned arbitrary arrest and detention as contrary to universal human rights, such declarations did not create a *specific* norm with *binding* effect, but rather only stated broad, nonbinding principles at a "high level of generality." *Id.* at 736 n. 27, 124 S. Ct. 2739; *see also id.* at 732, 124 S. Ct. 2739 (citing *United States v. Smith*, 5 Wheat. 153, 163–80, 5 L.Ed. 57 (1820)) (emphasizing specificity with which piracy was defined by law of nations). In other words, the *Sosa* majority found that there was insufficient agreement among nations as to the *precise* conduct that would constitute a violation of an *enforceable* rule against arbitrary arrest and detention. Thus, while *Sosa* interprets the ATS to confer upon federal courts limited discretion to recognize new causes of action for violations of the law of nations, it also holds that arbitrary arrest and detention are not among the causes of action cognizable under the statute.

Importantly, *Sosa* counsels the federal courts to engage in "vigilant doorkeeping" when determining whether to recognize a cause of action under the ATS for five reasons, each of which relates to the need for judicial restraint in importing international norms (if such exist) into American law in the absence of explicit

---

7 Nevertheless, if the ATS were strictly jurisdictional, recognizing only existing common law causes of action, then the claims recognized under it would presumably also be cognizable under the other grants of jurisdiction to the federal courts. This, however, is not the case: no court has held that claims alleging violations of the law of nations are cognizable under other grants of subject-matter jurisdiction in the absence of ATS jurisdiction. Thus, irrespective of the statute's terms, *Sosa* is best read to conclude that the ATS is not strictly jurisdictional. *See* Curtis A. Bradley, Jack L. Goldsmith & David H. Moore, Sosa, *Customary International Law and the Continuing Relevance of* Erie, 120 Harv. L. Rev. 869, 892 (2007) ("If modern position proponents are correct about *Sosa*, and [customary international law] automatically has the status of federal law, CIL would provide a basis for federal question jurisdiction.").

8 These sources included the Restatement (Third) of Foreign Relations Law of the United States, Brownlie's treatise on public international law, cases of the International Court of Justice, and an academic survey of the laws of various nations. *See* 542 U.S. at 736 n. 27, 737, 124 S. Ct. 2739.

legislative authorization or guidance. 542 U.S. at 729, 124 S. Ct. 2739. First, *Sosa* explains that the common law is no longer understood, as it was at the time of the ATS's enactment, to be a "'transcendental body of law outside of any particular State but obligatory within it unless and until changed by statute.'" *Id.* at 725, 124 S. Ct. 2739 (quoting *Black and White Taxicab & Transfer Co. v. Brown and Yellow Taxicab & Transfer Co.*, 276 U.S. 518, 533, 48 S. Ct. 404, 72 L.Ed. 681 (1928) (Holmes, J., dissenting)). Instead, it is now recognized that "the law is not so much found or discovered as it is either made or created," and that reliance on international norms for the generation of a new common law cause of action would require "a substantial element of discretionary judgment." *Id.* at 725–26, 124 S. Ct. 2739. Accordingly, *Sosa* suggests that just as the understanding of the role of common law has changed, so should courts' willingness to look to international norms to determine the content of that common law. Second, *Sosa* notes that the Supreme Court's watershed decision in *Erie Railroad Co. v. Tompkins*, 304 U.S. 64, 58 S. Ct. 817, 82 L.Ed. 1188 (1938), denied the existence of any federal "general" common law, thus emphasizing the importance of "look[ing] for legislative guidance before exercising innovative authority over substantive law." *Sosa*, 542 U.S. at 726, 124 S. Ct. 2739. Third, *Sosa* teaches that recent Supreme Court decisions evince a reluctance to infer the existence of an implied federal cause of action where the statute does not explicitly create a cause of action. *Id.* at 727, 124 S. Ct. 2739 (citing *Correctional Services Corp. v. Malesko*, 534 U.S. 61, 68, 122 S. Ct. 515, 151 L.Ed.2d 456 (2001); *Alexander v. Sandoval*, 532 U.S. 275, 286–87, 121 S. Ct. 1511, 149 L.Ed.2d 517 (2001)). Fourth, *Sosa* suggests that courts should impose a "high bar" in creating new private causes of action for violations of international law norms because of the risk of "impinging on the discretion of the Legislative and Executive Branches in managing foreign affairs." *Id.* Finally, *Sosa* notes that Congress has repeatedly declined to provide the courts with a "mandate to seek out and define new and debatable violations of the law of nations." *Id.*

It is clear, then, that *Sosa* does not incorporate customary international law ("CIL") into the body of federal common law in a wholesale manner. Indeed, Sosa directs the federal courts to consider carefully the "practical consequences of making [a] cause of action available to litigants in the federal courts." 542 U.S. at 729, 732–33, 124 S. Ct. 2739. If, as some commentators suggest, federal common law automatically incorporates CIL,[9] then such considerations would be entirely inapposite.

---

9 *See, e.g.*, Martin S. Flaherty, *The Future and Past of U.S. Foreign Relations Law*, 67 LAW & CONTEMP. PROBS. 169, 173 (2004) (concluding that Sosa "confirm[s] that international custom was part of judicially enforceable federal law even in the absence of a statute"); Ralph G. Steinhardt, *Laying One Bankrupt Critique to Rest:* Sosa v. Alvarez-Machain *and the Future of International Human Rights Litigation in U.S. Courts*, 57 VAND. L. REV. 2241, 2259 (2004) ("[CIL] remains an area in which no affirmative legislative act is required to 'authorize' its application in U.S. courts."); *The Supreme Court, 2003 Term—Leading Cases,* 118 HARV. L. REV. 226, 453 (2004) (reading *Sosa* to indicate that "all customary international law has been included within federal common law").

See Curtis A. Bradley, Jack L. Goldsmith & David H. Moore, Sosa, *Customary International Law, and the Continuing Relevance of* Erie, 120 HARV. L. REV. 869, 892 (2007) (hereinafter Bradley, et al., 2007) (concluding that the analysis prescribed by *Sosa* is inconsistent with the view that CIL is an inherent part of federal common law); Gerald L. Neuman, *The Abiding Significance of Law in Foreign Relations*, 2004 Sup. Ct. Rev. 111, 130 (same). Put another way, if CIL were an inherent component of federal common law, there would be no occasion for the federal courts to exercise their "vigilant doorkeeping" duty as envisaged by the Sosa majority.[10]

Moreover, *Sosa* affirms the well-settled rule that when Congress defines the relevant norms of international law by legislative enactment, courts are bound by that determination. Specifically, *Sosa* quotes, with approval, the traditional pre-*Erie* formulation that

> *where there is no treaty, and no controlling executive or legislative act or judicial decision*, resort must be had to the customs and usages of civilized nations; and, as evidence of these, to the works of jurists and commentators, who by years of labor, research and experience, have made themselves peculiarly well acquainted with the subjects of which they treat.

542 U.S. at 734, 124 S. Ct. 2739 (quoting *The Paquete Habana*, 175 U.S. 677, 700, 20 S. Ct. 290, 44 L.Ed. 320 (1900)) (emphasis added).[11] Moreover, as *Sosa* notes,

---

10 In addition to being inconsistent with *Sosa*, wholesale incorporation of CIL into federal common law would raise a significant constitutional problem. Specifically, it would represent an unconstitutional delegation of federal lawmaking power to foreign persons or entities not constitutionally competent or authorized to exercise that important power. *See* Michael Stokes Paulsen, *The Constitutional Power to Interpret International Law,* 118 YALE L.J. 1762, 1806 (2009) ("[T]he power to interpret, apply, and enforce international law *for the United States* . . . is not possessed by, and cannot authoritatively be exercised by, non-U.S. actors."); *Cf. Wayman v. Southard*, 23 U.S. (10 Wheat.) 1, 2, 6 L.Ed. 253 (1825) (unconstitutional delegation of federal lawmaking power to state legislatures avoided by construing federal statute not to incorporate post-enactment state legislation). *See generally* John O. McGinnis, Medellin *and the Future of International Delegation,* 118 YALE L.J. 1712 (2009) (identifying problem of international delegations and analyzing potential constitutional limitations);

It is important to note, however, that it is far from clear that the *Sosa* majority adequately addressed the risk of unconstitutional delegation of lawmaking power. To be sure, the *Sosa* majority's careful attempt to cabin the phrase "law of nations," and its salute to the "vigilant doorkeeping" duty of federal courts, may partially address this issue. But in the end, whether the unconstitutional delegation problem is avoided will depend on the wisdom and restraint of federal judges and Justices. It goes without saying that the Founders and members of the Congress that passed the ATS would have been surprised, and indeed dismayed, to learn that the ATS could be used as a vehicle for directly and unconstitutionally incorporating into American law principles and notions from the amorphous body of CIL.

11 *See also* PAULSEN, *supra* note 10, at 1803 ("[E]ven under the strongest reading of the force of customary international law, it may always be displaced . . . by any official action within the constitutional powers of the federal government. The opinion in The Paquete Habana is explicit on the point, and the Supreme Court has never suggested anything to the contrary.");

Erie and cases since then have further reduced federal courts' discretion to create new federal common law in the absence of legislative guidance. *Id.* at 726–27, 124 S. Ct. 2739. Accordingly, reference to secondary sources to define the "law of nations" is appropriate only insofar as Congress has not itself defined the relevant norms.

Three cases decided by the Supreme Court since Sosa emphasize the power of Congress and the courts to declare, authoritatively, the content of international law for the United States. In *Hamdan v. Rumsfeld*, 548 U.S. 557, 625–35 (2006), trial procedures for a Guantanamo Bay detainee were found to violate the Uniform Code of Military Justice ("UCMJ"). The relevant provision of the UCMJ conditioned the military commission's authority on compliance with the "law of war." 10 U.S.C. § 821. *Hamdan* held that the petitioner had an enforceable right to challenge the trial procedures as contrary to the Geneva Conventions because Congress had implicitly incorporated the treaty's provisions into the authorizing statute by referring to the law of war.[12] 548 U.S. at 625–35, 126 S. Ct. 2749. In other words, when one act of Congress (the UCMJ) referred generically to a body of international law (the law of war), *Hamdan* incorporated the norms of international law provided by Congress in the Geneva Conventions.

Moreover, it is clear that federal courts are to interpret international treaties ratified by Congress in much the same way they interpret any other act of Congress, namely by determining congressional intent through careful examination of the text of the enactment. In *Sanchez-Llamas v. Oregon*, a case involving the scope of foreign nationals' rights to consular communication under the Vienna Convention on Consular Relations ("VCCR"), the Supreme Court concluded that the International Court of Justice's ("ICJ") interpretation of the VCCR deserved "respectful consideration," but did not compel reconsideration of prior Supreme Court decisions interpreting the VCCR that contradicted the ICJ's conclusion. 548 U.S. 331, 333, 126 S. Ct. 2669, 165 L.Ed.2d 557 (2006). In other words, the final determination of the content of the international treaty belonged to U.S. courts, not an international tribunal. *Id.* at 353, 126 S. Ct. 2669 (quoting *Marbury v. Madison*, 1 Cranch 137, 177 (1803)). Finally, in *Medellin v. Texas*, 552 U.S. 491, 128 S. Ct. 1346, 1360 (2008), at issue was the state's failure to inform Mexican nationals on death row of their consular notification rights under the VCCR. The ICJ ruled that this

---

NEUMAN, THE ABIDING SIGNIFICANCE OF LAW IN FOREIGN RELATIONS, 2004 Sup. Ct. Rev. 111, 132 ("Where Congress has not provided explicit direction, courts ease the interaction between the domestic and international legal systems by recognizing and incorporating international norms, to the extent that they can be harmonized with other federal law.").

12 A concurrence, written by Justice Kennedy and joined by three other Justices, focused even more explicitly on Congress's affirmative steps to define the law of war through ratification of the Geneva Conventions and the War Crimes Act of 1996, discussed *infra.* 548 U.S. at 642–43, 126 S. Ct. 2749 (Kennedy, J., concurring); *see* Bradley et al., 2007, at 931–32 (discussing post-Sosa emphasis on finding legislative incorporation of international law as exemplified in *Hamdan*).

failure constituted a violation of the VCCR. Yet, the Supreme Court held that the ICJ's determination was not "automatically enforceable federal law." *Id.* In so holding, the Supreme Court emphasized that whether treaties are self-executing is a question of U.S. law for the courts of the United States to decide, and the analysis proceeds, as usual, through determination of congressional intent through examination of the treaty's text.[13] *Id.* at 1364–65. In summary, these cases support the proposition that when Congress has defined the relevant international legal norms, federal courts must follow Congress's lead. And, where Congress has not spoken on the content of international law, U.S. courts must define the applicable legal norms independently of the determinations of international tribunals and foreign bodies, but they may accord those determinations an appropriate level of "respectful consideration." Sanchez-Llamas, 548 U.S. at 333.

Thus, although *Sosa* permits the assertion of claims for violations of the "law of nations," the case sets a high bar for causes of action to clear in order to be cognizable under the ATS. To constitute an actionable violation of the "law of nations" within the meaning of the ATS, plaintiffs must allege violations of international law norms that (i) are universally recognized, (ii) have specific definition and content, and (iii) are binding and enforceable, rather than merely aspirational. Moreover, federal courts must examine whether Congress has itself defined the relevant international law norm by legislative enactment; if so, federal courts are bound by that determination. Only in cases where Congress has not spoken on the content of the law of nations is it appropriate for federal courts to consider the conclusions contained in the decisions of international tribunals and in widely-accepted treatises of international law. Yet, even then they must do so carefully because of (i) the potentially serious practical consequences of recognizing such a cause of action, and (ii) the modern understanding of the limited discretion of federal courts to create new federal common law causes of action in the absence of clear legislative guidance. These principles and Sosa's norm-specific analysis govern plaintiffs' war crimes and summary execution claims.

A. War Crimes Claims

Claims for violations of the international norm proscribing war crimes are cognizable under the ATS. By ratifying the Geneva Conventions, Congress has adopted a precise, universally accepted definition of war crimes. Moreover, through enactment of a separate federal statute, Congress has incorporated this precise definition into the federal criminal law. 18 U.S.C. § 2441. Thus, Congress has clearly defined the law of nations to include a binding prohibition on the commission of war crimes. Given this, and given Sosa's teachings, it follows that an allegation of a war crime states a cause of action under the ATS.

---

13 It is worth noting that *Medellin* also held that the President of the United States lacked the power to convert, by order, the ICJ's ruling into a binding federal rule of decision because the Constitution vests such authority exclusively in Congress. 128 S. Ct. at 1368–69.

Specifically, it is a "grave breach" of the Fourth Geneva Convention intentionally to kill or inflict serious bodily injury upon innocent civilians during the course of an armed conflict.[14] The treaty has been ratified by the United States and every other nation in the world. *See* U.S. Dep't of State, *Treaties in Force* 435-37 (2009). Thus, every country in the world, including the United States, has agreed to precisely the same definition of war crimes.[15] Moreover, this specific universal norm is binding on nationals of the vast majority of nations in the world. Indeed, nationals of 110 states—including Australia, Canada, Japan, Mexico, and all of Western Europe—are criminally punishable in the International Criminal Court (ICC) for precisely these grave breaches as defined in the Geneva Conventions. Furthermore, many of the countries that have not ratified the treaty establishing the ICC have nonetheless passed laws criminally punishing grave breaches of the Geneva Conventions in their own courts.[16] Importantly, the United States is among this group of countries, having incorporated the Geneva Conventions into its domestic criminal law through the War Crimes Act of 1996, which criminalizes grave breaches of the Conventions committed by or against a national of the United States. 18 U.S.C. § 2441. Thus, Congress has directly and explicitly stated that the Geneva Conventions contain the binding international norms that govern the definition of war crimes in federal courts. *See Hamdan*, 548 U.S. at 642, 126 S. Ct. 2749 (Kennedy, J., concurring) (concluding that by ratifying the Geneva Conventions and enacting the War Crimes Act of 1996 Congress has with "no

---

14 The Fourth Geneva Convention, which concerns the protection of civilians during armed conflicts of an international character, deems a "grave breach" of the Convention acts against "protected persons" consisting of "willful killing, torture or inhuman treatment, including biological experiments, [or] wilfully causing great suffering or serious injury to body or health." Geneva Convention Relative to the Protection of Civilian Persons in Time of War, Aug. 12, 1949, art. 147 [hereinafter Fourth Geneva Convention]. Moreover, protected persons are "those who, at a given moment and in any manner whatsoever, find themselves, in case of a conflict or occupation, in the hands of a Party to the conflict or Occupying Power." *Id.* art. 4. The "in the hands of" language is interpreted extremely broadly, and includes any time that a civilian is in territory controlled by a party to the conflict. *See* Jean S. Pictet, *Commentary on Geneva Convention Relative to the Protection of Civilian Persons in Time of War* 46-47 (1958). Indeed, in a 2004 memorandum, the Office of Legal Counsel of the U.S. Department of Justice opined that all noncombatant Iraqi nationals qualified as protected persons under the Fourth Geneva Convention. *See* Jack L. Goldsmith III, *"Protected Person" Status in Occupied Iraq Under the Fourth Geneva Convention* 5–7 (2004), *available at* http://www.usdoj.gov/olc/2004/gc4mar18.pdf.

15 Compare *Sosa*, in which the Supreme Court majority concluded that various national prohibitions on arbitrary detention demonstrated that such an international norm existed, but that differences in these state laws indicated that "the consensus is at a high level of generality." *Sosa*, 542 U.S. at 736 n. 27, 124 S. Ct. 2739. This is not true where, as here, all of the nations of the world agree to precisely the same language in the course of defining a grave breach of international law.

16 For an exhaustive list of laws and regulations enacted by states to enforce international human rights law, *see* International Committee of the Red Cross, *International Humanitarian Law—National Implementation*, at http://www.icrc.org/ihl-nat.nsf/.

doubt" defined the law of war by the content of the Geneva Conventions). Accordingly, applying the principles of *Sosa*, the ATS confers subject-matter jurisdiction over properly stated claims of war crimes.[17]

Defendants argue that even assuming that war crimes claims are cognizable under the ATS, such claims are not cognizable against defendants. In this regard, defendants first contend that as a general rule, the ATS only recognizes claims against state actors. Yet, it is quite clear that the language of the ATS is not self-limiting to claims against state actors. Thus, defendants' argument may have merit only insofar as it is supported by *Sosa* or by recognized norms of international law. It is supported by neither.

Indeed, *Sosa* explicitly acknowledges the existence of a developing consensus that non-state actors may violate certain norms as defined by the law of nations. Because *Sosa* clearly indicates that the reach of ATS liability to non-state actors should be determined with regard to the specific norm alleged to have been violated, it is clear that there is no *per se* rule that the ATS does not reach private actors. In particular, footnote 20 of *Sosa*, which defendants cite in support of their argument, comments that

> [a] related consideration [to the determination of whether a norm is sufficiently definite to support an ATS cause of action] is whether international law extends the scope of liability for a violation *of a given norm* to the perpetrator being sued, if the defendant is a private actor such as a corporation or individual. Compare *Tel-Oren v. Libyan Arab Republic*, 726 F.2d 774, 791–95 (D.C.Cir. 1984) (Edwards, J., concurring) (insufficient consensus in 1984 that torture by private actors violates international law), with *Kadic v. Karadzic*, 70 F.3d 232, 239–41 (2d Cir.1995) (sufficient consensus in 1995 that genocide by private actors violates international law).

Id. (emphasis added). Contrary to defendants' argument, this language makes clear that the analysis for non-state actor liability is norm-specific. Moreover, the parenthetical explanations of the citations to *Tel-Oren* and *Kadic*, emphasizing the eleven-year gap between the two decisions and the distinct claims alleged—torture in *Tel-Oren* and genocide in *Kadic*—suggest that a consensus may now exist that at least some ATS claims reach non-state actors.[18] Thus, there is no support for

---

17 While the Court of Appeals for the Fourth Circuit has yet to confront the question, all of the circuit courts to have considered the issue post-*Sosa* have reached this same conclusion. *See Sinaltrainal v. Coca-Cola Co.*, 578 F.3d 1252, 1266–67 (11th Cir.2009) (recognizing ATS claims of war crimes); *Abdullahi v. Pfizer, Inc.*, 562 F.3d 163, 175–87 (2d Cir.2009) (citing *Kadic v. Karadzic*, 70 F.3d 232, 240 (2d Cir. 1995)) (concluding that medical experimentation on nonconsenting human subjects is a sufficiently universal and definite norm to be covered by the ATS); *Sarei v. Rio Tinto*, PLC, 487 F.3d 1193, 1202 (9th Cir.2007) (rev'd in part en banc on other grounds) (allowing war crimes claims to proceed under the ATS, noting that such claims "form the least controversial core of modern day [ATS] jurisdiction").

18 It is worth noting that the two opinions cited in Sosa's footnote 20 are consistent with one another. Tel-Oren acknowledges that private actors are liable for some violations, just not torture, and Kadic in fact requires state actors for torture and summary execution claims, but

defendants' argument that ATS claims, as a general matter, are cognizable only against state actors. Nevertheless, the question remains whether war crimes claims, in particular, are cognizable against private actors. They clearly are.

The relevant provisions of the Geneva Conventions and their incorporating federal criminal statute, the War Crimes Act, clearly do not, by their terms, limit their applicability to state actors. While other prohibitions contained within the Geneva Conventions, such as the ban on summary executions, discussed *infra*, require that the conduct be committed by a party to the armed conflict, there is no such requirement for grave breaches such as the murder of protected persons.[19] Instead, the grave breach is defined in terms of the status of the victim, *not* the status of the perpetrator. *See* Fourth Geneva Convention art. 146 ("Grave breaches . . . shall be those involving any of the following acts, if committed against persons or property protected by the present Convention."). Indeed, the War Crimes Act, in codifying the Geneva Conventions' "grave breach" provisions into federal criminal law, subjects all United States nationals to liability with no reference to color of law or status as a party to the armed conflict. *See* 18 U.S.C. § 2441(b).[20] Accordingly, the courts of appeals to consider the question since *Kadic* have recognized that ATS war crimes claims are cognizable against non-state actors. *See Sinaltrainal v. Coca-Cola Co.*, No. 06-15851, 2009 WL 2431463, at 10 (11th Cir. Aug. 11, 2009) ("[W]ar crimes . . . negate the need for state action."); *Abdullahi v. Pfizer, Inc.*, 562 F.3d 163, 173 (2d Cir.2009) ("ATS claims may sometimes be brought against private actors . . . when the tortious activities violate norms of universal concern that are recognized to extend to the conduct of private parties—for example, slavery, genocide, and war crimes" (internal quotation marks omitted).); *Doe I v. Unocal Corp.*, 395 F.3d 932, 945–46 (9th Cir.2002) ("[C]rimes like slave trading, genocide or war crimes . . . by themselves do not require state action for [ATS]

---

not for genocide and war crimes. *See Tel-Oren*, 726 F.2d at 795; *Kadic*, 70 F.3d at 244–45. Indeed, Judge Edwards's Tel-Oren opinion, cited in Sosa, acknowledges an emerging consensus that CIL reaches non-state actors, and merely concludes that there was not yet, in 1984, sufficient consensus that torture was "among the handful of crimes to which the law of nations attributes individual responsibility." 726 F.2d at 795. A recent D.C. Circuit opinion, which defendants cite, also supports this conclusion. *Saleh v. Titan Corp.*, 580 F.3d 1, 15 n. 13 (D.C.Cir.2009) (dismissing torture claims on state actor grounds, but assuming without deciding that war crimes claims may be cognizable against non-state actors) ("Even if torture suits cannot be brought against private parties—at least not yet—it may be that 'war crimes' have a broader reach.").

19 Defendants cite Kadic as requiring that the conduct be performed by a party to the conflict. Defs.' Mots, to Dism. at 11 (citing *Kadic*, 70 F.3d at 242–43). Kadic, in turn, derives the language from Common Article 3 of the Geneva Conventions, which applies to armed conflicts not of an international character. Because the conduct at issue here allegedly occurred during an armed conflict of an international character, the "party to the conflict" language of Common Article 3 is inapposite.

20 Moreover, as plaintiffs note, U.S. Department of Defense regulations also require contractors operating in foreign countries to notify their employees that they are subject to criminal liability under the War Crimes Act. *See* 48 C.F.R. § 252.225-7040(e)(2)(ii) (2009).

liability to attach."). Thus, defendants offer no basis to conclude that war crimes claims under the ATS are cognizable only against state actors.

Defendants further argue that conduct constitutes a war crime only if it is perpetrated in furtherance of a "military objective" rather than for economic or ideological reasons. Although this argument sweeps too broadly, it is true, as defendants suggest, that plaintiffs must allege a nexus to the armed conflict in order to state a valid claim for war crimes under the ATS. Accordingly, in order to state a valid claim for war crimes, plaintiffs must allege that the conduct constituting war crimes occurred in the context of and in association with an ongoing armed conflict.

No doubt, a more substantial relationship must exist between the armed conflict and the alleged conduct than the mere fact that the conduct occurred while an armed conflict was ongoing. Otherwise, the ATS would create a cause of action in federal court for any murder committed anywhere in the world as long as (i) there was an armed conflict happening in the country at the time and (ii) the murder victim was not a national of the United States. Allowing all such claims would swing open U.S. courthouse doors to plaintiffs alleging conduct far short of being one of a "'handful of heinous acts—each of which violates definable, universal, and obligatory norms.'" *Sosa*, 542 U.S. at 732, 124 S. Ct. 2739 (quoting *Tel-Oren*, 726 F.2d at 781). Thus, the duty of "vigilant doorkeeping" that Sosa assigns federal courts requires that there exist a substantial nexus between the armed conflict and the alleged conduct constituting war crimes. *Id.* at 729, 124 S. Ct. 2739.

Indeed, courts have generally required such a nexus. The Second Circuit in *Kadic* required that acts be "committed in the course of hostilities" in order to constitute a war crime. 70 F.3d at 242. Similarly, the Eleventh Circuit, citing *Kadic*, recently held that alleged war crimes must occur "during the course" of the armed conflict, clarifying that such a showing would require that the conduct occurred "because of or "in the course of the conflict. *Sinaltrainal*, 578 F.3d at 1267. In *Sinaltrainal*, Colombian nationals alleged that the defendant corporations hired paramilitaries to torture and murder leaders of a trade union in order to eliminate the union's presence at the corporations. A civil war was raging in Colombia at the time, and plaintiffs argued that defendants were able to resort to such openly violent means precisely because of the ongoing armed conflict. The Eleventh Circuit concluded that this relationship between the conflict and the alleged conduct was insufficient. Indeed, a rule allowing those claims would have allowed war crimes claims whenever an ongoing armed conflict contributed substantially to the alleged perpetrator's ability to carry out the unlawful acts, and because armed conflicts, by their nature, increase the degree of disorder in a country, this requirement would normally be met.

Nor are these decisions the only support for a nexus requirement. Congress and the Executive Branch have also adopted a nexus requirement in defining war crimes in related contexts. Specifically, for conduct committed during a non-international armed conflict to constitute a war crime punishable pursuant to federal criminal law, Congress requires that the conduct occur "in the context of and in association with" the armed conflict.[21] 18 U.S.C. § 2441(c)(3), *amended by* Military Commissions Act of 2006, Pub. L. No. 109-366, 120 Stat. 2633 (2006). Similarly, the Secretary of Defense requires that the willful murder of protected persons by enemy combatants "took place in the context of and was associated with armed conflict" in order to constitute violations of the law of war triable before military commissions. 32 C.F.R. § 11.6(a)(1)(i)(2009).[22] Thus, the Legislative and Executive Branches have defined the law of nations to require a nexus of context and association to the armed conflict in order for conduct to constitute a war crime. Moreover, adopting the nexus requirement here serves to limit the scope of the ATS consistent with Sosa's concern for the "possible collateral consequences of making international rules privately actionable." 542 U.S. at 727, 124 S. Ct. 2739.

Instead of the context and association requirement adopted here, plaintiffs propose a rule that the conduct must be "'shaped by or dependent upon the environment—the armed conflict—in which it is committed.'" Pl.'s Mem. in Resp. at 36 n. 12 (quoting *Prosecutor v. Kunarac*, Nos. IT-96-23 ¶ 58 (Int'l Crim. Trib. for the Former Yugoslavia June 12, 2002)). This argument is unpersuasive. Adopting this amorphous standard would keep few—if any—ATS claims from coming through federal courthouse doors. Indeed, interpreting the ATS to recognize any war crimes claim for conduct that was "shaped" by the environment of the armed conflict would have the consequence of allowing nearly any claim alleging murder when

21 It should be noted that this provision only governs criminal prosecutions for alleged violations of Common Article 3 of the Geneva Conventions for conduct arising during a non-international armed conflict. Because the claims in these cases do not allege violations of Common Article 3 and did not arise during a non-international armed conflict, the nexus requirement of the War Crimes Act would not directly apply in a criminal prosecution for the conduct alleged here. The Military Commissions Act of 2006 did not modify any other sections of the War Crimes Act.

22 This regulation further defines the context and association element to require a nexus that

> could involve, but is not limited to, time, location, or purpose of the conduct in relation to the armed hostilities. . . . This element does not require a declaration of war, ongoing mutual hostilities, or confrontation involving a regular national armed force. A single hostile act or attempted act may provide sufficient basis for the nexus so long as its magnitude or severity rises to the level of an "armed attack" or an "act of war," or the number, power, stated intent or organization of the force with which the actor is associated is such that the act or attempted act is tantamount to an attack by an armed force. Similarly, conduct undertaken or organized with knowledge or intent that it initiate or contribute to such hostile act or hostilities would satisfy the nexus requirement.

32 C.F.R. § 11.5(c) (2009). It is worth noting that the Military Commissions Act of 2006 authorizes military commissions for murders, committed by enemy combatants, of persons protected pursuant to the Geneva Conventions without any reference to a nexus requirement. 10 U.S.C. § 950v(b)(1). Nevertheless, the 2007 Manual for Military Commissions, issued by the Secretary of Defense to implement the Military Commissions Act, reiterates the required context and association element for the murder of protected persons. U.S. Dep't of Defense, *Manual for Military Commissions*, at IV–3 (2007).

the perpetrator, for reasons unrelated to the conflict, merely takes advantage of the civil disorder that invariably accompanies an armed conflict.

While plaintiffs' proposed rule is overbroad, defendants' is too narrow. Defendants would require that the conduct allegedly constituting a war crime be committed in direct furtherance of a "military objective." Under this standard, an ATS action would not lie where defendants were motivated by ideology or the prospect of financial gain, as plaintiffs allege here. Indeed, under defendants' proposed rule, it is arguable that nobody who receives a paycheck would ever be liable for war crimes. Moreover, so narrow is the scope of this standard that it would exclude murders of civilians committed by soldiers where there was no legitimate "military objective" for committing the murders. It is true that acting with a purpose related to the objectives of the armed conflict is evidence of the alleged conduct's association with the armed conflict. But purpose cannot be the only factor to consider, nor can it be defined as narrowly as defendants propose. Other factors such as temporal and geographic proximity to the armed conflict, the nature of the conduct, and the identity of the victims must also be considered. Thus, some nexus must be shown between the conduct and the armed conflict. Accordingly, to state a valid ATS claim for murder or infliction of bodily injury as a war crime, plaintiffs must plead that the alleged conduct was perpetrated in the context of, and in association with, the armed conflict.

Defendants next argue that the ATS does not permit a claim to proceed on a theory of vicarious liability against a corporation. Plaintiffs respond that they do not allege a theory of vicarious liability for their ATS claims. Rather, they allege that Xe defendants, acting as "alter egos" of defendant Prince, are directly liable for the commission of war crimes. Pl.'s Mem. in Resp. at 44–45; Hearing on Deft.' Mots, to Dism. Tr. at 40–41.[23] Accordingly, there is no need here to reach the question whether a corporation may be held vicariously liable for the war crimes of its employees.

Defendants also argue that corporations can never be held liable under the ATS. This argument is unavailing. Nothing in the ATS or *Sosa* may plausibly be read to distinguish between private individuals and corporations; indeed, *Sosa* simply refers to both individuals and entities as "private actors." 542 U.S. at 732 n. 20, 124 S. Ct. 2739. Moreover, there is no identifiable principle of civil liability which would distinguish between individual and corporate defendants in these circumstances. While it is true, as defendants note, that criminal liability for war crimes

23 During the course of the hearing on defendants' motions to dismiss, plaintiffs, by counsel, explicitly disclaimed any theory of vicarious liability under the ATS:

> THE COURT: Do you allege vicarious liability?
>
> MS. BURKE: No, Your Honor. What we are alleging is that the person who is responsible for these deaths is Mr. Prince and that he has set up a series of shells to give the appearance that there are these companies but that they do not have their own corporate weight.

Hearing on Deft.' Mots, to Dism. Tr. at 40–41.

is generally limited to private individuals, it is also true that a "private corporation is a juridical person and has no *per se* immunity under U.S. domestic or international law." *Presbyterian Church of Sudan v. Talisman Energy, Inc.*, 244 F. Supp. 2d 289, 319 (S.D.N.Y.2003). Accordingly, all courts to have considered the question have concluded that "the issue of whether corporations may be held liable under the [ATS is] indistinguishable from the question of whether private individuals may be."[24] *Khulumani v. Barclay Nat'l Bank Ltd.*, 504 F.3d 254, 282 (2d Cir. 2007) (Katzmann, J., concurring with *per curiam* opinion, joined by Hall, J.); *see Abdullahi v. Pfizer, Inc.*, 562 F.3d 163 (2d Cir.2009); *Romero v. Drummond Co.*, 552 F. 3d 1303, 1314–16 (11th Cir.2008); *Presbyterian Church of Sudan v. Talisman Energy, Inc.*, 374 F. Supp. 2d 331, 336 n. 10 (S.D.N.Y.2005) ("[T]here is no principled basis for contending that acts such as genocide are of mutual and not merely several concern to states when the acts are performed by some private actors, like individuals, but not by other private actors, like corporations" (citations omitted).); *In re Agent Orange Prod. Liab. Litig.*, 373 F. Supp. 2d 7, 58–59 (E.D.N.Y. 2005) ("Limiting civil liability to individuals while exonerating the corporation directing the individual's action through its complex operations and changing personnel makes little sense in today's world."). Accordingly, claims alleging direct corporate liability for war crimes are cognizable under the ATS.

In sum, Congress, by ratifying the Geneva Conventions and by enacting the War Crimes Act, has defined the international law norm governing war crimes. This norm is binding, universal, and precisely defined. Accordingly, the ATS recognizes a cause of action alleging war crimes, and claims arising under this cause of action are cognizable against non-state actor defendants, including corporations. This cause of action requires plaintiffs to show that defendants (i) intentionally (ii) killed or inflicted serious bodily harm (iii) upon innocent civilians (iv) during an armed conflict and (v) in the context of and in association with that armed conflict. The analysis next turns to whether plaintiffs have properly stated a claim for relief under this cause of action.

For ATS claims alleging a cause of action for violations of the law of nations, the analysis pursuant to Rule 12(b)(1), Fed. R. Civ. P., is merged with that of whether plaintiffs have properly stated a claim upon which relief can be granted under Rule 12(b)(6), Fed. R. Civ. P. In other words, if plaintiffs have failed to state a claim

---

24 Defendants note that the Second Circuit's recent decision in *Presbyterian Church of Sudan v. Talisman Energy, Inc.* assumes without deciding that corporations may be held liable under the ATS for aiding and abetting in the commission of genocide, war crimes, and crimes against humanity. 582 F.3d 244 (2d Cir.2009). In that case, the Second Circuit affirmed the district court's grant of summary judgment for the defendants because the evidence did not support the requisite elements to prove aiding and abetting liability pursuant to the law of nations. Accordingly, the Second Circuit did not need to address the question of whether the ATS allowed aiding and abetting claims against corporations. In any event, that is not the question at issue here. The Second Circuit's decision is entirely inapposite to the question of whether defendants in these cases may be held directly liable for war crimes under the ATS.

validly alleging a violation of the law of nations within the meaning of the ATS, then federal subject-matter jurisdiction under the ATS is lacking. *See Sinaltrainal*, 578 F.3d at 1270 (dismissing ATS claims for lack of subject-matter jurisdiction due to failure to allege facts creating plausible entitlement to relief).

The Supreme Court recently declared that threshold dismissal for failure to state a valid claim must be granted unless the complaint "contain[s] sufficient factual matter, accepted as true, to 'state a claim to relief that is plausible on its face.'" *Ashcroft v. Iqbal*, 129 S. Ct. 1937, 1949, 173 L.Ed.2d 868 (2009) (quoting *Bell Atl. Corp. v. Twombly*, 550 U.S. 544, 570, 127 S. Ct. 1955, 167 L.Ed.2d 929 (2007)). It follows that a complaint must contain "more than an unadorned, the-defendant-unlawfully-harmed-me accusation." *Id.* at 1949. And in this respect, it is also true that "the tenet that a court must accept as true all of the allegations contained in a complaint is inapplicable to *legal* conclusions." *Id.* (emphasis added). Thus, "[t]hreadbare recitals of the elements of a cause of action, supported by mere conclusory statements, do not suffice." *Id., quoted in Walker v. Prince George's County, Md.*, 575 F.3d 426, 431 (4th Cir.2009) (O'Connor, J.). Justice Kennedy succinctly summarized these principles by noting that

> a court considering a motion to dismiss can choose to begin by identifying pleadings that, because they are no more than conclusions, are not entitled to the assumption of truth. While legal conclusions can provide the framework of a complaint, they must be supported by factual allegations. When there are well-pleaded factual allegations, a court should assume their veracity and then determine whether they plausibly give rise to an entitlement to relief.

Iqbal, 129 S. Ct. at 1950. Moreover, *Iqbal* reinforced the axiom that in ruling on threshold motions to dismiss for failure to state a claim, courts should consider only the factual allegations made in the complaint itself.[25] *See, e.g., id.* at 1949–54 (emphasizing repeatedly that factual content of the complaint controls the 12(b)(6) ruling).

Accordingly, plaintiffs must allege facts in their complaints that give rise to a plausible entitlement to relief for claims alleging war crimes pursuant to the ATS. In other words, the facts alleged in the complaint, assumed to be true, must create a plausible inference that each of the elements required to state a claim for war crimes under the ATS is met. *See id.* at 1937. Thus, in order to prevail on defendants' motions, the complaints must state facts that would allow a trier of fact plausibly to infer that defendant Prince (i) intentionally (ii) killed or inflicted serious bodily harm (iii) on innocent civilians (iv) during an armed conflict and (v) in the context of and in association with that armed conflict. Plaintiffs have failed to meet this burden as to the ATS war crimes claims in each of the five cases.

---

25 A narrow exception applies to materials that are integral to the complaint and appended thereto. *See generally* 5A Wright & Miller § 1327. No such materials were appended to the complaints in these cases.

In this respect it must be noted at the outset that the content of all the complaints contained within the sections entitled "Count One—War Crimes" is not entitled to the presumption of truth normally afforded a complaint's factual allegations on a motion to dismiss. Those sections do not contain factual allegations, but instead offer only "threadbare recitals of a cause of action's elements, supported by mere conclusory statements." *Iqbal*, 129 S. Ct. at 1940 (quoting *Twombly*, 550 U.S. at 555, 127 S. Ct. 1955). Specifically, this portion of the complaints merely asserts that defendants engaged in acts that were "deliberate, willful, intentional, wanton, malicious and oppressive and constitute war crimes," that the acts occurred "during a period of armed conflict," that the war crimes were committed against the decedents "and others," that defendants are liable for the war crimes, and that the misconduct caused "grave and foreseeable" injuries to the plaintiffs. Compl., No. 1:09cv615, ¶ 37–42; Compl., No. 1:09cv616, ¶¶ 32–37; First Am. Compl., No. 1:09cv617, ¶¶ 75–81; First Am. Compl., No. 1:09cv618, ¶¶ 89–94; Compl., No. 1:09cv645, ¶¶ 22–27. These sections allege no facts, but merely recite the elements, as plaintiffs understood them, for claims of war crimes under the ATS. Accordingly, the "conclusory nature of [the] allegations . . . disentitles them to the presumption of truth." *Iqbal*, 129 S. Ct. at 1951 (rejecting as conclusory, in a *Bivens* action, allegation that defendants "knew of, condoned, and willfully and maliciously agreed to subject" plaintiff to harsh conditions "solely on account of his religion, race, and/or national origin"). Whether plaintiffs have validly stated claims therefore depends on the factual content of the complaints, and not these conclusory statements.

The complaint in the first case, No. 1:09cv615, fails to allege any facts that create a plausible entitlement to relief on the war crimes claim against any of the defendants. As discussed *supra*, in No. 1:09cv615, Andrew Moonen, then a guard employed by Xe defendants, allegedly became severely intoxicated at a Christmas party, became lost, and, "stumbling drunkenly around Little Venice," shot and killed the decedent. Compl., No. 1:09cv615, ¶ 22. Plaintiffs allege that Xe defendants' employees were present at the Christmas Eve party and failed to prevent Moonen from leaving despite his visibly intoxicated state. This assertion does not support the war crimes claim for three reasons. First, plaintiffs have stated that they are not proceeding under the ATS on a theory of vicarious liability. Thus, the conduct of Xe defendants' employees is not pertinent to the question of the liability of Prince or Xe defendants. Second, failure to restrain an intoxicated person from leaving a party may support a plausible inference of negligence or recklessness, but it does not support an inference of intentional killing. Finally, these factual allegations do not support a plausible inference that the nexus requirement is met with respect to this claim.

Plaintiffs further allege that Prince, acting through Xe defendants, knowingly armed people he knew to be alcoholics. This factual allegation also does not support a plausible inference that Prince intentionally killed the decedent in No. 1:09cv615. First, plaintiffs do not allege that Moonen himself is such an alcoholic. Thus, the factual allegation that Prince armed alcoholics does not tend to support the conclusion that Prince caused the decedent's death in this case. Second, even if Moonen were an alcoholic and Prince was aware of it, these facts do not give rise to a plausible inference that by arming Moonen, Prince intentionally caused the decedent's death. Instead, such facts would at most support a conclusion that Prince was negligent or reckless in entrusting Moonen with a weapon. Thus, while the conduct alleged in No. 1:09cv615, if true, is reprehensible, it does not give rise to a plausible inference that any of the defendants committed a war crime. Accordingly, plaintiffs have failed to state a claim of war crimes that is cognizable under the ATS. The federal claims in No. 1:09cv615 should therefore be dismissed for lack of subject-matter jurisdiction.

The four remaining cases, Nos. 1:09cv616, 1:09cv617, 1:09cv618, and 1:09cv645, allege similar factual bases. In all of these complaints, innocent Iraqi civilians are alleged to have been shot or severely beaten without reason by guards who, at the time of the alleged incidents, were working for Xe defendants. As in No. 1:09cv615, the complaints in the other four cases support a plausible inference of recklessness or negligence by defendants, but not of intentional killing or infliction of serious bodily harm. Indeed, the complaints accuse defendants of "a pattern and practice of recklessness in the use of deadly force." Compl., No. 1:09cv616, ¶ 18; First Am. Compl., No. 1:09cv617, ¶ 49, First Am. Compl., No. 1:09cv618, ¶ 81; Compl., No. 1:09cv645, ¶ 14. Plaintiffs allege that defendants knew that some of their guards were working while under the influence of chemical substances, that they hired known mercenaries, that they "created and fostered a culture of lawlessness," and that they refused to discipline guards who used excessive force. Compl., No. 1:09cv616, ¶¶ 18–24; First Am. Compl., No. 1:09cv617, ¶¶ 49–57; First Am. Compl., No. 1:09cv618, ¶¶ 81–86; Compl., No. 1:09cv645, ¶¶ 13–21. Even assuming that these allegations are sufficiently non-conclusory under *Iqbal* and *Twombly* to be entitled to the presumption of truth, they do not give rise to a plausible inference that defendant Prince intentionally killed or severely harmed innocent Iraqi civilians. Specifically, plaintiffs do not allege any facts which would create a plausible inference that Prince possessed the requisite intent to kill or inflict serious bodily injury. At most, the factual allegations presently contained within the complaints would allow for a plausible inference that Prince was negligent or reckless. Finally, plaintiffs have not alleged facts creating an inference that the alleged conduct was committed in the context of and in association with an armed conflict. Accordingly, plaintiffs have not stated valid claims of war crimes cognizable under the ATS in these four cases. The claims should therefore be dismissed for lack of subject-matter jurisdiction.

In their responses to defendants' motions to dismiss, and at oral argument, plaintiffs represent that they have a sufficient factual basis to plead, consistent with Rule 11, Fed. R. Civ. P., that Prince ordered or otherwise directed the killings of innocent Iraqi civilians. During the course of the hearing held on August 28, 2009, plaintiffs, by oral motion of counsel, requested leave to amend the complaints as necessary to cure defects and provide additional detail. Such leave should be denied as futile as to No. 1:09cv615, but granted as to the other four cases.

Prior to trial, leave to amend is "freely given" in accordance with Rule 15(a), Fed. R. Civ. P. In this circuit, such leave is denied "'only when the amendment would have been prejudicial to the opposing party, there has been bad faith on the part of the moving party, or the amendment would have been futile.'" *Laber v. Harvey*, 438 F.3d 404, 426 (4th Cir.2006) (en banc) (quoting *Johnson v. Oroweat Foods Co.*, 785 F.2d 503, 509 (4th Cir.1986)); *see also Sciolino v. City of Newport News*, 480 F.3d 642, 651 (4th Cir.2007) (applying Oroweat Foods standard to post-dismissal context). There is no indication, at this early stage in these proceedings, that allowing plaintiffs leave to amend would cause any significant likelihood of prejudice to defendants. Moreover, there is no evidence to suggest that plaintiffs acted in bad faith by failing to plead factual allegations which meet the standard of *Iqbal* and *Twombly*. Thus, leave to amend may only be denied if amending the complaint would be futile. In other words, if the complaints as amended would nonetheless fail to state a claim upon which relief could be granted, then leave to amend may properly be denied. *See Steinburg v. Chesterfield County Planning Comm'n*, 527 F.3d 377, 390–91 (4th Cir.2008) (upholding denial of leave to amend because plaintiff "has pointed to no material in his proposed amended complaint that would have changed the analysis conducted by the district court").

In No. 1:09cv615, it is pellucidly clear that plaintiffs' proposed amendment would not cure the present defect in the complaint. During the course of the hearing held on August 28, 2009, plaintiffs suggested that the Christmas party at which Moonen became intoxicated was a "Blackwater party," that it may have been "part of his employment" to attend, and that management in some way "played a role in encouraging him . . . to continue to carry his weapon after he was visibly intoxicated." Hearing on Defs.' Mots, to Dism. Tr. at 13–14. The addition of these vague factual allegations to the complaint would not remedy the defects or alter the analysis of the claims in this case. The mere fact that the party was sponsored by his employer or that attendance was within the scope of his employment is inapposite to the question whether defendants intended to kill the decedent. As amended, the complaint in No. 1:09cv615 would fail to allege facts giving rise to a plausible inference that Prince engaged in any conduct with an intent to kill, let alone that this conduct proximately caused the decedent's death. Moreover, the allegation that Xe defendants allowed or encouraged Moonen to continue to carry his weapon after he became intoxicated does not create a plausible inference that defendants intentionally caused the decedent's death in this case. Indeed, the lengthy chain of inferences that would be required to trace such conduct back to Prince's alleged directive to his employees to kill Iraqi civilians is so tenuous that it does not even approach the plausibility standard articulated in *Iqbal* and *Twombly*.[26]

---

26 Indeed, plaintiffs, through counsel, acknowledged during the hearing that No. 1:09cv615 "is the weakest" of their cases. Hearing on Defs.' Mots, to Dism. Tr. at 14. Moreover, plaintiffs acknowledged that they are unsure "[w]hether Moonen and that particular shooting fits within the rubric [of the war crimes] that we have learned about." *Id.*

Accordingly, plaintiffs' oral motion for leave to amend the complaint in No. 1:09cv615 must be denied on grounds of futility. *See Steinburg*, 527 F.3d at 391.

In the other four cases, it is at least possible that plaintiffs will be able to cure the defects in their complaints. More specifically, it seems possible that the complaints in Nos. 1:09cv616, 1:09cv617, 1:09cv618, and 1:09cv645 could be amended to add factual allegations that would permit plausible inferences that Prince and Xe defendants ordered killings of innocent Iraqi civilians, during an armed conflict, in the context of and in association with that armed conflict, and that defendants' conduct proximately caused the injuries or deaths to plaintiffs. Thus, leave is appropriately granted to plaintiffs to amend their complaints in these four cases. The onus remains on plaintiffs to plead facts, rather than conclusory statements, establishing a plausible inference that each of these required elements is met. Of course, if plaintiffs choose to amend their complaints in these four cases, defendants will be free to renew their Rule 12 motions to dismiss as to any or all of the re-pleaded claims.

B. Summary Execution Claims

In two of the cases, Nos. 1:09cv617 and 1:09cv618, plaintiffs also claim that defendants directed summary executions in violation of the law of nations. To be sure, there is support for the existence of an international norm prohibiting *official* summary executions. Indeed, Congress has confirmed that such a norm exists. In creating a federal civil cause of action for extrajudicial killing in the Torture Victim Protection Act (TVPA), Congress required that the individual alleged to have violated the TVPA acted "under actual or apparent authority, or color of law, of any foreign nation." Pub. L. No. 102-256, § 2(a), 106 Stat. 73, 73 (1992). Moreover, it is clear that by enacting the TVPA, Congress codified its understanding of the international law norm governing the commission of summary executions. The TVPA's definition of extrajudicial killing closely tracks the language employed in the Geneva Conventions.[27] Moreover, the TVPA's definition expressly exempts "any such killing that, under international law, is lawfully carried out under the authority of a foreign nation." Finally, the report that accompanied the TVPA to the Senate floor unambiguously states that "the TVPA incorporates into U.S. law the definition of extrajudicial killing found in customary international law."[28] As noted above, *Sosa* reaffirmed the rule that when Congress defines the international law norms at issue, courts are bound by its determination. *See Sosa*,

---

27 *Compare* TVPA § 3(a) (defining extrajudicial killing as "a deliberated killing not authorized by a previous judgment pronounced by a regularly constituted court affording all the judicial guarantees which are recognized as indispensable by civilized peoples"), *with* Fourth Geneva Convention, art. 3 (prohibiting "the carrying out of executions without previous judgment pronounced by a regularly constituted court, affording all the judicial guarantees which are recognized as indispensable by civilized peoples").

28 S.Rep. No. 102-249, at 6 (1991).

542 U.S. at 734, 124 S. Ct. 2739. Because Congress has, by legislative enactment, expressed its understanding of the international law governing extrajudicial killings, judicial resort to the customs and usages of other nations is not appropriate.[29] Moreover, even assuming that the TVPA does not directly address the issue, plaintiffs would not find support in universally accepted international laws for the proposition that extrajudicial killings by non-state actors violates the law of nations, as the Geneva Conventions only prohibit executions without judicial process when they are committed by a party to an armed conflict.[30]

Yet, plaintiffs themselves assert that the alleged executions "were not carried out under the authority of any country or court." Compls., Nos. 1:09cv6171 ¶ 83, 1:09cv618 ¶ 96. Instead, they argue that in addition to being liable for war crimes, non-state actors are liable for summary executions committed during the course of war crimes. In making this argument, plaintiffs misread *Kadic* to create an exception to the normal rule requiring state actors for a cognizable claim for summary executions. In fact, *Kadic* merely acknowledges that the conduct alleged in a claim for summary executions, which would require state actors, could also be sufficient to state a claim of war crimes, which is cognizable against non-state actors. *Kadic*, 70 F.3d at 244.[31] Thus, because summary execution claims require state action, and none is alleged here, the summary execution claims must be dismissed without leave to amend.

---

29 It is worth noting that the fact that Congress has defined the applicable norms of international law in this area does not compel the conclusion that the TVPA implicitly repeals all or part of the ATS or that the entire field of laws governing civil remedies for extrajudicial killing is preempted by the TVPA. Indeed, most courts have held that the TVPA supplements the ATS, and does not preempt it. *See Sinaltrainal v. Coca-Cola Co.*, 578 F.3d 1252, 1266–67 (11th Cir.2009) (analyzing torture and summary execution claims separately under ATS and TVPA); *Chavez v. Carranza*, 559 F.3d 486 (6th Cir.2009) (same); *Sarei v. Rio Tinto, PLC*, 550 F.3d 822 (9th Cir.2008) (same); *Khulumani v. Barclay Nat'l Bank Ltd.*, 504 F.3d 254 (2d Cir.2007) (same). But *see Enahoro v. Abubakar*, 408 F.3d 877 (7th Cir.2005) (concluding that TVPA occupies the field of civil remedies for claims of torture or extrajudicial killing). Because plaintiffs do not state a claim of summary execution cognizable under either the ATS or the TVPA, the question need not be decided here.

30 *See* Geneva Convention Relative to the Protection of Civilian Persons in Time of War, Aug. 12, 1949, art. 3. Accordingly, courts have consistently required state action to prove an ATS claim for summary execution. *See, e.g.*, *Sinaltrainal*, 578 F.3d at 1266–67; *Abdullahi v. Pfizer, Inc.*, 562 F.3d 163, 203 (2d Cir.2009) (quoting *Kadic*, 70 F.3d at 243); *Tel-Oren v. Libyan Arab Republic*, 726 F.2d 774, 791 n. 20 (D.C.Cir.1984).

31 *See also Kadic*, 70 F.3d at 243 ("Torture and summary execution—when not perpetrated in the course of genocide or war crimes—are proscribed by international law only when committed by state officials or under color of law."). Indeed, the Second Circuit held that plaintiffs would have to prove the specific elements required to establish genocide and war crimes. *Id.* at 244; *see also Sinaltrainal*, 578 F.3d at 1266–67 (concluding that plaintiffs' ATS claims are not cognizable as summary execution claims due to absence of state action and not cognizable as war crimes despite "war crimes exception" to state action requirement due to absence of nexus with armed conflict).

C. Exhaustion

Defendants further contend that plaintiffs should be required to exhaust their remedies in Iraq before they can bring their ATS claims in federal court. While the text of the ATS itself offers no basis for this argument, Sosa expressly reserves judgment on whether the ATS requires exhaustion of domestic remedies. 542 U.S. at 733 n. 21, 124 S. Ct. 2739 ("We would certainly consider [an exhaustion] requirement in an appropriate case."). Indeed, at least one court of appeals has applied a prudential exhaustion doctrine to ATS claims. *Sarei v. Rio Tinto, PLC*, 550 F.3d 822 (9th Cir.2008). While it is far from clear that an exhaustion requirement is appropriate in this case,[32] even if it were, it would not prevent plaintiffs' claims from proceeding.

It is pellucidly clear that neither domestic nor international law requires exhaustion of an unavailable remedy.[33] Moreover, the Supreme Court has recently confirmed that failure to exhaust is an affirmative defense, and thus, defendants bear the burden to prove the existence of available, unexhausted remedies. *Jones v. Bock*, 549 U.S. 199, 212–14, 127 S. Ct. 910, 166 L.Ed.2d 798 (2007). Accordingly, in order to prevail in their exhaustion defense, defendants must show that plaintiffs may bring claims in Iraqi court against defendants arising from the conduct alleged in these cases.

Defendants cannot meet this burden because they agree with plaintiffs that Coalition Provisional Authority ("CPA") Order No. 17 shields defendants from liability in Iraqi courts for claims arising out of the conduct alleged in these cases. More specifically, Order No. 17, which was subsequently incorporated into Iraqi law, immunizes contractors from "Iraqi legal process with respect to acts performed

32 In Sarei, the Ninth Circuit implemented a prudential exhaustion requirement for cases lacking a "significant United States 'nexus.'" 550 F.3d at 831. Specifically, in a case involving a "foreign corporation's complicity in acts on foreign soil that affected aliens," the plaintiffs were required first to exhaust their remedies in their home country. *Id.* Unlike the claims at issue in Sarei, these cases involve the conduct of U.S. citizens and entities who were working under contract with the U.S. Government in a country that was at the time occupied by the United States. Thus, the instant cases are quite meaningfully distinguishable from Sarei and at the very least present a far less compelling reason to impose a prudential exhaustion requirement. In any event, because the parties essentially agree that there is no available remedy in Iraq, the question whether an exhaustion requirement should be imposed upon ATS claims like these is essentially moot and need not be answered here.

33 *See Woodford v. Ngo*, 548 U.S. 81, 92, 126 S. Ct. 2378, 165 L.Ed.2d 368 (2006) ("In habeas, state-court remedies are described as having been 'exhausted' when they are no longer available, regardless of the reason for their unavailability."); *Sarei v. Rio Tinto, PLC*, 550 F.3d 822, 830 (9th Cir.2008) (adopting prudential exhaustion requirement for ATS claims) ("A core element of the exhaustion rule is its futility, or denial of justice exception, which excuses exhaustion of local remedies where they are unavailable or inadequate."); Restatement (Third) of Foreign Relations Law § 703 cmt. d (1987) (noting domestic remedies are exhausted for purposes of international law claims if no domestic remedy is available or it would be futile to pursue such remedy).

by them pursuant to the terms and conditions" of a government contract. CPA Order No. 17 § 4(3). All of the Iraqi legal experts retained by the parties agree that Iraqi courts would most likely read Order No. 17 to bar claims against defendants for the conduct alleged in these cases.[34] Indeed, defendants acknowledge that Order No. 17 "appears to preclude plaintiffs from litigating their claims in Iraqi courts." Defs.' Consol. Post-Hearing Br. at 1. In arguing for dismissal, defendants merely recite the truism that one does not know for certain how a court will rule on an issue until it does so. *Id.* at 2 (quoting Defs.' Exp.'s 2d Supp. Rep. ¶ 5) (noting that "there is no guarantee" how an Iraqi court would rule). Defendants' assertion is plainly insufficient to meet their burden. Accordingly, defendants have not shown that plaintiffs failed to exhaust available Iraqi legal remedies and the claims therefore should not be dismissed on those grounds.

D. Availability of Punitive Damages

Defendants assert that punitive damages are not available under the ATS. Yet, they offer no support in the case law or from recognized international treatises for this proposition. Indeed, a note in the current *Restatement of Foreign Relations Law* states that punitive damages are available under international law for the commission of international crimes. *Restatement (Third) of Foreign Relations Law of the United States* § 901 rep. n. 5 (1997).[35] Accordingly, courts have consistently awarded punitive damages for ATS claims.[36] Thus, punitive damages, if proven, are available for plaintiffs' ATS claims.

---

34 In federal courts, questions of foreign law are legal issues judicially determined upon consideration of any relevant material or source, including testimony. Rule 44.1, Fed. R. Civ. P.; *S.E.C. v. Dunlap*, 253 F.3d 768, 777 (4th Cir.2001).

35 In full, the note, titled "Punitive or exemplary damages," states that

> [i]f a violation is not merely a delict but an international crime, *see* Reporters' Note 1, punitive damages may be awarded. In fixing the amount of an award, some international tribunals have taken into consideration the seriousness of the offense and included an element of punishment in the award. Borchard, The Diplomatic Protection of Citizens Abroad 419 (1915); *see* the case of The I'm Alone, 1935, 3 R.Int'l Arb. Awards 1616, 1618 (1949) ("as a material amend in respect of the wrong, the United States should pay the sum of $25,000" to Canada). For a contrary view, *see* Judge Parker's opinion in Lusitania Cases (United States v. Germany), 1923, 7 R. Int'l Arb. Awards 32, 38–44 ("counsel has failed to point us to any money award by an international arbitral tribunal where exemplary, punitive, or vindictive damages have been assessed against one sovereign nation in favor of another presenting a claim in behalf of its nationals"). In the United States, the Foreign Sovereign Immunities Act excludes punitive damages against a foreign state, but allows them against an agency or instrumentality of the foreign state. 28 U.S.C. § 1606.

Restatement (Third) of Foreign Relations Law of the United States § 901 rep. n. 5 (1997).

36 *See, e.g.*, *Chavez v. Carranza*, 559 F.3d 486 (6th Cir.2009); *Abebe-Jira v. Negewo*, 72 F.3d 844 (11th Cir.1996); *Hilao v. Estate of Marcos*, 103 F.3d 767 (9th Cir.1996); *Licea v. Curacao Drydock Co.*, 584 F. Supp. 2d 1355 (S.D.Fla.2008); *Doe v. Rafael Saravia*, 348 F. Supp. 2d 1112 (E.D.Cal.2004); *Chiminya Tachiona v. Mugabe*, 216 F. Supp. 2d 262 (S.D.N.Y.2002); *Cabello Barrueto v. Fernandez Larios*, 205 F. Supp. 2d 1325 (S.D.Fla. 2002); *Mehinovic v. Vuckovic*,

III.

RICO affords a civil remedy for those who suffer property damage as a result of a violation of the criminal RICO provisions. 18 U.S.C. § 1964(c). To prevail, civil RICO plaintiffs generally must show that the defendant violated a provision of 18 U.S.C. § 1962, and that this violation caused damage to the plaintiffs' property.

Certain plaintiffs in Nos. 1:09cv617 and 1:09cv618 allege that they suffered damage to property as a result of defendant Prince's violations of RICO §§ 1962(b) and 1962(c). Section 1962(b) prohibits the acquisition or maintenance of an interest in or control of an enterprise engaged in interstate or foreign commerce through a pattern of racketeering activity. 18 U.S.C. § 1962(b). Thus, to prevail on a claim alleging a violation of § 1962(b), the RICO plaintiffs must prove (i) that Prince engaged in a pattern of racketeering activity, (ii) that through this pattern, he acquired an interest in, or control of, an enterprise (iii) that engaged in activities affecting interstate or foreign commerce, and (iv) that this acquisition of an interest or control caused property damage to the RICO plaintiffs. *See Danielsen v. Burnside-Ott Training Ctr., Inc.*, 941 F.2d 1220, 1231 (D.C.Cir.1991); *Smithfield Foods, Inc. v. United Food & Commercial Workers Int'l Union*, 633 F. Supp. 2d 214 (E.D.Va.2008) (Order); *Davis v. Hudgins*, 896 F. Supp. 561, 567 (E.D.Va.1995); *see also* Gregory Joseph, *Civil RICO: A Definitive Guide* § 13 (2000).

Plaintiffs have not made factual allegations sufficient to give rise to a plausible inference that Prince engaged in a pattern of racketeering activities as defined by RICO. A racketeering activity is defined as an act indictable under certain provisions of Title 18 of the United States Code, or

> any act or threat involving murder, kidnapping, gambling, arson, robbery, bribery, extortion, dealing in obscene matter, or dealing in a controlled substance or listed chemical . . . , which is chargeable under State law and punishable by imprisonment for more than one year.

18 U.S.C. § 1961. Plaintiffs claim that the "Prince RICO Enterprise" has committed violations of several federal statutes enumerated in § 1961. Specifically, plaintiffs allege violations of 18 U.S.C. § 1512(c) (destruction of evidence); 18 U.S.C. § 1956 (money laundering); 18 U.S.C. §§ 2251, 2251A, 2252, 2260 (sexual exploitation of minors); and 18 U.S.C. § 1952 (racketeering). Plaintiffs also allege that the "Prince RICO Enterprise" committed murders and kidnappings. Yet, plaintiffs do not accuse Prince himself of committing these predicate acts, as required for Prince to have violated § 1962(b). Moreover, plaintiffs do not allege that Prince acquired an interest in, or control of, an enterprise as a result of his pattern of racketeering activity. 18 U.S.C. § 1962(b). Indeed, the complaints are completely

---

198 F. Supp. 2d 1322 (N.D.Ga.2002); *Xuncax v. Gramajo*, 886 F. Supp. 162 (D.Mass.1995); *Filartiga v. Pena-Irala*, 577 F. Supp. 860 (E.D.N.Y.1984); *see also* 21 C.O.A.2d § 327 ("Punitive damages are likely warranted in any ATS case in which the plaintiff prevails on the merits [because ATS claims generally require wanton and willful misconduct].").

devoid of any factual allegations suggesting that Prince acquired control over his "RICO Enterprise" through his racketeering activities. *Id.* Instead, plaintiffs merely plead that Prince's enterprise engages in illegal acts. This is plainly insufficient to prove a violation of § 1962(b). *See Toucheque v. Price Bros. Co.*, 5 F. Supp. 2d 341, 350 (D.Md.1998) ("[Section 1962(b)] prohibits acquiring control of an enterprise through a pattern of racketeering activity, and requires that the pattern of racketeering activity be the cause of the acquisition of control" (citing *von Bulow v. von Bulow*, 634 F. Supp. 1284, 1307 (S.D.N.Y.1986); *In re* VMS Sees. Litig., 752 F. Supp. 1373, 1403–04 (N.D.Ill.1990)).).

Finally, plaintiffs do not establish a plausible basis for recovery for violations of § 1962(b) because they do not allege that they were injured as a result of Prince's acquisition of an interest in, or control of, the enterprise. The civil RICO provision requires that the injury occur "by reason of a violation of section 1962." 18 U.S.C. § 1964(c). The violation, for purposes of § 1962(b), is the acquisition of control of the enterprise through the pattern of racketeering activity. Thus, it is well-settled that proving causation under § 1962(b) requires proof of an "acquisition injury." *See, e.g., Fischbein v. Sayers*, No. 04-CIV-6589, 2009 WL 2170349 (S.D.N.Y. July 16, 2009); *DeFazio v. Wallis*, 500 F. Supp. 2d 197 (E.D.N.Y.2007); *In re Am. Honda Motor Co.*, 941 F. Supp. 528 (D.Md.1996). Plaintiffs have not alleged that it was Prince's acquisition of control over the alleged RICO enterprise that caused their injuries; rather, they state that the predicate acts themselves caused the property damage they allegedly suffered. Accordingly, the RICO claims predicated on an alleged violation of § 1962(b) should be dismissed. Moreover, because plaintiffs' theory of RICO liability—that the alleged commission of predicate acts caused physical damage to plaintiffs' property—is inconsistent with the § 1962(b) requirement of an acquisition injury, granting leave to amend the complaints would clearly be futile. Accordingly, such leave must be denied. *Steinburg v. Chesterfield County Planning Comm'n*, 527 F.3d 377, 390–91 (4th Cir.2008). Plaintiffs can only state a valid claim for civil RICO relief, if at all, to the extent that it is predicated on an alleged violation of § 1962(c).

Section 1962(c) is violated where a person associated with an enterprise engaged in interstate or foreign commerce conducts or participates in the enterprise's affairs through a pattern of racketeering activity. 18 U.S.C. § 1962(c). Thus, the RICO plaintiffs state a valid claim for damages resulting from a § 1962(c) violation if they plead factual allegations creating plausible inferences (i) that Prince is associated with an enterprise (ii) that engages in or affects interstate or foreign commerce, (iii) that Prince conducted or participated in the conduct of the enterprise's affairs (iv) through a pattern of racketeering activity, (v) and that this pattern of racketeering activity caused the property damage to the RICO plaintiffs. *See Sedima, S.P.R.L. v. Imrex Co.*, 473 U.S. 479, 496, 105 S. Ct. 3275, 87 L.Ed.2d 346 (1985); *AvalonBay Cmtys., Inc. v. Willden*, No. 1:08cv777, 2009 WL 2431571 (E.D.Va. Aug. 7, 2009); *see also Gregory*, Civil RICO § 14 (2000).

The RICO plaintiffs in Nos. 1:09cv617 and 1:09cv618 have alleged facts that create a plausible inference that the first three elements for a violation of § 1962(c) are met. They allege that Prince is associated with an enterprise—Xe defendants—that engages in interstate or foreign commerce by virtue of its contracting activities in Iraq. Moreover, the RICO plaintiffs allege that Prince wholly owns and controls this enterprise. Yet, the RICO plaintiffs fail to allege any facts relating to the final two elements required to show a violation of § 1962(c). As discussed above, plaintiffs do not allege that Prince himself has engaged in a pattern of racketeering activity, as required under § 1962(c). Rather, they only allege that the "Prince RICO Enterprise" has committed the predicate acts which would constitute a pattern of racketeering activity.

Moreover, in order for a pattern of racketeering activity to cause injury, the predicate acts constituting racketeering activity must themselves proximately cause the injury. *See Sedima*, 473 U.S. at 497, 105 S. Ct. 3275 ("[T]he compensable injury necessarily is the harm caused by predicate acts. . . ."). In this matter, the only predicate acts which the RICO plaintiffs allege to have caused the injuries in question—damage to motor vehicles caused by the discharge of weapons—were murders. To qualify as RICO predicate acts, under § 1961, the murders must be "chargeable under state law." 18 U.S.C. § 1961. Thus, a RICO claim based on a predicate act committed in violation of state law "would fail if the state where the conduct occurred did not criminalize such conduct." *United States v. Le*, 316 F. Supp. 2d 355, 360 n. 11 (E.D.Va.2004) (citing *United States v. Marino*, 277 F. 3d 11, 30 (1st Cir.2002)). Yet, plaintiffs do not show how murders committed of any state. Specifically, the complaints offer no factual allegations giving rise to a plausible inference that the conduct constituting murder occurred within the territorial jurisdiction of a U.S. state. Thus, plaintiffs have failed to allege a pattern of racketeering activity which proximately caused the damage suffered by the RICO plaintiffs. Accordingly, the RICO claims predicated on an alleged violation of § 1962(c) should be dismissed.

In their briefs and in the course of the hearing on defendants' motions, plaintiffs represented that they have a good-faith basis to plead that Prince committed murders that are chargeable under state law. Specifically, plaintiffs state that they are prepared to plead, consistent with Rule 11, Fed. R. Civ. P., that Prince ordered or directed the killings allegedly committed in Iraq from within the United States, and that such conduct proximately caused the damage allegedly suffered by the RICO plaintiffs. If plaintiffs state nonconclusory factual allegations which give rise to plausible inferences that the elements of a violation of § 1962(c) are met, and that the violations proximately caused the damage suffered by the RICO plaintiffs, then they will have met the pleading requirements for this claim under *Iqbal* and *Twombly*. Accordingly, the RICO claims should be dismissed pursuant to Rule 12(b)(6), Fed. R. Civ. P., without prejudice and with leave to amend the claims predicated on violations of 18 U.S.C. § 1962(c).

Defendants further argue that, assuming the facts alleged in the complaints to be true, the RICO claim of plaintiff Al Rubae in 1:09cv618 is time-barred. The Supreme Court has held that civil RICO claims are subject to a four-year limitations period, and that this period begins to run no later than when the injury is discovered. *Rotella v. Wood*, 528 U.S. 549, 554, 120 S. Ct. 1075, 145 L.Ed.2d 1047 (2000). According to the complaint, the injury alleged—damage to Al Rubae's car caused by gunfire—occurred in March 2005, and such damage would have been immediately apparent, since Al Rubae was allegedly in the car at the time. Thus, the applicable statute of limitations would have expired in March 2009, prior to the case's June 2, 2009 filing date. Accordingly, Al Rubae's RICO claim, being clearly time-barred, should be dismissed without leave to amend.

Defendants also argue that plaintiffs are not entitled to punitive damages or injunctive relief on their RICO claims. Indeed, is it well-settled that the statutory civil remedy for RICO violations—three times the value of damage to property—is exclusive. *See SouthStar Funding, LLC v. Sprouse*, No. 3:05cv253, 2007 WL 812174, at 5 (W.D.N.C. Mar. 13, 2007); *Toucheque v. Price Bros. Co.*, 5 F. Supp. 2d 341, 350 (D.Md.1998); *see also Humana Inc. v. Forsyth*, 525 U.S. 299, 313, 119 S. Ct. 710, 142 L.Ed.2d 753 (1999); *Johnson v. Collins Entnm't Co.*, 199 F.3d 710, 726 (4th Cir.1999). In their response to defendants' motions, plaintiffs do not offer any argument that they are entitled to such relief on their RICO claims. Accordingly, it is clear that the only relief to which plaintiffs may be entitled is for alleged RICO violations is the statutory remedy of treble damages.

IV.

A necessary consequence of dismissal of all of the federal claims in Nos. 1:09cv615, 1:09cv616, and 1:09cv645 for lack of subject-matter jurisdiction is that the remaining claims in those cases must also be dismissed. This conclusion follows from the fact that the ATS claim is the sole federal claim alleged in those cases and there is, given the current complaints, no basis for either diversity jurisdiction under 28 U.S.C. § 1332, or supplemental jurisdiction under 28 U.S.C. § 1367.

It is well-established in this circuit that "state citizenship for purposes of diversity jurisdiction depends not on residence, but on national citizenship and domicile." *Axel Johnson, Inc. v. Carroll Carolina Oil Co.*, 145 F.3d 660, 663 (4th Cir.1998). Plaintiffs do not plead that defendants are citizens of a U.S. state. Instead, they only plead that defendant Prince is a resident of Virginia; the complaints also provide addresses in Virginia and North Carolina at which the defendant entities are allegedly "located." *See, e.g.*, Compl., No. 1:09cv615, ¶¶ 7–14. These facts, assumed to be true, are plainly insufficient to establish subject-matter jurisdiction under the federal diversity statute. Moreover, diversity jurisdiction does not exist in any case in which there are foreign citizens on both sides. *See Slavchev v. Royal Caribbean Cruises, Ltd.*, 559 F.3d 251, 254 (4th Cir.2009) (concluding that jurisdiction under § 1332(a)(2) is lacking in a suit between a citizen of Bulgaria and a corporation incorporated in Liberia with a principal place of business in Florida). Plaintiffs acknowledge that defendant Graystone is incorporated in Barbados and therefore is a citizen of Barbados. Accordingly, because all plaintiffs are Iraqi citizens, there are foreign nationals on both sides of the case. Thus, diversity jurisdiction does not exist in any of these cases.

Plaintiffs request leave to amend to cure any defects in jurisdiction under § 1332. They indicate that if leave is granted, they will amend the cases to remove Graystone. Because it appears that plaintiffs may be able to cure the jurisdictional defect at issue here by (i) removing Graystone and (ii) stating the citizenship of all the defendants, such leave should be granted in all five of the cases as to the nonfederal claims.

Second, supplemental jurisdiction is also lacking in the three cases alleging only ATS claims. Federal courts may only exercise supplemental jurisdiction over nonfederal claims if they form part of the same case or controversy as claims "of which the district courts have original jurisdiction." 28 U.S.C. § 1367. As discussed above, federal subject-matter jurisdiction is lacking over the ATS claims in Nos. 1:09cv615, 1:09cv616, and 1:09cv645. Moreover, plaintiffs have not alleged any other claims in those cases over which original jurisdiction exists. Accordingly, the nonfederal claims must be dismissed. Because all federal claims in No. 1:09cv615 are dismissed without leave to amend, leave to cure the jurisdictional defect under § 1367 as to the nonfederal claims in that case would be futile. Yet, as to Nos. 1:09cv616 and 1:09cv645, if plaintiffs amend the complaints to state claims cognizable under the ATS, then the jurisdictional hurdle of § 1367(a) will be cleared in those cases as to nonfederal claims that form part of the same case or controversy.[37] Accordingly, leave should be granted to replead the nonfederal claims alleged in Nos. 1:09cv616 and 1:09cv645 to state properly the existence of supplemental jurisdiction pursuant to 28 U.S.C. § 1367.

V.

Defendants argue that all of the claims in these cases raise nonjusticiable political questions and therefore must be dismissed. The analysis of the political question argument begins with *Baker v. Carr*, 369 U.S. 186, 217, 82 S. Ct. 691, 7 L.Ed.2d 663 (1962). In *Baker*, the Supreme Court declared that courts should not exercise jurisdiction over cases where one of six circumstances is present.[38] Defendants contend that one of those circumstances is present here, namely that the questions presented in this matter involve issues that are constitutionally committed to the Executive Branch. This argument is unavailing.

---

37 Decision is deferred as to whether such claims should nevertheless be dismissed under 28 U.S.C. § 1367(c).

38 Specifically, the six circumstances in which a claim is nonjusticiable pursuant to *Baker* occur when: (i) there is a textually demonstrable constitutional commitment of the questions to be determined to the political branches, (ii) there is a lack of judicially discoverable and manageable standards for resolving the question, (iii) the question could not be decided without an initial policy determination clearly meant for nonjudicial discretion, (iv) judicial determination would necessarily express a lack of the respect due the coordinate branches of government, (v) there is an unusual need for unquestioning adherence to a political decision already made, or (vi) there is the potential of embarrassment resulting from multifarious pronouncements by various political branches on one question. 369 U.S. at 217, 82 S. Ct. 691.

The political question doctrine, applied in the national security context, prevents judicial second-guessing of the battlefield decisions of the U.S. government. *See Gilligan v. Morgan*, 413 U.S. 1, 10, 93 S. Ct. 2440, 37 L.Ed.2d 407 (1973). Applying this principle, the Fourth Circuit has concluded that courts should not "dictate to a branch of the Department of Defense how it should react when it faces unknown and potentially hostile aircraft." *Tiffany v. United States*, 931 F.2d 271, 278–79 (4th Cir.1991). In *Tiffany*, the North American Aerospace Defense Command (NORAD), a component of the U.S. Department of Defense, scrambled aircraft in response to an unidentified civilian airplane that had failed to file a valid flight plan. A military aircraft subsequently collided with the civilian plane, killing everyone on board the civilian plane. The widow of the pilot of the civilian craft brought suit against the government. Relying on the principles enunciated in *Baker v. Carr*, the Fourth Circuit concluded that the matter was nonjusticiable.

Tiffany is plainly distinguishable from the present matter. Specifically, *Tiffany* involved litigation against the United States over decisions made by federal employees acting within the scope of their federal employment. Indeed, the Fourth Circuit repeatedly emphasized the importance of the fact that the suit was against the government and required judicial evaluation of the procedures and plans of a government agency on a question of national security. *See id.* at 275–78 (applying discretionary function exception to Federal Tort Claims Act), *id.* at 278 (emphasizing that NORAD is "a branch of the Department of Defense"); *id.* at 279 (noting that alleged tortfeasors are "government agents"); *id.* at 281–82 (discussing discretion left to NORAD under military regulations). On the rare occasion when claims against government contractors have been deemed nonjusticiable, it has been because the claims depended critically on battlefield policies and procedures of the United States government. *Carmichael v. Kellogg, Brown & Root Services, Inc.*, 572 F.3d 1271 (11th Cir.2009), on which defendants rely, is an example of such a case. In *Carmichael*, the plaintiff brought suit against a government contractor for injuries suffered while serving as a military escort in the contractor's truck as part of a larger U.S. government convoy in Iraq. The plaintiff was injured when the truck crashed. He alleged (i) that the contractor's employee was negligent for operating the vehicle at an unsafe speed, for failing to keep a proper lookout, and for failing to inspect the vehicle, and (ii) that the contractor was negligent in its hiring, supervision, and entrustment of the employee. On these facts, the Eleventh Circuit concluded that the military had made virtually every essential decision related to the convoy, including the speed of the vehicle, the date and time of departure, the decision to travel along a particular route, how much fuel was to be transported, the number of trucks necessary for the task, the distance to be maintained between vehicles, and the security measures in place. *Id.* at 1281 ("There is not the slightest hint in the record suggesting that KBR played even the most minor role in making any of these essential decisions."). Thus, adjudicating Carmichael's claims of negligence would have required direct reevaluation of many of the military's decisions concerning the convoy. In other cases more analogous to this matter, courts—including the Eleventh Circuit, which decided the case on which defendants rely—have concluded that decisions made by government contractors during wartime are not shielded by the political question doctrine.[39]

In this matter, defendants have not shown that adjudicating plaintiffs' claims would require second-guessing the battlefield procedures, plans, or decisions of the United States Armed Forces, or of any government entity. Indeed, plaintiffs' allegations do not indicate that the claims depend in any way on any determinations made by the federal government. The United States has appeared as an interested party and argues that if defendants committed the alleged conduct, they were not acting as employees of the United States when they did so. Moreover, the government states that its contracts with defendants "provided for multiple layers of [Xe defendants'] management to oversee the day-to-day operations" of its employees and that the employees were under the direct supervision of Xe defendants' management when the alleged conduct occurred. Gov't's Consol. Br. in Opp. at 12, 55–56. Thus, there is no indication that adjudication of plaintiffs' claims would require judicial determination of any issues committed by the text of the Constitution to the political branches. Accordingly, the political question doctrine does not bar these claims.[40]

VI.

Defendants contend that plaintiffs' nonfederal claims should be dismissed on *forum non conveniens* grounds. This argument is without merit. In considering whether dismissal for *forum non conveniens* is appropriate, courts must determine, as a threshold matter, "whether there exists an alternative forum." *Piper Aircraft Co. v. Reyno*, 454 U.S. 235, 254 n. 22, 102 S. Ct. 252, 70 L.Ed.2d 419 (1981). Specifically, if defendants are not "'amenable to process'" in the foreign jurisdiction, then *forum non conveniens* dismissal is not appropriate. *Id.* (quoting *Gulf Oil Corp. v. Gilbert*, 330 U.S. 501, 506, 67 S. Ct. 839, 91 L.Ed. 1055 (1947)).

---

39 *See Lane v. Halliburton*, 529 F.3d 548, 558–60 (5th Cir.2008) (conduct of contractor for allegedly negligent conduct in Iraq did not necessarily require evaluation of military decisions and thus not shielded from judicial review); *McMahon v. Presidential Airways, Inc.*, 502 F.3d 1331, 1358–61 (11th Cir.2007) (concluding that claims against Blackwater and related companies are justiciable because they do not necessitate second-guessing decisions by U.S. government); *Al Shimari v. CACI Premier Tech., Inc.*, 657 F. Supp. 2d 700 (E.D.Va.2009) (political question doctrine does not bar claims of contractor misconduct in the course of detaining captured Iraqi combatants).

40 Because the political question doctrine is jurisdictional in nature, it may be raised at any time. If, upon further development of the record in this cases, it appears that adjudication of plaintiffs' claims would require judicial evaluation of decisions constitutionally committed to the Executive Branch, defendants may renew their motions for dismissal on this ground. *See McMahon*, 502 F.3d at 1365 (affirming denial of motion to dismiss on political question grounds at pre-discovery stage, but noting that the defendant "remains free to assert the argument at any time").

Moreover, the burden is on the party seeking dismissal to show the adequacy of the alternative forum. *See Fidelity Bank PLC v. N. Fox Shipping N.V.*, 242 Fed. Appx. 84, 91–92 (4th Cir.2007) (reversing forum non conveniens dismissal because defendants failed to establish that Nigerian courts would take jurisdiction over a claim for wrongful arrest that occurred in the United States). Accordingly, unless defendants show that Iraqi courts would hear claims arising out of the conduct alleged here, then these cases cannot be dismissed on *forum non conveniens* grounds.

The parties agree that CPA Order No. 17 shields defendants from liability in Iraqi courts for claims arising out of the conduct alleged in these cases. As noted previously, Order No. 17 specifically immunizes government contractors from "Iraqi legal process" for all claims arising from conduct pursuant to the contracts. CPA Order No. 17 § 4(3). All of the parties' experts on Iraqi law agree that this language protects defendants from civil liability in Iraqi courts on the claims alleged in these cases. In their brief on the *forum non conveniens* issue, defendants merely qualify their previously absolute position that plaintiffs lack a remedy in Iraq by noting that "'there is no guarantee'" an Iraqi court would agree with their expert. Defs.' Consol. Post-Hearing Br. at 2 (quoting Defs.' Exp.'s 2d Supp. Rep. ¶ 15). Defendants are correct. Indeed, there is never a guarantee that a court will agree with a party's contention on a given matter. The assertion that a mere possibility exists that a court would disagree with a legal argument is plainly insufficient for defendants to meet their burden to establish the existence of an available alternate forum for adjudication of these claims.[41] Accordingly, the claims should not be dismissed on grounds of *forum non conveniens.*

VII.

Defendants argue that plaintiffs' nonfederal claims should be dismissed for a variety of reasons. Specifically, they argue (i) that Iraqi law grants defendants immunity from claims arising there, (ii) that Iraqi law does not recognize vicarious liability, the tort of spoliation of evidence, or punitive damages, (iii) that the negligent hiring and training claims are barred by the government contractor defense, (iv) that the negligent hiring and training claims are barred by the doctrine of absolute immunity, (v) that the estate plaintiffs are not properly qualified under applicable law, and (vi) that certain nonfederal claims are barred by the applicable statute of limitations.

Because the resolution of these issues depends in part on whether and how plaintiffs replead their claims, and in light of the obvious difficulties associated with ascertaining the content of Iraqi law at the threshold motion stage, it is appropriate

---

41 Moreover, defendants have declined to request that the United States exercise its power to waive any immunity they may possess in Iraqi courts pursuant to Order No. 17.

to defer ruling on defendants' motions to dismiss the nonfederal claims until a later time.

VIII.

In sum, plaintiffs have failed to state valid federal claims in these cases. Moreover, they have not properly pleaded the facts necessary for diversity jurisdiction to exist over the nonfederal claims, nor does supplemental jurisdiction exist as to the nonfederal claims in cases only alleging invalid ATS claims. Yet, the claims do not raise nonjusticiable political questions, nor should they be dismissed on grounds of *forum non conveniens*. Accordingly, plaintiffs may amend their complaints to re-plead claims to cure their present defects to the extent that such amendment would not be futile.

Appropriate Orders will issue.

I. INTERNATIONAL LAW IN GENERAL

3. *Jus Cogens*

MIGUEL LOPEZ
v.
OFFICER RICHARDSON OF THE CITY OF ATLANTA POLICE DEPARTMENT

647 F. Supp. 2d 1356 (N.D. Ga. 2009)
Decided August 12, 2009

Erik John Meder, Ave Maria Legal Services, LLC, Smyrna, GA, Jerome D. Lee, Hernan Taylor & Lee, Norcross, GA, for Plaintiff.

Michael John O'Hagan, Lowendick Cuzdcy Ehrmann Wagner & Stine, Dennis McRay Young, Office of Atlanta City Attorney, Atlanta, GA, for Defendants.

OPINION AND ORDER

J. OWEN FORRESTER, Senior District Judge.

This matter is before the court on Defendant City of Atlanta's motion to dismiss [4].

I. Background

A. Procedural History

Plaintiff filed suit against Defendants, Officer Richardson of the Atlanta Police Department in his individual and official capacities, and the City of Atlanta, pursuant to 42 U.S.C. § 1983, alleging Fourth and Fourteenth Amendment constitutional violations arising out of an incident outside of the "Peek-A-Boo" club in Atlanta, Georgia. In addition to the constitutional violations, Plaintiff also alleges violations of the law of nations, specifically, torture; cruel, inhumane, and degrading treatment of a minor; and arbitrary detention. Finally, Plaintiff raises state law claims of assault, battery, and intentional infliction of emotional distress. Plaintiff seeks punitive damages under his federal and state law claims. In an order dated December 16, 2008, the court held that Plaintiff could proceed without a guardian ad litem despite the fact he is a minor. The court also ruled that Plaintiff could not proceed anonymously and directed Plaintiff to amend his complaint accordingly.

B. Facts

In his complaint, Plaintiff alleges that Officer Richardson was called to the scene to respond to a dispute Plaintiff was having with the cashier of the club. Plaintiff avers that during his interaction with Officer Richardson, the officer struck Plaintiff on the wrist with his patrol baton and then kicked and punched Plaintiff repeatedly while he was on the ground. Plaintiff contends Officer Richardson grabbed Plaintiff's head by the hair and repeatedly shoved Plaintiff's face into the pavement. Plaintiff eventually lost consciousness but was handcuffed and dragged to Officer Richardson's police car. Officer Richardson then drove Plaintiff into DeKalb County to an unlit parking lot and stopped the car. Officer Richardson pulled Plaintiff out of the police cruiser, removed the handcuffs, and dumped Plaintiff in the parking lot. Plaintiff stumbled to a nearby apartment building where a resident saw Plaintiff and called an ambulance and the police. Plaintiff was taken to Grady Hospital and admitted for treatment. *See* Cmplt., ¶¶ 14–74.

Plaintiff's complaint labels his causes of action without specifying the defendants to which these claims are applicable. *See generally* Complaint. He alleges that Defendant Richardson "acting under color of law" violated norms of international law. *Id.,* ¶ 78. He then separates his international law claims into Count I: Torture, Count II: Cruel, Inhuman, Degrading Treatment or Punishment of Minor; and Count III: Arbitrary Detention. He goes on to aver that Defendant Richardson was "a public official and/or acting in an official capacity" when he "intentionally caused the Plaintiff severe physical and mental pain." *Id.,* ¶¶ 92–93, 113–14, 131. Plaintiff also refers only to acts of Defendant Richardson in his state law counts.

The only specific reference he makes to the City of Atlanta is with respect to his federal § 1983 claims under the Fourth and Fourteenth Amendments. There, Plaintiff alleges:

> that the violation of his constitutional rights were [*sic*] caused by implementation of a custom, policy, or official act of Defendant City of Atlanta including but not limited to: a police department custom or policy of tolerance of physical mistreatment of Spanish-speaking immigrants; failure to properly screen applicants for the position of police officer with the City of Atlanta; failure to supervise police officers; failure to train police officers in dealing with minors and Spanish-speaking immigrants; failure to investigate allegations of misconduct similar to that alleged in this Complaint; failure to discipline police officers who engage in conduct similar to that alleged in this complaint.

Id., ¶¶ 150, 161 (similar allegations with respect to Fourteenth Amendment). In all other respects, Plaintiff's complaint refers only to the actions of Defendant Richardson.

C. Contentions

In this litigation, Defendant the City of Atlanta and Defendant Officer Richardson are represented by different counsel. Although the City of Atlanta has filed a motion to dismiss, Officer Richardson has not done so and has filed an answer to Plaintiff's complaint. In its motion to dismiss, the City of Atlanta argues that (1) the official capacity claims raised against Defendant Richardson should be dismissed as redundant because they are in reality claims against the City of Atlanta; (2) although Plaintiff alleges both Fourth and Fourteenth Amendment claims concerning the use of excessive force against him, those claims arise only under the Fourth Amendment and not the Fourteenth; (3) Plaintiff makes no allegations of how any custom or policy of the City of Atlanta led to his constitutional injuries and therefore the § 1983 claims against Atlanta should be dismissed; and (4)(a) Plaintiff's complaint does not raise state law or international law claims against the city; and (b) even if the complaint is read as raising such claims, Plaintiff's allegations do not rise to the level of a violation of international law and Plaintiff's state law claims against the City fail because the City is entitled to sovereign immunity.

Plaintiff responds that he can raise both Fourth and Fourteenth Amendment claims because he was not "seized" at the time Defendant Richardson utilized excessive force against him. Further, because there is no heightened pleading requirement with respect to municipalities, his mere allegation in the complaint that his injuries were sustained as a result of the City's customs and policies, Plaintiff argues, is sufficient to survive a motion to dismiss. Finally, Plaintiff argues that corporations, such as the City of Atlanta, can be held liable for violations of international law.

II. Discussion

A. Preliminary Matters

Because Plaintiff did not respond to Defendant Atlanta's motion to dismiss state law claims on the basis of sovereign immunity, the court grants that portion of Defendant's motion and dismisses state law claims against the City of Atlanta. *See Reese v. City of Atlanta,* 261 Ga.App. 761, 762, 583 S.E.2d 584 (2003). Further, Plaintiff did not oppose Defendant Atlanta's assertion that the claims against Defendant Richardson in his official capacity should be dismissed as redundant of his claims against the City of Atlanta. Therefore, the court finds that Plaintiff's claims against Defendant Richardson will proceed in his individual capacity only.

B. Source of Constitutional Injury

The parties dispute whether Plaintiff's claims should proceed on the basis of the Fourth Amendment only or also under the Fourteenth Amendment. Plaintiff's complaint clearly alleges that Defendant Richardson used improper physical force against Plaintiff during the altercation in front of the nightclub.

In *Mercado v. City of Orlando,* 407 F.3d 1152 (11th Cir.2005), the Eleventh Circuit addressed whether the Fourteenth Amendment covered a plaintiff's allegation of excessive force. There, the plaintiff and his wife became involved in an argument when she told him she wanted to end their marriage and return to Puerto Rico.

The plaintiff threatened suicide and even wrapped a telephone cord around his neck and attached the other end to a ceiling vent. He used a kitchen knife to make cuts on his arm.

The wife called the City of Orlando Police Department and reported the attempted suicide. Officers arrived at and entered the apartment. The plaintiff would not respond to the officers' requests to drop the knife and eventually the officers fired a Sage SL6 Launcher at the plaintiff in an attempt to subdue him. The Sage Launcher device has the force of a professionally-thrown baseball and is a device designed to protect persons from self-inflicted injury. Although the officer aimed at the plaintiff's shoulder, the launcher hit the plaintiff in the head, fracturing his skill and resulting in brain injuries. The plaintiff sued the officers *inter alia* under the Fourth and Fourteenth Amendments. The Eleventh Circuit analyzed the plaintiff's claims under the Fourth Amendment. Under these circumstances which the court agreed did not involve a "criminal arrest," the court stated that Plaintiff's "alternative" Fourteenth Amendment argument

> is without merit because there is no question that [plaintiff] was in custody at the time of the seizure. A suspect is in custody whenever an officer "restrains the freedom of a person to walk away, he has seized that person." *Tennessee v. Garner,* 471 U.S. 1, 7, 105 S.Ct. 1694, 85 L.Ed.2d 1 (1985) (citing *United States v. Brignoni-Ponce,* 422 U.S. 873, 95 S.Ct. 2574, 45 L.Ed.2d 607 (1975)). Because the police surrounded [plaintiff] and there was no way for him to escape, he was "seized" for the purposes of the Fourth Amendment. Even if [plaintiff] was not seized at the point when he was surrounded by police, he was seized at the time he was struck by the projectile from the Sage Launcher. *See Carr v. Tatangelo,* 338 F.3d 1259, 1268 (11th Cir.2003).

Id. at 1154 n. 1.

In *Carr,* 338 F.3d 1259 (11th Cir.2003), the plaintiffs also had an altercation with the police. One plaintiff was shot by an officer and the other was on the scene but not injured. The Eleventh Circuit held that the claims of the plaintiff who was shot were covered by the Fourth Amendment, but the Fourteenth Amendment substantive due process analysis applied to the other plaintiff "because he was not impacted physically in the shooting." *Id.* at 1267 & n. 15.

The court quoted *Graham v. Connor,* 490 U.S. 386, 395, 109 S.Ct. 1865, 104 L.Ed.2d 443 (1989), for the proposition that

> *all* claims that law enforcement officers have used excessive force—deadly or not—in the course of an arrest, investigatory stop, or other 'seizure' of a free citizen should be analyzed under the Fourth Amendment and its 'reasonableness' standard, rather than a 'substantive due process' approach. Because the Fourth Amendment provides an explicit textual source of constitutional protection against this sort of physically intrusive governmental conduct, that Amendment, not the more generalized notion of 'substantive due process,' must be the guide for analyzing these claims.

Id. (noting also that *Graham* court found "seizure" occurs when government actors through physical force or show of authority have restrained the liberty of a citizen);

see also Wilson v. Northcutt, 987 F.2d 719, 722 (11th Cir.1993) ("a non-seizure Fourteenth Amendment substantive due process claim of excessive force survives *Graham*"). The court also noted that an intentional seizure "readily bears the meaning of a laying on of hands or application of physical force to restrain movement, even when it is ultimately unsuccessful." *Id.* (quoting *California v. Hodari D.,* 499 U.S. 621, 626, 111 S.Ct. 1547, 113 L.Ed.2d 690 (1991)).

Because Plaintiff's complaint contains allegations that Defendant Richardson used excessive physical force on him, the court concludes Plaintiff was "seized" and his federal constitutional claim arises under the Fourth Amendment and not the Fourteenth Amendment.[1]

C. Section 1983 Claims Against City of Atlanta

In *Monell v. Department of Social Services,* 436 U.S. 658, 98 S.Ct. 2018, 56 L.Ed.2d 611 (1978), the Supreme Court held that municipalities (and other local government entities) are "persons" within the meaning of 42 U.S.C. § 1983. The Court, however, consistently has declined to hold municipalities liable under a theory of respondeat superior. *See, e.g., Pembaur v. Cincinnati,* 475 U.S. 469, 479, 106 S.Ct. 1292, 89 L.Ed.2d 452 (1986). Rather, a plaintiff must demonstrate a municipal "policy" or "custom" that caused the plaintiff's injury in order to establish a municipality's liability. *See, e.g., Canton v. Harris,* 489 U.S. 378, 389, 109 S.Ct. 1197, 103 L.Ed.2d 412 (1989). The plaintiff must also show that "through its deliberate conduct, the municipality was the 'moving force' behind the injury alleged." *Board of Comm'rs v. Brown,* 520 U.S. 397, 404, 117 S.Ct. 1382, 137 L.Ed.2d 626 (1997) (emphasis in original). To impose liability on the City of Atlanta for failing to act to preserve a constitutional right under section 1983, Plaintiff must show (1) that his constitutional rights were violated; (2) that the City of Atlanta had a policy or custom that constituted a deliberate indifference to his constitutional rights; and (3) that the violations were caused by the policy or custom. *See Canton,* 489 U.S. at 388, 109 S.Ct. 1197.

There is no heightened pleading requirement with respect to municipal defendants in § 1983 litigation. *See Leatherman v. Tarrant County Narcotics Intelligence & Coordination Unit,* 507 U.S. 163, 113 S.Ct. 1160, 122 L.Ed.2d 517 (1993). Even under *Bell Atlantic Corp. v. Twombly,* 550 U.S. 544, 127 S.Ct. 1955, 167 L.Ed.2d

---

1 Plaintiff's citation to *United States v. Lanier,* 520 U.S. 259, 272 n. 7, 117 S.Ct. 1219, 137 L.Ed.2d 432 (1997), is unavailing. *Lanier* states that not all physically abusive claims arise under the Fourth or Eighth Amendments but that *Graham* holds only if a constitutional claim is covered by either the Fourth or Eighth Amendment, the claim must be analyzed under the standard of that particular provision and not under the broader standards of substantive due process. As the court explained above, *Graham* clearly holds that under the circumstances described by Plaintiff in his complaint, his excessive force claims are covered by the Fourth Amendment and, therefore, *Lanier* instructs it would be improper to proceed to a Fourteenth Amendment analysis.

929 (2007), a complaint must only contain "enough facts to state a claim to relief that is plausible on its face." *Id.* at 1964.

Here, Plaintiff has alleged:

> that the violation of his constitutional rights were [*sic*] caused by implementation of a custom, policy, or official act of Defendant City of Atlanta including but not limited to: a police department custom or policy of tolerance of physical mistreatment of Spanish-speaking immigrants; failure to properly screen applicants for the position of police officer with the City of Atlanta; failure to supervise police officers; failure to train police officers in dealing with minors and Spanish-speaking immigrants; failure to investigate allegations of misconduct similar to that alleged in this Complaint; failure to discipline police officers who engage in conduct similar to that alleged in this complaint.

Id., ¶¶ 150, 161. These allegations meet the elements of municipal liability set forth in *Canton;* that is, Plaintiff suffered constitutional injury, the City had deficient policies, and those policies were the cause of Plaintiff's injuries. Therefore, the court cannot dismiss Plaintiff's municipal liability claims against the City of Atlanta at this stage in the litigation. *Grech v. Clayton County,* 335 F.3d 1326 (11th Cir.2003), cited by Defendant Atlanta, was before the court on a motion for summary judgment, and therefore, does not apply to pleading requirements at the motion to dismiss stage. The court denies Defendant City of Atlanta's motion to dismiss § 1983 claims.

D. Violations of International Law

Plaintiff's claims under international law raise a host of complicated issues that neither party has fully explored in their short briefs. The first issue—and one that has not been explored at any length in case law—is the extent to which a domestic actor, such as a police officer or city government, can be held liable under the Alien Tort Statute. The second issue is whether the facts as alleged by Plaintiff rise to the level of a violation of "the law of nations."

Briefly stated, the Alien Tort Statute, codified at 28 U.S.C. § 1350 (formally known as the Alien Torts Claims Act), states: "The district courts shall have original jurisdiction of any civil action by an alien for a tort only, committed in violation of the law of nations or a treaty of the United States." The Alien Tort Statute was enacted as part of the Judiciary Act of 1789 and went largely unnoticed for 200 years, until the Second Circuit held in *Filartiga v. Pena-Irala,* 630 F.2d 876 (2d Cir.1980), that deliberate torture under the color of authority violated human rights law and that such a violation of human rights law could constitute a violation of domestic law arising under § 1350.

Notably, the Alien Tort Statute fails to describe the potential group of defendants. A related statute, the Torture Victim Protection Act, passed in 1991, does describe the potential group of defendants. That statute, appended as a statutory note to the Alien Tort Statute at 28 U.S.C. § 1350, creates a cause of action for damages against "[a]n individual who, under actual or apparent authority, or color of law, of *any foreign nation* . . . subjects an individual to torture." *Id.*, § 1350 note (a)(1) (emphasis added); *see also Aldana v. Del Monte Fresh Produce, N.A., Inc.*, 416 F.3d 1242, 1246–47 (11th Cir.2005). Plaintiff, here, however, specifically disavows any claim under the Torture Victim Protection Act, and such a claim would not be viable as Defendants are not acting under the color of law of any foreign nation. The court's analysis, therefore, focuses on the Alien Tort Statute.

The court finds it telling that of the significant amount of litigation conducted pursuant to § 1350 since the Second Circuit's opinion in *Filartiga,* there is no reported case that directly discusses whether domestic actors can be held liable under the Alien Tort Statute. Rather, the cases primarily focus on (1) whether the Alien Tort Statute is more than simply jurisdiction granting, (2) what torts are actionable under the Alien Tort Statute, (3) whether foreign individuals can be sued under the Alien Tort Statute in U.S. Courts, and (4) whether and how U.S. corporations operating in foreign countries can be held liable under the statute for acts committed by foreign governments or agents of foreign governments when the corporation is allegedly acting in some manner in concert with the governments.

The very few cases brought against domestic U.S. actors go straight to a sovereign immunity or merits analysis without considering whether a cause of action against a domestic actor can—or should— be brought under the Alien Tort Statute. For example, in *Mora v. New York,* 524 F.3d 183 (2d Cir.2008), the plaintiff foreign national filed a civil rights action against officials of the State of New York alleging a violation of Article 36 of the Vienna Convention on Consular Relations because those officials did not notify the plaintiff that he could contact his consulate after he was arrested in New York and that such failure to notify violated customary international law such that it constituted a tort of unlawful detention under the Alien Tort Statute. The court ultimately determined that the plaintiff's allegations were not sufficient to amount to a tort in violation of customary international law. *Id.* at 208; *see also Koohi v. United States,* 976 F.2d 1328, 1332 n. 4 (9th Cir.1992) (noting that Alien Tort Statute does not constitute a waiver of sovereign immunity); *Goldstar (Panama) S.A. v. United States,* 967 F.2d 965, 968 (4th Cir.1992) ("[A]ny party asserting jurisdiction under the Alien Tort Statute must establish, independent of that statute, that the United States has consented to suit"); *Sanchez-Espinoza v. Reagan,* 770 F.2d 202, 207 (D.C.Cir.1985) (same); *Canadian Transp. Co. v. United States,* 663 F.2d 1081, 1092 (D.C.Cir.1980) (same); *El-Shifa Pharmaceutical Indus. Co. v. United States,* 402 F.Supp.2d 267 (D.D.C.2005) (same and Administrative Procedures Act does not waive sovereign immunity); *Jama v. United States Immigration & Naturalization Service,* 22 F.Supp.2d 353 (D.N.J.1998) (same).

While there is nothing in the language of the Alien Tort Statute that precludes its use against domestic U.S. actors, there are obvious reasons why allowing domestic actors to be held liable under the Alien Tort Statute would result in a significant change to the legal landscape. If courts were to recognize the applicability of § 1350 to domestic situations, then every encounter of an alien with a police officer will become not just a "federal case," but an "international case." This would require federal courts to not only determine whether a plaintiff's cause of action against police officers, to take one example, states a federal constitutional claim— a complicated exercise in itself— but also whether the actions state a claim under international law.[2]

The Supreme Court, in part, recognized this danger in *Sosa v. Alvarez-Machain,* 542 U.S. 692, 124 S.Ct. 2739, 159 L.Ed.2d 718 (2004). There, the plaintiff, Alvarez, a Mexican national, alleged that he was abducted in Mexico by U.S. Drug Enforcement Agents and transported to the United States to face murder charges. After being acquitted on those charges, Alvarez filed suit pursuant to the Alien Tort Statute and the Federal Tort Claims Act, against the United States, the agents, Mexican policemen, and Mexican civilians, alleging that the defendants violated his civil rights. The Court considered whether Alvarez's claim of arbitrary detention fit within the "torts" contemplated by the Alien Tort Statute. The Court stated:

> Alvarez thus invokes a general prohibition of "arbitrary" detention defined as officially sanctioned action exceeding positive authorization to detain under the domestic law of some government, regardless of the circumstances. Whether or not this is an accurate reading of the Covenant, Alvarez cites little authority that a rule so broad has the status of a binding customary norm today. He certainly cites nothing to justify the federal courts in taking his broad rule as the predicate for a federal lawsuit, for its implications would be breathtaking. His rule would support a cause of action in federal court for any arrest, anywhere in the world, unauthorized by the law of the jurisdiction in which it took place, and would create a cause of action for any seizure of an alien in violation of the Fourth Amendment, supplanting the actions under Rev. Stat. § 1979, 42 U.S.C. § 1983, and *Bivens v. Six Unknown Fed. Narcotics Agents,* 403 U.S. 388, 91 S.Ct. 1999, 29 L.Ed.2d 619 (1971), that now provide damages for such violations. It would create an action in federal court for arrests by state officers who simply exceeded their authority; and for the violation of any limit that the law of any country might place on the authority of its own officers to arrest. And all of this assumes that Alvarez could establish that Sosa was acting on behalf of a government when he made the arrest, for otherwise he would need a rule broader still.

Id. at 736–37, 124 S.Ct. 2739. Not only does this passage demonstrate a concern for overreaching under the Alien Tort Statute, but it also speaks directly to the court's concern about whether the law should reach to the Alien Tort Statute when Plaintiff's claims here are clearly cognizable under the Fourth Amendment. It is

---

2 The intersection of customary international law with domestic law is complicated and highly debated. The Supreme Court's opinion in *Sosa v. Alvarez-Machain,* 542 U.S. 692, 124 S.Ct. 2739, 159 L.Ed.2d 718 (2004), provides some insight into this debate, as does a series of law review articles. *See, e.g.,* Harold Hongju Koh, *Is International Law Really State Law?,* 111 HARV. L. REV. 1824 (1998), and Curtis A. Bradley & Jack L. Goldsmith, *Customary International Law as Federal Common Law: A Critique of the Modern Position,* 110 HARV. L. REV. 815 (1997).

not to ignore the serious nature of Plaintiff's claims to state that they are not a matter of "international law" when they are clearly covered by federal constitutional law. *See also Romero v. Drummond Co.,* 552 F.3d 1303 (11th Cir.2008) (under "the Alien Tort Statute, state actors are the main objects of the law of nations, but individuals may be liable, under the law of nations, for some conduct, such as war crimes, regardless of whether they acted under the color of law of a foreign nation," and thus implying involvement of a foreign nation is generally expected under Alien Tort Statute).

In sum, the court finds that Defendants Richardson and City of Atlanta are not appropriate defendants under the Alien Tort Statute with respect to injuries resulting from an allegedly constitutionally deficient interaction between the alien and a police officer.

In the alternative, the court considers whether Plaintiff's allegations are sufficient to state a cause of action under § 1350. To state a claim under the Alien Tort Statute, a plaintiff must (1) be an alien, (2) suing for a tort, which was (3) committed in violation of international law. *See Aldana v. Del Monte Fresh Produce, N.A., Inc.,* 416 F.3d 1242, 1246 (11th Cir. 2005). In his complaint, Plaintiff alleges three torts under the "law of nations": (1) torture, (2) cruel, inhuman, and degrading treatment or punishment, and (3) arbitrary detention. In its motion to dismiss, the City of Atlanta contends that the facts as alleged in Plaintiff's complaint fail to raise a claim under international law. Plaintiff points to no specific source of international norms in response to Defendant's motion to dismiss, but rather simply argues that § 1350 is jurisdictional and permits Plaintiff to raise *jus cogens* claims under international law.

In *Sosa,* the Supreme Court explained that although the Alien Tort Act is jurisdictional in nature, it also provides a cause of action "for the modest number of international law violations with a potential for personal liability at the time [of its enactment]." *Sosa,* 542 U.S. at 724, 124 S.Ct. 2739.[3] The Court, however, warned that federal courts should exercise "great caution" when considering new causes of action and maintain "vigilant doorkeeping . . . thus [opening the door] to a narrow class of international norms [recognized] today." *Id.* at 728–29, 124 S.Ct. 2739. The Court explained that the "collateral consequences of making international rules privately actionable argue for judicial caution" and that to provide a cause of action under the Alien Tort Statute, a tort under customary international law must meet a "high bar" for recognizing new causes of action in that it must be both specific and well-accepted. (*Id.* at 715, 720, 725, 124 S.Ct. 2739 (holding that alleged tort must be "defined with a specificity comparable to the features of the

3 This statement is a bit of an oversimplification. *Sosa* discusses this issue at great length. While the Court held that § 1350 is jurisdictional, it also concluded that the "jurisdictional" statute brings along with it the ability to raise a narrow range of claims under international law similar to those that existed at the time of enactment of the statute.

18th-century paradigms" of torts in violation of the law of nations—such as violations of safe conduct, offenses against ambassadors, and piracy and that these examples involve torts "principally incident to whole states or nations and not individuals seeking relief in courts")). *Sosa* also instructs that whether to find a tort actionable under the Alien Tort Statute "involve[s] an element of judgment about the practical consequences of making that cause available to litigants in the federal courts." *Id.* at 732–33, 124 S.Ct. 2739.[4]

The Eleventh Circuit applied *Sosa* in *Aldana v. Del Monte Fresh Produce, N.A., Inc.,* 416 F.3d 1242, 1246–47 (11th Cir. 2005), where Guatemalan labor unionists sued the U.S. corporate owner of a Guatemalan banana plantation alleging the owner participated in torture and other human rights violations against the unionists. The court specifically rejected the notion that "cruel, inhuman, degrading treatment or punishment" could be a violation under the Alien Tort Act. *See* 416 F.3d at 1247. The court explained that this violation arose out of the International Covenant on Civil and Political Rights, but that *Sosa* holds that the Covenant did not "create obligations enforceable in the federal courts." *Id.* The *Aldana* court also rejected the idea that the plaintiff could raise a claim for "arbitrary detention," finding that under *Sosa,* "a single illegal detention of less than a day . . . violates no norm of customary international law so well defined as to support the creation of a federal remedy." *Id.*

Aldana would seem to provide sufficient precedential basis for a conclusion that Plaintiff's cruel, inhuman, degrading treatment or punishment and arbitrary detention claims are not sufficient to establish a violation of a norm of customary international law. Plaintiff, however, claims that international law protection under these two notions is broader for minors, which he was at the time of his interaction with Officer Richardson. Without citation in his complaint, and without any additional briefing in response to Defendant's motion to dismiss, Plaintiff claims that international law protections are broader for minors than adults. Therefore, despite the fact that *Sosa* and *Aldana* rejected claims of arbitrary detention and cruel, inhuman, degrading treatment or punishment under the Alien Tort Statute, Plaintiff argues the protections are still available for minors.

The court can locate no specific support for this contention with respect to these two potential violations of the law of nations. Further, the Supreme Court has noted in general that the United States has not ratified the United Nations Convention on the Rights of the Child, which might arguably give broader human rights protection to minors. *See Roper v. Simmons,* 543 U.S. 551, 576, 125 S. Ct. 1183, 161 L.Ed.2d 1 (2005). *Sosa* holds that violations of the laws of nations brought under § 1350 must be specific and well-accepted. *See* 542 U.S. at 715,

---

4 Although it did not so hold, the Supreme Court also suggested in *Sosa* that exhaustion might be a requirement before bringing a claim under the Alien Tort Statute. *See* 542 U.S. at 733 n. 21, 124 S.Ct. 2739 (citing to brief of amicus European Commission).

720, 725, 124 S.Ct. 2739. Plaintiff has not demonstrated that his claims of arbitrary detention of a minor and cruel, inhuman, degrading treatment or punishment of a minor meet this high bar.

In contrast, the *Aldana* court did recognize that "state-sponsored torture" "likely violates international law and is therefore actionable under the Alien Tort Act." *Aldana,* 416 F.3d at 1247–48. In construing the state action requirement, the court should look "to the principles of agency law and to jurisprudence under 42 U.S.C. § 1983." *Id.* (citing *Kadic v. Karadzic,* 70 F.3d 232, 245 (2d Cir.1995)). Further, state-sponsored torture under the Alien Tort Act "may be based on indirect liability as well as direct liability." *Id.* The court, however, concluded that the plaintiffs had not sufficiently plead that the torture was "state sponsored" because they only alleged that Guatemala had registered and tolerated the private security forces accused of harming plaintiffs. *Id.* at 1248. Further, "police inaction" in response to events not occurring within their plain sight was not sufficient to establish state action. *Id.* The court did find, however, that the plaintiffs sufficiently pled a claim against the Mayor of Morales District because he was alleged to be an "armed aggressor" and not merely an observer. *Id.* at 1249. The mayor's involvement could be sufficient to establish state action. *Id.*

Aldana then went on to define "torture" under "international law" such that it could be raised via § 1350. The court referred to the Convention Against Torture and Other Cruel, Inhuman or Degrading Treatment or Punishment which defines torture as

> any act by which severe pain or suffering, whether physical or mental, is intentionally inflicted on a person for such purposes as obtaining from him or a third person information or a confession, punishing him for an act he or a third person has committed or is suspected of having committed, or intimidating or coercing him or a third person, or for any reason based on discrimination of any kind, when such pain or suffering is inflicted by or at the instigation of or with the consent or acquiescence of a public official or other person acting in an official capacity. It does not include pain or suffering arising only from, inherent in or incidental to lawful sanctions.

Id. at 1251. The plaintiffs in *Aldana* alleged that they were captured by the security force and were threatened with imminent death because of their work with the labor union. Several were filmed with a video camera and told to give their "last messages." They were also told that a member of the security forces wanted to take a "clear photo" of their faces before he killed them. Numerous other threats were made to the plaintiffs by heavily armed members of the security forces. The plaintiffs alleged they continued to suffer from extreme and severe mental anguish and emotional distress. Based on these allegations, the court denied Defendants' motion to dismiss for failure to state a claim of torture.

The Eleventh Circuit has not undertaken a more exhaustive consideration of what constitutes "torture" for the purposes of the Alien Tort Statute. Other circuits considering the Torture Victim Protection Act, which also draws its definition of torture from the Convention on Torture, note that "only acts of a certain gravity shall be considered to constitute torture." *See Price v. Socialist People's Libyan Arab Jamahiriya,* 294 F.3d 82, 92 (D.C.Cir. 2002) (holding that "severity requirement" of statute is "crucial to ensuring that the conduct proscribed by the Convention and the [Torture Victim Protection Act] is sufficiently extreme and outrageous to warrant the universal condemnation that the term 'torture' both connotes and invokes"). The *Price* court further noted that the

> critical issue is the degree of pain and suffering that the alleged torturer intended to, and actually did, inflict upon the victim. The more intense, lasting, or heinous the agony, the more likely it is to be torture. *See* S. Exec. Rep. No. 101-30, at 15 ("The United States understands that, in order to constitute torture, an act must be a deliberate and calculated act of an extremely cruel and inhuman nature, specifically intended to inflict excruciating and agonizing physical or mental pain or suffering.") (internal quotation marks omitted). *This understanding thus makes clear that torture does not automatically result whenever individuals in official custody are subjected even to direct physical assault. Not all police brutality, not every instance of excessive force used against prisoners, is torture under the [Foreign Sovereign Immunities Act applying Convention Against Torture].*

Id. at 93 (emphasis added) (dismissing torture claim even where complaint alleged "kicking, clubbing, and beatings" because no way to determine severity from those statements alone). Other cases note that "torture is a label that is usually reserved for extreme, deliberate and unusually cruel practices, for example, sustained systematic beating, application of electric currents to sensitive parts of the body, and tying up or hanging in positions that cause extreme pain." *See Simpson v. Socialist People's Libyan Arab Jamahiriya,* 326 F.3d 230, 234 (D.C.Cir.2003) (allegations that Libyan authorities forcibly removed victims from cruise ship, held them captive for months, threatened them with death, held them incommunicado from one another, while "reflecting a bent toward cruelty," were not sufficient to satisfy high bar of "torture"). *Compare Abebe-Jira v. Negewo,* 72 F.3d 844, 845 (11th Cir.1996) (detaining victim, forcing her to undress, binding her legs and arms, and whipping her on legs and back with wire and threatening her with death constituted torture); *Kiobel v. Royal Dutch Petroleum Co.,* 456 F.Supp.2d 457 (S.D.N.Y.2006) (plaintiffs stated claim for torture where they alleged they were shot, raped, beaten with various instruments, stripped of their clothing, tied up, forced to lie for hours in tropical sun, sprayed with chemicals and denied adequate food, medical care, and sanitary facilities).

Based on this review of case law, the court concludes that Plaintiff's allegations here are not sufficient to constitute "torture" under the Alien Tort Statute. Again, this is not to state that Plaintiff's allegations are not serious and as alleged are sufficient get beyond the motion to dismiss stage under the Fourth Amendment, but, rather, states only that they are not sufficient to state a claim of "torture" under the law of nations. Therefore, the court grants Defendant's motion to dismiss Plaintiff's "law of nations" claims.

In sum, Plaintiff's official capacity claims against Defendant Richardson are dismissed. Plaintiff's state law claims against Defendant City of Atlanta are barred under sovereign immunity. Plaintiff's complaint sufficiently pleads § 1983 liability against the City of Atlanta. Plaintiff's federal constitutional claims under § 1983 against both Defendants City of Atlanta and Defendant Richardson arise only under the Fourth Amendment and not the Fourteenth. Plaintiff's complaint fails to state a cause of action for torture; arbitrary detention; or cruel, inhuman or degrading treatment, and thus, his "law of nations" claims are dismissed.

III. Conclusion

The court GRANTS IN PART AND DENIES IN PART Defendant City of Atlanta's motion to dismiss [4].

I. INTERNATIONAL LAW IN GENERAL

4. The Foreign Commerce Clause

UNITED STATES
v.
JULIO ADRIAN MARTINEZ

599 F. Supp. 2d 784 (W.D. Tex. 2009)
Decided February 27, 2009

J. Brandy Gardes, Assistant U.S. Attorney, El Paso, TX, for Plaintiff.

Tyrone Thelonious Mansfield, Federal Public Defender's Office, El Paso, TX, for Defendant.

ORDER

KATHLEEN CARDONE, District Judge.

On this day, the Court considered "Defendant's Motions for Dismissal and for Bill of Particulars" ("Defendant's Motion") (Doc. No. 23) and "Government's Response to Defendant's Motion to Dismiss Indictment and for Bill of Particulars" ("Government's Response") (Doc. No. 26). For the reasons set forth herein, Defendant's Motion is DENIED.

I. Background

The following facts are alleged in the Probable Cause Statement appended to the Criminal Complaint. (Doc. No. 1). On September 23, 2008, deputies from the El Paso County Sheriff's Office ("EPCSO") responded to a kidnapping complaint in Vinton, Texas, in the Western District of Texas. When the deputies arrived at the scene, they interviewed Maria Villalobos ("Villalobos"), who stated that her minor cousin ("JC"), had been staying with her while JC's mother was at work.[1] Just after 6 p.m. on that day, a vehicle arrived at Villalobos's residence. Villalobos told JC to see who it was. A few minutes later, Villalobos looked out the window and saw Defendant forcing JC into a brown Kia Sephia. Villalobos stated that it seemed to her that JC was attempting to get away, but Defendant pushed JC into the vehicle with his body. Once JC was in the car, the vehicle drove off.

EPCSO deputies also interviewed Lucy Guillen ("Guillen"), JC's mother. Guillen stated that on September 23, 2008, she had taken her other daughter to the hospital

1 JC was fifteen years old at the time of the Complaint.

emergency room and had left JC with Villalobos. Just after 7 p.m., when Guillen arrived at Villalobos's house to pick up JC, Villalobos informed Guillen that Defendant had taken JC. Guillen stated that JC had been dating Defendant for three months. Guillen also stated that she feared for her life and her family's lives because of everything that had happened. Guillen filed kidnapping charges on behalf of JC.

On September 24, 2008, EPCSO issued an AMBER Alert[2] for suspected kidnap victim JC and Defendant in a brown Kia Sephia.[3] Later that same day, JC was recovered while crossing from Juarez, Mexico, to the United States.

In a subsequent interview, JC stated that she was eating outside the Villalobos residence on September 23, when she saw Defendant pull up in the brown Kia Sephia and park in front of the residence. Defendant then got out of the car, grabbed her by her arm and pushed her into the vehicle. JC stated she tried to fight back, but Defendant hugged her from behind and forced her into the backseat of the car, tearing her shirt in the process. Defendant then jumped in after JC and told the driver to go.

As the car drove off, Defendant asked JC why she did not want to be with him. She stated that he was just a friend, and Defendant got angry. The car then dropped her and Defendant off in the downtown area, where they were picked up by another driver in a different vehicle. They then drove around in the area of Defendant's aunt's house, but never stopped because Defendant thought he saw police in the area.

After an hour, JC and Defendant were dropped off near a bridge from El Paso, Texas to Juarez, Mexico. Defendant then grabbed JC's arm and led her across the bridge into Juarez. Once in Juarez, Defendant took JC in a taxi cab to a house that Defendant was able to unlock with a key. Defendant told JC that the house belonged to his aunt and that she was not home. Once inside, JC laid down on the couch and Defendant sat down beside her. Defendant started to touch JC's leg, but she told him to get away. Initially, Defendant stopped, but after a few minutes he came back and got on top of JC. Defendant pulled JC's pants down while he held JC hands above her head. Defendant then raped JC. JC struggled to push Defendant

---

2 The term "AMBER" means "America's Missing: Broadcast Emergency Response." An AMBER Alert is

> a voluntary partnership between law-enforcement agencies, broadcasters, transportation agencies, and the wireless industry, to activate an urgent bulletin in the most serious child-abduction cases. The goal of an AMBER Alert is to instantly galvanize the entire community to assist in the search for and the safe recovery of the child.

See U.S. Department of Justice: Office of Justice Programs, AMBER Alert: America's Missing Broadcast Emergency Response, *available at http://www.amberalert.gov/* (last visited Feb. 18, 2009).

3 Defendant is 20 years old.

off and repeatedly told Defendant to get off of her. JC continued to struggle and Defendant stopped a few minutes later.

The next day, September 24, 2008, at approximately 9 a.m., JC and Defendant were watching television and saw the ABER Alert that had been issued for JC. JC suggested that Defendant let her go, but Defendant said that things could not get any worse. Defendant also stated that he believed that no one could find them in Juarez. Later that morning, Defendant received a telephone call regarding a work opportunity. Defendant told JC that he would be back in half an hour and that JC should not do anything stupid. Defendant then locked the door and left.

Once Defendant had left, JC found an open window and climbed out of the house. JC then made her way towards the border by following road signs. When she arrived at the border, JC begged for the money needed to pay the toll and cross over the bridge. Once JC had received enough money, she crossed back into the United States and informed Customs and Border Protection that she was the female in the AMBER Alert.

On October 8, 2008, a bench warrant was issued for Defendant, pursuant to a Criminal Complaint filed on that same day. (Docs. No. 1, 4). The Criminal Complaint charged Defendant with knowingly transporting a minor in foreign commerce with the intent to engage in illicit sexual conduct, in violation of Title 18, United States Code § 2423(a). Compl. 1. On November 25, 2008, Defendant was arrested and held without bond.

On December 10, 2009, a Grand Jury sitting in the Western District of Texas returned a seven-count Indictment against Defendant, charging Defendant with:

> Count 1: Transportation of a minor with intent to engage in criminal sexual activity, in violation of 18 U.S.C. § 2423(a).
>
> Count 2: Travel with intent to engage in illicit sexual conduct, in violation of 18 U.S.C § 2423(b).
>
> Count 3: Engaging in illicit sexual conduct in foreign places, in violation of 18 U.S.C. § 2423(c).
>
> Count 4: Coercion and enticement, in violation of 18 U.S.C. § 2422(a)
>
> Count 5: Coercion and enticement, in violation of 18 U.S.C. § 2422(c)
>
> Count 6: Transportation, in violation of 18 U.S.C. § 2421.
>
> Count 7: Kidnapping, in violation of 18 U.S.C. § 1201(a).

Indictment 1-4.

On January 14, 2009, Defendant filed the instant Motion. In his Motion, Defendant argues that the charges in the Indictment are multiplicitous, and that the Government should be compelled to elect the Counts it chooses to prosecute and to dismiss the others. Def.'s Mot. 2-6. Defendant also argues that the Court lacks jurisdiction over Defendant's underlying alleged illicit sex acts in Counts 1, 2, and 3, because such actions took place in Mexico, and applying the laws in these Counts to Defendant violates principles of international law. *Id.* at 8–16. Defendant also argues that Count 3 must be dismissed because 18 U.S.C. § 2423(c) violates the Commerce Clause of the United States Constitution. *Id.* at 16–18. Defendant also requests the Court to order the Government to produce the minutes of the Grand Jury proceedings and to file a bill of particulars. *Id.* at 7–8; 18–22.

On January 27, 2009, the Government filed its Response to Defendant's Motion.

II. Standard

Federal Rule of Criminal Procedure 12(b)(2) states that "[a] party may raise by pretrial motion any defense, objection, or request that the court can determine without a trial of the general issue." FED. R.CRIM.P. 12(b)(2); *United States v. Lankford,* 196 F.3d 563, 569 (5th Cir.1999). A party must raise before trial "a motion [that] alleged a defect in the indictment or information—but at any time while the case is pending, the court may hear a claim that the indictment or information fails to invoke the court's jurisdiction or to state an offense[.]" FED.R.CRIM.P. 12(b)(3).

When challenging the constitutionality of a statute, a defendant may challenge the statute either on its face, or as the statute is applied to a defendant's particular circumstances. *See United States v. Luna,* 165 F.3d 316, 319–22 (5th Cir.1999) (analyzing the constitutionality of 18 U.S.C. § 922 both facially and as applied); *United States v. Robinson,* 119 F.3d 1205, 1213–15 (5th Cir.1997) (holding the Hobbs Act to be constitutional both facially and as applied to the defendant). Outside of the First Amendment context, a plaintiff may only succeed in a facial challenge to the constitutionality of a statute by "establishing that no set of circumstances exists under which the Act would be valid."[4] *Washington State Grange v. Washington State Republican Party,* ___ U.S. ___, 128 S. Ct. 1184, 1190 & n. 6,

---

4 *See also United States v. Salerno,* 481 U.S. 739, 745, 107 S. Ct. 2095, 95 L.Ed.2d 697 (1987) ("A facial challenge to a legislative Act is, of course, the most difficult challenge to mount successfully, since the challenger must establish *that no set of circumstances exists* under which the Act would be valid.") (emphasis added). This Court notes, however, that there is an ongoing disagreement among the justices of the United States Supreme Court regarding the validity of the *Salerno* standard to determine the facial validity of a legislative act. *See Washington State Grange v. Washington State Republican Party,* ___ U.S. ___, 128 S. Ct. 1184, 1190 & n. 6, 170 L.Ed.2d 151 (2008) (citing *Washington v. Glucksberg,* 521 U.S. 702, 739–40 & n. 7, 117 S. Ct. 2258, 138 L.Ed.2d 772 (1997)). In fact, several of the justices have called into question the validity of this portion of the *Salerno* opinion. *Glucksberg,* 521 U.S. at 739–740, & n. 7, 117 S. Ct. 2258 (Stevens, J., concurring in judgments) (citing inter alia Michael C. Dorf, *Facial Challenges to State and Federal Statutes,* 46 STAN. L.REV. 235, 239–240 (1994)).

The uncertainty surrounding the authority of the *Salerno* holding is significant. *Chicago v. Morales,* 527 U.S. 41, 55 n. 22, 119 S. Ct. 1849, 144 L.Ed.2d 67 (1999) (plurality opinion) (Stevens, J., Souter, J., and Ginsburg, J.) ("To the extent we have consistently articulated a clear standard for facial challenges, it is not the *Salerno* formulation, which has never been the decisive factor in any decision of this Court. . . .").

170 L.Ed.2d 151 (2008) (citing *United States v. Salerno,* 481 U.S. 739, 745, 107 S. Ct. 2095, 95 L.Ed.2d 697 (1987)); *Center for Individual Freedom v. Carmouche,* 449 F.3d 655, 662 (5th Cir.2006).

III. Discussion

A. Multiplicity of Counts

Defendant first argues that a number of the Counts in the Indictment are multiplicitous. Def.'s Mot. 2. Specifically, Defendant argues that several of the Counts, though charged under different statutes or statutory subsections, require proof of the same facts, and therefore expose Defendant to multiple punishments for the same act. *Id.* Defendant argues that Counts one and six are multiplicitous, and Counts four, five and seven are multiplicitous. *Id.* at 3–7. Defendant argues that the Government should be compelled to elect the Counts it chooses to prosecute and to dismiss all other Counts. *Id.* at 2.

"The rule against multiplicitous prosecutions stems from the Fifth Amendment's proscription against double jeopardy." *United States v. Planck,* 493 F.3d 501, 503 (5th Cir.2007) (citing *United States v. Kimbrough,* 69 F.3d 723, 729 (5th Cir.1995)). "The rule prevents the Government from charging a single offense in more than one count of an indictment." *Id.* (citing *United States v. Heath,* 970 F.2d 1397, 1401 (5th Cir.1992)). The rule "is intended to prevent multiple punishments for the same act." *Kimbrough,* 69 F.3d at 729 (citing, inter alia, *United States v. Brechtel,* 997 F.2d 1108, 1112 (5th Cir.), *cert. denied,* 510 U.S. 1013, 114 S. Ct. 605, 126 L.Ed.2d 570 (1993)).

While multiplicity often involves charging a defendant with multiple counts under the same statute, multiplicity may also arise when a defendant is charged with violating different statutes, but "Congress intended the same conduct to be punishable under two criminal provisions." *Kimbrough,* 69 F.3d at 730 n. 5 (citing *Blockburger v. United States,* 284 U.S. 299, 304, 52 S. Ct. 180, 76 L.Ed. 306 (1932)). In *Blockburger,* the Supreme Court held that "where the same act or transaction constitutes a violation of distinct statutory provisions, the test to be applied to determine whether there are two offenses or only one, is whether each provision requires proof of a fact which the other does not." *Blockburger,* 284 U.S. at 304,

---

Most recently, in *Washington State Grange,* Justice Thomas, writing for the majority, recognized this criticism of *Salerno. Washington State Grange,* 128 S. Ct. at 1190 & n. 6. The Court in *Washington State Grange* applied both the *Salerno* standard as well as the more deferential "plainly legitimate sweep" standard and held that the statute in question survived the facial challenge under either standard. *Id.* at 1190. Nevertheless, though there may be uncertainty surrounding the authority of the *Salerno* holding as the proper analysis for considering facial challenges to the constitutionality of a statute, the Fifth Circuit has clearly stated that the "no set of circumstances" standard applies to facial challenges outside of the First Amendment context. *Center for Individual Freedom v. Carmouche,* 449 F.3d 655, 662 (5th Cir.2006) (citing *Salerno,* 481 U.S. at 745, 107 S. Ct. 2095). Because this Court must follow Fifth Circuit precedent, the Court will apply the *Salerno* no-set-of-circumstances standard to the instant case.

52 S. Ct. 180 (citation omitted); *see also United States v. Ogba,* 526 F.3d 214, 233 (5th Cir.2008); *United States v. Buchanan,* 485 F.3d 274, 278 (5th Cir.2007). In applying this test, a court must not examine the particular facts of the case or the circumstances involved, but rather must compare the statutory elements of each offense argued to be multiplicitous. *See Lankford,* 196 F.3d at 577–78 (citing *United States v. Soape,* 169 F.3d 257, 266 (5th Cir.1999); *United States v. Singleton,* 16 F.3d 1419, 1422 (5th Cir. 1994)). The appropriate remedy for allowing a jury to return convictions on multiplicitous counts is to order the government to "dismiss[ ] the counts that create the multiplicity." *United States v. Saks,* 964 F.2d 1514, 1526 (5th Cir.1992) (quoting *United States v. Moody,* 923 F.2d 341, 347–48 (5th Cir.1991)).

However, "[w]hile the Double Jeopardy Clause may protect a single defendant against cumulative *punishments* for convictions on the same offense, the Clause does not prohibit the State from *prosecuting* [a defendant] for such multiple offenses in a single prosecution." *Ohio v. Johnson,* 467 U.S. 493, 500, 104 S. Ct. 2536, 81 L.Ed.2d 425 (1984) (emphasis added). Indeed, "a draftsman of an indictment may charge crime in a variety of forms to avoid fatal variance of the evidence. He may cast the indictment in several counts where the body of facts upon which the indictment gives rise to only one criminal offense or to more than one." *United States v. Universal C.I.T. Credit Corp.,* 344 U.S. 218, 225, 73 S. Ct. 227, 97 L.Ed. 260 (1952). The Supreme Court "has long acknowledged the Government's broad discretion to conduct criminal prosecutions, including its power to select the charges to be brought in a particular case." *Ball v. United States,* 470 U.S. 856, 859, 105 S. Ct. 1668, 84 L.Ed.2d 740 (1985). Accordingly, the Government may prosecute a defendant under separate statutes even when conviction and punishment under multiple statutes may not be appropriate. *Id.; see also United States v. Thomas,* 810 F.2d 478, 479 (5th Cir.1987).

Nevertheless, the Fifth Circuit has identified two dangers arising from a multiplicitous indictment. *United States v. Smith,* 591 F.2d 1105, 1108 (5th Cir.1979). First, "[t]he chief danger raised by a multiplicitous indictment is the possibility that the defendant will receive more than one sentence for a single offense." *Planck,* 493 F.3d at 503 (quoting *United States v. Swaim,* 757 F.2d 1530, 1537 (5th Cir. 1985)). However, this danger is only inchoate at the time of charging and does not become full-fledged until after sentencing on purportedly multiplicitous counts. Accordingly, an indictment charging multiplicitous counts does not require dismissal, and any compelled election of counts before sentencing is in a court's discretion. *Smith,* 591 F.2d at 1108.

In deciding how to exercise its discretion, the Court notes that an additional danger may arise from a multiplicitous indictment: "namely an adverse psychological effect on the jury may result from the suggestion that several crimes have been committed." *Smith,* 591 F.2d at 1108 (citing *United States v. Hearod,* 499 F.2d 1003 (5th Cir.1974)); *see also United States v. Alexander,* No. 06-60074-01, 2008 WL 4790125, at 2 (W.D.La. Oct. 31, 2008). Therefore, an election of counts may be ordered if the Defendant can show prejudice from being charged with multiplicitous counts. *Cf. United States v. Pacheco,* 489 F.2d 554, 560 (5th Cir.1974) (allowing for an election of counts under Rule 14 of the Federal Rules of Criminal Procedure when "prejudice would result from a joinder of offenses or of defendants for trial."). However, "the burden of demonstrating prejudice is a difficult one, and the ruling of a trial judge will rarely be disturbed upon review." *Id.* Defendant has made no attempt at demonstrating prejudice from being charged with multiplicitous counts. Accordingly, no prejudice from the Counts will be inferred.

The Court therefore need not reach the issue of whether the Counts charged against Defendant are multiplicitous. Any such argument is premature and will only be addressed once these matters have been brought to trial.

B. Request for the Minutes of the Grand Jury Proceedings

Included in Defendant's multiplicity argument is a request for the grand jury minutes regarding certain counts in his Indictment. Def.'s Mot. 7-8. Specifically, Defendant argues that "[i]f the Government elects to pursue . . . distinct legal theories [in Counts Four, Five, and Six], it is requested that it be ordered to produce the grand jury minutes and validate the grand jury proceedings in this case, as well as to insure Governmental compliance with grand jury referral obligations." Def.'s Mot. 8.

"Federal courts long have recognized that secrecy is essential to maintaining the integrity of the grand jury system." *In re Grand Jury Testimony,* 832 F.2d 60, 62–63 (5th Cir.1987) (citing *Douglas Oil Co. v. Petrol Stops Northwest,* 441 U.S. 211, 222, 99 S. Ct. 1667, 60 L.Ed.2d 156 (1979); *United States v. Procter & Gamble,* 356 U.S. 677, 682, 78 S. Ct. 983, 2 L.Ed.2d 1077 (1958)). However, such secrecy "is not an absolute," *id.,* and Federal Rule of Criminal Procedure 6 states, in relevant part, that "[t]he Court may authorize disclosure—at a time, in a manner, and subject to any other conditions that it directs of a grand jury matter: . . . (ii) at the request of the defendant who shows that a ground may exist to dismiss the indictment because of a matter that occurred before the grand jury[.]" Fed. R.Crim.P. 6(e)(3)(E). Moreover, "case law has established that a district court may properly order release of grand jury materials where a party demonstrates with particularity a 'compelling necessity' for the materials." *Izen v. Catalina,* 256 F.3d 324, 329–30 (5th Cir.2001) (quoting *In re Grand Jury Testimony,* 832 F.2d at 62–63 (quoting *Procter & Gamble,* 356 U.S. at 682, 78 S. Ct. 983)). Disclosure of grand jury minutes falls to the court's discretion. *Id.* at 329.

To demonstrate "compelling necessity" for grand jury materials under Rule 6(e), a party must show (1) that the material they seek is needed to avoid a possible injustice in another judicial proceeding, (2) that the need for disclosure is greater than the need for continued secrecy, and (3) that their request is structured to cover only material so needed. *In re Grand Jury Testimony,* 832 F.2d at 62 (citing *Douglas Oil Co.,* 441 U.S. at 222, 99 S. Ct. 1667).

Defendant's argument for access to grand jury proceedings arises out of his argument that the Counts in his Indictment are multiplicitous. The Court has held that any argument of multiplicity is premature and that the Defendant has failed to show any irregularity in the manner in which the Government has drafted his Indictment. Moreover, Defendant has failed to show a need pursuant to the factors outlined in *In re Grand Jury Testimony* or an otherwise "compelling necessity" for the requested materials. *See id.* Accordingly, Defendant's request for grand jury materials is denied.

C. Lack of Jurisdiction Based on International Law Principles

Defendant next argues that this Court lacks subject-matter jurisdiction over the offenses alleged in Counts One, Two, and Three, because the underlying illicit sexual activity took place in Mexico. Def.'s Mot. 8-9. Specifically, Defendant argues that the statutes which Defendant is charged with violating—18 U.S.C. §§ 2423(a)-(c)— cannot be applied extraterritorially, because to do so would violate Congressional intent, principles of international law, and would otherwise be unreasonable under international law. *Id.* at 9–16. Accordingly, Defendant argues that Counts One, Two and Three should be dismissed as a matter of law. *Id.* at 16.

Defendant is charged in Count One of the Indictment with violating 18 U.S.C. § 2423(a). Defendant is charged in Count Two with violating § 2423(b). Defendant is charged in Count Three with violating § 2423(c). 18 U.S.C. § 2423 states, in relevant part:

> (a) Transportation with intent to engage in criminal sexual activity.—A person who knowingly transports an individual who has not attained the age of 18 years in interstate or foreign commerce, or in any commonwealth, territory or possession of the United States, with intent that the individual engage in prostitution, or in any sexual activity for which any person can be charged with a criminal offense, shall be fined under this title and imprisoned not less than 10 years or for life.
>
> (b) Travel with intent to engage in illicit sexual conduct.—A person who travels in interstate commerce or travels into the United States, or a United States citizen or an alien admitted for permanent residence in the United States who travels in foreign commerce, for the purpose of engaging in any illicit sexual conduct with another person shall be fined under this title or imprisoned not more than 30 years, or both.
>
> (c) Engaging in illicit sexual conduct in foreign places.—Any United States citizen or alien admitted for permanent residence who travels in foreign commerce, and engages in any illicit sexual conduct with another person shall be fined under this title or imprisoned not more than 30 years, or both.

18 U.S.C. § 2423(a)-(c).[5]

---

5 The statute further states that "the term "illicit sexual conduct" means (1) a sexual act (as defined in section 2246) with a person under 18 years of age that would be in violation of

The Court initially notes that the Fifth Circuit has held that the criminal act required for 2423(b) is not the subsequent exploitation of a child but "the foreign travel with an illicit intent." *United States v. Bredimus,* 352 F.3d 200, 210 (5th Cir. 2003) (citing *United States v. Gamache,* 156 F.3d 1, 8 (1st Cir.1998); *United States v. Hersh,* 297 F.3d 1233, 1245–46 (11th Cir.2002)). Accordingly "the prohibited conduct [in § 2423(b)] occurred in the United States[.]" *Id.* Similarly, in the instant case, Defendant is charged in Count Two of the Indictment with travelling from the United States to Mexico with the intent to commit an illicit sexual act. Indictment 2. Accordingly, no discussion of extraterritorial jurisdiction is necessary for this Count.

The reasoning in *Bredimus* regarding § 2423(b) also appears to apply *a fortiori* to Defendant's charge under § 2423(a), given that Defendant is charged with travelling from the United States to Mexico with a similar criminal intent. *Compare Bredimus,* 352 F.3d at 210 *with* Indictment 1. The criminal act in Count One also took place in the United States, and there is no need to consider the application extra-territorial jurisdiction.

The foregoing analysis therefore applies primarily to Count Three, namely Defendant's alleged violation of § 2423(c), because the criminal act—illicit sexual conduct with a minor—allegedly took place extraterritorially. The Court notes, however, that the analysis can apply similarly to any extraterritorial elements remaining in Counts One and Two.

1. Section 2423 and Congressional intent

"Generally, there is no constitutional bar to the extraterritorial application of the United States penal laws." *United States v. Felix-Gutierrez,* 940 F.2d 1200, 1204 (9th Cir.1991) (citing *Chua Han Mow v. United States,* 730 F.2d 1308, 1311 (9th Cir.1984), *cert. denied,* 470 U.S. 1031, 105 S. Ct. 1403, 84 L.Ed.2d 790 (1985); *United States v. King,* 552 F.2d 833, 850 (9th Cir.1976), *cert. denied,* 430 U.S. 966, 97 S. Ct. 1646, 52 L.Ed.2d 357 (1977)). It is further undisputed that "the legislative authority of the United States over its citizens extends to conduct by Americans. . . even within the territory of other sovereigns." *United States v. Mitchell,* 553 F.2d 996, 1001 (5th Cir.1977) (citing *Steele v. Bulova Watch Co.,* 344 U.S. 280, 73 S. Ct. 252, 97 L.Ed. 319 (1952); *Foley Bros. v. Filardo,* 336 U.S. 281, 69 S. Ct. 575, 93 L.Ed. 680 (1949); *Vermilya-Brown Co. v. Connell,* 335 U.S. 377, 69 S. Ct. 140, 93 L.Ed. 76 (1948); *Blackmer v. United States,* 284 U.S. 421, 52 S. Ct. 252, 76 L.Ed. 375 (1932); *Cook v. Tait,* 265 U.S. 47, 44 S. Ct. 444, 68 L.Ed. 895 (1924); *United States v. Bowman,* 260 U.S. 94, 43 S. Ct. 39, 67 L.Ed. 149 (1922)). Moreover, "international law principles do not constrain this

chapter 109A if the sexual act occurred in the special maritime and territorial jurisdiction of the United States; or (2) any commercial sex act (as defined in section 1591) with a person under 18 years of age." 18 U.S.C. § 2423(f). Chapter 109A comports with 18 U.S.C. §§ 2241–49.

legislative authority, because citizenship alone is generally recognized as a relationship sufficient to justify the exercise of jurisdiction by a state." *Id.* (citations omitted). In determining whether Congress intended for a law to apply extra-territorially, the court considers two principles. *Id.* The first is whether the law itself speaks to being applied extraterritorially:

> (Some laws) are such that to limit their locus to the strictly territorial jurisdiction would be greatly to curtail the scope and usefulness of the statute and leave open a large immunity for frauds as easily committed by citizens . . . in foreign countries as at home. In such cases, Congress has not thought it necessary to make specific provision in the law that the locus shall include the . . . foreign countries, but allows it to be inferred from the nature of the offense.

Id. (quoting *Bowman,* 260 U.S. at 98, 43 S. Ct. 39); *see also United States v. Baker,* 609 F.2d 134, 136 (5th Cir.1980) ("Absent an express intention on the face of the statutes to do so, the exercise of [extraterritorial jurisdiction] may be inferred from the nature of the offenses and Congress' other legislative efforts to eliminate the type of crime involved.").

However, "if the nature of the law does not mandate its territorial application, then a presumption arises against such application." *Mitchell,* 553 F.2d at 1001 (citing *Bowman,* 260 U.S. at 98, 43 S. Ct. 39). "To overcome that presumption and to apply the statute beyond the territory of the United States, the Government must show a clear expression of congressional intent." *Id.* (citations omitted); *see also Boureslan v. Aramco,* 857 F.2d 1014, 1016 (5th Cir.1988) (recognizing a presumption against the extraterritorial application of statutes absent Congressional intent); *Chitimacha Tribe of La. v. Harry L. Laws Co.,* 690 F.2d 1157, 1168 (5th Cir.1982).

A plain reading of § 2423 demonstrates that it is designed to have extraterritorial application. First, all three operative subsections (under which Defendant is charged) refer to a defendant's travel in "foreign commerce" as a nexus for prohibiting the criminalized behavior. *See* § 18 U.S.C. § 2423(a)–(c). This term alone evinces Congressional intent for the statute to be applied extraterritorially. *See United States v. Montford,* 27 F.3d 137, 139–40 (5th Cir.1994) ("Congress intended foreign commerce to mean travel to and from, or at least some form of contact with, a foreign state."); *United States v. Hill,* 279 F.3d 731, 739 (9th Cir.2002) (inclusion of a "foreign commerce" provision "strongly suggests that Congress intended to cast a broad net and apply the statute to all offenders, whether or not they are found in the United States."). While a strained reading of the statute may support an argument that the statute only criminalizes illicit sexual behavior when a defendant has travelled from *outside* the country *into* the United States, nothing in the statute indicates it was designed to punish behavior going only one direction. Indeed, such a reading would "greatly . . . curtail the scope and usefulness of the statute and leave open a large immunity for [crimes] as easily committed by citizens . . . in foreign countries as at home." *Mitchell,* 553 F.2d at 1001 (quoting *Bowman,* 260 U.S. at 98, 43 S. Ct. 39).

Moreover, it may also "be inferred from the nature of the offenses and Congress' other legislative efforts to eliminate the type of crime involved" that extraterritorial jurisdiction was part of the legislative scheme. *See Baker,* 609 F.2d at 136. On July 5, 2000, President William Jefferson Clinton signed the Option Protocol to the United Nations Convention on the Rights of the Child on the Sale of Children, Child Prostitution, and Child Pornography ("Optional Protocol").[6] Optional Protocol, May 16, 2000, 39 I.L.M. 1285, 2000 WL 33366017. The Senate ratified the Optional Protocol on December 23, 2002, and it entered into force in January of 2003. *See* Optional Protocol (signatories) at 9, *available at http://www.unhcr.org/ refworld/pdfid/3ae6b38bc.pdf* (last visited Feb. 5, 2009).[7] The Optional Protocol states in its preamble that the States Parties to the present Protocol are "*[g]ravely concerned* at the significant and increasing international traffic of children" and that the parties were "*[d]eeply concerned* at the widespread and continuing practice of sex tourism[.]" *Id.* Preamble (emphasis in original). In relevant part, the Optional Protocol calls upon each signatory to criminalize, "as a minimum," the sale and sexual exploitation of a child as it relates to child prostitution "whether these offences are committed domestically or transnationally or on an individual or organized basis[.]" *Id.* art. 3 ¶ 1. The Optional Protocol also calls upon its signatories to "take such measures as may be necessary to establish its jurisdiction over the offences" when the offender is a national of the state in question, and when the victim is a national of the state in question. *Id.* art 4. ¶ 2. The Optional Protocol also "does not exclude any criminal jurisdiction exercised in accordance with internal law." *Id.* art. 4 ¶ 4.

One of the statutes that Congress enacted to implement the Optional Protocol was § 2423, which was part of the Prosecutorial Remedies and Other Tools to End the Exploitation of Children Act of 2003 (the "PROTECT Act"). Pub. L. 108-21, 117 Stat. 650 (2003); *see also United States v. Frank,* 486 F. Supp. 2d 1353, 1356–60 (S.D.Fla.2007) (discussing Optional Protocol, the PROTECT Act, and the extraterritorial effect of § 2423(c)). As part of the House Conference Report accompanying the PROTECT Act, the House stated that its proposed modification to § 2423

---

6 The Convention on the Rights of the Child, to which the Optional Protocol is appended, defines a "child" as "every human being below the age of eighteen years unless under the law applicable to the child, majority is attained earlier." *See* Convention on the Rights of the Child, G.A. Res. 44/25 (Sep. 2, 1990), *available at http://www.unhchr.ch/html/menu 3/b/k2crc.htm* (last visited Feb. 6, 2009). The United States is a signatory to the Convention, and Mexico has both signed and ratified the Convention. *See* Status of Ratifications of the Principal International Human Rights Treaties 7, 12, *available at http://www.unhchr. ch/pdf/report.pdf* (last visited Feb. 6, 2009).

The Mexican federal Civil Code also denotes that "majority begins at 18 years of age." Codigo Civil Federal (Federal Civil Code) C.C.F. § 13.04 (Mexico), as stated in 1-1 MEXICO LAW DIGEST 13.04.

7 Mexico also signed the Optional Protocol on Sep. 7, 2000, and ratified it on Mar. 15, 2002. *See id.*

"addresses a number of problems related to persons *who travel to foreign countries* and engage in illicit sexual relations with minors." H.R. Conf. Rep. 108-66, 108th Cong. 1st Sess. 2003, reprinted in 2003 U.S.C.C.A.N. 683, 686 (emphasis added). Given that § 2423 was passed to enforce a multilateral treaty designed to protect children from *transnational and domestic* child sex prostitution and "sex tourism," and given that the House Conference Report specifically mentions the statute's application to persons travelling in foreign countries, the Court concludes that Congress intended § 2423 to apply extraterritorially. *See also United States v. Strevell,* 185 Fed. Appx. 841, 844–45 (11th Cir. 2006) (unpublished) (holding that § 2423(c) was designed to apply extraterritorially).

2. Section 2423 and general principles of international law

Defendant also argues that an extraterritorial application of § 2423 violates principles of international law. The Court notes initially that "international law," *qua* law, is not a fixed set of legal mandates or legally cognizable statutes with independent authority in United States courts. Indeed, there is no authority in *international* law that United States *national* courts must recognize, except insomuch as Congress or the President incorporates some part of it through constitutional channels into national law. *See, e.g., Medellin v. Texas,* ___ U.S. ___, 128 S. Ct. 1346, 1357, 170 L.Ed.2d 190 (2008) (neither decisions of the International Court of Justice nor non-self-executing treaties create domestically enforceable law); *Hamdan v. Rumsfeld,* 548 U.S. 557, 610, 126 S. Ct. 2749, 165 L.Ed.2d 723 (2006) (applying protections recognized by customary international law only as they have been adopted and incorporated into federal law), *superseded by statute on other grounds as stated in Boumediene v. Bush,* ___ U.S. ___, 128 S. Ct. 2229, 171 L.Ed.2d 41 (2008); *see also United States v. Davis,* 905 F.2d 245, 248 (9th Cir.1990) ("International law principles, standing on their own, do not create substantive rights or affirmative defenses for litigants in United States courts."). Moreover, "[i]n enacting statutes, Congress is not bound by international law. . . . If it chooses to do so, it may legislate with respect to conduct outside the United States, in excess of limits posed by international law." *United States v. Pinto-Mejia,* 720 F.2d 248, 259 (2d Cir.1983); *see also Rainey v. United States,* 232 U.S. 310, 316, 34 S. Ct. 429, 58 L.Ed. 617 (1914). Nevertheless, when "determining whether a statute applies extraterritorially, [courts] presume that Congress did not intend to violate principles of international law." *United States v. Vasquez-Velasco,* 15 F.3d 833, 839 (9th Cir. 1994) (citing *McCulloch v. Sociedad Nacional de Marineros de Honduras,* 372 U.S. 10, 21–22, 83 S. Ct. 671, 9 L.Ed.2d 547 (1963)); *see also Murray v. Schooner Charming Betsy,* 6 U.S. 64, 2 Cranch 64, 2 L.Ed. 208 (1804) ("[A]n Act of Congress ought never to be construed to violate the law of nations if any other possible construction remains. . . ."); *United States v. Thomas,* 893 F.2d 1066, 1069 (9th Cir.1990) ("Although Congress is not bound by international law in enacting statutes, out of respect for other nations, courts should not unnecessarily construe a congressional statute in a way that violates international law.") (citations omitted). Therefore, the Court will next look to see if an extraterritorial application of § 2423 violates certain principles of international law.

International law recognizes several principles under which a statute may be applied extraterritorially. These include the "territorial" principle, where jurisdiction is based on the place where the offense is committed; the "national" principle, where jurisdiction is based on the nationality or national character of the offender; the "protective" principle, where jurisdiction is based on whether the national interest is affected; the "universality" principle, where jurisdiction is based on the physical custody of the offender; and the "passive personality" principle, where jurisdiction is based on the nationality or national character of the victim. *See Rivard v. United States,* 375 F.2d 882, 885–86 (5th Cir.1967); *United States v. Roberts,* 1 F. Supp. 2d 601, 607 (E.D.La. 1998).

Upon review, § 2423 withstands scrutiny under several principles of international law. First, Defendant is charged as a United States citizen. *See* Personal Data Sheet (Doc. No. 12). As stated previously, citizenship alone grants Congress the right to enact laws with extraterritorial application, thus authorizing jurisdiction under the "national" principle. *See Mitchell,* 553 F.2d at 1001; *see also Rivard,* 375 F.2d at 886; *Hill,* 279 F.3d at 740; *Thomas,* 893 F.2d at 1069; *United States v. Clark,* 315 F. Supp. 2d 1127, 1131 (W.D.Wa.2004), *aff'd,* 435 F.3d 1100 (2006). In addition, the Government asserts that the victim in the instant case—JC—is also an American citizen. Gov't's Resp. 17-18. Jurisdiction may also therefore be appropriate under the "passive personality" principle. *See United States v. Yousef,* 327 F.3d 56, 96–97 (2d Cir.2003) (finding jurisdiction was consistent with the passive personality principle when the crime involved a plot to bomb United States-flag aircraft that would have carried United States citizens); *United States v. Neil,* 312 F.3d 419, 422–23 (9th Cir.2002) (passive personality principle applied when defendant sexually molested American girl in Mexican waters); *Hill,* 279 F.3d at 740 (failure to make child support payments to American citizens satisfies passive personality principle). Finally, Defendant is charged with travelling in foreign commerce from the United States to Mexico. *See* Indictment 1-2. The alleged facts also state that once the victim had escaped from Defendant's control, she made her way back into the United States, where authorities were engaged in a manhunt for both Defendant and JC, and an AMBER Alert was in effect. These facts are sufficient to support jurisdiction under the "territorial" principle. *See Neil,* 312 F.3d at 422 (sexual molestation of an American victim prompting FBI investigation, followed by arrest of defendant in the United States enough to satisfy territorial principle); *Hill,* 279 F.3d at 739–40. Given that extraterritorial jurisdiction is plainly appropriate under the national, passive personality, and territorial principles of international law, the Court need make no holding with regard to whether § 2423 is appropriate under any other international law principles found in *Rivard.*

3. Section 2423 and the "unreasonableness" standard

It has also been held that the extraterritorial application of jurisdiction must not be "unreasonable" under international law. *See, e.g., Boureslan,* 857 F.2d at 1024 (King, J., dissenting); *Vasquez-Velasco,* 15 F.3d at 840; *Clark,* 315 F. Supp. 2d at 1132. These opinions that hold to an "unreasonableness" standard each cite the Restatement (Third) of Foreign Relations Law § 403, which sets forth a list of factors in determining the reasonableness of applying a law extraterritorially.[8]

Unlike the other principles of international law cited above, there is no Fifth Circuit precedent making these factors a mandatory part of the threshold inquiry to determine whether a statute may be applied extraterritorially.[9] The Court declines to do so here. Assuming, however, that the "unreasonableness" standard outlined in the Restatement bears on whether § 2423 may have extraterritorial jurisdiction, an evaluation of the statute reveals no conflict with an "unreasonableness" determination, given the almost universal condemnation of illicit sex with minors in the international community (including Mexico),[10] the fact that both the victim and

---

8 These factors are:

> (a) the link of the activity to the territory of the regulating state, i.e., the extent to which the activity takes place within the territory, or has substantial, direct, and foreseeable effect upon or in the territory;
>
> (b) the connections, such as nationality, residence, or economic activity, between the regulating state and the person principally responsible for the activity to be regulated, or between that state and those whom the regulation is designed to protect;
>
> (c) the character of the activity to be regulated, the importance of regulation to the regulating state, the extent to which other states regulate such activities, and the degree to which the desirability of such regulation is generally accepted.
>
> (d) the existence of justified expectations that might be protected or hurt by the regulation;
>
> (e) the importance of the regulation to the international political, legal, or economic system;
>
> (f) the extent to which the regulation is consistent with the traditions of the international system;
>
> (g) the extent to which another state may have an interest in regulating the activity; and
>
> (h) the likelihood of conflict with regulation by another state.

RESTATEMENT (THIRD) OF FOREIGN RELATIONS LAW § 403(2).

9 Judge King notes in her dissent in *Boureslan* that "[n]o court has applied the reasonableness test as part of the threshold inquiry to determine whether a statute may, as a general matter, be applied extraterritorially. The Restatement, however, notes that the reasonableness test may serve the same purpose as the traditional tests for deciding whether a statute may be applied extraterritorially." *Boureslan,* 857 F.2d at 1025 (King, J., dissenting) (citations omitted). Since Judge King's dissent, the Fifth Circuit has made no mention of the Restatement factors in any published or unpublished opinion.

10 *See* Convention art. 34 ("States Parties [shall] undertake to protect the child from all forms of sexual exploitation and abuse. . . ."); Optional Protocol Arts. 1-3 (calling for the criminalization of child prostitution and exploitation); Second World Congress against Commercial Sexual Exploitation of Children, The Yokohama Global Commitment 2001 ("We reaffirm, as

Defendant in the instant case are alleged to be United States citizens, and the direct link that the charged crimes have with United States territory. *See Clark,* 435 F.3d at 1106. (holding application of § 2423(c) extraterritorially was not "unreasonable" pursuant to international law principles).

Defendant nevertheless argues that applying § 2423 is unreasonable because Defendant was travelling to Mexico to engage in sex, and "the age of consent in Mexico is established by law as 12 years of age depending [sic] the laws of the individual state." Def.'s Mot. 15. The Court fails to see how the target country's law is relevant in the foregoing analysis, given the nationality of the parties and the fact that the statute specifically applies federal law to determining the legality of the predicate sexual conduct. *See* 18 U.S.C. § 2423(f). Moreover, the Court notes that the "illicit sexual conduct" alleged in this case is not consensual sex with an underage child, as Defendant implies in his Motion, but forced sex with a child, which is specifically prohibited in chapter 109A of the United States Criminal Code, and is thus incorporated into § 2423. *See* 18 U.S.C. § 2423(f) (incorporating § 2241(a) (Aggravated Sexual Abuse by Force or Threat)). This crime is also illegal in Mexico, both under Mexican federal law, and the laws of the state of Chihuahua. *See* Codigo Civil Federal (Federal Civil Code) C.C.F. Titulo 15, Capitulo 1, art. 262 (prohibiting forced sex with a minor); Codigo Penal del Estado de Chihuahua (Chihuahua State Code), Titulo 5, Capitulo 1 ("Violacion"), arts. 171–175. Defendant has therefore failed to demonstrate any likelihood of conflict with Mexico that would exist if the United States regulates this activity.

Accordingly, this Court holds that pursuant to the Indictment and the alleged facts of the instant case, the extraterritorial application of § 2423 does not violate the plain language of § 2423, Congressional intent, or general principles of international law.

D. 18 U.S.C. § 2423(c) and the Commerce Clause

Defendant's final substantive argument is that § 2423(c) is unconstitutional because it violates the Commerce Clause. Def.'s Mot. 16-18. Specifically Defendant argues that "[i]in punishing an action that may be entirely legal in the host country and at best loosely connected to a channel of commerce, section 2423(c) reflects an unprecedented use of Commerce Clause authority." *Id.* at 18.

The Constitution grants Congress the authority to "regulate Commerce with foreign Nations, and among the several States, and with Indian Tribes." U.S. CONST. art. I, § 8, cl. 3. The Constitution also grants Congress the authority to "make all laws which shall be necessary and proper for carrying into execution the foregoing power[.]" *Id.* art I., § 8, cl. 18. When reviewing an act of Congress passed under

---

our primary considerations, the protection and promotion of the interest and rights of the child to be protected from all forms of sexual exploitation. . . ."), *available at* http://www.uniceforg/events/yokohama/outcome.html (last visited Feb. 6, 2009).

the Commerce Clause, we review the statute under the rational basis standard. *Bredimus,* 352 F.3d at 203 (citing *Groome Resources, Ltd. v. Parish of Jefferson,* 234 F.3d 192, 203 (5th Cir.2000)). In applying this deferential standard, "due respect for the decisions of a coordinate branch of Government demands that we invalidate a congressional enactment only upon a *plain showing* that Congress has exceeded its constitutional bounds." *Bredimus,* 352 F.3d at 203 (quoting *Groome,* 234 F.3d at 216) (emphasis in quoted text).

Courts have generally recognized three distinct sets of authority under the Commerce Clause, depending on whether Congress seeks to regulate interstate commerce, foreign commerce, or commerce with Indian tribes. *See Clark,* 435 F.3d at 1112–1113 (reviewing Congress's authority under each provision, and the extent of that authority). For much of the 20th century, "the scales of the federal courts' [interstate] Commerce Clause jurisprudence tipped more towards according to Congress considerably greater latitude in regulating conduct rather than to maintaining a distinction between 'what is truly national and what is truly local.'" *Bredimus,* 352 F.3d at 204–05 (quoting *United States v. Morrison,* 529 U.S. 598, 608, 617–18, 120 S. Ct. 1740, 146 L.Ed.2d 658 (2000); *United States v. Lopez,* 514 U.S. 549, 567–68, 115 S. Ct. 1624, 131 L.Ed.2d 626 (1995)). However, the Supreme Court heralded essentially a "new era" of interstate Commerce Clause jurisprudence with the decisions of *United States v. Lopez,* and *United States v. Morrison,* which "clarified the legal standards applicable to a constitutional challenge under the [inter-state] Commerce Clause." *Id.* These cases, and their progeny have determined the "outer limits" of Congress's power to enact legislation, and provide the framework for any analysis of interstate Commerce Clause questions. *Id.* (citing *Lopez,* 514 U.S. at 556–567, 115 S. Ct. 1624); *United States v. Ho,* 311 F.3d 589, 596 (5th Cir.2002).

In *Lopez,* the Supreme Court held that a statute making it a federal crime to have a gun within 1,000 feet of a school exceeded the "outer limits" of Congress's authority under the interstate Commerce Clause. *Lopez,* 514 U.S. at 561, 115 S. Ct. 1624 (holding 18 U.S.C. § 922(q)(1)(A) unconstitutional). In holding the gun-control statute unconstitutional, the Court in *Lopez* outlined three broad categories of activity that the Constitution allows Congress to regulate under its interstate commerce power: (1) "the use of the channels of interstate commerce," (2) "the instrumentalities of interstate commerce, or persons or things in interstate commerce, even though the threat may come only from intrastate activities," and (3) "activities having a substantial relation to interstate commerce, i.e., activities that 'substantially affect' interstate commerce." *Id.* at 558–59, 115 S. Ct. 1624; *see also Bredimus,* 352 F.3d at 206. Subsequent Supreme Court cases have further elaborated on the *Lopez* framework. *See, e.g., Gonzales v. Raich,* 545 U.S. 1, 22, 125 S. Ct. 2195, 162 L.Ed.2d 1 (2005) (applying a rational basis test to whether activities in question substantially affect interstate commerce); *Morrison,* 529 U.S. at 617, 120 S. Ct. 1740 (holding that Congress cannot regulate violent criminal conduct based solely on its aggregate effect on interstate commerce).

The Fifth Circuit has not determined whether § 2423(c) violates Congress's authority under the Commerce Clause. However, the Fifth Circuit recently held in *United States v. Bredimus* that § 2423(b) ("Travel with intent to engage in illicit sexual conduct") did not violate the Commerce Clause. *See Bredimus,* 352 F.3d at 205–06; *see also United States v. Tykarsky,* 446 F.3d 458, 470 (3d Cir.2006); *United States v. Han,* 230 F.3d 560, 562–63 (2d Cir.2000); *Gamache,* 156 F.3d at 8. The court in *Bredimus* held that the language of § 2423(b), and that other laws comparable to § 2423(b), all contain an element of criminal intent that the defendant must have travelling in foreign commerce, thus making the crime one that Congress may regulate. *See Bredimus,* 352 F.3d at 205–07 (comparing § 2423(b) to 18 U.S.C. §§ 1958, 2261, and 2262(a)). The court in *Bredimus* added that because § 2423(b) "only criminalizes foreign travel when the travel is done with an illicit intent, [the statute] does not impermissibly burden the fundamental right to travel." *Id.* at 210.

In contrast to § 2423(b), § 2423(c) has no intent element. An offender may therefore travel in foreign commerce with no intent to commit an illicit sex act, arrive in a foreign locale, commit the act, and still violate § 2423(c). In fact, when Congress passed the PROTECT Act in 2003, the House Conference Report accompanying the Act explained that § 2423(c) was added to the pre-existing law (which is substantively identical to § 2423(b)) so that "the government would only have to prove that the defendant engaged in illicit sexual conduct with a minor while in a foreign country." H.R. Rep. No. 108-66 at 51, 2003 U.S.C.C.A.N. at 686. In other words, § 2423(c) was added so that the Government does not have to prove intent. Because the court in *Bredimus* dealt with a statute containing an intent element absent from the statute at issue in the instant case, and because the court in *Bredimus* based its analysis in part on this intent element, the analysis in *Bredimus* is not dispositive of § 2423(c)'s constitutionality.[11]

Perhaps more on point, the Ninth Circuit more recently held in *United States v. Clark* that "Congress acted within its constitutional bounds in criminalizing commercial sex acts committed by U.S. citizens who travel abroad in foreign commerce" pursuant to 18 U.S.C. § 2423(c). *Clark,* 435 F.3d at 1109. In *Clark,* an American citizen travelled to Cambodia and engaged in sex acts with underage boys, whom he had promised to pay. *Id.* at 1103. The Court in *Clark* held that because the defendant had travelled in foreign commerce and engaged in a *commercial* sex act, "[t]he rational nexus requirement is met to a constitutionally significant degree." *Id.* at 1114–17.

---

11 The Court reiterates that the Fifth Circuit in *Bredimus* held that the criminal act in § 2423(b) is not the ultimate sex exploitation "but rather the foreign travel with illicit intent." *Bredimus,* 352 F.3d at 210. The criminal act in § 2423(c), meanwhile, is the illicit sexual act itself, after the defendant travelled in foreign commerce. *See, e.g., United States v. Armstrong,* EP-07-CR-2276-DB, 2007 WL 3171775, at 3–4 (W.D.Tex. Oct. 26, 2007).

As in *Bredimus,* however, the court in *Clark* based its decision in part on an element conspicuously absent from the instant case. The court in *Clark* specifically analyzed the second prong of "illicit sexual conduct," under § 2423(f), namely "any commercial sex act . . . with a person under 18 years of age." *See Clark,* 435 F.3d at 1105 ("it is this second 'commercial sex act' prong that is at issue in Clark's appeal."). Describing child prostitution as a "pernicious 'species of commercial intercourse,'" (*id.,* quoting *Gibbons v. Ogden,* 22 U.S. 1, 193, 9 Wheat. 1, 6 L.Ed. 23 (1824)), the court in *Clark* made its constitutional analysis dependent on the *commercial* element of the definition. *Id.* at 1114–15; *see also id.* at 1110 n. 16 ("We do not decide the constitutionality of § 2423(c) with respect to illicit sexual conduct covered by the non-commercial prong of the statute, such as sex acts accomplished by the use of force or threat.") (citations omitted).

In the instant case, the alleged illicit sex act is non-commercial and likely falls under the first prong of the definition of "illicit sexual conduct" in § 2423(f). Because the court in *Clark* made its conclusion dependent on the commercial nature of the sex act, its decision relies specifically on an element not present in the instant case. Accordingly, *Clark* is not dispositive.[12]

While neither *Bredimus* nor *Clark* deal with the constitutionality of § 2423(c) regarding non-commercial sex acts, both cases provide guidance in how to approach the issue. First, both courts note that the *Lopez/Morrison* framework set forth by the Supreme Court is a relevant starting point to analyzing the foreign commerce clause, and both recognize that some questions of foreign commerce may be answered simply by applying the framework. *See Bredimus,* 352 F.3d at 208 (applying the three-prong *Lopez/Morrison* framework to § 2423(b)); *Clark,* 435 F.3d at 1103 (citing *United States v. Cummings,* 281 F.3d 1046, 1049 n. 1 (9th Cir.2002) (analyzing the constitutionality of the International Parental Kidnapping Act, 18 U.S.C. § 1204(a), under *Lopez*'s three-category approach)). Using this framework, the Fifth Circuit has found § 2423(b) and the Ninth Circuit has found § 2423(c) to be potentially valid regulations of the "channels of commerce."

---

12 Even more recently, a federal court in the Southern District of Florida held that § 2423(c) was constitutional under the Necessary and Proper Clause in enacting the Optional Protocol. *See Frank,* 486 F. Supp. 2d at 1356–59. As in *Clark,* however, the court in *Frank* dealt specifically with the "commercial sex act" prong of § 2423(f) and did not address the constitutionality of the first prong of the "illicit sex act" definition, which is at issue in this case. *See Frank,* 486 F. Supp. 2d. at 1358 (defining the issue as "whether, under rational basis review, Congress could enact § 2423(c) under the Necessary and Proper Clause to implement the Optional Protocol and if so, whether the statute—insofar as commercial sex with minors is concerned— reasonably implements the Optional Protocol."). The Court in *Frank* therefore restricted its analysis to commercial sex acts, as the Optional Protocol does not contain specific language addressing the crimes outlined under the first prong of § 2423(f), but deals more specifically with child prostitution, child pornography, and other forms of sexual exploitation of children in regard to child prostitution, all of which fall under the second definition of § 2423(f). *See* Optional Protocol art. 3; *see also United States v. Bianchi,* No. 06-19, 2007 WL 1521123, at 5 (E.D.Pa. May 22, 2007) (holding § 2423(c) constitutional without discussion of whether defendant's sex acts were commercial in nature).

See Bredimus, 352 F.3d at 205–07 (comparing § 2423(b) to other statutes regulating the channels of interstate commerce); *Clark,* 435 F.3d at 1116 ("[N]onetheless, there is a good argument that, as found by the district court, § 2423(c) can also be viewed as a valid regulation of the 'channels of commerce.'").[13]

In addition, both the Fifth Circuit and Ninth Circuit go further in their analysis and hold that when regulating foreign commerce, Congress's authority is not constrained by the three categories in the *Lopez/Morrison* framework. The *Lopez/Morrison* framework "developed in response to the unique federalism concerns that define congressional authority in the interstate context." *Clark,* 435 F.3d at 1103 (citing *Lopez,* 514 U.S. at 557, 115 S. Ct. 1624); *see also Bd. of Trustees of Univ. of Ill. v. United States,* 289 U.S. 48, 57, 53 S. Ct. 509, 77 L.Ed. 1025 (1933) ("[T]he principle of duality in our system of government does not touch the authority of the Congress in the regulation of foreign commerce."). However, there exists in the realm of foreign commerce "the necessity that the nation speak with one voice." *Bredimus,* 352 F.3d at 208 n. 10. Accordingly, any statute that would be granted constitutional deference when it regulates interstate commerce is accorded even greater deference when Congress is regulating foreign commerce. *See Bredimus,* 352 F.3d at 208 ("The Supreme Court has long held that Congress's authority to regulate foreign commerce is even broader than its authority to regulate interstate commerce.") (citing *Japan Line, Ltd. v. Los Angeles County,* 441 U.S. 434, 448, 99 S. Ct. 1813, 60 L.Ed.2d 336 (1979)). "In fact, the Supreme Court has never struck down an act of Congress as exceeding its powers to regulate foreign commerce." *Clark,* 435 F.3d at 1113.[14]

Finally, for jurisdictional purposes, the court in *Clark* notes that the term "travels in foreign commerce" "unequivocally establishes that Congress specifically invoked the Foreign Commerce Clause." *Id.* at 1114. The term "foreign commerce" is also given a broad definition in Title 18 of the United States Code,[15] and courts have thus given the term an "expansive reach." *Id.* (citing *Montford,* 27 F.3d at 139–40; *Londos v. United States,* 240 F.2d 1, 6 (5th Cir. 1957)). In *Clark,* the defendant "got on a plane in the United States and journeyed to Cambodia. This act

---

13 Because a person may form the intent to commit the criminal act in § 2423(c) after all use of the channels of commerce cease, the Court expresses doubt that § 2423(c) may be constitutionally upheld simply as regulation of the channels of commerce.

14 The Ninth Circuit has gone even further than this Court does today in stating that "Congress's plenary authority over foreign affairs may also provide a sufficient basis for § 2423(c)." *Clark,* 435 F.3d at 1109 n. 14 (citing, e.g., *United States v. Curtiss-Wright Export Corp.,* 299 U.S. 304, 315, 57 S. Ct. 216, 81 L.Ed. 255 (1936) ("The broad statement that the federal government can exercise no powers except those specifically enumerated in the Constitution, and such implied powers as are necessary and proper to carry into effect the enumerated powers, is categorically true only in respect of our internal affairs."); *United States v. Belmont,* 301 U.S. 324, 331, 57 S. Ct. 758, 81 L.Ed. 1134 (1937) ("[C]omplete power over international affairs is in the national government. . . .")).

15 This section states that "[t]he term "foreign commerce", as used in this title, includes commerce with a foreign country." 18 U.S.C. § 10

is sufficient to satisfy the 'travels in foreign commerce' element of § 2423(c)." *Id.* In the instant case, Defendant allegedly climbed in a car and journeyed to Mexico, therefore similarly satisfying the foreign commerce element of § 2423(c).[16]

With these guideposts in mind, the Court turns to the only possible question of constitutional import in the instant case: whether Congress may regulate under the Commerce Clause non-commercial illicit sexual conduct that a defendant engages in after having travelled in foreign commerce. The Court finds the answer to this question in the principles set forth in one of the Supreme Court's more recent discussions of Congress's power under the Commerce Clause—*Gonzales v. Raich,* 545 U.S. 1, 125 S. Ct. 2195, 162 L.Ed.2d 1 (2005).

In *Raich,* the Supreme Court held that Congress had the authority under the Commerce Clause to prohibit the purely local cultivation and use of marijuana, even when that cultivation and use was in compliance with California Law. *Raich,* 545 U.S. at 9, 125 S. Ct. 2195. Pursuant to the Controlled Substances Act, 21 U.S.C. § 801 et seq. ("CSA"), Congress had made it unlawful to manufacture, distribute, dispense, or possess any controlled substance (including marijuana) except as permitted in the CSA. *Id.* at 13, 125 S. Ct. 2195 (citing 21 U.S.C. §§ 841(a)(1), 844(a)). Despite the purely local nature of the defendants' use and cultivation of marijuana for personal medical purposes, the Supreme Court nonetheless found the CSA constitutional, as such private use and cultivation was part of an economic "class of activities" that had "a substantial effect" on interstate commerce. *Id.* at 17–18, 125 S. Ct. 2195 (citing *Perez v. United States,* 402 U.S. 146, 150, 91 S. Ct. 1357, 28 L.Ed.2d 686 (1971); *Wickard v. Filburn,* 317 U.S. 111, 128–29, 63 S. Ct. 82, 87 L.Ed. 122 (1942)). Accordingly, "when a general regulatory statute bears a substantial relation to commerce, the *de minimus* character of individual instances arising under that statute is of no consequence."[17] *Id.* at 17, 125 S. Ct. 2195 (citations and quotations omitted) (emphasis in original). The Supreme Court stressed that it "need not determine whether respondents' activities, taken in the aggregate, substantially affect interstate commerce in fact, but only whether a 'rational basis' exists for so concluding." *Id.* at 22, 125 S. Ct. 2195 (citations omitted). The Supreme Court concluded that:

> "[g]iven the enforcement difficulties that attend distinguishing between marijuana cultivated locally and marijuana grown elsewhere, 21 U.S.C. § 801(5), and concerns about diversion into illicit channels, we have no difficulty concluding that Congress

---

16 The Court in *Clark* also held that § 2423(c) does not require that a defendant commit the illicit sex act while travelling in foreign commerce, and that an act committed two months after the travel was within the statute's meaning. *See Clark,* 435 F.3d at 1107–08; *see also United States v. Jackson,* 480 F.3d 1014, 1022 (9th Cir.2007). In the instant case, the period between foreign travel and the conduct in question was less than 24 hours. *See* Criminal Compl. 3-4.

17 The Supreme Court also noted that whether the market Congress is seeking to regulate is lawful or unlawful "is of no constitutional import." *Raich,* 545 U.S. at 19 n. 29, 125 S. Ct. 2195.

> had a rational basis for believing that failure to regulate the intrastate manufacture and possession of marijuana would leave a gaping hole in the CSA."

Id. (footnote omitted.).

As stated previously, the alleged illicit sexual conduct in the instant case is not itself commercial. However, a worldwide market exists for child prostitution, an activity that is "quintessentially economic" in nature, and that falls within foreign trade and commerce. *See Clark,* 435 F.3d at 1115.[18] As the Optional Protocol states, there is both "significant and increasing international traffic of children for the purpose of the sale of children, child prostitution and pornography," as well as "the widespread and continuing practice of sex tourism[.]" Optional Protocol (Preamble).[19]

The PROTECT Act, which contains § 2423(c), was passed to implement the Optional Protocol, and contains specific language criminalizing commercial sex with minors. *See Frank,* 486 F. Supp. 2d at 1356–60. Section 105 of the PROTECT Act, where § 2423(c) and § 2423(f) are found, is entitled "Penalties Against Sex Tourism," further evincing the statute's overall economic nature. *See* H.R. CONF. REP. 108-66. Incidentally, a year prior to the passage of the PROTECT Act by both houses of Congress, an almost identical statute was passed only in the House of Representatives called the Sex Tourism Prohibition Improvement Act of 2002. *See* H.R.REP. No. 107-525, 107th Cong., 2nd Sess. 2002, 2002 WL 1376220. This piece of legislation contains a statute that is substantively identical to what would later become § 2423(c) and § 2423(f). *Compare* H.R.REP. No. 107-525 *with* H.R. CONF. REP. 108-66 *and* 18 U.S.C. §§ 2423(c),(f). The House Report to this bill, in a section entitled "Background and Need for the Legislation" section, states:

> Many developing countries have fallen prey to the serious problem of international sex tourism. . . . Because poor countries are often under economic pressure to develop tourism, those governments often turn a blind eye toward this devastating problem because of the income it produces. Children around the world have become trapped and exploited by the sex tourism industry. . . . This legislation will close significant loopholes in the law that persons who travel to foreign countries seeking sex with children are currently using to their advantage in order to avoid prosecution.

H.R. Rep. 107-525 at 2–3.

Accordingly, the language of the PROTECT Act, the Optional Protocol that § 2423(c) was designed to implement, and the language accompanying § 2423(c)'s legislative forerunner all demonstrate that § 2423(c) is primarily designed to

---

18 The Court notes here, as did the Ninth Circuit in *Clark,* that "foreign trade or commerce includes both goods and services." *Clark,* 435 F.3d at 1115 n. 18.

19 For a closer look at the billion-dollar child sex tourism industry, its component parts, and its economic impact both at home and abroad, *see* Christine L. Hogan, Note, *Touring Commerce Clause Jurisprudence: The Constitutionality of Prosecuting Non-Commercial Sexually Illicit Acts Under 18 U.S.C. § 2423(c),* 81 St. John's L. Rev. 641, 646 (2007).

combat the human suffering and economic evils of worldwide sex tourism and child prostitution. Similar to *Raich,* there is a rational basis for concluding that leaving non-commercial sex with minors outside of federal control could affect the price for child prostitution services and other market conditions in the child prostitution industry. *See Raich,* 545 U.S. at 19, 125 S. Ct. 2195. Therefore, the Court has no difficulty concluding that Congress had a rational basis for believing that failure to regulate the non-commercial sexual abuse of minors "would leave a gaping hole" in the PROTECT Act and its ability to regulate the commercial industry of child prostitution. *See id.* at 22, 125 S. Ct. 2195.

In conclusion, given the almost complete deference federal courts have shown towards Congress in enacting laws regulating foreign commerce, the extensive powers that the Constitution affords Congress in regulating international affairs, and the unambiguous jurisdictional language in § 2423(c), this Court holds that Congress was acting well within its authority to "make all Laws which shall be necessary and proper" to "regulate Commerce with foreign Nations" when it made both the commercial and noncommercial illicit sexual conduct in § 2423(c) and § 2423(f) unlawful. At best, there has been no *"plain showing* that Congress has exceeded its constitutional bounds." *Bredimus,* 352 F.3d at 203. Accordingly, Defendant's Commerce Clause argument against § 2423(c) fails.

E. Request for a bill of particulars

Defendant also seeks a bill of particulars regarding his Indictment. Def.'s Mot. 18-21. A bill of particulars is a "formal, detailed statement of the claims or charges brought by . . . a prosecutor." BLACK'S LAW DICTIONARY 177 (8th ed. 2004). Federal Rule of Criminal Procedure 7(f) states that "[t]he court may direct the government to file a bill of particulars. The defendant may move for a bill of particulars before or within 10 days after arraignment or at a later time if the court permits." FED. R. CRIM. P. 7(f). Once the government provides a defendant with a bill of particulars, it is bound by the information in that bill and may not present materially different information at trial.[20] 24 JAMES WM. MOORE ET AL., MOORE'S FEDERAL PRACTICE ¶ 607.07[1] (3d ed. 2008).

"The purposes of a bill of particulars are to obviate surprise at trial, enable the defendant to prepare his defense with full knowledge of the charges against him, and to enable double jeopardy to be pled in case of a subsequent prosecution." *United States v. Mackey,* 551 F.2d 967, 970 (5th Cir.1977); *see also United States v. Shepard,* 462 F.3d 847, 860 (8th Cir.), *cert. denied,* 549 U.S. 1099, 127 S. Ct. 838, 166 L.Ed.2d 671 (2006). However, most requests for bills of particulars are denied. *See* MOORE'S ¶ 607.07[1]. A court must consider a defendant's need for information while mindful that the bill of particulars "is not designed to compel the

---

20 It should be noted that the government may nevertheless "amend a bill of particulars subject to such conditions as justice requires." FED. R. CRIM. P. 7(f).

government to detailed exposition of its evidence or to explain the legal theories upon which it intends to rely at trial." *United States v. Burgin,* 621 F.2d 1352, 1359 (5th Cir.1980). Whether to grant a bill of particulars is within a trial court's sound discretion; for practical purposes, the trial court's decision is almost invariably final.[21] *See Mackey,* 551 F.2d at 970; *see also United States v. Davis,* 582 F.2d 947, 951 (5th Cir.1978) (determination of whether bill of particulars is needed is "seldom subject to precise line drawing").

Having reviewed the Indictment, Defendant has presented no compelling reason for this Court to require the Government to provide Defendant with a bill of particulars. Accordingly, Defendant's request is denied.

IV. Conclusion

Defendant has prematurely argued that the counts in his Indictment are multiplicitous. Moreover, he has failed to demonstrate that an extraterritorial application of § 2423 is contrary to the intent of Congress, the plain language of the statute, or that it otherwise violates any principle of international law. In addition, Defendant has failed to make a plain showing that § 2423(c) violates the Commerce Clause of the Constitution.

Accordingly, Defendant's Motion for Dismissal in his Motions for Dismissal and For Bill of Particulars (Doc. No. 23) is DENIED.

Defendant's request for a bill of particulars contained in his Motion (Doc. No. 23) is DENIED.

Defendant's request for grand jury materials contained in his Motion (Doc. No. 23) is DENIED.

SO ORDERED.

21 To overturn a denial of a defendant's motion for bill of particulars, a defendant must demonstrate actual surprise at trial and prejudice to his substantial rights as a result. *See United States v. Marrero,* 904 F.2d 251, 254 (5th Cir.), *cert. denied,* 498 U.S. 1000, 111 S. Ct. 561, 112 L.Ed.2d 567 (1990).

I. INTERNATIONAL LAW IN GENERAL

5. The Protective Principle*

* Cases are indexed under this subject. The full text of these cases is published on the pages indicated.

UNITED STATES
v.
ALBERTO ANGULO-HERNÁNDEZ

576 F.3d 59 (1st Cir. 2009)
Decided August 7, 2009

Timothy R. Henwood, Nelson J. Perez-Sosa, German Rieckehoff, US Attorney's Office, San Juan, PR, for United States of America.

Rafael Anglada-Lopez, San Juan, PR, for Alberto Angulo-Hernández.

Jorge Enrique Rivera-Ortiz, Law Office of Jorge E. Rivera Ortiz, Manati, PR, Rafael Andrade-Ravelo, Joseph C. Laws, Federal Public Defender's Office, San Juan, PR, for Eusebio Estupinan-Estupinan.

Jedrick H. Burgos Amador, Trujillo Alto, PR, for Gustavo R. Brito-Fernandez.

Frank D. Inserni Milam, Frank D. Inserni Milam Law Office, Hato Rey, PR, for Jose Luis Casiano-Jimenez.

Before LYNCH, Chief Judge, TORRUELLA, BOUDIN, LIPEZ and HOWARD, Circuit Judges.

ORDER OF COURT

Defendant José Luis Casiano-Jiménez's petition for rehearing is denied.

Defendants Alberto Angulo-Hernández, Eusebio Estupinan-Estupinan, and Gustavo Rafael Brito-Fernández's petitions for rehearing having been denied by the panel of judges who decided the case, and the petitions for rehearing en banc having been submitted to the active judges of this court and a majority of the judges not having voted that the cases be heard en banc, it is ordered that the petitions for rehearing and the petitions for rehearing en banc be denied.

TORRUELLA, Circuit Judge (Dissenting from the denial of en banc review).

In this case, defendants challenge their convictions under the Maritime Drug Law Enforcement Act ("MDLEA"). 46 U.S.C. §§ 70501–08. The Coast Guard found a large quantity of drugs banned under United States law on board the defendants'

Bolivian vessel in the Caribbean, en route from Colombia to the Dominican Republic. Neither the defendants nor any other crewmembers are U.S. nationals, and there is no other specific suggestion of any tie to the United States. I dissent from the denial of en banc review on two grounds set forth below.

I. Sufficiency

Up to now, the rule in this circuit has been that a defendant's mere presence at the scene of a discovery of a quantity of illegal drugs is, without additional evidence, insufficient to establish a defendant's knowledge of the presence of those drugs. *United States v. Steuben*, 850 F.2d 859, 864 (1st Cir.1988). As a result of the panel opinion, that rule is now substituted by one that allows a jury to speculatively link presence to entrustment, and then link entrustment to knowledge. *United States v. Angulo-Hernández*, 565 F.3d 2, 13–18 (1st Cir.2009) (Torruella, J., dissenting). I would grant en banc rehearing as to this issue as to crewmembers Casiano-Jiménez and Brito-Fernández to correct this error.

II. Extraterritorial Jurisdiction

Additionally, I would grant en banc rehearing as to all defendants to allow this court to reexamine and correct our law on the extraterritorial reach of the MDLEA. The defendants, foreign nationals on a foreign-flag ship in waters not subject to U.S. jurisdiction, have challenged the application of the MDLEA to them in this prosecution. In the panel decision, I concurred in this application, because our circuit precedent clearly forecloses their argument. *Id.* at 19.

But our precedent has missed an important logical link in its decision to uphold the MDLEA against a due process challenge on similar facts. And, as explained below, a convincing argument can be made that due process aside, Congress lacks the power to proscribe the instant conduct, which lacks a nexus with the United States. Both legal strands lead to the same conclusion: we should follow the Ninth Circuit and impose a requirement that a prosecution under the MDLEA establish a nexus between the criminal conduct and the United States.

A. Due Process

In an earlier decision addressing whether the MDLEA included a nexus requirement, *United States v. Cardales*, we agreed with the Ninth Circuit that MDLEA defendants had a due process right not to be subject to this country's law enforcement in a manner that was "arbitrary or fundamentally unfair." 168 F.3d 548, 553 (1st Cir.1999) (citing *United States v. Davis*, 905 F.2d 245, 248–49 (9th Cir.1990)). But we concluded that the MDLEA, even without a nexus requirement, was neither arbitrary nor unfair. *Id.* We reasoned that through consent of the flag nation, the MDLEA comported with the territorial principle of international law, which provides that a "'state has jurisdiction to prescribe and enforce a rule of law in the territory of another state to the extent provided by international agreement with the other state.'" *Id.* (quoting *United States v. Robinson*, 843 F.2d 1, 4 (1st Cir.1988)).

We also rejected a nexus requirement as we found application of the MDLEA consistent with the "the protective principle of international law because Congress has determined that all drug trafficking aboard vessels threatens our nation's security." *Id.* These conclusions are both suspect. The consent of the flag nation is not material to a due process analysis focused on our government's power over a foreign individual defendant. And the protective principle is simply inapplicable on these facts.

1. The Protective Principle

I will address the latter rationale first. Justifying the reach of the MDLEA under the protective principle is not convincing on facts where there is no nexus between the drug trafficking vessel and the United States. *Cf. Robinson*, 843 F.2d at 3–4 (Breyer, J.) (observing problems with that principle and so relying only on the territoriality principle). Since the drugs at issue in this case were heading for the Dominican Republic, not the United States, there is not the kind of direct threat to the United States required to trigger the protective principle. *See United States v. Perlaza*, 439 F.3d 1149, 1162 (9th Cir.2006) ("Our circuit has recognized the 'protective principle' as part of its consideration of whether nexus exists, not as a substitute for it.").

The only response to this argument is that drug trafficking, generally, is such a global threat that the United States is justified in protecting itself by prosecuting traffickers anywhere, regardless of the destination of the drug shipment. *See* 46 U.S.C. § 70501 (generally finding trafficking to be a threat to the United States). But this broad proposition is not consistent with international law. *See* Restatement (Third) of Foreign Relations Law § 402 cmt. f (1987) (defining the scope of the protective principle as allowing prosecution of "offenses directed against the security of the state or other offenses threatening the integrity of governmental functions that are generally recognized as crimes by developed legal systems," such as counterfeiting currency). Relying on the protective principle without any nexus would be to conclude that Congress could allow for arrests and prosecutions of drug traffickers on the other side of the world, even without flag-nation consent. This cannot be and is not the correct result; the protective principle requires a showing that the "particular conduct endangered the United States." Eugene Kontorovich, *Beyond the Article I Horizon: Congress's Enumerated Powers and Universal Jurisdiction over Drug Crimes*, 93 Minn. L. Rev. 1191, 1229–31 (2009) (rejecting, in the context of analyzing Congress's Article I powers, the argument that the MDLEA could be justified under the protective principle because drugs not destined for United States markets do not fall into the "limited class of offenses . . . directed at the security of the State," since that principle "refers to the safety and integrity of the state apparatus itself (its 'government functions' or 'state interests'), not its overall physical and moral well-being"); *see also Robinson*, 843 F.2d at 3 (identifying, but not resolving, this argument). Such interpretation would result in a protective principle which swallows the principle of universal jurisdiction. Kontorovich, *Beyond the Article I Horizon*, *supra*, at 1231.

2. The Territorial Principle

Relying on the consent of the flag nation, the "territorial" argument could justify our government's exercise of power under international law. But this does not mean that all due process concerns are automatically satisfied. In other words, we erred in *Cardales*, and subsequent precedent, by assuming due process was satisfied if international law was satisfied.*

Rather, compliance with international law is necessary but not sufficient. Under the doctrine of personal jurisdiction, principles of due process and comity between the states preclude one state from exercising jurisdiction over non-forum-state individuals where that person lacks sufficient contacts with the forum state. *See Helicopteros Nacionales de Colombia, S.A. v. Hall*, 466 U.S. 408, 414, 104 S. Ct. 1868, 80 L.Ed.2d 404 (1984) (finding no personal jurisdiction over a foreign defendant in a suit based on a foreign helicopter crash where there were no "certain minimum contacts with [the forum] such that the maintenance of the suit [did] not offend 'traditional notions of fair play and substantial justice.'" (quoting *Int'l Shoe Co. v. Washington*, 326 U.S. 310, 316, 66 S. Ct. 154, 90 L.Ed. 95 (1945))). The same result should be applied when our government attempts to exercise criminal jurisdiction over foreign nationals—due process limits one State's power to seize the citizen of another State, absent a nexus between the seizing State and the seized individual. *See Perlaza*, 439 F.3d at 1168 ("The nexus requirement is a judicial gloss applied to ensure that a defendant is not improperly haled before a court for trial. . . . [It] serves the same purpose as the minimum contacts test in personal jurisdiction." (internal quotation marks omitted)); *United States v. Caicedo*, 47 F.3d 370, 372 (9th Cir.1995) ("A defendant would have a legitimate expectation that because he has subjected himself to the laws of one nation, other nations will not be entitled to exercise jurisdiction without some nexus."); *see also* Restatement (Third) of Foreign Relations Law § 403 (explaining that extraterritorial exercise of jurisdiction must be reasonable, and basing a reasonableness inquiry on eight factors, many of which relate to the nexus between the activity and the jurisdiction). Considered in this way, I fail to see how the fact that the flag nation has consented to a search and potential arrest aboard its vessel in international water has any bearing on the sufficiency of contacts between a defendant and the United States. Thus, consent of the flag nation, while relevant to establishing statutory jurisdiction, should not automatically establish that due process is satisfied. *See Perlaza*, 439 F.3d at 1169.

---

* This position is well-made in a Ninth Circuit decision:

> International law principles may be useful as a rough guide of whether a sufficient nexus exists between the defendant and the United States so that application of the statute in question would not violate due process. However, danger exists that emphasis on international law principles will cause us to lose sight of the ultimate question: would application of the statute to the defendant be arbitrary or fundamentally unfair?

Davis, 905 F.2d at 249 n. 2 (citation omitted).

B. Constitutional Power

In addition to the due process problem, a separate basis supports vacatur here: the MDLEA, as applied without a nexus requirement, is beyond Congress's power. *See* Kontorovich, Beyond the Article I Horizon, *supra*; Eugene Kontorovich, The "Define and Punish" Clause and the Limits of Universal Jurisdiction, 103 Nw. U.L. Rev. 149 (2009).

The MDLEA, as applied without a nexus requirement, cannot be legitimately based on the "Piracy and Felonies" clause, which gives Congress the power to "define and punish Piracies and Felonies committed on the high Seas and Offenses against the Law of Nations." U.S. Const. art. I, § 8, cl. 10. The term "Felonies" has not been read to include all felonies, but rather only felonies with an adequate jurisdictional nexus to the United States. *See, e.g., United States v. Furlong*, 18 U.S. 184, 197, 5 Wheat. 184, 5 L.Ed. 64 (1820). The *Furlong* decision rejected a prosecution for murder of a foreigner by another foreigner on a foreign vessel. *Id.* In so doing, the Court effectively distinguished between "Felonies," which are not subject to universal jurisdiction, and "Piracy," which is. *Id.* at 196–198, 5 Wheat. 184 ("If by calling murder piracy, it might assert a jurisdiction over that offence committed by a foreigner in a foreign vessel, what offence might not be brought within their power by the same device?"). This understanding is also demonstrated by congressional hesitance to prohibit the slave trade unless there was a nexus between the defendant and the United States. *See* Kontorovich, *Beyond the Article I Horizon, supra*, at 1207–17.

Even though the term "Piracy" has evolved to include other crimes that are universally condemned (as the slave trade has since become), the drug trade is not subject to universal jurisdiction. *See id.* at 1223–27.** As explained above, the protective principle also does not support exercise without nexus. *Id.* at 1229–31. Nor can the

---

** As explained in the article, the United Nation Convention on the Law of the Seas, Article 105 allows every State to "seize a pirate ship or aircraft, or a ship or aircraft taken by piracy and under the control of pirates, and arrest the persons and seize the property on board." The same convention, Article 108, only recognizes that States may cooperate to eliminate the drug trade. A Second Circuit decision is also of note:

> The historical restriction of universal jurisdiction to piracy, war crimes, and crimes against humanity demonstrates that universal jurisdiction arises under customary international law only where crimes (1) are universally condemned by the community of nations, and (2) by their nature occur either outside of a State or where there is no State capable of punishing, or competent to punish, the crime (as in a time of war).

See United States v. Yousef, 327 F.3d 56, 103 05 (2d Cir.2003) (finding certain terrorist acts not subject to universal jurisdiction); *see also* Restatement (Third) of Foreign Relations Law § 404. Drug trafficking does not rise to the required level of universal condemnation:

> While there is no firm agreement on the precise set of crimes subject to UJ, there is a general consensus that they are egregious, violent human rights abuses. Not a single UJ offense, or indeed widely recognized international crime, is a so-called victimless offense. All U.S. courts that have considered the issue have held that narcotics traffic falls outside UJ.

Kontorovich, *Beyond the Article I Horizon*, supra, at 1224 (footnotes omitted).

consent from other nations be deemed some form of extension of legislative power by treaty.*** *Id.* at 1227–29, 1238–48. Further, no other Article I powers save the MDLEA. *Id.* at 1237–51 (explaining that treaty power does not apply and that foreign commerce clause power does not apply absent a nexus). Thus, the exercise of Congressional power in enacting the MDLEA is not consistent with the Constitution, which limits Congress's power to proscribe crimes on the high sea to crimes of universal jurisdiction and crimes with a U.S. nexus.

III. Conclusion

On the sufficiency issue, the panel opinion uproots our precedent. On the question of the extraterritorial reach of the MDLEA, the panel opinion rests on substantial circuit precedent, which, in my view, is in need of serious reexamination. Each of these is adequate justification for en banc review. For the reasons stated, I respectfully dissent from the refusal to grant en banc review.

*** In this regard, it is important not to confuse consent by a flag nation with true statelessness, where the analysis may be quite different. *Id.* at 1229; *see also Caicedo*, 47 F.3d at 372–73.

UNITED STATES
v.
ERIK BANJOKO

590 F.3d 1278 (11th Cir. 2009)
Decided December 23, 2009

Elsie Mae Miller, Carlos Alfredo Williams, Frederick W. Tiemann, Fed. Pub. Defenders, Mobile, AL, for Defendant-Appellant.

Richard H. Loftin, Steven E. Butler, Mobile, AL, for Plaintiff-Appellee.

Before EDMONDSON, BIRCH and BLACK, Circuit Judges.

PER CURIAM:

Erik Banjoko appeals his conviction for stowing away on a vessel that entered United States jurisdiction, in violation of 18 U.S.C. § 2199. On appeal, Banjoko argues § 2199:(1) should be interpreted as requiring a knowing and voluntary act, and (2) does not clearly manifest an intent to overcome the presumption against applying a statute extraterritorially. After review, we conclude the district court did not err in instructing the jury, and affirm.[1]

I.

Banjoko contends although 18 U.S.C. § 2199 does not specify the intent required, it should be interpreted as requiring a knowing and voluntary act. Banjoko analogizes from our interpretations of 8 U.S.C. § 1324 and § 1326, which require the Government to prove knowledge of entry or bringing an alien into the United States even though the statutory text does not explicitly require proof of this mental state.

---

1 We review the district court's jury instructions *de novo* "when determining whether [the instructions] misstate the law or mislead the jury to the prejudice of the objecting party." *United States v. Bender,* 290 F.3d 1279, 1284 (11th Cir.2002) (quotation omitted). "We give the district court wide discretion as to the style and wording employed in the instructions, ascertaining that the instructions accurately reflect the law." *Id.* "Whether a criminal statute reaches a defendant's conduct is reviewed *de novo.*" *United States v. Lopez-Vanegas,* 493 F.3d 1305, 1311 (11th Cir.2007).

Section 2199 of Title 18 provides:

> Whoever, without the consent of the owner, charterer, master, or person in command of any vessel, or aircraft, with intent to obtain transportation, boards, enters or secretes himself aboard such vessel or aircraft and is thereon at the time of departure of said vessel or aircraft from a port, harbor, wharf, airport or other place within the jurisdiction of the United States; or
>
> Whoever, with like intent, having boarded, entered or secreted himself aboard a vessel or aircraft at any place within or without the jurisdiction of the United States, remains aboard after the vessel or aircraft has left such place and is thereon at any place within the jurisdiction of the United States. . . .

18 U.S.C. § 2199.

Before trial, Banjoko submitted a proposed jury instruction for defining the crime, with the following elements: (1) boarding a vessel, (2) with the intent to obtain transportation without the consent of the owner or master of the ship, (3) remaining aboard after the ship left port, and (4) with the intent to be transported into United States jurisdiction. The district court did not instruct the jury that the Government was required to prove Banjoko had the intent to enter United States jurisdiction.

Banjoko's claim the district court's jury instruction was erroneous is without merit because the statutory language shows intent to be transported to the United States is not an element of the offense. Section 2199 explicitly requires proof of intent "to obtain transportation" from a vessel without consent. 18 U.S.C. § 2199. Although the government must prove the defendant is on the vessel "at any place within the jurisdiction of the United States," the statute does not require proof of the defendant's knowledge or intent regarding United States jurisdiction. *Id.* The district court did not err by refusing to incorporate Banjoko's proposed jury instruction into the jury charge because it misstated the law by ignoring the plain reading of the statute. *United States v. Bender,* 290 F.3d 1279, 1284 (11th Cir.2002).

Banjoko's reliance on this Court's interpretations of § 1324 and § 1326 of Title 8 is also without merit. Banjoko argues this court has defined the elements of those statutes to include an alien knowingly entering or another person knowingly bringing an alien into the United States even though the statutory text does not impose these requirements. In his examples, proof of *mens rea* was required for the essential violation criminalized. *See* 8 U.S.C. § 1324 (prohibiting smuggling illegal aliens into the United States); *id.* § 1326 (prohibiting re-entry of deported illegal aliens). The essential violation criminalized by § 2199, however, is the act of stowing away, which does require proof of *mens rea.* 18 U.S.C. § 2199. The fact the vessel is within the jurisdiction of the United States is the reason the United States is involved, not the normative wrong punished by the crime. Therefore, the jurisdictional element of § 2199 is not analogous to the essential elements of § 1324 and § 1326.

II.

Banjoko argues the prohibition on stowaways contained in 18 U.S.C. § 2199 does not clearly manifest an intent to overcome the presumption against applying a statute extraterritorially, and the other provisions of § 2199 prohibit conduct that originates in or effects the United States. Even assuming § 2199 is intended to apply extraterritorially, Banjoko maintains due process requires compliance with one of the five essential principles of international law to criminalize his conduct.

Generally, a statute "is presumed to apply only domestically." *United States v. Lopez-Vanegas,* 493 F.3d 1305, 1311 (11th Cir.2007).

> [S]tatutes may be given extraterritorial application if the nature of the law permits it *and* Congress intends it. Absent an express intention on the face of the statutes to do so, the exercise of that power may be inferred from the nature of the offenses and Congress' other legislative efforts to eliminate the type of crime involved.

Id. at 1311–12 (citation and quotation omitted, emphasis in original). "Congress, under the protective principle of international law, may assert extraterritorial jurisdiction over vessels in the high seas that are engaged in conduct that has a potentially adverse effect and is generally recognized as a crime by nations that have reasonably developed legal systems." *United States v. Rendon,* 354 F.3d 1320, 1325 (11th Cir. 2003) (quotation omitted). "[T]he protective principle does not require that there be proof of an actual or intended effect inside the United States." *United States v. Marino-Garcia,* 679 F.2d 1373, 1381 n. 14 (11th Cir.1982).

Banjoko's argument Congress did not intend to apply the statute extraterritorially is without merit. The statute criminalizes stowing away "within or without the jurisdiction of the United States." 18 U.S.C. § 2199. Use of this language shows Congress's intent to apply the statute extraterritorially. *Lopez-Vanegas,* 493 F.3d at 1311. Additionally, the statute complies with international law by acting to protect the United States from stowaways. *Cf. Rendon,* 354 F.3d at 1325 (holding the United States may assert jurisdiction over vessels in international waters to prevent "potential adverse effects" in the United States). Moreover, United States jurisdiction does not rely on intent to affect the United States. *Marino-Garcia,* 679 F.2d at 1381 n. 14. Therefore, the district court correctly interpreted § 2199 when instructing the jury.

AFFIRMED.

UNITED STATES OF AMERICA
v.
MARCO ANTONIO SALCEDO-IBARRA

Case No. 8:07-CR-49-T-27TGW (M.D. Fla. 2009)
Decided July 6, 2009

ORDER

JAMES D. WHITTEMORE, District Judge.

BEFORE THE COURT is Defendant's Motion to Dismiss Count Three of Superseding Indictment (Dkt. 70) and the Government's Response in Opposition (Dkt. 74). Upon consideration, Defendant's Motion to Dismiss is DENIED.

Count Three of the Superseding Indictment charges Defendant with conspiracy to possess with intent to distribute five (5) kilograms or more of cocaine while on board a vessel subject to the jurisdiction of the United States, in violation of 46 U.S.C. §§ 70503(a) and 70506(a) and (b), and 21 U.S.C. § 960(b)(1)(B)(ii). (Dkt. 7). Defendant contends that he was never on board a vessel subject to the jurisdiction of the United States and therefore is not subject to prosecution under the Maritime Drug Enforcement Act (MDLEA), as codified in Title 46 of the United States Code. He contends that the "Define and Punish" clause of the United States Constitution,[1] which authorizes Congress to define and punish piracies and felonies committed on the high seas, does not grant extraterritorial jurisdiction over a foreign national who was never "on board" a vessel subject to the jurisdiction of the United States, and whose alleged conduct otherwise had no nexus to the United States.

Defendant's contentions, although premised on an accurate recitation of the history of the Define and Punish Clause, as well as the limitations on extraterritorial jurisdiction embodied in the Constitution, are mistaken. As a general proposition, district courts have subject matter jurisdiction over all offenses committed against the United States. U.S. Const. art. III, § 2; 18 U.S.C. § 3231; *United States v. De La Garza*, 516 F.3d 1266, 1271 (11th Cir. 2008). It follows that an individual

1 Art. I, § 8, cl. 10, United States Constitution, often referred to as the "Piracies and Felonies Clause." *See United States v. Estupinan*, 453 F.3d 1336, 1338 (11th Cir. 2006).

against whom an indictment is returned which alleges a violation of federal law is subject to the jurisdiction of the district courts. *United States v. Rendon*, 354 F.3d 1320 (11th Cir. 2003), *cert. denied,* 541 U.S. 1035 (2004).

Defendant is charged in Count Three with having conspired with others on board a vessel subject to the jurisdiction of the United States, to possess with intent to distribute cocaine. The alleged conspiracy is a violation of federal law. 46 U.S.C. § 70506(b). The object of the charged conspiracy, the possession of cocaine with intent to distribute while on board a vessel subject to the jurisdiction of the United States, is expressly proscribed by the MDLEA. Just as one who possesses cocaine with the intent to distribute while "on board" a vessel subject to the jurisdiction of the United States violates the MDLEA, one who conspires with those "on board" the vessel likewise violates the MDLEA. Just as the extraterritorial reach of the MDLEA is constitutional as to those on board the vessel, its reach is likewise constitutional as to an individual like Defendant, who allegedly conspired with those on board the vessel.[2]

Under the MDLEA, the jurisdictional component is identical with respect to those "on board" the vessel, and those who conspire to commit an MDLEA offense:

> Therefore, for a district court to have adjudicatory authority over a charge that a defendant "knowingly or intentionally . . . possess[ed] with intent to manufacture or distribute a controlled substance" in violation of 46 U.S.C. App'x § 1903(a), the Government must preliminarily show that the defendant was "on board a vessel subject to the jurisdiction of the United States." *Id.* Furthermore, for a district court to have adjudicatory authority over a charge that a defendant conspired to violate the substantive crime defined in subsection (a), the Government must preliminarily show that the conspiracy's vessel was, when apprehended, "subject to the jurisdiction of the United States." *Id.*;

De La Garza, 516 F.3d at 1271–72 (citing *United States v. Tinoco*, 304 F.3d 1088, 1107 (11th Cir. 2002))

To the extent Defendant complains that there is no "nexus" between his wholly extraterritorial conduct and the United States, and that his due process rights are violated by subjecting him to prosecution in the United States, his argument is unpersuasive. The Circuits disagree on whether a nexus between conduct ostensibly proscribed by the MDLEA and the United States is required. *United States v. Estrada-Obregon,* 270 Fed. Appx. 978, 981, n.1 (11th Cir. 2008). This Circuit, and others, require no such nexus in a prosecution under the MDLEA. *See United States v. Portocarrero*, 182 Fed. Appx. 889, 893 (11th Cir. 2006)("Moreover, we have noted that 'this circuit and other circuits have not embellished the MDLEA

---

2 This case is therefore distinguishable from *United States v. Lopez-Vanegas,* 493 F.3d 1305 (11th Cir. 2007). There, there was no evidence that the defendants had ever agreed to possess cocaine in the United States, the requisite nexus under 21 U.S.C. § 841(a)(1), under which they were charged.

with a nexus requirement.'") (citing *United States v. Rendon, supra); United States v. Cardales,* 168 F.3d 548, 552–53 (1st Cir.), *cert. denied,* 528 U.S. 838 (1999); *United States v. Martinez-Hildago,* 993 F.2d 1052, 1055 (3d Cir. 1993), *cert. denied,* 510 U.S. 1048 (1994); *United States v. Perez Oviedo,* 281 F.3d 400, 403 (3d Cir. 2002).

In those jurisdictions which require a nexus, the Government must demonstrate that there exists "a sufficient nexus between the conduct condemned and the United States" such that application of the statute would not be arbitrary or fundamentally unfair to a defendant. *United States v. Medjuck,* 156 F.3d 916, 918 (9th Cir. 1998); *United States v. Zakharov,* 468 F.3d 1171, 1177 (9th Cir. 2006); *United States v. Yousef,* 327 F.3d 56, 111 (2d Cir. 2003). In *Medjuck*, although the conspirators did not intend to deliver the drugs directly into the United States, "both economics and geography dictate that at least some portion of the hashish would at some point be found in the United States," and the requisite nexus was accordingly found to have been established. 156 F.3d at 919.

To the extent due process requires a nexus between the alleged conduct of Defendant and the United States in this MDLEA prosecution, a sufficient nexus between the alleged conduct and the United States exists. The affidavits filed in support of the Government's Response proffer facts which refute Defendant's contention that the crime charged in Count Three "had no effect or intended effect on the United States." (Dkt. 74-2, at ¶¶ 21). Although the ultimate facts supporting Count Three remain to be proven, it cannot be seriously disputed that shipments of cocaine interdicted in the Eastern Pacific on stateless vessels are destined, at least in part, for the United States. Once the conduct giving rise to subject matter jurisdiction occurs, those who conspire to commit that act are subject to prosecution under the MDLEA. The prosecution of one who participates in the underlying agreement to transport cocaine on board stateless vessels is not, therefore, arbitrary or fundamentally unfair, considering the underlying purpose of the MDLEA and its constitutional reach.

The MDLEA is a constitutional exercise of extraterritorial jurisdiction pursuant to the Define and Punish Clause, under the "protective principle" of international law. *Tinoco,* 304 F.3d at 1110. Likewise, as applied to foreign nationals such as Defendant, the MDLEA is constitutional. *Estrada Obregon,* 270 Fed. Appx. at 979. International drug trafficking, as proscribed by the MDLEA, is universally condemned as an offense against the "Law of Nations" and presents a specific threat to the security and societal well-being of the United States. *United States v. Estupinan-Estupinan*, 244 Fed. Appx. 308 (11th Cir. 2007). Just as trafficking in narcotics on the high seas is considered an offense against the "Law of Nations," including the United States, likewise, conspiring to traffic in narcotics on the high seas constitutes such an offense.

Defendant makes no compelling argument that international law would be violated by his prosecution. Indeed, a nation is permitted "to assert jurisdiction over a person whose conduct outside the nation's territory threatens its national security." *Cardelas*, 168 F.3d at 553. Simply put, for purposes of jurisdiction under the MDLEA, there can be no meaningful distinction between those individuals found "on board" stateless vessels laden with cocaine and those who planned, organized or funded those ventures.[3]

Defendant contends that the Eleventh Circuit has "expressly recognized that Congress did not intend for the conspiracy portion of the MDLEA to apply to wholly extraterritorial conspiracies." (Dkt. 70, p. 14). This contention is a misreading of *De La Garza, supra.* The reference in *De La Garza* to whether Congress intended the MDLEA "to apply to wholly extraterritorial conspiracies" is in a footnote in the opinion. The court did not definitively address the issue. Rather, it only identified and paraphrased "arguments touched upon, though not explicitly raised, in De La Garza's brief . . . ." *De La Garza*, 516 F.3d at 1272, n.4.

The footnote in *De La Garza* cites *United States v. MacAllister,* 160 F.3d 1304, 1307 (11th Cir. 1998). In *MacAllister,* the Court discussed "whether 21 U.S.C. § 963 may be applied extraterritorially, and if so, whether its application to MacAllister's case is appropriate." 160 F.3d at 1306. Recognizing that "[f]ederal criminal statutes may properly include extraterritorial effects," the Court examined "whether 'language in [§ 963] . . . gives any indication of a congressional purpose to extend its coverage beyond places over which the United States has sovereignty or has some measure of legislative control.'" *Id.* at 1307. Acknowledging that §§ 953 and 963 do "not expressly provide for extraterritorial application," the Court nonetheless found the requisite Congressional intent inferred from "the nature of the offense." *Id.*

> Under this rule, the district court properly concluded that drug smuggling is an offense where extraterritorial application is inferred. "[B]y its very nature [drug smuggling] involves foreign countries, and . . . the accomplishment of the crime always requires some action in a foreign country . . . ."(citation omitted). Logic dictates that Congress would not have passed a drug conspiracy statute that prohibits international drug smuggling activities, while simultaneously undermining the statute by limiting its extraterritorial application.(citation omitted).

160 F.3d at 1308.

The MDLEA, like the Comprehensive Drug Abuse Prevention and Control Act of 1970 discussed in *MacAllister*, is intended to apply to international drug smuggling. Unlike the Comprehensive Drug Abuse Prevention and Control Act of 1970, however, the MDLEA expressly provides for extraterritorial application to those possessing narcotics with the intent to distribute while on board vessels subject to the jurisdiction of the United States. Defendant's contention that Congress did not

---

3 To the extent Defendant suggests that his prosecution intrudes the sovereign territory of Colombia, suffice it to say that Colombia consented to Defendant's extradition for prosecution under the MDLEA. (Dkt. 74-3).

intend to apply the conspiracy provision of the MDLEA to one who conspires with others found on board a vessel subject to the jurisdiction of the United States, and that application of the MDLEA to him would be contrary to international law is unpersuasive, particularly considering the reasoning in *MacAllister.* There, application of the Comprehensive Drug Abuse Prevention and Control Act of 1970 was approved based upon "the objective territorial principle." The court found that "the defendant's actions . . . produced some effect in the United States . . . ." *Id.* at 1307. Extraterritorial application of the statute was therefore reasonable, based on the principle that "[d]rug smuggling is a serious and universally condemned offense," and therefore, "no conflict is likely to be created by extraterritorial regulation of drug traffickers." *Id.*

Here, extraterritorial application of the conspiracy provisions of the MDLEA to Defendant, who was not found on board a vessel subject to the jurisdiction of the United States, but allegedly conspired with those on board, is justified on the objective territorial principle. "The protective principle permits a nation to assert jurisdiction over a person whose conduct outside the nation's territory threatens the nation's security or could potentially interfere with the operation of its governmental functions." *United States v. Romero-Galue,* 757 F.2d 1147, 1154–55 (11th Cir. 1985) (citing *United States v. Marino-Garcia*, 679 F.2d 1373, 1381 n.14 (11th Cir. 1982), *cert. denied*, 459 U.S. 1114 (1983)); *United States v. Columba-Colella*, 604 F.2d 356, 358 (5th Cir. 1979); *Rivard v. United States*, 375 F.2d 882, 885, n.7 (5th Cir. 1967), *cert. denied*, 389 U.S. 884 (1967) ("There is nothing in the objective territorial principle announced in *Strassheim, Ford* and *Marin* hich creates a jurisdictional distinction between a substantive offense and a conspiracy.").

As discussed, the substantive act proscribed by the MDLEA, the possession of narcotics while on board a vessel subject to the jurisdiction of the United States, has a sufficiently deleterious effect within the United States to justify this country in prohibiting that conduct. *See United States v. Estupinan,* 453 F.3d 1336, 1339 (11th Cir. 2006)("Indeed, as the Third Circuit has recognized, '[i]nasmuch as the trafficking of narcotics is condemned universally by law-abiding nations, we see no reason to conclude that it is 'fundamentally unfair' for Congress to provide for the punishment of persons apprehended with narcotics on the high seas.'"). Just as "it is not fundamentally unfair to prosecute those 'apprehended with narcotics on the high sea,'" it is not fundamentally unfair for Defendant to be prosecuted for conspiring to engage in such conduct. Defendant's Motion to Dismiss Count Three is accordingly DENIED.

DONE AND ORDERED

CUNZHU ZHENG
v.
YAHOO! INC.

Case No. C-08-1068 MMC (N.D. Cal. 2009)
Decided Dec. 2, 2009

ORDER GRANTING DEFENDANTS' MOTION TO DISMISS PLAINTIFFS' THIRD AMENDED COMPLAINT UNDER RULE 12(B)(6); VACATING HEARING

MAXINE M. CHESNEY, District Judge.

Before the Court is defendants Yahoo!, Inc. ("Yahoo!") and Yahoo! Hong Kong, Ltd.'s ("Yahoo! HK") (collectively, "Yahoo! Defendants") "Motion to Dismiss Plaintiffs' Third Amended Complaint Under Rule 12(b)(6)," filed August 7, 2009.[1] Plaintiffs Cunzhu Zhen, Liu Guokai, Tao Jun, and the China Democracy Party have filed opposition, to which the Yahoo! Defendants have replied. Having read and considered the papers filed in support of and in opposition to the motion, the Court finds the matter suitable for decision on the parties' respective submissions, VACATES the hearing scheduled for December 4, 2009, and rules as follows.

BACKGROUND

In the Third Amended Complaint ("TAC"), plaintiffs allege that Yahoo! China disclosed to the Peoples Republic of China ("PRC") "specific personal information" about plaintiffs, in particular, "Internet user information" and "specific identifying information about the [p]laintiffs and their electronic communications" (*see* TAC ¶¶ 14, 27), and that, as a result of the disclosures, plaintiffs were subjected by the PRC to "serious injuries, including torture, detention, imprisonment, degrading and/or humiliating treatment and emotional distress" (*see* TAC ¶¶ 22, 52) and, additionally, incurred "serious economic damages" (*see* TAC ¶ 52).[2] According to

1 A third defendant, the Peoples Republic of China, has not appeared.

2 Plaintiffs allege that each individual plaintiff is a citizen of the PRC who presently lives in exile in the United States. (*See* TAC ¶¶ 3, 4, 6.)

plaintiffs, Yahoo! HK was, at the time of the alleged disclosures, the "parent company" of Yahoo! China and was "responsible for operating and managing Yahoo! China" (*see* TAC ¶¶ 11, 15), while Yahoo!, as the "parent company" of Yahoo! HK, "exercised functional control and supervision over important aspects of Yahoo! China," including "supervision and control of policy and legal decisions made by Yahoo! China's legal team," such as "review[ing] and approv[ing]" Yahoo! China's "decision to disclose Internet user information" to the PRC (*see* TAC ¶¶ 11, 14).

Based on the above allegations, plaintiffs allege that the Yahoo! Defendants violated the Electronic Communications Privacy Act ("ECPA"), 18 U.S.C. §§ 2517–2712, and, based on such "unlawful act," violated § 17200 of the California Business & Professions Code as well.[3]

DISCUSSION

"In 1986, Congress passed the [ECPA], which was intended to afford privacy protection to electronic communications." *Konop v. Hawaiian Airlines, Inc.*, 302 F.3d 868, 874 (9th Cir.2002) (internal citation omitted). "Title I of the ECPA amended the federal Wiretap Act, which previously addressed only wire and oral communications, to address the interception of electronic communications." ki (internal citation, quotation, and alteration omitted). "Title II of the ECPA created the Stored Communications Act (SCA), which was designed to address access to stored wire and electronic communications and transactional records." ki (internal citation, quotation and alteration omitted). In sum, the ECPA, by amending the Wiretap Act, prohibits interception of electronic communications, *see* 18 U.S.C. § 2511(1), and, by creating the SCA, prohibits, *inter alia,* unauthorized access to certain electronic communications, *see* 18 U.S.C. § 2701(a)(1), and, subject to specified exceptions, the divulging of the contents of electronic communications during such time as the communications are electronically stored, *see* 18 U.S.C. § 2702(a). The ECPA also provides a private cause of action for persons injured by a violation of the ECPA. *See* 18 U.S.C. §§ 2520, 2707.

Here, as discussed above, plaintiffs assert Yahoo! China's alleged disclosures of plaintiffs' electronic communications and other information to the PRC were in violation of the ECPA, and that the Yahoo! Defendants can be held liable therefor. Specifically, plaintiffs allege violations of §§ 2511, 2701, and 2702. (*See* TAC ¶¶ 48–50.) The Yahoo! Defendants argue plaintiffs' claims under the ECPA and

3 As pleaded, plaintiffs' § 17200 claim could be interpreted as alleging that the Yahoo! Defendants engaged in additional unlawful acts, specifically, by violating the Alien Tort Statute, the Torture Victims Protection Act of 1991, and/or the United Nations Convention Against Torture. (*See* TAC ¶ 65.) Subsequent to the filing of the TAC, however, plaintiffs have clarified those specific alleged violations are not "predicate offenses" alleged under § 17200 against the Yahoo! Defendants, but rather, are only alleged against the PRC. (*See* Pls.' Opp. to Mot. to Dismiss Under FRCP 12(b) (1) and (7), filed October 19, 2009, at 2:21–24.)

plaintiffs' derivative claims under § 17200 are subject to dismissal because, defendants argue, the ECPA does not apply outside of the United States.

It is a "longstanding principle of American law that legislation is presumed to apply only within the territorial jurisdiction of the United States unless the contrary affirmative intention of Congress is clearly expressed." *See ARC Ecology v. U.S. Dep't of the Air Force,* 411 F.3d 1092, 1097, 1103 (9th Cir.2005) (holding plaintiffs failed to state claim against federal agency for alleged violations of CERLA at military bases in Philippines, where plaintiffs failed to overcome "statutory presumption against extraterritoriality"); *cf. Chua Han Mow v. United States,* 730 F.2d 1308, 1311 (9th Cir.1984) (finding "clear" congressional intent to "give extraterritorial effect" to statute prohibiting manufacture of drugs, where statute explicitly provided it was "intended to reach prohibited acts committed outside the territorial jurisdiction of the United States"). "[C]ourts must resolve restrictively any doubts concerning the extraterritorial application of a statute." *See ARC Ecology*, 411 F.3d at 1097.

Although it does not appear that any court has expressly considered whether the ECPA applies outside the United States, the Ninth Circuit, as the Yahoo! Defendants note, has held that the version of the Wiretap Act in existence prior to its amendment by the ECPA had "no extraterritorial effect." *See United States v. Peterson,* 812 F.2d 486, 492 (9th Cir.1987) (rejecting argument that wiretapping of telephones in Thailand could violate Wiretap Act; holding Wiretap Act "has no extraterritorial effect"). In so holding, the Ninth Circuit cited two Second Circuit decisions, each of which, in turn, cited the reasoning set forth in *United States v. Toscanino*, 500 F.2d 267 (2nd Cir.1974). In finding that the pre-ECPA version of the Wiretap Act had "no application outside of the United States," the Second Circuit, in *Toscanino,* relied on a statement in the legislative history that "[t]he term 'wire communication,' as used in the [Wiretap Act], is intended to refer to communications 'through our Nation's communications network,' " *see id.* at 279 (quoting 1968 U.S.C.C.A.N. 2178), and the fact that the Wiretap At, in "prescribing the procedures to be followed in obtaining a wiretap authorization," made "no provision for obtaining authorization for a wiretap in a foreign country." *See id.; see also Stowe v. Devoy*, 588 F.2d 336, 341 (2nd Cir.1978) ("[T]he federal statute governing wiretapping and eavesdropping, 18 U.S.C. § 2510, et seq., has no application outside the United States .").

Plaintiffs point to no language in the ECPA itself, nor to any statement in the legislative history of the ECPA, indicating Congress intended that the ECPA, unlike the version of the Wiretap Act then in effect, apply to activities occurring outside the United States. *See, e.g., Smith v. United States*, 507 U.S. 197, 204, 113 S. Ct. 1178, 122 L.Ed.2d 548 (1993) (holding, where plaintiff alleging claim under Federal Tort Claims Act based on act in Antarctica failed to offer "clear evidence of congressional intent to apply the FTCA to claims arising in Antarctica", plaintiff failed to show FTCA applied to claims arising in Antarctica). Nor is any such intent apparent.

First, no language in the ECPA itself suggests an intent that its provisions apply to interceptions and disclosures occurring in other countries. The ECPA did not amend the portion of the Wiretap Act that made no provision for obtaining authorization for wiretaps in a foreign country, nor did the ECPA, in amending the Wiretap Act and creating the SCA, reference in any manner activities occurring outside the United States.

Further, the available legislative history not only fails to include any statement indicating Congress intended the ECPA to apply outside the United States, the legislative history, specifically, Senate Report No. 99-541, clearly expresses Congress's intent that the ECPA not apply to interceptions outside the United States:

> Subparagraph (D) [of the ECPA] specifies that wire, cable or similar connections furnished or operated by any person engaged in providing or operating such facilities for the transmission of "communications affecting interstate or foreign commerce," are within the definition of a "wire communication." This language recognizes that private networks and intra-company communications systems are common today and brings them within the protection of the statute. However, that language is not meant to suggest that the [ECPA] applies to interceptions made outside the territorial United States. Like the Omnibus Crime Control and Safe Streets Act of 1968 which it revises, the [ECPA] regulates only those interceptions conducted within the territorial United States.

See 1986 U.S.S.C.A.N. 3555, 3566.[4]

Notwithstanding the above, plaintiffs argue the Court can extend the application of the ECPA outside the United States for "policy reasons," specifically, for the reason that the "protective principle of jurisdiction" should be applied, under the theory that threats to persons advocating democracy in the PRC constitutes a threat to the United States. (*See* Pls.' Opp. at 11:11–12:16.) In support of this argument, plaintiffs rely on *Peterson,* in which the Ninth Circuit, in addition to holding the then-existing version of the Wiretap Act did not apply outside the United States, held that 21 U.S.C. § 955a(c), a statute then in effect that prohibited the manufacture and distribution of controlled substances, applied to "the high seas," i.e., outside the territorial boundaries of the United States, because § 955a(c) "specifically" included a provision applying the statute to the high seas. *See Peterson*, 812 F.2d at 493. The defendant in *Peterson* then argued that if § 955a(c), as a matter of statutory construction, applied to conduct on the high seas, the statute was "an improper and unconstitutional exercise of extraterritorial jurisdiction." *See id.* The Ninth Circuit rejected the defendant's argument, finding Congress may prevent "drug trafficking" under the "protective principle of jurisdiction" because drug

4 The Senate Report's reference to the "Omnibus Crime Control and Safe Streets Act of 1968" is a reference to the Wiretap Act as it existed before it was amended by the ECPA. *See Peterson*, 812 F.2d at 492.

trafficking "presents the sort of threat to our nation's ability to function that merits application of the protective principle of jurisdiction." *See id.* at 493–94.

Plaintiffs' reliance on *Peterson* is unavailing. Where Congress makes clear its intent that a statute is to apply outside the United States, extraterritorial application of such statute is, under some circumstances, subject to judicial "restriction[ ]," for the reason that any such "application of the statute to the acts in question [must] not violate the due process clause of the Fifth Amendment." *See United States v. Davis*, 905 F.2d 245, 248–49 and n. 2 (9th Cir.1990) (citing cases holding "extra-territorial application" of statute was justified by "protective principle"). Here, by contrast, there is no extraterritorial application to either enforce or restrict. As discussed above, Congress has not made clear an intent that the ECPA apply outside the United States, and, indeed, the available legislative history clearly reflects the congressional intent that the ECPA not apply outside the United States. Consequently, no issue regarding whether extraterritorial application would comport with due process is presented by the instant case.

Lastly, plaintiffs argue that the Yahoo! Defendants have "email servers around the globe," and that when a Yahoo! user in one city in the PRC sends an electronic communication to a Yahoo! user in another city in the PRC, the communication "may" travel through the Yahoo! Defendants' network, which is located, in part, in the United States. (*See* Pls.' Opp., filed October 19, 2009, at 11:3–10.) Consistent with this theory, plaintiffs, in the TAC, allege that the Yahoo! Defendants acquired "communications sent and/or received by [p]laintiffs through the use of an electronic device" that is a "part of, and utilized in, the Yahoo! Defendants' electronic communications system, which exists, in part, in the United States." (*See* TAC ¶ 50.) Plaintiffs further allege, however, that the acquisitions and subsequent disclosures to the PRC were made "locally" by Yahoo! China. (*See* TAC ¶ 14.) Because the alleged interceptions and disclosures occurred in the PRC, the ECPA does not apply to them, even if the communications, prior to their interception and disclosure, traveled electronically through a network located in the United States. *See, e.g.*, *Stowe*, 588 F.2d at 341 and n. 12 (holding, where official in Canada intercepted telephone call made from United States to Canada, Wiretap Act did not govern legality of interception "even though the intercepted phone conversations traveled in part over the United States communication system"); *United States v. Cotroni,* 527 F.2d 708, 711 (2nd Cir.1975) (holding Wiretap Act inapplicable to communication intercepted in Canada that had "traveled in part" over "United States communication facilities"; citing legislative history indicating "Congress sought by [enacting Wiretap Act] to regulate interceptions, not wire communications").[5]

5 In light of the Court's findings with respect to the applicability of the ECPA outside the United States, the Court does not decide whether plaintiffs' claims against the Yahoo! Defendants are subject to dismissal for the additional reasons set forth in the instant motion.

In sum, plaintiffs' claims that the Yahoo! Defendants violated the ECPA are subject to dismissal with prejudice, for the reason that the ECPA does not apply outside the United States. Further, because plaintiffs' claim that the Yahoo! Defendants violated § 17200 is based on the theory that defendants violated the ECPA, the § 17200 claim likewise is subject to dismissal with prejudice.[6]

Accordingly, the Yahoo! Defendants' motion to dismiss for failure to state a claim will be granted.

CONCLUSION

For the reasons discussed above, the Yahoo! Defendants' motion to dismiss the Third Amended Complaint for failure to state a claim is hereby GRANTED, and plaintiffs' claims against the Yahoo! Defendants are hereby DISMISSED with prejudice.

IT IS SO ORDERED.

---

6 The § 17200 claim is also alleged against the PRC, and is, to such extent, based on conduct other than alleged violations of the ECPA. Consequently, the instant order is inapplicable to the § 17200 claim against the PRC.

II. TERRITORIES, TRUSTEESHIPS, BOUNDARIES & NAVIGABLE WATERS

1. Territories in General

DELAWARE RIVER & BAY AUTHORITY
v.
JAN D. KOPACZ

584 F.3d 622 (3d Cir. 2009)
Decided September 25, 2009

Mary E. Reeves, Esq. [ARGUED], Donna Adelsberger & Associates, Glenside, PA, Counsel for Appellant/Cross Appellee.

E. Alfred Smith, Esq. [ARGUED], E. Alfred Smith & Associates, Wayne, PA, Counsel for Appellee/Cross Appellant.

Before: RENDELL, STAPLETON and ALARCON*, Circuit Judges. ALARCON, Circuit Judge, dissenting.

* Honorable Arthur L. Alarcon, Senior Judge, United States Court of Appeals for the Ninth Circuit, sitting by designation.

OPINION OF THE COURT

RENDELL, Circuit Judge.

In this appeal from the District Court's award of declaratory judgment in favor of defendant Jan Kopacz, and against plaintiff Delaware River & Bay Authority ("DRBA"), we are called upon to decide two issues of admiralty law: (1) whether commuter seamen, who eat and sleep on land, are entitled to "maintenance and cure"—payment from a shipowner to a seaman to cover medical, food, and lodging expenses during the seaman's recovery from illness or injury; and (2) if so, whether a shipowner is relieved of its maintenance and cure obligation when the injured seaman receives Social Security disability benefits and long-term disability payments provided by the shipowner. Relying on our opinions in *Barnes v. Andover Company, L.P.*, 900 F.2d 630 (3d Cir. 1990), and *Shaw v. Ohio River Company*, 526 F.2d 193 (3d Cir. 1975), the District Court concluded that commuter seamen are entitled to maintenance and cure, independent of other benefits paid to the seaman. Accordingly, the District Court awarded Kopacz maintenance of $50,790.00, plus prejudgment interest of $2,204.29, but denied Kopacz's claim for consequential damages, including lost wages, pain and suffering, and attorney's fees and costs. Both parties timely appealed.

DRBA's central contention on appeal is that payment of maintenance would produce a "double recovery," because Kopacz's wages already enabled him to procure food and housing on land, and because Social Security disability and long-term disability payments made to Kopacz adequately covered his living expenses. DRBA argues, further, that the award of prejudgment interest was punitive and thus impermissible. The sole argument advanced in Kopacz's cross-appeal is that consequential damages were improperly denied. Finding no error in the District Court's thoughtful resolution of these issues, we will affirm its order.

I. Background

Maintenance is the payment by a shipowner to a sailor for the sailor's food and lodging costs incurred while he is ashore as a result of illness or accident. *Barnes*, 900 F.2d at 631. A common law remedy, maintenance, derived from medieval maritime codes, was incorporated into American jurisprudence nearly two centuries ago. *Harden v. Gordon, 11 F.Cas.* 480, 482–83, F. Cas. No. 6047 (C.C.D. Me. 1823) (No. 6,047); *see The Osceola,* 189 U.S. 158, 175, 23 S. Ct. 483, 47 L. Ed. 760 (1903). Its original purpose was clear and compelling—to ensure injured seamen funds adequate to cover basic living expenses during their recovery. The imposition of such a duty, it was felt, would benefit both shipowners and seamen, by encouraging shipowners to implement appropriate Safeguards to protect sailors, and by encouraging seamen to undertake hazardous voyages:

> Seamen are by the peculiarity of their lives liable to sudden sickness from change of climate, exposure to perils, and exhausting labour. They are generally poor and friendless, and acquire habits of gross indulgence, carelessness, and improvidence. If some provision be not made for them in sickness at the expense of the ship, they must often in foreign ports suffer the accumulated evils of disease, and poverty, and sometimes perish from the want of suitable nourishment. . . . If these expenses are a charge upon the ship, the interest of the owner will be immediately connected with that of the seamen. The master will watch over their health with vigilance and fidelity. . . . Even the merchant himself derives an ultimate benefit from what may seem at first an onerous charge. It encourages seamen to engage in perilous voyages with more promptitude, and at lower wages. It diminishes the temptation to plunderage upon the approach of sickness; and urges the seamen to encounter hazards in the ship's service, from which they might otherwise be disposed to withdraw.

Barnes, 900 F.2d at 633 (quoting *Harden*, 11 F.Cas. at 483).

Since *Harden* was decided almost 200 years ago, the lot of the "poor and friendless" seaman has improved considerably. As we noted in *Barnes*, union contracts may guarantee sailors a host of benefits, including overtime and premium pay, vacation allowances, disability pensions, and various amenities, including televisions and washers and dryers. 900 F.2d at 637. The emergence of these contractually-guaranteed benefits, however, has not diminished our historic solicitude toward seamen, who continue to be viewed by the law as "wards of the admiralty." *Id.* at 636–37. Accordingly, maintenance, a duty that is "annexed to the employment contract," that "attaches once the seaman enters the service of the ship," and that "no private agreement is competent to abrogate," has retained its vitality in the modern era. *Id.* at 636.

DRBA guarantees many of the benefits discussed above to its seamen. The interaction of these benefits and the maintenance obligation lies at the heart of this appeal.

A permanent full-time employee of DRBA who suffers an injury on the job is entitled to full wages for the first 90 days of disability. Thereafter, the employee is entitled to benefits equivalent to 60% of his wages, which are paid through a long-term disability ("LTD") policy funded wholly by DRBA, and administered by Hartford Insurance Company ("Hartford").[1] The personnel manual provided to Kopacz sets forth the purpose of LTD benefits—to "provide a continuing income should the employee's ability to earn a living be interrupted or terminated by a prolonged disability." A. 6–7.

The duty to provide LTD benefits stems from a provision in the collective bargaining agreement between DRBA and its marine employees, providing that, "Employer agrees to continue to provide all permanent full-time employees long-term disability plans that are offered to . . . employees generally." A. 7. The agreement makes no mention of maintenance payments, and DRBA does not maintain an insurance policy specifically to cover its maintenance obligation to seamen.

In the event of a delay in the payment of LTD benefits, an injured sailor also receives the value of his sick and annual leave. According to DRBA's risk manager, Bonnie Miller, the payment of annual leave is distinct from maintenance and is merely a stop-gap to enable an injured seaman to cover his living expenses during the pendency of his LTD application.

Kopacz suffered a debilitating back injury in December 2004 and was subsequently deemed unfit to return to duty by DRBA. As a full-time permanent employee, Kopacz received his full wages for 90 days following the date of his disability, equivalent to approximately $9,900. Kopacz also received the value of his sick and annual leave, equivalent to approximately $4,600. Thereafter, Hartford paid Kopacz monthly LTD benefits of $2,192 for 17 months, beginning in April 2005 and ending in September 2006.[2] DRBA did not make separate maintenance payments to Kopacz, nor did Kopacz request them.

---

1 Hartford calculates an employee's monthly LTD benefit by: (1) multiplying the monthly income loss by the benefit percentage; (2) comparing the result with the maximum benefit; and (3) deducting other income benefits, including Social Security disability payments, from the lesser amount.

2 DRBA also mistakenly transmitted three checks, totaling $1,770.00, to Kopacz. Miller explained that this was done because the prior plan administrator required DRBA to pay seamen "maintenance wages" in the amount of $450 per month, or $15 daily—payments which were then deducted from the LTD benefit paid to seamen. Accustomed to making these payments, DRBA inadvertently sent Kopacz checks with notes indicating that the payments constituted "maintenance wages" for the period between April 2005 and July 2005, and that the payments offset Kopacz's LTD benefit.

Because Hartford also required injured seamen to apply for Social Security disability ("SSD") benefits, which, if approved, would be deducted from monthly LTD benefits, Kopacz submitted an application for SSD benefits in October 2006. After approval of Kopacz's application, the Social Security Administration transmitted a check to him in the amount of $17,142.00, representing his total benefits retroactive to July 2005, and thereafter provided monthly payments of $1,167.00.

Upon discovering the payment of $17,142.00, Hartford demanded reimbursement of slightly less than this sum[3] and advised Kopacz that his LTD benefit would thereafter be reduced by the amount of his monthly SSD payment. After Kopacz refused to reimburse Hartford, it suspended payment of LTD benefits. Shortly thereafter, Kopacz advised DRBA that it, not he, was required to reimburse Hartford for this sum; when DRBA declined to do so, this suit followed.

DRBA sued Kopacz in the United States District Court for the District of Delaware, seeking a declaratory judgment that DRBA did not owe Kopacz maintenance and cure. After a one-day bench trial, the District Court concluded that Kopacz was entitled to maintenance in the amount of $50,790.00, plus prejudgment interest of $2,204.29. However, the District Court denied Kopacz's claim for consequential damages, including lost wages, pain and suffering, and attorney's fees and costs.[4] Both parties timely appealed.[5]

DRBA contends that commuter seamen, who eat and sleep ashore, are ineligible for maintenance. It also argues, in the alternative, that the District Court should have deducted other payments made to Kopacz, including LTD and SSD, from the amount of maintenance owed to Kopacz—a result that, DRBA maintains, is necessary to avoid double recovery. Further, DRBA contends that the award of prejudgment was punitive, rather than compensatory, and thus impermissible. Kopacz's cross-appeal urges that the District Court improperly denied his claim for consequential damages.

---

3 The amount of reimbursement requested—$16,607.92—was slightly less than the lump sum amount received from the Social Security Administration due to differences in the eligibility dates under the Hartford policy and the Social Security disability program.

4 The parties stipulated that Kopacz's monthly living expenses were $2,190.00 in the time period beginning in January 2005 and ending in April 2007, that Kopacz attained his point of maximum medical improvement on the latter date, and that the monthly SSD benefits of $1,167.00 represented Kopacz's sole source of income since October 2006, with the exception of interest earned on a money market account. All of Kopacz's documented medical expenses have been paid, and Kopacz has made no claim for cure.

5 The District Court had subject matter jurisdiction over this admiralty action under 28 U.S.C. § 1333. We have appellate jurisdiction over the final judgment of the District Court under 28 U.S.C. § 1291. We review the District Court's findings of fact under a clearly erroneous standard. *See Sheet Metal Workers Local 19 v. 2300 Group, Inc.*, 949 F.2d 1274, 1278 (3d Cir. 1991). However, our review of the District Court's application of the law to these facts is plenary. *See Tudor Dev. Group v. United States Fidelity & Guar. Co.*, 968 F.2d 357, 359 (3d Cir. 1992).

II. Discussion

A. Commuter Seamen

DRBA asks the Court to adopt a *per se* rule denying maintenance to commuter seamen. DRBA observes that the rationale for maintenance—to provide seamen compensation equivalent to food and lodging received at sea—is inapplicable to commuter seamen, who eat and sleep ashore. DRBA argues, further, that the wages of commuter seamen are already computed with the expectation that they will pay for their own food and housing expenses on land and, therefore, an award of maintenance would produce an unjustified windfall. DRBA maintains that, based on these concerns, we left "open the question" of whether commuter seamen are entitled to maintenance in *Barnes*, 900 F.2d at 643.

Our inquiry begins with *Barnes*. There, we considered whether a blue water seaman, who maintained a home ashore, was entitled to include in his calculation of maintenance expenses incurred in connection with his permanent lodging, or whether he was solely permitted to recover the incremental costs attributable to his presence on land, including food, laundry, and gas. In approving Barnes's recovery of costs associated with his permanent lodging, we cited precedents awarding maintenance to commuter seamen:

> Many of the reasons given by the courts for awarding maintenance to land-based seamen who, by definition, ordinarily incur their own expenses for food and lodging are also applicable to inclusion in maintenance of the prorated costs of permanent lodging by a blue water seaman: the status of seamen as wards of the admiralty, *Weiss*, 235 F.2d at 313; *Duplantis*, 298 F.Supp. at 14–15 & n. 3; consistency with maritime tradition, *Weiss*, 235 F.2d at 313; *Duplantis*, 298 F.Supp. at 14–15[;] and the need to provide support to those who are ineligible for workman's compensation or other means of support. *Weiss*, 235 F.2d at 313.

Id. at 642.

Despite our reliance on these precedents in *Barnes*, DRBA insists, "This Circuit has left open the question of whether a commuter seaman, such as Kopacz, is even entitled to maintenance in the first place." Appellant's Br. at 14. Although *Barnes* acknowledged that there was "some logic" in denying maintenance to shore-based seamen, the court stressed that the "life of the law" is "experience," not "logic." *Id.* at 643. *Barnes* then reiterated Congress and the Supreme Court's "long-established solicitude" to seamen, the "liberal attitude" regarding the scope of maintenance, and the interpretative canon requiring that ambiguities in regard to maintenance be "resolved in favor of the seaman"—all considerations that, *Barnes* concluded, supported an expansive understanding of the right to maintenance. *Id.* at 637, 643 (citing *Vaughan v. Atkinson*, 369 U.S. 527, 532–33, 82 S. Ct. 997, 8 L. Ed. 2d 88 (1962)). *Barnes* also quoted at length from an opinion rejecting a position identical to that urged by DRBA:

> To deny [maintenance to a seaman] because he does not receive lodging and meals aboard ship raises problems that would distort the simple lines of the maintenance

> remedy. . . . Indeed, the rationale that maintenance is allowable only when meals would have been served aboard challenges the now well settled doctrine that the disabled seaman is entitled to be paid maintenance beyond the end of his voyage, for were maintenance to be allowed only for those days during which the ship would have served him meals, it would end when the voyage was over.

Id. at 642 (quoting *Hudspeth v. Atlantic & Gulf Stevedores, Inc.*, 266 F. Supp. 937, 943 (E.D. La. 1967)); *see Smith v. Del. Bay Launch Serv., Inc.*, 972 F. Supp. 836, 849 (D.C. Del. 1997); *see also Crooks v. United States*, 459 F.2d 631, 634–35 (9th Cir. 1972) ("[T]he maintenance remedy should be kept simple, uncluttered by fine distinctions which breed litigation, with its attendant delays and expenses.") (internal citation omitted). Hence, *Barnes* strongly suggested that commuter seamen are also entitled to maintenance.

Today, we make explicit what was implicit in *Barnes*: commuter seamen enjoy the same right to maintenance as their blue water counterparts. Although DRBA's concerns relating to other payments have merit, we do not write on a blank slate. *Id.* at 637 (noting the Court's "clear and frequent pronouncements" that seamen remain wards of the admiralty). Rather, our analysis is informed by nearly two centuries of jurisprudence "consistently expand[ing] the scope of the right [to maintenance]." *Id.* at 633. In *Vaughan*, decided over one hundred years after the introduction of maintenance into admiralty law, the Supreme Court stressed the continued status of seamen as "wards" of admiralty and the need for "liberal" interpretation of the maintenance obligation. 369 U.S. at 532.

Notwithstanding our dissenting colleague's vigorous argument that the maintenance and cure obligation does not arise when the seaman is a commuter, we find no such limiting principle—or inclination to curtail this historic remedy—in the applicable jurisprudence.[6] As much as we might have expected the Supreme Court in 1962 to modify the traditional maintenance obligation to reflect changes in the modern seaman's lifestyle, it did no such thing. To the contrary, the Court, stressing the expansive nature of this right, declined to fashion exceptions to the shipowner's longstanding duty to provide maintenance and cure:

> Admiralty courts have been liberal in interpreting this duty 'for the benefit and protection of seamen who are its wards.' We noted in *Aguilar v. Standard Oil Co.*, that the shipowner's liability for maintenance and cure was among 'the most pervasive' of all and that it was not to be defeated by restrictive distinctions nor 'narrowly confined.' When there are ambiguities or doubts, they are resolved in favor of the seaman.

Id. at 531–32 (internal citations omitted). And, in fact, DRBA cites no authority supporting withholding maintenance from commuter seamen. *See id.* at 642 (quoting *Weiss v. Central R.R. Co. of N.J.*, 235 F.2d 309, 313 (2d Cir. 1956)

6 Kopacz's claim rests upon the age-old common law doctrine of maintenance and cure, not the Shipowners' Liability Convention. Nothing in that Convention purports to alter the right Kopacz here asserts.

("We know of no authority . . . for holding that a seaman is not entitled to the traditional privileges of his status merely because his voyages are short, because he sleeps ashore, or for other reasons his lot is more pleasant than that of most of his brethren.")); *Bailey v. City of N.Y.*, 55 F.Supp. 699, 701 (S.D.N.Y. 1944), *aff.*, 153 F.2d 427 (2d Cir. 1946) (awarding maintenance to land-based seaman after finding no authority for narrow construction of the right); *see also Crooks*, 459 F.2d at 633 ("Thus we find the obligation of maintenance enforced even where maritime compensation did not include board and lodging-where the seaman was expected to pay for his meals out of his wages. No matter what the terms of his maritime employment were, during the period of his disability he was entitled to be provided with maintenance as well as cure."); *The City of Avalon*, 156 F.2d 500, 501 (9th Cir. 1946) (holding that seaman could recover cost of food as element of maintenance, even where shipowner had not paid for his meals).

In short, "[t]he Supreme Court has shown no inclination to depart from its long-established solicitude for seamen," despite the protections afforded modern seamen. *Barnes*, 900 F.2d at 637. Until it does so, we decline to depart from the "uniformly enforced" rule entitling deep water and commuter seamen to maintenance. *Weiss*, 235 F.2d at 313.

B. Long-Term Disability Benefits

Having established Kopacz's general eligibility for maintenance, we turn to DRBA's alternative contention—that LTD payments satisfied its maintenance obligation. *Shaw v. Ohio River Company* governs when other payments received by an injured seamen satisfy a shipowner's maintenance obligation. 526 F.2d at 200. There, we considered whether benefits paid to a seaman under a disability policy funded by the shipowner, and administered by Prudential Insurance Company ("Prudential"), relieved the shipowner of its maintenance duty. *Id.* We attached primary importance to the "character" of the benefit conferred. *Id.* We explained that where a benefit is part of the seaman's wage package, it will be deemed separate and independent of the shipowner's maintenance obligation; accordingly, payment of the benefit will not relieve the shipowner of its maintenance duty. Considerations supporting characterization of a benefit as "wages" rather than maintenance include that: (1) the benefit is mandated under a wage agreement between the employer and the seaman; (2) the absence of any contractual provision indicating that the benefit is in lieu of, or in satisfaction of, the employer's maintenance obligation; (3) the purpose of the benefit is to replace lost wages; and (4) the benefit is recoverable, even where the seaman does not satisfy the maintenance requirements. *Id.* In *Shaw*, all four factors supported classification of disability benefits as a substitute for wages: (1) the benefits were guaranteed in a collective bargaining agreement governing employee compensation; (2) the shipowner did not specify that disability payments were in lieu of maintenance; (3) employees were entitled to the benefits, even if they did not satisfy the conditions required to recover maintenance; and (4) the benefits, designed to replace lost wages, were not narrowly tailored to cover food and lodging expenses. *Id.*

Accordingly, we concluded that the payment of disability benefits did not relieve the shipowner of its maintenance obligation.

On the other hand, we concluded in *Shaw* that health benefits provided to the seaman *did* satisfy the shipowner's duty to provide "cure"—the payment of a seaman's medical expenses during his convalescence. Under the relevant policy, which was fully funded by the shipowner and administered by Blue Cross-Blue Shield, all of the injured seaman's medical expenses were covered. Because the benefits were narrowly tailored to satisfy the shipowner's "cure" duties, we concluded that additional payments to the seaman were not required.

Here, the District Court, applying the considerations discussed in *Shaw*, found that the LTD benefits were part and parcel of Kopacz's wage package. It specifically noted that: (1) DRBA extended LTD benefits to all permanent full-time employees, including personnel ineligible for maintenance at common law; (2) the employee manual characterized LTD benefits as "continuing income," not as payment for food and lodging; (3) the collective bargaining agreement did not expressly indicate that LTD benefits were in lieu of maintenance; and (4) disability benefits were awarded, even when the maintenance requirements were not met.[7] Nothing "connected" the insurance payments to food and lodging, or the maintenance offered as such. Accordingly, the District Court concluded that DRBA's maintenance obligation was not satisfied by the payment of LTD benefits.

DRBA attempts to distinguish the Prudential payments in *Shaw* from the LTD benefits paid here. DRBA insists that the collective bargaining agreement here is silent on LTD benefits. To the contrary, the document expressly provides, "Employer agrees to continue to provide all permanent full-time employees long-term disability plans that are offered to . . . employees generally." A. 7, 553, 563–64. The inclusion of this guarantee in the collective bargaining agreement thus supports classification of LTD benefits as a substitute for wages, not maintenance.

In *Shaw*, we scrutinized the record for clear written evidence that the shipowner intended disability benefits to satisfy its maintenance duty. We stated, "[T]he collective bargaining agreement in this case contained *no provision* specifying that payments from the insurance company under the benefits plan would be in lieu of maintenance. Undoubtedly a vessel owner could insure against his maintenance obligation by a benefits program tailored to that end but there is *no indication in the collective bargaining agreement* before us that this was done." 526 F.2d at 200 (emphasis added); *see also id.* at 199 ("It is clear that in the absence of an *explicit contractual provision* specifying that accumulated leave time pay or other wages is to be deemed a substitute for maintenance, there is no basis for crediting such earned wages against the vessel owner's maintenance obligation.") (emphasis added). Conceding that no such written evidence exists here, DRBA asserts that,

7 It is also worth noting that neither a seaman's actual nor his projected expenditures on food and lodging are factors in the computation of LTD payments and, therefore, LTD payments are not narrowly tailored to satisfy the shipowner's maintenance obligation.

instead, its evidentiary burden is satisfied by the existence of a "tacit and long-standing understanding" between the DRBA and its seaman that LTD benefits were in lieu of maintenance. Appellant's Br. at 20. DRBA relies on testimony offered by its risk manager, Bonnie Miller, that no employee had previously sued DRBA to recover both maintenance *and* disability benefits. This absence of suit, however, is readily explained—the prior plan administrator, Pennsylvania Manufacturer's Association, paid injured seamen "maintenance wages" of $15 daily. The absence of suit, therefore, is not indicative of a "tacit" understanding that LTD benefits would be provided in lieu of maintenance. In any event, speculation about why other DRBA employees refrained from suit is just that-speculation-and such circumstantial evidence is especially unpersuasive here, where all of the considerations identified as significant in *Shaw* support classification of the LTD payments as a wage substitute, not maintenance, and where LTD payments were not narrowly tailored to the essential purpose of maintenance—to cover food and lodging expenses during the seaman's recovery.

Unable to demonstrate that LTD payments were intended as maintenance, DRBA focuses on the underlying rationale for this right. DRBA contends that the historic purpose of maintenance—to provide an injured seaman funds adequate to cover basic living expenses—was met by the payment of LTD benefits, and that an additional award would produce an unjustified windfall for Kopacz. We considered-and rejected-a similar argument in *Barnes*, where we approved an award of maintenance to a unionized seaman, who received benefits similar to those afforded Kopacz:

> Andover is persuasive in arguing that today those seamen who are unionized are neither friendless nor improvident. The record in this case shows that the Seafarers International Union, to which Barnes belongs, has obtained for its members overtime and premium pay, vacation allowances, *disability pensions*, and amenities. . . . Furthermore, the adjectives friendless and helpless were generally used to describe sailors in foreign ports. Now, under union contracts ill or injured seamen are quickly repatriated. The changed circumstances of the unionized seaman may undercut the rationale supporting the traditional right to maintenance and cure, at least for unionized seamen. However, the Supreme Court has shown no inclination to depart from its long-established solicitude for seamen. Until it does so, we see no basis to assume the emergence of powerful seamen's unions, a development concerning which the Court has full knowledge, justifies our ignoring the Court's clear and frequent pronouncements that seamen remain wards of the admiralty.

Barnes, 900 F.2d at 636–37 (internal citations omitted) (emphasis added); *see also Vaughan*, 369 U.S. at 533 (rejecting double recovery argument and finding that income earned by an injured seaman at non-maritime position during his recovery did not offset the amount of maintenance due).[8]

---

8 DRBA also contends that requiring shipowners to pay maintenance, in addition to disability benefits, would discourage employers from offering such benefits. We disagree, and conclude, as the District Court did, that a shipowner may avoid "double" liability by specifying that disability benefits are intended to cover, in whole or in part, its maintenance obligation. *See Shaw*, 526 F.2d at 200.

Hence, we conclude that the LTD payments do not offset the amount of maintenance owed to Kopacz, a duty that is independent of DRBA's contractual obligations. *See Barnes*, 900 F.2d at 636; *see also Vaughan*, 369 U.S. at 532 ("Maintenance and cure differs from rights normally classified as contractual.").

C. Social Security Disability Benefits

Alternatively, DRBA maintains that Kopacz's receipt of SSD benefits satisfied its maintenance obligation, at least in part. For its position, DRBA relies on our statement in *Shaw* that a "vessel owner has no obligation to provide maintenance and cure if it is furnished by others at no expense to the seaman." 526 F.2d at 201.

In *Shaw*, discussed earlier, we held that Blue Cross-Blue Shield benefits satisfied the shipowner's cure obligation. We reasoned that these benefits, which covered the costs of the seaman's medical care and hospitalization, were the "exact[] equivalent" of "cure." *Shaw*, 526 F.2d at 201. Accordingly, we concluded that the parties intended the Blue Cross-Blue Shield payments be in lieu of, rather than in addition to, the "cure" owed to the injured sailor. However, we reached the *opposite* conclusion with respect to the Prudential disability benefits, which the record indicated were intended as a substitute for lost wages-not as payment for food and lodging-and which were owed to the seaman, independent of his eligibility for maintenance and cure. On that basis, we held that the Prudential payments did *not* offset the maintenance owed to the seaman. Distinguishing the Blue Cross-Blue Shield benefits from the Prudential payments, we explained,

> [I]t is also true that the vessel owner has no obligation to provide maintenance and cure if it is furnished by others at no expense to the seaman. . . . The *essential difference* between the Blue Cross-Blue Shield and the Prudential payments [which do not satisfy the maintenance obligation] is that the former provides the *exact equivalent* of maintenance and cure whereas the latter, at least under this collective bargaining agreement, constitutes a substitute for lost wages which are owed to a seaman even if he is ineligible for maintenance and cure.

Id. at 201 (emphasis added). The dispositive issue here, therefore, is whether SSD benefits provide the "exact equivalent" of maintenance, or whether the two differ in their scope, purpose, and conditions of eligibility. *Id.*

SSD benefits and maintenance are distinguishable in several important respects. First, distinct policy aims underlie maintenance and SSD payments. Whereas maintenance is "intended to provide for the cost of food and lodging comparable in quality to that the seaman is entitled to at sea," *Barnes*, 900 F.2d at 634–35, SSD benefits "aim[] to replace the income of beneficiaries when that income is reduced on account of retirement and disability." *Temple Univ. v. United States,* 769 F.2d 126, 130 (3d Cir. 1985); *see Barnes*, 900 F.2d at 634 (noting that maintenance does not entitle a seaman to a pension or a lump-sum payment to compensate for disability or lost earning capacity). Hence, SSD benefits are more closely analogous to LTD payments, which aim to replace lost wages, than to maintenance.

Second, the conditions of eligibility for maintenance and SSD payments differ substantially. Maintenance is available solely when a seaman: (1) is injured during the course of his employment or at a place where he is "subject to the call of duty," *Barnes*, 900 F.2d at 633 (citing *Aguilar v. Standard Oil Co.*, 318 U.S. 724, 732, 63 S. Ct. 930, 87 L. Ed. 1107 (1943)); (2) is incapable of performing "seaman's work," *Vaughan*, 369 U.S. at 531; and (3) has "actually incurred" food and lodging expenses during his recovery. *Barnes*, 90 F.2d at 642; *see Vaughan*, 369 U.S. at 531 (noting that maintenance is limited to food and lodging expenses incurred); *Gypsum Carrier, Inc. v. Handelsman,* 307 F.2d 525, 535 (9th Cir. 1962) ("Maintenance and cure is based upon need," and the seaman is under a duty to minimize expenditures). Maintenance, moreover, is available *immediately* upon the seaman's incapacitation, but *ceases* once the seaman attains "maximum cure," defined as the point at which he is either cured or his condition is diagnosed as permanent and incurable. *Barnes*, 900 F.2d at 633–34; *see Vella v. Ford Motor Co.*, 421 U.S. 1, 5, 95 S. Ct. 1381, 43 L. Ed. 2d 682 (1975); Crooks, 459 F.2d at 635 ("Payments must be promptly made, at a time contemporaneous to the illness or injury.") (internal citation omitted).

The conditions of eligibility for SSD benefits, by contrast, are both more-and less-stringent than those required to obtain maintenance. On the one hand, the SSD requirements are more onerous: a claimant must demonstrate that he has suffered a disability for a minimum period of five months, *Gaines v. Amalgamated Ins. Fund,* 753 F.2d 288, 290 (3d Cir. 1985); that his disability is permanent, having lasted, or been expected to last, for a continuous period of 12 months, *id.*; 20 C.F.R. § 416.909; and that his impairment precludes performance not only of his former job but also of any work "existing in significant numbers in the national economy," including "basic work activities." *McCrea v. Comm'r of Social Sec.*, 370 F.3d 357, 360 (3d Cir. 2004); *see* 42 U.S.C. § 423(d)(2)(A); 20 C.F.R. §§ 404.1520, 416.920.

On the other hand, the conditions of eligibility for SSD benefits are, in certain other respects, *less* burdensome than those required to receive maintenance. Claimants with non-occupational injuries may recover SSD benefits, 42 U.S.C. § 423(d)(1)(A),[9] and proof of actual expenditure of funds on food, lodging, or other expenses is not necessary to obtain benefits. Further, SSD payments need not be expended on food and lodging, and financial need is not a prerequisite to obtain assistance. *Mazza v. Sec. of Health and Human Servs.*, 903 F.2d 953, 956 (3d Cir. 1990). Further, a Social Security claimant is entitled to benefits, even if his condition is diagnosed as permanent or incurable. 42 U.S.C. § 423(a)(1).

---

9 The federal statute defines "disability" as: "inability to engage in any substantial gainful activity by reason of any medically determinable physical or mental impairment which can be expected to result in death or which has lasted or can be expected to last for a continuous period of not less than 12 months." 42 U.S.C. § 423(d)(1)(A).

These important differences support classification of maintenance and SSD payments as different, rather than "exact[ly] equivalent," benefits. *Shaw*, 526 F.2d at 201; *see Handelsman*, 307 F.2d at 537 (holding that payments received by sailor under state disability program do not offset amount owed under maintenance duty); *see also Barnes*, 900 F.2d at 637 (upholding seaman's right to maintenance, despite possibility of double recovery from his receipt of disability pensions, overtime and premium pay, and vacation allowances).

Nonetheless, DRBA attempts to analogize SSD payments to Medicare benefits, which at least one court of appeals has concluded may satisfy a shipowner's "cure" obligation. *Moran Towing & Transportation Co. v. Lombas*, 58 F.3d 24, 26–27 (2d Cir. 1995). In *Moran*, the Second Circuit Court of Appeals held that a seaman's receipt of Medicare-funded treatment relieved the shipowner of its duty to provide "cure." The court relied on our pronouncement in *Shaw* that "a vessel owner has no obligation to provide maintenance and cure if it is furnished by others at no expense to the seaman." *Id.* at 27 (quoting *Shaw*, 526 F.2d at 201). Significantly, *Moran* did not analyze a consideration that we identified as critical in determining whether "offset" was appropriate in *Shaw*—whether the payments received are the "exact equivalent" of cure. *Shaw*, 526 F.2d at 201. Because *Moran* omitted an aspect of the offset analysis that we deemed "essential" in *Shaw*, its holding lacks persuasive force.

Even if *Moran* were binding on this Court, *Moran's* core holding—that Medicare benefits may satisfy a shipowner's "cure" obligation—comports with the reasoning in *Shaw*. There, as discussed, we held that Blue Cross-Blue Shield benefits, which covered all of the seaman's medical expenses during his recovery, provided the "exact equivalent" of "cure." Likewise, the Medicare benefits in *Moran*, which covered the seaman's hospital bills during his convalescence, provided the equivalent of "cure." SSD benefits, by contrast, differ in scope and purpose from maintenance. Hence, *Moran's* conclusions with respect to Medicare benefits do not govern our analysis of SSD payments made to Kopacz.

Hence, we conclude that Kopacz's receipt of SSD benefits did not relieve DRBA of its maintenance obligation.

D. Prejudgment Interest

Next, DRBA contends that the District Court erred in granting Kopacz prejudgment interest on the amount of maintenance owed to him.[10] "The rule in admiralty is that prejudgment interest should be awarded unless there are exceptional circumstances that would make such an award inequitable." *Matter of Bankers Trust Co.,* 658 F.2d 103, 108 (3d Cir. 1981); *see Noritake Co. v. M/V Hellenic Champion*, 627 F.2d 724, 728 (5th Cir. Unit A 1980) ("Discretion to deny prejudgment

10 Kopacz sought-and was awarded-prejudgment interest from October 2006, when Hartford ceased payment of LTD benefits, to the date of judgment.

interest is created only when there are 'peculiar circumstances' that would make it inequitable for the losing party to be forced to pay prejudgment interest.") (internal citation omitted). In *Matter of Bankers Trust Co.*, we explained, "Generally, exceptional circumstances exist only when the district court concludes that the party requesting interest has (1) unreasonably delayed in prosecuting its claim, (2) made a bad faith estimate of its damages that precluded settlement, or (3) not sustained any actual damages." 658 F.2d at 108. An award of prejudgment interest, however, must be compensatory rather than punitive, *id.*, and is "left to the sound discretion of the district court," which will be disturbed only for abuse of discretion. *M & O Marine, Inc. v. Marquette Co.,* 730 F.2d 133, 136 (3d Cir. 1984); *see Socony Mobile Oil Co. v. Tex Coastal & Intern.,* 559 F.2d 1008, 1014 (5th Cir. 1977); *see also Skretvedt v. E.I. DuPont De Nemours*, 372 F.3d 193, 206 (3d Cir. 2004) (noting district court's broad discretion to award prejudgment interest). The District Court concluded that an award of prejudgment interest was "appropriate in this instance," citing our statement in *Deisler v. McCormack Aggregates Co.*, that such relief is "merely an element of a plaintiff's complete compensation." 54 F.3d 1074, 1087 (3d Cir. 1995).

DRBA does not identify an exceptional circumstance justifying withholding prejudgment interest. Rather, DRBA's sole contention on appeal is that other payments to Kopacz, including LTD benefits and the value of his sick and annual leave, adequately compensated him, and that the award of prejudgment interest was thus punitive. However, we earlier rejected this argument, concluding that other payments made to Kopacz did not satisfy DRBA's maintenance obligation. Having held that Kopacz has a separate and independent right to maintenance, we conclude that the District Court did not abuse its discretion in compensating Kopacz for losses stemming from DRBA's tardy discharge of its duty. *See Matter of Bankers Trust Co.,* 658 F.2d at 108 ("Its [prejudgment interest's] purpose is to reimburse the claimant for the loss of use of its investment or its funds from the time of such loss until judgment is entered."); *Skretvedt*, 372 F.3d at 208 ("As a general rule, prejudgment interest is to be awarded when the amount of the underlying liability is reasonably capable of ascertainment and the relief granted would otherwise fall short of making the claim ant whole because he or she has been denied the use of the money which was legally due." (quoting *Anthuis v. Colt Indus. Operating Corp.,* 971 F.2d 999, 1010 (3d Cir.1992))); *see also Deisler*, 54 F.3d at 1087 ("The Supreme Court has repeatedly held that prejudgment interest is merely an element of a plaintiff's complete compensation.").

E. Consequential Damages

In his cross-appeal, Kopacz argues that the District Court erred in denying his claim for consequential damages. In *Deisler*, we held that consequential damages arising from a shipowner's failure to provide maintenance and cure, including lost wages and pain and suffering, are generally recoverable. 54 F.3d at 1082–84. To establish an entitlement to such damages, however, a plaintiff must articulate, at minimum, a specific injury, and explain how that injury resulted from the shipowner's breach of its maintenance duty. *Id.* at 1082–83. Kopacz fails both requirements. In fact, Kopacz fails even to identify the kind of consequential damages that he seeks—lost wages, pain and suffering, or other relief. Nor does Kopacz specifically identify an emotional, physical, or economic injury resulting from non-payment of maintenance. To the contrary, Kopacz concedes that all properly documented medical costs were promptly reimbursed, and he does not allege, much less prove, that other payments, including SSD and LTD benefits, were insufficient to cover his basic expenses. Rather, Kopacz merely asserts that he "really needed the money." Appellee's Br. at 26. On this record, we conclude that the District Court did not abuse its discretion in denying Kopacz's claim for lost wages and pain and suffering.

The sole type of consequential damages that Kopacz expressly seeks—attorney's fees and costs—was properly denied by the District Court. Attorney's fees and costs are recoverable solely where a shipowner's refusal to pay maintenance and cure is unreasonable. *See Atlantic Sounding Co., Inc. v. Townsend*, _____ U.S. ______, 129 S. Ct. 2561, 2571, 174 L. Ed. 2d 382 (2009) (noting that award of attorney's fees is permissible for shipowner's "callous" and "willful and persistent" refusal to pay maintenance and cure); *Vaughan*, 369 U.S. at 530–31 (noting that attorney's fees are recoverable where shipowner's refusal to pay maintenance stemmed from a "wanton and intentional disregard" of the legal rights of the seaman); *Deisler*, 54 F.3d at 1087 ("Attorney's fees and costs differ from interest, lost wages and damages for pain and suffering because attorney's fees and costs cannot be recovered unless plaintiff can first establish defendant's bad faith or recalcitrance."). Here, DRBA, providing Kopacz almost $40,000 in wages, sick and annual leave, and long-term disability benefits, did not exhibit the requisite callousness. Further, Kopacz did not seek maintenance until over one year after his date of injury, when Hartford demanded reimbursement for the amount of SSD payments made to him. Although DRBA declined to pay maintenance, its decision, premised on a colorable legal theory, did not reflect a wanton and intentional disregard of Kopacz's rights. *See Deisler*, 54 F.3d at 1087 (requiring proof that denial of maintenance was "arbitrary or capricious" to recover attorney's fees and costs).

Accordingly, we conclude that the District Court properly exercised its discretion to deny Kopacz attorney's fees and costs.

III. Conclusion

For the foregoing reasons, we will AFFIRM the judgment of the District Court.

DISSENT

ALARCON, *Circuit Judge, dissenting*:

I respectfully dissent from the majority's opinion in this matter. The question presented for our review is whether a person who resides on shore and commutes to his or her job as a day laborer aboard a ferry is entitled to compensation for lodging and food, if he or she becomes incapacitated, in addition to receiving long-term disability benefits paid for by his or her employer that fully cover his living expenses.

In concluding that Mr. Kopacz is entitled to an additional payment for the cost of his lodging and meals, the majority, citing this Court's decision in *Barnes v. Andover Co., L.P.*, 900 F.2d 630 (3rd Cir. 1990), states as follows: "Although *Barnes* acknowledged that there was 'some logic' in denying maintenance to shore-based seamen, the court stressed that the 'life of the law' is 'experience,' not 'logic.'" Majority Op. at 9. In a subsequent passage, the majority states: "*Barnes* strongly suggested that commuter seamen are also entitled to maintenance." Majority Op. at 10. I disagree with this reading of *Barnes*. In fact this Court *expressly declined* to reach this question in *Barnes*. Instead, this Court stated:

> Whatever the merits of the double recovery objection for maintenance paid to land-based seamen, that argument is inapplicable to Barnes. Barnes was not *shore bound and Andover does not suggest that his wages were fixed in contemplation of his providing his own food and lodging*. Thus, the fact that Barnes chose to use his wages to maintain an on-shore residence rather than on entertainment or on some frivolity should not be used to reduce his recovery, *particularly since there is no question here of any double recovery as a result of land-based wages*."

Id. at 643 (emphasis added).

Moreover, the fact that "DRBA cites no authority supporting withholding maintenance from commuter seamen," Majority Op. at 11, does not logically support a conclusion that a commuter seaman is therefore *entitled* to maintenance without some showing that the equities favor this result. I cannot join the majority's number because I am persuaded that extending the maritime doctrine of maintenance to an employee who commutes each day from his shore-based home to his job as a day laborer on a ferry boat is contrary to both logic and experience.

I.

As noted in *Barnes*, this Circuit has not yet determined whether the doctrine of maintenance applicable to seamen who are incapacitated while on ships that sail to distant ports should be extended to commuter seamen.

In his brilliant Harvard Law School lectures, Justice Oliver Wendell Holmes explained the evolution of Common Law principles as follows:

> The object of this book is to present a general view of the Common Law. To accomplish the task, other tools are needed besides logic. It is something to show that the consistency of a system requires a particular result, but it is not all. The life of the

> law has not been logic: it has been experience. The felt necessities of the time, the prevalent moral and political theories, intuitions of public policy, avowed or unconscious, even the prejudices which judges share with their fellow-men, have had a good deal more to do than the syllogism in determining the rules by which men should be governed. The law embodies the story of a nation's development through many centuries, and it cannot be dealt with as if it contained only the axioms and corollaries of a book of mathematics. In order to know what it is, we must know what it has been, and what it tends to become. We must alternately consult history and existing theories of legislation. But the most difficult labor will be to understand the combination of the two into new products at every stage. The substance of the law at any given time pretty nearly corresponds, so far as it goes, with what is then understood to be convenient; but its form and machinery, and the degree to which it is able to work out desired results, depend very much upon its past.

Oliver Wendell Holmes, Jr., *The Common Law* 3–4, (John Harvard Library ed., Belknap Press of Harvard Univ. Press 2009) (1881).

The woeful experience suffered by seamen incapacitated on lengthy voyages to distant ports that led to the adoption of the maintenance doctrine was vividly described by Justice Story in 1823 in *Harden v. Gordon*, 11 F. Cas. 480, F. Cas. No. 6047 (C.C.D. Me. 1823) (No. 6,047).

> Seamen are by the peculiarity of their lives liable to sudden sickness from change of climate, exposure to perils, and exhausting labor. They are generally poor and friendless, and acquire habits of gross indulgence, carelessness, and improvidence. If some provision be not made for them in sickness at the expense of the ship, they must often in foreign ports suffer the accumulated evils of disease, and poverty, and sometimes perish from the want of suitable nourishment. Their common earnings in many instances are wholly inadequate to provide for the expenses of sickness; and if liable to be so applied, the great motives for good behavior might be ordinarily taken away by pledging their future as well as past wages for the redemption of the debt. In many voyages, particularly those to the West Indies, the whole wages are often insufficient to meet the expenses occasioned by the perilous diseases of those insalubrious climates. On the other hand, if these expenses are a charge upon the ship, the interest of the owner will be immediately connected with that of the seamen. The master will watch over their health with vigilance and fidelity. He will take the best methods, as well to prevent diseases, as to ensure a speedy recovery from them. He will never be tempted to abandon the sick to their forlorn fate; but his duty, combining with the interest of his owner, will lead him to succor their distress, and shed a cheering kindness over the anxious hours of suffering and despondency.

Id. at 483. Justice Story's opinion in *Harden* was written in his capacity as the Circuit Justice for the District of Maine.

In 1903, the United States Supreme Court referred to Justice Story's decision in *Harden* as the first case in this country that adopted the doctrine of maintenance and cure. *The Osceola*, 189 U.S. 158, 172, 23 S. Ct. 483, 47 L. Ed. 760 (1903). The Court summarized Justice Story's opinion as follows:

> Justice Story held that a claim for the expenses of cure in case of sickness constituted in contemplation of law a part of the contract for wages, over which admiralty had

> a rightful jurisdiction. The action was *in personam* against the master and owner for wages and other expenses occasioned by the sickness of the plaintiff *in a foreign port in the course of the voyage*, which were allowed.

Id. (emphasis added). The Court held in *The Osceola* that, upon reviewing English and American authorities, the law

> may be considered as settled upon the following proposition[]: . . ."[t]hat the vessel and her owners are liable, in case a seamen falls sick or is wounded in the service of his ship, to the extent of his maintenance and cure, and to his wages, at least as long as the voyage is continued.

Id. at 175. The Court also held "[t]hat the seaman is not allowed to recover an indemnity for the negligence of the master, or any member of the crew, but is entitled to maintenance and cure, whether the injuries were received by negligence or accident." *Id.*[1]

In each of the cases in which the Supreme Court has applied Justice Story's analysis of the experiences of seamen that support application of the doctrine of maintenance and cure, the facts demonstrate that the seaman was incapacitated while he served as a member of a vessel traveling to distant ports. In *Calmar S.S. Corp. v. Taylor,* 303 U.S. 525, 58 S. Ct. 651, 82 L. Ed. 993 (1938), the Court defined the terms "maintenance" and "cure" as follows: "The maintenance exacted is comparable to that to which the seaman is entitled to while at sea and 'cure' is care, including nursing and medical attention, during such period as the duty continues." *Id.* at 528 (internal citations omitted).

In *Aguilar v. Standard Oil Co. of New Jersey*, 318 U.S. 724, 63 S. Ct. 930, 87 L. Ed. 1107 (1943), the injured seaman was a messman on a steamship engaged in coastwise trade between New Orleans and East Coast and Gulf Coast ports. While the vessel was moored in a port in Philadelphia, the seaman was injured as he left the ship on shore leave. *Id.* at 725. In a consolidated companion case, a seaman on shore leave was injured as he walked back to his ship by the driver of a motor vehicle not owned, operated or controlled by the ship owner. *Id.* at 725–26.

Citing Justice Story's decision in *Harden*, the Court in *Aguilar* explained its holding that the seamen were entitled to cure and maintenance as follows:

> From the earliest times, maritime nations have recognized that unique hazards, emphasized by unusual tenure and control, attend the work of seamen. The physical risks created by natural elements, and the limitations of human adaptability to work at sea, enlarge the narrower and more strictly occupational hazards of sailing and

---

1 In 1920, Congress enacted the Jones Act. Its current text provides as follows:

> A seaman injured in the course of employment or, if the seaman dies from the injury, the personal representative of the seaman may elect to bring a civil action at law, with the right of trial by jury, against the employer. Laws of the United States regulating recovery for a personal injury to, or death of, a railway employee apply to an action under this section.

46 U.S.C. § 30104. Thus, under the Jones Act, a seaman can now recover for lost wages and compensation for medical expenses in a civil action against his or her employer.

> operating vessels. And the restrictions which accompany living aboard a ship for long periods at a time combine with the constant shuttling between unfamiliar ports to deprive the seaman of the comforts and opportunities for leisure, essential for living and working, that accompany most land occupations. Furthermore, the seaman's unusual subjection to authority adds the weight of what would be involuntary servitude for others to these extraordinary hazards and limitations of ship life.
>
> Accordingly, with the combined object of encouraging marine commerce and assuring the well-being of seamen, maritime nations uniformly have imposed broad responsibilities for their health and safety upon the owners of ships. In this country these notions were reflected early, and have since been expanded, in legislation designed to secure the comfort and health of seamen aboard ship, hospitalization at home and care abroad. The statutes are uniform in evincing solicitude that the seamen shall have at hand the barest essentials for existence. They do this in two ways. One is by recognizing the shipowner's duty to supply them, and the other by providing for care at public expense. The former do not create the duty. That existed long before the statutes were adopted. They merely recognize the preexisting obligation and put specific legal sanctions, generally criminal, behind it.

Id. at 727–29 (footnotes omitted).

In *Vaughan v. Atkinson*, 369 U.S. 527, 82 S. Ct. 997, 8 L. Ed. 2d 88 (1962), the plaintiff served as a seaman on the respondent's vessel from November 26, 1956 to March 2, 1957. He was discharged on the termination of a voyage. On March 2, 1957, the ship's master furnished the seaman with a certificate to enter a United States Health Services Hospital. He was examined five days later at the hospital. He was admitted as a patient on March 18, 1957 and treated for tuberculosis. He was discharged to an outpatient status on June 6, 1957. He continued to receive treatment in that status for over two years. *Id.* at 528.

The ship owner declined to provide the seaman with maintenance because he "never complained of any illness during his four months' service." *Id.* The seaman hired a lawyer to enforce his right to maintenance. He also requested an award of attorney's fees. The District Court denied his request for the payment of his attorney's fees. The Court of Appeals affirmed the denial of attorney's fees and held that the amount he earned as a taxi driver had to be deducted from the amount he was entitled to for maintenance and cure. *Id.* at 529.

Relying on its decision in *Calmar S.S. Corp. v. Taylor*, and Justice Story's opinion in *Harden*, the Supreme Court held in *Vaughan* that "[i]t is difficult to imagine a clearer case of damages suffered for the failure to pay maintenance than this one." *Id.* at 531.

The Supreme Court has not extended the maritime doctrine of maintenance and cure to persons who commute to work aboard vessels that do not sail to distant ports. Instead, the Court has continued to adhere to Justice Story's explanation of the policy underlying that duty in *Harden*. For example, in *Vaughan*, the Court stated:

> *The reasons underlying the rule, to which reference must be made in defining it, are those enumerated in the classic passage by Mr. Justice Story in Harden v. Gordon,*

> *Fed. Cas. No. 6047 (C. C.)*: the protection of seamen, who, as a class, are poor, friendless and improvident, from hazards of illness and abandonment while ill in foreign ports; the inducement to masters and owners to protect the safety and health of seamen while in service; the maintenance of a merchant marine for the commercial service and maritime defense of the nation by inducing men to accept employment in an arduous and perilous service.

369 U.S. at 531 (quoting *Calmar S.S. Corp. v. Taylor*, 303 U.S. at 528) (emphasis added).

The undisputed facts in this matter demonstrate that Mr. Kopacz was employed by the DRBA as a deckhand on its ferries. It was his day job. He commuted from his home. He did not receive lodging or meals from his employer. He reported an on-the-job injury on December 24, 2004. He was found to be unfit for duty on DRBA's ferries on January 5, 2005.

Mr. Kopacz received benefits through a long-term disability policy paid for by his employer which provided for the payment of his full wages for the first ninety days of his disability, and 60% of his wages thereafter so that he would continue to be provided an income in the event his ability to earn a living was interrupted or terminated by prolonged disability.

Mr. Kopacz received his full pay for ninety days. Thereafter he was paid $2,192 per month. The parties stipulated that his monthly living expenses totaled $2,190 per month.

Mr. Kopacz applied for Social Security Administration ("SSA") disability payments. SSA approved his application in October of 2006. SSA sent him a check in the amount of $17,142 which represented his benefits retroactive to July 5, 2005.

Thereafter, Mr. Kopacz received SSA benefits of $1,167 monthly. The DRBA's long-term disability benefits policy provided that SSA benefits are an off-set to those provided by the policy. Hartford, the long-term disability insurer, requested that Mr. Kopacz repay the overpayment of $16,607.92 which arose when Mr. Kopacz was awarded SSA payments retroactively. Mr. Kopacz refused. He insisted that DRBA repay the Hartford $16,607.92 and the $1,100 per month that Hartford was deducting.

DRBA filed this action in the District Court seeking a declaration that it had fully met its obligations to Mr. Kopacz. The District Court concluded that DRBA was required to make payments to Mr. Kopacz for his maintenance to cover the cost of his lodging and food, notwithstanding the fact that DRBA had provided monthly living expenses benefits through a long-term disability policy.

The foregoing facts do not meet the requirements for the application of the doctrine of maintenance set forth in *Harden* and adopted by the Supreme Court in *The Osceola*. As the Court instructed in *Vaughan*, the "reasons underlying the rule to which reference must be made in defining" the doctrine of maintenance are those enumerated by Justice Story in *Harden*. *Vaughan*, 369 U.S. at 531. In awarding maintenance in this matter, the District Court failed to set forth the experiences encountered by a commuter seamen that define his or her entitlement to maintenance.

There is no evidence in the record that Mr. Kopacz is a poor, friendless, and improvident person. He was not subjected to the perilous hazards and sudden illnesses that can be incurred from the change of climate while sailing on the high seas. He was not subject to being abandoned in a distant port - without wages, or the means of providing for his own maintenance. Therefore, he clearly did not qualify for maintenance.

In extending the doctrine of maintenance and cure to day laborers who work on ferries and who do not face the hazards described by Justice Story, the District Court ignored Justice Holmes's admonition that we must look to real-life experience in creating new rules of law. The fact that the Supreme Court has categorized seamen as "wards" of admiralty does not justify an extension of the maintenance doctrine to seamen who commute to work each day, and in addition, receive benefits through disability insurance and social security that were unavailable to Justice Story's hapless seamen who depended on their masters to provide their lodging, food, and medical care. In my view, an award of maintenance under these circumstances clearly results in an impermissible double recovery for Mr. Kopacz.

II.

Perhaps an even stronger argument that an award of maintenance and cure does not apply to a commuter seaman who does not sail to distant ports, and does not receive lodging and food aboard his employer's ferry boats, is that such a rule is contrary to the Shipowners' Liability (Sick and Injured Seamen) Convention. *See* Convention Between the United States of America and Other Members of the International Labor Organization Respecting Shipowners' Liability in Case of Sickness, Injury, or Death of Seamen, October 24, 1936, 54 Stat. 1693, 40 U.N.T.S. 169, attached hereto. The Shipowners' Liability Convention, proclaimed by the President on September 29, 1939, provides in section 1 of Article 4 that: "The ship owner shall be liable to defray the expense of medical care and maintenance until the sick or injured person has been cured, or until the sickness or incapacity has been declared of a permanent character." 54 Stat. 1693, art. 4, § 1.

In section 3 of Article 4, the Convention also provides that:

> if there is in force in the territory in which the vessel is registered a scheme applying to seamen of compulsory sickness insurance, compulsory accident insurance or workmen's compensation for accidents, national laws may provide–
>
> > (a) that a shipowner shall cease to be liable in respect of a sick or injured person from the time at which that person becomes entitled to medical benefits under the insurance or compensation scheme.

Id. at art. 4, § 3. The United States of America adopted the Convention subject to the understanding that "the United States understands and construes the words 'maritime navigation' appearing in this Convention to mean navigation on the high seas only." *Id.* at 1704, U. S. ratification subject to understandings.

The Senate of the United States gave its consent on June 13, 1938 to the ratification of the Convention by the President of the United States. President Franklin D. Roosevelt declared on September 29, 1939 that he "caused the said convention to be made public to the end that the same and every article and clause thereof may be observed and fulfilled in good faith by the United States of America and the citizens thereof . . . subject to understandings above recited . . . ." *Id.* at Final Proclamation.

Extending the doctrine of maintenance and cure to commuter seamen, as adopted by the United States in ratifying the Convention, is in direct conflict with its limitation to seamen incapacitated on voyages on the high seas.

CONCLUSION

The Supreme Court's decision in *The Osceola* limited the application of the doctrine of maintenance and cure to seamen incapacitated during voyages to distant ports where the record shows the following facts:

> One. Because of the length of the voyage, the shipowner has provided the seaman with lodging and food.
>
> Two. The shipowner has ceased paying wages to the seaman because of his unfitness for duty.
>
> Three. The shipowner has failed to compensate the seaman for his food or lodging, for which he is unable to work because of his injury.
>
> Four. The shipowner has failed to pay for the seaman's medical care and hospitalization.
>
> Five. The seaman has been abandoned in a foreign port without funds to pay for his medical treatment and transportation to his home.

Mr. Kopacz has not been subjected to any of these deprivations. His ferry boat did not sail to distant ports on the high seas. Because he commuted to his work assignment each day from his home, he did not eat or sleep aboard the shipowner's ferry boats. He was not abandoned in a distant port without compensation for his living expenses and medical care. The shipowner paid for disability insurance that was sufficient to cover his monthly living expenses.

I am sure Justice Story would be astonished to learn that a commuter seaman, whose monthly living expenses were provided for by his shipowner, must also be furnished additional funds to pay for lodging and food that he was not entitled to receive during his eight-hour shift, *solely* because he is a ward of admiralty.

While I am not sure Justice Holmes had the doctrine of maintenance and cure in mind when he instructed us that experience plays a dominant role in the evolution of the Common Law, I doubt seriously that he would have concluded that the relatively bland experience of a commuter seaman, as compared to one whose work takes him or her to distant parts on the high seas, would justify an extension of the doctrine of maintenance to seamen who do not encounter the conditions described in the Supreme Court's decision in *The Osceola*.

It is also troubling that an award of maintenance to a commuter seaman is contrary to a Convention that the United States has entered into with other maritime nations. In relying on the absence of authority supporting the withholding of maintenance from commuter seamen to reach its conclusion that such seamen are therefore entitled to maintenance, Majority Op. at 11, the majority has failed to set forth the "reasons underlying the rule to which reference must be made in defining" the doctrine of maintenance as enumerated by Justice Story in *Harden. Vaughan*, 369 U.S. at 531. Until the Supreme Court addresses this novel question, I believe the lower federal courts must faithfully comply with the limited reach of the maintenance rule announced by the Supreme Court in *The Osceola* as the supreme law of the land.

Accordingly, I would reverse the double recovery awarded to Mr. Kopacz in the District Court's judgment.

ATTACHMENT

CONVENTION BETWEEN THE UNITED STATES OF AMERICA AND OTHER MEMBERS OF THE INTERNATIONAL LABOR ORGANIZATION RESPECTING SHIPOWNERS' LIABILITY IN CASE OF SICKNESS, INJURY, OR DEATH OF SEAMEN, OCTOBER 24, 1936, 54 STAT. 1693, 40 U.N.T.S. 169

October 24, 1936

Convention between the United States of America and other members of the International Labor Organization respecting shipowners' liability in case of sickness, injury, or death of seamen. Adopted by the General Conference of the International Labor Organization, twenty-first session, Geneva, October 24, 1936; ratification advised by the Senate of the United States, subject to understandings, June 13, 1938; ratified by the President of the United States, subject to the said understandings, August 15, 1938; ratification of the United States of America registered with the Secretary-General of the League of Nations October 29, 1938; proclaimed by the President of the United States September 89, 1939.

By the President of the United States of America

A PROCLAMATION

Whereas a draft convention (No. 55) with regard to the liability of the shipowner in case of sickness, injury, or death of seamen, was adopted on the twenty-fourth day of October nineteen hundred and thirty-six, by the General Conference of the

International Labor Organization at its twenty-first session held at Geneva October 6-24, 1936, a certified copy of which draft convention, communicated by the Secretary-General of the League of Nations, acting in conformity with the requirements in the nineteenth Article of the Constitution of the International Labor Organization, to the Government of the United States of America as a Member of the said Organization, is, in the French and English languages, word for word as follows:

[Editor's Note: Only the English language version of this convention has been reproduced below.]

The General Conference of the International Labour Organisation,

Having been convened at Geneva by the Governing Body of the International Labour Office, and having met in its Twenty-first Session on 6 October 1936, and

Having decided upon the adoption of certain proposals with regard to the liability of the shipowner in case of sickness, injury or death of seamen, which is included in the second item on the Agenda of the Session, and

Having determined that these proposals shall take the form of a Draft International Convention, adopts, this twenty-fourth day of October of the year one thousand nine hundred and thirty-six, the following Draft Convention which may be cited as the Shipowners' Liability (Sick and Injured Seamen) Convention, 1936:

ARTICLE 1

1. This Convention applies to all persons employed on board any vessel, other than a ship of war, registered in a territory for which this Convention is in force and ordinarily engaged in maritime navigation.

2. Provided that any Member of the International Labour Organisation may in its national laws or regulations make such exceptions as it deems necessary in respect of:

(a) persons employed on board,

(i) vessels of public authorities when such vessels are not engaged in trade;

(ii) coastwise fishing boats;

(iii) boats of less than twenty-five tons gross tonnage;

(iv) wooden ships of primitive build such as dhows and junks;

(b) persons employed on board by an employer other than the shipowner;

(c) persons employed solely in ports in repairing, cleaning, loading or unloading vessels;

(d) members of the shipowner's family;

(e) pilots.

ARTICLE 2

1. The shipowner shall be liable in respect of:

(a) sickness and injury occurring between the date specified in the articles of agreement for reporting for duty and the termination of the engagement;

(b) death resulting from such sickness or injury.

2. Provided that national laws or regulations may make exceptions in respect of:

(a) injury incurred otherwise than in the service of the ship;

(b) injury or sickness due to the wilful act, default or misbehaviour of the sick, injured or deceased person;

(c) sickness or infirmity intentionally concealed when the engagement is entered into.

3. National laws or regulations may provide that the shipowner shall not be liable in respect of sickness, or death directly attributable to sickness, if at the time of the engagement the person employed refused to be medically examined.

ARTICLE 3

For the purpose of this Convention, medical care and maintenance at the expense of the shipowner comprises:

(a) medical treatment and the supply of proper and sufficient medicines and therapeutical appliances; and

(b) board and lodging.

ARTICLE 4

1. The shipowner shall be liable to defray the expense of medical care and maintenance until the sick or injured person has been cured, or until the sickness or incapacity has been declared of a permanent character.

2. Provided that national laws or regulations may limit the liability of the shipowner to defray the expense of medical care and maintenance to a period which shall not be less than sixteen weeks from the day of the injury or the commencement of the sickness.

3. Provided also that, if there is in force in the territory in which the vessel is registered a scheme applying to seamen of compulsory sickness insurance, compulsory accident insurance or workmen's compensation for accidents, national laws or regulations may provide—

(a) that a shipowner shall cease to be liable in respect of a sick or injured person from the time at which that person becomes entitled to medical benefits under the insurance or compensation scheme;

(b) that the shipowner shall cease to be liable from the time prescribed by law for the grant of medical benefits under the insurance or compensation scheme to the beneficiaries of such schemes, even when the sick or injured person is not covered by the scheme in question, unless he is excluded from the scheme by reason of any restriction which affects particularly foreign workers or workers not resident in the territory in which the vessel is registered.

ARTICLE 5

1. Where the sickness or injury results in incapacity for work the shipowner shall be liable—

(a) to pay full wages as long as the sick or injured person remains on board;

(b) if the sick or injured person has dependants, to pay wages in whole or in part as prescribed by national laws or regulations from the time when he is landed until he has been cured or the sickness or incapacity has been declared of a permanent character.

2. Provided that national laws or regulations may limit the liability of the shipowner to pay wages in whole or in part in respect of a person no longer on board to a period which shall not be less than sixteen weeks from the day of the injury or the commencement of the sickness.

3. Provided also that, if there is in force in the territory in which the vessel is registered a scheme applying to seamen of compulsory sickness insurance, compulsory accident insurance or workmen's compensation for accidents, national laws or regulations may provide:

(a) that a shipowner shall cease to be liable in respect of a sick or injured person from the time at which that person becomes entitled to cash benefits under the insurance or compensation scheme;

(b) that the shipowner shall cease to be liable from the time prescribed by law for the grant of cash benefits under the insurance or compensation scheme to the beneficiaries of such schemes, even when the sick or injured person is not covered by the scheme in question, unless he is excluded from the scheme by reason of any restriction which affects particularly foreign workers or workers not resident in the territory in which the vessel is registered.

ARTICLE 6

1. The shipowner shall be liable to defray the expense of repatriating every sick or injured person who is landed during the voyage in consequence of sickness or injury.

2. The port to which the sick or injured person is to be returned shall be-

(a) the port at which he was engaged; or

(b) the port at which the voyage commenced; or

(c) a port in his own country or the country to which he belongs; or

(d) another port agreed upon by him and the master or shipowner, with the approval of the competent authority.

3. The expense of repatriation shall include all charges for the transportation, accommodation and food of the sick or injured person during the journey and his maintenance up to the time fixed for this departure.

4. If the sick or injured person is capable of work, the shipowner may discharge his liability to repatriate him by providing him with suitable employment on board a vessel proceeding to one of the destinations mentioned in paragraph 2 of this Article.

ARTICLE 7

1. The shipowner shall be liable to defray burial expenses in case of death occurring on board, or in case of death occurring on shore if at the time of his death the deceased person was entitled to medical care and maintenance at the shipowner's expense.

2. National laws or regulations may provide that burial expenses paid by the shipowner shall be reimbursed by an insurance institution in cases in which funeral benefit is payable in respect of the deceased person under laws or regulations relating to social insurance or workmen's compensation.

ARTICLE 8

National laws or regulations shall require the shipowner or his representative to take measures for safeguarding property left on board by sick, injured or deceased persons to whom this Convention applies.

ARTICLE 9

National laws or regulations shall make provision for securing the rapid and inexpensive settlement of disputes concerning the liability of the shipowner under this Convention.

ARTICLE 10

The shipowner may be exempted from liability under Articles 4, 6 and 7 of this Convention in so far as such liability is assumed by the public authorities.

ARTICLE 11

This Convention and national laws or regulations relating to benefits under this Convention shall be so interpreted and enforced as to ensure equality of treatment to all seamen irrespective of nationality, domicile or race.

ARTICLE 12

Nothing in this Convention shall affect any law, award, custom or agreement between ship-owners and seamen which ensures more favourable conditions than those provided by this Convention.

ARTICLE 13

1. In respect of the territories referred to in Article 35 of the Constitution of the International Labour Organisation, [FN:4 TS 874, ante, vol. 2, p. 251 (art. 421).] each Member of the Organisation which ratifies this Convention shall append to its ratification a declaration stating:

(a) the territories in respect of which it undertakes to apply the provisions of the Convention without modification;

(b) the territories in respect of which it undertakes to apply the provisions of the Convention subject to modifications, together with details of the said modifications;

(c) the territories in respect of which the Convention is inapplicable and in such cases the grounds on which it is inapplicable;

(d) the territories in respect of which it reserves its decision.

2. The undertakings referred to in sub-paragraphs (a) and (b) of paragraph 1 of this Article shall be deemed to be an integral part of the ratification and shall have the force of ratification.

3. Any Member may be a subsequent declaration cancel in whole or in part any reservations made in its original declaration in virtue of sub-paragraphs (b), (c) or (d) of paragraph 1 of this Article.

ARTICLE 14

The formal ratifications of this Convention shall be communicated to the Secretary-General of the League of Nations for registration.

ARTICLE 15

1. This Convention shall be binding only upon those Members of the International Labour Organisation whose ratifications have been registered with the Secretary-General.

2. It shall come into force twelve months after the date on which the ratifications of two Members have been registered with the Secretary-General.

3. Thereafter, this Convention shall come into force for any Member twelve months after the date on which its ratification has been registered.

ARTICLE 16

As soon as the ratifications of two Members of the International Labour Organisation have been registered, the Secretary-General of the League of Nations shall so notify all the Members of the International Labour Organisation. He shall likewise notify them of the registration of ratifications which may be communicated subsequently by other members of the Organisation.

ARTICLE 17

1. A Member which has ratified this Convention may denounce it after the expiration of ten years from the date on which the Convention first comes into force, by an act communicated to the Secretary-General of the League of Nations for registration. Such denunciation shall not take effect until one year after the date on which it is registered.

2. Each Member which has ratified this Convention and which does not, within the year following the expiration of the period of ten years mentioned in the preceding paragraph, exercise the right of denunciation provided for in this Article, will be bound for another period of ten years and, thereafter, may denounce this Convention at the expiration of each period of ten years under the terms provided for in this Article.

ARTICLE 18

At the expiration of each period of ten years after the coming into force of this Convention, the Governing Body of the International Labour Office shall present to the General Conference a report on the working of this Convention and shall consider the desirability of placing on the Agenda of the Conference the question of its revision in whole or in part.

ARTICLE 19

1. Should the Conference adopt a new Convention revising this Convention in whole or in part, then, unless the new Convention otherwise provides,

(a) the ratification by a Member of the new revising Convention shall ipso jure involve the immediate denunciation of this Convention, notwithstanding the provisions of Article 17 above, if and when the new revising Convention shall have come into force;

(b) as from the date when the new revising Convention comes into force this Convention shall cease to be open to ratification by the Members.

2. This Convention shall in any case remain in force in its actual form and content for those Members which have ratified it but have not ratified the revising Convention.

ARTICLE 20

The French and English texts of this Convention shall both be authentic.

AND WHEREAS it is provided in Article 14 of the said draft convention that the formal ratifications thereof shall be communicated to the Secretary-General of the League of Nations for registration and in Article 15 that the convention shall come into force twelve months after the date on which the ratifications of two Members of the International Labor Organization have been registered with the

Secretary-General of the League of Nations and that thereafter the convention shall come into force for any Member twelve months after the date on which its ratification has been registered;

AND WHEREAS the said draft convention was duly ratified on the part of the United States of America subject to understandings as follows:

> "That the United States Government understands and construes the words 'vessels registered in a territory' appearing in this convention to include all vessels of the United States as defined under the laws of the United States.
>
> "That the United States Government understands and construes the words 'maritime navigation' appearing in this Convention to mean navigation on the high seas only.
>
> "That the provisions of this convention shall apply to all territory over which the United States exercises jurisdiction except the Government of the Commonwealth of the Philippine Islands and the Panama Canal Zone, with respect to which this Government reserves its decision."

AND WHEREAS the ratification of the said draft convention by Belgium was registered with the Secretary-General of the League of Nations on April 11, 1938, subject to subsequent decisions regarding application to the Belgian Congo and the territories under Belgian Mandate and the ratification thereof by the United States of America, subject to the understandings above recited, was registered with the Secretary-General on October 29, 1938;

AND WHEREAS by such registrations the said draft convention became a formal convention between the United States of America and Belgium on October 29, 1938, which, pursuant to Article 15 thereof, will come into force as between the United States of America and Belgium on October 29, 1939, twelve months after the date on which the ratification of the United States of America was registered with the Secretary-General of the League of Nations, and pursuant to the same Article, will come into force, for other Members of the International Labor Organization whose ratifications may have been or hereafter may be registered with the Secretary-General of the League of Nations subsequent to October 29, 1938, twelve months after the date on which the ratification has been or may be registered in each case;

NOW, THEREFORE, be it known that I, Franklin D. Roosevelt, President of the United States of America, have caused the said convention to be made public to the end that the same and every article and clause thereof may be observed and fulfilled in good faith by the United States of America and the citizens thereof, on and from October 29, 1939, subject to the understandings above recited and to any exceptions and any limitations of liability in accordance with the provisions of the convention which may be made by legislation or regulations on the part of the United States of America.

IN TESTIMONY WHEREOF I have hereunto set my hand and caused the Seal of the United States of America to be affixed.

DONE at the city of Washington this twenty-ninth day of September in the year of our Lord one thousand nine hundred and thirty-nine and of the Independence of the United States of America the one hundred and sixty-fourth.

[SEAL]

FRANKLIN D. ROOSEVELT

By the President:

CORDELL HULL

Secretary of State:

Printed and bound in the UK by
CPI Antony Rowe, Eastbourne

The manufacturer's authorised representative in the EU for product safety is Oxford University Press España S.A. of El Parque Empresarial San Fernando de Henares, Avenida de Castilla, 2 - 28830 Madrid (www.oup.es/en or product.safety@oup.com). OUP España S.A. also acts as importer into Spain of products made by the manufacturer.
Printed and bound by CPI Group (UK) Ltd, Croydon, CR0 4YY
14/09/2026
02216290-0015